SCENES FROM THE HIGH DESERT

Scenes from the High Desert

Julian Steward's Life and Theory

VIRGINIA KERNS

UNIVERSITY OF ILLINOIS PRESS
URBANA AND CHICAGO

© 2003 by the Board of Trustees
of the University of Illinois
All rights reserved
Manufactured in the United States of America
C 5 4 3 2 1

∞ This book is printed on acid-free paper.

Library of Congress Cataloging-in-Publication Data
Kerns, Virginia, 1948–
Scenes from the high desert : Julian Steward's life and theory /
Virginia Kerns.
p. cm.
Includes bibliographical references and index.
ISBN 0-252-02790-6 (alk. paper)
1. Steward, Julian Haynes, 1902–1972. 2. Anthropologists—United
States—Biography. 3. Archaeologists—United States—Biography.
4. Indians of North America—West (U.S.)—Social life and customs.
I. Title.
GN21.S78K47   2003
301'.092—dc21   2002008814

In memory of Terry
and the western years

CONTENTS

Illustrations follow pages 122 and 234

PREFACE

During the twelve years that I spent learning about Julian Steward's life and his theory, cultural ecology, I came to see that many of his ideas were rooted in memories of particular places and encounters with particular people. Only Steward's name appears on the title page of most of his books and articles, but when I read them now I see the names and faces of many other people who figured in his life and his memories in important ways. Sometimes as I read, even the rather abstract passages on resources and technology, a high desert landscape comes to mind. In a similar way, this book is very much a product of places I saw and the people I met in the course of working on it—and during the years before I ever thought of writing it.

The process of learning about Julian Steward's career has shown me that American anthropology—as a profession, not only an intellectual discipline—itself merits ethnographic study. Writing this book has also deepened my sense of the fragility of life and the transience of our labors and ideas. At the same time, I have experienced again and again how people and their ideas live on in our memories as well as in words written by them and about them. Some of the people I thank below, including Jane Steward, Dorothy Nyswander, Gordon Willey, and Robert Murphy, have died since I began working on this project. Others, whom I had hoped to talk to about Julian Steward, have also died in recent years, before I had the opportunity to meet them. They include Elman Service, Robert Manners, Omer Stewart, Cora Du Bois, and Eric Wolf.

Of those I had the good fortune to meet, my first thanks are to Jane Cannon Steward. But for her generosity and candor this would be a different book, and no doubt a much shorter one. Her emotional honesty helped me from the outset to see Steward as a whole person rather than a personage. Although her untimely death cut short our collaboration, in the week we spent together it became clear that telling about her husband's life and work required giving attention not only to the obvious successes, but also to the apparent contradictions, conflicts, and struggles. These were closely connected.

Michael and Gary Steward kindly allowed me to use and quote from their parents' journals from the 1930s. The two journals proved invaluable as I reconstructed several journeys in the American West and South America that Jane and Julian Steward made during the early years of their marriage. Reading their own words also greatly enriched my understanding of their life together and its relationship to Julian Steward's work during that important period.

I owe a great deal as well to the late Dorothy Bird Nyswander, Julian Steward's first wife. Because of her willingness to talk about the seven years when she knew Steward—which she did with frankness and without any trace of bitterness—I was able to confirm many inferences I had made based solely on scattered evidence in records and other documents. She also told me a great deal about her life before and after their marriage. Curiously, her own very different career took her to many of the same places where Steward worked and traveled, and during the same era, in the late 1930s and 1940s. Her recollections clarified, in unexpected and indirect ways, some aspects of Steward's life and work in those places and those times. Dorothy Nyswander's own life, I should add, is worthy of far more attention than I have been able to give it here.

Herbert Reich, who knew Steward during their student years at Deep Springs, a private school in California, and later at Cornell University, helped me reconstruct a time and a place that were pivotal in Steward's work as an anthropologist. Trained in physics and engineering, he had detailed memories of the technical side of life at Deep Springs, including the many quirks of the ranch's irrigation system and mechanical equipment. An entire saga centered on the temperamental semidiesel engine, a Fairbanks-Moss, that for many years provided power for the ranch. He also remembered exploring Deep Springs Valley and beyond, and prospecting for silver with his friend. Even fifty years after leaving the valley, the two men mentioned some of its landmarks in letters to each other.

During my two visits to Deep Springs, and in ensuing conversations and letters, students and faculty members kindly assisted me in various ways. Brandt Kehoe and L. Jackson Newell, both former Deep Springs students who later served as president of the college, offered perspectives on the school that helped me understand its enduring influence on Steward. Although he too returned to Deep Springs, to his lasting regret he never managed to remain for more than a few days or weeks at a time.

Many of Steward's students and colleagues contributed their memories of the man and their thoughts about him as an anthropologist and theorist. I am especially grateful to Sidney W. Mintz, the late Demitri B. Shimkin, and the late Robert F. Murphy for their perceptive essays on Steward's work and for telling me about Steward as they knew him during the 1940s and later in his life. The names of others who contributed memories and impressions of Steward appear in the list of interviews. Some of them offered ideas about how Steward had or had not influenced his students and how other scholars had supported or challenged some of Steward's work. Tracing those connections, a worthy but enormous task, would require another volume, or several, and is regrettably beyond the scope of this one.

This book itself has grown far beyond what I originally planned. I imagined writing something rather brief, drawing on a limited amount of documentary material. Steward's own papers, which Jane Steward deposited in the University of Illinois archives after his death, cover the entire span of his career, but with emphasis on the later years. I eventually located correspondence and records in other collections that added balance. This material helped me verify what I learned in interviews about Steward's early life and the first years of his career and allowed me to reconstruct that period in far greater detail than I had thought possible.

The more I learned about his experiences during those formative years, the more I realized how greatly they had affected his work as a theorist. Initially, I had doubts about including some events mentioned in interviews, events that seemed very relevant, yet highly personal and perhaps difficult to document. I wondered whether cultural anthropologists' efforts to protect the privacy of the people they write about should remain in force even after the deaths of those people. I was inclined to think so, although our usual technique for protecting privacy—the use of pseudonyms—was not an option in this case. Finding correspondence and records that supported or confirmed what I had been told, and in certain cases added more detail, clarified the issue. I saw no point in remaining silent about material that was freely available in public archives and that would come to light sooner or later. It did not seem amiss, in other words, to write about what was *already* in writing, especially since it enhanced understanding of Steward's life and work.

The process of piecing together evidence—from documents, interviews, and my own observations of places where Steward lived and worked—led me to set aside a number of ideas I had at the outset of this project. The introduction summarizes the book's guiding questions, the way I approached the research, and some of the ideas that emerged about the influence of autobiographical memory on Steward's theoretical work. The conclusion locates the theoretical approach that he called cultural ecology in the context of Steward's lived experience, autobiographical memory, and personal construction of meaning. His concept of the patrilineal band emerges as central to his intellectual work, emotionally meaningful, and unquestionably grounded in his own social experience and memories of place.

Twelve intervening chapters provide the supporting evidence, a detailed account of his life both before he studied anthropology and after. Eight chapters deal with the first half of Steward's life, and only four with the last half, reflecting the greater importance of those early years to his theoretical work. What might at first glance seem needless detail (his mother's and sister's employment histories, for example, or his sister's wages during the Great Depression) helps illuminate the links between Steward's own social experience as a man in midcentury, middle-class America and his theoretical ideas.

The documentary material relating to Steward, while surprisingly abundant, is also scattered and uneven in certain respects. Resisting both impulse and fashion, I have not filled the gaps by inventing or imagining any details about people, places, or events. Although I have tried to avoid too much conjecture, I *have* engaged in what I think of as informed inference, while giving respectful attention to the evidence and remaining aware of its limitations. I believe that this is somewhat in keeping with Steward's approach to empirical data, although I do not share his faith, widespread during his era, in an easily achieved objectivity. My own biases will no doubt be apparent, but I hope that the respect and goodwill are just as obvious.

That said, I am aware that circumstances of my own life, past and present, have shaped the very questions that I pose, besides informing my interpretation of Steward's early life, career, and theoretical work. A range of events and experiences has affected my angle of vision in many ways, just as surely as a variety affected Steward's. In my own case, some of these relate to growing up during America's postwar years and undergoing a series of dislocations that heightened my awareness of regional contrasts. Entering the academic world in the 1970s, at a point when very few women had yet found a place in it, was also a formative experience. While too complex to summarize here in a few sentences, it did show me a division of labor by gender that I now see had a long history in American anthropology, including the years of Steward's career from the mid-1920s to the early 1970s.

To cite a more recent experience, a puzzling illness that remained undiagnosed during most of the period that I worked on this project affected how I viewed Steward's reports of sickness. I took his reports seriously and examined them closely. Details of context and timing finally led me to conclude that some of the episodes before his 1938 trip to the Andes, where he contracted a parasitic infection, may well have been largely psychological in origin. If so, they were an expectable outcome of certain difficult events of his childhood, as recounted in chapter 1. His ill health after 1938 may have had as much to do with the effects of lingering infection as with his lifelong anxiety about illness. The prolonged hospital stay in 1949 and 1950, mentioned in chapter 10, signaled the beginning of a medically documented decline in health marked by repeated surgery. Although many of his colleagues considered Steward a hypochondriac, I believe that this obscures the emotional significance of illness in his life and that he did have a diagnosed, but not effectively treated, medical condition from the age of thirty-six.

Steward, who had scant interest in folklore and mythology, is himself the subject of several folktales within the profession. The somewhat unflattering stories of this oral tradition cannot be documented, suggesting that such folklore may reveal more about the fault lines of the profession than about the man himself. In the course of reading published works, I have also encountered many errors about particular details of his life. These range from incorrect dates to mistaken notions about his early life and later research. Unlike the folklore that has grown up around Steward, the errors in published sources do not denigrate, but rather tend to magnify or mythologize aspects of his life and work. (He did not attend a school for gifted students, in the sense that that term is used today, and Paiute villages did not exist in Deep Springs Valley when he lived there. He was not a student of Franz Boas, and he did not teach the first course in anthropology offered at the University of Michigan. He never carried out ethnographic or archaeological fieldwork in South America, in the usual sense of the term *fieldwork*. The Great Basin fieldwork in 1935 extended over a period of months, not a year or more. And so on.)

I initially intended to point out and correct these and other factual errors in the endnotes, but as those endnotes multiplied, I finally abandoned that plan. I do note, perhaps too erratically, errors that have appeared repeatedly in print, a few of which can be traced to Steward himself. The structure of his professional world, especially the perpetual struggle for prestige and status, no doubt explains personal mythologizing just as it accounts for disparaging folklore. Anthropology's long tradition of celebrating in print a few men as founders and leaders—a tradition it shares with many other academic fields—also contributes to mythologizing, the propensity to gild just a few lilies. As I found, however, the actual events of Steward's life are far more compelling than any embellished version.

The breadth of Steward's interests and the variety of people and places he wrote about have taken me into new territory again and again in the process of writing this book. I have many guides to thank: colleagues who answered questions and suggested books and articles to read. They corrected many of my own errors and misunderstandings, but they are not responsible, of course, for those that remain. I am especially grateful to the following scholars who read and commented on the manuscript, either in full or on specific portions of it: Robert L. Carneiro, Sally Cole, Catherine S. Fowler, Ronald A. Hallett, the late Dorothy B. Nyswander, William J. Peace, Antonio Lauria-Perricelli, Sidney W. Mintz, Gordon R. Willey, and Rita P. Wright.

Many other scholars, whose names appear in the endnotes and list of references, also provided guidance through their writings. They range from archaeologists and cultural anthropologists to geographers, historians, cognitive psychologists, and psychoanalysts. I refer to them in endnotes rather than directly in the text in order to avoid confusing readers with the names of hundreds of people, from historical figures to contemporary scholars. In general, only those who knew Steward—as teacher, student, colleague, relative, or friend—are mentioned in the text.

I am grateful to the following institutions for providing assistance with documentary research and, when necessary, permission to quote unpublished material: the Bancroft Library, University of California, Berkeley; Columbia University Archives; Cornell University Archives; Deep Springs College, California; Family History Center, and Historical Department, Church of Jesus Christ of Latter-day Saints, Salt Lake City; First Church of Christ, Scientist, Boston; National Archives, Washington, D.C.; National Anthropological Archives, Smithsonian Institution; Telluride Association, Ithaca, New York; University Archives, University of Illinois, Urbana; University of Michigan Archives, Ann Arbor; University of Utah Archives, Salt Lake City; the Utah Museum of Natural History; and the Utah State Historical Society.

Financial support from the Virginia Foundation for the Humanities and from the College of William and Mary made it possible for me to begin research and complete the manuscript, respectively. During the intervening years, I was fortunate to have seven outstanding students as research assistants: Christie Borum, Catharine Dann, Allison Keller, Elizabeth Lane, Susan Smyre, Patricia Takach, and Karen Taylor. At the University of Illinois Press, I wish to thank Elizabeth G. Dulany for her encouragement and support over the course of many years. My final thanks are to Ronald Hallett for conversation and good counsel on the journey.

SCENES FROM THE HIGH DESERT

INTRODUCTION

A map of Julian Steward's life, charting his journey as an anthropologist and theorist, would surely center on the high desert of eastern California. During the years he lived in that borderland, a place of harsh beauty and grand scale, Steward explored its mountains and valleys on horseback and on foot. Landmarks on a map of his early life would include White Mountain, Birch Mountain, and much of the Sierra Nevada, Deep Springs Valley, Owens Valley, Eureka Valley. He knew many other places just as well, some with evocative names that hold fast to memory: the Last Chance Range, Chocolate Mountain, Horse Thief Canyon. In a region called the "land of little rain," Wyman Creek and Owens River stand out as conspicuous features on the map, however ordinary their names.[1]

Steward first entered that country in 1918 at the age of sixteen, after a childhood spent in the East. Long before his death in 1972, he had emerged as a leading figure in American anthropology, perhaps best known for his theoretical approach, cultural ecology. His theoretical ideas, which had a long gestation, began to take shape even before he returned to the high desert, home ground, for fieldwork in 1935. During some of the worst years of the Great Depression, a time when he, like many other Americans, had no steady employment, Steward started to develop the approach that he eventually called cultural ecology.

Although other anthropologists had given some attention to the natural environment, I think it is fair to say that Steward was the first to focus consistently and systematically on the intersection between culture and the natural world. He had a distinctive voice in midcentury anthropology, in part for the attention he gave to the land: to the landscape itself and to the animals, plants, and water that sustain human life. Specifically, Steward emphasized the relationship between technology—especially the tools that humans use in pursuit of subsistence—and certain environmental features. Climate, water sources, the contours of the land, its soils, plants, and animals all were "crucial," he wrote. In practice, he gave greatest attention to environmental resources, especially water and food. The years that he spent living in the high desert, living on the land, had taught him something about how water scarcity affects both the supply of food and the structure of social life. This became a prominent theme in his later writings.

Along with technology, Steward stressed a second key cultural feature: the organization of work. Put simply, he argued that how people use tools and organize work to wrest a living from the land affects "other aspects of culture," ranging from settlement patterns to land tenure to kinship structures. In his most succinct definition, he characterized cultural ecology as "environment plus technology and the social arrangements entailed thereby." Robert Murphy, one of Steward's students at Columbia University during the late 1940s, aptly called Steward's cultural ecology a rather "open-ended theory dealing with human labor in its natural setting."[2]

In a book published in 1938, Steward took some of his first visible steps in the direction of cultural ecology. Based on field research in the West with Paiute and Shoshone Indians, his book offered a highly detailed, place-by-place account of traditional subsistence practices. In the last three pages, a section titled "Ecology in Cultural Studies," he argued that the "force of purely cultural and psychological determinants" cannot be understood "if the ecology which conditions and delimits them is unknown." He would spend many years working out his ideas about what he later called the "method," not theory, of cultural ecology.[3]

The book itself, titled *Basin-Plateau Aboriginal Sociopolitical Groups*, received a positive review in the *American Anthropologist* but limited attention in the early years after publication. The cumbersome title revealed nothing about Steward's unusual approach; perhaps more to the point, his junior status in the profession did not guarantee a wide readership. Specialists working in the Great Basin—a vast desert region that stretches between Utah's Wasatch Range and California's Sierra Nevada—formed the book's first audience. Over time, however, as Steward's ideas gained currency, *Basin-Plateau* became something of an ethnographic classic; it appeared again in print decades after its initial publication. Another landmark work, *Theory of Culture Change,* published in 1955, has remained in print for forty-five years, with only a brief hiatus. A collection of essays, more than half of them previously published, *Theory of Culture Change* immediately brought his ideas to a much broader audience.[4]

By now, generations of anthropologists and their students have read Steward's essays. I first read them myself as a student in a course on theory, and I recall finding many of his ideas original and persuasive but others puzzling. His language, always concise, usually precise, and markedly scientific in tone, sometimes resulted in perplexing abstractions. The meaning of "functional interdependency of features in a structural relationship" was not immediately apparent to me. Yet a propensity for the concrete characterized most of his work. He used an impressive array of ethnographic and archaeological evidence to support a range of creative, generalizing conclusions about how, in his own words, "similar subsistence activities had produced similar social structures."[5]

I also vividly remember encountering the casual claim in two essays that "innate male dominance" helped account for certain features of social life. Although deeply skeptical of that view, the twice-repeated phrase left me, as a woman, with an uncomfortable feeling. The fact that the book was an assigned text and I was the sole woman in the small class only increased my discomfort. Steward provided little in the way of explanation or evidence, a rather common practice at the time because the idea was widely accepted. It remained noncontroversial in many quarters, in fact, until years after his death.[6]

Looking back, I now see that Steward's words expressed a core assumption of disciplinary knowledge—I would read similar claims again and again—and described the tenor of gender relations in the academic world during the mid-twentieth century. Still, at the time, this particular assertion seemed at odds with Steward's general approach, especially his obvious concern with empirical evidence. At first, I simply wondered why he claimed that male dominance was innate. Eventually, I wondered why he chose to say it in print, twice, during a specific period of time, the mid-1930s, and to leave that language intact in the mid-1950s when the essays were republished, one of them in revised form.

Years later, rereading *Theory of Culture Change*, I was again struck by the language, but for still other reasons. Steward routinely used words such as *fact, determinant, cause,* and *scientific,* words that had nearly disappeared from the lexicon of cultural anthropology, although not from that of archaeology. Steward is now often labeled, rather accusingly, as a positivist, but in some sense this misses the point, or at least oversimplifies the man and his ideas. In common with critics of positivism, for example, he was skeptical of all grand theory, any metanarrative: in his own private vocabulary, any ism. Whatever his philosophical reasons, he also had highly personal ones, which led to an intense commitment to scientific method and empirical research and to an equally intense dislike of dogma.

Steward identified wholly as a scientist, and this distinguished him from some of his colleagues in cultural anthropology. From the beginning of his career, he viewed anthropology as a value-neutral science, similar to the natural sciences. Its goal was to develop explanations about the causes of cultural change and other cultural phenomena and to test specific hypotheses about observable "regularities" in social life. He always assumed that cultural phenomena could be studied empirically through fieldwork in exactly the same way as objects in the natural world.[7] In the era that followed, however, the language of positivism began to give way to a rather different vocabulary in cultural anthropology, and the goals of ethnographic research started to shift in other directions.

Other questions, some old and some new, came to me as I reread the essays. How had Steward happened to look for specific connections between the natural and the cultural world? Why did he always make such a sharp distinction between culture and nature? Why did he think that he could discover laws governing cultural change? What had led him to a strictly materialist approach that treated religious belief, for example, as a "peripheral" feature of culture? As Robert Murphy later told me, Steward had no analytical interest in religion beyond "priesthoods and temples," which is to say religion's political and material dimensions. And why did Steward call cultural ecology a concept and a method, not a theory or a theoretical approach? This seemed especially odd because the word *theory* figures so prominently in the title of his best-known book and because many anthropologists consider cultural ecology his major achievement. As Murphy himself wrote, "Julian Steward's greatest contribution to anthropology was his earliest: the theory of cultural ecology."[8]

I wondered also what accounted for the strongly masculinist quality of his ideas, not unique to his times but certainly marked in his case and obvious in his writings. Steward showed an enduring concern not so much with "human labor in its natural setting," to borrow Murphy's phrase, but specifically with men's labor: men working together outdoors, men procuring food and other necessities from the land. Indeed, he emphasized hunting by men in what he referred to as his first theoretical essay, "The Economic and Social Basis of Primitive Bands." Published in 1936, the essay drew primarily on secondary sources rather than on his own fieldwork. Some twenty years later Steward divided his essay on hunting bands into two parts, "The Patrilineal Band" and "The Composite Band," revised both, and included them as two chapters in *Theory of Culture Change.* The original essay and its incarnations, especially "The Patrilineal Band," became some of his best-known works, contributing to what was later called, often critically, the "Man the Hunter" model of foraging societies.[9]

The concept of the patrilineal band, with its emphasis on men and hunting, was the first to emerge when Steward began to think along the lines of cultural ecology. It remained *the* foundational concept in his thinking, and always guided his ideas about social organization—a point that has not been recognized in the extensive and often excellent commentary on his published work.[10] I saw this myself only by degrees, and only by reconstructing his early life and later research in as much detail as possible, and then placing his published writings in the context of his social experiences and relationships, personal as well as professional. As I was to discover by giving attention to his own life, the concept of the patrilineal band always held great personal meaning for him, and it stimulated his most important fieldwork, in the Great Basin, as well as later work and travel in other places.

Ironically, some of Steward's first findings from fieldwork suggested that Northern Paiute and Western Shoshone women, not men, had once provided the major share of subsistence, gathering most of the seeds, roots, and nuts that comprised the daily diet. The earliest evidence of that finding probably came to light in the late 1920s when Steward did field research with Owens Valley Paiute, collecting long lists of plant names and asking questions about the use of plants as food. He learned at least this much about gathering: "Women, working in groups, gathered seeds by beating them from plants with seed beaters." He certainly understood the importance of their labor by 1935. Soon after undertaking fieldwork, and just two weeks after completing his essay on hunting bands, he reported on his initial findings. "This comes near to being a woman's economy," he remarked, a phrase that never saw print.[11]

I wondered why Steward had almost entirely excluded women from his writings, not only from the texts, but even from the bibliographies.[12] That question, along with the others, raised a more general one in my mind about how a social theory develops. Is it an intellectual construct and primarily a product of intellectual filiation? Does it result largely from reading the works of leading scholars and perhaps training with them as graduate students? This "genealogical" point of view—which assumes some degree of patrilineal transmission, from (fictive) father to son—is often implicit in writings about theorists, including those about Steward.

I resorted to this patrilineal model myself at the outset, but cast it aside almost immediately as I realized the importance of other people and a specific place in Steward's life and ideas. Eventually, however, I concluded that a modified version had merit. Anthropology's "patrilineal" structure, which became increasingly visible to me as I learned about Steward's career, did directly affect the transmission of his ideas and indirectly their creation. There was little interest at the time in "a woman's economy," especially among the recognized scholars in his field, a category that scarcely included any women. This probably reinforced Steward's own strong inclination to ignore women's labor, even while giving attention to the products of their labor, the essential food that they provided.

A few professionally prominent men—Alfred Kroeber, Robert Lowie, and geographer Carl Sauer, three of his graduate teachers at Berkeley—often receive credit for influencing Steward's theoretical ideas. Steward himself, however, privately denied that his teachers—with the slight exception of Lowie—had affected the direction of his thought. His unpublished writings suggest that he saw practically no connection between his graduate training and his ideas; he considered himself a maverick and freethinker, not anyone's disciple. (He was not at all unique in this regard. Lowie himself declared in print that no one in his own field, including his graduate teacher, Franz Boas, had been a "source of inspiration" for him.)[13]

Robert Murphy also cited Steward's fieldwork with the Western Shoshone, and the depression era when he worked, as major influences. His field research, however, did not entail cultural immersion or prolonged contact with informants; he spent as much time or more observing the land as he did interviewing elderly men and a few women about how they had lived on it in the past. And his central ideas, as I came to see, reached back years before the depression and his 1930s field research.[14]

Steward made scattered comments in letters and other unpublished writings about some people and events that influenced his work as an anthropologist. He never made a direct and detailed statement about how he developed cultural ecology as a theoretical approach. In this, he resembles most other theorists in anthropology. Accounts of fieldwork abound, perhaps in part because nearly every anthropologist undertakes fieldwork, a defining aspect of the discipline. Far fewer anthropologists have created a social theory, or reflected deeply on how they did so. The process of theory making in anthropology remains largely unexamined, either by theorists themselves or by others.[15]

* * *

Although he usually denied that his family background or his teachers at Berkeley had exerted any important influence on his work, Steward did credit his early education with provoking what he called "an intellectual awakening." In middle age, when he wrote those words, he remembered the last years of adolescence as "the turning point" in his life. At that juncture, he wrote, "I was subjected to the most profound influence of my career."[16] That "profound influence" was a highly unusual school in a most unlikely place, both of which made an indelible impression on him and, in turn, on his theoretical approach. That is to say, autobiographical memory—as cognitive psychologists use the term, meaning "memory for information relating to the self"—directly inspired many of Steward's theoretical ideas. His image-laden personal memories, especially those of self in relation to other people and to a place, provided much of the source material for cultural ecology.[17]

In 1918, at the age of sixteen, Steward left his childhood home in Washington, D.C., in the wake of his parents' separation. He journeyed west on his own, traveling cross-country by train to his destination, a new and innovative private school in eastern California. Located in the high desert near the California-Nevada border in Deep Springs Valley, the school included a working ranch run by about twenty male students and a few ranch hands, all under the supervision of a ranch manager.

Steward had spent a month during the previous year working on a farm in Virginia, but he arrived in the West knowing nothing directly about ranch life. Still, he did have some romanticized images of the West and life on the range, gained mostly from reading not schoolbooks but westerns. The young Julian Steward was already a longtime fan of Zane Grey, whose romances of western life included the best-selling *Riders of the Purple Sage* and many others. Grey's stories of the Wild West were serialized in newspapers and magazines, sold millions in book form, and appeared on the silent screen.[18]

Several staples of the western novel were absent from life at Deep Springs. There were no gunslingers, no cattle rustlers, no lawlessness. Order prevailed, with the young cowboy-students abiding by a strict regimen that included long hours spent in disciplined labor. Working outdoors each afternoon, after a morning in classes, Julian Steward learned not only from books but also directly from the land around him. Unlike most anthropologists of his era, who spent their formative years in eastern, urban settings, he spent three memorable years living and learning and working in a remote desert valley. His direct engagement with the land offered lessons that books and formal study, first of geology and zoology and later of anthropology, would reinforce and complement.

Deep Springs left visible marks on Steward's life and his theory. Memories of what he saw and experienced in the high desert during those years found later expression in cultural ecology. They comprised only one element, but perhaps the most crucial one, in a theory that drew on many aspects of Steward's own life. I first suspected that his theoretical ideas in some way recalled his early life experiences when I visited Deep Springs Valley myself and had the immediate sense that I had entered the laboratory of cultural ecology. It took years, however, to see exactly how autobiographical memory had shaped certain aspects of Steward's theory; to see that required reconstructing his life both before and after his years at Deep Springs.

While the valley itself presented the first clues, a photograph album that I found at the school, now Deep Springs College, offered others. The photographs, taken by Julian Steward during his student days, constituted a record of what he saw and what he thought important enough to capture on film. They provided portraits of the people and the place from the point of his arrival to his departure a few years later. At the time of that first visit, I had not yet talked to anyone who knew details of Steward's early life, and so the photographs were my first window on his world.

One afternoon, as I searched through some unsorted papers in a cardboard box in the school library, I happened across the old album, its dark cover dusty and frayed. Turning the fragile pages, I saw someone's visual record of the ranch and school during its early years. Many of the faded black-and-white snapshots showed students at work, branding calves and feeding livestock, or lined up for the annual school photograph. Others showed the faculty members, several sober-faced men, none of them at home on the range to judge from the dark suits and stiff-collared white shirts. Scattered in the album were a few photographs of an Indian man and woman. In one, a man named Captain Harry gazes intently at the camera; in another he kneels on the ground, skinning a coyote. As I later learned, Captain Harry and his wife, Mary, worked briefly at the school, he as irrigator and she as laundress.

The landscape surrounding the ranch and school had also drawn the eye of the photographer. Again and again he captured the wide sweep of the valley, dotted with sagebrush, framed by long horizons of mountain and sky. Some of those scenes reminded me of illustrations in Steward's 1938 book on the Great Basin. I recalled that the photographs in that book showed only places, in photographs and in maps, and not the Paiute and Shoshone people, who for countless generations had gathered seeds and hunted in those places. I had wondered about their absence. By contrast, pictures of people filled this album. Many had names written underneath: "Henry Hayes," "Reich," "Bob," "Windsor Putnam," and others, but no "Julian" or "Steward." Eventually I began to wonder whether the photographer, shown in a few pictures labeled "Me," might not be Steward. The only portraits I had seen of him at that point, from late middle age, bore slight resemblance to the much younger "Me" of the album. It was those landscape shots, more than any of the other pictures, that made me think of him.

Deciding to trust intuition, I left Deep Springs the next day and drove south through Owens Valley, headed for Los Angeles to buy the photographic equipment I needed to copy the contents of the album. Along the way, I crossed and recrossed the aqueduct that carries most of the valley's water to the same destination, hundreds of miles away. In the early 1900s, in one of the West's most famous water disputes, the expanding and thirsty metropolis of Los Angeles began secretly buying up the water rights to the Owens River, the main source of water for the valley. Constructing an aqueduct to transport the water across the desert, over more than two hundred miles of severe terrain, took six years of hard labor and technical ingenuity. As a result of this engineering feat, Los Angeles, a city surrounded by desert, continued to grow and prosper while Owens Valley did not.[19]

Steward first arrived in Owens Valley in 1918, just five years after the Los Angeles aqueduct began draining its water. Over time, the green patchwork of irrigated fields would disappear, replaced by stands of sagebrush. Owens Lake, startlingly blue and a haven for thousands of waterfowl, would slowly lose color and life as the water that once fed it flowed elsewhere. In 1918 its sparkling blue water still drew the attention of travelers. As a student, Steward painted a small picture of the lake, capturing the colors of water and sky on canvas. But in 1935, when he returned to the vicinity for fieldwork, Owens Lake was no more than a place-name marking a windswept salt flat.[20]

Over a period of some twenty years, first as a student at Deep Springs and then on frequent visits, Steward saw Owens Valley gradually lose its economic base and much of its population along with the water. In his later work, he would write about the links between irrigation, economy, and population in early civilizations, citing archaeological evidence from far-flung sites ranging from Mesopotamia to the Andes of South America. As I eventually reconstructed Steward's many trips to Owens Valley, and returned again myself, I began to wonder whether his own memories of the valley had provided his original model, or at least had guided his thinking, consciously or not.

Returning through Owens Valley on that first trip, long before I knew enough about Steward's life or the valley's history to detect any parallels, I stopped at the lake bed. A bleak site where clouds of alkali dust rose up in a gust of wind, it embodied the valley's loss. Back at Deep Springs, I examined the several irrigated fields with new interest. Emerald green and glistening with water, they had the lush look of a small oasis in a pale brown land; and in the distance I could see several students at work, tending the irrigation system as in Steward's day.

Water for the fields still came from the same creek, a source too small and too distant to have suffered the same fate as the Owens River.

Before leaving Deep Springs I made copies of all the photographs in the album, including the few pictures from Owens Valley. I later learned that my supposition was correct: the photographs were in fact taken by Julian Steward. A few years before his death, and near the end of his long exile from the West, he finally sent the album back to Deep Springs. There it remained until I happened to find it almost twenty years later.[21]

The photographs show what Julian Steward saw. More importantly, they show what he remembered clearly for the rest of his life with the help of the visual record: how he worked together with his friends and the ranch hands, maintaining the irrigation system, harvesting the crops, caring for the livestock. These were tasks essential to survival in a high desert valley. The students did their work day by day, from one season to the next, in a place that offered few distractions from the land and from their labor. Each day offered lessons about technology, labor, and environmental resources such as water, the constellation of elements on which his later theory rested. Working with his hands, doing manual labor on a daily basis, was an unusual experience for a young man of his class background. It helps to explain the uncommon emphasis on labor in his theoretical work, one largely missing in anthropology, unless derived from Marxism, during his era.

The ranch in Deep Springs Valley occupied a place where Indians had once led a very different way of life, using other tools. Evidence of that way of life and remnants of those tools remained, in the form of the petroglyphs that Julian Steward photographed and the stone arrowheads he collected during his student days. In just decades following the entry of white settlers, and within the memories of Captain Harry and Mary, life in Deep Springs Valley had changed dramatically. In even less time, the diversion of water from nearby Owens Valley to Los Angeles had begun to transform the way of life that white settlers had brought with them. The very landscape, the look of the land, changed along with it: silvery sagebrush replaced green pasture and field; an expansive blue lake simply vanished.

Years later, memories of his experiences at Deep Springs and in Owens Valley resurfaced in Steward's theory of cultural ecology, reworked and recast in the language of anthropology. Land, water, food, technology, and the work of men: these, along with cultural change, formed the central and enduring themes of his research and writing. Vivid memories from adolescence, personal memories of a particular time and place, provided the template for his later intellectual work as an anthropologist.[22]

* * *

As I examined and reexamined the photographs from Steward's album, I found the near absence of women striking. The students, faculty members, and most of the school's staff were men; and unlike the men, the few women who lived at the ranch did not do outdoor work. To put this another way, Julian Steward had experiences then available only to men, as witnessed by the contrasting ones of the woman who became his first wife. She grew up on a large, company-owned ranch along the California-Nevada border, just north of Deep Springs. She felt at home on horseback, explored the desert freely as a child, and knew many of the ranch hands, most of them Northern Paiute and Washo Indians and all of them men. But there any similarities end. She never had Steward's experience of ranch life: the daily experience of working outside on the land alongside peers. Any ranchwoman who did outdoor labor, sometimes by preference, but often by desperate necessity, violated custom. More to the point, she did not work with her peers, other women.[23]

In contrast, Steward had detailed memories of the time he spent outdoors on the ranch, working with other men (both white and American Indian), and these are embedded in his theoretical approach. Although he developed it years later, in the course of reconstructing the precontact cultures of American Indians, it had its genesis in the *Anglo*-American West, where Indians constituted a minority, and in the decidedly masculine social world in which he spent the later years of adolescence. I would even argue that during his era *only* a man was likely to have conceived of cultural ecology. Most women simply did not have the sorts of social experiences and personal memories that inspired Steward's particular vision of culture.[24]

By reconstructing Steward's early life in detail, I began to see that his personal memories of other experiences and relationships had also influenced his theoretical work in various ways. For example, his own words confirm that his mother, Grace Steward, encouraged his appreciation of landscape and interest in natural history and provided opportunities for him to follow those interests. But she and her son never reached agreement, or even a truce, on the subject of science and religion.[25] She was passionate and outspoken about her religious beliefs, which she embraced in adulthood as a convert to a new religious sect. Her son came not only to reject her beliefs but also to scorn religion. He avoided giving attention to it in research, and it had practically no place in his theoretical work.

Steward's abiding fascination with technology and technological change just as surely derived to some degree from his early relationship with his father. Thomas Steward, then examiner-in-chief of the U.S. Patent Office, introduced his young son to the automobile and to memorable driving adventures at a time when the horse and buggy still prevailed. As a child, Julian Steward took part in the transition from the old mode of transport to the new. He witnessed the myriad social and economic effects of this technological change as well.

His father's secure position in the federal service, and his acquaintance with government scientists and top-ranking officials, also meant that Steward began life in a rather privileged class position and with valuable social connections. He spent his childhood among the socially conservative, educated, and professional middle class of Washington, D.C.; but after his parents separated, he experienced years of financial insecurity, unlike his friends from the same background. The contrast seemed to heighten the salience of his financial problems. A preoccupation with subsistence found its way into his theory, as did others that developed later in his life, based on personal memories of his experiences with other people and places.

* * *

What I saw on my first trip to Deep Springs and Owens Valley gave me some sense of the importance of place in Steward's theory, an understanding that deepened with successive visits. It also led me to travel to other areas where he lived and worked, in order to see what he had seen, and, still later, to structure the chapters of this book around a series of places significant to him. To judge from his photographs, Deep Springs Valley has changed rather little in the eighty-five years since Steward arrived there. A paved road now runs through it, replacing the original rutted track; otherwise the valley appears much the same. Many areas of the Great Basin that were uninhabited, or sparsely inhabited, during the 1920s and 1930s remain so due to their limited water supply. Anyone traveling through them today can see a landscape that retains the look of wildness, a landscape that Julian Steward knew well, not just intellectually but viscerally.

Other places have changed almost beyond recognition. Las Vegas was still a sleepy desert outpost at the time of Steward's fieldwork in the mid-1930s. Lake Mead and Boulder Dam, then under construction, soon transformed the nearby town, providing the water and electicity to create a city of neon lights. Salt Lake City, at the foot of the Wasatch Range, sprawled forth over the years to fill more and more of the valley floor. Most grievous to Julian Steward, the open land around San Francisco and Berkeley, especially in Marin County and the Berkeley Hills, disappeared under roadways and dense suburban development. So much growth took place between the 1930s and the early 1960s that he finally surrendered any hope of returning there to live.

Examining old photographs of Deep Springs and searching through its records helped me to reconstruct a bygone social world and to detect some lingering traces of it in the present. During a spell of observation at Deep Springs, I learned firsthand about its work program, which has changed rather little since its inception. Twenty-five years as an anthropologist in the academic world, which may qualify here as (retrospective) participant observation, helped me to understand Steward's professional milieu. Interviews with people who knew him, sometime between his arrival at Deep Springs in 1918 and his death fifty-four years later, added details about the person and the events of those years.

I count myself especially fortunate to have known two women whose memories of Julian Steward spanned most of his adult life. Jane Cannon Steward, to whom he was married for nearly forty years until his death, was his companion in field research in the West in the 1930s. His first wife, Dorothy Bird Nyswander, met Steward in Berkeley soon after he began graduate work in anthropology at the University of California. She was completing a doctorate in psychology at the time. They collaborated briefly on a research project with Ute Indians after they married, then separated a year later. Steward married Jane Cannon in 1933.

I first met Jane Cannon Steward by chance, a few years after her husband's death. In her midsixties at the time, she struck me as having unusual energy, a certain ageless quality, and an infectious laugh. When we met again fifteen years later, she was living in Hawaii, where she had moved several years after the death of her husband. During the week we spent together talking about the past, I had much the same perception of her as before. Jane laughed easily and often. Then nearly eighty years old, she remained open to life and continued to meet it on her own terms. Her untimely death only a few months later left me with many unasked questions and with the particular sadness of losing a friend just met.

Long after talking to Jane, and when I had reached the midpoint in writing this book, including the portions dealing with Julian Steward's first wife, I unexpectedly located Dorothy Nyswander. The last references to her that I had seen in print placed her in California in the 1950s and India in the 1960s. I had already tried to contact her daughter, a well-known psychiatrist, a few years earlier, but I learned she had died in New York at the age of sixty-seven. To my surprise, I found that Dorothy Nyswander, a centenarian, still lived in California in the late 1990s. She felt some faint surprise herself when she received a brief handwritten note from me explaining that I was writing a book about Julian Steward and that I would like to meet her before returning to the East. Very generously, she said yes, thereby agreeing to reopen a long-closed chapter in her life. Her marriage to Steward had ended sixty-five years earlier.

Meeting Dorothy Nyswander a week later was illuminating, not least because she shared certain striking qualities with Jane Steward. Despite their many differences, Julian Steward's two wives each showed an engaging warmth and openness toward other people and a buoyant optimism about life as it is. It helped me immeasurably that they had such detailed memories of the distant past and that so many of their perceptions and memories coincided. I was later able to document nearly all of the names, dates, and professional events that they mentioned and many personal ones as well. The first interview with Dorothy, along with subsequent conversations and interviews, added nuance and detail to the years between 1926, when Julian and Dorothy met in Berkeley, and the early 1930s, when they separated in Salt Lake City. Dorothy Nyswander, who achieved great success herself in a different field, did not follow Steward's work in anthropology and never suspected that she might have figured in it in any way.[26]

I had decided early on to use interviewing, observation, and other field methods—instead of relying solely on written records and published material—so that I could approach Steward's life from the perspective of an ethnographer. I also adopted the framework of a life history instead of following the format of a traditional biography. Ethnographers have long drawn on individual life stories to illuminate a culture or a specific aspect of culture. In a similar way, I wanted to use Steward's life as a vehicle for examining theory making in anthropology, perhaps illuminating in the process the professional culture in which he worked. As I began to see evidence of personal memories in Steward's theory, I turned to works by cognitive psychologists and psychoanalysts to help me understand the importance of autobiographical memory to his work.

I did not intend at the outset to write a full-scale biography of a notable anthropologist, although Julian Steward certainly attained that status. Writing such a book would require giving attention to the entire range of his publications and to aspects of his professional life that I mention largely in passing. These include his diverse activities at the Smithsonian Institution and at the five universities where he held faculty appointments. Rather than detailing those, I have tried to keep the focus on a specific set of theoretical ideas, against the background of some important social experiences in his early life and later in his long professional career.

Since I could not speak directly with the subject of my study as ethnographers traditionally do, I talked to people who had known him, especially Jane Steward and Dorothy Nyswander but also his students and colleagues. Although each person saw Julian Steward from a different angle of vision, their memories yielded an unexpectedly consistent portrait of the man.[27] Jane Steward and Dorothy Nyswander alike recalled his commitment to science and aversion to religious dogma, which seemed to him the antithesis of scientific inquiry; his deep attachment to the mountains and deserts of the West and his warm memories of boyhood days spent exploring them in eastern California; and his usually serious manner that could dissolve suddenly in a flash of humor. Both women also remembered the dark moods that gripped him and the times when he retreated into himself.

More than a few of Julian Steward's colleagues and students, especially those who knew him later in life, remarked that they found him complex and rather enigmatic. They remembered him as intensely committed to his theoretical approach, but also uncommonly willing to question his own ideas. Some commented on his mercurial moods, adding that, given his professional stature, he was oddly withdrawn from professional life. Despite being so well known in his field, Steward remained a highly elusive figure to many.[28]

To let Steward speak for himself, I turned to his published and unpublished writings. Reading his many publications—books, monographs, edited works, articles, and reviews—helped me see how his ideas developed over time. Unpublished material, including letters, journals, and notes, provided clues about the links between his own experiences and memories and his theoretical ideas.

As I sifted through thousands of pages written in his own hand or composed at his typewriter I had a long, if necessarily one-sided, conversation with Julian Steward.

Documents also helped me reconstruct events of his early life in far greater detail than any other means would have allowed, and they enabled me to chart his travels with great precision. Given his intellectual bent toward the material conditions of social life, I tried to learn as much as possible about those of his own life. Here again, documents offered a great deal of detail, though they did not provide much in the way of personal memories recorded by Steward. Some of these I had to infer, primarily on the basis of striking parallels between his own life experiences and his ideas. "Secondhand" memories, such as what Jane Steward remembered about her husband's recollections, also provided some guidance.

The weight of this diverse evidence suggests that emotion- and image-laden memories and personal meaning played a highly creative role in what Steward thought of as purely "scientific" and "objective" lines of argument. Personal memories from his early life made certain ideas real to him, imbuing them with felt truth. His theory also provided a way of ordering and making sense of his social experiences as a man, especially those that took place during a critical time in his life, which he remembered as a period of transformation and self-definition.[29]

In saying this, I am not asserting that cultural ecology was "subjective" and "unscientific" because Steward, like everyone, had values and beliefs that made complete "objectivity" unlikely. Rather, my aim is to demonstrate that autobiographical memory and the personal construction of meaning had a direct and creative influence on Steward's intellectual work as an anthropologist, most obviously by channeling his attention, sensitizing him to certain aspects of human social life, and deflecting his attention from others. Like every person, his vision was highly selective, as were his memories, and this necessarily influenced his theoretical work. My main point is that his work was not simply an act of the imagination nor primarily a product of empirical research; instead, his most important concepts and ideas derived largely from autobiographical memory. Memory images of known people and places and events from his own life, *not* images of imagination, played the major part in the construction of cultural ecology.[30]

* * *

What began as a type of life-history project—examining Steward's life to understand how a social theory develops—took on a life of its own and evolved finally into a hybrid form: part life history and intellectual biography, part exploration of autobiographical memory and theory making, part ethnography of the profession during its classic era. Giving attention to gender relations in the profession at midcentury, and in Steward's social world before he entered anthropology, proved especially instructive. His theoretical perspective on human social relations unmistakably expressed and gave greater meaning to his own memories and social experience of manhood. The exclusion of women from full participation in the social worlds that men inhabited—in Steward's case, the ranch and school at Deep Springs, the universities he attended, and his profession—helped to define manhood during that era. Not surprisingly, this exclusion of women from the center, their relegation to the social margins, also found expression in his theoretical ideas.

I catch glimpses of Julian Steward's world in his letters and journals and in Jane Steward's and Dorothy Nyswander's personal memories—from a time when just a handful of anthropologists, few of them women, had worked in the Great Basin; when anthropology was still a "guild occupation," and several hundred, not thousands, of people gathered for the yearly meetings of the American Anthropological Association; when California had a population of three million, not more than thirty million.[31] In later life, Steward expressed dismay at many of the changes, especially the loss of the California he had known so well as a young man. Owens Valley had a new economy based on tourism. West of the Sierra Nevada, the once open land along the Pacific Coast had been bulldozed, subdivided, and paved to accomodate the relentless population growth.

A few years before he died, and after decades spent living in the East and Midwest, Steward confessed to feeling "terribly homesick" whenever he looked at his photographs of the desert and the Sierra Nevada.[32] Professional ambition had led him back to the East some thirty-five years earlier, at the age of thirty-three, but he had returned with ambivalence, entering what he supposed a temporary exile. Commitment to his chosen field, one offering few chances for professional mobility, however, meant that he could exercise little choice about where he lived. He remained east of the Mississippi River for the rest of his life, save for some westward travel. But the desert West remained always in his mind's eye, the source of his most original ideas, the subject of much of his writing.

By his late sixties, beset by failing vision and declining health, Steward had given up his plan to move back to California. He continued to live on the prairie, a flat and spacious land where the immense sky arcs down to an earth horizon. To Steward, the prairie presaged the scale and colors of western terrain and sky, especially in the deserts. If it was a place too far removed from the mountains of the West, he found it happily distant from the East, the scene of his childhood years.

AN EASTERN CHILDHOOD

In 1902, the year of Julian Steward's birth in Washington, D.C., one of that city's most famous residents, John Wesley Powell, died. Powell had set out from his home on the Illinois prairie in the late 1860s to explore the Rocky Mountains. Departing from Wyoming Territory in 1869, he and a small band of men made one of that century's most celebrated journeys of exploration. After launching their wooden boats into the swift current of the Green River, they were soon swallowed up by the wilderness and within weeks were reported lost. But Powell and his companions survived their long journey, which took them through the fierce rapids and white water of the Green and Colorado Rivers and into the heart of uncharted territory. The journey ended when the men emerged from the Grand Canyon; they were the first explorers to reach it by water.[1]

Powell had spent his life up to then living in the East and Midwest, regions that showed a certain uniformity over large areas. By contrast, he saw a striking degree of variety in the West, in altitude, terrain, climate, and soil. As a native of the well-watered lands to the east, the aridity of the American West impressed him deeply as well. These themes, of variety and aridity, ran through his *Report on the Lands of the Arid Region of the United States,* submitted to the government in 1878. The renowned explorer was not only a geologist and a founder and director of the U.S. Geological Survey but also a self-taught anthropologist. In his early western journeys he encountered Shoshone, Ute, and Paiute Indians and began studying their languages and cultures. Eventually he founded the Smithsonian Institution's Bureau of Ethnology, later called the Bureau of American Ethnology. Powell remained director of the bureau until the time of his death. Three decades later, Steward would join the bureau as a research ethnologist, specializing in a portion of the vast area that Powell called the Arid Region.[2]

Alfred Kroeber, who would become Steward's teacher and a dominant figure in American anthropology, offered his first course, on North American ethnology, in 1902. (He had a new position as instructor at the University of California in Berkeley, where he taught for nearly forty-five years.) In the same year, the American Anthropological Association was established, with Kroeber and Powell among its founding members. Many of the members of this new scientific society specialized in North American ethnology and archaeology, and, in common with Kroeber and Powell, had worked in the American West. Very few members had graduate training in anthropology, which was still a fledgling academic discipline. In 1902 Kroeber was one of only nine men who had earned a Ph.D. in anthropology from an American university. Like Powell, many of the founding members were not academics, and their interest in North American Indians and anthropology grew out of a background in the sciences, especially natural history, which encompassed botany, zoology, and geology, as well as ethnology and archaeology by some definitions.[3]

Steward's own path into the field, which began with a boyhood interest in natural history, followed an early and authentically American tradition in anthropology. It was a native American tradition in a double sense, one dating back at least to Thomas Jefferson's excavations of an Indian site in Virginia, not far from his home at Monticello. Powell, still widely remembered as an explorer/ scientist during Steward's childhood years, belonged to the same tradition. Steward's graduate training would introduce him to a European-influenced anthropology, as taught by Franz Boas. Boas had emigrated to the United States from Germany in the 1880s, later joining the faculty of Columbia University, where he offered graduate training in anthropology; Kroeber was his first student at Columbia to earn a Ph.D.[4]

In 1902 anthropology was thus the preserve of a select number of men and a very few women, the most eminent of whom was Alice Fletcher. The only woman invited to the founding meeting of the American Anthropological Association, Fletcher was a contemporary of Powell's and had worked for many years with Omaha Indians and the Nez Percé. Later she lived in Washington, D.C., not far from a neighborhood where Steward's parents happened to reside for a year or two before his birth. Fletcher was drawn to the city because of her work in anthropology. Washington, along with Cambridge, Massachusetts, was one of two organizational centers for anthropology in nineteenth-century America. At the turn of the century, the federal capital retained its place as a center of the new field.[5]

Anthropology would remain practically unknown to the general public until decades later. The first generation of university-trained anthropologists, nearly all of them men and easterners, went west to study what they believed were the dying cultures of American Indians, and they published their research in monographs and journals that few people other than scholars read. In 1902 the West that captured the popular imagination was the one Owen Wister portrayed in his newly published and best-selling novel, *The Virginian,* as a land of cowboys without Indians. The many popular writers who soon followed Wister, adopting the genre of the western novel, wrote about a cowboy way of life that had nearly vanished by the early 1900s.[6]

Remnants of these earlier Wests remained, however, in the high desert of eastern California, a place where cowboys and Indians still lived. Most of the cowboys, in fact, were Indians, as Julian Steward would discover when he arrived there at age sixteen.

* * *

Julian Haynes Steward was the second child of Thomas and Grace Steward. At the time of his birth, on January 31, 1902, his parents had been married for six years. The marriage later ended in divorce. The years preceding the divorce were marked by Thomas Steward's gradual withdrawal from family life and at least one lengthy separation. Steward later wrote simply, "my father and I were not close." Behind those few words, however, lay a complex family history that presented Steward with opportunities as well as difficulties. Notably, his family background prepared him for professional success by providing important social connections and by fostering ambition and a strong work ethic.[7]

At the time of his marriage in 1895, Thomas Steward was thirty-seven years old and an examiner in the U.S. Patent Office. Grace Garriott was twenty-six when they married and, unusual for the times, also was a federal employee, having worked for nearly six years as a "lady clerk" in the Pension Office. Both the Pension and Patent Offices were then part of the Department of the Interior and were located only a few blocks from each other on F Street. How the couple met is unknown, but perhaps her brother, Edward Garriott, introduced them. Like Thomas Steward, Edward Garriott was rising rapidly through the ranks of the civil service in the 1890s.[8]

Grace Garriott's employment ended when she married. She gave birth to their first child, a daughter named Marion, in December 1896. When Julian, their second and last child, was born five years later, Thomas Steward, then in his midforties, had already been promoted to examiner-in-chief at the Patent Office. He remained there until he left the civil service in 1917, at the age of sixty, to practice as a patent attorney.

Julian Steward usually denied that his family background had influenced his career as an anthropologist. "My forebears," he wrote, "had little direct influence upon my scientific career." He did concede that his father "obviously had considerable aptitude in science," since "without a college education and through his own studies, he became Chief of the Board of Examiners of the United States Patent Office." It is a curious statement, and one that he evidently made to colleagues as well. The archaeologist Gordon Willey remembered that Steward, in speaking of his father sometime during the 1940s, "referred to him as a man of considerable intellectual potential who, had he been given the advantages of a university education, would have gone much farther."[9]

Although Thomas Steward did not have a college education in the sense of training in the liberal arts, he had earned an engineering degree and two law degrees from reputable universities. Highly educated for someone of his generation, he also achieved great success in his work, rising to a senior, secure position in the federal government. Indeed, he reached the top of his chosen profession and could have advanced further only by being appointed commissioner of patents. In keeping with his professional stature, Thomas Steward counted many distinguished scientists among his acquaintances and close associates. His name appeared with theirs, and with others prominent in the professions and business, in an early volume of *Who's Who in America*. Julian Steward did occasionally allude to his father's accomplishments—he wrote, for example, "His achievements, I suppose, made me implicitly assume that I, too, would pursue some profession"—but he still denied any influence. Perhaps he tended to diminish his father's professional success and influence because he saw him refracted through the lens of unhappy childhood memories.[10]

* * *

Thomas Gifford Steward, born in 1857 in New York State, came from a family line of New Englanders, Baptist ministers, and abolitionists. In 1876, two years after graduating from high school, he moved to Plano, Illinois, a small town thirty-five miles southwest of Chicago, where his father established a church. The Stewards had relatives in Plano, including a cousin who was a business associate of William Deering, of the Deering Harvesting Machine Company. That company later merged with four other harvesting machine companies, forming the industrial giant, the International Harvester Company, in 1902.[11]

Thomas Steward began to work as a machinist at the age of nineteen. He found employment in Plano soon after he arrived, very likely with the Deering Harvesting Machine Company. During the late 1870s, a time of economic depression, skilled workers at harvesting machine companies saw their wages fall at a rate that exceeded cost-of-living declines. This, along with periodic layoffs, may explain why Thomas Steward looked elsewhere for employment. After three years as a machinist, he moved to Washington, D.C., having been appointed from Illinois to the federal service. Family connections and political affiliations probably played a role in his appointment, as they so often did in that era before the introduction of competitive examinations for civil service positions. At twenty-two he began his long career with the government, initially as a clerk in the General Land Office of the Department of the Interior.[12]

At twenty-four, he earned a degree in civil engineering and entered the Patent Office, where he worked for six years as an assistant examiner. During that time he earned both a bachelor's degree and a master's degree in law.[13] No doubt like many ambitious young men in the capital, Thomas Steward saw that he could combine well-paid employment in the civil service with the opportunity for higher education and professional training. A law degree offered the prospects of professional mobility, higher social status, and financial security. During that era, young men who worked as clerks in government offices by day often attended university classes at night, and local universities assisted them by scheduling all classes after 4 P.M., when government offices closed for the day. Thomas Steward conformed to the profile for law students in Washington, D.C., in the 1880s: male, Anglo-Saxon, and a federal employee.[14]

His legal training, as well as his previous experience as a machinist, surely helped him rise through the ranks of examiners at the Patent Office. In 1887, at the age of thirty, he was appointed principal examiner; ten years later, on the recommendation of the commissioner of patents, President William McKinley appointed him examiner-in-chief. As examiner-in-chief, he ascertained whether claimed inventions met the three tests of patentability still used today: novelty, utility, and invention.[15]

Thomas Steward held a position in the Patent Office from 1881 until 1917, years of dramatic technological change in which many significant inventions were patented in the United States. Shortly before he began to work as an examiner, Alexander Graham Bell invented the telephone (in 1876) and Thomas Edison invented the incandescent lamp (in 1879). During his tenure in the Patent Office, many new technologies that transformed twentieth-century life received patents: automobiles, aircraft, radio, motion pictures, and the phonograph, to name only a few. Thomas Steward's career roughly coincided with a growth in American technology following electrification; the new technologies virtually created a second industrial revolution by fostering new industries and changing production processes in old industries.

Ten years after Thomas Steward joined the Patent Office, it celebrated its hundredth anniversary. Held in Washington, D.C., in April 1891, the centennial commemorated both the founding of the Patent Office and a century of significant technological innovation. Employees of the Patent Office, including Thomas Steward, and many luminaries attended the centennial and heard one of the speakers, a senator, declare that seven American inventions surpassed the pyramids of Egypt as wonders of the world: " 'The cotton-gin; the adaptation of steam to methods of transportation; the application of electricity in business pursuits; the harvester; the modern printing press; the ocean cable [transatlantic telegraph], and the sewing machine.' "[16] Whatever their merits as judged against the pyramids, these new technologies did transform the American economy and social life.

Visitors to the Patent Office building could see display models of many significant American inventions.[17] In addition, in the mid-nineteenth century the Patent Office also carried out scientific research and, for many years, was responsible for some functions later assumed by the Department of Agriculture, the Smithsonian Institution, and the Weather Bureau. Because it sponsored scientific expeditions, the Patent Office accumulated a large collection of specimens and artifacts, much of which related to North American natural history and native peoples. A patent commissioner in the 1850s considered the collection too significant to keep in storage, and he convinced Congress to appropriate money to display the collection. A trip to the Patent Office soon became requisite for visitors to the city. William Henry Holmes, who later became a prominent anthropologist, visited the museum around 1871, when he saw effigies of two Indian "chiefs" in traditional dress, an arresting sight that he later called his "'first lesson in ethnology.'"[18]

If the young Julian Steward ever saw this collection, it may have provided his own first lesson about scientific expeditions, and not only about ethnology. A career as an explorer/scientist appealed to him even before he chose anthropology as his profession. In childhood and adolescence, he knew of government scientists who had taken part in expeditions to the remote reaches of the American West. The museum at the Patent Office exhibited the type of material that Steward would later collect in that very region.

Perhaps his father, whose office was in the same building, took him to see the museum or, more likely, his mother did. She had an enduring attraction to the American West, and although this centered on landscape, she did appreciate the Indian arts.[19] Those interests might have drawn her to the museum as early as the 1880s, when she worked at the nearby Pension Office.

* * *

Grace Garriott was born near St. Louis, Missouri, in 1869, a few months before Powell and his men set off on their river journey to the Grand Canyon. In that same year, the transcontinental railroad was completed, opening up the West to a flood of settlers from the East and Midwest. Her father, P. Addison Garriott, a Virginian, claimed French Huguenot and English ancestry. As a child, her mother, Maria Bennett Garriott, emigrated with her family from England. Maria and her husband were living near Cincinnati when their son, Edward Bennett Garriott, was born in 1853. Four of their children reached adulthood: Edward, the eldest, and three daughters, of whom Grace was the youngest.

Grace's family had wandered slowly westward in the years before her birth in the wake of the advancing frontier. Moving westward across Indiana, the family settled briefly in southern Illinois. They reached the Mississippi River in the 1860s, coming to rest in the small town of Kirkwood, Missouri, where Grace was born.[20]

Her father established himself in Kirkwood as "a moderately successful businessman," to use Steward's own words about his grandfather. The family's prosperity allowed it to provide Edward with a good education. After leaving primary school, he attended a preparatory school for a year, then enrolled for three years at an academy of Washington University in St. Louis. He continued his education at an academy in Chicago, earning a bachelor of science degree. By 1874, at the age of twenty-one, Edward was living in Washington, D.C., employed as an assistant weather observer by the Signal Corps, a precursor of the U.S. Weather Bureau. He had evidently been appointed to federal service from Chicago, and he remained a legal resident of Illinois for the rest of his life. His career in meteorology, then a new science, would span about thirty-five years. Before his untimely death in 1910, he had reached the top of his profession and held the position of chief forecaster for the Weather Bureau. His death was reported in the *New York Times*.[21]

Edward was sixteen years old when Grace was born, and he probably left for Chicago within a year or two. Grace spent her childhood in Missouri, where she attended primary school and graduated from high school. She continued her education at a "normal school" in St. Louis that trained teachers; after graduating she taught in a primary school for a year. By 1889, at the age of twenty, she had moved to Washington, D.C., probably with her parents. Grace worked briefly as a schoolteacher but then found a better-paying position with the federal government in the General Land Office. After several months there, she accepted employment as a "lady clerk" with the Pension Office, where she worked for six years, from 1889 until she married.[22]

The prospect of federal employment may well have drawn her to Washington, just as it attracted so many young men. Female clerks in government offices earned among the highest salaries then available to women. They earned less than male clerks, but much more than women employed as public schoolteachers, one of the few occupations then open to educated, middle-class women. Grace's salary as a clerk in the Pension Office was three times the average salary of a schoolteacher during that era. The term *clerk* now has somewhat different connotations, but until the beginning of the twentieth century it referred within the federal government to the more highly paid positions.[23]

In 1890 the federal government employed several thousand women as clerks. Their number had grown dramatically since the Civil War, when the shortage of male labor led the Treasury Department to hire a few women. Before the war, and before the invention of the typewriter, several women had held irregular positions as clerk-copyists in the Patent Office, where they made "fair copies" of letters and documents.[24] After the war, in 1873, the gunsmith E. Remington and Sons manufactured and sold the first widely used typewriter. The federal government quickly adopted this new technology, with the Patent Office appropriately in the lead. By the late 1870s, the commissioner of patents had already installed a typewriter in his own office. Soon, and despite loud protests, he ordered them put into all divisions of the Patent Office as quickly as typists could be hired.[25]

When the Civil Service Commission was established in 1883, typewriters were common in government offices, and the Commission began to require tests for typist positions and others. Women thus had the chance to qualify for some of the same positions as men by taking tests that measured their skills in a stan-dardized way. The new system of hiring, based on competitive examinations, superseded the old system of patronage, which had largely excluded women. Because women could not vote, they could not directly repay political patron-age.[26]

Grace presumably took the civil service examination that was required for many positions with the federal government after 1883. She never learned to type, and did other sorts of clerical work instead. Like her, most of the women who worked as federal clerks during the latter part of the nineteenth century were single, white, and from middle-class backgrounds. They routinely listed family financial need as their reason for seeking employment with the government. Sometimes the need was urgent and exteme, especially for households without a male wage earner due to disability, desertion, or death.[27]

Grace's father, still alive but in his late sixties, probably no longer earned an income. She undoubtedly worked to help support her parents and herself. Un-like so many of the women employed by the federal government, however, she enjoyed a measure of security because of her brother's professional success. Edward Garriott, rising steadily through the ranks of the federal service, had already been promoted from assistant weather observer to meteorological clerk. He would soon attain the position of forecaster. In 1890 Grace and her parents lived with Edward and his family on Corcoran Avenue, NW.[28]

Perhaps her own ambitions, as well as family financial needs, led Grace to leave teaching and, following her brother's example, to seek employment with the federal government. Few middle-class women worked outside the home in the 1890s, either before or after marriage, and women who did so risked social disapproval. Middle-class women had limited means of earning income aside from teaching school or taking in boarders. Even after she married Thomas Steward, who held a secure and well-paying position in the Patent Office, she showed a marked interest in earning money. In 1900, five years after they mar-ried, the Steward household included three boarders.[29]

When Grace gave up her position with the Pension Office she was probably responding to some combination of personal, social, and political circumstances. In the 1890s, during two periods of economic depression, the number of women in federal service suddenly dropped and the number of men rose sharply. Grace may have had to leave government employment during the hard times of Presi-dent Grover Cleveland's second administration: a financial panic soon after Cleveland took office in 1893 brought in its wake a serious depression. Even more likely, her impending marriage required her to give up her position, for reasons of social convention, government policy, or both. She resigned in October 1895, the same month that she married Thomas Steward. The competition for gov-ernment jobs in Washington had grown so intense that some departments pro-hibited the employment of more than one member of a family.[30] Both Grace and Thomas worked for the Department of the Interior.

Grace Garriott Steward lived during an era when it was thought unseemly for women to have ambitions for themselves and when they had few opportunities to advance in life except through marriage. She married a man who, at least in outward respects, closely resembled her own brother. Thomas Steward was roughly the same age as Edward, he worked in the civil service, and he had professional and social connections to prominent scientists and senior bureaucrats in Washington. It seems, however, that he also had a temperament and an approach to life that she finally found incompatible with her own.

The principle that opposites attract may have brought the couple together, but their differences finally drove them apart. Thomas Steward appears to have been a rather taciturn and practical man who appreciated the logic of machines and legal principle. Grace Steward, in contrast, was a voluble and sociable woman, deeply religious and remembered as "quite firm in her ways." She was drawn to the arts and admired the beauty of the natural world. It was in part a passion for landscape that attracted her to the Far West. She also held the unshakable conviction that her life would improve vastly if only she lived there, a certainty perhaps rooted in the "geography of hope," to borrow an apt phrase.[31]

The young Grace Garriott might have preferred to go west when she left Missouri, or perhaps her intense longing for life in the Far West was simply a reaction against an unhappy marriage and her life in the East. Whatever her personal ambitions and regional preferences, they would have been difficult for a young woman to sustain before marriage and equally difficult after marrying a successful federal bureaucrat. Thomas Steward remained a resident of Washington throughout his career. Grace Steward eventually left him, however, and left for the West, along with their children. She had already transferred many of her own interests and ambitions, as well as a very middle-class work ethic, to both children.

* * *

Julian Steward rarely spoke about his childhood. Robert Murphy remembered that although Steward liked to reminisce, he rarely mentioned his earliest years and expressed no fondness for Washington. When he was in his forties and working at the Smithsonian, Steward told Gordon Willey that the Washington of his childhood had the qualities of a small town, with nearby woods and ravines where he liked to play. Jane Steward, Steward's second wife, recalled hearing him talk about the pleasures of spending weeks at a camp on the Chesapeake Bay in summer, living the outdoor life. An enthusiastic Boy Scout, Steward was an Eagle Scout by the age of fifteen. He had a deep interest in the natural world, in all branches of natural history, but he confessed to a certain indifference toward most of his schoolwork.[32]

Over the many years of their marriage, he occasionally spoke about other memories. A difficult relationship with his mother, which Jane Steward knew about firsthand, dated from early childhood. He remembered his father as very remote and recalled that as his parents' marriage slowly deteriorated his father retreated more and more from family life, spending most of his time at work and at the Cosmos Club, a private men's club he joined in 1904. His brother-in-law, Edward Garriott, joined the Cosmos Club in 1900 and may have acted as his sponsor for membership.[33]

Founded in 1878, the Cosmos Club was yet another of Powell's organizational ventures.[34] As director of the newly created U.S. Geological Survey, Powell knew many of the scientists in government service, and he hoped that the Cosmos Club would help to bridge some of the divisions then emerging in American science. The Cosmos Club provided a place where Washington's scientists and other intellectuals could meet to exchange ideas informally and sociably. By 1882 the club had moved to comfortable quarters in Lafayette Square, occupying a house that had once belonged to Dolly Madison. It remained there for the next seventy years. The Cosmos Club quickly became a meeting place for men who belonged to the city's intellectual elite and the venue for meetings of Washington's learned societies.[35]

In many respects, Thomas Steward and Edward Garriott typified the Cosmos Club's membership.[36] Most of the members—male, Anglo-Saxon, highly educated, and well established in their professions—had achieved prominence by engaging in some sort of scientific work. From the beginning, scientists in government service formed the core of the Cosmos Club, although many of the members also served on the faculties of the city's universities. According to the bylaws, club membership was restricted to men who had done "meritorious work in science, literature, or the fine arts" or who were "distinguished in a learned profession or in public service." High-ranking government officers, such as Thomas Steward, qualified on the basis of public service.[37]

As his marital problems grew worse, Thomas Steward spent more and more of his time in the company of such men at the Cosmos Club. The club maintained a dining room and sleeping quarters for members, and these amenities aided his retreat from family life. (By coincidence, the writer Zora Neale Hurston worked there briefly as a waitress when she was young, while he was a member. Later, at Columbia University, she studied anthropology with Franz Boas; but as an African American woman, she was largely excluded by the academic world.)[38]

Even before Thomas Steward's final retreat began, he and his son had already had one lengthy separation from each other. Between the ages of six and eight, from 1908 to 1910, Julian lived in St. Louis with his mother and maternal relatives and attended primary school there.[39] In 1909, Julian's maternal grandmother, Maria Garriott, died at the age of eighty. Less than a year later, in 1910, his uncle, Edward Garriott, died unexpectedly in Washington; he was fifty-seven years old. In 1911 his maternal grandfather died, and in that same year, at the age of forty-two, Grace Steward became a Christian Scientist. Her son was just nine years old. Perhaps the loss of three family members in three years made

Grace receptive to new ideas about the nature of life, illness, and death and influenced her to join the Church of Christ, Scientist. Mary Baker Eddy, known as the discoverer and founder of Christian Science, also died in 1910, in the period between the deaths of Grace Steward's brother and father.[40]

Despite her unwavering commitment to the tenets of Christian Science, neither her children nor her husband ever shared her religious beliefs or joined the church. Thomas Steward listed his political and religious affiliation in the 1910 edition of *Who's Who* as "Republican. Baptist." Those two words, given their context, read as a strong assertion of identity; many of the entries that precede or follow his are silent on the matter of religion and politics. His family's abolitionist background probably explains the strong affiliation with the Republican party. (Julian Steward, in contrast to his father, and perhaps in reaction against him, was a lifelong Democrat.) The family's commitment to the Baptist faith had also remained firm for generations.[41]

Christian Science, founded in 1879, is probably most widely known for its radically antimaterialist perspective and the practice of spiritual healing. According to the tenets of Christian Science, the usual, materialist perception of the world is in error; matter is not "real" but is a limited mode of human perception; and disease is delusion, a product of false belief in the world of matter. While it appears to depart from orthodox Christian theology in some respects, Christian Science represents a profound break with scientific materialism. Grace Steward probably could not have chosen a religion more at odds with her husband's direction in life, his intense interest in science and technology.[42]

Thomas Steward paid scant attention to Christian Science, always preferring plain science instead. To use Eddy's own terms, he accepted "material science" rather than "Divine Science." He may well have agreed with archaeologist J. Walter Fewkes, a fellow member of the Cosmos Club and a government scientist who served as director of the Bureau of American Ethnology. Fewkes considered the religion of his own wife, a devout Christian Scientist, as "neither Christian nor scientific." This view prevailed widely at a time when the membership of the Church of Christ, Scientist was growing rapidly and gaining converts from other denominations.[43]

Despite opinion to the contrary, Grace Steward, like others of her new faith, certainly considered herself a Christian. She had joined a religious sect that continued to stir controversy, however, and not only because of its unusual tenets about sickness and healing. Mary Baker Eddy had also written extensive commentary on the Book of Genesis, affirming the equal worth of men and women; and she had established a church that allowed women to participate with men at every level. Only a few years earlier, Mark Twain had mounted a caustic attack against Eddy; and Willa Cather had helped write a widely read biography of the woman who controlled what Cather called "the largest and most powerful organization ever founded by any woman in America." It was to become a worldwide religious denomination.[44]

Unlike Twain, Cather showed some sympathy for Eddy's ambition and even a trace of admiration for her success. But she considered the denial of materiality a philosophical absurdity, describing it as "the revolt of a species against its own physical structure; against its relation to its natural physical environment. . . ." And she also viewed Christian Science as highly suspect because of the economic opportunities it offered followers, many of whom were women: specifically, the chance to gain a livelihood as a spiritual healer. (Grace Steward never attained the status of a practitioner, who helps patients heal by using prayer, but she did eventually earn some income as a Christian Science nurse.)[45]

Like his father, Steward never joined the church, but his mother's religious beliefs did have a great influence on him during childhood and later in life. The effects included an abiding interest in what his mother seemed to deny: to borrow Cather's words again, the human "relation to its natural physical environment." That interest took root very early despite, or in reaction against, his mother's beliefs. What Steward remembered most clearly years later was her repeated insistence that microbes were "not real" and that he should disregard what he had learned at school. His teacher had presented the general findings of well-known scientists, men such as Louis Pasteur, Edward Jenner, and Robert Koch, who helped to revolutionize scientific understandings of disease. By the early twentieth century, scientists had offered empirical evidence that microscopic pathogens caused a range of often fatal illnesses, from smallpox and tuberculosis to malaria and yellow fever—conclusions that were very much at odds with Grace Steward's convictions.

One day, as part of a science lesson at school, Julian Steward saw bacteria with the aid of a microscope. Unlike his classmates, he faced a troubling dilemma as a result of using that microscope: he could believe what he saw with his own eyes or he could believe what his mother told him; he could identify with his father, who endorsed science and technology, or he could identify with his mother, who did not. His parents' conflict, and his own inner conflict, mirrored then prevailing cultural notions that associated science, technology, and intellect with men, and religion, morality, and emotion with women. A family conflict that overtly centered on science and religion thus involved—perhaps unconsciously and more profoundly—gender relations and gender identity.[46]

In Steward's memory, his mother asserted rather than explained her views, invoking the authority and the words of Eddy. She often recited a passage known as the "Scientific Statement of Being" from Eddy's book about prayer-based healing, *Science and Health: With Key to the Scriptures:* "There is no life, truth, intelligence, nor substance in matter. All is infinite Mind and its infinite manifestation, for God is All-in-all. Spirit is immortal Truth; matter is mortal error. Spirit is the real and eternal; matter is the unreal and temporal. Spirit is God, and man is His image and likeness. Therefore man is not material; he is spiritual."[47]

It is certainly true that many followers of Christian Science devote years to studying the writings of Eddy, in order to grasp complex and subtle ideas about the nature of reality and the material world. The ideas are not necessarily explained easily or understood readily. Perhaps Grace Steward resorted to quoting from *Science and Health* for that reason, or because she had a nineteenth-century sensibility about teaching children, or because faith, not intensive study, had led her to accept the tenets of Christian Science. Or she may simply have followed the guidance offered in *Science and Health:* "The entire education of children should be such as to form habits of obedience to the moral and spiritual law, with which the child can meet and master the belief in so-called physical laws, a belief which breeds disease."[48]

Her newfound religious beliefs also influenced how she treated her son when he felt ill. Christian Science teaches that spiritual healing does not depend on experience or age, and that prayer can heal infants and small children as readily as adults.[49] Beginning at some point in his childhood and continuing over the years, Grace Steward routinely insisted that only prayer led to healing. She had no use for medicine, a product of material science, of mortal error. Under those circumstances, a sick child, especially one not raised in the faith but abruptly introduced to it, might well give more attention to his mother's actions, or apparent inaction, than to her words. It might seem to him that she placed more importance on her religious beliefs than on taking care of him. He could not fail to notice that his classmates and friends, who belonged to other religious denominations, received medical treatment when they fell ill.[50]

Julian Steward eventually intellectualized, displaced, and denied what appear to have been painful and conflicting feelings involving childhood fears about sickness and loss of care and his parents' disagreements.[51] Despite some early, telling memories about his mother—specifically, of inattention and absence even before she converted—he blamed and rejected her religion. Not surprisingly, given his parents' opposing views and the times, he thought in terms of science versus religion, adopting a framework then current among supporters and opponents of Darwin's theory of evolution. By the time the controversy about evolution escalated into the well-known Scopes trial in 1925, Steward had resolved the issue of science and religion, at least intellectually, by concluding that an "inherent moral order of the universe is a philosophical fiction."[52]

He would always equate religion with dogma and irrationality. When his skepticism, his habit of questioning, collided again and again with his mother's certainty and habit of quoting Mary Baker Eddy, he angrily concluded that she accepted dogma at the expense of reason.

* * *

By Steward's own admission, put in writing more than once, he was a "mediocre" student in primary school and high school, "quite undistinguished owing to lack of motivation."[53] From 1907 until 1912, when he was ten years old, the Steward family lived on Monroe Street, NW, and he attended the John Eaton School. In 1912 or 1913, they moved to Macomb Street in Cleveland Park, then a prosperous suburb favored by families of Washington's professional and upper middle classes. In 1915 his sister, Marion, left Washington to attend the University of Michigan, and Julian entered Central High School. He continued there until his junior year in 1918.[54]

Although an indifferent student, he found much to interest him outside of school. The woodlands and open fields around Washington, which had not yet yielded to concrete and asphalt, gave children countless places for escape and exploration outdoors. Rock Creek Park, which was only blocks away, offered high cliffs and forested ravines, and a winding, narrow creek that eventually spilled its waters into the Potomac River. A favorite park of Theodore Roosevelt, it remained largely in a wild state. Julian's mother encouraged his interest in the natural world, and especially an appreciation of its beauty. He began to draw and, despite having no formal training in art, developed a good eye for line and color in nature. Western landscapes would inspire his best artistic works—and his most lasting intellectual works.[55]

Later in life, Steward wrote that he was led to a career in science in part because of "a love of nature and the out of doors acquired most likely through the influence of my mother." He amended that in another draft of the essay, eliminating any mention of his mother and saying simply that as a child he had "a very generalized interest in natural history." He credited other, unnamed people more than his parents with influencing his life. In both primary school and high school, as he recalled, he had known the children of congressmen and professionals. His contact with the children of such successful men, he decided, gave him an "aspiration toward an intellectual professional life."[56]

From a rather young age, play seems to have taken second place to work in Julian Steward's life. He earned money for several years by delivering two daily newspapers and establishing a route for the *Saturday Evening Post* and other magazines. At the age of fifteen, he found a summer job with the Department of Agriculture and was assigned to the dairy division of the Bureau of Animal Industry. He also spent a month in 1917, soon after the United States entered World War I, working on a farm in Virginia.[57]

Years later, Steward called 1918 "the turning point" in his life. Events of the previous year, while difficult to reconstruct, led to some decisive changes. In 1917 Marion left the University of Michigan after studying there for two years, and she never returned to complete her undergraduate degree. She held a temporary civil service appointment with the U.S. Post Office before finding a position as a clerk and typist in the fall with the Office of the Quartermaster General. Thomas resigned from the Patent Office in July 1917, at the age of sixty. He immediately established a patent law practice with another attorney. Julian was employed all summer, returning to high school in the fall. Grace began looking for employment herself; by November 1917, because of vacancies created by clerks moving to the War Department, she had secured a position in the Department of Agriculture.[58]

After twenty-two years of marriage, Grace and Thomas Steward separated sometime in 1917, largely at her instigation. Their religious differences influenced her decision to some degree. Despite Eddy's prescriptive words against divorce ("After marriage, it is too late to grumble over incompatibility of disposition," and "The nuptial vow should never be annulled"), Grace may have fastened on one particular sentence: "Separation never should take place, and it never would, if both husband and wife were genuine Christian Scientists." She undoubtedly also knew that Eddy had divorced one of her husbands, a fact that critics rarely failed to mention, although they did not always explain the circumstances.[59]

Apparently, Grace and Thomas reached a financial settlement that involved selling the house on Macomb Street, with part or perhaps all of the proceeds going to Grace. Thomas did not make regular financial contributions to support his son in the years that followed; the settlement apparently included funds for that purpose.[60] Grace seems to have concluded very quickly, however, that she might need most of it to support herself. Her son's own words suggest this, as do some of her actions during that period. Even before he had turned sixteen, Julian wrote that he wished "to become self-supporting as soon as possible," a rather singular wish for someone of his age and social class. He made that statement in a letter expressing his interest in Deep Springs, a newly established college preparatory school, improbably located in an obscure desert valley directly north of Death Valley.[61]

Sometime during 1917, Grace Steward had heard about Deep Springs and urged her son to apply for admission. The school charged no tuition, provided room and board, and offered college scholarships for a select number of young men, most of whom were from socially or professionally prominent Anglo-Saxon families.[62] Its purpose was to recruit young men of good character, ability, and intelligence and to train them for a life of humanitarian service, a life in which they would, in the words of school founder L. L. Nunn, "'uplift mankind from materialism to idealism, to a life in harmony with the Creator.'"[63] No doubt the expressed purpose of the school, as well as its financial benefits and location in the West, appealed to Grace. She may also have seen Deep Springs as an opportunity for her son because her own brother had attended a preparatory school, a prelude to further education and his highly successful career with the federal government.

Julian Steward wrote a letter of application in early January 1918, just before his sixteenth birthday. "At the suggestion of Mr. Sidney Walcott," he began, "I am writing to you for information in regard to your school and to find out what prospect there is for me to be admitted and how soon I can hope to enter."[64] The Walcotts were a prominent family in Washington. Sidney S. Walcott was the son of Charles D. Walcott, a geologist, a paleontologist, and the leading member of Washington's scientific community. Charles Walcott had served for more than a decade as the head of the U.S. Geological Survey after Powell's retirement in 1894; he served as secretary of the Smithsonian Institution for twenty years, directing it from 1907 until his death in 1927. Walcott, a longtime member of the Cosmos Club, and once its president, undoubtedly knew Thomas Steward. He also counted Nunn as a close friend.[65]

Sidney Walcott belonged to Telluride Association, an educational foundation established by Nunn in 1911, six years before Deep Springs opened its doors to students. In 1918, Walcott was informally recruiting students for Deep Springs from the families of Washington's professional and upper middle class.[66] A report on the school in the early 1920s noted: "Deep Springs offers free tuition, not that the parents may be spared the burden of their son's education, but for the favorable reaction it arouses in the student's mind. . . . There is an obligation to fulfill a trust. People of means are more responsive to this than are the poor. Wealth is not a *sine qua non,* but it is a further qualification."[67]

Steward's family, while not wealthy, did belong to the socially conservative and financially secure middle class that comprised the upper ranks of Washington's bureaucracy. His father's professional status and membership in the Cosmos Club gave the family certain social connections that led Nunn and his associates to take note of Julian's letter. His parents' marital problems were not yet generally known. (Their separation, once made public, compromised the family's social position at a time when divorce was very rare and highly stigmatized within the white middle class; it also spelled the end of the children's financial security.) Julian soon received a reply suggesting that he send more information about himself and promising an interview with Nunn or a colleague by March 1918. His enduring and unhappy memory of the event centered not on the interview itself but on his mother's anxious demands that he make a good impression. He probably did not understand that the outcome of the interview—successful, as it happened—had such a direct bearing on her own financial concerns.[68]

In May 1918, even before his school term had ended, Julian Steward boarded a train bound for California in Washington's Union Station. His mother had arranged for him to have a lower berth by a window because she wanted him to see the landscape, and she also presented him with a camera.[69] Within weeks of his departure, Grace Steward requested a transfer from her position with the Department of Agriculture in Washington to one with the branch office in Los Angeles. Soon after, Thomas Steward, who was no longer a federal employee but surely retained some of his connections with high-ranking bureaucrats, interceded on her behalf. He explained to Department of Agriculture officials that his son was "living in the vicinity of Los Angeles" (in truth, more than two hundred miles away) and that his wife wished to live nearby.[70]

Finding that there was little prospect of a position in the Los Angeles office because she had no skills as a typist or stenographer, Grace Steward adopted a different strategy. She requested a transfer from the Department of Agriculture to the Department of the Interior, specifically to a field position in the West with the Indian Service. This unusual request unleashed a flurry of memoranda between the departments, most of which blandly cited "personal reasons" to explain why she wanted to transfer and government policy to explain why the transfer was impossible. Finally, in October 1918 Grace Steward broke the impasse by claiming that her request came "at the suggestion of her physician." This was probably a veiled illusion to divine guidance since she placed her faith in spiritual healing and enjoyed remarkably good health throughout most of her life.[71]

Somehow she won the sympathy of officials at the Department of the Interior. At the end of that month, having been offered a clerk's position at Klamath Agency in southern Oregon, she resigned from the Department of Agriculture. A report on her resignation was silent on the matter of her health, stating tersely that "Mrs. Steward . . . is tendering her resignation as, for personal reasons, she finds it impossible to live in Washington." Estranged from her husband and eventually divorced, Grace Steward may have found it impossible to remain in the socially conservative setting of Washington because of the stigma attached to her irregular marital status. The various employment forms she filled out during this period suggest this. The forms routinely asked for marital status, giving "married" or "single" as the only choices. She simply drew a line through the blank space as if the question was irrelevant.[72]

By mid-November 1918, less than two weeks after resigning from the Department of Agriculture, Grace arrived at Klamath Agency, headquarters of a reservation for Klamath Indians near the Oregon-California border. Taking the new position as assistant clerk with the Indian Service had meant accepting a lower salary, but her living expenses would be far less there than in a city. Meanwhile, Marion took up residence in San Franciso, following a transfer from her position as a clerk-typist at the Office of the Quartermaster General in Washington to a branch office of the War Department at Fort Mason. Julian, in the middle of his first year at Deep Springs, lived on a ranch in a remote valley several hundred miles from San Francisco, three thousand miles and a world away from Washington.[73]

Grace Steward's will, her ambition for her own life, and a fearlessness perhaps drawn from her new faith, had carried them all west.[74]

* * *

Any account of Julian Steward's childhood can be only a very partial one. The people who knew him well as a child are no longer alive, and most of the surviving records pertain to his adolescent years. Even Jane Steward's secondhand knowledge of his early life was quite limited because her husband so rarely spoke of the years before he went to Deep Springs. The details she offered do suggest that he retained unhappy memories of a difficult family life in Washington. Yet some of his childhood experiences, the ones he remembered in a positive light, appear to have affected his later theoretical work quite directly, defining its general focus: take, for example, the emphasis on technology (the family business, so to speak) and close attention to the natural world.

A very unhappy set of experiences also had a direct result: the splitting off of religion, which always remained peripheral in Steward's thought. To say this another way, denying religion a central place allowed him to avoid thinking deeply about it. The same experiences, and not only his later training in the natural sciences, probably helped incline him toward the use of observation, and an emphasis on the observable, in his work as an anthropologist. He trusted what he saw with his own eyes; he distrusted any system of ideas that he judged had the look of dogma. And he did not merely ignore those ideas but objected to them (and their adherents) with obvious feeling, ranging from scorn to anger. Still other remembered experiences of childhood influenced his intellectual direction in more or less subtle ways.

One of the few comments that Steward made in writing about his early life concerned leaving Washington, and in it he alluded to his parents' separation. "In 1918, at the age of 16," he wrote, "my home in Washington broke up and, having been selected as one of the"—and there the sentence abruptly ends. The next paragraph begins: "In 1918, at the age of 16, I was fortunate to be selected as one of the 7 or 8 new students at Deep Springs who would spend three years there and study. I left Washington where my grammar school and high school career had been mediocre to say the best, and left my home and family to which I was never to return."[75]

His own circumstances as he went west in 1918 might have produced a strong sense of kinship with the unnamed cowboy hero of Owen Wister's popular novel. The Virginian was "the standard American orphan, dislocated from family, church, and place of origin." Like the central character in so many of the westerns that he read over the years, the young Julian Steward was on his own, soon to inhabit a western landscape of desert and mountains and work in the company of other men. The world of westerns was, like the school and ranch that awaited him, Anglo-American and male, a world in which the few women and Indians occupied the social margins.[76]

Steward's departure for the West marked the end of what he always remembered as a rather forlorn childhood in the East.

CHAPTER 2

WEST TO DEEP SPRINGS

Julian Steward boarded a train at Union Station and left Washington in late May 1918. Arriving several days later in Reno, Nevada, he proceeded to nearby Mina, the northern terminus of the Carson and Colorado railway line. There he caught the narrow-gauge *Slim Princess,* a small and sturdy engine that pulled freight cars and a few diminutive coaches along narrow tracks. The rail line extended three hundred miles from its northern point in Nevada to Keeler, California, on the eastern shore of Owens Lake.[1]

From the swaying coach car, Julian saw the desert reaches of Nevada give way to the rich farming and ranching lands of eastern California's Owens Valley (see map 1). As the small train slowly made its way down the valley, he watched a passing landscape of lush fields of alfalfa and herds of sheep and cattle grazing in the valley's green pastures. He passed orchards filled with apple and peach trees and fields of newly planted potatoes and corn. The valley's irrigation system, and the abundant waters of the Owens River, had created this oasis in a desert land.[2]

The journey proceeded slowly with stops at Benton, Hammil, Piute, Laws, and finally a small station named Zurich. Little more than a train platform, Zurich stood two miles east of the town of Big Pine. Julian got off the train there and waited on a dusty platform for a truck from Deep Springs to meet him. From his vantage point in the valley, he saw the Sierra Nevada in full majesty to the west, with snow-swept peaks towering to fourteen thousand feet. To the east lie the massive White Mountains, which also rise to fourteen thousand feet, the highest range in the Great Basin, and south of them, the Inyo Mountains. In the years to follow, he and some of his friends from Deep Springs would climb peaks in both the Sierra Nevada and the White Mountains, in one instance trying to earn a place in the record books of California mountaineering.[3]

A fellow student from the East who had arrived months earlier remembered wearing a new suit for his journey. Herbert Reich, soon to be one of Julian's close friends and a partner in adventure, waited at the Zurich station for several hours. An old truck finally pulled up and the driver told him to get busy, new suit or not, loading freight for the ranch. Hoisting sacks of cement into the truck was his introduction to ranch life. The final leg of the trip, twenty-eight miles by road, took him across Westgard Pass at nearly seventy-three hundred feet. Looking west as the road wound upward, he could see the section of the Sierra Nevada known as the Palisades, with splintered peaks reaching higher than fourteen thousand feet. From Westgard Pass, the road descended some two thousand feet into Deep Springs Valley, high desert country, then deteriorated to "two ruts in the sand." Another student who arrived at Deep Springs at about the same time recalled very little about the road trip except that his blue serge suit had turned "dusty grey" by the time they reached the ranch.[4]

L. L. Nunn had bought the ranch only about a year before Julian Steward arrived there in 1918. A previous attempt to establish an innovative school had ended in failure in the East, less than two hundred miles south of the Stewards' home in Washington. In 1916, Nunn had purchased an estate that included a large tract of wooded land with a mansion set on the bluffs of the James River in Surry County, Virginia, near the town of Claremont. The house was to provide a temporary dormitory and classrooms for students—of whom there were nineteen when the Telluride Institute of Virginia was established in November 1916—but the school quickly foundered. In spring 1917 the United States entered World War I, and most of the students left to enlist as soldiers.[5]

Even without the war, the Telluride Institute might well have failed for reasons of structure and location. Nunn had envisioned a self-governing student body but the results proved "far from satisfactory," and within four months half of the young men had resigned. The others dropped out one by one until the school was finally disbanded in May 1917. Some conflict seems to have centered on a controversial ban on the use of alcohol and tobacco, a policy that many of the students ignored.

The school's proximity to the distractions of town life (notably, young women) posed another problem, at least in the eyes of Nunn, a lifelong bachelor. Some students evidently ignored the school's isolation policy, which prohibited them from going to town for social purposes. Although Surry County had, and retains to this day, a very rural character, the county seat was only about twelve miles away and Claremont was even closer at hand. As one student remembered, Nunn "didn't want us to mix up with the local girls," for fear of the effects on students' academic work and other consequences. Nunn wrote to this student and another in May 1917, "Reports of conditions at the house since I left indicate disregard by you of your obligations to me." He then grew specific: "No more girls are to be brought to the house."[6]

Yet another problem with the school's location involved its work program. Nunn bought land with the intention of having students do agricultural and mechnical work as well as academic study. He had grown up on a farm himself and had experienced the rigors and benefits of manual labor. As he envisioned the school at Claremont, students would devote five hours a day to outdoor work and the rest to classes and study. But the wet winter weather in eastern Virginia reportedly interfered. Day after day of fine, misting rain saturated the earth and, along with the pinching chill, discouraged outdoor work. The students spent most of the winter indoors and they began remodeling the house, which they did not find at all satisfying.[7]

The school at Claremont had precursors in the West, where Nunn had developed student training programs at the electric power plants he established as part of his Telluride Power Company. Nunn chose to return to the West in the year that the Telluride Institute failed. In 1917 he purchased a cattle ranch in a remote valley in Inyo County, California, near the Nevada border. The nearest towns, Big Pine and Bishop, were respectively located twenty-eight miles west and forty miles northwest of the ranch over a difficult road that was nearly impassable in some seasons. To the east, Goldfield and Tonopah, Nevada, lay sixty-five and ninety-five miles away. Aside from the ranch, Deep Springs Valley remained virtually uninhabited, assuring the isolation of students at this school.[8]

Besides the contrast in isolation, Claremont and Deep Springs could not have differed more in landscape and history. Claremont is situated near the southern boundary of the Tidewater region of Virginia. As the name implies, water defines this region of expansive salt marshes and broad tidal rivers that spill out into the Chesapeake Bay. Flat, well-watered, and thickly wooded, Tidewater was the site of the first permanent English settlement in North America. Jamestown, dating from 1607, lies across the James River from Surry County, only a few miles downriver from Claremont.

Before the English arrived, horticulture, hunting, and fishing had supported a large and sedentary population of Powhatan Indians. English settlers, and the Africans they brought to Virginia as slaves, quickly displaced most of the Indians, and profit-making enterprises soon transformed the landscape. The settlers established plantations along the rivers, replaced forest with permanent fields, and built spacious brick houses. They set about subduing the wilderness and reaping nature's bounty in the new colony, sending back reports that praised the land's fertility. By 1916 when Nunn bought the estate at Claremont, nearly all of the people in the area and throughout Tidewater were white and African American. The region's few Indians lived several counties away from Claremont. No wilderness remained, only a patchwork of open fields and new forests.[9]

Although Steward never visited Claremont, the region would have seemed familiar to him. He had grown up in Washington not far from the Potomac River, a tidal river that flows into the Chesapeake Bay, where he had spent several summers at camp. An avid naturalist, he could identify many of the trees, birds, and other wildlife of the eastern woodlands. Unlike Claremont, however, Deep Springs Valley offered a striking contrast to everything he had seen of the natural world to that point. Leaving the train station at Zurich, climbing up to the pass between the White Mountains and the Inyo Range, and then descending to Deep Springs Valley, he looked out on an alien landscape, the western border of the Great Basin.[10]

* * *

A vast expanse of sagebrush and mountains framed by a relentlessly blue sky, the Great Basin extends from the eastern face of the Sierra Nevada in California to the Wasatch Range near Salt Lake City. In a matter of days, Julian Steward had left the well-watered and wooded flatlands of the East far behind and found himself living in an arid, mountainous land of spare, even severe, beauty. Deep Springs Valley is just one of the countless high desert valleys that comprise the Great Basin, a region striking not only for its immense scale but also for the hundreds of mountain ranges that march north and south across it. Many of the ranges have peaks rising above ten thousand feet, and in this high country, even the valley floors may lie five or six thousand feet above sea level.[11]

Deep Springs Valley, at an elevation of about five thousand feet, is roughly oval in shape and encircled by mountains. Fifteen miles long and five miles wide at its maximum points, it encloses an area of some fifty square miles. The valley takes its name from a number of springs that border a shallow salt lake at its lower, southwestern end, miles away from the ranch at the upper end. The sparse vegetation runs to sagebrush, Indian rice grass, rabbitbrush, and salt grass. Among other wildlife, deer and antelope, jackrabbits, badgers, coyotes, mountain lions, bighorn sheep, and rattlesnakes live in the valley or surrounding mountains. All but the deer were new to the young easterner.[12]

The valley has also provided a home to people for at least three thousand years. Prehistoric sites give evidence of small groups of foragers who subsisted on wild plants and game. During the early historic era, Indians followed a way of life similar to their ancestors of a thousand years before. In the mid-nineteenth century, white miners arrived but soon left; a few ranchers replaced them. From 1917 most of the inhabitants lived at the valley's only ranch, the site of Nunn's unusual school. Indians continued to live in the valley while working at the ranch through the 1920s and perhaps the 1930s.[13]

According to one of the first students to arrive at Deep Springs in 1917, "There really wasn't much to see from the pass, . . . just a clump of trees." Shady cottonwoods surrounded the corrals and the weathered ranch buildings, which included several sheds and barns, most of board-and-batten construction. The house occupied by a previous owner and his family had been turned into the new school's dining room. A smaller building, converted for use as a kitchen, had been extended by means of a tent, and two Chinese cooks prepared meals there. Facing the improvised kitchen was a bunkhouse where the ranch superintendent and a cowboy lived. Another small building functioned as an office. Lacking a suitable building to use as a dormitory, for several months the students slept two to a bed in tents.

Along with the ranch, Nunn had also purchased the water rights to Wyman Creek, the valley's main source of fresh water. The creek, which rises in Wyman Canyon, provided water for the cattle and for irrigating the alfalfa fields, as well as for drinking and washing. The first students took their water directly from a ditch that ran behind the ranch buildings—"a poor arrangement," one of them recalled, "in that the cattle got it first. However, we thought little of this and, needless to say, survived." (But just two years later, another student remarked in a letter to his parents that "Phil drank from one of the irrigation ditches below the ranch and is now very sick with typhoid fever.")

During the first academic year at Deep Springs, 1917–18, about ten students lived at the ranch and helped build the school. They assisted carpenters, stonemasons from Salt Lake City, and various construction workers, more than thirty men hired that year. While the stonemasons set about quarrying stone, some of the students began transporting lumber, nails, and other building supplies from the railroad station at Zurich. The need for haste, the poor state of the road, and the steep incline from Westgard Pass made this a rather harrowing proposition. The trucks' brakes wore out so often that finally the student drivers grew tired of replacing them, and learned to drive without using brakes, saving them "for emergencies only." Chester Dunn, one of the drivers, ruefully remembered the day when he was "coming down the big wash . . . in a cloud of dust, at a God-awful speed and who should be waiting to meet me there but Mr. Nunn. He could really chew a fellow out when he caught him dead wrong."

The construction of the school began on a site about a quarter of a mile from the old buildings, which came to be known as the "lower ranch." One afternoon in 1917, Nunn drove around the area in his Buick, and then, as Dunn later recalled, he "finally stopped on a rise above the ranch, stuck his heel down on the ground, and said that the school would be built" there. He pointed out where he wanted the main building (housing the students' quarters, classrooms, a living room, and the library), the boardinghouse (dining hall and kitchen), and cottages for faculty members. These were built around a circular driveway and lawn, at the base of granite foothills, an area soon known as "the circle." By the time that other students arrived in late October 1917, the roof of the main building was under constuction, along with the walls of the boardinghouse and one cottage.[14]

By December the main building was moving toward completion. Sturdily constructed of masonry and stone, it had a sloping roof and broad, sheltering eaves that extended over the generous veranda at the front. The students left their tents and moved into the section of the main building that eventually housed the library. They sealed off one end of the space and used it at first for a dormitory, and then for a classroom as well. The room was furnished very simply with a carpet, a large table, and beds. Although the building still lacked plumbing, the students had two bathtubs and various other amenities, including an oil-burning stove for heat. That winter proved bitterly cold, with more snow than usual; but the temporary quarters, however warm, felt too confining for some of the students, who chose to sleep in the unfinished part of the building. It was a difficult winter for the livestock, and the students had to bring the cattle in from the range periodically to feed them from the haystacks.

At least one of the faculty members had arrived in fall 1917, prepared to teach, but he found no classrooms available. Classes finally began on January 2, 1918. Herbert Reich remembered courses in Spanish, social science, and public speaking, with weekly lectures in history. The students struggled to make up for lost time, in one case covering two years' worth of language study in six months. Their days were divided in two, with academic study and outside work each occupying half, six days a week. In letters home, they reported doing a variety of work outdoors: "digging ditches, taking down fence, digging post holes, cleaning up the garden area, chopping down willows, feeding cattle, and rolling rocks downhill for a new building."[15]

By spring 1918, following a memorable, knife-wielding quarrel between the two Chinese cooks, both men had departed. Three white women took their place, and one of them soon began to work as the laundress, replacing an Indian woman named Mary Harry. According to one of the early students, Mary Harry "did our laundry for us and did a very good job." Her husband, Captain Harry, served as irrigator for the ranch, and later did occasional odd jobs. Their son-in-law worked as a ranch hand, or cowboy. The family was Northern Paiute, and they were the first American Indians Julian Steward met. His acquaintance with Mary Harry would extend over nearly twenty years.[16]

When Julian Steward arrived at Deep Springs in May 1918, Captain Harry and his wife, together with their daughter, son-in-law, and a grandchild, were living outside the gates of the lower ranch, in what the students considered a makeshift shelter. The ranch manager, Mr. Woodhouse, and other staff members occupied living quarters at the lower ranch or in the boardinghouse. Except for the two Chinese cooks, whose tenure was brief, and the few Indian ranch hands, all other residents of the ranch were white, and they were newcomers to the valley.[17] Captain Harry and his family had lived there before the students arrived in 1917. The ranch probably occupied a very small place in their geography of the valley, which they called by two names, each one indicating an area around water. The lower end, with the springs and salt lake had a name meaning "Salt Place," while the upper end of the valley near Wyman Creek was Willow End. The valley had yet another name, translated as Lake Water.[18]

Mary Harry had grown up in other valleys in the region. She and her parents and brother left her childhood home after her maternal grandfather fell from a cliff while hunting eagles in the White Mountains. Following custom, the family expressed sorrow at his death by moving away. They went to live in Fish Lake Valley, across the White Mountains from Owens Valley. At about the age of six, she remembered, she heard of whites for the first time. As Steward later wrote, a report that "two white men with pack animals were passing through the country so frightened her people that they fled to the mountains and hid." Bitter experience had taught them that safety lay only in hasty retreat.[19]

Ten years later, when she was sixteen or seventeen, Mary met Captain Harry, then about thirty years old, at a festival. He was both Northern Paiute and Shoshone, and his first wife, a Shoshone, had died. After their families exchanged the prescribed gifts, Mary and her new husband went to live at a place near the current site of Oasis in Fish Lake Valley, along the California-Nevada border. By this time, white people had entered the valley and established several ranches.

Throughout the Great Basin, the introduction of grazing livestock always signaled a profound change in ecology, as the animals quickly decimated the native food plants that had sustained generations of native people. By late in the nineteenth century, gathering and hunting no longer provided full sustenance, and making a living required earning some money. As was then common among Northern Paiute and Shoshone men, Captain Harry found work at one of the ranches, but after several years he and Mary decided to move with their three children to Deep Springs Valley "to live, hunt, and gather seeds." They may have lived near the springs or Wyman Creek, at some distance from the ranch, until Captain Harry began to work there occasionally, irrigating the alfalfa fields.[20]

At some point, the family moved just outside the gates of the ranch. Students commonly referred to their living quarters as a *hogan* or *shack*, both misnomers, but Steward later used the term *camp*. The shelter that they built looked nothing like a Navajo hogan but may have followed traditional Northern Paiute principles of design and construction. The doorway was low, and one of the students remembered that he had to stoop to enter the house. Perhaps it bore little outward resemblance to traditional shelters because Mary and Captain Harry had built it from old boards, tar paper, and other leftover materials they found at the ranch. They did not bother to gather natural, less durable but more flexible, materials.[21]

The many years that they had spent subsisting as gatherers evidently helped them to see value and use in what their middle-class neighbors regarded as worthless. One student remarked that "[Captain] Harry treasured an old hammer" and used it to remove nails from the discarded boards that he found lying about the ranch.[22] It seems that some of what he gathered found use in the family's shelter. Despite the boards and nails, it was not very substantial in construction, probably because he and Mary, following tradition, did not regard it as permanent when they built it. As a child, Mary had lived in a grass house, a willow-frame structure covered with bundles of wild grass, which her parents abandoned after her grandfather's death. People also left shelters behind and built new ones during seasonal moves to other areas to gather wild seeds, roots, and pine nuts, and to hunt.[23] A change in Mary's circumstances would soon lead once again to a change in residence.

* * *

In almost every respect, Mary and Captain Harry's camp stood in telling contrast to the students' living quarters. By the time Julian Steward reached Deep Springs, the city-bred students had begun to enjoy some comforts. When the three women were hired to cook and bake and serve meals, the students got out "all the china, silver, tablecloths, and napkins" and began "eating in style," as one of them recalled, pleased to find the food far better than the previous fare. Months later, following the completion of the main building, the living room was furnished with leather chairs, mahogany tables, a piano, and oriental rugs and tapestries, most of which had been shipped to Deep Springs from Claremont along with the linens and silver.[24]

Many of the students came from comfortable, even affluent, families and from homes that may have had similar furnishings, but in this remote desert valley the living room seemed the height of luxury. Resolutely middle class and house-proud, they kept it in good order. Nunn's bookkeeper, Mr. McKay, soon learned not to toss his hat on one of the tables as he made his way to the office in the main building. Reich remembered that one day the students collected some thirty hats and scattered them on the chairs, tables, and piano. Then they sat down and waited for the culprit to appear. After this object lesson, McKay's hat never again appeared on a table.[25]

Julian Steward arrived at Deep Springs just as the students were completing the swimming pool, perhaps more aptly described as a swimming hole. Working on Sundays, they hitched a team of four horses to a Fresno scraper and dug a rectangular pit that they then filled with water from an adjacent irrigation ditch. They finished the pool in early June, as the desert heat began to escalate from merely intense to searing. "When we filled it for the first time," one of the students recalled, "we had a celebration: all the boys got into a big scrap and threw each other in." Julian used his camera to document the event, both the hard labor and the rowdy aftermath.[26]

By this time, the buildings around the circle had running water, brought from an irrigation ditch by an engine-driven pump. One of the students had to get up at five every morning to start the engine that drove the pump. Although the water often tasted of sheep dip, it seemed a major step forward to have tap water. The completion of the power plant followed in about six months. Even many years later, Steward remembered his own contribution—the installation of electrical wiring in the main building—with obvious satisfaction. Soon after arriving at Deep Springs he had been assigned to work as assistant to the electrician hired to put in the wiring, but after teaching him the bare essentials the electrician abruptly quit. Nunn instructed him to continue the work, which he did at first with a deep sense of trepidation and then with growing confidence. When he finally threw the switch, the lights went on.[27]

Sometime during fall 1918, a worldwide epidemic of influenza reached even the remote valley of Deep Springs. By the time it ran its course, a half million Americans and at least twenty million people elsewhere in the world had died. Several students, including Steward, came down with the flu, but none fell seriously ill. The students took care of one another. One of them, Cabot Coville, remembered that a Greek carpenter who had great difficulty speaking English worked at the ranch, and it soon became "very clear that he had a bad case." Along with Harvey Gerry, another student who had recovered quickly from the flu, Cabot cared for the carpenter and others who had fallen sick. They kept the carpenter isolated in a building at the lower ranch, and he died there one day while Harvey was with him.[28]

Responsibility was probably the most important of the lessons that Nunn sought to teach. By all accounts, he possessed a stern moral sense, highly idealistic but also pragmatic. He had bought the cattle ranch intending to give students a major role in running it, to teach them responsibility not simply as an ideal but as a lived, daily experience. He also limited the number of students admitted to Deep Springs to about twenty so that each might have a responsible position there. They learned quickly that evading an assigned duty had direct and harmful effects on their small community. If they neglected to milk the cows early in the morning, they had no milk for breakfast. If they forgot to split wood for the woodstove, they had no cooked food for dinner. If they failed to bring in the hay in summer, the cattle would go hungry in the winter.[29]

Early records from the school suggest that teaching responsibility through the work program was a constant concern. The work program itself constituted a central pillar in the school's unusual structure, which promoted student self-government. In one of his monthly academic reports to the student body in 1920, a faculty member reminded the students, "There has been a pile of rubbish outside the laundry door for two weeks. . . . The stove woodboxes must be filled on Sunday as well as other days. . . . The library needs constant attention." Although he did not name names, each task belonged to a particular student. Work assignments, which rotated periodically, were made by the labor commissioner, a position held by one of the students. Coville remembered being the first to hold this position at Deep Springs. As labor commissioner he also had dealings with the ranch manager, in order to coordinate the work of the students and the ranch staff.[30]

Nunn aimed to "educate the man as a whole," not only intellectually, and he conceived of the work program not in any sense as vocational training but rather as life training. Its purpose was to instill in students not only a deep sense of responsibility but also self-confidence, discipline, cooperativeness, and a certain kind of practical creativity. The students learned to work with their hands, to find solutions to mechanical and other everyday problems by using their own wits and any tools available. The isolation of Deep Springs together with the school's ethos meant that they had to depend on themselves and work together to solve problems. This sort of training, Nunn believed, would produce men well suited to lead others and to serve their country, educated men who would direct their careers toward a life of public service rather than simply material gain.[31]

Ironically, his conviction grew out of experiences that he had in the course of accumulating a large fortune. Born on a farm in northeastern Ohio in 1853, Nunn trained as a lawyer before he went to Colorado in 1880 at the age of twenty-seven. He settled in Telluride, a small mining town in western Colorado, north of Durango, where he soon prospered as a lawyer and businessman. Together with a few partners, he acquired several mines near Telluride but quickly discovered that they were expensive to operate. Transporting coal to the mines, located above the timberline, was prohibitively expensive, but transmitting electricity to them seemed impossible: direct current, although generated at Telluride, could not be transmitted over long distances. Nunn eventually found a way to provide his mines with electricity, soon after George Westinghouse built the world's first alternating current motor.[32]

Alternating current and long-distance transmission of electricity led Nunn into a new industry, generating hydroelectric power. Besides building the first plant to operate at Niagara Falls in upstate New York, he formed the Telluride Power Company and operated power plants throughout the West, from Colorado to Montana. Finding it difficult to recruit suitable engineers from the East to isolated outposts in the West, especially because they demanded high wages but often lacked physical stamina and practical skills, Nunn decided to hire promising young men with no more than some high school education and to train them himself. Most of his young employees had grown up in the remote areas around the power plants, and Nunn apparently realized that one way of attracting and retaining such "superior young men" was to offer them educational opportunities not otherwise available.[33]

His training program grew along with the Telluride Power Company and slowly took on an academic cast. Nunn became deeply interested in what motivates young men to learn and to work effectively together, and he came to believe that an isolated setting enhanced learning by keeping students away from the distractions of the larger world. He eventually concluded that a work-study program of education produced better results than the traditional, purely academic one: giving young men responsible jobs and an education led them to take more mature attitudes toward both. Robert Aird, who attended Deep Springs and became one of Julian Steward's close friends at Cornell, noted that Nunn's ideas about "community responsibility and public service naturally developed from this background."[34]

By 1905 the young employees at his power plant in Olmsted, Utah, spent several hours a day studying physics, mathematics, English, German, and history. Eventually, Nunn decided to offer college scholarships to his more promising employees, and he established Telluride Association at Cornell University in 1911. He had built a large house on the campus in 1910, and he gave this to Telluride Association as part of its trust. Cornell offered a rather fitting site for the association; unlike other Ivy League universities, its educational program had once combined manual work with academic study.[35]

Over the years, Nunn grew more interested in his educational ideas than in business pursuits, and by the time he established the schools at Claremont and Deep Springs he had sold the Telluride Power Company and devoted most of his attention and considerable fortune to education. When Julian entered the school, none of Nunn's students was a former employee. Many of the young men at Claremont had previously worked in his power plants in the West and were of age to enlist in military service when the United States entered the war in 1917. Julian and his fellow students were younger, fifteen and sixteen years old, and, Nunn hoped, less likely to become involved with the war unless it continued on for years. (It ended in November 1918, six months after Julian arrived.) Perhaps because of the students' age, the ban on alcohol and smoking did not pose a problem as it had at Claremont.[36]

The Deep Springs and Claremont students evidently differed in other ways as well. It seems that when Nunn established Deep Springs he wanted, as Aird put it, "to obtain more highly selected students (not just from the region of his power plants)." The early bias toward "superior young men of the West" from modest backgrounds gave way to a more conventional elitism, one that gave precedence to social class. If Nunn's original idea had been to hire and train a cadre of promising young Anglo-Saxon men, resembling the protagonists of Horatio Alger novels, by 1917 his interest had turned in a somewhat different direction. As Steward said many years later, Nunn wanted to train "a special group who would be, in the British sense, an obligated aristocracy, [and who would] become 'trustees of the nation.'"[37]

The first students at Deep Springs, unlike their predecessors at the power plants, came from the East and from families that belonged to the educated and professional middle class or upper middle class.[38] The greatest number appear to have come from Washington, D.C., where many of them attended the same high school. Like Julian Steward, they were the sons of high-ranking civil servants and members of Washington's scientific community. A disproportionate number of the fathers were geologists.

Nunn's friendship with the geologist Charles Walcott, secretary of the Smithsonian Institution, accounts for this. Sidney Walcott drew on his father's professional circle to recruit Steward and about ten others to Deep Springs between 1918 and the early 1920s. Carlyle Ashley, Harvey Mansfield, and Jim Mansfield were the sons of geologists employed by the U.S. Geological Survey. Jim Holmes's father was head of the federal mining service (perhaps the Bureau of Mines). Frederick Coville, Cabot's father, a botanist, was curator of the National Herbarium at the Smithsonian Institution. He and Charles Walcott were friends as well as colleagues, sharing broad interests in natural history and field experience in the West.[39]

Frederick Coville had, in fact, taken part in a government expedition to California's Death Valley in 1891, and soon after published an article on the Indians of nearby Panamint Valley, focusing on how they procured food in that harsh environment. His article, which appeared in an early volume of the *American Anthropologist*, anticipated Steward's later work in the region. Coville observed that "the desert Indians' means of subsistence is a subject of unusual interest." "The very first necessaries of life appear to be absolutely wanting," he wrote, "and this state of affairs exists not for one mile only, nor for ten miles, but for hundreds." Steward would cite this article repeatedly in some of his later publications.[40]

Other students at Deep Springs, among them Henry Hayes, Elbridge Gerry, Harvey Gerry, and Charles Schaaf, also came from Washington, D.C. Quite a few, including Cabot Coville and the Gerry brothers, had attended Central High School. Some of the families knew one another, and, as Coville later pointed out, they shared a great deal in common, having gone to Washington "in the great days" of the late nineteenth century when the federal government sponsored so much scientific work. Steward's own father belonged to that group, and was certainly known to, if not actually part of, "the Walcott circle."[41]

* * *

Surrounded by peers from Washington and elsewhere, Julian Steward quickly fell into the routines of the school. He used his camera to record a wide range of work scenes as well as the surrounding landscape of desert and mountains. The photographs in his album show the students rounding up cattle, branding calves, milking the cows, feeding the other livestock, cutting firewood, and harvesting hay. He and his fellow students spent upward of twenty hours a week doing "outside work," as it was always called.[42]

The photographs document not only the students' work but also their free time, much of which they spent outdoors: ice skating in the winter when the lake froze, riding horses, climbing mountains, and prospecting for silver. Herbert Reich wrote to his parents one spring, "The prospecting fever has hit the school. Julian Steward and I are partners in seven claims, staked out on Sundays." Two months earlier he had reported in a letter to his parents, "People are starting to prospect for silver in our valley." A faculty member soon admonished the students that "Great 'strikes' and 'findings' in the hills around our institution must not be in any way the cause of excitement or of interference with our program. If you 'strike it rich' . . . remember to keep your head. On the whole a mining boom in our valley will benefit us, unless we let the glamour and excitement upset our purpose."[43]

This sober view does not seem to have dampened the students' enthusiasm. Steward's own photographs show a claim that he and his partner worked. None of the students made a strike, and they eventually lost interest in mining, but fifty years later some of them still remembered the sites of their claims. (In 1969 Reich returned to Deep Springs to teach, and he wrote to his old prospecting partner, "One of the first walks I took after getting here was up Soldier Pass to see whether I could locate our mining claim.")[44]

The early history of Deep Springs Valley had a close connection with mining, but by the time the first students arrived at the ranch, the valley's mining days existed only in memory. The nearby Tonopah district in Nevada, the last of the great bonanza silver districts in the Great Basin, had been discovered more recently, around the turn of the twentieth century. Mines still operated there and would, in fact, continue to do so for decades. At the time the students succumbed to prospecting fever the Tonopah district mines were producing far less than they had at first, and evidently there was some renewed interest in Deep Springs Valley itself.[45]

As Julian Steward must have learned soon after arriving in the valley, the first white settlers there had been miners. During the 1860s, a mining settlement named White Mountain City stood on a site about four miles from where the school was built only fifty-five years later. Steward photographed the ruins, as well as much earlier evidence of human settlement in the valley. His album includes snapshots of petroglyphs, drawings and carvings on rock made by Indians in the past. (His interest in petroglyphs, which began at Deep Springs, culminated a decade later in one of his first publications, on the petroglyphs of California and adjacent regions.) He also collected arrowheads, which remain at Deep Springs as part of the school's teaching collections.[46]

Perhaps during these years he also saw his first prehistoric archaeological sites. A winter village occupied by Indians had stood on the eastern side of Deep Springs Lake at the lower end of the valley, and fragments of pottery and flint littered the ground by some rock shelters near Wyman Creek. Steward probably noticed these sites as a student at Deep Springs; he returned to the valley as a graduate student to do some archaeological research. His third article, published just seven years after he left the school, drew on that research, probably the first archaeological work carried out in Deep Springs Valley.[47]

Photographs of Captain Harry and his family offer a vivid reminder that Indians continued to live in the valley, and that Julian Steward knew them. Because Mary Harry and her husband worked on an irregular basis at the ranch, they must have earned very little money and perhaps subsisted in part by gathering some of their food. That was primarily women's work. Captain Harry, once known as a "good hunter," had probably stopped hunting by 1918. A few years earlier a horse had kicked him, badly injuring his elbow. He told one of the students about consulting a doctor who refused him treatment because he had no money to pay for it. As a result, he had nearly lost the use of that arm. In any case, the photograph that shows him skinning a coyote offers no real evidence that he still hunted for food. He or another ranch hand or a student may have trapped or shot the animal as "vermin," or to earn a bounty, but coyote was rarely eaten.[48]

To judge from the photographs and what the students wrote about them, Captain Harry and Mary lived between two worlds, between the traditions of the past and a new way of life that arrived when whites took over their territory. Besides their own language, they spoke what the students considered a rudimentary form of English, memorialized in Captain Harry's retort, "White man, he too damn smart!" This constituted his stock response to what he regarded as the odd and foolish ways of his white neighbors. He and his wife must have learned English as adults. Mary spoke very little, but their daughter spoke fluently and had clearly learned English early in life.

Captain Harry usually dressed in overalls, a shirt, and a pair of large leather boots that he had salvaged and patched. His daughter appears in a photograph wearing an ankle-length skirt, a large sweater, and a wool cap. Mary wore a long skirt and a long-sleeved blouse. While she knew how to weave the traditional twined baskets, and sometimes earned money by selling them, her daughter owned a sewing machine. Mother and daughter thus embodied cultural change quite visibly in their labor and use of technology, and with respect to language.[49]

The ranch's own technology, especially the irrigation system, also illustrated the process of cultural change, a major theme in Steward's later research and writing as an anthropologist. The system of water control obviously made a greater impression on him than changes in language or women's work and their use of technology, which always lay outside the scope of his interest.[50] He worked directly with irrigation and paid close attention to its operation and the immediate effects of water control. Deep Springs Valley also offered evidence of fundamental changes that occur with irrigation, illustrating how technology influences settlement pattern. (Steward probably saw this clearly only with hindsight. Years later he promoted the study of settlement patterns in archaeology, complaining that archaeologists spent too much time classifying potsherds and not enough studying how and why settlement patterns changed through time.)[51]

As he may have realized even during his student days, the Indians who once lived in Deep Springs Valley had by necessity situated their winter villages or camps near natural sources of water. In contrast, the ranch, with its irrigation system, stood at some distance from both the springs and Wyman Creek. The valley offered very concrete examples of how, in one instance, people must live near one of the desert's widely scattered sources of fresh water, and in another, how technology can allow people to live in a place removed from the source of water. By 1917, Captain Harry and his family had moved to the ranch and made camp next to one of the irrigation ditches; like the first students, they took their water from it.

The ranch's system of flood irrigation had its own peculiarities, but like most water supply systems it required well-coordinated labor to keep it going. Wyman Creek provided the water carried by pipe into ranch buildings and by irrigation ditches to the fields. Harvey Mansfield remembered that the water followed the creek bed to a small dam where some of it, destined for the pipes, was diverted to a pressure box. The pressure box, "a rectangular wooden structure with pipe coming out of the other end of it" settled the sand and silt from the creek water. The pipe often froze in the wintertime, interrupting the ranch's water supply. As Mansfield recalled, "We were forever having to dig out sections [of pipe], thaw it with a blow torch to get the water flowing again," then patch the holes that they inadvertently made with the blowtorches. Students also had the daily task of cleaning the screens that kept the pipes from clogging.[52]

The problem of frozen pipes in the winter gave way to others in the summer, when the students irrigated the alfalfa fields. One student recollected covering a field with water, looking in another direction, and then glancing again at the field, only to find that "the water had all disappeared and it was coming out of gopher holes in the next field."[53] Whatever the season, the problem of water, and water control, was an inescapable part of life at Deep Springs. Every day offered vivid lessons in how water scarcity affected where and how people lived, where crops could be planted, how far the cattle ranged. Years later, Steward drew on his personal memories of Deep Springs when he began to think in a serious and systematic way about how the water supply affects human social life. The question would remain a lifelong preoccupation, emerging again and again in his writings.[54]

* * *

During these years at Deep Springs, Julian Steward also experienced what he called "an intellectual awakening." Oddly enough, or most appropriately, it happened during an afternoon spent working on the irrigation system, when he suddenly realized, he later told his wife Jane, that "he could think, and could think for himself." The certainties pressed on him in childhood may have discouraged free and creative thinking. Whatever the case, years later he wrote, "I experienced an intellectual awakening, caused partly by the system of individual instruction, partly by the deep skepticism of a member of the faculty. I have managed to cling ever since to the determination to draw my own conclusions about things."[55]

The faculty member he referred to, Professor Srager, taught mathematics and science. His teacher spent an afternoon with him during his second year at the school, "questioning the basic purposes of education in general and Deep Springs in particular." The school has always favored a Socratic approach to teaching, and it seems that Srager employed it in this instance. Steward remembered that afternoon as "a vivid and crucial experience; for it made me aware that I could think for myself, in spite of all educational procedures and ratings. It was this rather sudden unleashing of my mind far more than the moralistic philosophy [of the school] that enabled me to use my inherent abilities."

The "sudden unleashing" came sometime after the encounter with his teacher, during a spell of solitude as he worked outside. His intellectual abilities had not been evident before, not to himself or, it seems, to his previous teachers. A teacher at his school in Washington had even challenged him about a poem he submitted for an assignment, questioning whether he wrote it. Steward never forgot that painful episode. "I have no idea," he concluded years later, "what I would have become without the Deep Springs experience."[56]

He also attributed his interest in anthropology to Deep Springs, not to the school itself but to the three years he spent living in the valley. Nothing in the curriculum, which was devoted to the traditional liberal arts, directly encouraged an interest in anthropology, then a new and relatively unknown discipline. The students took courses in history, English, French, Spanish, and Latin. In the sciences, they studied mathematics, biology, and geology. A course in public speaking was required, as Nunn believed that leaders must be able to speak well.[57] Although the records show that Steward usually did well in public speaking, he disliked it; and his later experiences, even when successful, did nothing to change that. Twenty-five years afterward, he credited "such miscellaneous things as a great love of the Deep Springs country . . . and a real dread of public speaking" to his years at the school.[58]

Julian Steward was one of about twenty students at Deep Springs, but he was the only one who responded so immediately and directly to his surroundings by becoming an anthropologist. Only three students did so in the school's first thirty years.[59] Most of Steward's fellow students went on to careers in law, business, and various academic fields.[60] It seems that even before reaching Deep Springs he was receptive to what he would see there, from its austere landscape and open sky to his Northern Paiute neighbors. His mother, on account of what Jane Steward called her "passion" for the West, encouraged her son to appreciate all things western; and once he arrived at Deep Springs, she urged him to travel and see other western landscapes. One of those trips took him to visit her at the Klamath Indian reservation in southern Oregon.

* * *

During June 1919, at the end of his first year at Deep Springs, Julian Steward left the ranch to spend six weeks with his mother at Klamath Agency. He went first to visit his sister, Marion, in San Francisco, where, as the photographs in his album attest, they saw some of the major sights, mainly outdoors. He and Marion took a ferry across the bay to Marin County, where they walked through Muir Woods and ascended Mount Tamalpais. In San Francisco they toured Golden Gate Park and walked on the beach along the bay. "We took in most of the town, including Chinatown and the various parks," he wrote in a letter several weeks later. "The trees in Muir Woods were the first redwoods I had ever seen, so they seemed quite wonderful." Mount Tamalpais, he added, usually provided "a fine view of the ocean, bay, and San Francisco," but on that day a veil of fog had obscured the city and ocean below. Both his photographs and the letter suggest that he saw San Francisco, city and environs, with a naturalist's eye.

The trip to San Francisco had taken him across the Sierra Nevada, from the desert on the eastern side to the well-watered western side. After spending a year in the high desert, coastal California presented a striking contrast: awash in mist on some days; on others, drenched in sunlight, a study in brilliant color, not the desert's shades of brown and gray. Continuing on his journey to Oregon, Julian traveled northward through the Sacramento Valley, the upper reaches of the Central Valley. The abundant waters of the Sacramento River supported a rich agricultural area of fields and orchards covering much of the broad valley floor.

Approaching the far north of California, he entered a darkly green and forested land, crosscut by wild and rushing rivers. En route he passed the frozen peaks of Mount Lassen and Mount Shasta, each standing luminous and alone in the distance. Volcanic mountains, massive and solitary, they offered his first glimpse of the Cascade Range, entirely different from the Sierra Nevada in look and, as he would later learn in geology courses, in formation. He crossed the border into southern Oregon and continued on to Klamath Agency, located near Crater Lake National Park.

He soon set to work in a temporary job probably arranged by his mother. In the middle of July, Julian wrote to an official of Telluride Association, "I am now working on the Agency farm for four dollars a day. I believe I have to do about everything I had to do at the ranch. . . . We are haying now." (His wages, which rivaled his mother's, more than paid for the cost of his trip and daily expenses that summer; at seventeen he was entirely self-supporting.) In his reply, the official inquired rather kindly if this summer job did not constitute something of a busman's holiday. "I am wondering," he asked, "whether or not you are getting the best result from your vacation in doing work which is very similar to that which will occupy your attention throughout the Winter."

Although the work seemed much the same, the place bore no resemblance to the ranch and environs of Deep Springs Valley. Tall pine trees and lush green fields surrounded Klamath Agency, a cluster of simple frame buildings. Located in the Klamath Basin, the largest expanse of wetlands west of the Mississippi River, Klamath Agency stood amidst vast marshlands and lakes. Pumping plants and canals carried water away in the Klamath Basin, draining the marshes to create farmland, the opposite of what Julian had seen in Owens Valley, where canals carried water from the river and creeks to farm fields. The plentiful water not only supported swarms of mosquitoes, which made life difficult day and night, but also supported the stands of towering trees that distinguished the land around Klamath Agency from Deep Springs Valley. "It is heavily wooded with pines," Julian wrote, "some of which are six feet through."[61]

He had at least one break from work, joining his mother and other agency staff for an excursion to nearby Crater Lake on the Fourth of July. He took several snapshots of the lake, an arresting sight in terms of both beauty and geological history. The icy, azure waters fill the deep crater of a volcano that lost its peak thousands of years ago in an cataclysmic explosion. Sheer cliffs of lava, some rising nearly two thousand feet, form an almost circular rim around the lake, which stretches six miles from one side to the other. "The weather was very warm," Julian remarked in a letter, "but there were still snow drifts as low as at eight thousand feet. The lake was supposed to be [at] nine thousand [feet] and there was a drift there that was about eight feet deep." After just a year at Deep Springs, he was already keenly aware of how elevation affected what he saw around him.[62]

Whether he had very much contact with Klamath Indians during that summer is unclear. "The Indians on the reservation are very wealthy," he wrote, "[because they] own great tracts of timber and land." He added that they were "throw[ing] away their money" by gambling "and in other ways and have nothing to show for it."[63] In this remark, he echoed the firmly middle-class values of his family and Nunn's own perspective on money management. Students at Deep Springs received an allowance of fifteen dollars a month and had to account for their expenditures, down to the last cent, with the school's bookkeeper.[64] The traditional economy of the Klamath Indians did not center on money, and their views on exchange obviously differed.

Julian left Klamath Agency in the middle of August to return to school, and Grace departed just four months later, in December 1919. Writing from San Francisco, she asked for a three-month leave without pay in order to decide whether "to request a transfer to another location, or to resign." As she remarked pointedly in her letter to the agency superintendent, "It is hardly likely that I shall return to Klamath Agency again." The superintendent had apparently suggested a transfer or resignation because he considered her, in his own words, "too advanced in age to learn quickly and adapt herself to a new occupation." She was fifty years old.[65] After hearing that her request for a leave had been denied, she resigned in spring 1920. In San Francisco she found temporary work as a Christian Science nurse, providing home care. Any such position was always temporary; the city did not yet have a nursing home operated by the First Church of Christ, Scientist, which might have offered ongoing employment and a regular income.[66]

When Grace left for California, she took along some baskets that she had collected in Oregon. Whatever she thought about certain aspects of life at Klamath Agency, she clearly admired Klamath Indian basketry, regarding it as a traditional art. (Julian, in contrast, would see Indian baskets as artifacts, obtaining them as specimens for the scientific collections of museums.) A photograph of Grace taken by her son a year or two later shows her inside the cottage where she and Marion then lived in San Rafael, a quiet village in Marin County. She is wearing a long, dark skirt and a blouse with a high collar. The baskets stand on a shelf behind her.[67]

* * *

Sometime in 1919 or 1920, Captain Harry died. As was customary after a death, Mary burned their camp at the ranch and all of his possessions; also following tradition, she left the area. She moved twenty-eight miles west to Owens Valley and settled in Big Pine, once the site of a Paiute village. Her daughter's family lived there, and Mary joined them. She was still living in Owens Valley in the mid-1920s when Julian Steward did field research there during the summer, and in 1935, at the beginning of his well-known Great Basin fieldwork. Mary Harry served as one of his informants.[68]

When Mary left Deep Springs, Julian still had at least another year ahead of him as a student at the school, and his fieldwork lay far in the future. His life in the valley over the course of those three years, between 1918 and 1921, would mark his later professional work in various ways. To choose just one example, Steward's interest in ecology and his attention to water clearly had roots in his experience of a particular western landscape. In the spacious and stark reaches of Deep Springs Valley, as elsewhere in the Great Basin, there is nothing to distract the eye from the land, and the effects of limited water stand out in bold relief. He spent three years looking at that arid landscape, photographing it, exploring it with friends, and learning its natural history.

His final, firsthand lessons about the land came in summer 1921, at the end of his student years at Deep Springs. He remained at the ranch until late June, after most of the other students had already left for the summer break. He and three others had stayed on "to help them through the haying," as he later reported, adding that "practically four-fifths had been stacked" by the time he and his companions left. Two of the students, Henry Hayes and Charles Schaaf, planned to return to Deep Springs in the fall, while he and Windsor Putnam had completed their studies there and expected to enter the University of California, Berkeley in August. The four friends left the ranch during the last week in June and began an overland trek to San Francisco through the High Sierra. "We had two burros," Julian wrote, "and spent fifteen days in the hills, walking over two hundred miles."[69]

His mountaineering adventures, this one and others, became field trips of sorts where he could see firsthand the effects of the geological processes he read about in books. He had recently taken a brief course in geology, but he left Deep Springs with more than book knowledge. The Sierra Nevada, an immense and splintered mass of granite carved by glaciers, offered some of the most memorable lessons. The highest range in the United States, and the outstanding geographic landmark of California, it sprawls for nearly four hundred miles from north to south. The steep eastern face, a product of faulting and tilting, rises sharply above Owens Valley and looks out over the dry Great Basin. Geological features of the Owens Valley region are remarkably well exposed, dramatic, and diverse, and provided a kind of outdoor laboratory for him. Beyond any intellectual interests, Steward developed an enduring love for the Sierra Nevada during the years he spent living in the desert and exploring the mountains. Its snowcapped crest, visible from Deep Springs Valley despite an intervening mountain range, was within his daily field of vision.[70]

The signal event of his journey across the Sierra Nevada in 1921 took place high above Owens Valley, where Julian and Windsor succeeded in scaling Temple Crag, a towering peak at over thirteen thousand feet. Because the mountain's north face thrusts up vertically for two thousand feet, they skirted to the south and then climbed to a saddle below the eastern face. By crossing the head of a chimney rising from the south, they reached the summit. From that vantage point, the view of the Palisades was "incomparably fine," Julian wrote. Although he and Windsor thought they had made the first recorded ascent, in fact another party had preceded them fifteen years before. (Steward may not have known that. Later in life, he always kept a photograph of the mountain by the desk in his study at home.)[71]

Continuing northward on their journey, Julian and his friends arrived at the base of Mount Humphreys a few days later. Nearly a thousand feet taller than Temple Crag, Mount Humphreys offers exceptional views of the entire region to climbers who negotiate the final perilous section to reach a small and rocky summit. Julian and Windsor reported "no great difficulties" in ascending from the western side of the mountain. Mount Whitney rose up fifty miles to the south, and Mount Ritter, their next climbing destination, forty miles to the north. From the sheer drop-off on the northeastern side of Mount Humphreys, they could see Owens Valley nearly ten thousand feet below, a spreading blanket of green.[72]

The aqueduct completed just eight years earlier by the city of Los Angeles already carried away much of the valley's water, yet enough still remained to irrigate the alfalfa fields, expansive pastures, and orchards planted with tens of thousands of fruit trees. Apples and honey from the valley often won prizes at San Francisco's Mid-Winter Fair. Ranchers owned some twenty-five thousand head of cattle, moving them from the valley to summer ranges in the Sierra, and then driving them back down each fall. The extensive system of irrigation, and the plentiful water provided by the Owens River, gave Owens Valley a lush and fertile look, in distinct contrast to Deep Springs Valley.

In merely a few years, Owens Valley would lose most of its water to Los Angeles, hundreds of miles to the south. The city had nearly doubled in size between 1910 and 1920, and its continuing growth and insatiable appetite for water did not bode well for farming and ranching in the valley.[73] But in the summer of 1921, as Julian and his friends made their way through the bordering mountains, Owens Valley remained a land of plenty, if only on account of snowmelt from the Sierra and irrigation. Precipitation averages just six inches a year in the valley because the Sierra Nevada captures moisture carried inland from the Pacific, casting an enormous rain shadow to the east.

After leaving Mount Humphreys, the four friends walked in a northwesterly direction, reaching Mount Ritter several days later. On the Fourth of July, Julian, Windsor, and Henry climbed a glacier between Mount Ritter and Banner Peak, and then proceeded to the precipitous cliffs that form the eastern face of Mount Ritter. Slowly and cautiously they made their way to the top. The redoubtable John Muir had first ascended the mountain in 1872, as he later described in a rather harrowing account well known to Sierra mountaineers, including Julian and his friends. From the summit, they could see most of the northern High Sierra extending into the far distance, to a point where mountains merged with sky. Ten long hours after setting out on the most strenuous climb on their journey, they finally returned to their camp.[74]

The next day, crossing into Yosemite National Park, more than a thousand square miles of wilderness, they found themselves on the western flank of the Sierra, which slopes toward the Central Valley about fifty miles from the crest. In Yosemite they entered a land of spectacular wild beauty and water: a place of rushing rivers and streams, cascading waterfalls, and pristine glacial lakes. In terms of its water source and the presence of people, it could not have differed more from the valley they had recently left. Unlike Yosemite, which owes its lushness to the natural cycle—the rainfall and snowmelt that fill its many rivers and streams—Owens Valley depended on irrigation, on human effort and technology, to harness the waters of the Owens River. Unlike Yosemite Valley, which presents a stunning display of the force of nature, Owens Valley in 1921 still embodied the problem of aridity and the transforming power of technology. This experience constituted one more lesson among many in Steward's outdoor education.

He and his friends spent a few days in the park before traveling on to San Franciso. After living the outdoor life for two weeks, and relishing their freedom and solitude, the four students finally reached the city in mid-July. There they parted ways.

* * *

The three years that Steward spent at Deep Springs were formative ones, and they were the fortunate years of his young life. He not only had an "intellectual awakening" at Deep Springs but also caught glimpses of happiness there. Years later, what would impress Robert Murphy most strongly about Steward was his "enormous inner tension and conflict" and a tendency to "shift from sociability to isolation swiftly." Murphy saw this as a source of creativity, but some of Steward's teachers at Deep Springs considered him too withdrawn and subject to spells of "pessimism and gloom." In a monthly report written in 1920, one teacher remarked, "During the past week there has been improvement, but there is much to be done and perhaps this is the biggest task that this student must face while he is here." It seems likely that Steward felt a sense of loss and lingering unhappiness about the breakup of his childhood home, as suggested by elliptical comments he made forty years later. He seems not to have confided in anyone at the school, perhaps because of the stigma then associated with divorce.[75]

Exactly seventy years after he made the long and lonely journey to Deep Springs, Jane Steward examined a photograph of her husband taken during his student days, one of the few pictures of him in his album. "Oh, but he looks so happy!" she exclaimed. She paused, then said, "You know, this is a very unusual photograph of him. He was such a serious, quiet man." Later she said that she thought he had struggled with depression repeatedly in his life.[76]

In the photograph, the young Julian Steward stands with arms folded, looking directly at the camera, smiling broadly.

CHAPTER 3

UNIVERSITY YEARS,
EAST AND WEST

As soon as he arrived in San Francisco, Julian Steward set about trying to locate summer work, but he found it very scarce. San Francisco, a city where men had long outnumbered women, retained something of its frontier character, with saloons and boardinghouses that catered to longshoremen and merchant sailors. There was work at dozens of docks along the Embarcadero and the southeastern waterfront, and in the many businesses that served the shipping industry; but in midsummer 1921, the city offered nothing for a new graduate of a preparatory school.[1]

When Steward learned that Nunn was in the city and not at his home in Pasadena, he immediately went to see him. "I found him living within a block of where I am staying," he reported. Grace Steward, then living in a residential hotel on O'Farrell Street, had given up the cottage in San Rafael and moved back to the city. It seems she was not employed. Marion Steward had left her position at Fort Mason when the government reduced the clerical staff after World War I. Like her mother, she chose to resign from federal service in order to avoid a transfer and to live in San Francisco, but her decision would prove costly in several respects. She did find work, but she earned a lower salary as a Dictaphone operator and typist with the U.S. Rubber Company, a private firm.[2]

The previous year, Steward had been elected to membership in the Telluride Association, and in 1921 the association awarded him a three-hundred-dollar scholarship. Many of his classmates at Deep Springs received full scholarships of over seventeen hundred dollars to Cornell University, where tuition alone cost nearly three hundred dollars. Most of the remainder went for room and board at Telluride House, an imposing and well-appointed house on the Cornell University campus.

Penniless except for his scholarship, Steward enrolled at the University of California, Berkeley. It cost far less to attend than Cornell, a private, Ivy League university; as a state resident, he paid no tuition at the University of California. "I am not quite decided what studies I will take," he wrote to Dean Thornhill at Deep Springs, "but I incline rather strongly toward law, for I believe that by taking that up, I will be better able to carry out the purpose of Deep Springs." "I realize my shortcomings in dealing with people," he continued, "but feel confident that with a determined effort I can overcome them."[3] His letter marked the beginning of a campaign for acceptance that continued for nearly a year and ended in success.

Finances remained a problem despite his scholarship. "I don't know how well $300 will support me," he told Thornhill, "but with what I can earn between now and then, and what extra work I can do while studying, I will probably be able to get along very well." As it turned out, his father provided some unexpected assistance. This seems to have been the first support he received directly from his father after leaving Washington in 1918. In 1920, when he was eighteen, he referred to himself as "practically self-supporting for two years at Deep Springs."[4]

By August 1921 Steward was living in Berkeley, at first on Dwight Way and later on Durant Avenue. He enrolled in a variety of courses during the fall semester, including physics. Of them all, he looked forward most to the science course. "I have been very anxious to take physics this year," he wrote to Thornhill, "not only for its own sake but to help me decide whether I want to go into science or law later on. . . ." The problem of finding his lifework, and the question of whether it would center on science, now loomed larger than ever before. By October he wrote that he had given up the idea of studying engineering and would probably pursue law. "But in case I should want some scientific line of work," he added, "I am now taking a rather mixed course [of study]."[5]

His first, rather negative, impressions of the university may have reflected disappointment at finding himself in Berkeley instead of at Deep Springs or with his former classmates at Cornell.[6] The University of California differed in nearly every respect from Deep Springs, from the size of the student body, more than twelve thousand, to its inclusion of women in about the same numbers as men. The university, founded in the late 1860s, had soon begun to admit women as students. By the turn of the century, many women attended and earned degrees, but only one woman held a faculty position. When some male students showed open hostility to young women who tried to take part in campus life, they established separate clubs for themselves.[7] Well into the twentieth century, women had a place in university life perhaps best described as separate and marginal.

Phoebe Apperson Hearst—a former schoolteacher, widow of a mining and railroad magnate, and major donor to the university in the early years of the century—encouraged the administration to provide clubhouses for the women students and to hire women as faculty members. Because of her great wealth, and her position on the board of regents, her words carried weight, although she had to pay the salary of the first woman employed as a member of the faculty. (Hearst also provided the funds to establish anthropology at the University of California, giving three hundred thousand dollars in the first five years, an enormous sum at that time.) Eventually, the few women who taught at the university found themselves largely relegated to home economics, where they offered courses not generally taken by men. Steward probably never had a course taught by a woman from the time he reached Deep Springs until he finished his graduate course work ten years later. This was not uncommon at the time, and it contributed to his later expectation that having an academic career meant having only male colleagues.[8]

Near the end of his first semester in 1921, he reported finding the course in physics "instructive," but he had decided that the subject of "man and society" was more important. "I have definitely (or nearly so) renounced scientific work," he wrote. He continued his struggle to reconcile the ideals and expectations of his elders with his own interests, a conflict that he would finally try to resolve by choosing anthropology as his profession. His deeply religious mother looked askance at scientific materialism, and Nunn and some teachers at Deep Springs had urged him toward a life of humanitarian service that would "promote the highest well-being."[9]

Exactly what those words meant continued to puzzle Steward throughout his life. More than thirty years after leaving Deep Springs, he wrote that he had taken "the humanitarian principle with extreme seriousness," but that, even as a student, Nunn's notion of a "moral order of the universe" had perplexed him. As he explained it, Nunn had assumed that "there is a moral order of the universe that is as real as the physical order and that people have an inborn moral faculty that is as real as the physical senses." Students referred to this concept, so central to Nunn's educational mission, as the "M.O.U." It was a concept that Steward eventually rejected as "a philosophical fiction," but only after considerable thought, study, and inner struggle.[10]

Later in life, Steward remarked that he took his first anthropology course at Berkeley by chance, but the letters he wrote that year suggest that his choice was not serendipitous. He was searching for a field that would allow him both to pursue his interest in science and to help humanity in some way. At Deep Springs, what he described as his "vague interest in natural history" had become focused on the "exact sciences," although the school offered only mathematics, biology, and a single course in geology. At Berkeley he continued his education in science with the course in physics and one in mathematics, but finding the latter "a waste of time" because of his uncertainty about a career, he chose a replacement for spring semester 1922. That course was Anthropology 1b, the popular General Anthropology: Origin and Development of Civilization, taught by Alfred L. Kroeber, Robert H. Lowie, and Edward W. Gifford. The university catalog described the subject of the course as the "source and growth of institutions, arts, customs, industries, language, and religion."[11]

* * *

In 1922 Kroeber, Lowie, and Gifford constituted Berkeley's department of anthropology. Kroeber, then in his midforties, had held a position at the University of California since 1901. He had gone to California directly from Columbia University, where, after earning a B.A. and an M.A. in English literature, he studied anthropology under Franz Boas. In 1899, at the age of twenty-three, Kroeber spent a few months in the West doing fieldwork, producing a doctoral dissertation on the decorative symbolism of the Arapaho Indians. He was appointed instructor in anthropology at the University of California in 1901, and by 1919 he had attained the rank of professor. When Steward enrolled in Anthropology 1b in 1922, Kroeber was chair of the department, a position he had held from 1909, when the founding chair, Frederic Ward Putnam, retired. From the early 1920s until his retirement in 1946, Kroeber and Lowie alternated serving as department chair.[12]

Both men, already well established in the new discipline of anthropology, would achieve eminence over the course of their long careers. In such a small field, their influence was disproportionately strong. By 1922 only a few dozen men in the United States had earned Ph.D.'s in anthropology; one of the first women to do so, Ruth Benedict, was just finishing her dissertation at Columbia. Kroeber had already published a range of articles in the *American Anthropologist* and elsewhere, many of them dealing with California Indians. He had also recently written the brief *Three Essays on the Antiquity and Races of Man*, which he was expanding into his textbook, *Anthropology*, published in 1923; it would serve as the bible of the discipline for generations of anthropology students. Kroeber's master work, *Handbook of the Indians of California*, appeared in print just two years later.[13]

Lowie, then thirty-nine and an associate professor, had recently left the American Museum of Natural History in New York City to join Kroeber at the University of California. He too was a student of Boas. Lowie had lately published his second book, *Primitive Society*, with a third book, *Primitive Religion*, soon to follow. Despite what he modestly termed the "defects" of *Primitive Society*, the book quickly became a classic and would remain his best-known work. Lowie's first fieldwork, in 1906, had been with Northern Shoshone Indians in Idaho. By 1922, when Steward first encountered him, Lowie had also carried out fieldwork with Crow and Hopi Indians.[14]

The third, and junior, member of the department, Gifford, served as associate curator of the University of California's Museum of Anthropology and had recently been appointed lecturer in anthropology. Unlike Kroeber and Lowie, both New Yorkers, Gifford was a Californian. Also in contrast to his colleagues,

Gifford began his career in anthropology with strong interests in natural history, rather than an inclination toward literature and philosophy. After graduating from high school in Oakland, he made field trips to Mexico and the Galapagos Islands to study wildlife. He was appointed assistant curator of the Museum of Anthropology in 1912.

Remembered as a modest and unassuming man, Gifford never attended college, although he taught several generations of university students. He was one of the few self-taught anthropologists to gain a foothold in the academic world, and perhaps the only one to do so without any university study or degree.[15] The professionalization of anthropology was well underway by the time Steward enrolled in Anthropology 1b. The small fraternity of anthropologists, always rather exclusive, would grow even more exclusionary as the field expanded: the number of trained men increased, and a few women began to pursue graduate study and to compete for fellowships, but employment remained scarce.

Although a beginning student, Steward had already had direct contact with Northern Paiute Indians in Deep Springs Valley and Owens Valley, and with Klamath Indians in Oregon. He must have readily connected what he heard in lectures with his own experiences. Given anthropology's major focus at the time on American Indians, the field probably held an immediacy for him that was rather rare among college students. Yet despite earning high marks in the course, whatever he thought of it and his instructors did not persuade him to stay at the University of California. Cornell offered nothing in the way of anthropology, but by April 1922 he had decided to enroll there in the fall. At the age of twenty, joining his friends on the other side of the continent held far more appeal than living near his sister and mother and studying anthropology at Berkeley. In fact, he planned to earn a law degree at Cornell.[16]

The particular lure of Cornell for Steward, as he readily admitted, was Telluride House, where his classmates from Deep Springs lived. At the University of California, Windsor Putnam had remained a good friend, but otherwise Steward felt adrift in a sea of strangers. His plan to transfer to Cornell did not include living at Telluride House, which was far too expensive; he simply wanted the chance to associate with his friends. With credits from Deep Springs and the University of California, he hoped to transfer as a junior and to begin law courses immediately. Entering as a junior rather than a sophomore would save a year's tuition and living expenses.[17]

He left Berkeley in June 1922 and returned to the East after a four-year absence. "I have an invitation from Herbert Reich to spend the summer with him," he wrote. His friend, already a student at Cornell, had gone there directly from Deep Springs on full scholarship. He and Steward planned to attend the annual convention of Telluride Association, scheduled for June on the Cornell campus in Ithaca, New York, and then to look for summer work.[18]

This was the first Telluride convention that Steward attended. In letters he wrote a month beforehand to Thornhill and to F. C. Noon, chancellor of Telluride Association, he mentioned his plans to attend Cornell despite being "not too well fixed" financially, his wish to study law, and his high regard for Telluride Association. At the beginning of the convention, he submitted a list of his courses and grades at the University of California to the association's scholarship committee, which promptly awarded him one of twelve full scholarships to Cornell. The scholarship of $1,770 paid for tuition, which cost $270, and living expenses at Telluride House, estimated at $1,200. The award also included a three-hundred-dollar stipend for the year, an amount equal to the entire scholarship that Telluride Association had granted him the previous year to attend the University of California and about twice his allowance at Deep Springs. (To put the value of his scholarship in perspective, his sister earned twelve hundred dollars that year—about the same as the average public schoolteacher—in her new position as a clerk and typist at a bond-brokerage firm.)[19]

When the convention ended in late June 1922, Steward and Reich left Ithaca for Staten Island. Reich's parents had gone to Europe for the summer, and he and Steward shared the family's house with a reporter who worked for the *New York Times*. After looking for temporary work in and around New York City, they finally found jobs with a furnace company and spent weeks doing a survey of Staten Island residents to find out which houses did not have central heating. Sometime that summer, Steward also saw his father, probably for the first time since leaving Washington. Thomas Steward had traveled to New York City on business and Steward went to visit him at his hotel. This appears to have been the last time he saw his father, who died fourteen years later.[20]

At the end of the summer, Steward and Reich made a road trip together to the Adirondack Mountains in northeastern New York, bordering Vermont and Canada. A region covering thousands of square miles, much of it remained isolated and in a natural state, a lure to two young men who had relished life on the range and treks in the High Sierra. Whatever Steward thought of the area— a wild place of deep gorges, lakes, and low, weatherworn mountains bristling with balsam, spruce, and birch trees—is unknown. The intense greenness and the waterfalls spilling off cliffs might have been a striking sight after his experience of desert life. But he made no comment about it in writing, and it seems that he never returned.[21]

* * *

In September 1922 Steward moved into Telluride House, occupying quarters often described as "sumptuous" and "luxurious." Nunn believed that it provided the proper surroundings in which to test some of his ideas on educating men. He intended to select promising young men, free them from material concerns while they were students, provide them with an excellent education, and expose them to stimulating thinkers. The last would be accomplished by having men on the Cornell faculty live at Telluride House and by inviting eminent men to

visit. The students, in return, had limited responsibilities beyond applying themselves to their studies.[22]

Although a precursor of Deep Springs, Telluride House differed fundamentally in lacking a work program and an isolation policy. In fact, the two differed
in nearly every aspect of substance and setting. Deep Springs was a working
ranch located in a remote desert valley in the West. Men's work, "outside work,"
structured daily life there. Telluride House, in contrast, was a large and imposing house surrounded by the green lawns and winding roadways of an Ivy
League campus in the East. Its staff did all of the housework, presided over by
one Bernt Olsson, remembered as "the perfect, self-effacing servant."[23]

These differences were not lost on Steward, who greatly preferred the masculine atmosphere of the ranch. In comparison to Deep Springs, Telluride House
had aspects of a men's finishing school, providing social and professional connections and practice in the social graces to help prepare the students for leadership positions. Twenty years later, Steward made no effort to disguise his contempt for the "plush life" that Telluride House offered. He wrote to students at
Deep Springs, "Personally, I am convinced that far more should go into scholarships and far less into lush living at the Cornell house." He clearly believed
that the experience of living at Telluride House ran counter to Nunn's aims,
leading some students in the direction of "lucrative professions" rather than
humanitarian service. "I would even sell the house," he continued. "More idealistic plans for helping humanity are cooked up by students in boarding house
bedrooms than ever came from that refined, upper-class atmosphere."[24]

Although he understood the practical advantages of attending a private university in the East, and had desperately wanted to join his friends there, Steward missed the ranch and the desert and the mountains. Moreover, he had left
Deep Springs Valley with what would prove a lifelong preference for living far
from cities. In his thinking, often polarized, he always seemed to equate ranch
life, the outdoors, and western wildlands with maleness, and eastern landscapes
and domesticated life in eastern cities with femaleness. This reflected his own
experience, growing up in the company of his mother and sister in Washington, D.C., and then separating from them at adolescence when he went to Deep
Springs to join a community of men. Life at Telluride House undeniably had a
domesticated quality, even if all the residents were male; and Ithaca, despite its
small scale and a population of less than twenty thousand, unfortunately
qualified as an eastern city. Streetcars ran up and down the steep streets between
the university and a busy downtown area of banks, shops, and office buildings.[25]

He must have noticed many other contrasts between well-watered upstate
New York and the high desert of eastern California, and perhaps this awareness
contributed to his abiding interest in the effects of water scarcity. Ithaca itself
lies in a cloud belt that extends south from Lake Ontario along the Appalachian
ridge, and the area qualifies as one of the most overcast in North America. When

Steward looked up at the sky in the high desert, he had seen a vast blue dome arching over the mountains; in Ithaca, he saw banks of clouds or leaden skies more often than not. The area receives six times as much precipitation as Deep Springs, much of it in the form of extravagant winter snowfalls.[26]

Besides contrasts in climate and daily weather, the difference in rainfall and snowfall produces very visible effects on the landscape. The mountains around Deep Springs thrust up from the desert floor, massive and high and sparsely vegetated, their rugged contours clearly exposed. Thousands of miles to the east, Ithaca stands on the shores of Cayuga Lake, the longest of New York's Finger Lakes. Deep gorges crosscut the Cornell campus, set on a wooded hill hundreds of feet above the water. Deciduous forests of birch, beech, and maple turn the surrounding land green in spring and summer, and cloak it in vibrant colors in fall. The region's thickly forested hills have a luxuriant beauty, but one in which Steward showed no interest. At Deep Springs he had taken time for hiking and exploring and for photographing and painting the landscape around him. But there is no record that he did any of these things in Ithaca.

Instead, he seems to have immersed himself in academic work. Whatever he learned about the local landscape probably came in the course of studying geology. His science classes at Cornell offered an intellectual framework that also helped him begin to make sense of what he had seen and experienced while living in the West. During just seven years, between 1918 and 1925, Steward crossed the continental United States four times, in an era when many people never traveled very far from their region of origin. Cross-country travel seems not only to have heightened his awareness of regional differences but also to have reinforced his preference for western landscapes.

In yet another contrast to his life at Deep Springs, while in Ithaca he apparently had no contact with the Indian peoples of the region. In his boyhood he had read James Fenimore Cooper's *The Last of the Mohicans,* one of his favorite books, and set on the New York frontier. Steward apparently did not read any ethnography during his student days at Cornell to counterbalance Cooper's romantic tale.[27] The early anthropologist Lewis Henry Morgan, a lawyer by training and an ethnologist by preference, had published his classic study of kinship, *League of the Ho-de-no-sau-nee, or Iroquois,* seventy years earlier, based on ethnographic work in upstate New York. The League of the Iroquois, originally a confederacy of five tribes—including the Cayuga—had once claimed a large territory. There is no record that Steward ever visited one of their nearby reservations, located just fifty miles north of Ithaca, even in the course of his summer travels. He spent his three years at Cornell, unlike the three years at Deep Springs, living a rather interior life.[28]

* * *

Cornell evidently denied him advanced standing, and Steward transferred as a sophomore, receiving credit only for his year at the University of California.

Unable to register for law courses, he instead took a variety of classes in the humanities and social sciences, including history and economics. Years later, he also remembered studying philosophy in order to clarify what he called his "religious and ethical orientations."[29]

He must have had extensive contact during this period with George Lincoln Burr, a faculty member and historian who lived at Telluride House throughout the 1920s. Burr, then a middle-aged widower and exactly the age of Steward's own father, was by all accounts a kindly, charitable man as well as a committed scholar and teacher. Besides bringing a roster of distinguished men to Telluride House as guests, "Poppy Burr," as many called him, provided a fatherly presence. He took uncommon interest in his students, and tried to help them with their struggles, intellectual or otherwise.

Given his own particular quest during that period, Steward may have been intrigued to meet a scholar whose interests centered on the history of science, including conflicts between science and theology. Burr did not oppose organized religion, only dogmatic theology. A Baptist by birth and a Unitarian by choice, he sometimes invited Quakers to Telluride House and sat with them in silent prayer. By his own example, he encouraged students to question dogma, not to abandon religion. Steward resolved the issue for himself by the end of his undergraduate years, turning away from all religious doctrine and practice. Perhaps because of Burr's influence, sometime during his first year at Cornell or early in the second, he decided to major in history. (Burr, one of two faculty members at Cornell who occasionally offered lectures on anthropology, may have encouraged his interest in that field as well.)[30]

At the end of his first year at Cornell, Steward again made plans to attend the annual convention of Telluride Association, held that year in Provo, Utah. Leaving the overcast skies of Ithaca behind, he headed west on his third cross-country trip in five years. He arrived in Provo in late June 1923, and at the convention he again received a full scholarship to Cornell and a three-hundred-dollar stipend for the next academic year.

Perhaps the generosity of the scholarship relieved him of looking for summer work. In any case, he spent time touring in the West after the convention ended, traveling south from Provo to see some well-known sites favored as highly by geologists as by tourists: Bryce Canyon and Zion National Park in southern Utah and the Grand Canyon in northern Arizona. Then he headed west to southern California, where he crossed the barren stretches of the Mojave Desert under a cloudless western sky.[31]

In San Francisco he stayed with his mother, then living on Broderick Street. Grace was working as a Christian Science nurse, providing home care. Marion still worked for the bond-brokerage firm Pierce-Fair Company. During the few weeks that he spent in San Francisco, Julian visited Nunn. "We went out to see Mr. Nunn yesterday," he wrote in July 1923. "His house is very old, magnificent and dignified, and he seems to be thriving in San Francisco air."[32] Nunn may have found the air beneficial, but he in fact suffered from advanced tuberculosis and had only two years to live.

Back at Cornell in fall 1923, Steward enrolled in a science course, his first since completing a year of physics so successfully at the University of California. He was twenty-one years old, a college junior, and finally eligible to take law courses, but he decided against enrolling in any. Instead, he chose a class in zoology and filled out the rest of his schedule with courses about "man and society" that he thought would help prepare him for the sort of work Nunn envisioned. They included one in psychology, his first and last, another in economics, and two in history. By the end of his college years, he had taken five courses in economics and five in history, nearly a minor in each. This foreshadowed the direction of his theoretical work, which was to be markedly historical and economic in emphasis.[33]

At Cornell, as at the University of California, Steward shared classrooms with women students. He found far fewer at Cornell, however, which had long limited women's numbers. The university severely restricted the admission of women to the professional schools, such as the law school, and even limited the number admitted to the college of arts and sciences, where Steward took nearly all of his courses. The small number of women, and the segregated nature of housing and social life on campus, meant that he had little in the way of daily, informal contact with them.[34]

He arrived on campus soon after a campaign led by some prominent male students called for reducing the number of women students and eventually barring them altogether. The national press picked up the story, but the active campaign soon died away, although "anti-coed" feeling lingered on in many fraternities. Indeed, it was something of a tradition at Cornell. The first men to attend the university had opposed the admission of women because they wanted Cornell to rival the status and prestige of Harvard and Yale, which accepted only men. In the 1920s, women retained their place on the margins, quite literally in the case of the university's new student union. Still under construction during Steward's years on campus, it opened in 1925. Women could not use the large central entrance or most of the building. Instead, they entered the union through a smaller side door and were confined to two nearby lounges.[35]

Although women attended classes at Cornell in the 1920s, few women taught them. Replicating his experience at the University of California, Steward evidently took courses given only by men. No woman achieved even the rank of assistant professor in an arts and sciences department until twenty years after he had left Cornell. (After a long and bitter argument in 1911, the nearly all-male faculty had voted that "while not favoring in general the appointment of women to professorships," it would not object to their appointment in the newly created department of home economics, a unit in the college of agriculture.)[36]

Anna Comstock, nationally recognized in the field of nature study and one of the few women who taught at Cornell, spent years there without even the lowest faculty rank. Her *Handbook of Nature Study*, first published in 1911 and still in print, offered methods for teaching young children to learn about and learn to love nature. The intellectual origins of the nature-study movement lay in natural history, but it also had a strongly spiritual dimension; the goal was not simply scientific observation. At the turn of the century, the movement especially attracted educated, middle-class women.

One of those women was the mother of Rachel Carson, who as a biologist and well-known writer would later emerge as a leading "witness for nature" with her landmark book, *Silent Spring*. Grace Steward almost certainly had some interest in the nature-study movement, especially given its spiritual aspect. In any case, many schools in the first years of the twentieth century, perhaps even Steward's, adopted "Comstock readers." He would eventually disavow any knowledge of nature study, a stigmatized field for a young man studying science, given its association with women and children, and the spiritual. From his perspective, not at all unique to the times, these associations were counter to his identity as a man and a scientist-in-training. They would have no place in his future theoretical approach.[37]

* * *

With his mother three thousand miles away, and contact limited to letters and a brief summer visit, he had slowly begun to follow his own interests, although not without struggle. By the second semester of his junior year, Steward had given up any idea of studying law, had changed his major from history to geology, and had felt "at last settled" about the direction of his future work. He had decided that he wanted to "go into work in exploration" when he left college. In order to prepare for that, he hoped to accompany Charles D. Walcott on one of his summer expeditions, serving as an assistant. (Walcott spent time nearly every summer doing paleontological research in the Canadian Rockies. Just fifteen years earlier, during the summer of 1909, Walcott had located the Burgess Shale, now recognized as containing paleontology's most important fossils.) Having taken courses in "geology, anthropology, and the basic sciences (with a little education)," Steward wrote in March 1924, he planned to finish college and teach for a year. He then hoped to "spend several years in exploration, and perhaps ultimately go back to teaching—probably geology or anthropology depending on the course of developments up to that time."[38]

The idea of teaching for a year had nothing to do with his own wishes and everything to do with duty. "The year's teaching stuck in after graduation," he explained, "would be for the first purpose of taking care of my mother for a year." He added that he also planned to use that time for "extensive reading and study." His plan conveyed a certain indifference about teaching, together with misjudgment of its demands. Clearly the primary motives were duty and his mother's financial need. Grace Steward had exhausted most of the funds from her divorce settlement within a few years, although she occasionally earned some money as a Christian Science nurse. Still, her financial situation remained so chronically precarious that her children helped support her. Grace and Marion often shared living quarters in San Francisco, but their disagreements inevitably led Marion to live apart for months or more at a time. Julian may also have sent his mother part of his scholarship stipend, as a contribution to her living expenses. The stipend would end, of course, with his graduation from Cornell.[39]

As it happened, Walcott decided not to undertake geological fieldwork during the summer of 1924. Having already accumulated so much material, he concluded that some of it had to be analyzed before he collected more. Julian Steward was advised to contact George R. Mansfield, father of Harvey and Jim Mansfield, his former classmates at Deep Springs. A geologist with the U.S. Geological Survey, Mansfield often organized summer expeditions to the West.[40]

Steward may have heard a great deal about exploration from his friends, especially the sons of government scientists. Several had fathers who had taken part in scientific expeditions in the American West and elsewhere. Coville's father, for example, had accompanied not only the government expedition to Death Valley in 1891 but also another to Alaska in 1899.[41] Although Steward's father always remained desk-bound in his work, his family could claim kinship with an explorer/scientist, and one who had made a famous expedition. John F. Steward, a relative of some degree, had accompanied John Wesley Powell as assistant geologist on his second trip down the Green and Colorado Rivers in 1871.

Born in Plano, Illinois, John Steward met Powell during the Civil War, in the course of the long seige of Vicksburg. The two men encountered each other while collecting fossils in the earthworks thrown up around the city. A few years later, Powell invited him to join the second expedition, devoted primarily to scientific work. John survived its hardships but left at the end of the first season, suffering from the effects of old war wounds. He returned to Illinois and resumed work at the Marsh Harvester Company. Years later, in 1908, one of his companions on the journey published *A Canyon Voyage,* a popular book that Julian undoubtedly read. He just as surely heard about John from his father, who had moved to Plano in 1876, only five years after the expedition.[42]

Nothing came of Julian's plans to spend the summer exploring western wildlands and searching for fossils. Instead, he and his roommate, Robert Aird, attended the annual convention of Telluride Association in Ithaca and then hitchhiked through New England and elsewhere in the East. That 1924 journey, like his trip through the Adirondacks, left no lasting impression.[43]

* * *

At the 1924 convention of Telluride Association, Steward had again been awarded a full scholarship, which would pay for his final year at Cornell. Back at Telluride House in the fall, his new position as editor of the *Telluride News Letter* kept him busy. That editorial work would teach him the value of having his name on the masthead (and, years later, the title page) of a publication; his stature in Telluride Association increased.

Near the end of the same semester, he applied to Telluride Association for a loan of one hundred dollars, citing "many obligations." He explained that he planned to work after graduating and would repay the loan then. "I have no assets to cover this loan," he continued, "other than certain Liberty Bonds which have been converted into good bonds in San Francisco (I believe Pacific Gas & Electric Co.) and are now held in my mother's name and could be used to cover the loan if necessary." The bonds probably paid interest on a quarterly or semi-annual basis to Grace, helping with her living expenses. They may have formed part of the settlement that his parents reached when their marriage ended and perhaps were originally intended to pay some of Julian's educational expenses. Or he may have bought the Liberty Bonds with his own earnings from his news-paper routes and summer jobs. In any event, Grace had possession of them.

At the time he sought a loan, the bond market had recently slumped, Pierce-Fair had gone out of business, and Marion had looked for work once again. She found a secretarial position with a paper company; whether the change in the bond market also directly affected Grace's finances is not clear. Soon after send-ing his letter, however, Julian wrote to say that he had "most unexpectedly and pleasantly come into the possession of a sum of money" that would suffice for the rest of the year. The source of those funds may have been his father. But the next month he wrote again to a Telluride official, asking for a loan to pay for visits to a dentist and oculist "and a number of other unexpected expenses."[44]

It was an odd request from a young man who had excellent eyesight; who had learned to keep careful account of his expenses during his years at Deep Springs, required as part of Nunn's training in financial responsibility; and who had a generous scholarship at Cornell. The expenses were probably his mother's. Any work that she found was only temporary; San Francisco still had no Christian Science nursing care facility, which might have provided her with a permanent position.[45] Her financial needs would remain erratic and unpredictable for many years: it was clearly a source of chronic anxiety for her son, and, less obviously but just as surely, important to him in an intellectual sense. His future theoretical work would give unusual attention to resource fluctuation, scarcity, and inse-curity, all of which he had experienced firsthand—and as a direct result of his mother's decision to divorce her husband, based at least in part on their reli-gious differences. From his point of view that decision had cost him dearly, in several senses.

Two days before his twenty-third birthday in January 1925, a record snowfall delivered more than twenty-five inches of snow in one day, with a temperature of twenty-two degrees below zero. It was an impressive display even for Ithaca. A few days later, Steward met with Livingston Farrand, president of Cornell University, to discuss his plans to live and work in the tropics. In the 1920s, the Philippines was still a territorial possession of the United States, and there was some prospect of a teaching position under the auspices of the American commissioner. He intended to do research while living in the Philippines, and he wanted to begin graduate study in anthropology before going there to teach.[46]

Many years later, Steward recalled how he had decided on anthropology as a career. "At Cornell I attempted to resolve my internal conflicts concerning my interest in science, the out of doors, and human well-being," he wrote. "In the first place, I felt that anthropology might satisfy my scientific interests. In the second place, since it involved field work it would satisfy my desire to travel and live in rural or primitive areas." The third, and primary, reason for choosing anthropology was that "some form of social science might satisfy my [scientific] interests while also dealing with social problems which seemed badly in need of understanding." He explained that he had taken the Deep Springs credo about humanitarian service very seriously. As a result, he said, "I turned my scientific interests from the physical and biological sciences to the social sciences."[47]

Had he felt free simply to pursue his own interests, he might well have chosen geology. He had taken more courses in that field than in any other science at Cornell, and he had desperately wanted to spend a summer working with Walcott, exploring and collecting fossils in the mountains of western Canada. Like a career in law, which he had previously considered, a career in geology probably seemed more familiar and accessible than anthropology. Besides his acquaintance with geologists who worked in the federal service, he had studied with geologists during his last years as an undergraduate. The only anthropologists he had encountered—and briefly, in one course he took as a freshman—were Kroeber, Lowie, and Gifford.

But Steward did happen to know of two men with interests in both geology and anthropology. One of them, John Steward, remained a lifelong student of natural history in the broadest sense. The self-taught geologist spent years learning about local history and the Fox Indians who had once lived in the region around his Illinois home. He finally wrote a book on the subject, but as an avocation. John Steward spent his working life in the employ of private firms in the vicinity of Chicago, eventually joining International Harvester, with which his family had close connections. His first expedition with Powell, as it turned out, was also his last.[48]

The second man, in contrast, had a career with all of the elements that Steward wished to combine in his own: exploration, scientific expeditions and research, and public service. That man was Powell himself. Powell's career had begun with training in geology and other branches of natural history, followed by a brief spell of teaching; then exploration and expeditions in the arid West, including the famous river journey in 1869 and its sequel; and finally a long period of public service, when he directed both the U.S. Geological Survey and the Bureau of American Ethnology. Powell's research had ranged from geology to anthropology, encompassing the lands of the arid West as well as the native peoples who lived there, especially Paiute and Ute Indians.[49]

Steward's own education and professional life would share some striking parallels with Powell's. Since he knew of Powell from childhood, some of these were probably not entirely by chance. His experiences in Deep Springs Valley, including an acquaintance with Paiute Indians, may have led him to identify even more closely with Powell, a man widely regarded during that era as the quintessential explorer/scientist.

*   *   *

Burr probably advised Steward to consult President Farrand about graduate study in anthropology. Although trained as a physician, Farrand had previously held an appointment as a professor of anthropology at Columbia University. After finishing his medical studies in New York City in 1891, he studied in Europe for two years and returned to the city in 1893 as a psychology instructor at Columbia. In 1903 he was appointed to a position in anthropology; Boas was his colleague in Columbia's department of psychology and anthropology. Farrand remained at Columbia until 1914 and spent the final years of his career serving as a university president. Although his active interest in anthropology was behind him when he and Steward met in 1925, he continued to correspond with former students and colleagues, including Kroeber and Lowie.[50]

Farrand, remembered as an exceptionally kind man, seems to have listened closely to Steward. He quickly understood that financial constraints made it impossible for this student to do graduate study at an Ivy League university. In 1925 few American universities offered any courses in anthropology, and even fewer offered graduate training in the field. Most of them—including Harvard, Columbia, Yale, the University of Pennsylvania, and the University of Chicago— were private and very expensive to attend. In contrast, the University of California, a public institution, charged only a nominal fee. Farrand probably also knew that Kroeber, the senior member of the department, had recently published on the Philippines, perhaps another factor that favored applying to the University of California.[51]

In early February 1925, Farrand wrote to Kroeber on Steward's behalf. "When I inquired as to his financial situation he said that was difficult," Farrand noted, mentioning that Steward was at Cornell on full scholarship from Telluride Association. "I am not in a position at this writing to say anything particular about him or his quality," Farrand added, "except that he strikes me as being a good student. He certainly makes an interesting and favorable impression in conversation."[52]

Steward did not immediately apply for admission, perhaps because of the press of work during his final semester at Cornell. He was taking the last classes needed for a major in zoology and geology, and he had enrolled in an introductory course in German, the foreign language considered most useful in science. Nunn died that semester, and as editor of the *Telluride News Letter*, Steward began to put together a commemorative issue in early April. But by the end of the month, he had found time to write to the department of anthropology at the University of California, providing details about his background in anthropology. While admitting to limited preparation in "social anthropology," he insisted that at Cornell he had "covered most of the work usually given" in an undergraduate major in anthropology. Either this statement reflected a misunderstanding of the field or a certain bravado. (Steward himself later wrote, critically, that Deep Springs gave him "a sense of being one of the chosen," which was, he added, "really smugness.")[53]

The tone of his letter also expresses how intensely he wanted to begin professional training, despite an utter lack of resources compared with his friends. The University of California, Berkeley—the public, coeducational institution he had chosen to leave three years earlier—offered his only hope. Some of his Telluride friends, in contrast, planned to enter Harvard, Princeton, and Yale: private, expensive, and highly exclusive institutions that admitted only men. Most of his classmates could count on financial help from their families, but he could not; moreover, he still had to worry about supporting his mother.[54]

As Steward explained in his letter, he had chosen anthropology as his "life work," but "for family reasons" had only one year at that point to spend in graduate study. He hoped to earn a master's degree and then find employment as a teacher in the Philippines. "I desire to take a position there," he wrote, "in order to both fulfill my family obligations and at the same time be in a region where I can do work toward the Ph.D." He concluded his letter by asking permission to write a master's thesis while taking courses. The reply he received warned about "attempting a very full programme for one year's work," but conceded that he could try. This constituted Steward's acceptance into the graduate program in anthropology, concluding a simple process strikingly unlike the highly formalized and complicated ones that developed later.[55]

The department did not offer financial assistance. Telluride Association, however, granted him a $500 "preferment" for graduate study at its 1925 convention, held in Ithaca in June. Steward must have known that he would be eligible for one of these scholarships, which had been awarded in previous years. His friend Reich, who planned to begin graduate study in physics at Cornell, also received one.[56]

* * *

After the convention, Steward spent about a month working outdoors in the Berkshires of western Massachusetts, a scenic region of rolling highlands presided over by Mount Greylock. His surroundings left him unimpressed, and he said nothing about its tallest mountain, less than thirty-five hundred feet in height and no rival to any of the Sierra peaks he had climbed. Anxious to supplement his scholarship, he had located a paying position as "nature study counsellor" at Camp Greylock for Boys. Nature study, with its spiritual overtones, obviously held no appeal for an aspiring young scientist, and he made it clear that he knew nothing about it. "I have found my chief occupation," he remarked in an unmistakable tone of irony, "to be to learn something of the subject myself."[57]

The Scopes trial, called "the trial of the century," took place during that very period, in July 1925. It can only have reinforced his sense that science and religion were fundamentally opposed, and that he was embarking on a career in the *science* of anthropology. The defendant, John T. Scopes, a schoolteacher in Tennessee, had broken state law by teaching evolutionary theory. His trial pitted Clarence Darrow, America's leading criminal defense lawyer and a man well known for his anticlerical views, against William Jennings Bryan, the prosecutor and a former presidential nominee, then leading a crusade against teaching evolution in public schools.

Scientists who prepared affidavits for the defense included a geologist, a zoologist, and the University of Chicago anthropologist, Fay-Cooper Cole—the three men representing, as it happened, Steward's undergraduate and graduate fields of study. Citing fossil evidence, they offered a detailed account of hominid evolution; and Cole mentioned a recent and dramatic find from Africa, described as a "'man-like ape'" (the first identified remains of the genus *Australopithecus*). Unswayed by the testimony of science, the jury returned a verdict of guilty after nine minutes of deliberation.[58]

The Scopes trial was a front-page story in all of the major newspapers, and one that Steward must have followed with keen interest and a deep sense of identification. The material evidence of science, which pointed in a direction at odds with prevailing religious belief, had been summarily rejected and the defendant found guilty. In many ways the trial encapsulated his running disagreement with his mother, and with all proponents of what he later labeled "-ism and ideology." The materialist perspective that would characterize his work in anthropology was already in place in 1925, reflecting his recent training in science, a hard-won but firm commitment to science, and an equally strong repudiation of religion in any form.

A defining feature of his materialist perspective—a perennial interest in subsistence—also had roots in his experiences in late adolescence. During his university years, in the East and in the West, Steward was preoccupied with making ends meet, supporting himself and helping his mother as needed. Not surprisingly, he felt chronically, and sometimes acutely, insecure, as he edged from one scholarship and temporary job to another. He never knew until the Telluride convention in late June each year whether he could pay for his tuition in August, and he never knew from one month to the next whether his mother would need financial help. In sharp contrast to his friends, despite sharing the same class background, he had no sense of financial security. Even as he readied to enter graduate school, it remained unclear whether he had the means to complete the first year.

From his perspective, some of his mother's life choices had led to the splin-

tering of his family, to her chronic financial problems, and thus to his predicament. Grace's failure to support herself, along with a casual way of handling
money, would pose problems for Julian and Marion for many years to come.[59]
Perhaps predictably, in his later professional life and research, Steward would
always devalue, or completely overlook, women's labor.

His own persistent concerns during this period foreshadowed his intellectual
focus on subsistence. Years later, speaking about her husband's research, Jane
Steward put it this way: "His interest was in subsistence, *always.*"[60]

CHAPTER 4

BERKELEY AND BEYOND

Julian Steward returned to the West in August 1925, arriving just before classes began at Berkeley. During his first two semesters, he stayed sometimes with his mother on Green Street in San Francisco, and occasionally with his sister Marion, who lived on Pine Street. He disliked this nomadic way of life and complained that it left him "a bit disorganized." Limited finances kept him from moving across the bay to Berkeley and renting a room in a boardinghouse as most graduate students did. His scholarship fell short of the usual cost of a year's study by several hundred dollars.[1]

Marion still worked as a secretary and Dictaphone operator for Zellerbach Paper Company, at an office on Battery Street. Grace was again trying to find work as a Christian Science nurse. There was no shortage of nurses in San Francisco, and in December 1925 she finally advertised her services in the *Christian Science Journal*. Her financial needs as well as his own may explain why Julian sent a letter to Telluride Association less than two months after receiving two hundred dollars, the first installment of his five-hundred-dollar scholarship, to say that he was "now absolutely broke." Writing from his mother's Green Street address, he explained that he had "just scratched along for the last several days on a few borrowed dollars," and asked for another one hundred dollars of his scholarship funds.[2]

He attributed his financial dilemma to the expense of starting graduate study at Berkeley ("fees, etc."), but the cost was in fact negligible. The University of California charged far less than other major universities, public or private; and graduate students, with the exception of those in the professional schools, paid no tuition.[3] Educational expenses did not wholly explain Steward's need for an advance payment of his scholarship, and his living expenses were also modest.

He had recently bought a car, although it cost very little to commute to Berkeley by ferry and streetcar. Owning a car during that era—even a bargain like his "little fifty dollar Chevrolet," vintage 1923—was expensive because of the high cost of gasoline and the need for frequent maintenance. (The mechanical skills he developed at Deep Springs did help him take care of most maintenance and many repairs himself.) Owning the Chevrolet, clearly an extravagance, had everything to do with leaving the confines of city life and escaping to remote and scenic places. Motor vehicles had already emerged as the transportation of choice for scientific expeditions. A car was a passport to outdoor adventure and discovery in the West in an era when the road system remained so rudimentary that obstacles and hazards lay just around the next turn, along with sweeping views.[4]

Since he still hoped to do two years' work in one, to finish the course work and thesis for a master's degree within the year, Steward did not look for work. Instead, he planned to subsist on the funds from Telluride Association. "Next year," he wrote, "I hope to break away from this hand to mouth existence, and have pretty definitely planned to go to the Philippines where, I find much to my delight, I will probably be able to carry on my anthropological work among the mountain tribes." As it turned out, however, he would stay at Berkeley for doctoral study, and his subsistence worries would continue.[5]

Like many of his fellow graduate students, Steward spent his graduate years trying to patch together a livelihood. But in contrast to most of them, he had to help support someone else as well. His scholarship, while rather generous for the times and intended to pay only his own expenses, dwindled at an alarming rate during his first year of graduate study. Adding to his anxieties, he needed to find a topic for his thesis, and complete it, at the same time that he was taking courses in a new field. It comes as no surprise that he appeared to be "a worrier" to Ralph Beals and others who knew him at Berkeley. Beals remembered that Steward often seemed anxious about his health and that the other students generally regarded him as "a hypochondriac."[6]

This view persisted despite how much his health obviously deteriorated during at least one term as a graduate student. Even Kroeber and Lowie discussed it, wondering whether he could stand up to the physical rigors of fieldwork. Grace Steward, in contrast, must not have been receptive to his anxiety about his health and his decision, sometime during his graduate years, to undergo surgery.[7] She saw prayer as the proper course of action, but her son had by then shed any religious beliefs and made no secret of it, to her or to other people. He argued openly with her about religion.[8]

Two of Steward's other worries during this period centered on understanding women and on finding a place to live in Berkeley. Beals remembered hearing him "complain loudly that he couldn't understand women," but this did not prevent him from having a very active social life. His uneven relations with Grace and Marion may have contributed to the complaint, but living among men at Deep Springs and in Telluride House probably reinforced his sense of women as alien and difficult to understand. Frustrated as well by his housing problems, Steward made a mock threat to move into the foyer of the anthropology building, where an Egyptian sarcophagus made of black granite rested on trestles. Underneath was a small space, known for several years thereafter as "Julian's house," testimony to his wish to live in Berkeley and his inability to pay rent.[9]

The search for a place to stay resulted in a fortunate encounter with Matthew Stirling, not long before he became director of the Bureau of American Ethnology. (He hired Steward about eight years later.) Only six years older than Steward, Stirling had already organized a major expedition, reputedly self-financed by means of some creative speculation in real estate. A fellow student had told Steward that Stirling's parents, who lived in Berkeley, "always had a spare bed for a wanderer." As Steward recalled to Stirling thirty years later, "[I] was sound asleep—probably in your bed—when you arrived home from your Smithsonian-New Guinea expedition. We introduced ourselves, as one may under the circumstances, and you kindly let me go to sleep again."[10]

The department of anthropology during that era occupied an odd-looking building, with roof and walls made of corrugated metal sheets. It had once served as a temporary, fireproof storage place for the Phoebe Apperson Hearst collections, which formed the basis of the University of California's Museum of Anthropology. In 1903 the museum collections had been moved to San Francisco, where they remained until 1931. The department took over the vacant warehouse, converting it for use as an academic building.[11]

Even decades later, Beals and Steward had vivid memories of the "tin shack," as the renovated warehouse was called. They remembered that the ends had been partitioned off and a balcony built around the entire building inside. In the mid-1920s, casts of heroic-size classical statuary still stood on the lower floor, along with the Egyptian sarcophagus. Strangely out of place, their size had probably made moving them to the museum too difficult. All anthropology classes and seminars were held in the building, which contained, besides two classrooms and the faculty offices, space for teaching and research assistants, graduate students, and editorial assistants. During the years when Lowie served as editor of the *American Anthropologist,* from 1924 to 1933, the building also provided the journal's editorial office.[12]

Students not only attended classes, worked, and consulted faculty members there but also had space to socialize and have discussions with one another. The isolated location of the building, next to the faculty tennis court and not far from the faculty club, and the fact that anthropology was wholly centered there, encouraged a certain closeness among the students. Steward made friends with some of the other anthropology students, especially Beals and William Duncan Strong. Ronald Olson, a former lumberjack, with some colorful stories when he arrived at Berkeley at age thirty-one, was also a good friend during those years. Other students in the graduate program included Anna Gayton, Forrest Clements, Theodora Kracow Brown, W. Lloyd Warner, Isabel Kelly, and Lila M. O'Neale. Some of them became friends of different degrees, and members of "the gang," also known as "the North Berkeley gang." In contrast to Deep Springs and Cornell, a number of the students were women and nearly all were westerners by origin.[13]

Among all the students, Steward had the most in common with Duncan Strong, who hailed from Portland, Oregon. Three years older, he was already an advanced graduate student when Steward entered the program. Both shared a background in the physical and biological sciences. Strong had first majored in zoology as an undergraduate student, but by the beginning of his senior year, he had changed his major to anthropology, largely because of his interest in archaeology. When he needed a job during his senior year, Kroeber hired him to classify prehistoric material from Peru. The German archaeologist Max Uhle had collected it years earlier, with financial backing from Hearst. After Strong finished the work, Kroeber used the results to write two reports and listed him as coauthor. He followed this practice with a number of students, although never with Steward.[14]

Strong had written to Kroeber to ask for a job just before beginning his senior year at Berkeley, citing "a sudden change" in his family's financial circumstances. The next summer, after graduating but before beginning graduate study, he wrote again to Kroeber about his financial problems, but this time he did not find a sympathetic ear. Kroeber advised him that he should simply borrow money and pay it back when he was "established." "If the thing that has primary weight in your mind is income," he wrote, "or keeping out of debt at all hazards, it is obviously unwise to go in for scientific work when you are still several years from your doctorate and can easily make two or three times as much outside the University as in it."

He reminded Strong of their previous conversations and remarked that perhaps he had not been entirely clear about "this basic principle" of a career in science, a principle that he had "just tried to express in its nakedness." As he concluded, "the problem is one to be decided wholly by yourself; whether you sufficiently want the anthropological work to pay the price for it which the next few years are likely to entail." The price was not only hard work and bare subsistence but also insecurity and risk, given the scarcity of professional positions for anthropologists. Kroeber's counsel to an aspiring graduate student, as apt now as then, grew out of observations during more than twenty years in the profession as well as his own life experience.[15]

The son of a prosperous businessman, Kroeber well understood the differences between the academic world and the business world, especially the contrasts in financial reward and opportunity. He had narrowly avoided unemployment himself early in his career, when he lost his position as curator of anthropology at the California Academy of Sciences after just one year. In 1901, with the academy unable to continue paying his modest salary, Hearst agreed to fund a new position for an instructor in anthropology at the University of California. She paid Kroeber's salary, as well as other expenses of the new department and museum of anthropology, for several years.[16]

Although Kroeber later achieved eminence and had an extraordinarily long career in anthropology—he remained active for sixty years—his promotions came slowly, and he obviously found some aspects of professional life difficult. Only a few years before he wrote to Strong, he had privately questioned whether to continue in anthropology. Kroeber's letters to Elsie Clews Parsons, a friend and colleague, convey the depth of his disillusion with anthropology and academic life at that point: "I live in the Faculty Club, detest the members as a mass," he wrote in 1919.[17]

Kroeber never experienced unemployment but, as he well knew, some less-fortunate colleagues struggled with extended periods of marginal employment, or none. Even his own teacher, Boas, had no steady work for more than a year in the mid-1890s, although Kroeber may not have known that.[18] The common practice in anthropology, as in many other academic disciplines, has been to conceal periods of unemployment or employment outside the academic world to avoid stigma within the profession. For most academics, professional success is defined in part by the appearance of a smooth career path.

Kroeber's colleague Lowie had also lost a position, after fourteen years at the American Museum of Natural History, when the museum balanced its budget by reducing the staff. Two anthropologists, Lowie and Herbert Spinden, left the employ of the museum.[19] (Many of the published accounts about the two men say only that they left the museum in 1921, without explaining the reason for their departure. This habit of silence, which extended to cases other than Lowie's and Spinden's, had the effect of concealing the straitened circumstances of the new profession.)

Kroeber managed to create a position for Lowie, but he certainly knew other anthropologists, including Berkeley residents such as Paul Radin and Edwin Loeb, who did not have continuing academic employment. Steward's peers, but disproportionately the women, would also encounter problems. Some, like Kelly, spent their professional lives outside the university; others, including O'Neale and Gayton, found positions in programs related to home economics.[20] The employment problems that plagued the new field in its early years would persist for most of the twentieth century.[21]

Perhaps Kroeber offered Steward the same advice he had given Strong, especially since Steward had chronic financial worries during these years, not just the occasional setback. The Telluride Association scholarship, and it alone, had made it possible for him to begin graduate study, but it did not cover all of his expenses. By the end of his first semester, he had already received the fourth, and presumably final, installment of his scholarship. Somehow he managed to make ends meet and finished the academic year.[22]

As the end of fall term approached in December 1925, Steward contacted the director of Deep Springs about visiting the school for a week in January. "I have been hoping ever since I left Deep Springs four years ago to get in a visit," he explained, "and now that I am leaving for the Philippines, in all probability, right after my work is over . . . I am going to try awfully hard to come up during this vacation." After returning to Berkeley, he wrote that "The boys showed me the most cordial hospitality and I felt completely at home. Deep Springs has always meant a great deal to me but I did not realize until I went back just how much."[23] He would find reasons to return there repeatedly during the next few years.

During the fall semester he had taken upper-division courses with Kroeber, Lowie, and Gifford.[24] In spring 1926, he took another upper-division course and two graduate seminars, and registered to work on his master's thesis. One of his seminars, with Lowie, was "Applied Methods." Despite the name, it was not a course on field methods. The topic, which apparently shifted from one semester to the next, was linguistics that semester. This provided Steward's only training in linguistics, which he always considered entirely peripheral to his research interests.[25]

The other seminar, "Culture Processes," his only graduate-level course with Kroeber, trained students to organize data. Steward remembered years later that he and another student, Theodora Kracaw Brown, were assigned to work together on the problem of element distributions in North American Indian field games. Theodora Brown, called "Krakie" by her friends, was twenty-nine years old and a widow with two young sons. Coincidentally, she had grown up in the mining town of Telluride, Colorado, where Nunn began his career, and she had childhood memories of him. By the end of the semester, she and Kroeber decided to marry, and she withdrew from the graduate program despite encouragement from her husband to continue. He thought of a doctorate as "insurance" for her, useful in case she ever had to seek employment. But she finally decided that even with household help, her responsibilities at home precluded further work for a Ph.D. Kroeber, then fifty years old, was a widower; his first wife had died of tuberculosis in 1913, after a long and difficult illness.[26]

At the end of the same semester, Steward finished his thesis, as he had planned, receiving his master's degree in anthropology in May 1926. The title of the thesis, "The Distribution and Use of the Tambourine in Shamanism," reflected a then major interest of American anthropology, the diffusion of specific cultural traits from a point of origin to other regions. It also displayed elements of his own distinctive approach, which he would develop further in his doctoral dissertation: a preference for generalization rather than particularism; a disregard for religious belief and the symbolic; a focus on the observable; and an interest in function and causality.

In his thesis, he identified psychological forces as causal, an unexpected emphasis since he had taken only a one-semester course in that discipline, at Cornell. Defining the tambourine as a hand drum, he remarked that other types of drums share the same functions as tambourines with regard to "dealing with supernatural powers." He emphasized the psychological effects of drumming. "In Siberia and North America," he wrote, "it is perhaps the most important means of producing that state of nervous frenzy [spirit possession] which is the sine qua non of shamanizing."[27]

By May 1926, when he finished his thesis, Steward had moved from San Francisco to Berkeley, where he shared quarters with Strong. His choice of thesis topic, involving the scientific study of a religious phenomenon, as well as his new address on Shasta Road asserted his independence from his mother and her way of life. He received a high evaluation for his first year's work, which included finishing his master's thesis in record time, and planned to enter the doctoral program without delay. "My Philippines trip has blown over," he wrote, explaining that the American commissioner had failed to provide the promised teaching position. That was "much to my satisfaction," he continued, "for I seem pretty well established in Anthropology now and and hope to continue toward a Ph.D. next year."[28]

* * *

Sometime during that first year he met Dorothy Nyswander, a graduate student in psychology. A woman of great warmth, intelligence, and determination, she understood her abilities and had no doubts about her direction in life. Before entering the University of California, she had studied mathematics at the University of Nevada in Reno, where she earned bachelor's and master's degrees. She married a mathematician at the University of Nevada, and they had a child. Several years later she divorced him and moved with her young daughter to Alameda, California, not far from Berkeley, where she taught mathematics at a high school. During the first summer in 1922, she took some classes at Berkeley, including a summer school course taught by Boas.[29]

Dorothy Nyswander had considered earning a doctorate in mathematics but soon decided that the field was "not very useful." Increasingly, she found that her interests centered on psychology, and specifically on learning. "How does learning occur? That question fascinated me," she said seventy-five years later, adding that educational psychology seemed "much more useful" to her than mathematics. She decided on psychology for a Ph.D., with mathematics as her minor. When she met Julian Steward, during his first year of graduate study and her last, she was finishing research for her dissertation. Highly skilled in experimental research, a practiced "rat-runner," she was carrying out a series of experiments with white laboratory rats, using mazes and studying patterns of learning. Her adviser, Edward Chace Tolman, a prominent neobehaviorist and theorist, later incorporated her findings in his well-known book, *Purposive Behavior in Animals and Man,* published in 1932.[30]

When Dorothy and Julian met, she was thirty-one years old, seven years his senior, and about to embark on a professional career. They had much in common intellectually, from training in science to some shared interests in anthropology. The psychology and anthropology departments maintained close ties at the time, and students studying in one department were encouraged to take courses in the other. Besides the summer school course with Boas, she had taken a seminar with Lowie, whom she came to regard as an exceptionally kind person and a friend. When she finished her degree in 1926, another friend gave a party for her; she recalled that Lowie attended and regaled her with German drinking songs in honor of the occasion. Still a bachelor at the age of forty-three, he often socialized with his students, unlike Kroeber.[31]

Julian's thesis, in progress during Dorothy's last months in Berkeley, showed a strongly psychological orientation, as would his doctoral dissertation. Years later, many of his students and other anthropologists found this puzzling, given his antagonism during the 1940s and later to psychological explanation in cultural anthropology, and they wondered at the source. Some, like Beals, credited anthropology's close ties with the department of psychology at Berkeley, but Steward took no psychology courses as a graduate student and only one as an undergraduate. Personal ties explain more about the direction of his work than interdepartmental relations. Dorothy clearly influenced his approach, one better and more specifically described as behaviorist. He always rejected psychological explanations of a nonbehaviorist type, regarding them as unscientific.[32]

Julian and Dorothy met just as he was beginning to study anthropology, with the goal of understanding human behavior in a scientific way. But his teachers, as he soon learned, and especially Kroeber, had no interest in that approach and did not encourage his attempts to generalize and to identify causes of cultural behavior. "I am interested in phenomena, not causes," Kroeber repeatedly told his young student.[33] Dorothy, in distinct contrast, used an experimental methodology to study behavior, including its causes, and she had trained under a neobehaviorist.

Behaviorism, first systematically stated by John B. Watson just ten years before she entered graduate school, had quickly gained acceptance in psychology. Rooted in positivism, it emphasized the observable, embraced the methods of science, and rejected any notion of a metaphysical, nonmaterial reality. Behaviorism thus represented a radical departure from earlier psychological approaches, which focused on consciousness and mental activity, using introspection as a primary method of study. Watson had identified the subject matter of behaviorism as the objectively observable actions of animals, nonhuman and human alike. In his framework, an animal responds to internal biological processes and also to stimuli, conditions set by the external "environment"—meaning not simply the natural environment but everything external to the organism. When the stimuli change, the animals' behavior changes, a process of stimulus and response, or cause and effect. Neobehaviorists, including Tolman, remained committed to Watson's objectivist method but tried to formulate laws of behavior.[34]

By her own account, Dorothy became "an all-out behaviorist" at Berkeley. She received training from Tolman and others, and, most memorably, had a summer course with Edward L. Thorndike, whose experimentally derived laws of learning came to hold a central place in learning theory.[35] Convinced of the value of a stimulus-response framework, she seems to have given Steward some specific advice as he worked on his thesis. Besides determining distribution, almost obligatory in anthropology at the time, he used a behaviorist framework in thinking about function and causality. Essentially, he argued that the beat of the tambourine constitutes a stimulus, which produces a behavioral response, spirit possession.

Dorothy and Julian had much in common besides a shared interest in behaviorism and science. She had grown up in Antelope Valley, along the California-Nevada border and north of Deep Springs and Owens Valley, where her father served as general manager of a large ranch. The owner, T. B. Rickey, something of a local land baron, had holdings that included thousands of acres in Owens Valley; he later sold that land to the city of Los Angeles, thus helping to seal the valley's fate.[36] As a child, Dorothy spent time exploring the desert in Antelope Valley, often on horseback. She knew many of the Paiute and Washo ranch hands and played with their children. Two of her good friends and schoolmates, Dewey and Ida Cornbread, were Washo Indians. Her childhood world, in other words, had some parallels to life at Deep Springs.

But there were also important differences in her experience of ranch life, involving both ranch work and the workers, which influenced the course of her later professional work and led her in a direction that differed from Steward's. As a young girl, and as the daughter of the general manager, she did no outdoor work herself. All of that was left to men, the ranch hands, most of them Indians. She knew them and their families from an early age, and from them learned a different way of being: the ability "to be quiet, and to enjoy quietness," as she put it. But their poverty and living conditions distressed her, and she admired her parents for offering them help, often by providing food. Many years later, she saw this as the source of her own lifelong interest in human welfare. Reflecting on her life and career, she remarked, "My value system is biased in favor of the poor." Early experiences—including growing up during the Progressive Era, which emphasized the ideals of service and social reform—had led her in the early 1920s to study something "more useful" than mathematics.[37]

After finishing her doctorate, Dorothy spent the summer of 1926 at Stanford University, working as a research assistant in animal behavior and carrying out more experiments on the learning ability of white rats. At the end of the summer, she prepared to move to Salt Lake City. With Tolman's sponsorship, she had been offered a position as assistant professor of education and psychology at the University of Utah. Her seven-year-old daughter, Mary Elizabeth (later called Marie), and her parents went with her. She would return to Stanford

during the next summer to assist again in a research project—and also to see
Julian.[38]

* * *

In June 1926 Steward spent a few days at Deep Springs, where he attended the
annual convention of Telluride Association. His former roommate from Cornell,
Aird, also attended, along with a number of the students he had known at Deep
Springs. Once again he received a $500 scholarship from Telluride Association
to continue graduate study in anthropology. Reich, still a graduate student in
physics at Cornell, also received funding, as did Putnam and Aird, to study law
and medicine, respectively, at Harvard.[39]

After the convention ended, Steward left California for northern Oregon to
begin his first extended fieldwork in archaeology. Aird, at liberty for the summer before beginning medical school, went with him. During July 1926, they
worked at archaeological sites in the Dalles-Deschutes River area along the
Columbia River, where it forms the border between Oregon and Washington.
As a natural pathway between the Northwest Coast and the Plateau-Great Basin areas, the region held interest for archaeologists. Strong had worked there
previously, together with a businessman-turned-anthropologist, W. Egbert
Schenk.[40]

Recalling his fieldwork in Oregon thirty years later, Steward remarked that
he was almost wholly untrained in archaeology. It was "curious," he added, that
Kroeber offered no courses on archaeology at that time. He taught no survey
course and provided no instruction on field method, either archaeological or
ethnographic, despite his own experience. "I improvised my Columbia River
archaeology," Steward continued, "which, like that of Strong and Schenck, was
unbelievably bad." This sink-or-swim approach to first fieldwork, not at all
unique to Kroeber, would prevail for years in anthropology, and longer among
cultural anthropologists than archaeologists.[41]

A letter from the field gives some sense of this first venture, with aspects of
misadventure, in archaeology. Writing to Gifford in mid-July from Moody,
Oregon, Steward explained that he had worked at five sites, all on Miller's Island in the Columbia River. The first was a burial, located at the foot of a cliff
with pictographs. "The skeletons were very old," he wrote, "and only three could
be exposed sufficiently for photographing. Then they blew away!" The other sites
included burials and a row of fifteen house-pits, but the work had gone so
quickly that he thought they could finish it in "only a week or so." They would
not be sorry to leave, he remarked, on account of the extreme heat and wind.[42]

A month later, he wrote a more detailed letter to Strong describing the trip
to Oregon and the fieldwork. Strong had accepted a position as assistant curator at Chicago's Field Museum of Natural History in 1926, which may have kept
him from taking part in the Oregon project in July. Steward reported that he
and Aird had reached Portland in two-and-a-half days in his "fifty dollar car,"

adding, however, that they drove eighteen hours a day. They had covered more than six hundred miles, averaging less than twenty miles an hour, not unusual for that time and place. Proceeding eastward along the Columbia River to a point near Miller's Island, they encountered a gale-force wind that made crossing the river in a small boat seem "sheer suicide." They survived the trip but still had to reckon with the wind. For the next three weeks it blew constantly, and they worked, ate, and slept in a violent swirl of dust. Despite the poor field conditions, and the ravages of too many relic hunters who had already visited some sites, they recovered a fair amount of material, much of which they shipped to Berkeley by rail.[43]

Before leaving Oregon, Steward summoned up what remained of his energy and, as he put it, "insanely climbed Mt. Hood," a peak in the Cascade Range located just east of the Deschutes River. "[I] was repaid by a glorious view," he added. Mount Rainier, a hundred miles to the north in Washington, "seemed only a step away." The return trip to Berkeley took them through redwood country along the northern coast of California. Traveling over a rutted road that followed the sea offered still more adventure and scenic pleasure: "We averaged three blow outs a day, and the car required more water than gas," Steward reported. "However, the trip [from] Crescent City [to] Eureka, despite hellish roads, was damned pretty."[44]

Despite problems of inexperience and haste, the summer's work in Oregon yielded material for a publication by Strong, Schenck, and Steward a few years later. Before that appeared in print, Steward had already published several articles of his own, including his first, "A New Type of Carving from the Columbia Valley," which appeared in the *American Anthropologist* less than a year after his summer research in Oregon. Steward had mentioned the bone carvings in his letter to Strong, remarking that he had found a few similar pieces in Strong's collection and planned to write a short paper. "I have heard rumors that Krieger has found something similar in the upper Columbia somewhere," he said, "and I would like to get the jump on him."[45]

In the brief article that resulted, Steward concluded that how the carved figures had been used was "purely conjectural." While conceding that they might have been religious "effigies," he saw no reason to assume a use other than ornamentation. This foreshadowed what became a pattern in his theoretical work: avoiding the subject of religion by denying its analytical significance. (Near the end of his career, Steward denied the charge of critics that he had overlooked religion in his writings on cultural ecology; he simply did not see what they saw.)[46]

Other articles soon followed, including a popular piece on petroglyphs in the magazine *Touring Topics* in May 1927, at about the same time his article appeared in the *American Anthropologist*. His family background helps to explain why he, more than some of his fellow students, so readily understood the professional importance of publishing and the value of having his name on a lengthy list of publications. His maternal uncle, the older brother whom his mother looked up to, was a published writer; and Grace encouraged both her children to write from an early age and to write for publication, for prestige, and, when possible, for profit. Julian was probably paid for the article in *Touring Topics*. His article in a professional journal brought no income but did change his status from student to fledgling published scholar.[47]

Marion, described later in life by her brother as "especially gifted as a writer," published two poems a few years before his first professional article appeared in print. Marion's poems, both written for the *Christian Science Journal,* were filled with imagery from the natural world; she too had been influenced by her mother's naturalist aesthetic, although it found a very different expression in Marion's writing than in her brother's. Nearly all of Julian's writing was molded after Edward Garriott's; his uncle was a government scientist and an author of monographs on topics in meteorology.[48]

* * *

As he began his second year of graduate study at Berkeley, Steward found changes in the department, reflecting the peripatetic nature of anthropologists and their work. The departure of his good friend Strong for Chicago and the Field Museum left a true void. Kroeber, accompanied by his new wife, had departed for Peru in June to do archaeological work on behalf of the Field Museum. He remained in Peru during the fall semester, his position at Berkeley filled by a Swedish anthropologist, Baron Erland Nordenskiöld of the University of Göteborg, whom Lowie had met in Europe in 1924.

The son of the famous explorer/scientist who discovered the Northeast Passage, Nordenskiöld had made several lengthy expeditions to South America. Besides excavating at sites in the Andes, he had carried out ethnographic research among Indians living in the Amazon and in the Gran Chaco. During the fall term at Berkeley, he offered two courses on South America, "Problems in the Anthropology of South America" and "Ethnography of South America." Steward enrolled in both courses, excelling in the former but doing so poorly in the latter that he received no credit. He also took part in a few days of archaeological fieldwork, joining Nordenskiöld and several students at a site in the northern San Joaquin Valley, south of Sacramento.[49]

Nordenskiöld's visit at Berkeley later proved significant for Steward. Two years before Nordenskiöld came to Berkeley, Lowie had talked to him and another European scholar, the French anthropologist Paul Rivet, about publishing a handbook on South American Indians "as a joint venture." The project finally came to fruition in the 1940s, some years after Nordenskiöld's death, and as an American initiative. Steward served as general editor and the Smithsonian as sponsor. The *Handbook of South American Indians* was to be one of his major contributions to anthropology, and one stimulus as well as a vehicle for his ideas on culture types and cultural evolution.[50]

Besides his courses on South America, Steward took another graduate seminar with Lowie that semester, again under the title "Applied Methods." The topic that term appears to have been primitive art, a subject that would never hold great interest for him, given his materialist and behaviorist bent. But it obviously helped him analyze the bone carvings he had brought back from Oregon, some in fragments, which required patient reconstruction. He enrolled in a course in zoology as well, "Heredity and Evolution," an upper-division course also recommended for undergraduate majors in anthropology. Graduate students in anthropology and other departments at Berkeley commonly took courses outside their discipline at the time. Beals thought that psychology was the required minor for the early doctoral students at Berkeley, but if this had been the policy previously, the department no longer enforced it when Steward entered the program in the mid-1920s. He chose geography as his minor despite the interest he showed in psychology in his master's thesis. Geography, with both physical and cultural branches, was the social science with closest ties to geology, Steward's major subject at Cornell. Perhaps more to the point, it had a long history of scientific exploration.[51]

The intellectual justification for requiring a minor was that it helped students to pursue their own special interests and develop in their own chosen directions. Anthropology at Berkeley was not doctrinaire, and self-consciously so. But a glance at the university catalogs of the 1920s suggests a highly practical reason for encouraging graduate students to take courses in other departments. The anthropology faculty comprised just two full-time positions, Kroeber's and Lowie's; a part-time one, Gifford's; and a temporary appointment, then held by Edwin Loeb. Born to a prominent New York family and educated at Yale, Loeb is remembered as a modest man, "a gentlemanly scholar and a scholarly gentleman." His research interests centered on religion and on Pomo Indians.[52]

Steward appears to have audited just one of Loeb's courses, in spring 1928. The topic was primitive religion, but lectures made passing mention of "modern religions," including Christian Science: "curing by self hypnotism—not an original religion—a combination of older elements," Steward recorded in his notes. He also learned, "Women just as religious as men—but they have never started religions," since Christian Science, among other examples cited, was merely a "composite" of old beliefs and practices. Moreover, while "women can be shamans & seers . . . [they] are never priests," he recorded. Generations of students would read textbooks and hear lectures in anthropology courses that similarly denied that women had any importance in religious life, in any known place or time. For Steward, the sweeping generalizations about religion and about women conformed to and confirmed some of his own views; and although those views derived from his own social and emotional experiences, they took on the authority of science.[53]

By the end of his second year, Steward had taken the few graduate seminars in anthropology, including his third and final seminar with Lowie, on theory.

In a course that Beals remembered as "a pretty thorough survey of the history of ethnological theory," Lowie gave careful attention to different theories of diffusion and strenuously criticized various theories of evolution. Beals recalled that Lowie also claimed that he was not opposed to the concept of cultural evolution, although in his book *Primitive Society* he had attacked nineteenth-century evolutionary ideas, especially those of Lewis Henry Morgan. His objection to existing evolutionary theories was primarily that they did not conform to new ethnographic data. If anyone could construct a theory that did fit the facts, Lowie said, he would happily embrace it. (Despite Steward's later efforts, Lowie preferred diffusionist explanations until the end of his career.)[54]

During the same semester, spring 1927, Steward also enrolled in three of the five geography courses that would constitute his minor. Carl Sauer taught two of them, both upper-division courses. The class in field geography met on Saturdays, in the Berkeley Hills and in nearby Marin or San Mateo Counties. The university catalog described the course as an "intensive field study of a rural area with detailed mapping of the elements that constitute the natural region and of the condition of its utilization." The second course centered on the different schools of thought in geography, a counterpoint to his seminar with Lowie. Students had to read original sources in a variety of languages, including German; and Steward, who had formally studied German for only one semester at Cornell, struggled with some of the assigned texts. "I am trying to learn German by summer," he wrote to Strong, "and do a million other things."[55]

German geographer Oskar Schmieder taught the third course, a graduate seminar on regional geography. The following semester, in fall 1927, he took two more courses with Schmieder. During the same years, graduate students from geography commonly enrolled in anthropology courses. One of them remembered having a seminar in the 1920s with Kroeber "in which any traces of geographical determinism I might have acquired were wiped out."[56]

Sauer, who had left the University of Michigan for Berkeley in 1923, was in many respects Kroeber's counterpart in the department of geography. Both men published prolifically, achieved international prominence, and, on home ground, kept a close rein on their departments. Like Kroeber, Sauer spent nearly all of his professional career at Berkeley and served as chair of his department for decades. There he assembled, as did Kroeber, a small cast of faculty members who played supporting roles and a sizable contingent of graduate students, training about twenty doctoral students over the years.[57]

Soon after his arrival at Berkeley, Sauer made Kroeber's acquaintance. Their relationship grew so strong over time that they offered seminars together, coordinated their research projects, and served as members of doctoral committees in each other's department. The two men shared many interests, particularly in culture history, as well as a strongly Germanic worldview. Both were bilingual, having grown up in families in which German was the language of the home. At one time they discussed the possibility of a joint department, and Loeb, billed an "anthropogeographer," taught in both departments on occasion. These ties eventually grew weaker as the two departments expanded, but for years some graduate students from anthropology considered geography a second home, and those from geography routinely took courses with Kroeber and Lowie.[58]

Schmieder, recruited by Sauer in 1925, taught at Berkeley as an associate professor before returning to Germany in 1930. Schmieder had been working in Argentina on settlement and agriculture before going to Berkeley, and he taught courses based on his work in the pampas and Andean South America. At least one of Steward's courses with Schmieder, which he took after having the two courses with Nordenskiöld, had a strong South American component. The university catalog described the seminar as "concerned with primitive cultural areas, in particular South America." Years later, Steward may have remembered this specific seminar when he wrote that he had always considered geography "essential to studies of rural, primitive peoples."[59]

As his second year of graduate study drew to a close, Steward's finances for the third and final year remained uncertain. He was working as an editorial assistant for the *American Anthropologist,* a paying, part-time position that he held for both semesters, along with another part-time position grading quizzes and tests for the introductory courses.[60] But then, unexpectedly, he received a loan of fifty dollars a month for the next twelve months from Max Rosenberg, a San Francisco businessman, a friend of Kroeber's and an occasional patron of anthropology at Berkeley. Kroeber undoubtedly helped to arrange the loan, which Steward took several years to repay. As it happened, Telluride Association awarded him five hundred dollars for the next academic year; and together with the loan, this brought his income to a rather comfortable level for a student at that time.[61]

His mother's financial situation had also improved, at least in one respect. After having lived apart for several years, Grace and Marion were again sharing quarters, this time at a new address on Jones Street. Grace, nearing the age of sixty, still had no regular employment and must have counted on her children for support. Marion, then thirty-two, had given up her previous position as secretary at the paper company for a new one with a firm that sold automobile accessories. She earned slightly more, but unfortunately her employer would go out of business during the next year.[62]

Julian planned to remain in California during summer 1927, in part because Dorothy was returning to Stanford. In March he had confided in Strong: "My chief interest in life, of course, is waiting for summer when Dorothy comes back. I am trying to get my degree a year from May—which may be insanity—so that we can get married." In an attempt to complete his dissertation by May 1928, he had buried himself in work. Life, he remarked to Strong, was "too busy to

live." He added, "The gang all think something is wrong with me for never going to parties but I can't be troubled now. Odd, the way love affects a man."[63]

* * *

Dorothy Nyswander arrived at Stanford soon after the spring term ended at the
University of Utah. The research project kept her occupied and largely confined
to Palo Alto, but Steward drove from Berkeley to see her several times during
June. In early July, he turned over his duties at the *American Anthropologist* to
Erna Gunther, a cultural anthropologist and the wife of Leslie Spier. (Spier held
a position at the University of Washington, but taught summer courses at Berkeley several times in the 1920s.) Relieved of his editorial work, Steward returned
to Owens Valley for the first extended visit since his student days at Deep Springs.
He was still driving the notorious fifty-dollar Chevrolet, and, as usual, reported
having "extensive car trouble."[64]

The official purpose of his travels was to collect baskets, pottery, and other
specimens for the University of California's Museum of Anthropology. But that
task offered him the opportunity to follow his own interests as well: surveying
petroglyph sites in eastern California and undertaking his first ethnographic research with Indians in Owens Valley. Months earlier he had told Strong that he
did not want "to get shunted so definitely into archaeology at the present time"
and intended to do some ethnographic fieldwork, perhaps with the Southern
Paiute. He added, "I have a strong hankering to actually talk to some Indians
and try my hand at that kind of thing." But he also mentioned that Gifford had
asked if he had any interest in doing archaeological work in the desert of southern Nevada. "I would, of course," Steward told Strong, "as I not only love the
country but have a feeling that some very interesting things might turn up." He
was to continue working in both archaeology and ethnology for years after leaving Berkeley.[65]

Anthropology students at Berkeley in the 1920s were required to write dissertations based largely on library research, not fieldwork. They were also expected to do field research of such quality that they could publish an article or
monograph based on it. Steward's first ethnographic fieldwork, in the summers
of 1927 and 1928, resulted in a monograph and two articles, but a few years passed
before he began working on those and another year or two before they found
their way into print. Other publications, archaeological in nature, appeared more
quickly: a brief note in the *American Anthropologist* on pottery from Deep
Springs Valley, published in 1928, and a monograph on petroglyphs that he
finished writing while working on his dissertation.[66]

His awareness of petroglyphs dated back to his student days at Deep Springs,
when he had visited a site in the valley not far from the ranch. Seeing petroglyphs
again at archaeological sites along the Columbia River in Oregon had renewed
his interest, and he immersed himself in the subject after returning to Berke-

ley.[67] Writing to Kroeber in July 1927, Steward mentioned some of the petroglyph sites he had visited before returning to the northern end of Owens Valley. Some of the sites, around Olancha, were south of Owens Lake. As he drove by the lake that summer, he saw a dry basin covered with chalky white dust, not the vividly blue water and vast flocks of waterfowl that he remembered. The lake had finally gone dry in 1924, the result of the Los Angeles aqueduct diverting all the water that fed it.[68]

In that same year, a band of men from Owens Valley broke into a warehouse in Bishop and stole three boxes of dynamite, using it to blow a hole in the aqueduct. Months later, some ranchers seized the spillway gates at the Alabama Hills, which controlled the main flow of water into the aqueduct, and for a few days turned the water back to the Owens River. Valley residents celebrated by taking picnic dinners to the site, and the cowboy film star Tom Mix, who was making a movie nearby, sent over an orchestra. The violence subsided, temporarily. Then, in late May 1927, just six weeks before Steward returned to Owens Valley, ranchers blew up the No-Name Canyon siphon and the power house at Big Pine. During the next month, they blew up other portions of the aqueduct. Los Angeles responded by sending in a trainload of guards armed with sawed-off shotguns, about a month before Steward arrived in the valley. He had undoubtedly read about all of these events in the newspapers; the Alabama Gates episode got international coverage, and California newspapers carried detailed accounts of the continuing water war in 1927.[69]

That summer, his own problems were more prosaic. The repairs that his car needed en route from Berkeley made money short once again. "Being nearly broke," he explained to Kroeber, "I did not attempt any ethnography on the way here." But when he reached Owens Valley he located a former ranch hand from Deep Springs, a man he considered "an excellent informant." (Steward later described him in print less favorably, as "John Sumerville, about 45 years old, half-white, a willing informant though not well informed.") He stayed with the Sumerville family, who lived about four miles from Big Pine. "Today I have gone over kinship terminology, tribal groups, seasonal habits, social organization & marriage," he wrote. "The points are, of course, far from complete but I had a good introductory sketch."[70]

In the meantime, he was trying to survive the summer heat ("over 100 degrees in the shade daily") while also collecting specimens for the museum. A few days after sending his first letter to Kroeber, he wrote again to say that he had just attended a meeting of Indians at which he was asked to speak. He had explained his purpose, saying, "I wished to record their stories and ways of living so that a thousand years from now their descendants could read about them, and that I wished also to collect specimens so that people could see them." The speech was well received, he added, and he had already purchased baskets and other artifacts. Kroeber replied quickly to his query about additional funds, beyond the $250 advance already provided by the museum. "Do not hesitate to continue to get specimens if they are good," he wrote, "especially pieces that have been in actual use."[71]

Steward stayed in the vicinity of Big Pine for nearly two weeks. He was probably still there in early August when the banks failed, an event that signaled Owens Valley's greatest defeat in the water war. The banks' owners, the aptly named Watterson brothers, had helped lead the effort to win back the valley's water supply. With the bank failure, many of the ranchers lost their life savings, and resistance to Los Angeles collapsed in the wake of this financial disaster. By the end of that year, the city of Los Angeles reportedly owned 85 percent of the valley.[72]

Despite the turmoil that summer, Steward kept his attention on work. Since some anthropologists considered the Paiute reticent, he felt fortunate to have located two "very willing workers" as informants. Although he collected many myths and learned about various dances and games, he found the topic of social organization puzzling and frustrating. "Apparently there has been none except families and blood relatives," he wrote to Lowie, "and it merges into political organization which is equally indefinite." He noted that "little has come from the east," presumably meaning that few culture traits had diffused from the Plains or the Southwest. "There is no sign of any of the societies, ceremonials or clubs. Nor have I been able to discover even the ghost dance," he concluded.[73]

The Ghost Dance, a millenarian movement, began in about 1870 among Northern Paiute Indians in nearby western Nevada. It predicted the end of white domination and the return of Indian ancestors. Suppressed by the government, it emerged again in 1890, inspired by a Nevada Paiute named Wovoka. As a religious phenomenon, it held little interest for Steward in 1927, and none thereafter, not even when he worked in Nevada. Wovoka and the Ghost Dance were destined to remain outside Steward's field of vision, an odd omission in the view of some later scholars, but entirely in keeping with his wholesale avoidance of religion.[74]

His perspective on Paiute social organization would change little over the years, at least in broad outline. The puzzlement Steward felt in 1927 may well have led him to think more critically about diffusion as an explanatory principle. That diffusion could not account for specific features of Owens Valley Paiute social organization—that in fact their social organization had an "indefinite" quality, the cause of which he did not yet understand—would encourage Steward to turn in another direction for understanding.

* * *

At the start of his third year of graduate study, in fall 1927, Steward still intended to finish his dissertation by spring 1928, an unrealistic deadline given his course work and other commitments. By the middle of the semester he was doing research for his dissertation, taking his final two courses in geography, working part-time, starting to write up his research on petroglyphs, and possibly studying for his Ph.D. examinations. He was also showing the symptoms of overwork.

At just that point, Lowie received a letter from Elsie Clews Parsons, writing from her estate in Westchester County, New York. She asked whether he or Kroeber could suggest a "promising" student to send to First Mesa in Arizona to observe some Hopi initiation ceremonies. The Southwest Society, based in New York City and largely financed by Parsons, would pay the student's expenses.[75] A sociologist-turned-anthropologist, Parsons's great wealth allowed her to travel extensively, usually for the purpose of fieldwork, and underwrite research by other anthropologists. The young discipline of anthropology already had an established tradition of depending on wealthy women for support; Hearst was only one in a series of such patrons.[76] But Parsons, unlike her predecessors, also used her wealth to establish a professional identity for herself in a field that very few women had yet managed to enter.

Parsons lived much of her life against the grain. Despite the opposition of her mother—who had only social, not intellectual, aspirations for her daughter—she studied sociology at Barnard. A few years later, in 1899, she earned a Ph.D. in education at Columbia University, highly unconventional for a woman of her social class during that era. Her deep dislike, even scorn, of social convention led to an intellectual project that centered on questioning it. Eventually her interest turned to ethnology. By 1919, when Parsons and Boas worked together at Laguna, one of the Keresan-speaking pueblos in New Mexico, she already had several years' research experience in the Southwest.[77]

Both Kroeber and Lowie wanted to send Steward, perhaps because of his experience with Paiute Indians in California. Although Hopi and Paiute speak related languages, Steward would find any cultural links less than obvious. Kroeber and Lowie apparently shared concerns about their student's visibly bad health and wondered whether he could withstand fieldwork under winter conditions in northeastern Arizona. Eventually they discussed it with some of the other graduate students. Everyone agreed, Beals remembered, that "despite the winter climate of First Mesa, what he needed most was relief from the pressures of graduate work."[78]

Lowie wrote back to Parsons to say that he and Kroeber recommended a "very good student, Julian H. Steward, who would be very glad to go to the Hopi in February, provided this does not involve too long a departure from Berkeley." Kroeber wrote soon after to inquire about the exact dates of the ceremonies at First Mesa, noting that Steward's time was limited. "He has two examinations to take and a thesis to write by May," Kroeber explained. "I wish he did not feel he had to hurry so much, but as the boy has had to borrow money to study and wishes to get to a point where he earns something, I cannot blame him." "He is thorough," Kroeber added, "and will do a good job."[79]

Finding out exactly when the ceremony would take place proved rather difficult. At the end of January 1928, Steward finally wrote to Lorenzo Hubbell, who had a trading post at New Oraibi, situated just below Third Mesa. He inquired when Powamu, the ceremony he wanted to see, would begin, explaining that the "University of California has asked me to go to First Mesa to observe [it]." Hubbell responded quickly by telegram, giving February 9 as the date. With only a few days to make the long journey from Berkeley to northern Arizona—more than seven hundred miles, much of it along rugged desert roads—Steward found to his disappointment that Powamu had already begun when he arrived.[80]

One of several ceremonies held in winter, Powamu precedes the planting season; beans and maize are ritually planted inside kivas (ceremonial rooms) in anticipation of a good harvest. In some years, in a long version of Powamu, children are initiated into kachina societies. Every Hopi is initiated into one or two of these societies, which are responsible for holding kachina dances. The kachinas, supernatural beings, bring rain and ensure well-being; kachina dances are public events, including performances by Hopi men who wear elaborate masks and costumes and appearances by ceremonial clowns.[81]

Two days after arriving, Steward was admitted to the kivas, although only to public performances. He apparently also fell ill with "grippe" (flu), but he soon wrote to Kroeber to say that conditions had improved: "I have partially recovered from my various ills, [and] my habitation is now several degrees above freezing," he remarked. He slept on the floor, he explained, where "only an inch or two of adobe and a couple of sheepskins separate me from the bedrock of the mesa. Your advice to bring my blankets was excellent as that is all the bedding I have." He found the food not to his taste but, as a matter of politeness, ate what he was served.[82]

Other difficulties beset him besides the unrelenting cold, the unfamiliar food, and his illness. He finally resolved the problem of a permit with the agent of the reservation, and also managed to locate an informant, a "Tewa man" (presumably Hopi-Tewa) who took active part in the ceremonies. Despite missing most of Powamu because of his late arrival and illness, Steward doubted that he would have been allowed to witness anything other than the public performances. He had not understood in advance that so much was secret. Following a common practice at that time in the Southwest, he met clandestinely with his informant and soon reported that he had learned a great deal about the initiation of boys and girls into the kachina societies. Still, they found it difficult to work together: "He tells me that people are constantly asking why I am here and he has to tell them I am just visiting. When anyone comes in we have to pretend that I am writing a letter!"[83]

Sometime in late February, about three weeks after his arrival, Steward left First Mesa abruptly, citing an "attack of pleurisy." He reported that he had gone to Salt Lake City to stay with friends and recuperate. Lowie sent a typically warm and supportive letter, advising his student to do no work unless he had the strength and not to worry about writing up the results of his fieldwork immediately. "Disagreeable as it undoubtedly is to defer your thesis work," Lowie wrote, "it may prove a blessing in disguise by giving you a long and much needed rest. So take it easy and let us know how you are."[84]

In the meantime, Kroeber wrote to Steward's benefactor to report that the trip to First Mesa had "left a trail of disappointments." He told Parsons that as soon as Steward had taken his Ph.D. examination and "got over the shock of it," he left for Arizona. But he was not in good physical shape and the strain of fieldwork, together with the extreme cold, had caused him to fall ill. "We knew he had overworked," Kroeber added, "but evidently did not realize to what degree, and thought as he did that the field work would put him on his feet again."[85]

*　*　*

Steward spent about three weeks in Salt Lake City, where he saw a physician and stayed with Dorothy and her family. Along with her daughter, Marie, her parents lived with her in Salt Lake City, as they had in Berkeley. Dorothy's mother, in the last stages of a long struggle with cancer, died that year. Julian's illness must have appeared rather slight in contrast; in any case, Dorothy had no lasting memory of it. She recalled only that they were engaged by this time, and that he gave her a Navajo ring. He had probably bought it during the fieldwork in Arizona. The ring, with three oval turquoise stones set in three linked silver bands, was striking in design, but it bore no resemblance to a conventional engagement ring. This suited them because they preferred not to announce their engagement. They kept their interest in each other so private that several years later even friends were surprised to learn of it. Julian confided only in Duncan Strong.[86]

Julian's relationship with Dorothy remained strong in March 1928, despite the nearly two years they had already spent living far apart. Their professional commitments, his in California and hers in Utah, had kept them from marrying; and Steward now had no hope of finishing his dissertation by May, as he had once planned. His ill health, which he later called a "crash" due to overwork, made that impossible, as did the problem of having to write something of substance for Parsons about the fieldwork at First Mesa. To judge from the report that he eventually wrote, Dorothy helped him define its focus.

In adulthood, Marie Nyswander spoke of her mother as a woman of exceptional energy, a perception that Dorothy's professional record supports. She had a long and varied research career, beginning with her work at Berkeley and extending for decades. Soon after finishing her dissertation, she published several articles, including one with Tolman, in psychological journals. But by the late 1920s, her primary interest had shifted from experimental research on learning using white rats to applied work on child psychology.[87]

One of her students at the University of Utah recalled a dictum in Nyswander's course on child psychology: "Give me a child until the age of six and

I will make of him or her anything I will." (Dorothy laughed when those words were read to her from a printed page sixty years later; she said that any sense of certainty that she had felt in her thirties had vanished in the course of a very long life.) Her former student, Fawn M. Brodie, who became well-known as a writer, found Nyswander's idea "arrogant at the time but breathtaking," and something of an intellectual watershed. A half century later Brodie still wondered about it. "But the concept," she wrote, "with all its ramifications developed in the psychological literature we read, was the beginning of freedom from the pervasive social ideas that genealogy and blood line were the crucial factors in determining a child's development, a theory that was then accepted almost without question by my parents."[88]

Nyswander's perspective on child development and child training was clearly rooted in her training in psychology, and specifically in behaviorism. It dovetailed in certain ways with ideas about race and culture that had begun to emerge in American anthropology in the early twentieth century, especially in the writings of Boas. By the 1920s, some prominent psychologists and anthropologists had already uncoupled biological differences—whether labeled "blood line" or "race"—from differences in behavior, individual or cultural. During the same era, however, the eugenics movement continued in full swing in the United States and Europe. To judge from some of their writings, Nyswander and Steward shared a general outlook on human behavior that stressed its plasticity and responsiveness to external circumstance and strongly opposed the assumptions of eugenicists. Steward's training in anthropology, under the tutelage of two students of Boas, undoubtedly helped introduce him to that perspective. His contact with Nyswander, a committed behaviorist, just as surely reinforced it.[89]

Although his fieldwork with the Hopi had been a near failure by almost any reckoning, he salvaged enough to write a credible report, which Parsons edited and the *American Anthropologist* published a few years later.[90] Another anthropologist might well have stressed the intricate religious beliefs associated with Powamu, but it comes as no surprise in hindsight that Steward avoided that topic. Instead, he chose to center much of the report on his observations of child initiation, a topic on which he would never again publish. The focus on children, which later puzzled some of his own students, and the behavioral emphasis suggest that Nyswander helped him organize his ideas about what he had seen at First Mesa. Whether her questions and comments about those observations had a more directing influence is unclear. At the least, she helped him recover something of value from the experience and turn it into a publication.[91]

* * *

Steward returned to Berkeley in early April. With no prospect of finishing his dissertation by May, he spent the rest of the term, as Kroeber told Strong, "getting himself in shape."[92] By early June, Steward had returned to the field, this time to do archaeological work with Ronald Olson on the California coast, near

Santa Barbara. From a site at Goleta they sent Gifford some specimens for the museum, then moved on to dig at the mouth of a river near Carpinteria, south of Santa Barbara. Steward described the site as a "splendid, big shell heap" but added that it had yielded almost nothing. Perhaps remembering the difficult field conditions of his first archaeological work, in Oregon's Columbia River Valley two summers earlier, he remarked that "camp life is great—sunny days, an ocean not a hundred yards away to swim in, cool nights . . ." Even the food had improved, he said, once Marie Olson, Ronald Olson's wife, arrived and began to act as camp cook. "Everybody is getting fat," Steward wrote. (Pleasant memories of that summer lingered. Forty years later, Steward wrote to colleagues in Santa Barbara and Los Angeles to inquire about Goleta and Carpinteria as places to retire.)[93]

Marie Olson appears to have been the sole woman in camp that summer, her presence permitted only because she was married to one of the men. By the unwritten rules of the profession, single women could not join archaeological crews unless a married woman was present to serve as chaperone. Luther Cressman, an archaeologist who routinely invited his male students to the field during the 1930s, remembered that his wife, who was not an anthropologist herself, urged him to include young women. Cressman agreed with her in principle but did not change his practice until years later.[94]

* * *

In early July 1928, after working at a few more sites around Santa Barbara, Steward left Olson and the others, who planned to remain until mid-August, and drove back to Berkeley. There he made final revisions on his petroglyph monograph, apparently at Kroeber's request. He departed for Owens Valley a few days later, to collect specimens for the museum and to continue the ethnographic work with Paiute Indians that he had begun the previous summer. By the time he arrived, the Watterson brothers, once successful bank owners, had been charged with embezzlement and grand theft and sentenced to ten years in San Quentin. Someone had posted a sign on the north side of Bishop that read "Los Angeles City Limit."[95] The long water war had ended, and most of the valley's irrigation system would soon fall into disrepair. Steward, however, was about to learn of another aspect of irrigation in the valley, previously unknown to anthropologists.

For the first several weeks he worked around Mono Lake and then about fifty miles south in Bishop, where he camped with Indians. Four older men served as informants during the four days he spent at Mono Lake, and about a dozen in Owens Valley, including one with posthumous status, Captain Harry ("died 1920, age about 90 years"). In an early instance of what became a habit of avoiding women as informants, Mary Harry was one of only three he consulted. He noted about Maggie Shaw, another informant, "little used but probably good." A photograph of Mary Harry using a metate, and another one showing her husband, seated, appear among the illustrations in the monograph that Steward later published.[96]

Steward had taken along some blank phonograph cylinders to use in recording songs, but within a few days he sent a telegram to Gifford asking for two dozen more. Once they arrived, he recorded dozens of songs, including some attributed to characters in Owens Valley Paiute mythology. He soon set about collecting more myths and secured a brief life history of an old man. Jack Stewart had been born a hundred years earlier at Big Pine according to Steward. An account of his long life, given through an interpreter, formed the first part of a later article, "Two Paiute Autobiographies." The life story of Sam Newland, born at Bishop and ninety years old, provided contrasts. Together, Steward said, the two illustrated "extraordinary individual differences" and provided "subjective data indicating psychological attitudes and social values implicit in the culture."[97]

Although he would never again show interest in the subject, Steward did seem to share some of the Paiute values he identified, ranging from admiration of good hunters to a deep interest in the land. Jack Stewart clearly impressed him with stories of his success as a hunter and as "a lady's man." He also showed remarkable physical vigor on a hot, midsummer day in 1928 by climbing thousands of feet up a mountain in Steward's company, in search of some specimens of medicinal plants for his young companion. In recording his life history, as well as Paiute songs and myths, Steward followed a trend of the time in ethnology, and then seized the chance to publish what he had collected. These topics did not interest him deeply, however, as his research was growing exclusively materialist and behaviorist in approach.[98]

By the end of July, he had turned in a different direction. "I am now attempting a kind of anthropogeographical study," Steward wrote to Kroeber, "of a sort which I think might win Sauer's approval." Using techniqes he had learned in Sauer's course on field geography the previous year, he had begun mapping the location of old Paiute settlements, seasonal camps, trails, and hunting and fishing territories around Bishop. "Also," he reported, "I am scouring the country for every kind of plant to ascertain its names and uses, and to plot the chief patches of it." He planned to extend "this more or less geographical study," as he termed it, to the entire Owens Valley. And he was collecting plants, he wrote, "hoping that some botanist will identify them for me." His training in biological science had been largely limited to zoology.[99]

His most intriguing discovery was that Owens Valley Paiute, who had no agriculture, had long practiced irrigation. This was the first known instance of the irrigation of wild food plants. The Paiute community of Bishop, the largest in the valley, had two fields, "each covering several square miles." A few miles above the fields, the Paiute made a dam across Bishop Creek and dug an irrigation ditch to each field. Every spring they diverted the water from the creek into one of the irrigation ditches and gathered the fish from it. Then, Steward explained, "an elected irrigator took charge & by a primitive method, irrigated the land during the summer." In the fall, they cut off the flow of water into the irrigation ditch and again gathered the fish from the ditch. The following spring and summer, they irrigated the other field, in order to avoid exhausting the soil by using the same field each year. "I saw and photographed the dam and one of the ditches," he added. In a brief reply, Kroeber acknowledged this example of irrigation as "a wholly new feature," previously unknown for nonagriculturalists.[100]

During his fieldwork in the summer of 1928, Steward came to believe that "the interest of the people [in Owens Valley] lay in their close relationship to nature rather than in social activities," such as their occasional festivals and ceremonies. During most of the year, he remarked to Kroeber, "the quest for food was paramount and this required an intimate knowledge of the country and its plants and animals." He had learned about the food quest not only by mapping their hunting territories and collecting plants but also through extensive interviewing and attempts to elicit the names of wild plants, the staples of the Paiute diet. "I have lived entirely with the Indians this trip," he concluded, "and have found them extremely hospitable and friendly." He had also enjoyed eating their foods; Paiute hospitality and cuisine offered, in his own words, "a pleasant contrast" to his experiences at First Mesa.

Kroeber sent a brief response encouraging this interest in "relations to the land." "In a subsistence area like the one you are in," he wrote, "it is bound to be a fundamental aspect of life; and it is one which we have all tended unduly to neglect as against those parts of culture which more easily crystallize into definite forms." He said much the same in print that year, observing that "the land, and those aspects of culture most directly dependent on it, economics and politics, have been slighted." As he explained, "They lend themselves less readily to systematization than society, ritual, tradition, and art, and their patterns are hence more plastic and harder to follow." Kroeber's own interests, unlike his student's, always centered on those cultural elements that did allow "systematization."[101]

Steward returned to Berkeley in August with notes on myths, life history material, recordings of songs, maps, photographs, lists of plant names, and plant specimens from Owens Valley. He filed all of it away for the future. His immediate concern was to finish a report on his fieldwork at First Mesa, send it to Parsons, and resume work on his dissertation.

* * *

The "more or less geographical study" that Steward described to Kroeber obviously owed something to his training outside of anthropology. His course in field geography had given him direct guidance in field research, far more than Kroeber or Lowie ever provided. Under Sauer's direction, he had spent time outdoors observing the California landscape, learning specific techniques, such as mapping, and recording his observations. He put those skills to use during the few weeks he spent around Bishop. Suggesting to Kroeber that his study "might win Sauer's approval" was, however, an attempt to win Kroeber's own approval for his unusual approach, not recognition of any intellectual debt to Sauer.

Nyswander's intellectual influence was less obvious but is unmistakable. Her experimental work, already underway the year she and Steward met, offered a perspective on behavioral research that he found much more compelling than any he encountered in the anthropology department. Her training in experimental method, including the emphasis on repeated observation—a staple part of empirical research—clearly impressed him with its rigor. Unlike behaviorist psychologists, however, Steward could not set up experiments, manipulate variables, and observe the outcome. Working outside a laboratory, like other field scientists such as geologists and geographers, he could only observe the world as it was and try to infer something about the past.

At the outset of his Owens Valley field research, he had not used observation. Instead, Steward followed the then standard procedure of working intensively with a few informants, asking questions about the past, and trying to reconstruct the precontact way of life. Cultural reconstruction was a central task of anthropology at that time. He and his fellow students, like their teachers Kroeber and Lowie, employed what Beals later called the "informant method."[102] During his last few weeks of fieldwork in Owens Valley, in contrast, Steward emphasized observation of the land and its resources. He continued to work intensively with a few informants, but he concentrated on asking questions about subsistence-related behavior in the past.

Years later, Robert Murphy pointed out that Steward's cultural ecology, with its emphasis on behavior patterns and observable activity, diverged from American anthropology's focus on culture traits as fundamentally symbolic and on jural rules. It was in this regard, although rarely noted and difficult to explain, Murphy remarked, that "Steward made one of his sharpest breaks with the past." This divergence seemed puzzling because the influence of behaviorist psychology on Steward's thinking was entirely unknown to Murphy, as was Nyswander in her role as mentor. She subscribed to the neobehaviorist idea of laws of learning, for example, which could explain behavior and predict behavioral change. This may well have encouraged what would become Steward's own abiding interest in what he called "the determination of cultural laws."[103]

His research around Bishop in 1928 marked a milestone in Steward's career as an anthropologist. It would prove far more important than his dissertation. Steward had gathered an enormous amount of material in a period of only five or six weeks because he knew the territory so well beforehand and because he felt deeply connected with it. His maps included many of the mountains he had climbed during his student days at Deep Springs and other places he knew firsthand. Mount Humphreys, Temple Crag, Lake Sabrina, and sites in Deep Springs Valley were all landmarks in his personal geography as well as named places in his ethnography of the Owens Valley Paiute. His own experiences and memories of place prepared him to recognize what he called the Paiutes' "close relationship to nature" and their attachment to Owens Valley.[104]

A few years later, writing in a tone that ranged from neutral to skeptical, he alluded to an informant's report of a visionary experience with Birch Mountain, which became his "power." Steward could not resist adding a sentence in a footnote about the mountain itself. Birch Mountain elicited these admiring and affectionate words: "one of the most magnificent of the Sierra Nevada peaks as seen from Big Pine, rising to more than 14,000 feet, or more than 10,000 feet above the valley."[105]

CHAPTER 5

FROM FAR WEST
TO MIDWEST

When Steward returned to Berkeley in August 1928, he found Anna Gayton, another graduate student, about to leave. She had just accepted a newly created but temporary position in anthropology at the University of Michigan, one that included part-time teaching and museum work. Forrest Clements had a temporary post as well, at the Yale Institute of Psychology, where he held a National Research Council fellowship. Even in the prosperous times of the late 1920s, full-time academic positions in anthropology, and research positions at museums, remained scarce. Graduate students had ongoing, worried discussions about finding employment.[1]

Gayton had defended her dissertation earlier that year, becoming the first woman to earn a Ph.D. in anthropology at Berkeley. Other women had earned master's degrees in anthropology, and Theodora Brown had planned to do doctoral study but dropped out when she married Kroeber. In common with the several other women students in her program, Gayton, then twenty-nine years old, was not married. She had completed her graduate training with her dissertation, "The Narcotic Plant *Datura* in Aboriginal American Culture."[2]

She received the informal offer of a one-year position from the University of Michigan early in the summer, just after learning that the National Research Council hoped to find funds to award her a fellowship. Kroeber had recommended her to the University of Michigan, and she felt that she had no choice but to take the temporary position on receiving a formal offer. It seems that she was following Kroeber's counsel, not her own wishes. He thought she should meet new colleagues and work in a new setting, although she had no teaching experience and a far stronger interest in research. As Kroeber conceded at the time, "Her real interest and I think greatest strength lie in pure research."[3]

The position that Gayton accepted marked a turning point for anthropology at the University of Michigan, the beginning of regular instruction in the discipline. A staff member in the university's Museum of Anthropology had resigned a few months earlier, in spring 1928, and funds for that position were diverted to create an instructorship in the new department of anthropology. Carl E. Guthe, a Harvard-trained archaeologist and director of the Museum of Anthropology, had a major hand in organizing the department and in hiring Gayton as the first instructor. Years later, he helped organize the Society for American Archaeology and a wide range of other professional ventures; during his long career, he worked actively in organization and administration at the local and national levels.[4]

Gayton planned to leave for Michigan in late August, but she fell seriously ill. She wrote to the National Research Council to say that she had given up the job in Michigan because of illness and would like to accept the fellowship if possible. Soon after, Kroeber sent a rather stern letter to her in Santa Cruz, where she was hospitalized. "I urge you strongly to make no further moves in any direction until you hear from me," he instructed.[5]

In the meantime, classes were due to begin at the University of Michigan in a few weeks, with a course in ethnology included on the schedule. Kroeber, in consultation with Lowie, decided to recommend Steward, perhaps in part because of his financial worries and the loan from Max Rosenberg, which he needed to repay. Steward received an offer from the University of Michigan in late September, and the next day he boarded a train for Ann Arbor. The term had already started at Berkeley, although not at Michigan.[6]

During his long train journey, he wrote to Strong, who had spent the previous winter in eastern Canada serving as anthropologist for the Field Museum's Rawson-MacMillan subarctic expedition. Strong stayed for months in Labrador with Montagnais-Naskapi caribou hunters, "a living Indian hunting culture," as he later put it. Traveling with hunters across the desolate terrain during a time of game shortage, he witnessed firsthand the effects of food scarcity. A foraging way of life that still existed in the subarctic had vanished from the Great Basin, resulting in very different field experiences for the two men. Strong, who directly observed a community of hunters, underwent the rigors of fieldwork in a remote, alien place, while Steward had worked briefly on home ground, trying to reconstruct a way of life that only a few elderly Owens Valley Paiute remembered. In future fieldwork, he too would see food scarcity, but caused by economic and political conditions—the Great Depression—rather than game shortage.[7]

Back in Chicago and newly married, Strong had resumed his duties at the Field Museum. They would soon be near neighbors, Steward explained, on account of the unexpected position at Michigan. About Gayton's illness, he wrote, "It was simply overwork, I guess, and if she can have a good rest and then get a fellowship, it may have all been for the best as far as she is concerned." He explained that overwork, resulting in illness, had interrupted his own progress in the spring. "But I hope to write my thesis this winter and take my degree next summer," he continued. "No, not married yet, either. But Dorothy and I are more in love than ever and if I can get some of my debts paid off this winter, we may be able to swing it next summer."[8]

The position that Steward had gained through serendipity, part-time lecturer in anthropology and part-time curator in the Museum of Anthropology, carried a salary of $2,500. His duties included teaching a course in ethnology, which he planned to model on the introductory course at Berkeley. On his arrival, however, he found that the class of fifteen had only three undergraduate students. Half the graduate students came from geography, the remainder from other fields. To add to his troubles, he had no equipment for the course: "no maps whatever, no slides, in fact nothing but a pair of callipers." And he had left Berkeley so hurriedly that his books were still there, not even packed for shipping.[9]

There were yet other problems. Steward found teaching the first classes difficult, although he tried to put up a brave front in his letters to Kroeber. "I have had three lectures and have gotten through the worst of it," he wrote. "I think I will not find the matter of lecturing very difficult." Two months later, he reported that his "feeling of incompetence" had vanished, replaced by self-confidence. In fact, however, his anxiety about public speaking would never diminish, and facing large classes always remained painfully difficult for him. He managed to conceal his discomfort, perhaps even from himself, by the time he wrote to Kroeber at the end of the term, and always from his students. They later remembered him as a skilled, highly organized speaker who seemed confident about his ideas.[10]

As he struggled through those first lectures, Steward felt both puzzled and displeased to see Guthe's name, not his own, listed as course instructor; he complained about it to Kroeber. Despite various problems, he also reported an unexpected stroke of good luck: the administration had created an anthropology department, "which Guthe had not at all intended," Steward told Kroeber. (Guthe's own account suggests otherwise.) Guthe planned to assume headship of the department, but only for the interim. Overall, prospects for the future appeared excellent.[11]

* * *

Kroeber may have had a sense of déjà vu when he read about Steward's situation at the University of Michigan. It showed many parallels with the early years of his own career, as well as the same great promise. In 1901, at the age of twenty-five, Kroeber had begun his teaching career as an instructor in the University of California's new department of anthropology. His senior colleague, Frederic W. Putnam, who directed the Peabody Museum at Harvard as well as the new department in California, periodically made the long cross-country trip by train from Cambridge, Massachusetts, to Berkeley. In 1909, having reached the age of seventy, Putnam retired, and Kroeber assumed the chairmanship of the department. An assistant professor, thirty-three years old at the time, he stood on the threshold of a notably long and distinguished career, one strengthened by his control of the department, one of the very few that then existed.[12]

Nearly twenty years later, when he received Steward's letter from the University of Michigan, Kroeber had already served as department head for many years, had hired the other faculty members, and was the undisputed leader of the department. Certain personal qualities had helped him achieve this position, including his impressive social skills and political instincts, as well as his psychological insight about others. He actually practiced as a lay psychoanalyst for several years, beginning in 1918, while remaining on the Berkeley faculty; according to his wife, he gave up his practice when he realized that without a medical degree he would never have control of that field. A later colleague, John Rowe, remembered Kroeber as very patient and tolerant, and "a good listener."[13]

He also had a difficult side. Years after his death, Theodora Kroeber spoke about it with some candor, remarking that she knew some people had found him difficult and had feared him. As one of his former students, she was certainly in a position to know that, but she also thought that he had changed over the course of his adult life from "a diffident and a difficult young man" to a person of great patience and tolerance. His experience in psychoanalysis and his practice as a lay analyst may have helped bring about some of those changes. Theodora Kroeber believed that marriage and fatherhood had also transformed her husband. They had children, and he adopted the two from her first marriage.[14]

Besides these personal qualities, his seniority in the department had given him control of hiring, which certainly helped him maintain a dominant position. And now his student Steward had just stepped into a parallel situation at Michigan, one that might benefit both men professionally. The benefits to Steward were obvious—he had a promising place at a major public university, one of Berkeley's peer institutions—but the position also offered the prospect of long-term benefits for Kroeber. His graduate program at Berkeley competed with those at private universities—Columbia, Harvard, Yale, the University of Chicago, and the University of Pennsylvania—in placing its new Ph.D.'s. Finding academic positions for them was vital to the success of the Berkeley program, to say nothing of Kroeber's own professional prestige, which increased with each hired Ph.D. Steward, now in a newly created department, might create employment or research opportunities for other Berkeley graduates. (Strong later did exactly that for Steward at the Bureau of American Ethnology in the 1930s and again in the 1940s at Columbia.)

There followed a series of encouraging letters from Kroeber to Steward. Kroeber gave Steward detailed advice on teaching the ethnology course and adapting it for graduate students who had never studied anthropology: "A course in pure theory is likely to seem sterile to the average student," he said. "The factual content serves as bal[l]ast." Whether or not Steward first learned this from Kroeber is debatable, but it did become his approach to teaching and writing. A mass of empirical evidence always provided the foundation for any theoretical point that he made.[15]

Kroeber also spoke well of Guthe, describing him as "kindly and fair," and carefully explaining why he, and not Steward, was listed as instructor of the course. Guthe had mentioned in a letter to Gayton that his name would appear as instructor, apparently because he thought some students might avoid enrolling in a course taught by a woman. As Kroeber told Steward, Guthe had questioned "how a woman in charge would draw [students] in an institution where sentiment is somewhat similar to that in Cornell." Evidently Kroeber and Steward had discussed prejudice against women, with reference to Steward's alma mater, sometime in the past. By implication, they agreed that institutional and professional prestige could be protected by excluding women or rendering them invisible: hence, the erasure of Gayton's name, with unintended consequences for the man who took her place.[16]

By early October, Gayton had left the hospital, and Kroeber mentioned that she had spent a day in Berkeley. "She looked pretty well," he wrote, "but I think it will be some time before they let her do any work." In the meantime, Steward had heard from her as well and reported that she seemed to be "in high spirits." Their ties as fellow students who had some shared interests—including ecological ones—would soon lapse, however, as they came to occupy the very different places available to women and to men in the profession.[17]

Sometime in 1928, Gayton received the National Research Council fellowship, apparently after giving up the position at Michigan. She held the fellowship until 1930, and in 1931 married Leslie Spier, whose marriage to Erna Gunther had ended. After many years without academic employment, she finally obtained a position in Berkeley's department of decorative art; originally part of home economics, nearly all of its faculty and students were women.[18] The death of Lila M. O'Neale, who earned a Ph.D. in anthropology soon after Gayton and Steward, left a position vacant in 1948, which Gayton filled. Both women are remembered as remarkably competent scholars whose achievements far exceeded the professional positions they held.[19]

Soon after sending his first letter from Michigan to Kroeber, Steward wrote to Lowie. As usual, he wrote a more personal and casual, even confiding, letter. "I miss my Berkeley friends like the devil," Steward confessed, "and were it not for a couple of friends of Dorothy's—who were at Utah last year—I should be quite forlorn as far as that goes." He added, "I miss the mountains of California, too." Guthe's intrusion in his course continued to rankle. "Ostensibly," he wrote, "Guthe is both 'giving' and 'supervising' the course. All I do is to appear before the class and do the dirty work." His duties also included the job of cataloging material in the museum collection.[20]

In the meantime, Steward continued to work on his dissertation, on the role of ceremonial clowns among North American Indians. His brief fieldwork at First Mesa, where he saw Hopi ceremonial clowns perform, made it more meaningful than a topic based solely on library research. A few weeks after arriving at Michigan, Lowie sent him a lengthy list of references for ceremonial clowning in southwestern and Plains Indian societies, remarking dryly, "This will probably suffice to keep you busy for the next 3 or 4 hours after receipt of my letter. More power to your elbow." Finding the time for research and writing already proved difficult, given the demands of teaching for the first time. Like many new instructors, Steward regarded this aspect of teaching with as much surprise as dismay: "I find that the course takes more time than I had ever dreamed," he wrote to Gifford six weeks after the term began.[21]

A month later, Steward reported that his dissertation was progressing "in a desultory fashion." Teaching remained very time-consuming, but he was determined to finish his dissertation by the summer. He hoped to see Strong, still at the Field Museum and, by midwestern reckoning, a rather near neighbor; and he mentioned meeting two prominent archaeologists who had visited the university, Sylvanus Morley and Alfred Kidder. Both were longtime colleagues of Guthe. Meeting Kidder, courtesy of Guthe, would prove a benefit a few years later.[22]

* * *

In December 1928 Steward traveled east to attend the annual meeting of the American Anthropological Association. In New York City, he met Parsons for the first time and saw Spier and Clements. He was disappointed, he told Kroeber, to find none of his other colleagues and friends from Berkeley in attendance. But in letters to Strong he mentioned that Dorothy had also attended the meeting, and that they had "a glorious time in N.Y."[23]

Steward presented a paper at the meeting, probably his first such experience. As he later told Kroeber, he had "the temerity to present a paper on diffusion." Framed as a brief analysis of the "logic" of diffusion and independent invention, and as a contribution to methodology, his paper also raised a theoretical issue. Steward questioned the prevailing view of diffusion as the major vehicle of cultural change, but he did so in a veiled way, and in the dispassionate language of science.

The paper constituted not only a tacit argument against Kroeber and Lowie's point of view but also an indirect protest. Steward thought that his teachers had failed to provide him with adequate training in research methods. Perhaps more obviously, the paper illustrates his own preoccupation with methodology; arguably a wish, if never openly stated, to match the rigor of the experimental method used by behaviorist psychologists. This preoccupation endured, and years later he consistently used the phrase "the concept and method of cultural ecology," not "the theory" of cultural ecology.

In "Diffusion and Independent Invention: A Critique of Logic," Steward suggested three principles "as logically valid formulations of the methodology employed" to solve problems of origins. That is, he developed what he considered a more rigorous methodology to help anthropologists determine whether diffusion or independent invention explained the presence of a particular cultural element. For example, he suggested that "the probability of independent invention is directly proportionate to the difficulty of communication between localities." He said almost nothing to Kroeber about how his colleagues in New York City greeted his ideas, commenting only that he was "at least not booed off the floor." Returning to Ann Arbor, he quickly submitted the paper to the *American Anthropologist*, still under Lowie's editorship.[24]

Privately, both before and after the meeting, Steward showed some anxiety about risking rejection by challenging orthodoxy, referring to his "short and silly paper" in a note to Strong, and to his "little paper" in a letter to Kroeber. Months later, when he received the galley proofs, he clearly had misgivings about putting his ideas in print. He had just about decided, he wrote to Lowie, that "it was not worth a damn" and should be withdrawn. (As editor, Lowie had accepted the article, but as a scholar he must have had reservations about it. He leaned toward diffusionist explanation even when great geographic distance—and thus "difficulty of communication," to use Steward's phrase—might argue against it.) Still hesitant, Steward sent the proofs to Strong instead: "I have cold feet about the thing but you might glance at it if you have time and send it back to Lowie."[25] Despite his last-minute reservations, the brief article attracted little notice when it finally appeared, no doubt because the author was an almost unknown newcomer to the field.

The ringing silence that greeted his first attempt in print to question prevailing theory—by offering a method to test the likelihood of diffusion in any particular instance—seems to have discouraged him. As a young scholar, he did not yet understand the singular importance of professional position in the world of academic writing: how professional position not just adds weight to words and ideas, sometimes unduly, but actually creates the audience for them. In any case, seven years passed before he published a paper that he thought made a strongly theoretical point, many more years before that paper attracted notice, and decades before he achieved the professional stature that gave him a larger and far more receptive audience.[26]

He continued to think about diffusion, but his comments grew muted. In the next few years, Steward published the first article on his field research with Owens Valley Paiute, a short paper entitled "Irrigation without Agriculture," and then a monograph, "Ethnography of the Owens Valley Paiute." In both works he considered three possible origins of the practice of irrigation in Owens Valley, two of them involving diffusion. The third possibility—that irrigation was a product of independent invention, probably inspired by the Paiutes' observation that plants grew more abundantly in the more moist, lowland areas of

Owens Valley—had theoretical implications that held far greater interest for him. It suggested that the Paiute might have been "on the verge of horticulture," Steward wrote, and also raised "the possibility of such an origin of horticulture elsewhere."[27]

Irrigation and agriculture, and their relation to cultural change, were to remain subjects that he returned to again and again in his theoretical work. He would always favor the idea of independent invention over diffusion. By the late 1930s, however, Steward had read nineteenth-century government reports that led him to qualify his original position on irrigation in Owens Valley. In an often overlooked, brief passage in *Basin-Plateau Aboriginal Sociopolitical Groups*, he remarked in passing that "there is some possibility that [irrigation] was introduced by Americans, who penetrated the valley after 1850, or by Spaniards who had settled at least the southern portion of it much earlier."[28]

Tellingly, Steward avoided the concept of diffusion when he cited evidence that irrigation might have originated outside Owens Valley. He distinguished himself from his teachers by suggesting a new source and means of origin. Unlike Kroeber, who had proposed the prehistoric Southwest as a probable source for the diffusion of irrigation, he now suggested American settlers of the previous century, or Spaniards, had introduced it when they entered the valley. (The issue remains unresolved some seventy years later, although historical evidence does not support the idea that American settlers introduced irrigation to Owens Valley; and as Steward himself noted, ranchers actually appropriated Paiute irrigation ditches.) By the end of his career, new evidence—although "not conclusive proof" in his view—led Steward again to propose that irrigation might be "aboriginal."[29]

The episode well illustrates Steward's approach to anthropology, which would not change measurably throughout his long career: a strong inclination to challenge accepted theoretical views; a firm commitment to scientific empiricism; and, in most cases, a willingness to examine new evidence, even if it meant revising or reversing his own position. He always accepted Cartesian doubt as a defining feature of scientific work, essential in anthropology just as in the natural sciences. Near the end of his career he wrote, "As I reexamine some of my own cross-cultural formulations, I note a long history of changing my mind." This did not trouble him. "There are perhaps others," he observed, "who . . . should also change their minds from time to time."[30]

Over the years, many would disagree with Steward's ideas; and others who shared his general perspective would find him far too willing to modify his views on specific issues when faced with any shred of evidence that appeared contrary. But few ever accused him of intellectual dishonesty.[31]

* * *

In January 1929 Steward turned his attention again to his dissertation research on ritual clowning. Although he was about to move in a rather different direction, his work appeared traditional in approach at that point; that is, he used a comparative and historical framework for his survey of native North American cultures, and he had nearly completed his reading on California Indians and had made good progress on Plains and southwestern Indians. But Steward also hoped to develop some ideas on "the extent to which the comic has been molded into patterns," ideas that would take an unusual, distinctly psychological turn.[32]

By April Steward had finished a draft of his dissertation. He sent it to Lowie, chairman of his committee, with an apology about its disorganized state, which he attributed to haste. A few weeks later, Lowie and Kroeber sent brief comments. Lowie commended him for clearly defining regional differences and for offering concise summaries of descriptive data. "The outstanding sin," Lowie wrote, "is one of omission rather than of commission. You have—I think, on the whole wisely—abstained from ambitious historical schemes, but you have not compensated by enough psychological interpretation." Steward had explicitly promised in that draft to provide a psychological analysis of humor, but he then failed to do so.[33]

Kroeber generally agreed with Lowie. He found the factual content excellent but conclusions almost lacking. "As I read," Kroeber explained, "I was under the impression that you were just warming up to the psychological discussion and then when I turned the leaf found the bibliography came next." He suggested that Steward take greater care to specify where specific culture traits related to ceremonial clowning were present or absent (for example, the use of inverted speech, the organization of clowns into a society, and so on). Kroeber conceded, however, that the topic appeared to resist a diffusionist, historical approach. He assured Steward that he welcomed a different perspective: "I am rather glad that we are again getting a thesis which is not primarily headed toward historical reconstruction."[34]

That approach would soon, in fact, become passé, as illustrated by Ronald Olson's dissertation. He defended it in spring 1929, only a few weeks before Kroeber wrote to Steward. His study "Clan and Moiety in Native America," well regarded at the time, appeared in print four years later, and shortly suffered direct attack—by former friend and colleague Steward, whose own work and professional life had taken a very different turn from Olson's.[35]

* * *

In spring 1929 the future must have seemed full of promise to both Olson and Steward. Only six months later, the shape of the future would change abruptly with the crash of the stock market in October 1929 and the onset of the Great Depression. But that was not yet on the horizon when Gunther wrote to Steward about Olson's upcoming defense and sent other news as well. She was living in Berkeley with her two young sons but working in Oakland, in a job unrelated to anthropology, while her husband, Spier, taught for the year at the University of Oklahoma. (Gunther had earned her Ph.D. from Columbia the year earlier.) She reported that Gayton had just left for fieldwork with the Yokuts and that Beals planned to work with the Southern Maidu during the summer. "I don't know any other gossip," she wrote in closing, "which shows that I am not a good anthropologist."[36]

In the meantime, Steward and Lowie had agreed to schedule his dissertation defense for August 1929, and Steward set to work again. As he explained to both Kroeber and Lowie, the draft he had sent them dealt only with "the historical aspect" of the topic. "I really had not worked out the psychological aspect at all," he wrote to Lowie, "and that last page was merely to indicate the direction of further research." He was searching the psychological literature, he continued, in the hope of finding out why humans laugh. Psychologists appeared to think that the answer remained unknown. Steward, however, believed that he would be able to "isolate certain things that are universally comic and infer a good deal from them; and find other things that are culturally determined and perhaps show why."[37] Questions of causality and an attempt to generalize dominated his thinking, although answers to his questions eluded him.

Sometime after the spring term ended, Steward left Ann Arbor for a long journey west. He had spent nine or ten months alone in a new place, far from friends and the California mountains he sorely missed. Aside from those few days in New York City with Dorothy Nyswander, his contact with her had been limited to letters. Nearly the only old friend he had seen was Reich, who had visited Ann Arbor that spring on his way from Ithaca to Urbana, Illinois, where he interviewed for a position at the University of Illinois. (He accepted the offer and taught at the university for many years and later moved to Yale.) Otherwise, Steward had seen little of friends, either from Deep Springs or from Berkeley, and little of the world beyond eastern Michigan.[38]

After that long first year in Ann Arbor, he must have looked forward to the trip, which took him first to Oklahoma and then on to Utah. In Oklahoma he collected specimens for the museum from Seminole and other Indians.[39] Soon after his arrival in Utah, he wrote to the anthropology department at Berkeley, giving Salt Lake City as his temporary address until early August, when he expected to leave for Berkeley. Julian stayed for nearly two months with Dorothy, whose household still included her father, now a widower, as well as her daughter, Marie. During that time, he finished his dissertation, a work decidedly psychological in approach, and one that included the psychological analysis that his advisers had thought missing from the previous draft.[40]

The many behaviorist elements in his dissertation, including an emphasis on conditioning, suggest that Dorothy offered a great deal of guidance. Almost seventy years later, she had no specific memory of the dissertation, but she did remember clearly that they "talked psychology" a lot in the years before and during their marriage. She recalled, in particular, her repeated comments about Julian's methodology and the rigor of the experimental psychologist's method in comparison to a cultural anthropologist's reliance on "one or two informants." She wanted him to take a "broader approach" in his ethnographic research, she said. If she questioned the quality of the ethnographic data that formed the body of his dissertation, she undoubtedly approved of the behaviorist framework taken from her own field.[41]

The dissertation defense was delayed for several weeks, which allowed him to linger in Salt Lake City. It finally took place on September 10. Besides Lowie and Kroeber, the other members included Sauer and Wolfgang Panzer of the geography department, and Margaret Trabue Hodgen, an assistant professor in the department of social institutions and one of the few women on the faculty. Steward had never had a course with Hodgen or Panzer and probably had not met them before. Panzer, a geographer from the University of Berlin, had a one-year appointment at Berkeley. Hodgen had some interest in anthropology and would soon publish an article in the *American Anthropologist*.[42]

The defense was open to other students and faculty and Beals attended. The psychological portion of the dissertation, as he remembered it, was not a great success. "Some people couldn't understand it at all," he recalled. Sauer asked a question, and then, after Steward answered it, responded, "'But that isn't what I meant.'" He finally gave up. Steward and Sauer never had a meeting of the minds, no doubt in part because of their very different intellectual styles and philosophical approaches to science. Sauer had a deep appreciation of German scholarship and literature and a disciplinary perspective rooted in German historicism. He was neither a positivist nor, as Steward understood the term, a scientist.[43]

Steward's own memories of his defense, which he shared with many of his students, centered on Kroeber's and Lowie's comments, and their sharp debate. Kroeber, he said, approved of the historical section in which Steward traced specific culture elements of ritual clowning; Lowie preferred the second part of the dissertation, in which Steward categorized the themes of humor and, finding that some themes ran across different cultural areas, tried to determine the psychological cause. Kroeber evidently considered the second section reductionist and did not support this attempt at "scientific generalization," as Steward later termed it. In his recollection of his defense, each of the two senior anthropologists eagerly seized the opportunity to defend his own theoretical position and to attack the other's, forgetting their student in the process. Steward remembered trying to move his chair outside their line of vision to avoid the debate.[44]

The maneuver evidently succeeded, and later in life he laughingly recommended it to many of his own students. Steward received the sixth Ph.D. in anthropology awarded at Berkeley.[45]

* * *

He returned to Ann Arbor in fall 1929 to learn that the introductory course had burgeoned from the 15 students he had found in 1928 to 130 students a year later. Writing to Kroeber soon after, Steward remarked, "I guess anthropology has really squirmed its way onto the campus." He wondered how he would manage to prepare the two new courses that were scheduled for the next year. But that same semester, Steward also offered an extension course for the first time, perhaps following the example of Nyswander, who routinely taught such courses to supplement a modest academic salary. Every Monday, he drove to Northern High School in Detroit, where he taught an evening course. He was still trying to work his way out of debt.[46]

The day after Steward wrote to Kroeber, the prosperity of the 1920s came to an abrupt end. The stock market, following its climb to new highs only a few months earlier, had begun a downward slide in early September that culminated in a crash on October 24, 1929. Remembered as Black Thursday, prices on stock shares dropped more quickly that day than ever before in history. The decline would continue for another two years as foreign trade fell sharply, banks failed, and factories closed. For months after Black Thursday, with the shape of the near future still unclear, some political leaders spoke hopefully about recovering prosperity. Instead, the Great Depression would hold sway through the 1930s.[47]

Steward's professional future still appeared bright in fall 1929, and he would continue to view it that way for a few more years, insulated from the early effects of the depression by what seemed a secure academic position. As a result of receiving his Ph.D., the university had promoted him and raised his salary by two hundred dollars. He now held the position of instructor rather than lecturer and earned $2,700 a year, as well as $300 for each extension course that he taught. But his letter to Kroeber betrayed his continuing ambivalence about the prospect of full-time teaching, an issue they had discussed by letter ten months earlier. If enrollment in anthropology increased, Steward had explained, there was "a fair chance that next year they will be able to have another man here." In that case, he would have to choose between full-time teaching or a position in the museum. "I have a strong hankering to do a lot of field work in the next few years," he wrote, "and would hate to think of having my winters all tied up for the rest of my life more or less."[48]

Kroeber's advice was cautious and, as usual, very astute. He pointed out that at a university "a teaching position should hold a greater future than a museum position," a lesson he had learned from his own experience at the University of California. His words had some effect, at least temporarily. A few weeks later, Steward wrote to Strong, "It rather looks now as tho I will go into full time teaching next year and be here indefinitely."[49]

Steward's hesitation about teaching may have stemmed from his interest in fieldwork and publication, not just his dislike of public speaking. With increasing commitments in the classroom, he found it more difficult to find time to write up the results of previous research. His monograph on petroglyphs had finally reached print after many delays, and he asked that copies be sent to several people, including his mother and Rosenberg, who had lent him the money he needed to finish his last year at Berkeley. He was working up the material he had collected on the mythology of Owens Valley Paiute, but the writing went more slowly than he expected, no doubt because of teaching.

Steward clearly saw research and publication as far more desirable than teaching. In this he subscribed to prevailing values in the academic world. (Kroeber had recommended a university position that involved teaching only for reasons of security and professional advancement. The memory of his fleeting research position at the California Academy of Sciences probably stimulated that advice, as much as his experience at the University of California.) But Strong would soon leave a research position at the Field Museum to teach anthropology at the University of Nebraska. He joined the department of sociology there. Just months before leaving Chicago, he wrote somewhat enviously to Steward, "There's a hell of a lot to be said for growing up with a department in a good university. I don't know much about universities, but I can assure you that a big museum is no bed of roses."[50]

During his few years at the University of Nebraska, Strong's students included Loren Eiseley, whom he encouraged to choose a career in anthropology, as well as Waldo R. Wedel, who earned a Ph.D. at Berkeley and became an archaeologist.[51] Despite his strengths as a teacher, Strong soon left university life and returned to full-time research, joining the Bureau of American Ethnology at the Smithsonian. There he had the time and resources in the early 1930s to complete research in Nebraska for what became a classic study. He reconstructed the culture history of Plains Indians by using both ethnological and archaeological evidence. His research showed that Plains Indians, historically well known as nomadic hunter-gatherers, had lived as sedentary farmers before the introduction of the horse.[52]

Strong would advocate this approach—reconstructing culture history by treating ethnological and archaeological evidence as complementary—for the rest of his career. Steward also actively adopted it in the mid-1930s; whether this was simply a legacy of his Berkeley training, as often suggested, is debatable. Strong's fieldwork with hunters, his Great Plains research, and his later work in South America provided a model that his slightly younger colleague would replicate to an uncanny degree. The two men remained in close contact during Steward's first twenty-five years in anthropology. Perhaps the fact that Strong's allegiance was primarily to archaeology, and Steward's to ethnology, helped to obscure the many parallels in their professional careers and research.

Steward's restlessness during fall 1929 was not strictly professional; it also had to do with missing friends, especially his fiancée. Surrounded by new acquaintances, he appears to have felt quite alone in Ann Arbor. Like most university instructors at the beginning of their careers, he found that taking an academic position required relocating to an unfamiliar place, one he had not chosen. He had simply accepted his only job offer, which happened to take him from the Far West to the Midwest. Certain features of professional positions in anthropology—their scarcity, scattered distribution, and often temporary and unpredictable nature—meant that he had little choice but to move, and quickly, to an unknown place two thousand miles away. (If "professional positions" are labeled "resources" in the preceding sentence, it has the ring of Steward's later writings on cultural ecology. Working in his own field prefigured what he would see during his research in "the field" in the desert West.)

As he told Strong, the prospect of remaining in Ann Arbor for the rest of his life was not appealing, but he considered the professional advantages presented by the University of Michigan too good to give up. His surroundings, other than the university, appear not to have impressed him in any way; he made no mention of Ann Arbor and environs in his letters to colleagues. His only comment on the region concerned its weather, reminiscent of Ithaca's: "Until today we had signs of spring here," he had written to Lowie in March, "but now it has reverted to type." Evidently, that meant leaden skies and more snow.[53]

A month after his letter to Kroeber in October 1929, Steward wrote again on a very different subject. "Recent developments," he began, "have thrown quite a new light on my plans for the future." The University of Utah's only anthropologist, Andrew A. Kerr, an archaeologist, had died a few months earlier in August. By October the president of the university, George Thomas, had decided to hire a replacement and had written to well-known anthropologists throughout the United States to ask for their recommendations. One of his letters went to Edgar L. Hewett, president of the Archaeological Institute of America and director of the School of American Research in Santa Fe, New Mexico.[54]

Hewett replied promptly to Thomas, requesting some information about the position and adding this final query: "May I ask also if you would consider a woman for the position? We have quite a number of young women who are becoming rather distinguished in this field." Thomas responded more directly to the last question than to the others Hewett raised about the exact scope of the work. "It is very doubtful whether a woman would be satisfactory," Thomas wrote, "because the instructor has to go out and make collections in the southeastern part of the state."[55]

Southeastern Utah remained sparsely settled and rather remote, but archaeologists had already carried out extensive research there. Steward himself later pointed this out to the president to explain his own limited work in the region. The area was far less remote, in any case, than western Mexico where Steward's fellow student, Isabel Kelly, would soon do archaeological work on her own, the first carried out in those parts. Southeastern Utah was also near at hand in comparison to Amazonia, where two other women, one unnamed and not an anthropologist, planned to travel. As briefly reported in the *American Anthropologist*, "Miss Elizabeth Steen, University of California, is making a journey into unexplored country in the state of Matto Grosso, [Brazil,] to search for Indians of the 'Tapirape' tribe, which has not heretofore been visited by white men." The notice continued: "Miss Steen will travel accompanied only by an Indian guide and a negro maid."[56]

By the time Steward wrote to Kroeber, Nyswander had already spoken to the president about the position in archaeology and about her fiancé at the University of Michigan. She enjoyed a very warm relationship with Thomas, whom she knew socially; they both belonged to a small group of administrators and faculty members who rode together every Friday afternoon. An experienced horsewoman, she had joined them soon after she arrived at the university in 1926. She remembered asking the president sometime during fall 1929, "Would you consider hiring the man I want to marry?" Thomas said that he would, "'providing he has the necessary credentials.'"[57]

Learning that Thomas planned to visit Berkeley and see Kroeber there, Steward wrote to Kroeber and ventured that he would appreciate his recommendation. He pointed out that Nyswander, whom he had long hoped to marry, taught at the University of Utah and was "quite firmly entrenched" there. He clearly understood Kroeber's advice about the professional opportunities that the University of Michigan offered and took a rather defensive tone. "It may seem madness to abandon the chance to build up a department here," he wrote. "On the other hand, I think the immediate offer there would probably be better than I could get here for a year or two." He also saw better prospects for fieldwork in Utah. Still hesitant, however, about leaving Michigan, unsure of the effects on his career, he ended his letter abruptly: "If you and Lowie think I am crazy, please tell me."[58]

Kroeber once again replied with a long letter and thoughtful advice. "First of all let me make it clear that I approve most highly of Dorothy," he wrote, "both as an individual and as a potential Mrs. Steward." That said, he pointed out some of the potential problems in marrying a woman with an academic career and one who taught at the same institution. Kroeber suggested first that Steward should request something in writing to the effect that their marital status would not ever exclude either his wife or himself from employment by the university. Alluding to nepotism policies, which prevented the employment of spouses and other near relatives, he pointed out that most universities refused to employ academic couples. (These policies would remain in effect at many universities for decades, usually preventing women from teaching at institutions that employed their husbands.)

At the University of Oklahoma, Kroeber explained, Spier could not hire his wife in even the most menial capacity. More to the point, Kroeber detailed the case of his cousin at the University of Texas. After marrying a woman with an established position in another department, she "was promptly canned the next year." Although the current administration at the University of Utah appeared willing to bend the rules, unwritten or otherwise, the state authorities might later insist on enforcement. "Even if the state rules are liberal now," Kroeber wrote, "there is no telling when the legislature might tighten them up."[59]

In fact, the depression would soon affect not only the employment of couples by some universities but more specifically the employment of married women.

Within a year after Kroeber wrote to Steward, Spier and Gunther separated, and Spier resigned from the permanent position that he held at the University of Washington. In the course of resigning, however, he negotiated a permanent position for Gunther. As the depression worsened and the University of Washington struggled to reduce expenses, including salaries, administrators chose to "purge" married women from the faculty in the early 1930s. Gunther, newly divorced and with custody of two small children, retained her position, apparently because she was regarded as self-supporting.[60]

Kroeber's warning thus proved very prescient. The cases that he mentioned might suggest that Steward's impending marriage posed a greater threat to his fiancée's academic career than to his. But Kroeber undoubtedly understood that their situation differed in important ways: Nyswander, not Steward, had the established position, along with higher rank and salary; and she, not he, enjoyed a warm and supportive relationship with the president of the university.[61]

Kroeber cautioned against giving up a promising situation at Michigan for several other reasons. He compared the University of Utah unfavorably with Michigan in terms of "contacts, prestige, connections, library facilities, and other opportunities" for professional advancement. Its geographic isolation created limitations that would be difficult to overcome. He implied that if Steward went to Utah, he might well remain there for the rest of his career, with little prospect of moving into a better position elsewhere. "I think it is well to realize," Kroeber explained, "that the scope of active competition is very much more limited in the academic field than in business or in most other professions." In other words, most academics have very few opportunities to move or to advance rapidly, and even a small misstep may carry grave professional consequences. He conceded, however, that Steward's decision was "a highly personal one in which no outsider can say what will be the ultimately wise thing to do."[62]

Kroeber replied to Steward's letter during the same week that Thomas visited Berkeley and met with him. Within a week, Thomas wrote directly to Steward, briefly describing the position at the University of Utah. The fall quarter, he explained, was devoted to developing the museum's collections, and the winter and spring quarters to teaching, but only two courses each term. Steward replied with a noncommital letter, which elicited a more detailed one from Thomas. The president made it clear that Steward would have about six months of the year, the summer and fall term, to devote to research, especially research that added to the museum's collections. He mentioned nothing about having to work in the southeastern part of the state. "I will say frankly," he added, "that from my survey up to date, if we can agree on terms, you are my first choice for recommendation to the faculty."[63]

To Steward, struggling with new courses and a surfeit of students, the position might have seemed attractive even for reasons other than those of the heart. The course load was extraordinarily low, about half of what Michigan required.[64] The position at the University of Utah also offered ample opportunity for fieldwork in the region around Salt Lake City, the eastern fringe of the Great Basin; he had worked in the westernmost region of the Great Basin during his summers in Owens Valley. His field activity at Michigan, in contrast, had so far consisted of a brief foray to faraway Oklahoma to collect museum specimens from American Indians about whom he had only reading knowledge, and, given their southeastern origins, no great interest. Michigan clearly felt like a kind of exile, not only with respect to his personal life but also in terms of his research interests and regional preference. (As a new instructor setting out on an academic career in anthropology, Steward's case was not at all unusual in those regards.)

Besides advantages in teaching and research, Utah promised to provide greater professional autonomy. While his relations with Guthe had reportedly improved with time, Steward clearly resented his senior colleague during the first year at Michigan. Guthe, only nine years older than Steward, actually appears to have exercised relatively little control over him, at least as compared to the situation in many academic departments, where senior faculty members constitute an entrenched majority. Still, Steward disliked his junior status at Michigan; at the University of Utah, he alone would comprise the department of anthropology and could run it as he saw fit. And, of course, the position offered a chance for more rapid promotion and a salary increase.

By late January 1930 Thomas offered Steward a position, noting that the rank, as yet undetermined, would be either assistant or associate professor.[65] The board of regents, scheduled to meet in February, would apparently have a voice in deciding rank, assuming that they accepted the president's recommendation, usually a pro forma matter. Steward held an appointment as instructor at Michigan, and the usual promotion would have been to assistant professor. (Associate professor was the next rank after assistant, and professor the highest.)

Thomas wrote promptly after the board meeting to offer the position formally, at a salary of $3,000. Steward replied just as promptly, accepting the position and inquiring about rank: "You do not state what the position will be but I assume that it is Associate Professor." The appointment, he soon learned, was as associate professor and head of the department of anthropology (the faculty consisting only of himself). This unusually rapid rise through the ranks owed much to Nyswander's powers of persuasion and good advice as well as to Kroeber's support. At twenty-eight, having earned his Ph.D. only six months earlier, and with less than two years of teaching experience, Steward had achieved a rank that typically took years to reach. Promotions would have come much more slowly at the University of Michigan. As Kroeber had pointed out, a "major institution" such as the University of Michigan simply did not promote faculty as quickly. His own promotion to associate professor had taken about ten years. Nyswander, in contrast, had joined the University of Utah faculty at the rank of associate professor.[66]

By the time Steward accepted the position, Kroeber was in the field in northern Mexico. Lowie knew about the possibility of an offer from the University of

Utah, but apparently doubted that Steward would throw over the position at Michigan simply to suit his personal life and regional preference. (Even fifty years later, Beals remembered that he and his friends were "astonished" by Steward's decision to leave the University of Michigan and thought it "mad" professionally.) Lowie first learned of it from Clements, who was still in search of regular employment and most interested in the impending vacancy at Michigan.[67]

"During the last week I had a letter from Clements," Lowie wrote, "and this was the first intimation that you were seriously considering the change to Utah." He expressed his hope that Steward would find the situation at Utah professionally satisfying. With half the year free for research, he said, Steward could certainly do important work in Utah. And he inquired about whether Clements might have a chance in obtaining the vacant position at Michigan.[68]

By the time Steward replied to Lowie's letter, he appeared to have no doubts about leaving the University of Michigan. He had seen Kidder again, he reported, and had received some advice about archaeological work. "I can see it is difficult," he remarked, "to avoid becoming too exclusively an archaeologist. For I imagine that kind of work will be expected of me. However, I shall not give up Basin culture!"[69]

* * *

As Steward's final semester at Michigan drew to a close, he wrote to Lowie about some promising students whom he had encouraged to pursue graduate study in anthropology at Berkeley. This was another advantage to Kroeber and Lowie in having their Ph.D. graduates placed at major universities: they could recruit more students for the graduate program at Berkeley. In the 1920s Kroeber and Lowie still drew most of the Ph.D. students from the ranks of their own undergraduate students. Steward described one of his best students as an undergraduate whom he considered independent and resourceful, "intellectually and temperamentally a perfect anthropologist." He had purposely set about recruiting her for anthropology: "She was majoring in geography," he wrote, "but I won her from that department, much to their disgust." Another prospect, a young woman in his extension course in Detroit, was "the cream of the crop" in that class. He also had a new anthropology major, "a fair student," who had shown some interest in Berkeley. "Terrible, isn't it," he concluded, "that they should all be women! Part of the modern trend, I suppose."[70]

Steward's own professional experiences made him quite aware of this trend: about half the doctoral students in his cohort at Berkeley were women, and he would soon marry a woman who held a doctorate in psychology and an academic position. But his private comments, and others' public and private statements, suggest that many men in anthropology believed that the entry of women into the profession posed a serious threat. They shared this fear of so-called feminization with male colleagues in some other disciplines.[71] But it seems to have been especially acute in the new and still-marginal field of anthropology.

Not surprisingly, women students—specifically, graduate students who planned to have professional careers—were treated with profound ambivalence. On the one hand, anthropologists with established positions needed them as students in order to advance anthropology as a profession (and hence their own careers). On the other hand, the presence of women in the profession was thought to undermine its prestige and deprive men of already scarce resources: primarily, fellowships and grants, and, potentially if rarely, professional positions.

Put simply, the few graduate programs in anthropology had to attract a certain number of qualified students for the programs to continue and the new profession to grow. Admitting women made that possible. The women's labor as scholars—their research and published writing—contributed not only to the growth of disciplinary knowledge but also to the very creation of the new discipline's knowledge base. Yet professional employment for anthropologists remained very scarce, and support for their research meager. As Kroeber had once tried to explain to Strong, embarking on a career in anthropology meant entering a profession that was defined by limited opportunity, modest pay, high demands, intense competition, and risk.

Established anthropologists, all of them men at that time, responded to this dilemma by accepting and sometimes actively recruiting a certain number of women into some graduate programs, but then restricting their training and professional opportunities in various ways.[72] The presence of women as students clearly helped to expand the number of graduate courses offered. Steward, who took at least one seminar with Theodora Brown and Sara Schenk, witnessed this, but perhaps never grasped its significance: that their presence actually benefited him, resulting as it did in a broader range of graduate courses. The two women helped fill the few seats in several small seminars. They were the sole students in a seminar that Lowie offered on the topic of symbolism; and they, along with Clements, made up the class in one taught by Kroeber. Neither woman earned a degree or ever sought employment in anthropology, but both published in the field. The seminar with Kroeber resulted in a publication by the three students on the statistical treatment of cultural relationships; Kroeber's culture element distribution survey, a source of employment for Steward in the mid-1930s, grew out of such earlier work.[73]

Very few women during this era—or in the following decades—managed to find continuing employment in the field, and even fewer attained positions of authority. Kroeber and many of his colleagues seem to have believed that the presence of more women would have detracted from the prestige and scientific credibility of the profession. Perhaps this explains some of the animosity later directed at Margaret Mead by many of her male colleagues, including Steward.[74] Arguably the most famous anthropologist of the twentieth century, and often in the public eye, her fame helped to perpetuate, if not create, a misleading image of anthropology as a field that welcomed women.[75]

The matter of professional prestige, along with the problem of competition for scarce resources, helps explain some of the practices related to training women in anthropology. As students, women found a place in classrooms during the 1920s, but their opportunities for training otherwise remained limited. Just a year before Steward wrote to Lowie about his best students, expressing regret about their gender, the Laboratory of Anthropology awarded field-training scholarships to fourteen graduate students. Only three went to women, which apparently did not reflect the proportion of female applicants. The announcement stated that "as there are at present open to women relatively few professional positions in anthropology, the number of scholarships granted to women should be limited." It further explained that "the conditions under which the investigations are being carried on during the summer of 1929 precludes the assignment of women to the ethnological and linguistic parties." The three women students, one of whom was Kelly, were assigned to the archaeology group. Published in the journal *Science* and in the *American Anthropologist*, the statement bore the names of three men, all prominent anthropologists: Fay-Cooper Cole of the University of Chicago, Roland B. Dixon of Harvard University, and Alfred V. Kidder of the Carnegie Institution.[76]

Parsons registered a quiet but pointed protest with Kroeber, slated to lead the ethnological group. His reply—uncharacteristic in sounding both scornful and defensive—did not invite further discussion.[77] Parsons did not respond to his insinuation that permitting more women to enter anthropology would damage its prestige as a profession. Her great wealth, and perhaps more specifically her role as a financial benefactor to anthropologists, gave her a protected position, one that allowed her to question her colleague's decision even if it did not guarantee a civil response. Having no need to compete with men for fellowships or employment, she pursued research and writing as she wished, with rather little interference. By virtue of her social prominence, wealth, and wits, she occupied a unique position in anthropology.

* * *

When Steward again wrote to Lowie, his letter concerned the position he was vacating. Clements and Guthe had been in contact, Steward reported, and the position would probably go to Clements if he wanted it. Neither he nor Lowie mentioned Gayton, then in her final year of the National Research Council fellowship. By that time, however, the position had lost its temporary status, making it highly prized.[78]

Clements, as it turned out, did not get the position, nor did any other graduate of the University of California. Credit for building the department went primarily to Leslie White instead. A young cultural anthropologist who had trained at the University of Chicago, he took Steward's place in 1930. White had a long, distinguished career in anthropology, although his intellectual position and political views led to ongoing conflict with University of Michigan administrators. Guthe kept a foothold in the department and, as a member of many committees and councils on campus, often acted as spokesman for anthropology, which reportedly displeased some members of the department.[79] His efforts in organizing anthropology at Michigan went largely unrecognized by the profession. Steward later claimed, and often received, credit for teaching the first courses in anthropology at the University of Michigan—but mistakenly, since others preceded the ones he offered.[80]

His position at the University of Michigan, however brief, gave Steward the opportunity to launch a successful career in anthropology. It offered a variety of benefits, not least a stable salary and the chance to free himself of accumulated debt. He gained teaching experience and learned directly that its demands distracted him from research and writing. His professional circle also broadened during these years. As a result of having a well-connected senior colleague and attending conferences in Ann Arbor and New York City, he met several men who occupied positions of prominence and power in his field. They included Edward Sapir, anthropology's foremost linguist, as well as Kidder and Morley. Lowie referred to such notables as "the important eastern men" and recommended that Steward meet as many possible.[81]

His distance from Kroeber and Lowie did not prevent a constant flow of counsel and sound advice, especially from Kroeber, but it did seem to heighten Steward's sense of intellectual independence. In any case, during this period he left behind what he later dismissed as the "descriptive, analytic, relativistic, and essentially aesthetic discipline" in which he had trained, American anthropology of the 1920s. His monograph on petroglyphs, research that he came to regard as "a completely futile sideline which had no bearing on my basic work or thinking," appeared in print at this very juncture. So too did his articles "Diffusion and Independent Invention" and "Irrigation without Agriculture." They indicated more about the direction of his future work.[82]

After spending less than two years in Ann Arbor, Steward left hurriedly in early June as soon as the spring term ended and headed west, driving a new green Dodge for the occasion. He and Dorothy Nyswander met in Denver and were married by a judge in a simple ceremony on June 14, 1930. They returned to Salt Lake City almost immediately, where summer school and other work awaited them.[83]

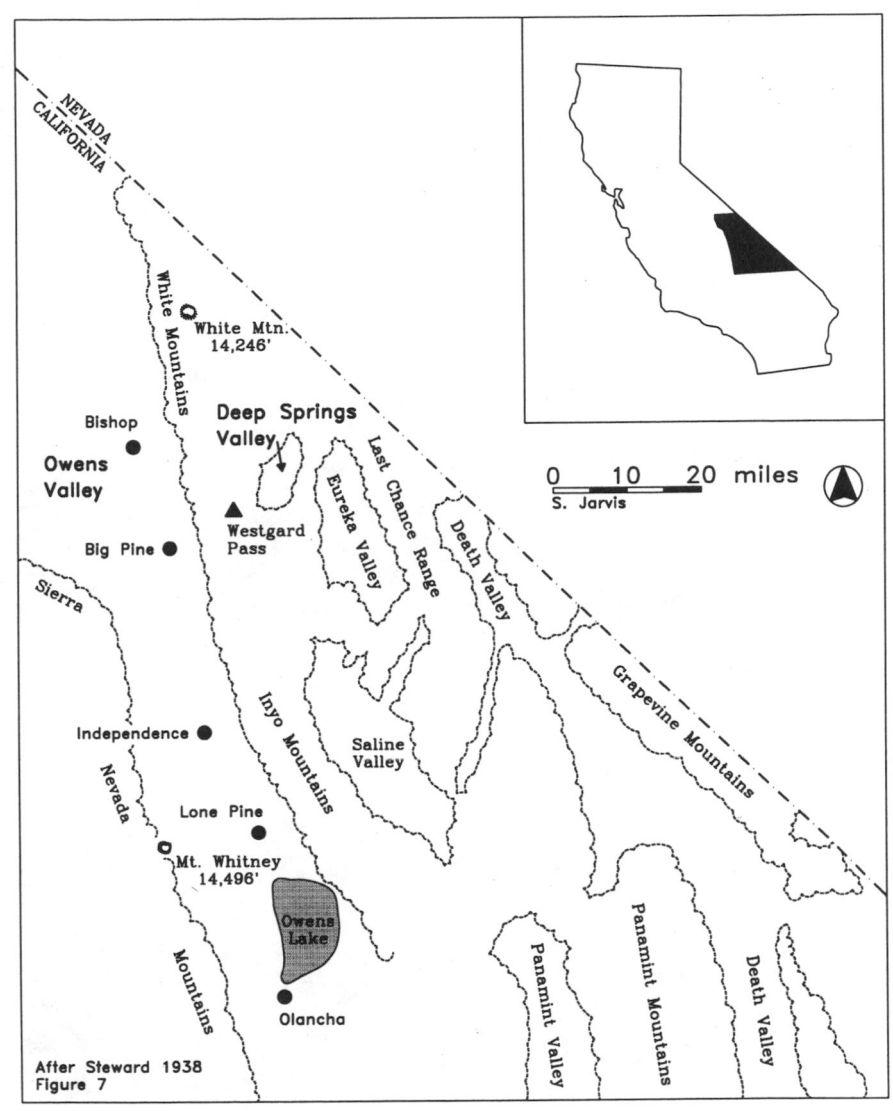

Deep Springs Valley and Owens Valley, eastern California. (Kerns 1999:2)

The ranch at Deep Springs, ca. 1918. (Deep Springs College)

Deep Springs Valley in winter. (Courtesy of the University of Illinois Archives)

L. L. Nunn. (Deep
Springs College)

Students and ranch hands branding cattle, ca. 1918. (Deep Springs College)

Julian Steward branding a calf. (Deep Springs College)

Julian Steward feeding calves. (Deep Springs College)

A happy moment. (Deep Springs College)

Students digging the swimming hole. (Deep Springs College)

Captain Harry. (Deep Springs College)

Captain Harry skinning a coyote. (Deep Springs College)

Paiute woman at the ranch.
(Deep Springs College)

Big Pine, California,
ca. 1918. (Deep
Springs College)

Grace Steward, ca. 1919.
(Deep Springs College)

Marion Steward, ca. 1919.
(Deep Springs College)

Telluride House, Cornell University. (Telluride Association)

Julian Steward (third row, left) with other residents of Telluride House, ca. 1923. (Deep Springs College)

CHAPTER 6

THE UTAH YEARS

Arriving in Salt Lake City in mid-June 1930, Steward settled in quickly. Just two years earlier in Ann Arbor, he had arrived as a stranger in an unfamiliar place. But now he experienced something of a homecoming, back in the West and again among intimates. Dorothy and her daughter, Marie, had been living in an apartment, but the new household of three soon moved to a comfortable two-story house on Twelfth East Street, near the university.[1]

With a population of 140,000, the largest city in the intermontane West, Salt Lake City had not yet fully felt the effects of the depression. The busy downtown area, crosscut by broad avenues and centering on Temple Square and the imposing Mormon Temple and domed Tabernacle, still had an air of prosperity. As always, city life held no appeal for Steward, but in this instance the surrounding landscape did. The city's natural setting—poised between desert and mountain at the eastern edge of the Great Basin—has a dramatic beauty, reminiscent of the western border region that Steward knew so well. Salt Lake City sits at the foot of the Wasatch Mountains, whose rain-catching peaks divide Utah into two arid regions. Steward would do fieldwork in both areas, but primarily on the western, Great Basin side.

The University of Utah, located a few miles from the downtown area and toward the mountains, had some four thousand students. With a student body less than half the size of the University of Michigan, it also had a much smaller faculty. Steward's colleagues at other universities considered it a lesser institution, in part because of its distance and isolation from the East, the epicenter of the academic world. They questioned whether the Mormon influence permitted free inquiry. (But students who attended during that era—writers Wallace Stegner and Fawn M. Brodie and anthropologist Omer Stewart, among others—remembered instructors and courses that opened their minds and re-directed their lives.)[2]

Steward set to work almost immediately, teaching a summer school course and reorganizing the small museum on the top floor of Park Hall, a stately build-ing that housed the president's office. He also outlined his research plans for the 1930–31 academic year, proposing that the 1930 field season (fall term at the university) be devoted to "archaeological explorations and excavations in the State of Utah." The university had eight hundred dollars available to support his research, and the president hoped to obtain a matching grant from the Smithsonian Institution.

Contrary to the president's comment to Hewett a year earlier ("the instruc-tor has to go out and make collections in the southeastern part of the state"), Steward did not plan to work intensively in southeastern Utah. His predeces-sor, Andrew Kerr, had concentrated on that area, an important one for archae-ologists interested in the development of Pueblo cultures in the Southwest. "As this region has been worked extensively by a number of institutions," Steward explained, "[it] is fairly well known." In contrast, archaeologists had hardly explored the western and northern areas and knew little about the nature of prehistoric relations between the southeast and these other areas of Utah.[3]

Steward planned to begin in September with a survey of the state, spending six weeks exploring Utah to learn about the distribution of archaeological sites. He intended to record information about the "geographical environment" of the sites, and to classify and plot them on maps. On the basis of this survey, he would then select one or two sites for excavation, preferably in central or south-western Utah, where little work had been done. The final analysis of material was to be carried out at the museum, which already had archaeological collec-tions from other sites in Utah.[4]

The Smithsonian approved of the plan and offered a matching grant. This gave Steward a total of sixteen hundred dollars for his work, an unusually gen-erous sum and equivalent to more than half of his salary. But even before learn-ing about the grant, Steward assured Kroeber that he was well satisfied with his new situation at the University of Utah. "The administration is very sympathetic toward anthropology," he wrote, "so with many advantages here over Michi-gan, I do not believe that I will ever regret the change." A passing comment about his personal life suggested that he found it harried but happy. "We are now enjoying married life as best we can," he remarked, "with teaching summer school, trying to get settled, and a hundred other things. After waiting four years for this, we are experiencing all the happiness we expected—and then some."[5]

During July, while teaching a summer school course, Steward surveyed the area around Salt Lake City, looking for archaeological sites. His most important find came at Grantsville, near the south shore of Great Salt Lake, where he lo-cated about twenty mounds. Regrettably, local pothunters had destroyed all of the large ones "beyond recovery," in his view. He made several weekend trips with some of his summer school students, and with them excavated a small mound that the looters had overlooked. Steward also learned about mounds in other areas but had no time to visit them that summer.[6]

In early August, after summer school had ended, he and Dorothy left Salt Lake City and headed toward the Uinta Mountains in northeastern Utah. She had agreed to take part in a small conference there, and he planned to survey a nearby area for archaeological sites. The three-day conference, held at Fort Duchesne, gave him his first glimpse of the Uinta Ute reservation. He planned to return to the reservation for fieldwork in the near future.

Dorothy was one of three speakers at the conference, which centered on child welfare. The other two speakers, a physician and a nurse from the University of Utah, discussed children's health, while she focused on child psychology. School officials and parents attended talks in the mornings and consultations in the afternoons. Her lectures to general audiences combined findings from the latest research on child psychology with practical advice. The titles of her talks at the Uinta conference and others convey her interest in applying scientific knowledge to the everyday problems of child rearing. Drawing on findings from experimental psychology, her talks included "What We Know About the Emotional Life of Children," "How to Form Desirable Habits in Children," and "The Laws of Learning That Parents Must Know."[7]

Dorothy Nyswander believed in using scientific knowledge to solve human problems and to improve the human condition. Having come of age during the Progressive Era, she also had a very deep reformist streak in her drive for humanitarian service. As her daughter, Marie, recalled, her mother was "'steeped in the ethic of the professional class.'" Marie Nyswander grew up to become a psychiatrist who worked primarily with drug addicts, reflecting that same ethic. "'When I was growing up,'" she said, "'I was drilled in the concept of noblesse oblige—the privilege and obligation of being of service to others.'"[8]

Dorothy and her new husband shared a commitment to science and to scientific research, and they identified themselves primarily as scientists. Perhaps at the beginning of their marriage they also thought they agreed on the meaning and importance of service. Nunn had certainly spoken about the value of humanitarian service, often in very idealistic terms, and his words had influenced Julian's choice of profession. But to Dorothy, service was not an abstract ideal or one that could be satisfied simply by teaching an academic subject. After arriving at the University of Utah, her interest turned exclusively to applied research as the best means of combining science and service. The idea of collaborative applied research appealed to her and, in fact, would characterize her career in future years.

Sometime after summer school ended, Julian and Dorothy left Salt Lake City for a three-week honeymoon. He had hoped to go to Alaska, but having only limited time and money, they went to the Rocky Mountains in northern Montana instead. At Glacier National Park they explored the mountain wilderness for a few days on horseback, but mainly on foot. Even sixty-five years later, she could recount exactly where they went and what they saw on that memorable journey. They carried their own food and equipment, she recalled, and hiked for days without meeting anyone else, finally passing over the border into Canada. Crossing immense alpine meadows, they reached small ice-blue lakes in the high country, tried their luck at fishing, and glissaded recklessly down steep snowfields. One morning they climbed up to a cliff before dawn, then lay hidden and still for hours, watching the wild mountain goats beneath them leap and play in the early spreading light.[9]

Like her husband, Dorothy relished outdoor life, especially camping and horseback riding. During the ten years of her childhood that she lived on a ranch in Antelope Valley, in the shadow of the Sierra Nevada, she grew to love the solitude and expansive beauty of desert and mountain terrain. Later, she introduced her own young daughter to the pleasures and adventures of outdoor life. Marie Nyswander remembered a time when, as a child, she and her mother camped alone in the mountains above Yosemite National Park in California, and a bear came into their camp. The terrified little girl saw her mother respond without any trace of fear: "My mother went up to [the bear], clapped her hands, told him to get away, and he did." Dorothy's own memory was of rattling some pans and shouting until it retreated.[10]

Of their many camping trips, Marie recalled another one, to the Grand Canyon, just as clearly. They pulled off a rugged road in the desert one night to pitch their tent, and she and her mother went to sleep quickly, wrapped in the immense solitude. The next morning they were awakened early by the sound of bells. Opening the tent flap, they found themselves surrounded by a flock of hundreds of sheep, and saw the sheepherder striding toward them, carrying a pan of warm biscuits to offer them for breakfast. In the last hours of her life, many years later, Marie remembered that scene: the vast expanse of open land, the milling sheep, the kindly sheepherder.[11]

* * *

Dorothy and Julian had much in common—far more than his friends, who privately held doubts about his marriage, ever understood. Both had a penchant for adventure, a taste for travel and for the remote, and warm memories of ranch life near the Sierra Nevada. They shared views about religion and politics. They also shared a strong professional drive and a willingness to center their lives around their work, a choice far more unusual for a woman than for a man in that era.

At the beginning of their marriage, Dorothy tried to support Julian's career while pursuing her own research and writing, teaching full-time, caring for her daughter, and running a household without any help. She also had many close friends and organized group outings that included them as well as Julian and Marie. This was a way of making the most of the limited time she had for a social life. Eventually, she realized that her husband went on these excursions reluctantly and that he resented sharing her attention. During their long and very private courtship, he had had her undivided attention when they were together, but this changed when he joined her household. "We were just so busy," Dorothy said repeatedly when speaking of those years.[12]

In that era, dual-career marriages such as theirs were quite rare; in Dorothy's recollection, they were the only couple with academic positions at the University of Utah. The sheer difficulty of meeting the demands of both careers, as well as myriad personal commitments, may have first led her to think about collaborative work. Working as a team would allow them both to be productive and, at the same time, to be together. But initially Dorothy simply tried to spend time with her husband as her own crowded schedule allowed. After they returned from their honeymoon, she and Marie accompanied Julian on his travels for a week or two. They took what he described as "a hurried trip south, visiting the [Harvard] Peabody Museum party in the field," then continuing on toward Mesa Verde in southwestern Colorado. Dorothy did most of the driving so that Julian could see the country. In Colorado they stopped at a site near Mesa Verde that archaeologists from the Field Museum were excavating. Returning to Salt Lake City, they arrived just as classes began at the university.[13]

Julian had the fall 1930 term to spend on his research, and he immediately set to work in the Salt Lake City area. In late July, he had visited a cave near Promontory Point, on the north shore of Great Salt Lake, spending four days there working with three companions. One of the three was Kilton Stewart, who had studied psychology with Dorothy at the university and had a growing interest in anthropology. Remembered as a free spirit and a gifted raconteur who never let the facts stand in the way of a good story, Kilton had already spent several years seeing the world, hopping freight trains and working his way from one foreign port to the next as a merchant seaman. (He later achieved recognition in some circles, notably among Jungian analysts, and notoriety in others for his cross-cultural studies of dreams.) Dorothy and Marie also went along with Julian and his field crew to camp at Promontory Point. Dorothy took along some of her own work. She recalled that Kilton, an exceptionally strong swimmer, usually swam by himself in the lake's briny water, and it was he who taught Marie to swim.[14]

Sometime during that summer, probably after spending those few days in July at Promontory Cave, Steward made a hasty trip to Gypsum Cave. A recently discovered site in southern Nevada, the cave had been occupied by prehistoric inhabitants of the Great Basin. Nothing had yet been published about the site, which he thought might be comparable in some ways to Promontory Cave. He saw the cave and took photographs and then returned to Salt Lake City.[15] Since Promontory Cave showed signs of disturbance, Steward resumed work at the site at the first opportunity, this time with four assistants in September 1930. Kilton Stewart saw to it that his younger brother, Omer, was hired as camp cook;

and this first experience of fieldwork convinced Omer that he wanted to be an anthropologist.[16]

Steward reluctantly limited his work to two weeks, but he hoped to resume it during the next field season, in summer or fall 1931. The trench he cut during September 1930 did not yield a good sample, and he planned to excavate a larger area when he returned. In the meantime, he wanted to follow his preliminary work at Promontory Cave with an archaeological survey of the southwestern part of the state. "There is so much to be done here," he told Kroeber, "that I scarcely know where to begin, but it is a wonderful field and I am fortunate in having the whole-hearted backing of the president and the university."[17]

Before beginning his survey, he returned briefly to San Juan County in south-eastern Utah, where Kerr had worked for six years during his tenure at the University of Utah. Steward had discovered some material in the museum that was "strictly Chaco in nature," but he could not locate any explanatory field notes written by Kerr. Hoping to learn more through firsthand research, he left Salt Lake City, crossed the Wasatch Mountains, and drove southeast through the desert to the small town of Blanding. From Blanding, he visited about twenty sites, including a number that Kerr had worked. Finally, at Whisker's Draw, a tributary of Cottonwood Canyon located twenty-two miles southwest of Blanding, he selected a site for excavation. Steward spent two weeks with a five-man crew working at what he described as a "large ruin." Before leaving the area, he also visited a cliff dwelling, which he photographed and mapped.[18]

Returning to Salt Lake City, Steward concluded that his trip had been "rather futile." He had hoped to publish something on the pots from San Juan County, but despite his work there he still lacked the field data he needed to do so. At the time, he underestimated the value of what was to be his only fieldwork in the heartland of southwestern archaeology. All of his other experience would be field research on the "periphery," in western Utah, together with visits in 1934 to important southwestern sites in Arizona and New Mexico. This work would culminate several years later in an article that many archaeologists regard as a classic, "Ecological Aspects of Southwestern Society." At least indirectly, it owed much to Steward's brief but intense reconnaissance of southeastern and western Utah.[19]

Words such as *reconnaissance, exploration, expedition, and terra incognita* pepper his letters and reports about this six-month period in 1930. The language makes it clear that "work in exploration," as he had once called it, still attracted him, drawing him toward the remote and the unknown. It also helps to explain why he made the difficult professional decision to leave Michigan for Utah and why he turned from southeastern Utah to western Utah for research. Although geographically remote, the San Juan area of southeastern Utah was scarcely unknown to archaeologists. Steward thus decided to dig in what he called "the comparatively virgin territory" of the Sevier Desert in western Utah. It also had the advantage of lying in the Great Basin, home ground in terms of his previous research and in a personal sense.[20]

In late October 1930, he left Salt Lake City and drove south to the small town of Delta, which he used as a base while carrying out his survey of the Sevier Desert. Finding a promising site on private property at Kanosh, south of Delta, he hired a crew of five men and began excavating in early November. Steward felt a sense of urgency about the site because the owner planned to begin work the next spring that would damage the archaeological remains, which included eight mounds. He and his crew continued the excavation, as weather permitted, for about three weeks. As he told Kroeber, the mounds were similar to those dug some years before by Neil Judd, one of several archaeologists who had preceded him at the University of Utah.[21]

Initially, Steward considered the site at Kanosh disappointing; he and his crew found nothing of significance, and the weather interfered with their work. They spent the last week "'shoveling more snow than dirt,'" he reported. But on their last day at Kanosh, Steward and his crew discovered two kivas. "'The importance of the find at Kanosh,'" Steward said several months later, "'is that Pueblo Indians lived throughout Utah in a manner like their southern neighbors, about 1300 to 1500 years ago. I have found evidence of the Pueblos at Grantsville and as far north as Brigham City'" (near the south shore and northeastern shore, respectively, of Great Salt Lake).[22]

In a report on the work at Kanosh, Steward explained that snowfall finally put a stop to the excavation. He planned to return during summer 1931, but as it happened, he would work elsewhere instead. Shortly after returning to Salt Lake City, he told Kroeber that he had found himself digging in snow at the site and suffering from chilblains: "so I finally had to come home," he wrote, "and settle down to enjoy married life."[23]

* * *

During winter term 1931, Steward taught two courses, wrote up a report of his work during the 1930 field season, and began analyzing archaeological material from the various sites. In mid-February, he prepared a lecture, "Ancient Cultures of the Desert," for a large university and community audience. He had made sure that his archaeological work was well publicized, with stories appearing in the local newspapers, the *Deseret News* and the *Salt Lake Tribune,* and in the university newspaper, the *Utah Chronicle.* The headlines of one *Tribune* story declared "Museum Reveals Dim Utah Tale"; a photograph shows Steward in jacket and tie, sporting the mustache he would wear for the rest of his life. He is pointing at an ancient skull, which he holds in his left hand (this in an era when archaeologists routinely excavated Indian burial sites and stored the skeletal remains in museums).[24]

Steward also outlined his research for the rest of the year, with hopes of obtaining funding from the Smithsonian Institution once again. He proposed continuing his work at Promontory Point during the summer, and then returning to the Sevier Desert to investigate other sites. During the fall, he planned to do research among Ute Indians of northern Utah (a collaborative project with his wife, although he made no mention of her). In the meantime, he intended to make a brief trip to the Uinta Ute reservation at the end of March to observe the annual Bear Dance. Just before departing he contacted Gifford to suggest that California's and Utah's anthropology museums trade some surplus specimens. In passing, he remarked that he liked his situation "tremendously" at the University of Utah. Conceding that it lay off the beaten path, thus limiting his professional contacts, he added: "But the administration is very good to me and I expect to accomplish a great deal."[25]

Steward left Salt Lake City on Friday, March 20. The seventy-mile trip east to Whiterocks, on the Uinta Ute reservation, took several hours, and the Bear Dance was scheduled to begin on March 21. At Whiterocks he found a room at the rustic hotel and settled in for the nine-day ceremony. None of his students from the university accompanied him, but at least one of them arrived in Whiterocks a few days before the Bear Dance ended. Kilton Stewart had just completed a master's degree in psychology and would soon resume his travels to other continents. Then twenty-nine, the same age as Julian, Kilton regarded both of his former teachers, Julian and Dorothy, as friends. Although he maintained a long friendship with Dorothy, one extending over decades, it was he who introduced Julian to Jane Cannon.[26]

Jane Cannon, twenty-two years old and single, belonged to a prominent Mormon family in Salt Lake City. Her father, Joseph Cannon, was a businessman who in 1931 became editor of the *Deseret News*, a newspaper owned by the Mormon Church (officially, the Church of Jesus Christ of Latter-day Saints). Jane had attended the University of Utah as a day student for two years, from 1926 to 1928, and then transferred unwillingly to Brigham Young University in Provo, Utah. Her father had insisted, in hope that she would find a suitable husband in Provo, where all of the students were Mormons. He considered the University of Utah "too worldly," offering too many temptations to his free-spirited and rebellious daughter. As a public institution, it had a more diverse student body; and he was well aware that some of the students used alcohol and tobacco, which Mormon doctrine forbids. Prohibition remained in effect throughout America, but Salt Lake City, like any other large city at that time, had illegal speakeasies that sold bootleg liquor.[27]

After an unhappy term in Provo, punctuated by repeated trips back to Salt Lake City, Jane left the university. She worked first at her father's business, Cannon Supply Company, then found a position as a stenographer with the ZCMI Department Store. ZCMI, Zion's Cooperative Mercantile Institution, founded in 1868 at the suggestion of the Mormon leader Brigham Young, was a Salt Lake City landmark and a major employer. (An advertisement in the early 1930s described it as "a vast merchandising organization, the largest in the Intermountain Country. . . . We manufacture the Famous Mountaineer Overalls with the Stop-Loss Pockets.") After a year or so with ZCMI, she took a position as secretary to the president of L. S. Gillham Company, an advertising agency with offices in the downtown Continental Bank Building.

One mild spring day in late March 1931, while she was still working at Gillham, she happened to read a few lines in the newspaper about a ceremony in progress at the Uinta Ute reservation. On the spur of the moment, she and a cousin and one of their friends decided to spend the weekend at Whiterocks, which had one small hotel: "just bedrooms, with one bathroom off the lobby," she recollected years later. The three young women knew practically nothing about the Ute. They simply wanted an excuse for an excursion after a long and tedious winter in Salt Lake City.[28]

Arriving in Whiterocks on Friday evening, March 27, Jane was surprised to see Kilton Stewart, a "former beau" from her years at the University of Utah. The weather, already inclement when the three friends left the city, took a turn for the worse as they checked in at the hotel. Jane recalled sitting in the lobby, playing bridge with Kilton and her companions, and ignoring the blizzard, when she heard the front door open. Turning, she saw a tall man emerge from the swirl of blowing snow. He wore a jacket with a sheepskin collar turned up for warmth, but what she noticed most of all were his very dark eyes and dark hair. She remembered trying not to stare at him, and explained, "To me, this man was exotic." Jane, with fair hair and blue eyes, came from a family and community of pale-skinned, light-eyed people.

She and Julian met that evening. The next day, Jane and her companions attended the Bear Dance, but finding it monotonous, they soon left. (Steward shared that view, later describing the dance as "hardly more than walking back and forth," but he dutifully stayed to watch it.) Sometime during that day, he and Jane saw each other again, and he helped her select a Navajo turquoise-and-silver bracelet from a trader, a birthday gift for her sister. Her sister Libby later returned it, as a memento of that first encounter on the reservation.[29]

The Bear Dance ended on Sunday, March 29, with what Steward described in a newspaper interview a few weeks later as "a grand beef barbecue." He returned to Salt Lake City with Uinta Ute specimens for the museum and notes for an article. The article on the Bear Dance was published in the *American Anthropologist* in 1932. It included a query about "the social behavior of the sexes," which seemed incongruous and which Steward never pursued.[30]

That query reflected his wife's interests and observations rather than his own. More than half a century later, Dorothy Nyswander well recalled some of the behavior she had observed on the reservation, which she thought might indicate social equality between Ute men and women. She still wondered about it.[31]

* * *

Throughout spring 1931, Steward continued to investigate sites in Salt Lake Valley and around Great Salt Lake, evidently with some sense of urgency. A letter from the president of the University of Utah to the Department of Interior at the end of April referred to "wholesale depredations by amateurs" at various sites. The president asked for a permit so that Steward could excavate in areas of public domain during the spring and summer. Permission was duly granted, and Steward began to assemble a crew so that he could start work at the end of June. In the meantime, he remained busy at the museum, which had been closed since December. When it opened again in early June, he described it as "the newly enlarged archaeological and ethnological museum." It not only occupied a larger space but also had been transformed. The exhibits now included ethnological material, including the specimens he had brought back from the Uinta Ute reservation.[32]

In mid-June, Dorothy and Julian left Utah for California. He planned to take part in a conference, "Early Man in America," presenting a paper on his research at Promontory Cave. The conference, sponsored by the American Association for the Advancement of Science, was held at the Southwest Museum in Los Angeles. Kroeber had other commitments and did not attend, but he invited Julian and Dorothy to visit him and his family on their return to Salt Lake City. By that time, the Kroeber family included not only Alfred, Theodora, and two sons by her first marriage but also a young son and daughter: Karl, who like his father and two brothers would become an academic, and Ursula, who as Ursula K. Le Guin would achieve great success as a science fiction writer.[33]

As it happened, both Julian and Dorothy were pressed for time and planned to return directly to Utah. A field crew was waiting for him in Salt Lake City, and Dorothy was trying to finish an article for publication. They declined Kroeber's invitation, but at the conference they did see some of Julian's friends from his Berkeley days. Strong, who was still teaching at the University of Nebraska, reported to Kroeber a week or so later, "Had a fine visit with Stew and his wife— he looks great. Is working hard and seems very happy." Beals also attended the conference. He remembered that he met Ruth Benedict for the first time, "then (as later) friendly, gracious and stimulating," and that both Steward and Strong presented papers.[34]

Dorothy recalled little about the event except for seeing Beals and Strong and feeling bored by the papers, perhaps because she knew so little about archaeology, including her husband's own work.[35]

* * *

Returning hurriedly to Utah, where his archaeological work was scheduled to begin on June 26, Steward met his crew and started work at Grantsville, about forty miles west of Salt Lake City. After spending a few weeks there, he moved on to excavate a cave about twenty miles from Salt Lake City (probably Black Rock Cave, near the south shore of Great Salt Lake). By September 1931, he had finished his archaeological research and was working on a collaborative project with his wife at the Uinta Ute reservation. It was to include "studies of Ute culture and mythology as well as psychological studies of the Indians through a series of mental tests."[36]

Dorothy and Julian spent two and a half weeks at the reservation doing a pilot study with twenty-five small children. She gave them "all the mental tests known to psychology" and he measured and photographed them. They hoped to continue and broaden the study during the following year. The project, as they envisioned it, embraced anthropology and psychology: Dorothy would administer psychological tests and study emotional conditioning while Julian did background work in ethnology. ("I never worried about boundaries," she recalled, alluding to her own double allegiance as an educational psychologist. "I never thought that boundaries were stretched enough.")[37]

Her enduring memories of the project, her first experience of field research, centered on physical hardship. "It was *hard work,*" she said emphatically. They stayed in a cabin at reservation headquarters, but had to clean it thoroughly to make it fit for their purposes. To get each of the Ute children, they drove ten to fifteen miles over rutted tracks that passed for roads, then returned to the cabin with the children and usually as many family members as the car could carry. After several hours of taking the children's measurements and administering a battery of tests, Dorothy offered her guests food. "If it was lunchtime," she explained, "it was just expected." She recalled cooking large quantities of rice, beans, and ground beef. After everyone had finished the meal, she collected the dishes. Then came another long trip to take the children home, the return to their cabin at headquarters, more time in the kitchen washing plates and pots and pans, and a spell of work in the evening going over the day's results.[38]

In the late 1930s and 1940s, collaborative work between anthropologists and psychologists would grow quite popular, but Dorothy Nyswander and Julian Steward were very much in the vanguard in 1931. (The later work brought together such anthropologists as Ruth Benedict, Cora Du Bois, Margaret Mead, and Rhoda Métraux with psychoanalysts and clinical psychologists, including Abram Kardiner, Max Wertheimer, and Erik H. Erikson.) Their own project was unusual in its behaviorist approach and the attempt to merge basic (or "pure") research and applied research. Steward's interests clearly lay more in the former and his wife's in the latter, but their plan of comparing their test results with those for white children, Steward suggested, promised to have a double significance. It would "not only have great theoretical importance but practical importance for [the] Indian Administration and the building of educational programs—if they will only use it!"[39]

The Indian agent at the Uinta Ute reservation had cooperated with them, and some of the local leaders helped them. The president of the university wrote to several leaders afterward, including John Duncan (who had provided many of the Uinta Ute specimens for the museum a few months before) and a man addressed as "Little Jim, Indian Doctor." President Thomas extended his thanks to them, saying that "Dr. and Mrs. Steward have just reported to me personally your kindness to them while they have been studying the young children of your tribe." He assured them that they wished to help, by informing the government about the condition of Ute children. "You may trust these people," he wrote, "for they do not desire in any way to interfere with your ways of thinking or living."[40]

The president's reference to Dorothy as "Mrs. Steward" rather than "Dr. Nyswander" expressed social understandings of the time. She had a conflicting social and professional status in the sense that the few women with professional careers were usually single. She was known as "Dr. Nyswander" at the university and in most of her professional dealings but as "Mrs. Steward" in any context that directly involved her husband. She had not changed her surname when they married because she had already published under that name and because she shared it with her daughter. She did, however, willingly answer to "Mrs. Steward." (To his lasting disgust, Steward was addressed as "Mr. Nyswander" more than once, but simply in error, by people who knew his wife but did not know of her previous marriage.)[41]

Returning from the Uinta Ute reservation, Steward set to work on his ethnography of the Owens Valley Paiute, which focused on the food quest and material culture (with some passing comments about "personality formation," probably the last time he wrote about psychological matters.) By the time he married, Steward had largely shifted away from topics such as mythology, preferring those that allowed him to take a strictly "objective"—that is, behaviorist—approach. His brief study of the Ute Bear Dance in 1931, along with his 1928 research at First Mesa, had given him the chance to observe directly the behavior he wrote about, perhaps the only two instances in which he ever did so. In each case he observed a ceremonial event, which never held interest for him; each was a publication opportunity but a virtual dead end as a research project, without follow-up.[42]

Methodology clearly remained an issue in most of his ethnographic work. In reconstructing "traditional" Paiute culture, he had to depend on what people told him during interviews about how they had once lived. He could not actually observe the past behavior they described, thus violating a sine qua non of behaviorism. Worse, he had had to depend on the memories of a very few informants, elderly men and women who had experienced an earlier, now vanished way of life. Dorothy Nyswander, years after the fact, remembered clearly that she questioned the results of his ethnographic fieldwork on methodological grounds. "Just one old man?" she recalled asking him more than once. "You're going to say how these people used to live based on what just *one* old man has *told* you?" (Steward did, in fact, generally work with several informants, usually older men.) Reflecting on that long-ago incident, she mused, "I suppose I'm too critical." She conceded that some of her later research experience, which involved intensive interviewing, taught her that achieving methodological rigor in laboratory experiments with white rats was one matter and working with people in their own territory, outside a laboratory, was quite another. In 1931, however, she was still a convinced behaviorist.[43]

Steward had finished more than half of the manuscript on the Owens Valley Paiute when he made plans to visit Deep Springs and the vicinity in early December 1931. He intended to spend a week in Owens Valley, "picking up odds and ends," as he put it, that he had missed during his fieldwork there in the summers of 1927 and 1928. He wanted to stop at Deep Springs for a week or so after leaving Owens Valley, and he offered to give a series of five lectures on the topic of civilization.[44]

The topic appeared timely, Steward said, in a period of worldwide economic crisis. Although the depression had worsened by the end of 1931, it had hardly affected his own life in any direct way. He viewed it in intellectual terms, from afar, and in the framework of his discipline. "Thinkers are questioning the very bases of civilizations," he wrote, "and wondering what the future will hold." The proposed lectures were to begin with one on human origins, and then move to the development of culture. The third lecture, on Owens Valley Paiute, would describe them as "the most primitive peoples of America," and suggest that their general way of life resembled that of Europeans twenty thousand years ago during the Stone Age. A lecture on the rise of civilization would follow, and then a final one titled "The Price of Civilization." "The glorification of 'production' is particularly characteristic of our western civilization," Steward wrote. "Our social life becomes each year less adjusted to our material culture, so that today we are faced with problems of labor, control of industries, class interests, marriage, in fact even how to secure for the individual a happy life in the face of a bewildering world."[45]

That Steward included marriage, along with conflicting class interests, in his list of social problems revealed more about his personal life in late 1931 than about his perspective on civilization. Only a month later, he sent a telegram to Kroeber, who was planning a cross-country trip by train; Steward wanted to meet him during the brief stop at Ogden, Utah, about thirty-five miles north of Salt Lake City. Kroeber wired back, giving the time and date when his train would pass through Ogden; it was scheduled to stop there for twenty minutes. Kroeber evidently suspected problems because he followed up his telegram with a lengthy letter about editorial matters, ending it abruptly with this prescient sentence: "I am writing this all to you now because I judge if you see me at Ogden, you would prefer to talk about other matters."[46]

Steward and Kroeber met at the train station in Ogden on the appointed date a week later, in January 1932. They talked business at least briefly; Steward asked Kroeber's advice on several editorial matters. But he also told Kroeber about his marital problems and raised the possibility of a separation. What Kroeber counseled is unknown, but he certainly understood the serious professional implications of separation or divorce and probably suggested caution. That, in any case, was the usual tenor of his advice to his sometimes impetuous student.[47]

Letters that Steward wrote to friends and colleagues in early 1932 gave little evidence of the looming crisis in his personal life. In several letters he exchanged with a friend who had become an official of Telluride Association, he referred to his psychologist wife and recommended the use of psychological tests to select Telluride members. Indeed, he even wrote to the *Telluride News Letter,* touting psychological tests as "tools of science" and mentioning in an aside that he had been "enjoying the status of matrimony" for nearly two years.

A passing comment that he made in spring 1932 implied that while he did enjoy having the status of a married man, he resented not having the attention of his very busy wife. Apologizing for the delay in sending some information about intelligence tests, he explained: "I mislaid your letter, still unfound, and Dorothy said in answering it she wanted to have your specific questions at hand, for they 'showed a very intelligent insight into the problems.' The other reason [for the delay] is that two professional people sometimes find it difficult to make their time coincide—and maybe this is more true when they are married!" His wife's myriad commitments—from teaching, writing, and giving public lectures to running a household and spending time with her daughter and friends—left less time for him than he wished. (Based on what he said about his first marriage, and on her own experience of marriage, his second wife concluded years later that he had wanted Dorothy's full attention.)[48]

Steward may have realized by this point that separating from his wife might mean leaving his position at the University of Utah. Kroeber, who understood the social conventions as well as the politics of academic life, certainly would have made that clear to him when they met at the train station in Ogden. The letter that Kroeber had written two years earlier, spelling out the many hazards of marrying an academic woman, said nothing about the consequences of a divorce. But as Steward already knew from firsthand experience, divorce carried a strong stigma, especially in socially conservative circles, whether government service or academe. His own father had resigned from the Patent Office in the wake of a separation. Kroeber, with his close ties to the field of psychology, and Steward, with his, must also have known about the case of John B. Watson, the well-known behaviorist. Watson had been forced to resign from Johns Hopkins University in the 1920s because of the scandal surrounding his divorce, which received national press coverage. Unable to find another academic position despite his professional eminence, he entered the field of advertising. His case was not exceptional, although some men did survive marital scandal by moving to another university.[49]

Perhaps this explains why Steward, writing to Ronald Olson at Berkeley just a few weeks after meeting with Kroeber in Ogden, inquired about news from the University of Washington. He added, "I begin to look somewhat yearning[ly] in that direction." Olson had recently left the American Museum of Natural History and accepted a position at Berkeley, one that Kroeber created for him. Because he had earned his undergraduate and master's degrees in anthropology at the University of Washington, he still had ties with the department there. But Olson could report nothing more than unsettling rumors that some type of reorganization was underway. He probably referred to the university's whole-sale dismissal of married women from the faculty, a cost-cutting measure in response to the depression. Erna Gunther, recently divorced, remained in the department of anthropology along with one colleague, Melville Jacobs. No position ever materialized there for Steward.[50]

* * *

In June 1932, Dorothy and Marie left Salt Lake City and drove to San Francisco to see Dorothy's sister, Margaret, who was ill. Dorothy planned to stay and take care of her and their father, who had gone to live with Margaret when Dorothy remarried. Her own words about that trip—"My family always had first call on me"—suggest that her husband's sense of coming second, or even third or fourth, in her life was not entirely unfounded. The trip across the Sierra Nevada into California proved harrowing, with a late snowfall that made driving haz-ardous and slow between Truckee and Sacramento. Dorothy had to stop the car repeatedly so that Marie could crawl up on the hood to clear the snow from the windshield. Speaking about that difficult journey many years later, she also re-called with absolute clarity the letter that she received from Julian a few days after she arrived in San Francisco. He wrote to say that he wanted a divorce. Stunned by the letter, Dorothy left immediately for Salt Lake City, while Marie stayed behind with her grandfather and aunt.[51]

Julian's comments in letters suggest that he regarded Dorothy's departure for San Francisco as the beginning of their separation, a perception she did not share on the day she left Salt Lake City in 1932 or sixty-five years later when she re-called her trip. In any case, during her absence, Steward had seen Jane Cannon again. More than a year after introducing Julian and Jane at the Uinta Ute Bear Dance, Kilton Stewart called Jane at home one Monday evening. He asked if she was free, explaining that he and two friends wanted her to join them that evening. She declined at first, thinking of work the next day; then, her curiosity piqued, she asked about the friends. He named a young woman and identified the other person mysteriously as "somebody else." Pressed, he finally said it was Julian Steward. When Kilton offered to stop by her house for her, she agreed.

As was common at the time, they went to a speakeasy, one disguised as a re-spectable-looking private home. They spent several hours sharing beer from a pitcher, eating potato chips, making small talk, and laughing. Jane learned, with a sense of dismay she tried to conceal, that Julian was married to Dorothy Nyswander (whose daughter she knew slightly because they took piano lessons from the same teacher) but that they had separated. When Julian took Jane home that night, he said he wanted to see her again, and she finally accepted, resolutely ignoring all of her reservations. As she explained with great candor so many years later, she said yes simply because she found his dark good looks compelling and his attention flattering, especially because of his status as a university professor. His being an anthropologist did not enter into it. She knew next to nothing about the field—"I didn't really know what anthropology *was*"—and she thought of him simply as a professor. Jane suggested that they see each other that weekend, but he persuaded her to meet him on Wednesday. They agreed that he would pick her up downtown, after work.[52]

On Wednesday they drove up into one of the canyons in the mountains near the city. Julian had brought a steak, and he grilled it over a campfire, made a salad, and fixed some coffee. His dinner companion, who had not yet learned how to cook, remembered that this impressed her. As the evening wore on, however, an unpleasant reality slowly sank in: she was deeply attracted to this man, but he did not qualify as an "eligible bachelor." She had thought of their dinner date as something of a lark and slightly bohemian, like smoking cigarettes and drinking bootleg alcohol. It took on an entirely different cast when she suddenly grasped the social implications, not only for herself but also for her family. She was in the company of a man who had separated from his wife, but in the eyes of her community and the law, he was still married. Finally, she reluctantly told him why she could not see him again. His reply startled her: "'Will you marry me?' he asked, and I just said . . . 'Yes.'" All those years later, she laughed at what struck her as the improbability of their marriage and its long duration.[53]

A few days after his impulsive proposal, Steward wrote to Kroeber to say that what he had "intimated" about his marriage had finally transpired. "The separation naturally does not come easily," he wrote, "but it seems to be the only thing to do." He reported that his estranged wife was in San Francisco, where he hoped that she would be able to find employment so that he could stay on at the University of Utah for another year, an impossibility if she returned to the university and others learned of their impending divorce. "We are not ready to let people know yet for many reasons," he remarked, "and I would especially like the Berkeley people not to know."[54] He referred to the many friends they shared among the anthropologists and psychologists on campus.

Judging from the language of Steward's letter, he was only beginning to realize that a divorce would not only cost him his position at the University of Utah but also might end his career. He faced unemployment at a time when the national economy remained sunk in depression. Academic positions in anthropology, always scarce, had simply disappeared. Beals, among others, remembered the early 1930s as a time when no employment could be found.[55]

Even such a prominent anthropologist as Leslie Spier was professionally adrift during this period after separating from his first wife, resigning from the University of Washington, and remarrying. The year before, Kroeber had taken it upon himself to write to colleagues in museums and anthropology departments, asking if they could find a temporary appointment or other salaried position for Spier, by then "completely out of a job." Kroeber recommended him as "one of the best men in anthropology and a definite leader of his generation." Spier, ten years ahead of Steward professionally, had an extensive list of publications to his credit. Nevertheless, he was to spend the 1930s in a series of temporary and courtesy appointments.[56]

The archaeologist Marshall Saville, a former president of the American Anthropological Association, also found himself entirely out of work during the early years of the depression. He had left his position at Columbia University to join the staff of the Heye Foundation in New York City. After the stock market crash, George Heye, the founder and director of the foundation, felt obliged to choose between purchasing more specimens for his museum and retaining his research staff, including Saville and Samuel Lothrop. He chose the specimens.[57]

Steward undoubtedly knew of these cases and others. His letter to Kroeber also suggests he knew that his wife, already well established as an educational psychologist, had far more opportunities for employment than he had as an anthropologist. Their later careers would confirm that. In the meantime, he asked Kroeber for advice and help in finding another position: "If you should have occasion," he wrote, "I would . . . appreciate your dropping the hint that a very good anthropologist would consider an offer." And, he added, he had learned something about keeping his professional and personal life separate, with the latter subordinate to the former. In his own words, he had twice "got off to a grand start and then had to quit for personal reasons" (leaving the University of Michigan in order to marry and leaving the University of Utah because of divorce). "It is perfectly plain," he concluded, "that hereafter personal matters cannot enter in!"[58]

His words may be read as a belated admission of error. By marrying Dorothy Nyswander and moving to Salt Lake City he not only had ignored Kroeber's warning but also had violated two of the most important social conventions of his conservative, largely male professional world. The first unwritten rule was that professional life and personal life must be treated as separate, with the former always taking precedence over the latter. Work-related duties and goals outweigh personal concerns, or should at least always appear to do so: in Steward's own words, "personal matters cannot enter in!" The second unwritten rule, that men lead and women follow, found perfect expression on the dance floor during that era. As it happened, Julian and Dorothy's courtship had begun when they danced together at Berkeley's Faculty Club; their first encounter conformed to social convention in a way that their marriage never would.

Steward had visibly broken both rules when he decided to marry. He broke the first when he seemed to give precedence to his personal life by resigning from his position at the University of Michigan to take one at a less prestigious institution. Although it offered a variety of professional advantages, in the eyes of most of his academic colleagues, prestige outweighed any other factor. Moreover, he followed his wife, moving a thousand miles to join her at her institution. "Of course, I was a first class idiot ever to have left Michigan," he later confessed ruefully to Strong. He also followed her in a more figurative sense, but one equally damaging at the time: she outranked him professionally, earned a higher salary, and surpassed him in her training in mathematics and behavioral science. He said nothing of that, but admitted that her achievements continued to impress him, even after separating. "I still have the highest regard for Dorothy and know of no woman comparable to her," he told Strong. "But that, of course, does not mean that marriage is going to be successful," he added. "Basically, I suppose, we really wanted quite different things out of life."[59]

His wife had tried to persuade him to follow her in yet another way, in the direction of collaborative, applied research. His ethnographic fieldwork, as she saw it, was methodologically flawed and, besides that, not very useful. Interviews offered only secondhand, and thus unreliable, behavioral data: what informants remembered and reported about the past. And reconstructing that past, in her view, was far less important than finding solutions to the pressing economic and social problems then facing Indian communities. Her childhood memories of how some impoverished Paiute and Washo families had lived in Antelope Valley remained vivid and strong.

Being called "Mr. Nyswander" on occasion, and feeling that other faculty members treated him as an arriviste, gave Steward the strong sense that he did not really belong at the University of Utah. As Jane Steward commented years later, "It was Dorothy's campus, not his."[60] He was there because of her, and everyone knew it, from other members of the faculty to his own colleagues in anthropology. Even establishing a separate identity and recognition as an archaeologist could not change that. A disregard for the rules of his conservative social world or his simple failure to reckon with the force of social convention had brought certain consequences. He would not make that mistake again.

* * *

Dorothy had returned by late June to Salt Lake City, where she stayed with close friends. She quickly learned about Jane. Still hoping for a reconciliation, she saw Julian and refused to grant a divorce. As she explained so many years later, she believed her husband might change his mind when the consequences of his actions began to unfold, when he saw the terrible social and professional costs to himself, to her, even to Jane and her family. And she worried about Marie, who had known Julian for six of her thirteen years, felt very attached to him, and would have a sense of loss nearly as great as her mother's if he left. "Jane Cannon was a beautiful girl," Dorothy said, "and I didn't blame Julian for falling in love with her." Her rival was fourteen years younger than Dorothy, who was then thirty-seven. Still, she recalled holding out hope that the crisis would pass, that she and Marie and Julian could resume their life together in Salt Lake City.[61]

Although he saw Jane Cannon a few more times, Steward escaped into his work that summer. Earlier in June, he had taken a group of students to a site in Willard, about forty-five miles north of Salt Lake City, where Neil Judd had previously excavated.[62] He spent most of July far away from Salt Lake City, searching for archaeological sites along the Colorado River, from the mouth of the Dirty Devil River in Utah to Lee's Ferry in Arizona. His journey, planned months before, covered 170 miles and carried him through Glen Canyon, along part of the route that Powell and his companions had first explored some sixty years before. John Steward had accompanied Powell on the second of his famous trips from the Green River in northeastern Utah to the Grand Canyon in Arizona. In the 1930s, Glen Canyon remained "virtually unknown archaeologically," Steward remarked. Whatever its scientific merits, the journey also offered him the chance to retreat from Salt Lake City and the myriad complications of his personal life, and, not least, to see the wild, rugged terrain of southern Utah.[63]

He left Salt Lake City with four companions on July 1, carrying two collapsible canvas boats, camping equipment, and three weeks' provisions in a large trailer. His companions included Charles Kelly of Salt Lake City and Hoffman Birney of Philadelphia, writers and amateur historians who would soon publish a book about the Mormons and who wanted to explore the river "for things of pioneer and historical interest"; Byron Hughes, a student and instructor in anthropology at the University of Michigan; and John Shoemaker of Philadelphia. Hughes had training in archaeology, and Kelly had some field experience, having assisted Steward at sites in the Salt Lake City area.[64]

Driving through the small community of Torrey, in south-central Utah, the group passed through the Capitol Reef area, named for an enormous ridge of rock about twenty miles long, then continued through a desolate region of dunes and mesas. They finally reached Hanksville, an isolated settlement frequented by Butch Cassidy and his Robbers Roost gang in the 1880s and 1890s. Turning south, they continued along a rough road to a ranch near the Dirty Devil River. After loading their equipment in a wagon, the rancher drove them to the river; their cars would be driven to the terminus of their river trip, Lee's Ferry, at the confluence of the Colorado and Paria Rivers in north central Arizona.[65]

Their first, unexpected task was to rescue a man who had been marooned on the other side of the river for nine days. He and a partner had tried to cross the river on a log raft, but the swift current had sent them smashing into a rock, and his partner drowned. The man finally made it to shore but had no prospect of surviving a journey on foot to the closest settlement from that side of the river. Steward's party quickly set up one of the canvas boats and rowed across to him, whereupon he "fell to his knees," Steward remarked dryly, "muttering prayers of thanks" to heaven rather than his human rescuers.

After this unsettling prelude to their river journey, the five companions pushed off on July 6 with three men in the larger boat and two in the smaller. During the days that followed, they found themselves scanning the shore not only for archaeological sites but also for some sign of the drowned man. They never found his body. To their great relief, the river, which had shown no mercy to a log raft, was easily negotiated by the canvas boats; loaded to the gunwales with equipment and food for three weeks, the boats proved quite stable. Steward later reported that he had few doubts that they could safely run "the few spots of rough water." He and his companions avoided the more dangerous sections of the Colorado River by entering it below the turbulent waters of Cataract Canyon in Utah and leaving it above the treacherous rapids of Marble Canyon in Arizona.

Because the current ran so swiftly, the men could have reached their destination quite easily in six days. But they limited travel to ten miles a day, stretching their river journey out to nineteen days and stopping often to investigate sites and record archaeological features. During the first few days, they saw cliff dwellings, petroglyphs, and pictographs, as well as cabins long abandoned by settlers. At Hall's Crossing, Steward reported finding several gold miners, "the last people we saw," he wrote, "until we reached Lee's Ferry."

Continuing downriver, they repeatedly passed unscalable cliffs and box canyons, "the kind of topography," Steward noted, "that almost defies cross country travel." Archaeological sites grew scarce, leading him to conclude that Glen Canyon had been uninhabited even in the distant past. The tributary canyons appeared more promising, but to their disappointment, the four men found the outlets blocked with quicksand. The trip yielded no major finds in terms of archaeology. As Steward conceded, its most memorable aspect was spending day after day in the presence of a "magnificent" and singular landscape: "Mile after mile of buff, red and creamy sandstone formations . . . beautifully formed and colored."[66]

Exactly what Steward and others saw of Glen Canyon in the century after Powell and his companions explored it is known only from written accounts, old photographs, and the memories of a few people. Years after Steward's journey, the river was flooded in the course of creating Lake Powell, a vast stretch of water unaptly named for the explorer/scientist who charted that part of the Arid Region.[67]

* * *

Steward continued to avoid Salt Lake City that summer. In the spring he had obtained an archaeological permit not only for Glen Canyon but also for the region around the Paria, Kanab, and Virgin Rivers in southern Utah. He initially planned to spend five or six weeks exploring that area, but he decided to confine his work to the lower Paria River and Johnson Canyon. Again with four companions, including Hughes, who had accompanied him in Glen Canyon, he made a pack trip through scenic country that he had first read about as a boy, in the Zane Grey classic, *Riders of the Purple Sage*. His party set off a few miles from Pahreah (now shown as Old Paria on most maps), skirting the Vermilion

Cliffs and ending their journey near Kanab. Steward located about 140 sites in the course of the trip.[68]

Leaving the desert solitude and finally returning to Salt Lake City, he confronted a tangle of personal and professional problems. In June he had told Kroeber that he planned to spend about six weeks during the fall term, his field season, doing ethnographic work in Nevada. But his marital problems, and perhaps Jane Cannon's situation as well, led him to leave Utah for California. Before departing, he saw his wife and asked again for a divorce, telling her that he intended to marry Jane. He spent most of the fall in Berkeley, writing up his summer research, with two weeks at Deep Springs in late October and November, where he offered some classes in anthropology.[69]

During Steward's absence that summer, Jane Cannon's father first learned of their relationship. Joseph Cannon, whose own father had played a prominent part in Mormon history, had a certain prominence himself as the new editor of the *Deseret News*. Founded in 1850, three years after Brigham Young led the first Mormon settlers into Salt Lake Valley, the *Deseret News*'s past editors had included George Q. Cannon, Joseph Cannon's father, who held the position in the 1860s. George Q. Cannon also served as first counselor to several presidents of the Mormon Church, prospered in his business ventures, and achieved notoriety outside Utah as a polygamist. Married to five wives and the father of thirty-three children, he was one of several Mormon leaders forced into hiding and later arrested during the antipolygamy raids of the 1880s. (A full century later, as she spoke fondly of "George Q.," Jane Steward leafed through an old book to find her favorite photograph of her paternal grandfather. It showed a white-bearded man wearing prison stripes with an air of great dignity.) After his death in 1901, many Mormons remembered him warmly as "a strong advocate of the patriarchal family system."[70]

Some thirty years after his father's death, Joseph Cannon found himself in a difficult position as a father. Seen from the perspective of his times and his community, he had a social position and family reputation to defend against what threatened to become a scandal. But he was also a rather indulgent father to his daughters. While he did not approve of Jane's attachment to a non-Mormon, and one who was still legally married at that, he eventually accepted her decision to marry Julian, largely persuaded by his wife, Ramona, Jane's stepmother. (His first wife, Jane's mother, died in 1912, leaving three small children. Two years later, Joseph married Ramona Wilcox, a young schoolteacher.) He insisted, however, that his daughter leave Salt Lake City and not return until Julian obtained a divorce. She found herself exiled to California, where she lived with relatives for a year.[71]

With the prospect of divorce still uncertain, the economy worsening each day, and unemployment on the horizon, Steward seems to have suffered a brief failure of nerve about leaving his marriage and his academic position. During fall

1932, as he worked on several articles in Berkeley, he took no comfort from what he saw around him. "Paul Radin haunts the building daily," Steward reported a few months later to Strong, adding that he looked the worse for wear, altogether "forlorn." "It gave me the willies," he continued, "for I saw J.H.S. equally woe-begone next year!" Remarking on the number of doctoral students in anthropology, he wondered "what fate awaits the mob of them when they face the cruel world!"[72]

Meanwhile, the country sank ever more deeply into economic depression as fall passed. While Franklin D. Roosevelt campaigned for president against Herbert Hoover, banks failed on a daily basis, factories closed their doors, and the number of unemployed workers continued to rise. An estimated one-quarter of all workers were jobless, and a quarter of farming families had lost their farms. Roosevelt was swept into office at just about the time that Marion Steward, still living in San Francisco, lost a full-time clerical position with Remington Rand. Marion eventually found temporary work, but Julian pointedly told a colleague that his mother and sister were "entirely dependent" on him during this time. He may have lived with them during the term he spent at Berkeley. While it was undoubtedly true that he offered some support, it was equally true that asserting his status as a male provider underlined his need for employment at a time when he otherwise seemed to have no dependents. (He had also provided for Grace during the lengthy period she stayed with him and Dorothy in the previous year, a visit that stretched on for many months.)[73]

In late October 1932, Steward wrote to President Thomas at the University of Utah, ostensibly to tell him about his work in Berkeley. He had just finished three articles and was working on an archaeological report that the University of California would publish, "providing, of course, there is any money," he remarked. Only the closing words of his letter broached the subject of his marriage: "Strange to say," he wrote, "I find myself wishing I were back in Salt Lake with Dorothy and at the University."[74]

By this point, he could no longer deny the full reality of his situation. A divorce, and the scandal surrounding it, would quite likely cost him his career, especially given the depressed economic conditions that had led museums and universities to reduce their staffs. As he later put it to Strong, "the highly moral Salt Lake community cannot bear the thought of having us divorced. . . . Curious bit of irony connected with this. People have raised a great outcry until now because we were married and both teaching. They wanted one of us to quit. Now they cannot stand it to have us separated and one must quit!" Kroeber's judgment, once again, had proved flawless.[75]

The president replied to Steward's letter a week later, offering counsel both kind and stern. He acknowledged that he had heard "rumors," and after receiving Steward's letter had investigated them. "I am not going to preach to you," he began, "but I think what you need right now is a father's advice, and as I am old enough to be your father, I am going to say a word to you." His language was apt in a way President Thomas could not have known. Steward was completely estranged from his father by this time. "It appears to me," Thomas continued, "that you are foolish in what you are doing, and if you do not move more deliberately, you are going to ruin your home and your professional career." He urged Steward to seek a reconciliation with "Mrs Steward." "I am sure that this can be accomplished," he added, "and that she will meet you more than half way." Without a reconcilation, Steward's position at the University of Utah would be "impossible." "I hope that when you consider this matter carefully," he concluded, "you will make an adjustment and get together again with this splendid, sweet, lovable woman."[76]

Two weeks later, Dorothy Nyswander submitted a request for a six-month leave of absence, beginning January 1, 1933. The president already knew that she had an offer of a salaried research position in New York City, but he evidently hoped that she and Steward would reconcile and both remain at the university. She, however, had heard nothing from her estranged husband and finally decided to accept the temporary appointment with the American Child Health Association in order to give Steward another six months at the university. She understood that finding employment in anthropology would prove difficult. As it turned out, the position in New York City marked an important step on a path that would lead to her later, widely recognized work in public health education. Marie Nyswander, who had fallen sick from tuberculosis, spent much of the year recuperating in a sanitarium near Los Angeles.[77]

In mid-November 1932, Steward returned from his trip to Deep Springs and found the president's letter waiting for him in Berkeley. He sent a lengthy reply. "A thousand times I have wished for a father's advice," he wrote. "And now I wish it more than ever, for while the situation is entirely clear to me, the solution is by no means obvious." The situation, as he explained it, was that he and his wife had found living together difficult from the beginning and had "experienced one crisis after another" in their relationship until they had finally decided to separate. (His wife did not share this perception of events, as attested by her reluctance to grant a divorce and her memories of their marriage many years later.) "The whole thing gives me a sense of bitter failure," Steward continued, adding that he had twice begun building academic programs only to leave them and start over again.

Thomas replied in late December in a terse letter informing him that "Mrs. Steward left for the East last Thursday," asking him to report to the university immediately, and directing him to submit a letter of resignation, which would take effect at the end of the academic year. Steward submitted the letter a week later, in early January 1933.[78]

* * *

Steward spent the winter and spring terms teaching, applying for fellowships, and inquiring informally about academic positions elsewhere. He had applied to the Social Science Research Council and the National Research Council for fellowships, and Kroeber sent letters of support, commending Steward in one of them for his "quite unusual originality." The same letter, written soon after Steward had separated from his wife, characterized him as "somewhat temperamental," but Kroeber hastened to add that "he is generally regarded as a highly presentable young man." Kroeber also praised Steward's ethnography of the Owens Valley Paiute, recently accepted for publication by the University of California, for its novel approach, "the relatively new angle of viewing the whole culture through its subsistence mechanisms."[79]

By late March, the Social Science Research Council had turned down Steward's application, and he doubted that the National Research Council would offer him a fellowship. With no employment prospects in sight, he wrote to Kroeber that he felt "resigned to a year of poverty." He wondered whether he should explain to colleagues elsewhere the "real reason" he was leaving the University of Utah and whether he should write to Clark Wissler at the American Museum of Natural History, among others, to inquire about positions. And he added, "I should very much like to get into the South American field. Is there any chance of raising funds for a field trip?" He undoubtedly planned to take Jane Cannon with him, although he made no mention of her in letters to Kroeber until after their marriage.

Kroeber responded to his questions, advising him not to discuss the circumstances of his leaving the University of Utah. "Everyone will assume that it is part of the universal economy wave," he said. "Other good anthropologists have preceded you in being let out." Although Kroeber did not recommend writing to Wissler and others, he conceded that the times were unusual: "The man who applies [now] is presumably out of luck, whereas in normal times he is a failure. So there is much less loss of prestige than would normally be the case."[80]

Later that spring, as students learned that Steward had resigned, they sent a petition to the board of regents, expressing their "most sincere protests at the release of Dr. J. H. Steward from this university for any reasons whatsoever and the subsequent closing of the Department of Anthropology." The administration solved some of the university's budgetary problems, serious ones during those depression years, by not replacing any faculty members who resigned. As the sole member of his department, Steward's resignation meant its termination.

The petition continued: "The dismissal of a teacher whose ability is so widely recognized, who has brought such favorable notice to the university's archaeological museum, and who is so well-liked by both students and members of the faculty would be entirely inconsistent with any unbiased management policy, and such dismissal could be based only on reasons that should not be matters of University concern." One hundred forty-four students signed the petition, Grant and Libby Cannon (Jane's brother and half-sister) among them. The board of regents read the petition at its April meeting during discussion of the university's budget. Thomas informed the board members that Steward had filed a letter of resignation, and the board voted to accept it.[81]

It appears that Steward had no part in the petition and that he held out no hope for reinstatement at the university. Weeks passed before he learned about the board's decision, but in the meantime he wrote again to Kroeber. He could see only two possibilities for the near future: fieldwork, if he could secure any funding for "a little work among the Shoshonean tribes of Nevada"; or, if he could borrow money, a year of self-financed postdoctoral study either in Europe or at Harvard or Berkeley (as important for the contacts it would provide as for a learning opportunity). "The last recourse," he wrote, "would be a commercial job, but I should hate to have to take one for I have the feeling that it would not only be a year wasted, but would make it a little more difficult to get back into anthropology."[82]

Kroeber agreed, knowing well that in a profession with an acute shortage of positions and a surplus of qualified applicants, entering the business world usually meant leaving academic anthropology for good. He encouraged Steward to borrow money rather than give up his research and writing, but he added that Max Rosenberg, Steward's former benefactor, had died two years earlier. His advice about how Steward should present himself as he searched for employment or research support was shrewd. He suggested offering "a frank admission that you are out of a job because your department has been abolished at Utah. No one will in the least hold this against you in these times." "The sum and substance of my suggestions," he concluded, "seems to be to seize anything you can get and then hang on to it like a bull dog until something better comes along."[83]

As his time at the University of Utah drew to a close, however, Steward wrote a rather impassioned plea to the president to continue the anthropology program. The president replied with a certain asperity that such decisions lay with the administration and the board of regents, commenting, "Some things have to be sacrificed." (The University of Utah reinstated anthropology later in the 1930s, but as a joint department with sociology.)[84]

At the end of June, Steward again wrote to Thomas from Los Angeles, where Jane Cannon was then living with relatives. In this final letter, he asked who would be in charge of the Museum of Anthropology, explaining that he wanted to send instructions about how to care for some specimens that appeared in danger of deteriorating. That marked the end of any formal relationship with the University of Utah, although he would visit Salt Lake City and the Cannon family repeatedly in the future and would consult with former colleagues at the university about his Great Basin research.[85]

Dorothy Nyswander returned to Utah from New York City in fall 1933, but after a year or so of teaching, she took an extended leave of absence from the university. She served as a state director of some WPA projects in Utah and then moved to San Francisco, where she held a position as a regional director for eleven states in the West. The Work Projects Administration, or WPA, created by executive order, had quickly become one of the most important agencies of Roosevelt's New Deal. Reporting informally to Eleanor Roosevelt, on one memorable occasion she also met the president. The demands of work consumed all of her thought and energy, leaving no time for regret or recrimination: "I had too much responsibility," she explained, "and I just didn't have time for personal things if they weren't going well."[86]

In 1936 Dorothy resigned from the University of Utah and the WPA to accept a long-term research position in New York City. During an exhausting year as a regional director, she had spent almost every day working and many nights traveling, usually between states in the West, but periodically to Washington, D.C. She was near physical collapse when she and her daughter, Marie, left San Francisco for New York City, traveling by ship so that she could rest. The journey took them along the rugged Pacific coastline, through the Panama Canal, and then across calm Caribbean waters to the Atlantic. Dorothy saw almost none of it, rarely venturing outside the cabin she shared with Marie. She remained in bed recuperating for most of the trip.[87]

* * *

When Steward left the University of Utah in 1933, he left behind the most direct results of his work in archaeology. That material remained in the museum's collections. But he did take with him the notes and diagrams and photographs he needed in order to write a series of reports, most of which appeared in print during the 1930s. Along with his research at the Columbia River sites in northern Oregon, his Utah work gave him some credentials as an archaeologist. Nonetheless, he would never again carry out archaeological fieldwork—despite seeking close, if informal, collaborative relationships with a number of archaeologists in the 1940s, and despite writing a series of theoretical articles that influenced the direction of American archaeology.[88]

A complicated mixture of personal motives and professional incentives led Steward to pursue archaeology actively during the Utah years but not in the years that followed—to the puzzlement of many of his later students and colleagues. Institutional priorities, unusually generous funding, and the museum's extensive collection of archaeological material encouraged him to focus on archaeology. And archaeology did not so obviously present the methodological problems that his colleague-wife pointed out about retrospective ethnographic research based on the informant method. It had the virtue of providing visible and tangible evidence about the past in the form of material remains, although the evidence was by nature limited and fragmentary, and past behavior could only be inferred from it. The dilemma for an aspiring behaviorist anthropologist thus remained: he could not directly observe what he wished to study. Nevertheless, working intensively in archaeology during this period reinforced Steward's materialist leanings, his knowledge of arid environments, and his interest in the process of cultural change. All of these would have a prominent place in his theoretical work.

Once he left Utah and his first marriage, the professional incentives for pursuing archaeology vanished, along with all of the personal ones. His work as an archaeologist had offered Steward full autonomy because his wife had neither knowledge of nor interest in the subject. Despite accompanying him to several sites in Utah, she later insisted, repeatedly and with an unmistakable air of boredom, that she knew "*nothing*" about archaeology, including her former husband's own work during the early 1930s.[89] Steward's archaeological research had also provided another benefit: it affirmed his separate professional identity, which had been undermined by joining his wife's institution—or so he had concluded soon after arriving at the University of Utah.

His seven-year relationship with Dorothy Nyswander, which began in Berkeley and unraveled in Salt Lake City, just as surely reinforced his objectivist bent and his commitment to scientific method as the foundation for theory. Any doubts that he had about how to address questions of cultural causality—questions that Kroeber had simply dismissed—dissolved in her presence. Her confidence, her energy, and her counsel all had a buoying effect during his graduate years and at the beginning of his career. She believed in scientific social science, behaviorism, and the rigor of experimental method and standardized testing. "Science was my religion," she said with a faint smile as she recalled her sense of mission during that period in her life.[90]

It turned out, however, that Steward was not her first convert, as she may have thought. He was a fellow believer from the start, plagued by self-doubt but intent on finding his way to a scientific anthropology. Like her, he crossed disciplinary boundaries, but silently, becoming an undeclared behaviorist in search of a method to study the causes of cultural change. As he well knew, behaviorist psychologists studied change at the individual level, making repeated observations of behavior and manipulating variables in controlled laboratory environments over a period of days or weeks. He wanted to study behavioral change at the cultural level, change that occurred over the course of centuries or millennia. Since he could not cause or directly observe changes in behavior, as was possible in a laboratory, he would have to infer them from what he observed of the material world, both human-made and natural. His experience as a student of geology and geography prepared him to observe the natural environment and to think about change over long periods of time.

Each of Steward's next projects, his 1934 field observations in the Southwest and his research on patrilineal bands, was to constitute this sort of naturalistic "experiment." It appears that he made no conscious connection between that approach and what he had learned about behaviorism and its possible application to anthropology from his first wife. In 1933, as in later years, he privately denied that he had gained anything of value from their relationship, regarding it as a complete detriment to his career and the scandal surrounding their di-

vorce as yet another injury inflicted by organized religion: in this case Mormonism rather than Christian Science.

Their collaborative research with Ute Indians left few traces. Given Nyswander's near erasure from official documents at the outset of the project, only
a few letters and her personal memories would attest that she took part in it.
Her final status, in terms of that unfinished project and the interrupted marriage, was not silent partner but rather silenced partner. Evidence of their marriage disappeared from Steward's own professional records, and he almost never
made mention of it.[91]

CHAPTER 7

SOUTHWESTERN SIGHTS

In mid-October 1933, Julian Steward married Jane Cannon in a civil ceremony in Mexico. They could not legally marry in the United States because Julian's first wife, Dorothy Nyswander, still refused to proceed with a divorce. Julian had finally obtained one in Mexico although "Mexican divorces," Jane remembered, "were under some shadow at the time." After their wedding they returned to California, still awaiting news about Julian's employment.[1]

Julian had remained in Los Angeles during summer 1933 and continued looking for work, unsuccessfully. Jane, who was living there with an aunt and uncle, had a secretarial job and earned a small but steady income. In July, at Kroeber's urging, Julian had gone to Sacramento to take a scheduled civil service examination. Months passed with no word about the results and no offer of employment.[2]

After Jane and Julian returned from Mexico, they moved to Berkeley to begin married life. Next to Deep Springs, Berkeley was the place he most considered home and the place where he had personal contacts—not only with Kroeber and Lowie but also with their former students—that might help him find another position in anthropology. There was no further news about the civil service position, but Julian continued to search for work and apply for grants and fellowships.[3]

Soon after arriving in Berkeley, Julian Steward wrote to an acquaintance at Telluride Association about his "scheme" to convince Albert Mussey Johnson, a wealthy insurance executive from Chicago, to finance an ethnographic study of the Shoshone Indians in Death Valley. Steward knew him slightly; Johnson, who had visited his friend Nunn at Deep Springs, had investments in Death Valley. In the mid-1920s, he and Walter Edward Scott, known as "Death Valley

Scotty," collaborated on a venture to build a Moorish mansion in the desert, later a famous structure known as "Scotty's Castle." Although the funds supposedly came from a secret mine that Scott owned, Johnson in fact provided two million dollars for the project. Construction stopped in 1931 as the depression worsened.[4]

Steward evidently knew nothing about Johnson's financial reverses, and, in any case, he estimated that it would cost only five hundred dollars to support several months of research. "In view of his long interest in Death Valley," he wrote, "[Johnson] should consider it no less than a favor to endow science in this manner." He continued in that ironic vein: "I am aware, of course, of his religious convictions, but it should not be difficult to show, if he wishes, that the Indians are really Baptists who have given up baptizing simply because they could not find water in that parched land."

Steward added that he had "just married a perfectly swell girl," and felt "so happy that the closed purses of universities don't seem very important." His new marriage had lifted his spirits; despite having no immediate prospects for employment, he said that he remained optimistic. In the same buoyant tone, he explained that he and Jane planned to go to Deep Springs in a few months, where he would teach in exchange for room and board: "[I] look forward with such pleasure to going to Deep Springs that I'm really glad there is nothing to prevent it. Unless, therefore, someone hands us a million dollars, we shall go in February. In fact, we shall probably go anyhow."[5]

Besides this creative avenue, Steward explored more conventional sources of funding for fieldwork. Although the Social Science Research Council had turned down his application for a fellowship the year before, he applied to the council in early January for a grant-in-aid to study Shoshone ecology. Both Lowie and Kroeber wrote in support of his project. Kroeber recommended him as having "imagination and originality" and "a sense of problem which is quite unusual." He continued: "The problem Dr. Steward is proposing I regard as important and promising—perhaps because I originally outlined it." (Kroeber said as much to Steward a few years later; it became a point of generally unspoken rivalry between the two men.) Most of his students, Kroeber explained, showed little interest in ecological data, preferring to deal with conventional topics. He gave Steward credit for discovering this particular approach while doing research with the Paiute. The present project was part of a larger one, an attempt to learn "what, if any, constant relations exist between ecology and culture." The plan would require a lifetime, Kroeber conceded, as Steward well knew. Still, he recommended the project as having merit in itself, besides being "part of a larger vision."[6]

This larger vision had begun to crystallize by the time Julian and Jane returned to Berkeley and while he was still unemployed. Having time for reflection, and greater intellectual autonomy, allowed him to think more deeply about his own ideas and how to pursue them in an orderly, scientific way. He developed a coherent plan for research, often referring to it as his "long-range plan" or "twenty-year plan." In Julian Steward's own words, it entailed "studying first the simplest societies I could find and working gradually into understandings of more complex societies in the hope that the latter would help illuminate contemporary affairs and trends."[7]

The stated goal, to "illuminate contemporary affairs," clearly derived from his education at Deep Springs, reflecting Nunn's emphasis on humanitarian service. The idea of proceeding from simple to complex appears to have been inspired by what Steward had learned as a student about the linguistic affiliation of Paiute Indians. As early as 1928, he remarked in print that the Paiute speak a Uto-Aztecan language; the linguistic stock, as the name indicates, also includes the language of the Aztecs, who developed a civilization. The striking differences in social complexity between hunter-gatherers of the Great Basin and their linguistic cousins, the imperialistic Aztec, seized Steward's attention at an early point.[8]

Gordon Willey, who worked with Steward at the Smithsonian during the 1940s, once heard him tell a colleague, "'You've got to plan your life. You can't just go along drifting into one kind of research, one kind of teaching, one kind of writing. It has to be a coherent whole.'" The colleague, who embraced the unexpected in life, rejected Steward's advice out of hand; and at the time, Willey himself wondered how closely Steward's counsel fit his own experience. In hindsight, however, some forty years later, he found a striking coherence and consistency in the body of Steward's research, perhaps indicating that there had indeed been a plan.[9]

Jane Steward, in fact, mentioned this plan in recalling the early years of her married life. She remembered her husband making "pronouncements," as she called them, about his twenty-year plan during the year they lived in Berkeley, in 1934. He also told her that the inspiration for his ecological approach had come from a chance meeting on Mount Tamalpais with a botanist who was doing a field study of plant ecology. After a brief exchange with the botanist, whom he did not know and never saw again, Steward continued on his way.[10]

During his years as a graduate student, he often walked on Mount Tamalpais, where for a brief time he felt freed from the press of city life and renewed by the sight of open landscape. From its summit, he could see a vast sweep of blue Pacific waters, the nearby Marin Hills, the Berkeley Hills rising up behind the San Francisco Bay, and far beyond, the shining white rim of the Sierra Nevada. It offered a view of nature writ large, and culture small—with human settlements, even San Francisco, dwarfed by the surrounding expanse of land and water and simplified by distance. Seen from Mount Tamalpais and the many other mountains that he climbed during his student days at Deep Springs and later, nature visibly intersected with culture in its material dimension. A mountain offered a fitting place, that is, for his particular epiphany.[11]

By Steward's own account, his brief conversation with the botanist soon led him to think about studying "human ecology," or what he finally termed "cultural ecology." He never mentioned the influence of his friend Strong, who had a deep interest in animal ecology during his student days and later in life and had just carried out fieldwork with descendants of hunter-gatherers when the two men met. Open-ended and ongoing conversations with Strong—about animal ecology, hunting, and other topics—were at least as likely a source of inspiration for Steward's cultural ecology as a fleeting exchange with a stranger about plant ecology.[12]

* * *

When Jane Steward recalled their year in Berkeley, she spoke of the difficulties, especially the financial uncertainty and the uncomfortable sense that their lives remained "in a state of flux," even though they were finally married. As she readily admitted, she had expected marriage to a university professor to offer a certain stability and security, not the rootlessness she felt during that first year and later. She still identified her new husband primarily as an academic and had only begun to meet other anthropologists, fellow members of his wandering tribe. In the spring, they rented a furnished apartment on Channing Street, and during the summer they lived in a "borrowed" house—the Kroebers'—on Arch Street in north Berkeley. Alluding to this state of transience, she told her sister Libby, "we consider twice before buying a light bulb, wondering if it will pack."[13]

Julian's plan of subsisting at Deep Springs probably held little appeal for her except as a last, desperate resort in hard times. City born and bred, Jane liked the sidewalks and streetcars of Berkeley. When temporary work materialized for her husband, he seized it, although it paid far less than the sum he had vowed it would take to keep him away from the ranch and the valley. Along with fellow anthropologist Paul Radin, who was in his fifties and also unemployed, Julian Steward found a job with the National Park Service, under the auspices of the Civil Works Administration. The Roosevelt administration launched the CWA, a temporary work-relief program, in the winter of 1933–34. In January 1934, while Steward was employed, the program reached a peak of four million workers. The government ended it abruptly three months later, throwing Steward out of work again; Radin, who often earned money by tutoring students in German, had already quit months before.[14]

Steward and, briefly, Radin worked in the area of museum research within the Field Education Division. They had been hired to plan museum exhibits for the National Park Service, and they probably reported to Ansel Hall, an administrator and educator who promoted national park museums and interpretive programs. Hall's National Park Service office was located on the Berkeley campus. Like Steward, he was an alumnus, and the two men also shared an interest in mountain climbing; both had climbed extensively in the Sierra Nevada and claimed a first ascent in the early 1920s. During these early months in 1934, Julian wrote up material on Blackfoot and California Indians. In the meantime, with Radin's help, Jane had found a secretarial position in the office of a neu-rosurgeon.[15]

By late April, when the government phased out the Civil Works Administra-tion and his job, Julian had accepted a temporary teaching position for the fall. He would replace Kroeber, who was to be on leave. Certain of having a roof over their heads that summer because of the Kroebers' generosity, and guaranteed a full salary in the fall, he and Jane decided to use their personal savings for a five-week tour through the Southwest. Julian planned to make field observations at a variety of archaeological sites and pueblos, primarily in northern Arizona and New Mexico, but also in southern Colorado and Utah. The trip would take him back to the Colorado Plateau, a vast and arid region of canyons and mesas, sur-rounded by mountains. He had first seen it briefly in 1923, when he traveled to the Grand Canyon after attending a Telluride convention in Utah; again in 1928, when he stayed at First Mesa in Arizona; and repeatedly in the early 1930s, when he excavated a site in southeastern Utah, visited other archaeological sites in the southern borderlands of Utah and Colorado, and made his trip down the Colo-rado River.

His 1934 field observations and conversations with archaeologists would con-stitute silent evidence in his essay "Ecological Aspects of Southwestern Society," written a few months after returning to Berkeley. What he had seen and heard would guide his thinking, but he made no reference to it in print—thus per-plexing later generations of readers, especially archaeologists, who wondered how a reading knowledge of southwestern archaeology and his brief experience in Utah, had resulted in such a complex, powerful line of argument. His obser-vations would also help prepare him to teach a course on the Southwest in the fall. The course, covering both archaeology and ethnology, centered on Pueblo cultures from the prehistoric period to the recent historic past.

The trip had a very practical side as well, extending the search for employ-ment. The National Park Service, his most recent employer, administered many of the archaeological sites, and a number of the private museums and founda-tions in the Southwest that Julian planned to visit likewise hired anthropolo-gists as staff members. Touring the sites—beginning with several in Arizona and ending at Mesa Verde in Colorado—would also provide a chance for personal contact with many prominent archaeologists, ranging from Byron Cummings to Alfred Kidder.

In a journal that they had just begun to keep, Julian recorded the following noteworthy event on May 1, 1934: "Jane quit work and is now a housewife for the first time in her life." Jane had charge of cooking by then, having learned the basics of campfire cooking, adapted to a kitchen, from her husband. Her new status as housewife did not mean keeping house, as she might have wished, but putting their few household effects in storage and accompanying her husband on a long, meandering trip of several thousand miles, part of it through the Sonoran Desert of Arizona, already simmering in late spring. After saying goodbye to Ralph and Dorothy Beals and other friends, Julian and Jane set off for the Southwest in early May.[16]

In Tucson, their first stop, they met Cummings and toured several nearby sites before moving on a few days later to Casa Grande and Montezuma Castle. Steward would see many such ancient pueblos during his travels. Unlike many archaeologists of the time, however, his primary interest lay in why and how the pueblos had developed, not why they had been abandoned and fallen into ruins. He viewed these prehistoric sites, which had had irrigation systems and sometimes populations in the thousands, as both precursors to cities and successors of simpler forms of social life. Archaeological evidence showed that before pueblos developed, people had lived in small settlements with their fields nearby. During the earliest period, they had subsisted as nomadic hunter-gatherers. His interest in southwestern prehistory thus represented another step in his long-range research plan, which called for "working gradually into understandings of more complex societies."[17]

On a hot and cloudless Sunday, Jane and Julian left Montezuma Castle for Flagstaff, Arizona, set at the foot of the towering San Francisco Peaks. At an altitude of nearly seven thousand feet, Flagstaff offered a sudden respite from the intense heat of the desert. Their first order of business on Monday morning was a visit to the Museum of Northern Arizona, which had recently been founded but already housed extensive collections of artifacts and Indian art. After arranging to meet the director, Harold Colton, on another day, they left for a guided tour of the environs, escorted by an archaeologist on the museum staff, Lyndon L. Hargrave.[18]

Their main destination lay about thirty miles north of Flagstaff, at Wupatki National Monument, a sprawling group of red sandstone ruins that date mainly from the twelfth to the early thirteenth centuries. The many pueblos at Wupatki differ from most others in the region in that they are freestanding, not built into cliffs or caves. With the San Francisco Peaks as a striking backdrop, the site offered some well-preserved ruins. In the company of the archaeologist who knew Wupatki best—Hargrave's excavations there ended that very month, in May 1934—Jane and Julian toured several pueblos.[19]

Hargrave and Steward shared many interests, as they must have immediately discovered. Hargrave had worked as a hydrographer in Arizona before finding his way into archaeology with the encouragement of Cummings. He had extensive experience in southwestern archaeology and had recently directed survey crews that located and mapped hundreds of prehistoric sites. Using ceramics as well as plant and animal remains, Hargrave managed to arrive at precise dates for some sites, allowing him to reconstruct the histories of specific cliff houses. He called his approach "human ecology." Its aim was to provide understanding of "the environmental factors which contributed to the shaping of the early cultures in the region."[20]

Jane Steward's cryptic journal entries said nothing about her husband's conversations with Hargrave or any of the other archaeologists they met on their journey; she did not follow their discussions closely, simply recording names and her impressions of the places they visited. Months later, however, Steward used the term *human ecology* in a grant proposal, writing that "Shoshonean tribes could be only very incompletely understood if one failed to recognize that the stark facts of human ecology in a most difficult environment are stamped upon them, that subsistence problems are the most important facts of their lives." Like Hargrave, he conceived of culture as an adaptation to environment, and he would soon use the term *human ecology* in print: in the opening and concluding pages of his well-known monograph on the Great Basin. (Hargrave, who left his position at the Museum of Northern Arizona five years later to pursue his interests in ecology, could find no support, and spent the next sixteen years working in business. For a complex set of reasons, including his marginal position in the profession, he did not receive wide recognition for his concept of human ecology nor the opportunity to develop it more fully.)[21]

Julian and Jane visited other museums on their journey, many of them at sites administered by the National Park Service. "More Park museums need attention," Jane remarked with detectable irony, having already seen a surfeit of exhibits on southwestern geology and prehistory. Her husband's insistence on touring all of the museums and, if possible, meeting the directors, had as much to do with his search for employment as with his research project. Before leaving the University of Utah, he had contacted Matthew Stirling at the Bureau of American Ethnology, expressing his interest in working at a research institution. "Although I know that you will answer me that the Bureau is now broke, you may nevertheless consider this an application for any opening from pot-washer up or down," he wrote. "Seriously, I am extremely anxious to get something for next year." He may have thought that he had far greater prospects of finding employment in a museum than a university. He had experience in collecting for museums, and much more interest in research than in university teaching.[22]

Before leaving Arizona, Jane and Julian visited the ruins at Canyon de Chelly, another national monument, and met "more Park people," as Jane put it. They crossed the border of New Mexico and continued on their journey, driving toward Santa Fe. Along the way they stopped at several pueblos, including Zuni and Santo Domingo. Like the ancient ruins with the status of national monuments, these still-inhabited pueblos were as well known to tourists as to anthropologists by the 1930s. Jane bought a pair of silver earrings in Zuni as a souvenir.[23]

In Santa Fe, their first order of business was to visit the Laboratory of Anthropology, which occupied a rambling adobe structure that housed offices and exhibit rooms. They learned that Jesse Nusbaum, the director, happened to be in conference with Alfred Kidder, who had spent many field seasons excavating a nearby site, Pecos. A few days later, having toured Taos Pueblo and Bandelier National Monument in the interim, Jane and Julian spent time at Pecos at

Kidder's invitation. He showed them around the ruins of what had been one of the largest pueblos in the Southwest.[24]

Julian and Jane left Santa Fe the next morning and began a hard day's drive west toward Chaco Canyon, in the northwestern corner of New Mexico, crossing the Continental Divide along the way. After traveling over miles of rough dirt track, they finally arrived at some of the most remote and dramatic ruins in the Southwest. It was yet another site administered by the National Park Service. So too was the next stop on their journey, Aztec Ruin, where they met Earl Morris, a specialist in southwestern archaeology. He had excavated the Great Kiva at Aztec Ruin.[25]

Continuing on their travels, they soon reached Mesa Verde, a short drive across the Colorado border from Aztec Ruins. One of the oldest national parks, dating from 1906, it was established to protect the many prehistoric cliff dwellings that lie within its boundaries. Julian and Jane arrived in time to see the museum and one of the most famous ruins, Spruce Tree House. The next morning they toured the accessible ruins, including Balcony House, before leaving at noon for Utah. Their visit to Mesa Verde, like the other southwestern sites, was brief. Julian had seen it a few years earlier, then in the company of his first wife.[26]

Heading toward Moab, in the southeastern corner of Utah, they drove through a landscape of contrasts, with "green farm lands and sheer red walls like Canyon de Chelly," Jane wrote. Technology, together with a natural resource (water) and human labor—the staples of Julian Steward's later cultural ecology—had created these contrasts. By building an extensive system of irrigation, which required cooperation and hard work, Mormon settlers had transformed large portions of the arid land they claimed and first called "Deseret." Taken from the Book of Mormon, the name referred not to the desert, as non-Mormons might suppose, but rather to honeybees, admired for their industry and cooperation.

What Steward saw in Mormon Utah, not only that day as they drove toward Moab but also repeatedly during the years he lived there, reinforced what he had first experienced at Deep Springs when he worked with the other students to maintain the irrigation system. Mormons, like Pueblo peoples, had not just survived, but prospered in the desert by controlling water and promoting cooperation. Even the drylands of southeastern Utah, with ancient red arches and spires and canyons carved by the natural elements, had bursts of startling green, products of human labor and design.[27]

By that day in June 1934, however, Utah's green fields had already begun to disappear in the face of relentless drought, which was curtailing irrigation, killing crops and livestock throughout the state, and compounding the hardships of the depression. The drought, which affected much of the nation, ravaged the Great Plains states lying directly to the east. Repeated storms, between November 1933 and May 1934, lifted hundreds of millions of tons of soil from the plains, leaving a devastated area that came to be known as the dust bowl. Julian and Jane were soon to see some of the many refugees who began to stream westward toward California, seeking food and work.[28] Centuries earlier, Pueblo Indians throughout the Southwest had also abandoned their homes, perhaps in response to devastating drought or other environmental change.

What Julian Steward saw during his 1934 travels—not only the archaeological sites but other southwestern sights as well—remained in mind as he tried to reconstruct the social and physical landscape of the distant past. His field observations, in other words, extended and amplified the always fragmentary evidence of archaeology. The conversations he had with dozens of colleagues during his journey clearly contributed as well, as much as or more than reading their publications. Given his particular angle of vision, Steward always found that talking to other archaeologists and cultural anthropologists about their field research proved even more useful than reading what they wrote. His field observations, however fleeting, raised questions in his mind that published research did not necessarily answer, questions that he pursued in conversations with colleagues. Those informal discussions also allowed him to learn more about the published data, and to test and refine his ideas repeatedly.

It was a collaborative, social approach to intellectual work—but not visibly so because of the informal and fleeting nature of so much of the contact. Following the standard practice of the time, in his own publications he cited only published works, regarded as the only authoritative sources. This practice had the effect of obscuring any contributions that others made to his theoretical work beyond simply providing data. It enhanced his image as a highly original thinker, but it also led one of his students, who collaborated with him in research, to conclude years later that Steward was "strictly oral and auditory," and did not read.[29]

It is more nearly accurate to say that he always made a habit of questioning colleagues closely and informally about their field research; that he profited from face-to-face intellectual exchange, but not from the win-lose battle of wits so common in academic life, including the professional meetings he disliked and came to avoid; and that he did not read widely outside of anthropology.

* * *

After spending one night in Moab, Jane and Julian canceled plans to visit some archaeological sites in the area and continued directly on to Salt Lake City to see her family. On arrival they found divorce papers; Dorothy had finally proceeded with a Utah divorce. To their consternation, they also learned that Jane's parents had planned a large reception in their honor: "Julian has the jitters," Jane wrote, "but no way out." The next few days included a busy round of social visits with old friends, culminating in the dreaded reception on a Friday evening. They "weathered" it, according to Jane, without benefit of cigarettes or strong drink (proscribed by her parents and their guests, all practicing Mormons). Afterward, she and Julian had a late-night drink with her younger brother and sister, Grant and Libby, and Libby's new husband. As she noted with humor and relief, "it was the only way to forget shaking hands with 200 people."[30]

Less than a week later Julian and Jane left Salt Lake City and returned to California, making the long trip across the Great Basin desert in just two days, despite delays caused by an overheated radiator on the first day and a flat tire in Reno, Nevada, on the second. Back in Berkeley, they moved into the Kroebers' spacious redwood house. Their new living quarters seemed lavish compared to the cramped apartment on Channing Street, to say nothing of the campsites, rented cabins, and improvised lodgings of their recent trip.[31]

In just days after their return, as they were still settling in, they learned that Marion Steward was "near breakdown" because she had lost her job. Several months earlier, Marion and her mother had moved across the San Francisco Bay to Marin County, an open landscape of rolling hills, pastures, and fields of wildflowers. Grace and Marion had lived briefly in San Rafael in the early 1920s. In the early 1930s, they bought a small cottage on Lovell Avenue in Mill Valley, a village not far from Mount Tamalpais and John Muir Woods.

At the time Julian had pointed out to Marion the "difficulties" of that decision, given the temporary and insecure nature of her work at Remington Rand. She would have to make a regular mortgage payment of twenty dollars a month, besides paying to commute by ferry five days a week to San Francisco. Marion also provided most of her mother's support in the period after her brother remarried. Resenting this unsolicited if sensible advice, she "took my head off," Julian wrote. Three or four months later, his worst prediction had come true, and Marion was completely out of work. But by the time he and Jane visited her and Grace in Mill Valley, Marion's spirits had improved although her job prospects remained slight. "No solution to M.'s problem," Jane wrote, adding, however, that "all seemed cheerful enough."[32]

Julian spent the next week finishing a paper for the annual meeting of the American Association for the Advancement of Science, held in June 1934 in San Francisco. When he presented it, the paper "received more comment & discussion than any other," in Jane's admiring view. "Day of days!" she exclaimed at the start of her journal entry, which chronicled the paper's success. Her words of praise gave no sign of the numbing boredom that Dorothy Nyswander recalled from the meeting in Los Angeles, where her husband read a paper on his Utah research.[33]

Titled "Ecological Aspects of the Patrilocate," Steward's 1934 paper appeared in print, revised and retitled, in 1936. "The Economic and Social Basis of Primitive Bands" was one of many essays that former students and colleagues contributed to a volume edited by Lowie and published in honor of Kroeber on his sixtieth birthday. Years later, Steward referred to it as his "first major theoretical work," and included a revised version, divided into two parts and renamed

"The Patrilineal Band" and "The Composite Hunting Band," in *Theory of Culture Change*. "The Patrilineal Band" became one of his best-known essays, stimulating and influencing work on hunter-gatherers by a later generation of anthropologists.[34] In it, he took the inductive approach that became his trademark as a theorist and that drew silently on his own field observations in desert environments. The patrilineal band was to constitute *the* foundational concept of Steward's cultural ecology. Its importance to his thinking and his subsequent work has not generally been understood—and cannot be overestimated.[35]

To judge from citations, Steward drew primarily on published secondary sources; he mentioned his own fieldwork with Owens Valley Paiute largely in passing. Strong's work on the "patrilineal clans" of southern California Indians, all hunter-gatherers, may well have been the most influential source. When the two men first met in 1925, Strong had just carried out field research with Cahuilla, Diegueño, and other desert-dwelling Indians; that fieldwork led first to an article and then to a lengthy monograph that appeared in print in the late 1920s. Gifford and Kroeber had also written, more briefly, about these groups, whose ancestral territories included land occupied in the twentieth century by residents of Riverside and San Diego Counties.[36]

Steward identified three types of bands in the opening paragraphs of his paper: patrilineal, composite, and matrilineal. Although he admitted the logical possibility of matrilineal bands, he said almost nothing about them, concentrating on patrilineal and composite bands instead. His interest clearly centered on the patrilineal band, defined by these characteristics: "land ownership, political autonomy, patrilocal residence, band or local exogamy, and patrilineal inheritance." His examples included Australian Aborigines, central African Pygmies, the Ona Indians of Tierra del Fuego, the Tehuelche of Patagonia, and some California Indians, among others.[37]

In a footnote, he pointed out that the "extraordinary frequency" of patrilineal bands had been noted by Wilhelm Koppers and other adherents of the German "culture historical school." They thought the patrilineal band had originated during the earliest stage of human life and then diffused widely. Steward suggested a different way of explaining its frequency: "I shall show that the patrilineal band is most common because it is produced by recurring ecological and social factors which may be formulated into something akin to cultural law." This was his first attempt in print to frame such a law.[38]

In Steward's view, the patrilineal band developed among hunter-gatherers in arid regions and other unproductive environments. Living by hunting and gathering in such environments resulted in low population density and small groups, averaging about fifty or sixty people. In such circumstances, Steward argued, men, as hunters, found advantage in remaining in their familiar home territory. This favored the development of male-centered bands, with patrilocal residence and patrilineal descent. He suggested as well that "innate male dominance"—which he treated as a fixed, psychobiological trait—helped explain the prevalence of patrilocal residence. Men's "greater economic importance" as hunters also contributed. "Patrilineal bands easily develop among hunters and gatherers," he wrote. "Matilineal bands may arise if women are economically of sufficient importance," he added, but did not provide examples.[39]

On the basis of his own fieldwork, Steward decided that the Owens Valley Paiute had formed larger, composite bands; to judge from published ethnographic evidence, he thought that Northern Algonquian and Athabaskan Indians of Canada had also lived in such groups, which, like patrilineal bands, were politically autonomous and landowning. Tellingly, however, he defined the composite band largely in negative terms, specifying what it lacked compared to the patrilineal band: "The composite band . . . does not have band exogamy, patrilocal residence, or land inheritance by patrilineal relatives." Certain "special factors" (such as demographic vagaries), which "have prevented consistent patrilocal residence, . . . will prevent the [composite] band from consisting of patrilineal relatives."[40]

His language throughout the essay suggests that Steward thought of the patrilineal band as the norm for hunter-gatherers. Other forms were, by implication, deviations. In his words, they "prevented" the patrilineal band or actually "destroyed" it by interfering with the practice of patrilocal residence. At least implicitly, he took part in a long tradition in anthropology: the effort to create a theory about the original form of human society. To Steward, the patrilineal band seemed to represent the most likely form for a hunting-based society to take.[41]

His own field research in Owens Valley, and his perplexity about Northern Paiute social organization, which did not resemble what Strong and others had found in southern California, may have first led Steward to read widely about other hunter-gatherers. What he found was disappointingly limited, as he admitted in the essay and elsewhere. In nearly every case, he had to qualify his statements: "Fragments of information now available indicate that the band is patrilineal." "There is some indication . . ." "The more or less inadequate information now available indicates . . ."

This did not prevent Steward from taking a creative leap and attempting to discover the cause of the patrilineal band. "Underlying this paper," he wrote, "is the assumption that every cultural phenomenon is the product of some definite cause or causes." (Ethnographic research carried out decades later, spurred in part by the later, revised version of this essay, provided the detailed information that Steward lacked on residence practices, kinship, and dietary patterns of hunter-gatherers. Those data did not support certain aspects of his argument, especially the gendered, social aspects such as the prevalence of patrilineality and patrilocality, with males acting as the primary providers of food.)[42]

Some of Steward's own life circumstances in 1934, including a heightened sense of identity as a man, seem to have informed aspects of the argument in this paper. In his second marriage, unlike his first, he thought of himself as the primary provider, in line with both prevailing social expectations of the time and his model of the hunter. In his second marriage, unlike his first, his wife followed him, conforming to social expectations; she gave up her own work to go with him when he returned "home" to Berkeley and, again, to travel with him in the Southwest, giving precedence to his work. Like a hunter's, his work had "greater economic importance," to borrow his words and convey his view. Perhaps this change in his social situation also gave new personal meaning to the notion of innate male dominance. He made explicit assertions about it in print twice in the 1930s, in articles written soon after divorcing his first wife—and senior colleague—and remarrying.[43]

It could be said that Steward had practiced a form of matrilocal residence when he married Nyswander and joined her household in Salt Lake City. As he later saw it, moving there had cost him his job and threatened his career. "This matrimony was rather expensive, wasn't it?" he remarked with more than a tinge of bitterness to Strong after resigning from the University of Utah while facing unemployment. When he married Jane Cannon and returned to Berkeley, Steward practiced a version of patrilocal residence in the sense that his "professional lineage," comprised largely of men, was established there. That his mother and sister lived in the area did not enter into his decision. Back in his home territory, Steward hoped to enlist help from his Berkeley colleagues as he searched for a particular type of scarce, valued resource: a secure position in anthropology.[44]

Throughout the AAAS meetings in San Francisco, he and Jane saw quite a few of his friends and colleagues, who had quickly become Jane's friends as well. Many members of the "North Berkeley gang" of Julian's student days still lived in Berkeley or visited there when conferences or other travel permitted. Ever sociable, Jane oversaw a busy calendar that summer. ("Lunch with the gang." "Dinner at Beals . . . Leslie Spier there too." "Radins for dinner." "Ralph [Beals] has a job with the Park Service so we celebrated at dinner with them.") A friend who knew them some years later recalled that "happy, down-to-earth Jane was the perfect counterpoise to the intense and temperamental Julian."[45]

* * *

At the end of June, a few days after the AAAS meetings ended, Julian began teaching two summer school courses: an introductory course with nearly fifty students and a course on American Indians that had a smaller enrollment. A week later, Jane was offered a secretarial position with the Strike Mediation Board, but she declined it, apparently in favor of another temporary position. Paul Radin, always resourceful, had helped her find secretarial work with an economist in charge of a large research project. In the meantime, a strike by longshoremen that had entered its seventh week was "assuming alarming proportions," she wrote, having "paralyzed shipping north of L.A." The longshoremen had struck all ports on the West Coast in May, closing down shipping along nearly two thousand miles of shoreline.

The rhythm of their own lives in Berkeley remained steady, untouched by labor unrest across the Bay. Both Julian and Jane had only temporary work, but with two incomes they managed to pay for their living expenses and keep up an active social life. On July 4, after having dinner with friends, Jane wrote, "Time filled with school and social things. Everything serene."[46]

But the next day, July 5, violence erupted on the waterfront in San Francisco. Business owners blamed the strike on Communist agitators, and many wanted to break it by using any means necessary, including force. The entire police force of San Francisco assembled on the waterfront, where thousands of longshoremen and other workers had gathered. Two workers were shot to death and scores of others were injured that day. The strikers, armed only with rocks and bolts, retreated in the face of bullets and tear gas, but the violence had only strengthened their resolve. The longshoremen's strike committee soon called for a general strike.[47]

A few days after this confrontation, when Jane and Julian went to San Francisco to view an exhibition of paintings, they saw "the militia holding down [the] waterfront." A week later, Jane wrote that the teamsters were on strike and that people had begun buying extra provisions, including candles in case the "utilities [workers] go out in sympathy." The following day she found the food supplies very limited in grocery stores: "Milk & bread still to be had but gasoline, canned milk, fruit, etc. very low." More than sixty unions were threatening to strike, but the mayor of San Francisco had promised to safeguard supplies of necessities ("food & gas & light & milk").[48]

In their last journal entry for 1934, written in mid-July, Julian described the strike as "pretty well full blast" in San Francisco and expected to spread soon across the Bay. The ferries continued to run, and "light, gas, newspapers, etc. still function," he wrote, but the food supply had been depleted for several days. "Meanwhile," he continued, "the full militia has been called, arriving even from L.A., to force thru necessities of [life] under armed guard." There was a generally tolerant attitude toward labor, but great suspicion toward Communists. The governor of California claimed that "they are back of all this." He added: "This is probably untrue, but there is reason to suppose that communism has gained considerably, being especially popular among young intellectuals" (presumably some of his university colleagues). He predicted that a settlement of the strike was near since "it is difficult to see how things can or will be endured more than a week—or two at the most."[49]

Four days later, workers accepted a government arbitration plan, and San Francisco's general strike ended. It was the most dramatic of some 1,800 strikes carried out across America in 1934, a year marked by labor unrest and class confrontation. Many young intellectuals, as Julian noted in his journal, found Marxism compelling, with its emphasis on class conflict and its call for political action and personal commitment. But Julian, never inclined toward activism or radical politics, did not join their ranks. He was a Roosevelt Democrat who held liberal political views during that time and in later years. He and his wife followed the strikes and other events with keen interest, but entirely from the sidelines.[50]

Although their life in Berkeley had an acutely contingent quality, and Jane longed to be "'put' for a time," they were not financially pressed. Their two incomes, she recalled, actually left them "flush" that summer. During those same depression years, millions of other Americans could find no work for months at a time, and they either went hungry or felt a deep sense of failure and shame when they finally applied for "the dole," or direct relief rather than work relief. As Jane pointed out years later, she and her husband never experienced that sort of hardship.[51]

Julian's teaching position at Berkeley would end in December, and throughout that summer they still could not predict their whereabouts more than a few months into the future. At some point, they met with the Russian consul in San Francisco about making a trip to Russia, the purpose of which had to do with research in Siberia, not politics. Jane mentioned the meeting in a letter to her sister Libby: "He [the consul] is writing to his friends for information for us but we can't expect to hear for at least 2 months, & then we merely begin to make arrangements if it seems possible to go." And Julian remarked in passing in a letter written in late August, "Next January we shall go to Fiji, Russia, Deep Springs or some other similar place."[52]

Most of Siberia lay within the Russian Republic, in what was then the Soviet Union. Steward had read an article by Waldemar Borgoras on the Chukchi, an indigenous Siberian people, some of whom still lived by hunting sea mammals and fishing, or by hunting and herding reindeer. Borgoras, a Russian revolutionary who was imprisoned and sent to Siberia in the 1880s, had spent his years in exile studying tribal peoples of the Arctic, including the Chukchi. Steward had also learned about another Siberian people, the Yakuts, and he remarked on their complex history of displacement: "Illustrates the ability to maintain culture in face of tremendous odds and splendid adaptation."[53]

Siberia seemed to offer Steward a place to continue with his twenty-year plan of studying the most "simple" cultures (especially hunter-gatherers) and their adaptive processes, and then more complex societies. Fieldwork in that remote region would also allow him to observe directly a community of hunters, just as Stong had done in Labrador. Few such opportunities still existed in the 1930s.

Nothing ever came of the visit to the consul, and the semester passed "uneventfully." At Julian's urging, Jane passed up employment that fall and sat in on several courses in anthropology, including his own on the Southwest and two others offered by Robert Lowie and by Ronald Olson. A remarkably popular instructor with undergraduates, Olson attracted record numbers of students to the introductory course, evidently as Kroeber had judged he would do. Omer

Stewart, Steward's former student at the University of Utah, had begun graduate study at Berkeley the previous year and eventually served as Olson's assistant. Steward avoided him, probably because Stewart knew a great deal about
his marital and professional problems in Salt Lake City. He wanted to keep the
entire episode out of the profession's rumor mill, realizing that it would only
hurt his employment prospects.[54]

During that same semester, Jane also tried taking Gifford's course on museums, but despite a new acquaintance with the subject matter, gained on location at museums in the Southwest, she found it too tedious to continue. The
other three classes constituted her "crash course" in anthropology, as she termed
it, preparation for assisting her husband in fieldwork, whether in the American
West or Siberia or some other place yet unknown to them.[55]

* * *

The new year found them not on their way to Fiji or Russia or Deep Springs, as
Julian had predicted, but still living in Berkeley. Jane located temporary work
in San Francisco through SERA, the State Employment Relief Administration,
in mid-January 1935. Like the Civil Works Administration, which had paid Julian to work for the National Park Service the previous year, SERA was a New
Deal program. Jane provided the couple's only income for the next three
months. Julian's sister also found employment through SERA in January. Marion worked as a clerk and typist in San Rafael, the county seat of Marin County,
earning fifteen dollars a week. That matched her wages for temporary work at
Remington Rand the year before, but it amounted to only about half the salary
she had earned as a secretary before the stock market crash in 1929.[56]

Continuing his own search for employment, Steward again took the civil
service examination, this time for a position as an anthropologist with the Bureau of Indian Affairs. He also wrote up a nine-page proposal, "Research Concerning the Present Status of Indians," summarizing the preliminary work that
he and Nyswander had begun with Ute Indians four years earlier. He did not
name her and referred to her only once, as "a member of the Department of
Psychology and Education at the University of Utah." Although Steward stated
that he was submitting the proposal to assist the government, he clearly hoped
that it would lead to a job offer. (Nyswander did not pursue the project on her
own when she returned to Utah from New York City, but sixty-five years later
she still wondered what had become of all the photographs and field notes from
their pilot study in 1931. "He probably destroyed them," she guessed.)[57]

During the next three months, Steward applied again to the Social Science
Research Council (SSRC) and another foundation for a small grant to do ethnographic research with Western Shoshone in Nevada. Both Kroeber and Lowie
provided letters of support for his project, Lowie remarking that it centered on
"a theoretical problem of great interest, the ultimate interrelation of ecological, economic and non-economic cultural factors." He added that Steward

"combines in unusual measure a feeling for theoretical problems and an interest in concrete fact."[58]

In late March 1935, Steward learned that the SSRC had awarded him a grant-in-aid for his fieldwork. Only he and Olson, among the forty-nine recipients, received funding for ethnographic research. Most of the awards went to historians and economists, who greatly outnumbered anthropologists and whose fields were firmly established and more liberally supported.[59] Kroeber offered to match the SSRC's stipend of five hundred dollars, which would allow Steward to extend his fieldwork by several months. Accepting those funds obligated him to take part in Kroeber's own research project, a "culture element survey" of American Indians in the West. Steward was to be one of about a dozen anthropologists who worked on the project in the 1930s.[60]

On the same day that the SSRC notified Steward, he also received a job offer, not from the Bureau of Indian Affairs, but from the National Park Service. Ansel Hall, who ten months earlier had been unable to hire Steward, now wanted him to take charge of archaeological research for the Rainbow Bridge/Monument Valley expedition. Steward had seen Rainbow Bridge three years before, on his trip down the Colorado River, describing it as an "almost perfect arch of exquisitely carved sandstone." Located in a remote, roadless area of southeastern Utah near the Arizona border, it had been first visited by an archaeologist in 1909. Byron Cummings, then at the University of Utah, and his Navajo guides reached it by horseback. (Monument Valley lies east of Rainbow Bridge, straddling the Utah-Arizona border.)[61]

The Rainbow Bridge/Monument Valley expedition, organized by Hall, was based on the model of the natural history expeditions of the late nineteenth and early twentieth centuries. Launched in summer 1933, it merged scientific research with exploration, a combination that had appealed to Steward from boyhood and had once led him to imagine a career as an explorer/scientist. The expedition's object of study, a territory called the Navajo Country, was known to Steward from his own travels and from reading. Located in the border area of southeastern Utah and northeastern Arizona, in the 1930s much of the region remained isolated and inaccessible except on foot or horseback. Although Zane Grey's novels had made it familiar to millions of readers, romanticizing the rugged landscape and the few Indian and white inhabitants, portions of the region were in fact poorly mapped and almost unknown to the outside world.

By 1935, when Hall contacted Steward, the expedition had already operated for two summers. Except for two women on the support staff, all of the scientists and other staff members were men. Male college students made up the crew. (Omer Stewart, newly graduated from the University of Utah, served as camp cook in summer 1933, then hitched a ride with Hall to Berkeley to begin graduate study.) For Hall, an important goal of the expedition was to provide young men with the opportunity to explore the outdoors and learn from the natural world. He organized a national network of university professors to recruit the students, and he set up an advisory board of prominent men who had worked in the Southwest. Besides Kroeber, the advisers included Harold Colton and Jesse Nusbaum, both of whom Steward had met on his recent tour of the Southwest. His trip, as he had hoped, had begun producing practical as well as scholarly results.[62]

The position that Hall offered Steward was not temporary but was an opportunity for a career with the National Park Service, with a salary between $2,400 and $4,000. "Not to insult him by answering 'no,'" Steward wrote the next day, "I said I'd think it over." It would provide security and a salary equivalent to an academic one, but taking it "would mean a government career & definitely giving up Anthropology." By "giving up Anthropology," he evidently meant his ambitious plan for research; "a government career" signified an administrative one. The summer work would also require lengthy separations from his wife. Both he and Jane quickly agreed to pass up the opportunity: "Jane is ready to endure more worry & semi-poverty," he averred, "to take a chance of getting a good anthropological job." She still held out hope for an academic position, happily imagining her husband as a professor once again and herself in the role of professor's wife.[63]

In the meantime, Steward finished a proposal for a Laboratory of Anthropology fellowship, sending it to Nusbaum in Santa Fe. He and Jane hoped it would provide the means for another year of ethnographic research in the Great Basin, and their own means of subsistence should he still be unemployed. His brief, two-page proposal, "A Study of Ute Economic Life," outlined the work he planned to undertake on "bands" in Utah, north of the area where Isabel Kelly had recently worked with Southern Paiute.

For the "Shoshonean tribes," he argued, "subsistence problems are the most important facts of their lives." (Here, again, the way he framed his research mirrored his own life circumstances.) Through his fieldwork, he intended to achieve "a thorough understanding of the essential facts of economic life," including how people had traditionally procured the food they needed to survive, how edible plants and animals were distributed across the landscape, and how this affected the distribution of human population. Rather than studying such topics as symbol, mythology, and ritual, the focus of so much ethnography, Steward proposed to show how the Shoshone survived "in this remarkably difficult environment and . . . the effect of the essentials of subsistence habits upon other traits."[64]

Many of his colleagues did not share Steward's interest in subsistence, including some who had meager and insecure livelihoods during the depression years. One of them, Spier, still without a permanent position but serving as editor of the *American Anthropologist,* declined to publish his paper, "Ecological Aspects of Southwestern Society." Under Lowie's editorship, Steward had already published seven times in that journal, including several research notes, articles, and a book review. It appears that everything he had submitted up to that point in 1935 had reached print.

Steward had written "Ecological Aspects of Southwestern Society" after returning from his trip and while teaching a course on the Southwest during fall 1934. Years later, in the 1940s, he referred to it as his "'most famous theoretical paper.'" (Almost twenty years after its first publication, he included it as a chapter in *Theory of Culture Change.*) Willey remembered that Steward said this half-jokingly, while also complaining that archaeologists had overlooked the significance of settlement patterns—and, by implication, his article on the subject. Despite what he perceived as long years of neglect, the paper came to be regarded in archaeology as a landmark study of settlement patterns.[65]

To support his argument that clans had developed from patrilineal bands, Steward marshaled evidence to show that Anasazi settlement forms had evolved in response to changes in subsistence, population size and density, and social and political organization. Once again, he proceeded by induction, assembling a dense mass of factual data—all pertaining to the directly observable material and social (behavioral) realms, none to the symbolic—and then seeking patterns, trying to reach a high level of generalization and establish cause and effect. He drew on his own work as an archaeologist in Utah but primarily, as became his standard practice, on secondary data taken from dozens of published reports and monographs by other ethnologists and archaeologists. His own informal observations of sites and what he learned in discussions with colleagues about their research also informed his argument, but silently.[66]

Spier's own caution in theorizing and his interest in cultural integration and patterning suggest that he probably had little sympathy for Steward's rather bold and frankly materialist approach. The paper, a frontal attack on diffusionist thinking, could also be read as a more oblique attack on some works by prominent colleagues, notably Kroeber (who had actively tried to find a permanent professional position for Spier, as Spier surely knew). Considering Steward's own employment status at the time, his paper could be seen as either quite brave or rather foolhardy.

Olson's monograph, *Clan and Moiety in Native America,* based on his dissertation, arguably received the most negative treatment. Steward directed his most favorable comment toward Lowie's *Primitive Society,* writing that Lowie had "paved the way for the treatment followed here by suggesting various economic interpretations of clan origins." (Lowie, however, would later confess to a general "neglect of the economic and technological aspects of life" in his scholarship.) The remarks Steward made in print, using the distant and detached language of scientific writing, were not a wholly dispassionate, intellectual appraisal of ideas.[67] They reflected some of his feelings about his colleagues during that period, as expressed privately to Strong.

His own reduced circumstances help explain why he resented Olson, once a fellow student and good friend, but now a rival and successful in the most important respect. Steward had no regular work, while Olson had a permanent position, thanks to Kroeber, and in the very place where Steward most wanted one. Kroeber was nearly inaccessible, Steward told Strong, now that he could leave "most of the dirty work to Olson," his willing lieutenant who took those duties (here a note of scorn) "very seriously." "Lowie, of course, is unchanging," Steward continued, shifting tone, "and with his big heart, took unto himself my woes in fatherly fashion."[68]

Once he learned that Spier had rejected his paper, Steward quickly sent it to Koppers, an editor of the Austrian journal *Anthropos*. He undoubtedly did so with Lowie's encouragement. Lowie, Viennese by birth and German-speaking, followed European scholarship closely and often reviewed books by German scholars, including Koppers. He must have realized that the article would have a better reception in Austria than in the United States. Steward may have suspected that as well. As in his paper on bands, he cited Koppers's 1921 monograph, which summarized the work of German anthropologists who saw features of the patrilineal band among peoples they regarded as the most primitive. The Vienna cultural-historical school of anthropology, founded by Wilhelm Schmidt, used a limited number of clusters of culture traits (*Kulturkreisen,* or culture circles) as a basis for classifying the cultures of the world. Schmidt himself visited Berkeley sometime in the early months of 1935, and he may well have advised Steward to submit his paper to *Anthropos*.[69]

Koppers and his associates evidently thought Steward's argument that clans had formed from patrilineal bands had merit, and "Ecological Aspects of Southwestern Society" appeared in print in *Anthropos* two years later, in 1937. It was to be Steward's sole publication in a European journal. Unlike Kroeber and Lowie, he had little interest in publishing outside the United States, and he seemed to think that his article in *Anthropos* had suffered a sort of exile, despite being published in English. Although this appears to have been his first, and perhaps only, article ever turned down by an editor, he often complained about it. Years later, the memory still rankled.[70]

During the early months of 1935, Steward, unemployed but hard at work, continued writing, still in pursuit of a secure position in anthropology. Nearly two years had passed since his resignation from the University of Utah. He had written several articles for publication and proposals for research; he had taken the civil service examination at least twice; he had held a temporary teaching position; and he had broadened his field of professional contacts, within academic anthropology and also beyond it. He had, in other words, invested ever more heavily in a career in anthropology, even though professional positions seemed to disappear as the depression, then in its fifth year, ground on.

He was not alone in his predicament. Ralph Beals had finished his Ph.D. in anthropology in 1930. Unlike Jane and Julian, however, Ralph and his wife Dorothy already had children to support. The Bealses spent the next three years in Mexico, in Sonora and Oaxaca, funded first by a National Research Council fellowship and then by a research grant from Elsie Clews Parsons. Returning to Berkeley, Ralph found a temporary position with the National Park Service—an event that called for a celebratory dinner with his friends the Stewards—and a one-semester teaching position at the university.[71]

Likewise, Isabel Kelly subsisted mainly on research stipends throughout the 1930s. After completing her Ph.D. at Berkeley in 1932, she received a postdoctoral fellowship to study the Southern Paiute Indians. Three years later, she went to Mexico to direct an archaeological project, supported by Berkeley's Institute of Social Sciences, which Sauer and Kroeber had founded. Returning to the university, she taught on a temporary basis in the department of geography, then went to Gila Pueblo in Arizona as a temporary research associate in archaeology. The following year, with only minimal funding, she returned to Mexico to carry out archaeological reconnaissance in a remote western area. (In 1940, Kelly gained Mexican residency, and she continued to live and work in Mexico for many years. She never held a permanent academic position.)[72]

The grim prospects for employment in anthropology, and the increasing number of unemployed anthropologists, led Kroeber to draw up a disclaimer of sorts, titled "Study for a Career in Anthropology," in the early 1930s. The graduate program at Berkeley continued to accept students during the depression years, and increasing numbers, in fact, applied for entrance. But Kroeber did forewarn them with a very frank statement about the "possibility" of a career in anthropology. "I am sorry to be so discouraging," he told one aspiring student, "but the truth seems to require it."[73]

In a few succinct paragraphs, he explained that no more than two hundred positions in anthropology had existed in the United States before the depression; that unlike most other academic disciplines, anthropology was taught only at a few major universities, rarely at colleges, and never in secondary schools, thus sharply limiting chances for employment; that "men of established repute and career" had lost their positions due to cutbacks at universities and museums; and that at least a hundred students were Ph.D. candidates or in course at the six universities that offered extensive training. "Only the best or luckiest of them can reasonably hope to secure a position," he cautioned, especially since any new openings would first be filled by "the older men now without a position." Kroeber's final words, written in the same year that Kelly received her Ph.D., proved prescient about her career prospects: "On account of the preference which most institutions give to men in filling positions, a woman's chances are on the average perhaps only one-third as great as those of a man of equal ability."[74]

Whatever his intentions, Kroeber's explicit warning to women may in fact have encouraged men, by implicitly assuring them that they would have priority in hiring. It is difficult to judge the full effects of his brutally honest words.[75]

* * *

In 1935 the ranks of the unemployed or marginally employed included Jane's and Julian's kin, as well as some of their colleagues and friends. In late March, Julian noted in their journal that Jane's brother Grant had arrived in Berkeley and was looking for work. Marion, his own sister, still had temporary work with SERA in Marin County, but she was, he remarked, "on, if not over, the verge . . . and the problem of her & mother as far from solution as ever." The "problem" as he cast it was that Marion did not live happily with her mother. Over the years she repeatedly tried to live on her own, only to move back in with Grace, sometimes after a matter of months. At the age of thirty-seven, she was once again residing with her mother.[76]

However complex the psychological dynamics, the financial reality of their relationship was starkly simple: Marion supported her mother for many years, and her wages for secretarial work always made it difficult to maintain two separate households. In 1935 her annual income was slightly more than seven hundred dollars, having shrunk by almost half since the late 1920s. She paid twenty dollars a month for a mortgage, leaving forty dollars for all other expenses for herself and Grace. Her earnings barely paid the basic expenses for one small household.

The insecurity of her income, not just its insufficiency, probably also pushed Marion to the edge. She repeatedly lost jobs during the depression, beginning around the time of the stock market crash. Her status as sole provider for herself and her mother—then sixty-six years old and a permanent dependent—was clearly another major source of insecurity. Grace remained deeply immersed in her religion but she no longer earned any income as a Christian Science nurse. Although her children, with whom she always had uneven relationships, were her main source of support, and although both struggled to find even temporary work as the depression wore on, this seemed not to worry her. (Christian Science explicitly regards fear as an obstacle to well-being, to be overcome through prayer.) Untroubled by personal problems or worldwide economic crisis, Grace enjoyed good health and good spirits. Jane did not remember that Julian contributed much toward his mother's living expenses during this period. In fact, he turned down the National Park Service position at the same moment he remarked that Marion was on "the verge."[77]

Julian and Jane probably had the same amount of income as Marion and Grace that spring, drawn entirely from Jane's SERA wages. It provided a very basic subsistence for a household of two adults: to borrow Julian's words, it supported their life of "semi-poverty." His fortunes had shifted dramatically in the few years since leaving his first marriage and the University of Utah, where he earned more than three thousand dollars a year; and Dorothy Nyswander—

remarkably, for the times—earned even more than her husband. In spring 1935, Julian and Jane had a level of household income equivalent to less than 15 percent of his and Dorothy's combined salaries.[78]

Still, in contrast to Marion's precarious situation they enjoyed a certain level of security even in those insecure times, one that allowed them to refuse Hall's offer of a National Park Service job. Their own household consisted of two wage earners, not one. They could count on each other for support, and during the first two years of their marriage, one or the other was always employed. Jane, in fact, never had great difficulty finding secretarial work. She was not competing for those jobs with men, who simply never applied for that sort of "women's work," not even during the worst days of the depression.[79] Moreover, she had already stopped working three times by choice: first to move to Berkeley, then to travel in the Southwest with her husband, and again, largely at his urging, to take courses in anthropology. During the several months when Julian was unemployed, her earnings supported them. And, as a last resort, Julian knew they could always go to Deep Springs, a place he had regarded as his surrogate home since arriving there at the age of sixteen, following the loss of his childhood home. Marion, however, had no such refuge. Entirely self-supporting, she found even a brief period of unemployment harrowing. In her desperation to earn income, she tried to sell some of her writing, but had little success in those hard times.

Her life differed fundamentally from her brother's in other ways as well. Without a university degree she had no prospect of a professional career; with a degree, she still would have found it difficult to enter any field other than those few open to women, and poorly paid, such as school teaching. By reason of gender she also earned less money during the depression. Even the federal government practiced wage discrimination during the 1930s, paying men on WPA projects five dollars a day, while women were paid three dollars. This policy, under which women received 60 percent of the rate given to men, may have reflected the prevailing view that women only supplemented household income, while working men supported families. Or perhaps it simply expressed a prevailing cultural view that women's labor, and the products of their labor, had far less value than that of men. Marion, the sole provider for her household, earned only fifteen dollars a week from SERA, possibly due to the same policy that governed WPA wages.[80]

Yet another source of anxiety for Marion was the widespread uncertainty about how long SERA would continue. A year earlier, Roosevelt had unexpectedly ended the Civil Works Administration after only four months, in the face of mounting criticism from political conservatives and over the protests of desperate workers. Some workers rioted and others went on strike or held demonstrations, but to no avail. Marion's brother, whose position with the National Park Service ended with the demise of the Civil Works Administration, took no part in the protests. He and his wife left a week later for the Southwest using

$170 of their savings, a sum equal to several months' wages for Marion. She continued as a temporary worker at Remington Rand, with no respite from her job until she lost it soon after Julian and Jane returned from their travels.[81]

In spring 1935 Marion might well have agreed that her problems were "as far from solution as ever." To put it directly, she eked out a living and provided for Grace, while her brother pursued his intellectual interests and career, and with the support of a young wife who would prove to be an exceptional helpmate. As an unmarried woman, and no longer young herself, Marion confronted a rather common fate in that era before the advent of the Social Security system. She, not her newly married brother, was the expected caretaker and provider for an older, widowed parent, a permanent dependent. (Most people assumed that Grace was a widow, an assumption she never bothered to correct. But as her children well knew, her financial dependence resulted from her own life choices, not from a husband's untimely death.) Some difficult years did, in fact, lay ahead for Marion, marked by marginal employment and repeated ruptures with her mother.

Julian paid scant attention to his sister's financial and employment problems. He regarded her difficulties as emotional in origin, a perspective not at all unusual for the times.[82] Just as he ignored the material conditions of Marion's life, as an anthropologist, he overlooked women's labor and contributions to subsistence, giving attention primarily to men's labor. The parallels between his own life and this aspect of his early theoretical work, which he began to put in writing during this period, are unmistakable. Women's gathering never commanded nearly as much attention as men's hunting, neither in his own work nor in the books and articles he consulted in the 1930s. In his own social experience, his sister and his wife earned enough income to put food on the table, but not much more. The fruits of their labor sustained their households but did not compare with what he and his unemployed colleagues were hunting: very scarce and valued—which is to say, more highly paid and prestigious—professional positions.

Julian Steward's interest in subsistence always centered on men's contributions—and, during this period in 1935, his own quest for employment. Meanwhile, the thousand dollars just provided by Kroeber and the Social Science Research Council offered a temporary livelihood. In April 1935 Jane Steward again gave up her work, this time with SERA in San Francisco, and prepared to follow her husband. They made ready to leave for the field, certain of the territory they wanted to cover but wondering when and where the journey would end.[83]

CHAPTER 8

RETURN TO
THE HIGH DESERT

Julian and Jane left Berkeley on a Saturday in mid-April 1935 and headed toward the desert of eastern California. Seven years had passed since Julian's summer fieldwork in Owens Valley, when he had come to think that "the quest for food was paramount," as he told Kroeber. In an effort to learn about the subsistence practices of Owens Valley Paiute, he had begun mapping their hunting territories and collecting plant specimens in the area around Bishop, California. The results of his research appeared several years later in a monograph that focused on the material conditions of their lives.[1]

In his return to the high desert, Julian Steward planned to extend that work throughout Owens Valley and beyond. The "ecological study" he envisioned included Shoshone and Paiute Indians in other, more remote parts of the Great Basin, where environmental resources—especially food and water—were far more limited. More specifically, he went in search of the patrilineal band, which he had not found among Owens Valley Paiute. As he recalled thirty years later, "I undertook my major work in the Great Basin after formulating the patrilineal band idea, and I fully expected to find it."[2]

By 1935 Owens Valley had actually come to resemble some of those distant desert areas that attracted Steward. Its transformation from a fertile, irrigated valley of prosperous farms and ranches to a high desert landscape of sagebrush and sand was nearly complete, hastened by the efforts of the city of Los Angeles. By the mid-1930s, Los Angeles owned 95 percent of the farmland, and its resolute campaign to erase the valley's recent past had wholly altered the look of that land. Orchards had been uprooted and farmhouses bulldozed. Roads leading to some of the former farms had been plowed up; other roads were bordered by lines of gray stumps, sad relics of the tall green trees that had once shaded them. Fields of alfalfa and grain had simply disappeared. Tourism in Owens Valley, by contrast, continued to grow, with the mountains and lakes of the Sierra Nevada as the main draw. Ironically, most of the tourists came from Los Angeles.[3]

Deep Springs Valley, by contrast, had not changed in such visible ways, either since Steward's student days or since his last visit there in 1932. The ranch and school remained a solitary outpost surrounded by open country that stretched to the bordering mountains. About twenty students, several male teachers—some married, some single—the ranch hands, and perhaps a small kitchen staff were still the sole inhabitants of the valley. Evangeline MacKenzie, the wife of a teacher, was one of the few women who lived there. Most of the women, whether visitors like Jane Steward or residents, were present only by reason of their marriage to men who worked at the school or had other ties to it. Life at Deep Springs thus had a certain "patrilocal" quality. Men's work—their employment at the school and ranch in this case—determined residence for married couples and dependent children, and it defined men's relations with one another.[4]

Soon after arriving, Steward gave several lectures on anthropology, as he had done on his previous visits. The school provided room and board for the next twelve days. Besides preparing for fieldwork, he also finished revising his paper on patrilineal and composite bands for the Kroeber festschrift volume. When he sent it to Lowie, he asked that "Pater Schmidt"—priest and anthropologist Wilhelm Schmidt, visiting from Austria—read it if he were still in Berkeley. The only event to interrupt the quiet rhythm of their days in the valley occurred when one of the teachers' wives suddenly suffered a miscarriage. Julian and Jane made a small grave in the desert, not far from the ranch, and took charge of the simple burial.[5]

In late April they left Deep Springs, crossed Westgard Pass, and made haste for Death Valley, ninety miles away. Spring would soon give way to the brutal heat of a Death Valley summer, when temperatures can exceed 130 degrees Fahrenheit. They planned to spend a few weeks locating and working with Western Shoshone informants in the area around Saline Valley, Death Valley, and Panamint Valley. On their return to Owens Valley, they hoped to find Northern Paiute informants for the southern and northern areas, and for Deep Springs Valley. Then they intended to leave eastern California and continue working with Western Shoshone and Southern Paiute, starting across the Nevada border at Lida, Beatty, and Tonopah, and continuing to other points farther north and east in Nevada.

Arriving in Death Valley, at an elevation several thousand feet below Deep Springs, they found that spring had already fled. On the second day Steward recorded, "Temp. outside about 100 degrees—in the car after being closed up, 135+ degrees." He and Jane immediately visited a small Indian camp, where he asked some questions of a Western Shoshone man, Wilbur Patterson. His sixty-year-old uncle, John Hunter, provided only "a few supplementary facts" about Saline Valley, his birthplace.[6]

Steward also ordered some specimens for museum collections from the two men. The Peabody Museum had given him one hundred dollars for collecting, and he mentioned to Kroeber that "Heye" had provided fifty dollars. This was undoubtedly George Heye, who let his research staff go during the first years of the depression in order to continue adding to his collections.[7]

"Reluctant informants," Steward later remarked about the men, dismissing the women as "speechless." But by the next day he had changed his mind, telling Kroeber that "the difficulty is not unwillingness nor hostility." Instead, as Steward put it with a trace of impatience, "The idea of reducing culture to definite statements is so novel that it must be pondered at some length."[8] These first informants were evidently perplexed by questions, perhaps rather abstract ones, relating to Steward's own research interests in band structure and political organization. Like every ethnographer, he would have to learn from hard experience how to frame questions that could be understood and then work to understand the answers.

Steward asked questions in English and needed replies in English, which may have contributed to the "pondering" that he reported. He was not at all exceptional in this regard. Cultural anthrologists of that era commonly worked with various language groups and did not devote time to intensive linguistic study, instead using English or employing interpreters. Virtually all of Steward's informants spoke English as a second language, and some, especially the elderly, had only limited command. This was true of the next Western Shoshone informant he sought out, George Hanson, who lived with his niece at a place called Indian Ranch in Panamint Valley, an arid, isolated area with few inhabitants. "Old Geo. greeted us & grunted 'yes' when we made our purpose known," Steward remarked. "Put up tent in his front yard and went to bed," he added.[9]

In the morning he spent some time working with Hanson, whom he judged to be about ninety and in good health except for his eyesight. ("Said he wanted to move because he can't see the rattlesnakes.") Steward found him knowledgable and cooperative but learned only a few details about how people had lived in Death Valley and northern Panamint Valley. He judged Hanson's English "insufficient for fine points without an interpreter." Lacking one, Julian and Jane left Indian Ranch shortly and drove through gusting wind and dust, the beginning of a prolonged dust storm. They traveled up Panamint Valley to Darwin, where they camped for the night. An old mining town on the wane, Darwin had only eighty remaining residents.[10]

The next day they visited an Indian camp and were given the names of three men who might serve as informants. Deciding on the third, George Gregory who lived at Olancha, they drove about sixty miles through the desert storm to see him. On the way, they passed through the town of Lone Pine, circled Owens Lake, where the blowing dust rose in billowing clouds, and continued on to

Olancha. Unlike Jane, who saw only a dusty salt flat as they drove by Owens Lake, Julian could remember its former dazzling blueness. In their travels up and down Owens Valley, they repeatedly crossed the cement-lined conduits of the Los Angeles aqueduct, a constant reminder that the waters of the Owens River now flowed to a faraway urban destination.[11]

Olancha, population seventy-five, was a small community shaded by cotton-wood trees. It stood near the southern end of Owens Lake, with towering Olancha Peak to the west; Indians had called their own village at that site by a name meaning "Water End Place." Julian already had an acquaintance with Olancha, where he had once stopped as a graduate student to collect specimens for the anthropology museum. He and Jane immediately went to see Gregory, a Western Shoshone man in his seventies, who agreed to work with them the next day. They also learned that Harold Driver, a Berkeley doctoral student who was working on Kroeber's project, had preceded them and collected a culture element list. (Driver received a Ph.D. in anthropology the next year, in 1936, but as the depression dragged on, he could only find employment in private indus-try. An unusual case, he succeeded in reentering the academic world ten years later, during the postwar period when universities expanded.)[12]

Backtracking three miles, they spent the night at Cartago, a drowsy hamlet that during its heyday in the 1870s had served as a landing for steamers cross-ing Owens Lake from the Cerro Gordo silver mines. By 1935, with the lake dry and the silver mines long exhausted, Cartago's population had dwindled to thirty. Julian and Jane rented "a shabby auto-cabin" there, with resident black widow spiders that he quickly dispatched. They "rejoiced in shelter from [the] wind," he wrote. After two days of breathing the smothering dust and carefully rationing their water, they embraced the luxury of four walls, a roof, and ample water for drinking and washing. This would prove to be the pattern for much of their fieldwork, especially in Nevada: several days on the road, camping out and roughing it, followed by a few nights of comfort "in town," defined as any place with a cabin to rent and a population of more than ten people.[13]

Returning to Olancha the next morning, Steward spent the day working with Gregory and his wife. He recorded his frustration with their answers, largely limited to "yes" and "no" and often contradictory. "I would never trust a trait list taken from him," he wrote after deciding not to waste his time on that task. Once again, he expressed impatience at the "unwillingness of these people to express themselves." With a large territory to cover—geographically and in terms of material covered in each interview—he felt pressed for time. Besides the lengthy culture element lists that he needed to collect for Kroeber, he had his own questions to ask. Taciturn replies and long silences seemed to impede his work. Those long silences may have had a different cultural meaning for his Shoshone and Paiute informants, however, indicating that they were giving his questions careful consideration. Years later, and in print, he would characterize most of them as "friendly, communicative, cooperative, and able to speak fair English."[14]

On his second day with Gregory and his wife, he asked about kinship terms, which he elicited with great difficulty, and then raised questions relating to his own research interests. "Finally got light on bands," he wrote at the end of that day. As he soon reported to Kroeber, he had learned that the people in the region around Death Valley (including Saline and Panamint Valleys and the Coso Mountains) "formed something of a single band." They were further divided into six to eight "sub-bands, each habitually utilizing [a] definite territory & apparently hunting rabbits & dancing together, and [each subband] also named." Intermarriage occurred often, and the subbands held "reciprocal gathering rights."[15]

Steward quickly realized that this did not qualify as a patrilineal band. He spent part of the next day asking more questions about bands, until he finally realized that the family was in desperate financial straits. The nine members survived on little more than four or five dollars a week. Two of the women earned that as laundresses, and a son who lived elsewhere sometimes contributed as well. The informant fee that Steward, and probably Driver before him, paid—two dollars a day—amounted to a windfall but nothing more. To put a weekly income of five dollars for nine people in perspective, Marion and Jane Steward each supported a household of two with SERA wages of fifteen dollars a week, a meager standard of living from their middle-class point of view.

"Took him to Independence [the county seat, forty miles away]," Steward wrote, "to see about SERA relief & after much to-do wound up with $5.00 grocery order and a promise to investigate him for SERA or county relief or old age pension." To his annoyance, the family said nothing. They "merely smiled at the sight of the groceries." His brief encounter with the Gregory family thus ended on a note of cultural misunderstanding.[16]

If Steward misinterpreted their silence, he did quickly grasp the subsistence problems that Paiute and Shoshone Indians faced during the depression. Few could find work to earn money, and few could find their way through the bureaucratic maze to collect relief from the government. For hundreds of Paiute Indians in Owens Valley, especially those without land, the depression compounded the ordeals they suffered when the valley's agricultural economy collapsed in the 1920s. Many of the men had worked as ranch hands or farm laborers, and women earned wages as laundresses or domestic workers. This was common throughout the region, which included nearby Antelope Valley, where Nyswander grew up, and Deep Springs Valley, where the first Indians Steward met, Captain Harry and Mary, worked as ranch hand and laundress. Owens Valley's loss of water, and the decline in agriculture and population, left many Paiute without work. Unlike their former employers—the white ranchers, farmers, and townspeople who packed up and left—the Indians stayed. They did not readily leave ancestral territory, even if rather few of them held recognized legal titles to the land.[17]

In 1935, as Jane Steward later remembered and as she and her husband occasionally noted in their journal, many Paiute and Shoshone men and women "lived off the country" in part, hunting and gathering some of their food. They used traditional knowledge and skills to get by in the new time of scarcity. When informants explained how they subsisted in the past, Jane said, they drew not only on memory but often on recent practice.[18]

* * *

The dust storm that had begun four days earlier continued for the following two days. "Wind still roars," Julian recorded, and "the Owens Lake salt bed is swept into the sky obliterating the mountains." Leaving Olancha, he and Jane drove about forty-five miles south through towers of swirling dust, past the hamlets of Little Lake and Brown, and on to Grapevine Canyon in the Sierra Nevada. Gregory had referred them to a man named Tom Spratt who lived there.

Steward collected a vocabulary of Panamint Kawaiisu from Spratt, noting his ancestry as one-quarter Shoshone, one-quarter Kawaiisu, and one-half white. He told Kroeber that he had collected five vocabularies, this in about ten days of fieldwork, although he never shared Kroeber's interest in language. Instead of classifying his informants on the basis of language or on a range of cultural traits, then standard practice, he focused on their environment.[19]

His own abiding interest in "ecological relations" would lead him to characterize the Northern and Southern Paiute and the Western and Northern Shoshone as "Basin-Plateau peoples." This "geographical term would appear more satisfactory," he wrote a few years later in the preface to *Basin-Plateau*. The term included all of the Great Basin as well as part of the Columbia Plateau in the north and part of the Colorado Plateau in the south. He considered limited water the hallmark of the region. "The important feature of the entire area," he asserted, "is its semiarid or steppe character."[20]

Steward spent his first ten days of fieldwork concentrating primarily on his own research. He had not yet collected any trait lists, he explained in a letter to Kroeber, because one of his informants had previously worked with Harold Driver and "there [seemed] little use in repeating." In fact, however, Steward thought the whole project was misguided, and he resented the time-consuming task of compiling lists of culture traits. As he complained privately in a journal entry, "The list merely enumerates more or less isolated items & is totally unsuited in classification for a descriptive ethnology." A few years later, he remarked pointedly in print that he had collected the culture element lists "somewhat incidentally" in the course of carrying out an ecological study of the Shoshone. His last reference to the culture element distribution survey, made near the end of his life and a decade after Kroeber's death, was blunt. He called it "a blind alley."[21]

Many of Steward's letters to Kroeber in 1935 and 1936 convey a sense of frustration with the trait lists, although he usually expressed his exasperation obliquely. He did not take the same care with his journal. ("Got a trait list from Tom & Mary at the same time. Exceedingly painful work." "Put in a full day . . . on the damned trait list.") He may also have resented the task because of his professional seniority; Driver, Stewart, and Demitri Shimkin, among others who worked on Kroeber's project, were still graduate students.[22]

As Steward noted many years later, Kroeber had rather little interest in "subsistence patterns, economics, social structure, and political forms," the very matters that engaged his own attention and that he highlighted in letters. "This comes near to being a woman's economy," Steward reported, "as seeds are almost the whole story." He wondered whether that might explain the greater frequency of matrilocal residence. Of the thirty marriages he recorded, more than half were matrilocal.

Kroeber does not appear to have replied, perhaps because he had limited interest in subsistence and economy, as Steward himself would later observe. Kroeber's silence did not encourage further discussion of the subject, however noteworthy: an economy as visibly based on the productive labor of women as of men. It was a subject foreign to Kroeber's and Steward's own class-derived social expectations, yet the subject resonated uncomfortably with Steward's personal experience: his unconventional, and unhappy, first marriage to a professional woman. (Kroeber also remained silent about significant aspects of women's lives that he learned of in his fieldwork with Yurok Indians. Perhaps these appeared as anomalous to him as the notion of women as providers. In any case, writing about such subjects would have brought no positive professional recognition.)[23]

Steward would find this "woman's economy" throughout the Great Basin. In the introduction to *Basin-Plateau,* he detailed the broad variety of plant foods in twelve pages of dense text and included lists of the names and uses of plants in the book's appendixes. Only a few sentences, however, dealt with food gathering by what he called "family units" (by his own account, usually women). There was, he noted, no need for cooperation in seed gathering: "A woman gathered as much, perhaps a little more, alone than she could in the company of others; and once gathered, all seeds were the exclusive property of the gatherer and her family." He did not question in print how this aspect of the subsistence pattern—that women's labor provided most of the food—affected social relations.

Despite acknowledging that "seeds and roots were the most important foods," Steward devoted far more attention to hunting: the animals sought, the weapons and other technologies used by men, and the social and political implications of hunting, especially organized hunts for rabbits and antelope. (These communal hunts, as he mentioned once in passing, actually involved women, and sometimes children, as well as men). The culture element lists likewise stressed hunting. Steward's own list for the Western Shoshone had twelve pages of text on hunting and one page on gathering. A glance at the names of his informants, and a close reading of journal entries, shows that he chose to work with men whenever possible, often resulting in the exclusion of women. And he did not always name women who had served as informants.[24]

Steward's search for links between subsistence and social organization was innovative and perceptive in many respects. But the focus on hunting and men's work reflected a highly traditional emphasis in anthropology that represented women primarily in relation to men, as their mothers and sisters, wives and daughters. By overlooking women's labor, this perspective implicitly presented women as the economic dependents of male providers.[25] This outlook remained firmly in place for another forty years, until increasing numbers of middle-class, married American women entered the labor market and began to contribute to household income."Woman the Gatherer" eventually, belatedly, joined "Man the Hunter" in anthropological thinking years after Steward's death.

* * *

Leaving Cartago behind, Jane and Julian drove twelve miles north to Lone Pine, a small town at the foot of Mount Whitney. Long before white settlers founded Lone Pine in the mid-nineteenth century, Owens Valley Paiute had had a village in the area, which they called by a name meaning "Yellow Pine Place." Since they had arrived in Lone Pine too late to locate any informants, Julian and Jane found a comfortable cabin in an auto camp and then "loafed, wrote, and went to a movie," Julian noted in their journal.[26]

Lone Pine, with a population of only 360, offered a striking range of amenities because of the many tourists who passed through. Most proceeded on to Mount Whitney, drawn by its fame as the highest mountain in the forty-eight states, or to other points in the high country. Visitors also included film crews from Los Angeles who stayed at the Lone Pine Hotel while they shot cowboy movies in the Alabama Hills and elsewhere in the Eastern Sierra. Later in the 1930s, the local theater probably showed a new western that held special interest for Owens Valley residents. Starring the young actor John Wayne as one of the Three Mesquiteers, *New Frontier* chronicled their rescue of the people of New Hope Valley, whose way of life was threatened by a water project for Metropole City.[27]

After relaxing on Saturday and seeing a movie, Jane and Julian spent part of Sunday trying to find an informant. They finally looked up a Paiute man Julian had met during his summer fieldwork in 1928, and whom he had considered "fairly reliable" as an informant. Andrew Glenn, then about fifty years old, remembered him and agreed to start work with him early on Monday morning. "He had relatives digging in his garden," Julian remarked in a journal entry, by way of explaining the delay. Although he gave no particulars, years later, a white resident of Owens Valley recalled that the Glenn family, who lived a few miles south of Lone Pine on the bank of Tuttle Creek, raised melons and vegetables and sold them in town. Their garden occupied a small corner of a ranch, she explained, but when the ranch was later sold, the new owner put up a fence, forcing the Glenns to move to a rocky area farther up the creek. "That ended their gardening," she said.[28]

With the next day's work settled, Julian and Jane left for Deep Springs, driving 150 miles roundtrip to collect their mail and, not incidentally, to have dinner with the MacKenzies and other friends. They also talked to Tom Stone, a Northern Paiute man in his late forties, who, in summer 1928 in Owens Valley, had served as one of Julian's best informants ("very communicative and with an extraordinary memory for old customs described by his grandfather"). "Visited with Tom Stone who was genuinely glad to see us," he recorded. Stone would soon serve again as an informant on Owens Valley and as an interpreter for an old acquaintance from Deep Springs.[29]

Andrew Glenn, Julian's informant in Lone Pine, was too "poorly informed" to be useful. They spent time during the afternoon trying to locate two other men, but they had no success. Julian devoted the rest of the day to writing letters, working on his notes, and "basking in the sun at the foot of Mt. Whitney (where they filmed 'Lives of a Bengal Lancer,' and several others)." The next morning, he and Jane drove fifteen miles north to Independence, where he had taken Gregory the previous week to inquire about relief. A town of four hundred people, Independence had once been the site of a Paiute village named after a plant that flourished there. Julian left Jane at the Eastern California Museum, which occupied the basement of the Inyo County Courthouse. Two librarians presided over a collection of books, newspaper files, and old documents and photographs, along with assorted artifacts. Jane spent the morning looking at material on Owens Valley Paiute, while Julian drove the few miles to nearby Fort Independence. As he told Lowie, "Jane has taken to the trip like a veteran and has been no end of help."[30]

Once a Paiute village of perhaps two hundred people, known by a Paiute word meaning Oak Place, the site bore the unapt but official name of Fort Independence. A military post had been built there in 1862, and its troops helped put down the Indian "uprisings" of the 1860s, a last stand against invading white settlers. At the turn of the century, the government set aside a portion of the land taken for the fort and reserved it for use by Indians; a few families also owned land outright. By the 1930s, only ruins remained at the former military site, nothing more than a dilapidated cabin that had long ago served as officers' quarters.[31]

Steward soon located George Robinson, a Paiute man then in his sixties, born only eight years or so after the fort was built. He owned a few acres planted with fruit trees, where he also grew vegetables and hay, and occupied "more imposing premises" than usual, in Steward's view. Although he had been busy plowing a field, Robinson agreed to stop, and they set to work at once. Steward found him helpful and fairly fluent in English, commenting that they "covered the outline of the band ecological material before lunch." Robinson, he added, had been born nearby at George's Creek and provided some insights about the George's Creek band. Steward drove back to Independence to have lunch with his wife, then returned with her to finish his work. "Kinship terms, as usual, were almost too much for all of us," he wrote in their journal.[32]

The next day he wanted to continue with another Paiute man, Dee Lacy. But Lacy happened to be working, and with Glenn's help Steward instead located a Shoshone woman in her fifties, Susie Shepherd, who came from Saline Valley. He spent the morning with her cross-checking the material he had collected from Gregory in Olancha. She supplied little new information. For three hours in the afternoon, her older sister, Patsie Wilson, recounted some myths, with Glenn serving as interpreter. Steward paid Wilson a dollar and paid Shepherd six dollars for what he judged "3 excellent winnowing baskets" for the Peabody Museum. Although he found Wilson knowledgeable and recommended her as an informant, he asked her only about myths.[33]

That evening he wrote up the myths, then went back the following day for more. Steward's motives appear to have been strictly pragmatic. Lacking any interest in symbol and meaning, given his behaviorist leanings and commitment to materialist explanation, he simply took the opportunity to add to his list of publications, the main route to professional advancement as Kroeber and Lowie had made clear.[34] But Wilson startled him when he returned the next morning, demanding more money for the previous day's work. "At the prices they sell baskets," he later observed, "they have worked at 3 to 5 cents an hour." Objecting neither to that rate for baskets nor to a higher informant fee for the day, he increased her wages: "Suspecting before that $1.00 was a little low for yesterday, I agreed on $1.50 for the morning and so paid her, altho she ran out of myths by 11:30."[35]

The standard rate for informants was twenty-five cents an hour, the same wage that restaurant workers earned in Berkeley during that period—and that graduate students earned by taking part in Kroeber's culture element distribution survey. Steward received the same sum, two dollars a day, that he paid his informants for a full day's work. It was not a salary, but a stipend for living expenses, with half of it often spent on lodging, unless he and Jane stayed at Deep Springs, and with no reimbursement for mileage (which he estimated at two thousand miles for the first five weeks). The hospitality at Deep Springs must have subsidized his research. His stipend, their only source of income, was too small to pay for gasoline, food, and lodging. As Steward told Strong, he had "no remunerative job," having turned down an offer from the National Park Service. "I am determined to stay with anthropological research," he explained.[36]

With Glenn acting as his interpreter, Steward went to see Lacy later that day to cross-check the information given by Robinson and to collect some genealogical material. That finished his work in Lone Pine, and he and Glenn parted ways. "As I left Andrew, bosom pals," Steward remarked tartly, "he inquired my name." He spent the next morning writing up his material on Owens Valley Paiute bands. After lunch, he and Jane drove down to the river so that he could look for archaeological sites. "Stuck in sand," he wrote. "Then found scattered site," he continued, which had pottery sherds and stone points, "& beach which delighted Jane." That night they saw another movie.[37]

The next morning they packed and drove back to Deep Springs, where they discovered that the trustees of the school had arrived for a meeting. Guest quarters were limited, and although Jane and Julian decided to spend the night, they left soon after breakfast on Sunday and drove back over Westgard Pass to Owens Valley. They went directly to Big Pine, becalmed as ever, where, belying its name, rows of tall oaks and maples shaded a few streets lined with houses and several stores. It was still the closest source of purchased food and supplies for the ranch.

Julian arranged to work the next day with Tim Stone and Captain Harry's widow, who still lived in Big Pine. Because she spoke Paiute ("English poor," he noted), and he did not, their communication must have been quite limited. Stone agreed to serve as an interpreter and as an informant himself, based on what he had learned about the past from his grandfather. With that settled, Julian and Jane drove to nearby Keogh's Hot Springs, a rustic resort with tourist amenities, where some hard bargaining produced a comfortable cabin for a weekly rate of just five dollars.[38]

On Monday, they spent most of the day in Big Pine. Julian called it "a pleasant relief" to work with Stone, praising him in his journal as intelligent, cooperative, "& more than friendly." Mary Harry was also friendly, but efforts to elicit the story of her life led nowhere that day, much to Julian's frustration. "We concluded," he wrote, "that the biographical approach was the wrong one, with her at least." He continued to work with her and Stone for the rest of the week, collecting a census and trait lists. "With lack of comprehension of questions & knowledge of answers, prob. ⅓ or more [of her] answers are unreliable," he guessed. Eventually he also pieced together a brief biography and a reconstruction of life in nearby Fish Lake Valley during her childhood, in about 1870, by his estimate.[39]

After spending five days working in Big Pine, on Saturday Jane and Julian drove fifteen miles north to Bishop, originally the site of a Paiute village. With a population of more than a thousand, Bishop remained the commercial center of Owens Valley. They talked with several people there, including Willie Chalfant, a writer and the editor of the *Inyo Register*. Then in his sixties and a longtime valley resident, Chalfant had just published a second, revised edition of his book on the region, *The Story of Inyo*. A few years earlier, when that edition was still in manuscript form, Julian had read it and acknowledged its "excellent ethnographic material on the Paiute." Chalfant gave them a copy of the new version, which detailed the events and effects of the valley's long struggle with Los Angeles over its water. That evening, back at Keogh's, the MacKenzies and another teacher from Deep Springs, Chuck Gilbert, arrived "for dinner and dance," Jane noted.[40]

Julian spent one more day working with Stone, then drove back to Bishop with Jane. He hoped to locate a Paiute man, Tom Sport, who had been born in Deep Springs Valley, in order "to get the Deep Springs band," as Julian put it. Before they could find him, he and Jane ran into a man called Deep Springs Johnny who remembered him from his student days in the valley. Deep Springs Johnny and his wife smiled so warmly, Julian wrote later that day, that "we used John [as an informant], his intelligent daughter translating." In a departure from his usual practice, he listed the daughter, Lizzie Babcock, as his informant. Before leaving, he bought a pair of moccasins for the Peabody Museum and a basket. He and Jane also sampled some roasted, ground wheat mixed with wild seeds, which Paiute women in Owens Valley continued to gather for food.[41]

A few days earlier, Julian had learned that the Laboratory of Anthropology in Santa Fe had awarded him a research fellowship, to begin in several months. The Laboratory had not yet notified him, but Ruth Benedict, a member of the selection committee, wrote informally to say that his proposal had been funded. A letter from Lowie conveyed the same news. "Which settles next year for us," Jane commented in their journal. The stipend of eighteen hundred dollars would cover expenses for twelve months' research in Utah, providing about the same level of support as they had at that moment. Although the distance meant that they would lose a subsidy in the form of free room and board at Deep Springs, in Utah they could count on staying with Jane's family as needed.

They had celebrated by taking a day off to drive up to Glacier Lodge, a small hotel near Big Pine, at the foot of the Palisades section of the Sierra crest. Julian painted what Jane praised in their journal as an "excellent picture of exquisite scenery there." With the certainty of a year's support and work ahead, they talked about taking time for a trip into the Sierra high country during the summer. By the middle of July, the snow would have melted and the wildflowers come into bloom. Because of the difference in elevation, flowers had already blossomed a month earlier in Panamint Valley, and the spectacle remained fresh in their minds. In midsummer they hoped to see the Sierra Nevada's version of the same event.[42]

Some promising news soon upset even these sketchy plans. After finishing work in Bishop and returning to Deep Springs to spend a few days, they found a letter from the Bureau of Indian Affairs (BIA) and another from Kroeber awaiting them. The BIA had four positions for ethnologists, and Kroeber urged Julian to apply, even if he wanted to avoid the applied anthropology "track." Having a rating for the position, Kroeber explained, might help in finding another one with the federal government. "Next year again unsettled," Julian noted in their journal.[43]

Before leaving for fieldwork in Nevada, Julian wrote to Lowie about his work in Owens Valley. "So far," he wrote, "the woman appears to be economically most important, which gives a preference for matrilocal residence, but census data show that always, in about half the cases, the man for some reason or other has things his way [that is, residence is patrilocal]. This makes the bands mixed." As he later wrote, "The Owens Valley Paiute were subdivided into true composite land-owning bands." The "degree of unity" in the bands varied, he explained to Lowie, "but always the extent of the band coincides rather closely with the minimum area which affords the necessary variety of foods." In other words, subsistence needs determined social and political boundaries.[44]

During their few days at Deep Springs, Jane took care of the laundry, and Julian, after catching up on correspondence, made repairs to the car. As Jane remarked years later, her husband had acquired a range of practical skills during his student years at Deep Springs, including many of the domestic arts; but their own division of labor as a married couple always followed very conventional lines.[45] In a similar way, his thoughts about women's labor would always mirror the experience of his second, and happier, marriage and conform to the prevailing, dominant views of his social class and profession.

* * *

When they left Deep Springs Valley, Julian and Jane drove east to Lida, Nevada, and then south to Beatty. Their journey of about a hundred miles took them into new country. Beatty, which in the 1930s was a small community of about two hundred, stands on the bank of the Amargosa River, which flows largely underground at the edge of the Amargosa Desert, directly across the border from Death Valley in California. "Different from the Sierra flanked Owens Valley," Julian wrote, "this country has real charm. Desert without end, virtually no water, but shining with color."[46]

Using a contact in Beatty, he quickly located several Southern Paiute and Western Shoshone informants who lived nearby. A few days later, in a letter to Kroeber, he alluded to bands and provided some other details about his fieldwork. Beatty itself impressed him as "one of Nevada's gems, where the main hotel consists of brothel, old time saloon and restaurant and where, in spite of the extremely small population, people get themselves shot, poisoned, blown up or wrecked every few days." He added that he had filled out the civil service application for the Bureau of Indian Affairs position, despite his reluctance, "since there seemed to be no permanent jobs to pluck from the sagebrush." He would worry about refusing it when the time came, he said.[47]

Jane and Julian left Beatty a few days later, departing soon after daybreak and arriving at Deep Springs before dusk. Several letters and telegrams awaited them. The Laboratory of Anthropology had been forced to reduce the stipend of fellowships from $1,800 to $1,500 and decrease the term of appointment from twelve months to ten months. Kroeber, who knew about this in advance, had written to say that he could contribute another $250 to pay for field expenses after July 1, when the fellowship had been scheduled to begin. Strong, in his second year at the Smithsonian's Bureau of American Ethnology, had sent a telegram about the closing date of applications for the BIA positions for ethnologists. "Sent them all telegrams to straighten it out," Jane said in summary. (Her husband's words in the proposal he had sent to the Laboratory of Anthropology just months earlier—that for the Shoshone of Nevada and Utah "subsistence problems are the most important facts of their lives"—described their own financial circumstances and ongoing insecurity.)[48]

Nearly two weeks later, Jane and Julian left Deep Springs, planning to spend the next six weeks in Nevada. Crossing the border, they drove to a place called Cow Camp, not far from Lida. At Cow Camp they located their first informant, a Western Shoshone man in his eighties named John Shakespeare. Finding him knowledgeable and intelligent, and with a fair command of English, Steward worked with him for several days in an effort to learn about the "Lida band." He eventually concluded that bands had not existed there, but rather "each family was the political unit" in the thinly populated country. Still sparsely inhabited and with only rudimentary roads, the terrain did not encourage travel back and forth to town. Julian and Jane made camp behind the house of Shakespeare's daughter and son-in-law, a white man by the name of Flint.[49]

Moving on a few days later, they reached Tonopah, a former mining town and desert metropolis, population two thousand, situated about sixty miles east of the Nevada-California border. There they located another Western Shoshone informant, but he proved uncooperative. With time on their hands and a county courthouse nearby, Julian and Jane decided to get married again, still uncertain about the legal status of their marriage in Mexico nearly two years earlier. They changed their clothes, picked up a marriage license at the courthouse, and within thirty minutes were married by a judge, "a pompous old boy," as Jane described him, who sported a "pair of big mustachios." After stopping for a drink to celebrate, they left town and drove 140 miles through the fierce summer heat to Schurz, a trading post and headquarters of the Walker Lake Indian Reservation.[50]

Unable to locate a cabin in Schurz, they drove on to Yerington, about twenty-five miles away, and spent the night there. Several hours' travel the next day took them to Carson City, Nevada, at the foot of the Sierra Nevada, where they tried to locate detailed maps of the state. Finding none, they continued on to Reno, thirty miles away, and searched there, again without success. They spent that night and the next day and night in Reno, while Julian made his own map and they bought tires for their car. Seeing a movie and watching the racy nightlife afforded a few hours of diversion. Then they drove back to the Walker Lake Indian Reservation where Julian spent two-and-a-half days working with a sixty-year-old Western Shoshone woman. He found her cooperative but not knowledgeable, having "spent most of her life among white people."[51]

Still hoping to find maps, and with other errands to do as well, Jane and Julian decided to return to Berkeley. Their trip took them past Lake Tahoe, straddling the California-Nevada border. The lake's cobalt blue waters, framed by dark evergreens along the shore, offered a vivid contrast to the dry and barren land they had just left.[52]

* * *

In Berkeley, they found that Jane's brother Grant had new roommates, including Joan London, daughter of writer Jack London, and a man whom Jane described cryptically as "head of Trotskyites." They spent the next few days visiting friends: Lloyd Warner, Lowie, Spier and his wife, among others. A foray into the city in search of maps yielded nothing of use, but they saw one of Julian's friends from his student days at Deep Springs, Henry Hayes, who worked in San Francisco. The three hastily planned a pack trip into the High Sierra in mid-July, just two weeks away. Boarding a ferry, Jane and Julian crossed the bay to Marin County, and drove to Mill Valley to see Marion and Grace Steward. Marion had no job, but she did have the prospect of work on a sewing project. "Her spirits good & outlook very reasonable," Jane wrote. "She and Mother now living together again."

They left Mill Valley the next day, Sunday, and drove to the Kroebers' country house, Kishamish, about fifty miles north. Set in the hills on the west side of Napa Valley, near St. Helena, Kishamish was the Kroebers' summer retreat. The property, which they had bought in 1930, included an old redwood house and barn. Each year, the day after school closed in June, they moved there for the summer. Their forty acres of land, once planted with grapes, had returned to pasture and brush and looked out over low hills covered with manzanita, madrone, chaparral, and pines. Jane and Julian stopped there to visit for a few hours, then drove eastward to Sacramento, where they spent the night.[53]

They crossed the Nevada border the next day, and by evening reached Fallon, a town of two thousand people about sixty-five miles east of Reno. Julian worked with several Western Shoshone informants there before moving on to Round Mountain, a wearing trip of 160 miles. The last sixty miles took them along a rutted dirt track, "Nevada's (and the world's) worst road," by Jane's account. Failing to find an informant, they gave up the chase without regret and headed west, reaching Deep Springs the following day.[54]

After spending a few days there, where they packed up and arranged shipment of the specimens they had collected, Jane and Julian left to spend a strenuous week of leisure, hiking in the Sierra Nevada. Near Independence they met Henry Hayes and his wife, Kit, who had come from San Francisco as planned. They had dinner with them and with Chuck Gilbert that evening. "After some persuasion," according to Jane, Gilbert "decided to come along." The party of five left the next morning from Oak Creek camp, a few miles from Independence, leading a string of burros that carried their gear.

Their route took them through Oak Creek Canyon, where a profusion of lupine, paintbrush, and other wildflowers covered the slopes, then along a narrow trail that began to climb steeply after several miles. They made camp for the night and continued on the following day until a rainstorm forced them to make camp again. On the third day, more than eight miles from their starting point and nearly seven thousand feet above it, they reached Baxter Pass, at approximately twelve thousand feet. A storm, this one with hail and lightning, again forced them to seek shelter. "We were all drenched to the skin," Jane wrote, adding that the rain had quickly turned to hail. "It took from 1 o'clock to 5 P.M. to get dried out," she continued. Then, with a certain asperity, she concluded that day's account: "Chuck exclaimed that the hail 'had made the trip for him.'"

On the following day, they reached a point where they could see a scattering of High Sierra lakes glinting silver in the strong, clear light. Descending, they made camp near one of them. That evening, Jane reported, they met "3 men from L.A. who had fished their limit [and] kindly pulled 30 brook trout out of the lake for us." Those provided their first and last taste of fresh food on the trip. The small burros, loaded with bulky packs, carried a week's supply of food and camping gear but no water, a departure from the practice on desert travels. The water, pure and plentiful, came from streams and lakes.

On the fifth day of their journey, they hiked around the high country. "Perfectly beautiful country & peaks," Jane wrote. At the height of summer, snow-fed streams rushed with water and the high country was awash in color: the deep greens of alpine meadows and trees, the bright blue of the sky, and everywhere the wildflowers igniting the slopes with red and yellow and purple. After their recent sojourn in the dry desert, then wearing its summer, monochrome hues, they saw the effects of abundant water everywhere they looked. The lush meadows, the swollen streams, the splashes of wildflowers all gave evidence of the power of water to transform the land. Over the years, Julian Steward had seen the power of water again and again in that border region of high mountains and high desert.

On the sixth day, their party broke camp early in order to cross Glen Pass; they soon reached an area that bore the signs of escalating tourism and too many careless visitors. "This place, while lovely," Jane observed, "is much more accessible & tin cans and campers' debris all over [the] place." They crossed Kearsarge Pass at 11,800 feet, and, after walking another five miles, arrived at Onion Valley in the afternoon of the seventh day. Jane and Julian soon parted company with Henry and Kit, with whom they had felt growing strain as the couple began to assume less and less of the work in making camp.

The trip had taken them in a loop, up from Independence into the High Sierra wilderness and then back down to a point less than ten miles from town. "The cars met us and we were out of the Sierras by 3," Jane recorded. Years later, she remembered her novice status in the venture and a strong sense of being put to a test. Even as she recalled the astonishing beauty of summer in the high country, she admitted leaving it with no strong wish to repeat their long trek and its various physical hardships.[55]

After two nights at Deep Springs, they left again for Nevada in late July, heading for Duckwater, more than two hundred miles northeast. Duckwater was little more than a ranch house on a dirt road with a view of the nearby White Pine Mountains, but it had once been the site of a Western Shoshone community, whose descendants still lived nearby, that bore a name meaning Red Top Grass. Although a flat tire delayed them, Julian and Jane arrived in time to locate an informant. They discovered that he was the younger brother of one of their informants in Fallon, but they decided to collect a trait list from him the following day.

Spending the night nearby in solitude, Jane confessed, "It is good to camp alone." A few days later they left Duckwater and drove toward Ely, some sixty miles east and not far from the Nevada-Utah border.[56]

* * *

When she recalled their desert travels years later, Jane still had vivid and gripping memories of the desperate people they met, refugees from the dust bowl. One day during the height of summer, when the air shimmered with heat, she and her husband drove past an old car by the side of an isolated road, miles from the nearest town. They stopped when they realized that the car had broken down but was not abandoned. The driver, a young woman, had no water, little money, and several children. She was traveling west, toward California, while Jane and Julian were headed east. Julian made some repairs and got the car running again, Jane gave her as much water as they could spare, and they both wished her luck. ("But whether she ever made it . . . ," Jane said, her voice trailing off.)

She also remembered seeing trains in the distance crossing open country and the small figures of men huddled on top of the cars, riding the rails to California.[57]

* * *

As soon as they reached Ely, population three thousand, Jane and Julian stocked up on food and water. Wayfarers in the desert, they had only secondhand knowledge about how to live off the land, gained from their Paiute and Shoshone informants. Since they bought all of their provisions, their food supply often affected the timing of trips to town. Campfire meals featured coffee, canned beans, and canned everything else once the potatoes and onions had been used up or had gone bad in the heat. Whenever they reached the limit with canned beans, they forgot frugality and had a steak dinner in town. Beef cost much more than beans, Jane remarked, but it was not such an extravagance as in the East.[58]

Ranches surrounded the town of Ely, Nevada, located in the broad and arid Steptoe Valley. Ely had begun as a gold-mining camp in the 1860s, and later gained prosperity from copper mining. The damaging effects of the mining industry, including the use of piñon wood for fuel, soon depleted the supply of pine nuts and nearly destroyed the native economy. But long before white miners entered the area, several Western Shoshone villages stood along Duck Creek and elsewhere in the valley. Julian and Jane found six informants in the area, probably at the ten-acre Ely Colony, and then spent ten days in late July and early August working with them.[59]

After leaving Ely in early August, Julian and Jane drove to the Utah border and continued on to Salt Lake City, covering about 250 miles. They spent a full week in Salt Lake City, "getting maps, having botanical specimens identified, doing errands, and drinking sloe gin fizzes with Stan at Maxie's." Walter P. Cottam, a botanist and ecologist at the University of Utah, identified the plant specimens that they had collected in their travels; a few years earlier he had identified material from Owens Valley for Julian. The night before leaving to continue fieldwork in Nevada, they stayed with Jane's sister Libby and her husband, "who [were] not getting on well," Jane observed. Libby had visited them about six months earlier in Berkeley, in the throes of marital problems. The next morning, Sunday, Jane and Julian left Salt Lake City and drove west to Wells, Nevada, about sixty miles from the Utah border. "No aged Amerinds in Wells," Jane reported, "so proceeded to Elko to start."[60]

Elko, population four thousand, stands along the banks of the Humboldt River at an elevation of five thousand feet. It had long served as a trade center for a vast territory of cattle ranches scattered across the high desert of northern Nevada. Many of the buildings on the main street dated from the 1880s and 1890s, and Victorian houses, with apple trees planted in the yards, lined some of the side streets. White settlers who began moving in around the 1860s had found Western Shoshone living along the Humboldt River and its tributaries. In the 1930s, some of the Western Shoshone descendants lived in an Indian colony on the north side of Elko.[61]

At the post office they picked up mail forwarded from Berkeley and unexpectedly found a letter and telegram from the University of New Mexico. It contained an offer of a one-year position as instructor and curator of the museum, with a salary of two thousand dollars. Both rank and salary were so low compared to the University of Utah, where Julian had earned more than three thousand dollars and held the rank of associate professor, that he and Jane quickly decided not to accept the terms. "We wired & wrote back we couldn't come for less than $2,500 and asst. prof.," Jane wrote in their journal. Before they received a reply, Matthew Stirling sent a telegram asking if Julian would accept a position at the Bureau of American Ethnology (BAE) for $3,200. "We said yes," Jane noted simply.[62]

Two days later another telegram arrived, this one from the president of the University of New Mexico, offering an assistant professorship and a salary of $2,500. Still unsure about the position with the BAE, they wired Stirling again. He replied that the position was "practically certain," but they wondered exactly how certain, given a recent and cautious letter from Strong. They decided to decline the position at the University of New Mexico, "preferring to gamble on Bureau job," as Jane put it in their journal. "Did not work at all today," she continued, "being too tense & tired to find a new informant."[63]

Fifty years after writing those words, Jane remembered the circumstances very clearly. They had not agonized over the decision, she said. Her husband thought he would find a certain colleague at the University of New Mexico difficult, whereas he considered Stirling and Strong friends as well as professional colleagues. The BAE salary was also higher, and the position offered far greater security and prestige. And finally, it would allow him to concentrate on the research and writing that he had planned; it involved no teaching. The single drawback was the BAE's location in Washington, D.C., where he had no wish to live again. Only a month earlier, Julian had ended a letter to Strong by writing, "Your swims in the Potomac sound good but as between Washington summers and the simmering desert, I still take the latter!" His reluctance to return had little to do, in fact, with summer in the city, and far more to do with his feelings about place.[64]

Aside from location, the choice between an academic post with heavy teaching duties in an undergraduate program and a research position at the Smithsonian Institution required no hard thinking. Ambition won out over place. Still, Jane admitted, at the time she felt a small stab of doubt about turning down a sure offer, and one from a university. Julian, she said, continued to believe that he would find a good position, even after two discouraging years of searching. He seemed not at all worried to her. "*I* was," Jane explained. "*He* was very confident because he had a sense of being part of an elite."

She saw that self-confidence as a legacy of his schooling at Deep Springs, but her unflagging admiration and support surely had an effect as well. In contrast to his former wife and his mother, Jane gave him her exclusive attention. He would always depend on her for encouragement and unqualified admiration, and he would increasingly resist spending time apart from her. The doubt and anxiety about career that he had privately expressed to Strong soon after leaving his first marriage were not in evidence in 1935: not to Jane, not in their journal, not in the letters he wrote.[65]

*   *   *

During the week they spent in Elko, Julian worked the most intensively with a Western Shoshone man in his sixties named Bill Gibson. Julian and Jane found him friendly and well informed, with an unusually keen historical sense. On their last day, Gibson recounted some myths and gave them "a clear picture of surrounding bands." The Western Shoshone of that region, like others, had not lived in patrilineal bands. That finished the work in Elko, and in mid-August they returned to California, where Julian began the tedious task of filling out the many forms required for federal employment. His impatience to finish them led him to schedule a medical examination before the needed form arrived. "By some miracle," Jane remarked in their journal, "[the tests] were the right ones."[66]

Although they still had not received final confirmation from the BAE, the position was due to begin in less than two months; they hastily packed most of the belongings they had left in Berkeley and took them to the wharf in San Francisco to have them shipped by sea to Washington. In the midst of preparing to leave California, they stayed with Marion and Grace in Mill Valley for a few days, and then with Grant Cannon in Berkeley. They still managed to keep up a frantic social schedule: "Visited with all the old friends there, an average of 3 social encounters a day," Jane wrote. On the day before they left Berkeley, they saw the Bealses, the Lowies, the Kroebers, the Radins, and several other colleagues and friends. Two years earlier, at the age of fifty, Lowie had married Luella Cole, a psychologist; Radin, exactly Lowie's age, had also recently married. Kroeber and his wife, cordial as always, wished them well; and Kroeber, ever generous with career advice, also offered good counsel about the professional situation that awaited in Washington.[67]

In early September 1935, Jane and Julian returned to Nevada. They stopped at Elko, planning to spend the night and to pick up their mail at the post office. To Jane's relief, they found formal confirmation of the BAE position. "That is settled," she commented, satisfied to think that they would soon give up their nomadic way of life. Julian had told Strong just two months earlier that Jane was helping him a great deal with his fieldwork and had taken "the heat, dirt, sleeping in the sagebrush, etc. like an old-timer." In truth, after many miles of desert travel and several months of physical discomfort, she looked forward to a rooted life and the amenities of city living.[68]

They left for Ruby Valley the next morning, driving eastward over dirt roads and then heading south, skirting the Ruby Mountains. The area, Julian later wrote, was "exceptionally fertile" for eastern Nevada. Unlike the arid valleys that lie to the east, Ruby Valley is blessed with water: myriad streams rushing down from the mountains fill two large lakes. To the west, the massive Ruby Mountains rise, with peaks reaching more than eleven thousand feet. As one of the tallest ranges in the Great Basin, with a spruce and aspen belt, mountain sheep, and glacial cirques, the mountain range has the look of the Sierra Nevada on a smaller scale. The Western Shoshone who lived nearby told Steward that they called the Ruby Mountains by a name that meant Snow Mountain. Jane and Julian spent about a week in Ruby Valley, where they camped at a ranch and worked with several informants.[69]

Returning to Elko, they found a letter from Jane's sister implying that divorce was on the horizon. Jane left immediately for Salt Lake City, planning to spend ten days there with her sister, while Julian drove about a hundred miles north to Owyhee, near the Nevada-Idaho border. Traveling over a road that was paved for about twenty-five miles, giving way to gravel, he crossed a remote country of mountains and valleys that offered expansive views of land and sky. Owyhee, set in a broad, fertile valley at the northern end of the Bull Run Mountains, served as headquarters for the Western Shoshoni Reservation. About four hundred Indians lived there, many of whom cultivated small farms along the Owyhee River.[70]

Writing to Lowie in mid-September, Steward praised his informants at Owyhee as "extraordinarily willing . . . and my interpreter the best yet." He had found Northern Shoshone and Western Shoshone men from areas of northern Nevada and Idaho, as well as Paiute from Nevada and Oregon. "I will have about two weeks total time here," he continued, "& expect to get a great deal." He worked with at least four older men, one of whom was a shaman; three were in their eighties and another was about sixty.[71]

At Owyhee, Steward learned about Western Shoshone who had lived along the Snake River in southern Idaho and Northern Paiute and Western Shoshone who had lived around the Humboldt River in nothern Nevada. His shaman informant, who had been born at Battle Mountain near the confluence of the Reese and Humboldt Rivers, proved to be one of his best informants and, he conceded, "particularly good on shamanism." Steward dutifully recorded what he learned about the presence or absence of various culture elements having to do with a shaman's powers, but his interest lay elsewhere. Later, and in print, he explained the cursory attention to religion by pointing out that various aspects of culture are not "equally amenable to tabulation," and religion among the least. In another publication, he asserted that the culture element lists did not qualify as full-fledged ethnographies. "Religion and shamanism especially require further study," he wrote, without adding that he left those subjects to others.[72]

After spending a week or so at Owyhee, Steward drove back to Elko to meet his wife at the train station. Then they returned to Owyhee for several days "& finished the field work for the 1935 season." But before leaving the West, one final task remained. The BAE had asked Steward to go to Pendleton, Oregon, "to do a little job," as he put it, which turned out to understate the task. In late September, he and Jane left Owyhee and drove hundreds of miles through Idaho, then crossed the rugged and remote high desert of eastern Oregon to reach Pendleton, located in the northeastern corner of the state.

In Pendleton, they spent long hours sorting through a private collection of five thousand photographic glass plates to select three hundred negatives by John K. Hillers. He had taken the photographs in the 1870s on expeditions in the West with John Wesley Powell. "A dirty & tiresome job," Jane wrote in their journal, "which we finished on Oct. 1, after working days & evenings." They left Oregon the next day, due in Washington, D.C., only two weeks later. Their work in Pendleton, despite its cost in time and tedium, would have professional benefits for Steward, yielding a publication about Hillers's photographs of Paiute and Ute Indians.[73]

* * *

Stopping in Salt Lake City for about four days, they found Libby in the midst of divorce proceedings: "consoled her & the family as best we could," Jane commented. Then she and Julian finished packing their belongings and left the boxes in her parents' basement, to be shipped later. Just five days before they were due in Washington, they left Salt Lake City and drove across Colorado, Kansas, and Missouri to St. Louis, where some of Julian's maternal relatives lived and where he had spent two years of his childhood. After paying them a hasty visit, Julian and Jane crossed the Mississippi River to East St. Louis, Illinois, and visited still more relatives.

Two days later, they left on the final leg of the trip. Their route through Kentucky and Virginia offered Jane her first glimpse of the Upper South. She was intrigued by the distinctive architecture and "cobbled streets" of the towns and cities, and by the African Americans who lived in them. Growing up in Salt Lake City, she had encountered only people of European ancestry. Most of the early Mormon converts were Americans of European descent, and others, including a few of her own ancestors, had emigrated directly to Deseret from Britain and northern Europe. Even her contact with Indians was rather recent. Although she would find many African Americans living in Washington, D.C., there would be little contact in that racially segregated city. "The feeling of the South is new and fascinating," she wrote during the last days of their long journey.

They finally reached Washington, three days late, and then had trouble finding a place to stay. "Circled the circles," Jane complained in their journal, adding that they had tried the Logan Hotel but considered it too expensive. Many years later, her dominant memory of that day was of seeing the Potomac River for the first time. As they drove across one of the city's bridges, she recalled, she stared transfixed at the broad river that flowed beneath them. It looked to her as if someone had opened the floodgate of an enormous irrigation canal and had then forgotten to close it. She had never seen such a sight in the West, and even the Mississippi River had not struck her as quite so ostentatious in displaying its wealth of water.[74]

Two days later, on Sunday afternoon, they spent a few pleasant hours with Duncan Strong and his wife, Jean. Their spirits revived, they moved into the Logan Hotel the next day, despite its expense. Once there, Jane noted an odd coincidence: their residence in Julian's birthplace, Washington, D.C., quite literally gave them a view of his birthplace. The hotel on Logan Circle stood within sight of the Iowa Apartments on 13th and O Streets, where he had been born thirty-three years earlier.[75]

While he spent his first day at the BAE, Jane, along with Jean, began to search for an apartment. Because of an acute housing shortage in Washington, the Strongs were also living in a hotel. The two couples had quickly decided during their Sunday visit to share an apartment for a few months until the Strongs left for fieldwork in Honduras. Having the advantage of Jean's previous searches, the two women found a place by the second day, but before they could sign the lease, Stirling cautioned against it. He thought it possible that Julian might be sent to Florida to direct a WPA archaeological project, an assignment that could last from six weeks to a year.

Before Julian learned of this further dislocation, he wrote to Lowie and, prematurely as it happened, expressed his relief at being settled: "At the end of the trek at last! And it is mighty good to look forward to a settled life for a time." By his third day at the BAE, he had met his other colleagues—including John Swanton, Truman Michelson, Frank H. H. Roberts, and the elusive linguist John Peabody Harrington—and found them cordial and welcoming. "For the present, at least," he continued, "my work will consist simply of writing up my Shoshonean researches—which seems too good to be true." To Kroeber, he likewise mentioned that he had "complete freedom to start immediately to work up the Shoshoni notes." That work came to an abrupt halt, however, a few weeks later. As Stirling had predicted, Julian and Jane left for Florida, uncertain whether they would return in a few months or stay for as long as a year.[76]

When they reached Miami in mid-November, they again moved into a hotel. Arriving there soon after a hurricane, they found the city still littered with all manner of debris, from fallen palm fronds to splintered yachts. With the tourist season due to begin in December, Miamians struggled to restore the city to some semblance of normalcy and order. In the meantime, Julian and his crew, described as "100 or so aged men," set to work at an archaeological site on Miami Beach ("off the mainland, on the northern & mostly uninhabited end"). Complications arose immediately, with Duncan Strong urging Steward to return to Washington to discuss a pending assignment at the Bureau of Indian Affairs and with Stirling disinclined to have him leave the WPA project.

As the tourist season approached, the price of housing soared, and Julian and Jane grew more disenchanted with their temporary home. They thought the city "much like southern California in atmosphere, artificial, a rich man's playground." With no regrets at all, they left balmy Miami after just a month and headed north in mid-December 1935. Strong had prevailed, and Julian was due to replace him at the BIA in January so that Duncan and Jean could leave for Honduras on schedule. Back in Washington, Julian was briefed about his upcoming work as a liaison between the BAE and the BIA, and Jane again searched for a place to live. The best she could find was a small, rather shabby apartment on Belmont Road, near Rock Creek Park and not far from the neighborhood where Julian had lived as a child. It was available for fifty dollars a month, which seemed an exhorbitant rent during the depression years. They moved in just before Christmas.[77]

* * *

The winter and spring months of 1936 passed in a blur. Julian, embroiled in complex internal politics at the BIA, largely neglected his own work. "Our time at home has been devoted to copying the trait list[s] for Kroeber," Jane mentioned in their journal, adding that Julian had worked on his own project whenever he found time. Kroeber had asked for the trait lists five months earlier, in October, but Julian had requested an extension, explaining that "many notes crept into the lists that are essential for my ecological study." In early November 1935, just before leaving for Miami, he finally began the tedious, time-consuming task of converting the notes into lists suitable for publication.[78]

By early February 1936, he had made little progress. As the deadline approached, he again asked Kroeber for more time to complete the lists: "Jane has agreed to work on them," he explained, "and I hope that between us we can put them in fairly decent shape." Kroeber quickly agreed, but added that "it strikes me as somewhat of a rough deal on Jane." He suggested that his own temporary staff of WPA workers could finish the chore very quickly: "Whenever Jane gets tired of carrying this baby, please have her remember that we are standing by, holding a fully equipped basinette." (Kroeber's metaphor proved strangely prescient: Jane conceived a few weeks later.)[79]

Julian had disliked the culture element project from the outset, and Kroeber's choice of a feminine metaphor, and perhaps especially the implication that his wife had charge of the lists, angered him. When he replied to Kroeber's letter, obviously in short temper, Julian insisted that he and his wife, not "your WPA hirelings," would finish the work. He and Jane had "slaved" on the lists every night, he wrote, working until midnight in hopes of finishing them very soon. Jane, an experienced typist, also spent long hours during the day typing final copy of the lists.[80]

True to form, Kroeber responded to this outburst with a cordial, if unusually delayed, letter. "I'm afraid you took casual praise for a slur," he said. He mentioned that he hoped to extend the trait list method to all of native North America, and he had tentative plans for a meeting in the East to discuss it with other anthropologists: "I hope you will be there. I always feel that when Julian Steward is convinced, the last legitimately doubting Thomas has been won over." Julian admitted to having doubts, but he suggested that the culture element approach might be of some use to archaeologists. He promised to send the lists within a week. Jane finally sent one of the lists to Kroeber almost two weeks later, a few days after her husband had left on a trip for the BIA.[81]

Besides dealing with the stresses of his job and the unremitting tedium of organizing and writing up the culture element lists, sometime in February 1936, Julian learned that his father had died. Thomas Steward, then seventy-nine, was not living in Washington at the time of his death. He and Julian had not had contact for years, perhaps for more than a decade. Rather than a definite break, a lengthening silence seems to have fallen between father and son. Julian did not attend the funeral. Jane, who felt great affection for her own father and who had what she described as a Mormon sensibility about the importance of family, was startled by his reaction, but the strain of his work concerned her more. Just two months after he started working at the BIA, she described Julian in their journal as "a wreck" from the "impossible situation" there.[82]

On March 8, Julian left on an extended trip to the West for the BIA, planning to return to Washington in six or seven weeks, at the end of April. Jane spent a few days in New York, visiting her oldest brother and his wife, and, according to a terse entry in their journal, she "had gala time but came home early. Julian returned." He was back well before the end of March, perhaps a sign of his growing reluctance to spend time apart from her, and certainly a harbinger of the many interrupted or canceled trips that were to puzzle his colleagues in the future. A few weeks later, Jane noted: "Disgusted with BIA & intending to get out. His health punk—nausea, weakness, dizziness, etc."[83]

His work with the BIA abruptly introduced Julian Steward to the sharp-edged politics of the federal bureaucracy. He arrived in Washington soon after passage of the Indian Reorganization Act, legislation that intended to change long-standing federal policies and practices that had assimilationist aims. The 1934 act called for restructuring tribal governments and creating reservations, in some cases. From the beginning, Steward took a dim view of granting federal recognition and providing reservation lands for groups of Western Shoshone living in Nevada. He opposed "segregating" them on reservations, not only because he believed it ran counter to their traditional way of life but also because it would impede assimilation. Despite the 1934 legislation, he regarded the assimilation of American Indians as inevitable and as the path to economic improvement. Some anthropologists and most of his fellow citizens shared that view in the 1930s.[84]

Others within the BIA saw it differently, and they prepared for battle while Steward turned his attention elsewhere and began preparing for summer fieldwork in the West. In May 1936, he told Kroeber that he had almost severed his ties with the BIA, choosing instead to spend more time on his research. He also mentioned plans to continue collecting culture element lists. This said more about his own research priorities than about his affiliation with the BIA, which, in fact, would pay for much of his upcoming fieldwork. The official purpose of that summer trip, made in the company of his wife, was to gather information for a report to the BIA on the issue of reservation lands.

In the meantime, Steward continued putting culture element lists in order and organizing notes for what he referred to as his "ecological paper." The patrilineal band still eluded him, but, partly as a result of systematically compiling the lists, he had gathered a massive amount of structured data on subsistence practices, population, and social groups. The BIA-financed trip would allow him to collect still more data.[85]

* * *

He and Jane left Washington in the middle of June 1936, planning to spend at least three months doing fieldwork in Idaho, Nevada, and Utah. They drove first to Utah, where they took a few days of annual leave in Salt Lake City. "Julian not feeling very well," Jane wrote in their journal. By contrast, she reported feeling "swell" in the third month of pregnancy. They left Salt Lake City in early July and drove to nearby Ogden, Utah, where they visited friends Maurice Howe and his wife. Maurice, who had joined Julian on his 1932 pack trip in southern Utah, had a new position as state director of the WPA Federal Writers' Project. In Ogden, both Julian and Jane also consulted a Dr. Seidner, who found Jane in good health. Julian, however, had an appendectomy about a week later, then convalesced quietly at the Howes' for two weeks. Although he had not had appendicitis, once "the useless organ" was removed, he reported, he felt better than he had in months.[86]

At the beginning of August, he and Jane left Ogden and drove to Pocatello, Idaho, about seventy-fives miles from the Utah border, to begin their fieldwork. They evidently went back to Ogden almost immediately because Julian felt unwell and had very little appetite. He saw Dr. Seidner again, "who assured him he was o.k.," Jane affirmed. "Has been eating more, gaining weight, and feeling much better. Was it couvade?" Thinking along the same lines, a colleague and anthropologist at the BIA wrote to Julian in jest, "I hope you have recovered from your slightly premature 'couvade.'" By the time he did recover, the period of research funded by the BIA had ended.[87]

Returning to Idaho, Julian and Jane spent several weeks in August and early September at the Fort Hall Indian Reservation near Pocatello. Surveying the plateau landscape, an arid and sagebrush-covered terrain, he thought that it resembled much of the Great Basin to the south and west. He set to work with a Northern Shoshone man named James Pegoga, who was eighty-five years old and had once lived in the mountains near the Lemhi River. As in his previous fieldwork, Steward wanted to know how people had lived on the land and how they had lived with one another, whether in patrilineal bands, other types of bands, or smaller groups.[88]

The Lemhi Valley, as Steward later described it, was the only area suitable for human occupation in the region. It was bounded by rugged, high mountains, the Bitterroot Range to the east, along the Montana border, and the Lemhi Range to the west. Northern Shoshone, and perhaps some Northern Paiute–speaking Bannock, entered the valley and lived in rather large villages along the Lemhi River and in several small, isolated villages in the mountains. They called themselves by a name meaning Salmon Eaters. Drawing on the journals of Lewis and Clark, who visited the Lemhi Valley in 1806, Steward characterized the valley people as "a loose band possessing many horses, hunting buffalo, and even engaging in some warfare under a true chief." The bands were clearly composite, not patrilineal. From several other male informants, he learned more about the importance of horses in the region.[89]

Judging from their accounts, Steward thought that Northern Shoshone and Bannock around Fort Hall had adopted the horse by the middle of the eighteenth century. Men hunted bison communally and on horseback, until the herds vanished from that area in the nineteenth century, perhaps due to the arrival of trappers and the use of firearms. As Steward later wrote, the horse "revolutionized [Northern] Shoshoni economy by making it possible to use new methods of hunting which yielded greater wealth in foods and hides and enabled people to live in large and comparatively permanent groups." By contrast, he pointed out, Indians living in the arid Great Basin saw horses as a source of food, not as a means of getting food. Horses had no use for hunting in areas without large game animals, and they grazed on the very grasses that women harvested for seeds.[90]

In the framework of cultural ecology, which he would not fully formulate until years later in an essay in *Theory of Culture Change,* horses represented a new food-getting tool in one environment. The use of horses entailed a new organization of labor along with other social and political changes. In a different environment, horses were not a tool but a resource, food. All of the elements of Steward's later cultural ecology—the interplay of environmental resources, technology, and labor, shaping the course of social and political change—were implicit in this account of the horse.

Leaving Idaho in early September, Julian and Jane returned to Utah, where they stopped briefly in Ogden and Salt Lake City. Two days later, they drove 150 miles south to the Kanosh Indian Reservation, citing BIA business as the reason for the trip. Kanosh, a small village of log houses built along a dirt road, stood only a few miles from the highway. "Very few (approx. 24) Indians left here, all young," Jane recorded. Several years later, Julian remarked that "a small remnant of Pahvant Ute live at Kanosh, Utah, but the people are so young and so intermixed with Southern Paiute that little reliable information is available from them."[91]

He and Jane returned to Salt Lake City and then continued north to Washakie, a community in northern Utah of fewer than two hundred Northern Shoshone. An outbreak of smallpox in the area had apparently caused them to delay going there after they left Fort Hall. Some sixty years earlier, the Mormon leader Brigham Young had granted the land at Washakie, and the Indians living there took up farming. In the 1930s, all the Indians were Mormons, although Julian reported "some friction" due to the church's opposition to shamans and the Indians' opposition to certain church policies.[92]

They spent about a week in Washakie, where Steward hired Seth Eagle, a shaman who was about fifty years old, as an interpreter. With his help, Steward worked intensively for four days with Old Diamond, a man in his eighties, and very briefly with Old Diamond's half-sister. Old Diamond told him about Northern Shoshone who had lived in Cache Valley, estimating that their band had comprised only twelve families. Steward, however, believed that the population of that exceptionally fertile valley had been greater before the infamous Bear River massacre took place in 1863.[93]

In his fieldwork, Steward sporadically had heard about instances of warfare. Because his interest lay in the precontact period, he gave some attention to armed conflict among groups of Indians. (He made only passing mention of postcontact conflict, which included the massacres perpetrated by whites, but also armed and organized resistance by Indians against whites.) Not surprisingly, Steward thought about warfare in cause-and-effect terms, as a factor that could produce unity among greater numbers of people, resulting in the consolidation of bands. "Warfare on a scale large enough to affect social cohesion," he eventually concluded, "was known only in the eastern part of the [Basin-Plateau] area." That, in turn, he believed, correlated closely with the possession of horses.[94]

Years later, he devoted more thought to warfare as a factor in political centralization, but he never gave it the same close attention he gave to irrigation. Ruminating about warfare—something entirely remote from his own direct experience—simply did not result in the insights and creative leaps that came from thinking about water scarcity or an uncertain food supply.

* * *

Julian and Jane returned to Salt Lake City in mid-September, and a few days later Jane boarded a train for Washington, D.C. Originally, she had planned to leave Utah at the beginning of September. Once in Utah, however, she and Julian had thought of staying in the West until the end of the year, after the baby's birth in December. Although it would have allowed two extra months of fieldwork, personal concerns argued against remaining. They had given up the apartment on Belmont Road, and just before leaving for Utah, they had signed a lease for a larger, more expensive apartment in Arlington, Virginia. It would have to be sublet if they did not return by early October when the lease began.[95]

Jane was almost seven months pregnant and had delayed her departure for the East by nearly a month when she finally left behind the punishing heat, bone-jarring roads, and other discomforts of her husband's nomadic style of fieldwork. Although they had not camped, instead staying in cabins during the course of their trip, she longed for the comfort and stability of home. It had come to seem a most elusive wish. During the first three years of marriage, she had followed her husband wherever his work took him, their residence pattern highly "patrilocal," dictated by his professional ties with other men. Wayfarers during those years, they had lived in four apartments, a borrowed house, and hotel rooms in three different cities—to say nothing of spending the night in countless cabins and camps throughout the West, and staying with an impressive array of relatives and friends across a major portion of the continental United States. When Jane left Salt Lake City in late September, she returned to Washington and their new apartment in Virginia with a detectable sense of relief.

Julian Steward remained in the West for another three weeks. As he later complained, those final few weeks were "pretty badly cut up." The day after his wife left he told Kroeber with obvious exasperation, "I have just received orders to look at some guano caves near Fallon which, as seen from Washington, is an inch away on the map, but is actually 500 miles from here!" On his way to Nevada, he stopped at the Skull Valley Indian Reservation to do some of his own work. The adjacent Great Salt Lake Desert had no water, no vegetation, and no inhabitants.[96]

Fewer than fifty Gosiute ("indistinguishable" from Western Shoshone, Steward observed) lived on the reservation, where they subsisted by herding a few sheep, gathering pine nuts from a nearby forest, growing some food, and renting grazing land to white ranchers. Steward stayed there for three days, working with an informant named Mudiwak, or Moody, a Gosiute man in his seventies. When he left Skull Valley, he turned south and then west, driving more than a hundred miles along rutted dirt roads to the Deep Creek Indian Reservation near the Utah-Nevada border. Once there he hired a Gosiute man in his sixties named Frank Bonamont to work as his informant for two or three days.[97]

The Gosiute territory was "true desert," he later wrote, and "one of the least favorable" areas among all those that Shoshone occupied. Sources of water were very scarce, and because water and food were so limited, he suggested, the human population was probably more sparse than in any other part of Western Shoshone territory. Predictably, there was no evidence of bands. "Gosiute culture and subsistence was fundamentally like that of other Shoshoni," he wrote, "but their environment is so exceptionally unproductive that their poverty was extreme." Many white explorers and travelers had commented to that effect, usually in the most unflattering terms.[98]

Steward continued on his journey, crossing into Nevada and heading northwest toward Fallon, where he hired a guide to take him into the guano caves. Taking the opportunity to see more of Southern Paiute territory, he drove hundreds of miles south to Las Vegas. He wanted to extend what he had learned from his informants in Ash Meadows, Nevada, a year before; and once in Las Vegas, he hired an informant for a day. Although it yielded rather little about the Southern Paiute of Las Vegas, his trip gave him another look at the town itself. Its population, then about eight thousand, would soon jump as the supply of water and electricity increased and the economy expanded.[99]

Nearby Boulder Dam, later renamed Hoover Dam, was widely viewed as the "eighth wonder of the world." Completed in 1936 at a cost of tens of millions of dollars, as well as some human lives, the dam's construction had proceeded quickly after the Colorado River was diverted around the site in the early 1930s. The government planned to recoup the cost of the dam by selling electricity to Los Angeles and other growing cities in water- and power-hungry southern California. After a long political struggle over water distribution, those faraway cities also captured some of the Colorado River's water. Years later, Steward would write about population growth, urbanism, and the politics and technology of water control in early civilizations. By the mid-1930s, through living and traveling in the American West, he had already witnessed many of the effects of water scarcity and control, both on the landscape and on human settlement.[100]

Returning to Utah, Steward hastily visited some Indian reservations in the southwestern part of the state before returning to Salt Lake City. In just a few months, he had driven thousands of miles in the desert, many of them over rough dirt roads, where he surveyed the landscape and questioned Indian men about how they had once lived. His field research during that summer and the previous one drew on the nineteenth-century survey tradition in anthropology, an approach also used by Powell. Steward had covered a vast area and had spent as much time observing the land as listening to people. The automobile and a growing network of roads across the American landscape had made it possible for him to do this in a matter of months. His own comments suggest that the pleasures of seeing the shifts in contours and colors and light, and the openness and remarkable scale of the landscape, compensated for difficulties with the human dimension of his work and the drudgery of compiling the culture element lists.[101]

Steward's approach to this fieldwork, while it had an undeniably geographic dimension, represented a reversal of Sauer's approach. Unlike Sauer, whose interest lay in how human activity transformed the landscape, Steward wondered how the natural environment had affected human activity, people's social behavior. His Great Basin research bore the unmistakable, but unrecognized, stamp of behaviorism in that it focused on how environment shapes behavior. In Steward's framework, however, the behaviorists' generalized concept of "environment" (the source of all stimuli external to the organism) had the specific meaning of the "natural environment," as he usually termed it. If he could not directly observe past behavior, in his travels through the desert he could at least see the environment that had, in some respects, shaped it.

Despite an exhaustive search, which had proven increasingly exhausting to his wife, Steward still had not found field evidence of the patrilineal band as his 1936 research drew to a close. As in 1935, he had learned that there were no bands, only family groups, in some areas; in others, people had lived in composite bands. Puzzled by the absence of the patrilineal band at the outset of his 1935 fieldwork, he had collected highly detailed information on subsistence and social life in each locality he visited. Compiling the culture element lists, while tedious, actually helped him in this effort by yielding an abundance of structured data. His ideas about ecological and social causes ("determinants") of sociopolitical organization thus drew on a wealth of localized detail, which would turn the projected "ecological paper" into a full-scale monograph.[102]

* * *

Eighteen years earlier, at the age of sixteen, Steward had boarded a train in Washington, D.C.; days later he stepped off another train in Owens Valley. To the west, he saw the gleaming white peaks of the Sierra Nevada and a valley that stretched out beneath the mountains and a brilliant blue sky. He stood at the western border of the Great Basin. Now, at the age of thirty-four and on the threshhold of a new stage in his career and personal life, he crossed the region's eastern border. Intent on pursuing his career and ambitious research plan, he left behind the mountains and deserts of the West and returned to the East, to the clouded skies and crowded city of his childhood.

Steward headed back to Washington in mid-October 1936, reaching his destination five days and twenty-four hundred miles later. He had covered more than seven thousand miles in a few months.[103] That journey marked the conclusion of his Great Basin fieldwork, if not the end of his search for the patrilineal band. Remembering and writing about the Great Basin would occupy him for years to come, but he would always write from a distance, drawing on his lived experience and personal memories of the region.

CHAPTER 9

WASHINGTON WAYS
AND MEANS

In late October 1936, when Steward resumed work in Washington, he faced the task of finishing his report for the BIA. Two months later, in December, the annual meeting of the American Anthropological Association was held in the city, but he did not attend. His first child, a son, had just been born and came home from the hospital in fragile health. Steward felt unwell himself after undergoing some minor surgery, which must have prompted more comments from his colleagues about couvade.[1]

He had felt ill throughout his unhappy year as consultant anthropologist with the BIA, and his health would worsen over time, particularly after his travels in South America in 1938. In December 1936, Steward felt especially unwell, perhaps because he had finally submitted his controversial report to the BIA, recommending against reservation lands for some Western Shoshone in Nevada. His recommendations put him in an adversarial position with the BIA, but he seemed to think that the findings of science, represented by his report, would inevitably prove convincing to misinformed policy makers.

Steward stated in his typewritten report, as he would in print, that most of the Western Shoshone had traditionally lacked any political groupings. From his ecological perspective, which he did not detail for the BIA but which he was working out in his ecological paper, this was due to the nature of their desert environment and food-getting techniques. Sparse and scattered resources, along with a simple and limited technology, had kept populations small and dispersed. As a result of these ecological conditions, Steward wrote, "the household was the independent political unit . . . among Western Shoshoni during most of the year."[2]

In his report, he argued that the fact that Western Shoshone had "a loose society, in which an individual's social horizon extended scarcely beyond his family" meant that reservations had no basis in tradition. He also regarded assimilation as inevitable. "I do not, of course, advocate enforced assimilation," he wrote, adding that "nature will take its course." Indeed, Steward reported that assimilation was already proceeding rapidly among younger people. He opposed "segregation on reservations," arguing that it would impede the process. His eighteen-page report made highly specific as well as general recommendations: for example, he opposed the suggestion of introducing "Navajo weaving, Hopi pottery, and other Indian arts" to Shoshone Indians as a way of earning income. "These industries are not understood, not wanted and would not have the necessary economic base to support them," he contended.

Describing Nevada Shoshone as "reasonably self-reliant and willing to work," Steward pointed out, "They are experienced as laborers, having worked on roads and at many odd jobs, and most of them are fairly competent ranch hands. In fact, they would probably be unusually successful in operating their own lands if they had them." As was common at the time, he used the word *they* in a general way, while in fact referring specifically to men. He excluded women, although their own subsistence and wage-earning activities certainly reinforced his point about the "willing[ness] to work." Steward also suggested that as ranch hands the Shoshone were not economic competitors with whites, but that as landowners they would be, with "race conflicts" a possible result.[3]

The commissioner for Indian affairs, John Collier, responded to the report in late December, just as the American Anthropological Association meetings got underway. His memorandum to an associate began with a list of objectionable excerpts from Steward's report. These provided a preface to Collier's comment that he did not view the report's contents "as factual reporting." "Even if some native traits could be preserved," Steward had written, "it is difficult to see what purpose they would serve." Another excerpt read, "Anything distinctively Indian about them merely brands them as queer and 'inferior'"—but this left out the final half of Steward's sentence. He had written, "Anything distinctively Indian about them merely brands them as queer and 'inferior' (rarely as picturesque) and enhances difficulties flowing from race prejudice." Still another excerpt—"Sincere devotion to the common good was completely foreign to Indian thinking"—was likewise a sentence fragment. Steward revealed something about his own outlook on humanity when he wrote, "But it is important to insist that sincere devotion to the common good was completely foreign to Indian thinking, in which respect they do not differ greatly from white men."[4]

Collier remarked at the end of his memorandum that he had found Steward "quite an attractive individual." He continued, "However, the shedding of light upon our complicated Indian problems needs something more." Collier concluded that this was yet another case in which expertise in a social science did not guarantee competence to deal with social problems. The memorandum was addressed to H. Scudder Mekeel, the anthropologist in charge of applied anthropology at the Office of Indian Affairs. A carbon copy went to Steward.[5]

Other memoranda followed, including one from Alida Bowler, superintendent of the Carson Agency in eastern Nevada. She commented on portions of the report that dealt with Shoshone living in Nevada and in Inyo County, California, encompassing the area from Owens Valley to Death Valley. She questioned the reliability of at least one of Steward's informants, as well as the accuracy of his census data, his definition of terms, and many of his observations. "The report presents a minimum of so-called 'facts,'" Bowler wrote, "and a maximum of 'interpretation' and recommendation based upon personal opinion." She concluded by saying that she planned to circulate a copy of her comments to those government workers who had read the Steward report and would soon go to "Nevada Shoshone country."[6]

Steward refused to amend his report or reply directly to Bowler's scathing memorandum. When he finally withdrew from the fray, he thought that his integrity and competence as a scientist had been called into question and his reputation as a scientist badly tarnished. Feeling that he had lost face, Steward carried away a sense of humiliation that would harden into an unshakeable disdain for applied anthropology. When he wrote to Kroeber a few weeks after the AAA meetings, he attributed his absence to ill health and said he had hoped to "break through the crowd" that inevitably surrounded Kroeber at professional meetings. But he had not even put in an appearance at the conference, perhaps reluctant to face Washington colleagues and others—including Kroeber—who might have heard about the unwelcome status of his report to the BIA.[7]

* * *

Sitting alone at his typewriter, he took his private revenge by writing two acts of a short play. Wickedly satirical, the play mocked the follies of prominent anthropologists, Indians in relation to the federal government, and selected BIA bureaucrats. Steward expressed disaffection with applied anthropology, contempt for BIA officials, and disdain for the established authorities of his field and their theories. Neither officials nor authorities would listen to him. By rejecting his report, BIA officials, from Collier to Bowler, had questioned his research and, at least indirectly, his new theoretical perspective on the Shoshone. At the same time, his essay "Ecological Aspects of Southwestern Society" had finally appeared in print, but it was exiled to an Austrian journal and greeted with silence.

With a certain grandiosity, Steward cast himself in the role of the good messenger who bears bad news, but who, in this case, cannot be vanquished. The short drama conveys his certainty that he was viewed as worse than hard-hearted by his critics at the BIA who wanted to help Indians resist assimilation. Steward, in contrast, saw himself as a hardheaded realist and scientist who harbored no illusions, including religious ones. Although his words can be read as a denial that the BIA episode had done him any real harm, his strong reaction suggests that he carried away a deep sense of injury.[8]

As he withdrew from the BIA, Steward increasingly found fault with Washington. To Lowie, he mentioned missing Berkeley and its informal intellectual debates: "The dangers of ossification in Washington," he wrote, "are now becoming apparent to me. And to keep ourselves alive, Duncan [Strong] and I are about to start a small discussion group." Whether his other colleagues at the BAE joined the group is not clear, but Steward's comment implied that they had succumbed to the very "ossification" he hoped to avoid. Most of the men were older, from their late forties to their sixties, compared to his thirty-five years, and had already spent years at the Smithsonian. (The professional staff, not surprisingly, included only men; the BAE sometimes supported research by women, but any affiliation was usually temporary.) His senior male colleagues stood at a very different point in their lives and their careers. Strong, in contrast, was just thirty-eight and, like Steward, a relative newcomer to the BAE.[9]

To judge from Steward's comment, in the wake of his BIA difficulties he regarded Washington as an intellectual backwater. Unlike Berkeley, a true university town, the federal government dominated Washington life. But the city had once been a major center of American anthropology, and when Steward arrived in the mid-1930s, it still had a sizable number of anthropologists employed by the Smithsonian, other federal agencies, and at least two universities, Catholic University and George Washington University.

The city was also home to the venerable Anthropological Society of Washington, founded in 1879 by Powell and others and the first sponsor of the *American Anthropologist*. Steward privately dismissed that group, however, with undisguised scorn. His choice of words, like the timing, was revealing: "The Washington Society, I may say, functions only to give popular lectures attended by fat and indolent females." His unsuccessful foray into applied anthropology had probably reminded him of the struggle during his first marriage to avoid being drawn exclusively into applied research with his wife. That struggle had also ended badly for him. Memories of her highly successful public lectures that applied behaviorist principles to child rearing—lectures sponsored by a Mormon women's organization—undoubtedly provoked his hostile words. He had likewise made assertions about male dominance, those now in print, immediately after his divorce.[10]

Most of the officers of the Anthropological Society of Washington and the speakers at its monthly meetings were men. Nearly all of those speakers, moreover, were professional anthropologists, many of them well known. Whatever Steward thought of the audience or the intellectual content of the lectures, attending the meetings gave him the opportunity to extend his professional contacts. He was elected to the board a few years later, in 1940. That same year, he served as chairman of the program committee for the annual meeting of the

American Anthropological Association, appointed by John M. Cooper, president of the association and a Washington colleague who shared some of his interests.[11]

"Father Cooper," as he was generally known, was a priest, chairman of the anthropology department at Catholic University, and editor of the journal *Primitive Man* (later called *Anthropological Quarterly*). He had a strong interest in North American hunter-gatherers, particularly Algonquian-speaking Indians in northeastern Canada and Great Plains Indians. He also published on South American ethnology, drawing on his extensive reading knowledge, as he had no field experience in the region. Very few North American anthropologists had firsthand knowledge of South America in the mid-1930s. Kroeber, who went to Peru twice in the 1920s to do archaeological work, qualified as one of those few.[12]

Steward's position at the BAE brought him many opportunities, the most important of which was editorship of the *Handbook of South American Indians*. He assumed that position about five years after joining the BAE and more than fifteen years after Lowie first discussed the project with Erland Nordenskiöld, the Swedish anthropologist who taught a course on South America during Steward's student days at Berkeley. Following those discussions and Nordenskiöld's death in 1932, the National Research Council appointed a committee of three members—Lowie, Cooper, and Spier—to plan the preparation of the *Handbook*. This small committee, appointed in the early 1930s, eventually grew to include other scholars.[13]

During Steward's first year at the BAE, and while he was still mired in liaison work with the BIA, he spoke of anticipating fieldwork in South America. In a letter to Kroeber, he pronounced himself "finished" with the Shoshone. This came at the same time that he declared himself finished with the BIA, which probably was not a coincidence. As he wrote to Kroeber, "I look forward now, as I think I told you, to the South American field." Nearly a year later, however, his plans for a trip to South America remained "vague and remote." In the meantime, he continued to work on his Great Basin monograph. "As far as I can tell now, I am through with the Basin for a while," he remarked to Kroeber, amending his sweeping vow of the previous year.[14]

By February 1938, Steward's South American travel plans had finally begun to take shape. "For a long time," he told Lowie, "the Araucanians have seemed to me a worthy objective. . . . And now it appears very possible that I shall be able to spend possibly 18 months in Chile." Exactly which group of Indians he would study remained undecided, but it appears that Steward hoped to study a functioning community of hunters, just as Strong had already done during a winter in Labrador. Still in search of the elusive patrilineal band, despite his disappointment in the Great Basin, he continued to believe that it had once been widespread in the world, and he thought he might discover evidence of it in Chile. Based on his reading, he had concluded that the Ona Indians of Tierra del Fuego, living in a cold and windswept land at the southern tip of South America, had once lived in such bands.[15]

The circumstances of the Ona were unknown to him. Most North American anthropologists of the time, Lowie as well as Cooper, had only reading knowledge of the continent, and the ethnographic sources were scattered, not easily accessible, of varying quality, and written in Spanish and several other European languages. The best published source on the Ona, by Martin Gusinde and written in German, convinced Steward to write to Gusinde, "who thanks to Herr Hitler, probably won't receive my letter," Steward complained. An associate of Wilhelm Koppers, Gusinde served with him as an editor of *Anthropos;* but Koppers, a severe critic of Nazi ideology, was stripped of his professorship at the University of Vienna in 1938 and left the country. He spent several years doing fieldwork with a tribal people in a remote region of India. Many scholars left Austria and Germany during those troubled times, perhaps including Gusinde.[16]

Steward also surmised that the Tehuelche Indians of Patagonia had previously lived in patrilineal bands. He had suggested in his 1936 article on bands that they developed larger and more complex groups, probably composite bands, after the introduction of the horse in the late eighteenth century.[17] In other words, the horse had changed the ecological conditions in which the Tehuelche lived in western South America, just as the horse had changed the way of life for Northern Shoshone living in the Lemhi Valley in western North America.

Groups such as the Tehuelche attracted Steward's attention in part because he thought that they had suffered less disruption in the course of European colonization than Indians in North America. The latter he privately characterized as "the broken-down Indian cultures of the United States." (As it happened, the very areas of cultural life that showed great continuity—religion, mythology, musical traditions, and so on—fell outside Steward's purview. These held the status of peripheral or secondary features in the ecological approach he eventually called "cultural ecology.") That the Tehuelche and neighboring Indians remained relatively unknown to North American anthropologists also attracted Steward, who told Lowie that Cooper considered one of the groups "ripe to be worked."[18]

Before he undertook any fieldwork, Stirling wanted Steward to spend about four months traveling from Colombia to Peru, "getting impressions of tribes along the eastern slope of the Andes," as Steward told Lowie. Stirling himself had worked briefly with the Jívaro in Ecuador six years earlier, giving him some idea of the region's research possibilities. His monograph on the Jívaro had just appeared in print as a BAE publication, and it, along with Strong's publications on Honduras, heralded the BAE's growing interest in Latin America.[19] As he had done from his first year at Berkeley, and always beneficially, Steward fell into step with Strong, his slightly older friend and more advanced colleague. From his earliest fieldwork in archaeology to his recent work on the patrilineal band, Steward had profited from following Strong's research very closely.

Steward hoped to learn from his own first trip to another continent "where the important problems and unstudied tribes lie," and then undertake intensive fieldwork. "I am somewhat loath to tackle South America in my present state of ignorance about the continent," he conceded. He had little choice, however, given the vagaries of the federal budget: funds were available and had to be used during the fiscal year, which ended shortly and thus made his departure imminent. The trip formed part of a long-term plan. As he explained to Lowie, "[My] future will be in South America. In short, I have eschewed, without too much regret, the sagebrush and the Shoshoneans."[20]

Other letters make it clear that Steward expected to find western South America very similar to western North America, in both its natural and its cultural landscapes. Perhaps this assuaged any regrets he had about leaving behind the mountains and deserts of his youth. It may also explain why the Araucanians, who lived in the shadow of a towering range of mountains, attracted his attention more than, say, Amazonian Indians. As he told Lowie, his hasty foray into South American ethnography suggested similarities "without end" between western North and South America. He was even intrigued to learn that one group of Araucanians, the Pehuenche, ate pine nuts. "Is there some destiny that draws me to pine nut eaters?" he wondered.[21]

A month before Steward's departure, his itinerary finally took shape. He had official approval to visit Ecuador, Peru, Chile, and Argentina, and plans to do archival work in Quito, Ecuador, and in Santiago, Chile. He also intended "to conduct certain ethnological researches" in the four countries, according to letters that Stirling wrote on his behalf. The main destination, however, was Chile and western Argentina, and the goal, fieldwork with Araucanian or neighboring Indians, whom he thought had once lived in patrilineal bands.[22]

Jane Steward's travel plans remained undecided until just weeks before departure. As Steward told Lowie, he did not know whether his wife would go along for the entire trip or join him in Chile at the end of his travels for fieldwork. "The question of finances will probably settle it definitely," he added. Among the reasons in favor of her making the entire trip was that she spoke Spanish, which she had learned while living in South America as a child. Official letters prepared for the upcoming trip listed her as "secretary and typist" and as "translator," noting that she would "assist in the research work and make necessary translations from the archives." Steward needed his wife's assistance, however, for more than archival work. He had only studied Spanish briefly himself, and many years earlier, as a student at Deep Springs.[23]

"I heed your remarks about my learning Spanish," he wrote to Lowie. "That shall be my first task."[24]

* * *

As it turned out, Jane, Julian, and their sixteen-month-old son left the United States together at the end of April 1938. The matter of finances had been settled just two weeks before their departure from Washington, with the BAE providing travel expenses for three and a generous stipend as well. They took the train to New York City, where they boarded a ship for South America. A small group of well-wishers crowded into their stateroom, including Julian's old friend Windsor Putnam, who practiced law in New York City, and Duncan Strong, who had recently joined the faculty of Columbia University.[25]

Julian had no previous experience of foreign travel, aside from brief forays across the Mexican border, where he had attended to the practical matters of getting a divorce and remarrying. Jane, however, had spent a year and half living in Colombia with her family, arriving when she was ten years old. Her father had a position managing a large cattle ranch, recently acquired by Utah investors, along the Río Magdalena. The family made a slow trip upriver by paddleboat along a broad corridor of water that wound its way through dense tropical forest. They settled in a Mompós, an old port town founded in the early sixteenth century, and were the only foreigners in residence there. Jane, always sociable, soon made friends with other children and learned to speak Spanish. Her stepmother, who had studied several languages herself and had lived briefly in Europe, helped her to retain her speaking ability when the family returned to Utah in 1919. The cattle business in Colombia had not proven profitable.[26]

Nine days after leaving New York City, the Stewards arrived in Guayaquil, Ecuador's main port and largest city. They traveled on to Quito, the capital, set at the foot of the volcanic mountain Pichincha, at an altitude of over nine thousand feet. Just days after arriving, their son ran a high fever, and within a few days Julian also had a fever, abdominal pain, and other symptoms. A physician told them that both father and son had amoebic infections, thus fulfilling Julian's worst fears about the "filthy" conditions he had complained of repeatedly during their brief time in Ecuador.[27]

Rest and medication helped his son, but Julian continued to feel unwell. Adding to their troubles, Jane discovered that she was pregnant, which only reinforced her wish to return home. Memories of her family's brief sojourn in South America—an idyllic time, as she remembered it—had not prepared her for the difficulties of a trip through the Andes in winter. In Colombia she had lived a settled and protected life, surrounded by her family. She recalled their comfortable house, a large and rambling structure, and the perpetual warmth of the tropical lowlands. But this time she felt like a wanderer, moving from one unknown place to another in a strange land, with a small child whose illness alarmed her. The unescapable chill and overcast sky in Quito, as well as a growing sense of exile, dampened her usually good spirits, and the prospect of eighteen months of transience did nothing to revive them. Her experience of summer fieldwork in the desert West, including those last four months during her first pregnancy, gave her some idea of what to expect—but this time in three foreign countries, in winter, and with one child in tow and another on the way.[28]

Six weeks after arriving in Ecuador, Julian Steward found himself unexpectedly alone there. He had finally managed to book passage for his wife and son to Panama, and then on to California. His own plans called for doing reconnaissance work on the eastern slope of the Andes, as Stirling had suggested, and continuing to Chile for fieldwork. But various problems, from travel logistics to language ("My Spanish seems not to progress at all," he wrote in his journal) discouraged him. Anxiety about his health increased, as did his unhappiness at being separated from his wife.

He traveled on to Lima, Peru, where he spent much of his time in the company of two visiting American archaeologists, Herbert Spinden and Wendell Bennett. Through them he met the prominent Peruvian archaeologists Julio Tello and Luis Valcárcel, who showed him various sites outside of Lima. One day they drove up the Rimrac Valley and explored agricultural terraces that extended several hundred feet up the mountain slope. Walls of stone, from one to fifteen feet high, supported the terraces, which ranged from six to thirty feet in width. Impressed by the labor needed to build and maintain the terraces, Steward mused about population growth during Andean prehistory: "It is difficult to understand why the Peruvian population, more than [others] elsewhere, expanded to the limits of production so as to be forced to such measures." His unusual awareness of population density and growth would underlie his thinking about the development of early civilizations. That awareness derived from his own experience and a personal preference for low population density, realized after he traded city living in the East for ranch life in the West.[29]

Steward also visited Pachacámac, located about twenty miles south of Lima. In a stark setting of desert and bare hills, Pachacámac had been the largest coastal city when the Spaniards arrived, looted the temples, and killed the priests. "Its size surpasses anything I imagined," Steward commented in his journal, adding a detailed description of the site. He observed with regret that modern looters had also been at work, leaving "rejected bones, textiles, and shards strewn about." He found the same evidence of looting at the ruins of the pre-Incan city of Cajamarquilla. As he approached the site with Tello, Steward saw "a large pyramid which loomed like a mountain through the heavy fog." Back in Lima that night, he discussed Peruvian archaeology with Bennett, who argued against some of Tello's interpretations. Steward also had many conversations about Andean archaeology with Spinden, often over dinner.[30]

Bennett and Spinden soon left Lima, and Steward departed as well. His trip to Cuzco, made partly by train, took him across the altiplano, a desolate and windswept plateau framed by the snow-clad peaks of the Andes. "Mostly arid," Steward wrote, "this being the dry season." He noted a scattering of small stone huts and villages, as well as "beautiful peaks with surprisingly large glaciers." As always in his travels, his best moments were spent observing a landscape of stark beauty and massive scale in which nature dwarfed culture. Arriving at Cuzco that evening, he checked into a hotel on the outskirts, feeling exhausted and unable to eat.

Steward had talked to several miners that day who told him about a "new and vicious variety" of malaria that had killed many people on the eastern slope of the Andes, in the very region he intended to visit. On the following day, his first in Cuzco, he contacted Bernard Mishkin, a young anthropologist in his midtwenties who had already earned a Ph.D. from Columbia University. Mishkin had just spent about seven months working in a Quechua village in the mountains, but he told Steward that he "had been afraid to go in" to the malarial areas of the wet, densely forested lower slope. "We spent the entire day discussing alternate plans," Steward wrote in his journal. "I finally went to sleep with nightmares of indecision."[31]

He soon concluded that the prevalence of malaria made the trip impossible and decided to abandon all exploratory travel and fieldwork with Araucanian Indians: "Chile is out," he wrote. Still feeling unwell, he spent several days in bed. One overcast afternoon he roused himself to go with a Peruvian acquaintance to see some Incan and pre-Incan ruins, including Sacsayhuamán, located above Cuzco. Returning to bed, Steward arrived at a new self-diagnosis: "The weakness, insomnia, [rapid] pulse, and indigestion are essentially nerves, which I now incline to regard as a cause rather than effect." The series of small catastrophes that had marred the trip, his persisting unease with an alien language and culture, his physical discomfort with the damp cold, and perhaps especially his wife's departure had left him feeling adrift and utterly alone.[32]

Yet during seven weeks in Peru, Steward had actually spent much of his time in the company of Americans, from Spinden and Bennett to various businessmen. Peruvian colleagues who spoke English had also repeatedly helped him and shown him many kindnesses. He had even enjoyed an unusual level of physical comfort, especially as compared to Mishkin, who had lived in a highland village for seven months. Still, his anxiety persisted. He worried about the "unbelievable filth" of the communal bathroom in his hotel in Cuzco; the possibility of contracting malaria, yellow fever, or another infectious disease; and the source of his continuously elevated heart rate, which he reported in one journal entry as 95 to 100 beats per minute. His Andean travels would, in fact, leave him with other, lingering health problems, having nothing to do with his racing heart, but the damage had probably already been done.[33]

The day after Steward saw one of his acquaintances in Cuzco in the grip of a malaria attack, he wrote to Stirling to inform him that there would be no trip to the eastern slope. He wondered about how to account for his aborted journey—an eighteen-month field trip reduced to a few months of travel—once he returned to Washington. "I have an idea that it will be hard to explain to the Smithsonian the fiasco of this trip, though my own conscience is clear," he concluded, "but it is good to know that whatever I do will be OK with Jane."[34]

When he arrived in California a few weeks later, Jane Steward could see immediately that her husband had lost a great deal of weight, at least twenty pounds. Just over six feet tall, he weighed only about 150 pounds. Months later, she remembered that he had looked "terribly thin and drawn and in need of good rest which he hasn't had yet—probably never will have."[35]

She had spent most of the summer in the Los Angeles area, staying with relatives. Originally she planned to go almost directly to San Francisco to visit Grace Steward and introduce her first grandchild, who bore her family name. (He was named Garriott Cannon Steward, and his parents later called him Gary.) Her relief at being in a warm, dry place was so great, Jane Steward remembered, and the hospitality so generous, that she delayed the trip. She and her son spent only a week in foggy San Francisco before returning to the cloudless skies and warmth of southern California. As she recalled it months later, "Our simple life there in the country was nothing more than a trip to the mail box for word from Julian, dishes to wash, and weeds to pull. So passed the rest of the summer."

After her husband arrived, they spent another two weeks in Los Angeles and probably visited his sister before she moved back to San Francisco. Marion and Grace Steward had lived apart during the previous year. Six months after taking a clerical position with the Social Security Board in San Francisco, Marion had applied for a transfer to the Los Angeles office. She moved there in fall 1937 and was living in a residential hotel when her sister-in-law and nephew arrived in June 1938. Grace had soon given up the cottage in Mill Valley and returned to San Francisco, where Jane visited her during July. Sometime in October, Marion moved back to San Francisco, citing her mother's health as the reason for requesting the transfer. She and Grace lived together on Stanyan Street for about a year, at which point Marion applied again for a transfer, this time to Santa Rosa, California. Grace remained in San Francisco.[36]

* * *

Jane and Julian left Los Angeles with their son in October 1938 and returned to the East. They stayed with friends in Virginia while they searched for a house that offered more room than an apartment for what would soon be a family of four. Two weeks later, they located an eight-room house on Marion Avenue in McLean, Virginia. After they moved in ("a family again," in Jane's words, to her obvious satisfaction), they spent three weeks putting the house in order and settling in to domestic life. Once reunited with his wife, Julian's depression had lifted and his health improved.[37]

Returning to work at the Smithsonian, he resumed a commute across the Potomac River and into Washington. More than two years earlier, he and Jane had given up the cramped apartment on Belmont Road, renting a larger, more expensive apartment on Key Boulevard in Arlington. Their move to the house in McLean, then a village surrounded by farmland, took them even farther from city center. This pattern would repeat itself in the future. Career demands and ambitions kept Steward near two major eastern cities, Washington and New York, for the next fourteen years, but he chose to live at a distance. A few months' residence in hotels in Miami and Washington and six months at the Belmont

Road address comprised his city living once he returned to the East. Always preferring open land to brick and concrete, he remained supremely indifferent to cities and any pleasures of urban life.[38]

Back at his desk at the BAE, where he kept notably casual hours rather than those of a civil servant, Steward turned his attention again to publication. He sent off several more manuscripts for various series sponsored by the Smithsonian. Like a number of papers written during this period, their value lay largely in being publishable, not in contributing to his long-term research plan. The topics were peripheral to his ecological interests, but he understood that the length of a list of publications contributed directly to professional success.[39]

Steward had submitted what stands as one of his major works—the "ecological paper" on the Great Basin, grown to the size of a monograph—before leaving for South America. It appeared in print as a BAE *Bulletin* in 1938, and soon after received positive notice in the *American Anthropologist.* The reviewer of *Basin-Plateau* did observe that Steward examined "social organization from the ecological perspective," but without defining his terms: "He is clear in his own mind, but he has not passed his clarity on to his readers. Such concepts are not yet standard enough to pass by without definition." While some readers might disagree with Steward's interpretation of field data, the reviewer continued, "his sincerity, sanity, and objectivity cannot be suspected. . . . Indeed, there is a ring of realism to all his people." Despite earning praise as "magnificent . . . [and] a genuinely scholarly job," *Basin-Plateau* attracted little immediate attention beyond a narrow circle of scholars. Decades passed before it gained wider recognition and the status of a classic ethnographic work. By the time the work was reprinted, Steward had attained the stature of a major scholar in his field, and he had spelled out his ideas about cultural ecology in greater detail—both of which retroactively enhanced the reputation of his book.[40]

The advantages of his position at the Smithsonian included ready outlets for publication as well as generous support for research and writing. As Steward himself admitted, he had rather few competing duties. Among them was replying to questions from the public. Frequent queries about petroglyphs passed across his desk, leading him to complain to a friend at Telluride Association that "we are continually plagued by letters [about petroglyphs] from every goof in the country."[41]

A few months after moving into the house in McLean, Jane Steward gave birth to their second son, Michael. He was their last child, his birth "completing our duties to posterity," his father remarked to Kroeber a month later. Because of complications with this pregnancy, Jane Steward was advised not to bear more children. She complied, and without regret, entirely happy with her two young sons and family life as it was.[42]

By spring 1939 the BAE had decided to sponsor the *Handbook of South American Indians,* even before Congress had approved funds for the project. Steward lobbied for the position of editor and was appointed, although there appear to have been other contenders. He had little to say in letters to colleagues about his travels in Ecuador and Peru. To Kroeber he commented simply, "You no doubt heard something of my trip. It was not highly successful from the point of view of field work but I did get some very vivid impressions of South America." Eventually, Congress passed a bill that granted funds to the BAE for the *Handbook* as part of its Good Neighbor policy toward Latin America.[43]

Steward spent quite a bit of time in 1939 laying the groundwork for the *Handbook,* conceived of as a five-year, two-volume project. He consulted with Father Cooper at Catholic University, traveled to New York City to discuss plans with Strong and other archaeologists, attended a small conference at the University of Michigan on Latin American bibliography, and made a trip to Berkeley to see Kroeber, Lowie, and Spier. At some point, he met with the committee that the National Research Council had created in the early 1930s to take charge of planning the *Handbook.* Steward and the committee outlined the contents in a preliminary way and drew up a tentative list of ninety contributors from North America, Latin America, and Europe. About forty Latin American scholars were eventually invited to contribute.[44]

This marked the beginning of a project that would consume far more of his time than Steward could foresee at that point, when even the funding had not yet been approved. Its ambitious goal, providing "a compendium of all [that was then] known about South American Indians," would result in the *Handbook* growing from two volumes, as first conceived, to six. Years later, Steward remembered this period at the BAE as one that required "many detours" in his long-range research plan and led him away from field research. But to put this another way, the *Handbook* gave him the "privilege," as he had once put it, "of not being in the field for a time." It accommodated his personal life. He disliked spending time away from his wife, and she, in turn, appreciated the trappings of settled life and domesticity, especially as the mother of young children.[45]

* * *

Steward carried out his last fieldwork, with Carrier Indians in western Canada, during summer 1940, just before Stirling appointed him as *Handbook* editor and two years after the failed field trip to South America. For the first time since his second marriage, he went alone. The BAE would not have paid his family's expenses, and experience had convinced him of the difficulties of fieldwork with small children. His younger son was just a year old, and his older son three, when he left for British Columbia in late May 1940. He spent about two months on his own, six weeks of it with the Carrier.[46]

One purpose of his Canadian fieldwork may have been to fulfill the vow made in his journal two years earlier: to compensate for what he privately called the "mess" of his South American journey by making a productive trip outside of the United States. The Carrier perhaps provided a substitute for the Araucanian

Indians he had set out to study in Chile or Argentina. And Canada qualified as a foreign country, albeit one that shared a border and language with the United States. This trip would also further his long-range research plan. Steward viewed the Carrier as "a people a little more complex" than the Shoshone. Unlike the Paiute and Shoshone, fish and game provided the major portion of the Carrier diet, and the men still hunted.

Steward had classified Carrier bands as composite in his 1936 essay, but he thought that the ecological conditions had "favor[ed] patrilineal or composite bands." It appears that Steward suspected a previous history of patrilineal bands; he was inclined to think of the composite band as a form that emerged when various factors "prevented" patrilocal residence. The Carrier had been recommended, among all of the Canadian Athabaskans, as the most accessible and most suitable for his study. In spring 1940, he wrote to Kroeber about his plans: "I am probably going to take a crack at Carrier and, if I have time, Tsimshian ecology this summer."[47]

Steward arrived in British Columbia at the beginning of June 1940. He had briefly visited western Canada ten years earlier on his honeymoon with his first wife and had some idea of what to expect. "The Carrier country," as he later described it, was "still a vast wilderness of lakes and forest-covered mountains." Although Carrier culture had changed fundamentally after white settlement, the land remained "unchanged by civilization," which undoubtedly explained a good part of its attraction for him. His field site, a village on the southern end of Stuart Lake, lay at the end of a road and forty miles from the rail terminus. While suitably remote, Fort St. James also offered a range of amenities. Steward later described it as "nearly ideal from the anthropologist's point of view." "Several hotels provide comfortable accommodations," he explained, "and stores and trading posts afford essential needs. The Indians are friendly and intelligent, most of them speaking English fluently, and many are excellent informants."[48]

He found lodging at the Hotel Fort St. James: "A country Hotel with modern conveniences, Moderate prices and home-like atmosphere," according to its letterhead stationery. Within days, Steward began working with Chief Louis Billy Prince, then in his midseventies and a "marvelous informant," as Steward described him to Stirling. He worked with him for several weeks, rarely consulting others except to verify specific points. Nyswander's once-challenging question about methodology—"Just *one* old man?"—no longer seemed to trouble him. He had worked out the fundamentals of what he later called "the method of cultural ecology" in his Great Basin fieldwork, and he seems to have used the same approach in western Canada. He concentrated on subsistence, labor patterns, and food-getting technology—aspects of what he eventually came to call the "cultural core."[49]

In advance, Steward had spent time studying a 200-page manuscript on the Carrier, recently obtained from Diamond Jenness, a well-known anthropologist. He recommended it highly to Stirling ("It is a perfectly swell job on social organization and religion"), and asked if the BAE could publish it. Jenness, he explained, had virtually "quit anthropology." He added that his sudden indifference toward "anthro is curious & inexplicable, being [due to] more than war work." Jenness, for many years an ethnologist with the National Museum of Canada, did intelligence work during the war years, and then retired from the museum after the war. What made his lack of interest in anthropology so curious in 1940 was his position as president of the American Anthropological Association in 1939.[50]

His manuscript, which Steward obviously admired, apparently remained unpublished and uncited, but it affected at least Steward's initial view of the Carrier. He also appears to have had an unpublished culture element list for the Carrier, collected for Kroeber's project. Like his informal discussions with colleagues and his field observations, unpublished manuscripts remained uncited in his publications. (This may have been a common practice at the time. Or perhaps he and others took Kroeber's well-known dictum—"What isn't published doesn't exist"—literally.)[51] As unacknowledged sources, their importance would go unrecognized by future readers.

Working intensively with his able informant, Steward accomplished a great deal in a short time. In a period of weeks, he managed to map hunting territories, compile genealogies, reconstruct the traditional subsistence pattern, and outline the major social and economic changes that had taken place. The Carrier, he concluded, had once lived in small bands and hunted together in the same territory. "There is insufficient evidence," he finally decided long after his fieldwork, "to know whether it was composite or patrilineal." Later, Carrier society took on matrilineal features, including matrilineal, exogamous clans, due to diffusion from the matrilineal Tsimshian. Still later, after the introduction of the fur trade and the arrival of Catholic missionaries, the clans broke down, along with matrilineal inheritance of hunting lands. "By the beginning of the present century," Steward wrote, "nearly every Carrier had his own land [for hunting and trapping] and used it exclusively to support his own family."[52]

Six weeks after arriving in British Columbia, a letter from the Smithsonian reached Steward at Fort St. James. Before returning to Washington, he was to proceed several hundred miles northwest to Ketchikan, on the southern tip of Alaska's coast, to examine an archaeological site. Steward left Canada for Alaska soon after, in late July, with material he used over a twenty-year period for several brief articles on the Carrier. The first of them seemed to argue against the central tenets of cultural ecology and to reverse his line of reasoning in "Ecological Aspects of Southwestern Society." He quickly concluded, for example, that Carrier social organization had changed profoundly from a system of bands to matrilineal clans, but in the absence of any material cause ("without any modifications of their economic basis of life"). Years later, he would reconsider some of his ideas about the Carrier in light of others' field research—Eleanor

Leacock's in eastern Canada and Robert Murphy's in Brazil—and reach somewhat different conclusions, at least about the causes of recent change.[53]

Steward's six weeks in British Columbia marked the end of his field research; he would never undertake extended fieldwork again. At the age of thirty-eight, he had reached a point common among midcareer anthropologists in university settings. Nine-month teaching schedules, along with other professional duties and the general scarcity of funds for field research, continue to have limiting effects on fieldwork. Steward's position at the BAE differed in many respects, however, from most academic positions. The BAE funded his research rather generously, and he did not teach, although he occasionally advised "other people's students" who found their way to the Smithsonian. In later years, he remarked that administrative and editorial tasks consumed nearly all of his time during his last years at the BAE.[54]

His editorial work on the *Handbook* actually served as a vehicle for his own research by providing a massive amount of empirical data. It had the advantage of eliminating the need to do fieldwork himself. One piece of proverbial wisdom in anthropology—that forgoing fieldwork enables theorists to do their work unencumbered by data—did not apply to Steward. He wanted empirical data, and the more the better; he did not want to spend long periods alone in the field gathering it by himself. The disappointing results of his study of Carrier ecology, close on the heels of his Andean travels, may have persuaded him to turn in that direction, away from further field research on his own. Steward had hoped to find hunters who gave evidence of a patrilineal past, but in South America he had not even glimpsed their territory. In British Columbia he had encountered a society whose former, matrilineal features he could explain only by resorting to diffusion.

A passage that he wrote years before he visited the Carrier reveals the nature of his expectations and his view toward matrilineality. In telling language, Steward wrote that "ecological conditions *favored* patrilineal or composite bands but allowed latitude for other patterns, and [the matrilineal] Northwest Coast influence seems to have *destroyed* the composite bands among most of the Western Athabaskans" (emphasis added). Matrilineality, which in his thinking presumed matrilocal residence, appeared aberrant, destructive, and almost without rational explanation (adjectives he might have used after the fact to describe his own experience of "matrilocal" residence in Salt Lake City). A society structured around men—the patrilineal band—made eminent sense to him, but one in which ties with women were primary could only be explained by the unpredictable vagaries of diffusion. He had mentioned the possibility of matrilineal bands in his 1936 essay on bands, but he removed any reference to them in the later, revised version in *Theory of Culture Change*.[55]

How much he learned about "ecological conditions" directly from his fieldwork in Fort St. James is unclear. Unlike his Great Basin research—carried out in an environment he knew intimately, and in which he spent as much time observing the land as talking to the people who lived on it—his Carrier fieldwork took place in a virtual terra incognita. Central British Columbia, a densely forested and well-watered region, was entirely new and alien to him; moreover, he spent only a few weeks there, and most of it, by his own account, working with one informant. Despite an early comment to the contrary—"The phratry, clan, and potlatch business complicates everything but makes it damned interesting from a theoretical point of view"—his 1940 fieldwork seemed to lead up a blind alley.[56]

Besides the discouraging results of his Carrier field research, personal concerns also constrained further fieldwork. In Steward's professional world, as a rule, men did not admit to such concerns, considering it "unprofessional" to let personal matters intrude into the workplace. But as Steward's life circumstances changed, the costs of fieldwork appear to have grown to a point where the professional rewards did not compensate. The trip to Ecuador in 1938 had complications and difficult moments, but it took a turn for the worse with the departure of his wife and their son. While Steward had a number of reasons for leaving Peru and passing up fieldwork in southern Chile, the prospect of a long separation from his wife clearly troubled him the most. After the early 1940s, he rarely spent more than a few days at a time away from home; whenever possible he worked at home rather than in his office. He seemed strangely unwilling to spend time apart from his wife, and over the years his dependence on her increased.[57]

By 1940 Steward had been happily married for seven years to a woman who supported his professional work and had followed him from place to place, but who did not find the wandering life agreeable. His wife had not expected to lead a nomadic life when she married a university professor who happened to be an anthropologist. He also had two children, secure employment, and a mortgage, the hallmarks of middle-class status and social maturity for men of his generation. Stated in terms they used themselves, whether or not in reference *to* themselves, Jane and Julian could finally begin to enjoy some of the advantages of sedentary life, their means of subsistence finally stable and secure.

The years of repeated dislocations—very common in the early stages of a career in anthropology—had taken a certain toll on Jane. Relentlessly cheerful, she did not openly complain about it, then or later. But nine moves in seven years, with twelve months on the road in the West and South America, had given their early married life a seminomadic quality. Jane embraced their new rootedness: they were finally "put," as she had wished from the first year of marriage. She and her family had just moved into a new house near Langley, Virginia, along a meandering country road not far from the Potomac River. The tumbleweed days were over.[58]

Whether or not Julian Steward made a conscious decision about it, he turned away from field research. Unlike Ralph Beals and Cora Du Bois, among others of his generation trained at Berkeley, he did not shift from the informant method of fieldwork to one based on cultural immersion and extended periods of participant observation. Instead, and for reasons that were not solely intellectual, he gave most of his attention to editorial work and to his own writing and theoretical interests, which kept him at his desk and at home. Back from the field in August 1940, he began work in earnest on the *Handbook of South American Indians.*

* * *

Along with his trip to Canada, the *Handbook* provided a way of compensating for the hapless trip to South America in 1938. Without it, Steward would have had little to show for the nearly five months he spent away from the BAE and the thousands of dollars in expenses. Editing the *Handbook* transformed his journey from a dead end into a "detour," as he put it, in his long-range research plan.[59] At some point, he realized that the editorial project could contribute to his goal of studying the whole range of human societies, from the simple to the more complex. The detour even offered a shortcut since it allowed him to bypass further fieldwork himself.

By editing the *Handbook,* he could capitalize on the labor of more than eighty other scholars, most of them archaeologists and ethnographers, who had carried out fieldwork documenting the full range of native societies in South America. They would provide an enormous amount of ethnographic and archaeological data, which he in turn could use, as he had in his work on bands and on the Southwest. Once again, he would attempt to synthesize a mass of empirical evidence, taking an inductive approach to find patterns and make generalizations about cause and effect. In this case, however, he did not have to settle for what happened to be available in print; instead, he could actually tailor it to suit his own research purposes.

Steward's position as editor allowed him to set the format for the articles, instruct authors to cover selected topics, and do so in a given order. These reflected his own theoretical leanings and a distinction between core cultural features and secondary ones. Leading the way in the cultural summaries were sections on subsistence, settlement pattern, technology, economy, and social and political organization. He relegated other, secondary topics—including life cycle, religion, mythology, and folklore—to the pages that followed. As Steward later explained, his synthesis and summary of *Handbook* material represented another step in his long-range research plan. Its very organization also constituted a step.[60]

During his six remaining years at the Smithsonian, he oversaw the complicated task of compiling the *Handbook.* He contacted potential contributors, explained the project and payment schedule, sent out contracts, dictated letters of reminder, found substitute contributors for those who failed to meet deadlines, arranged for translations of material written in languages other than English, and edited the final copy. The Central Translating Division of the Department of State did much of the translation, and his secretary, the able and engaging Ethelwyn Carter, assisted him with the ever increasing correspondence. (Steward, after hastily typing a letter to Lowie, one with its share of erratic punctuation and spelling errors, added a handwritten postscript: "Miss Carter . . . sends regards—and says don't blame this typing on her.") Two anthropologists, Alfred Métraux and Gordon Willey, also joined the staff of the BAE for several years to assist with the *Handbook*. Unlike Steward, both men had field experience in South America.[61]

Métraux, then in his late thirties, knew South America well. He had spent years of his childhood in Argentina, where his father practiced as a surgeon. After studying in Europe, with Nordenskiöld among others, he returned to Argentina and held a university post there for six years. By the early 1940s when he joined Steward at the BAE, Métraux had published extensively on South American ethnology. His articles, written in French, Spanish, and English, appeared in a variety of journals in Europe, Latin America, and North America. Fluent in several European languages, he read widely and had an unusual command of the literature on South America. Most of the ethnographic works in print at the time were in Spanish, Portuguese, Italian, French, and German. In Steward's own words, Métraux brought "an unsurpassed knowledge of South American ethnology" to the task of compiling the *Handbook*. Although only Steward's name appeared on the title page as editor, Métraux made such a major contribution that some of his colleagues considered him a coeditor, at least informally.[62]

Willey joined the project a few years after Métraux. Thirty years old at the time, Willey had earned a Ph.D. at Columbia University, working closely with Strong. He had served as Strong's assistant on an archaeological project in Peru two years earlier and had stayed on for seven months after Strong left, excavating at several sites. Just as Métraux brought firsthand knowledge of South American ethnology to the project, Willey provided direct experience from his archaeological work in Peru.

Both men not only helped Steward with the diverse tasks of producing the *Handbook* but also contributed text. Métraux may well have written more pages than any other contributor. Steward also pressed Willey into service almost immediately, asking him to write about the archaeology of the Argentine pampas. Never mind that Willey knew nothing about that region; a paper on the topic was long overdue, with no sign that the designated scholar in Argentina would produce it and the volume's deadline looming. With marching orders in hand, and some bibliographic suggestions from Steward, Willey set to work. After about a month of library work, he produced an article that duly appeared in the first volume. Many years later, Willey remembered that while Steward had high standards in scholarship, he was "not a perfectionist." These qualities, he added, served Steward well as editor, allowing the completion of the *Handbook*—and on schedule at that, despite the war.[63]

When the United States declared war on Japan in December 1941, Steward was nearly forty years old, beyond the age to be drafted or to enlist. He belonged to that small, fortunate cohort of American men who were slightly too young for military service during World War I, and slightly too old during World War II. He and many other anthropologists, women as well as men, undertook war-related work as civilians instead. They arrived in Washington "at the rate of about one a day," according to Steward, and took positions with a range of agencies.[64]

Still others, especially young men, enlisted or were drafted. Mishkin, whom Steward had met in Cuzco in 1938, was serving on a destroyer in the Atlantic when he submitted a manuscript for the *Handbook*. The young Claude Lévi-Strauss, who would later enjoy international prominence in anthropology, had left France for refuge in the United States, thus avoiding the German occupation and transport to a concentration camp. Finding himself eligible for the draft in America, he reportedly withdrew his papers for U.S. citizenship. Steward's comment to Lowie about this reveals something of his own values: "A drastic move," Steward wrote, "but nothing else could save [Lévi-Strauss] for work that is far more valuable than being a soldier." He referred here to scientific work, a term he often used. Ironically, twenty years later he would take aim at Lévi-Strauss's structuralism, calling it dogma rather than science.[65]

Steward clearly believed that his own work at the Smithsonian furthered science while supporting national interests during wartime. Funding for the *Handbook* and for a later project, the Institute of Social Anthropology, came from the Department of State. As part of the Good Neighbor policy, an aspect of Roosevelt's 1930s foreign policy, the federal government supported programs that fostered closer relations with Latin American countries. An obvious goal during the war years was to keep them aligned with the United States and, more broadly, the Allied forces.[66]

By coincidence, Steward's former wife also spent the war years in Washington and traveled frequently to South America in support of the same national purpose. Nyswander joined a new wartime agency, the Inter-American Education Foundation, in the early 1940s, where her duties included teaching courses on public health education in Ecuador, in both Guayaquil and Quito. Years later, she remembered her time in Ecuador—and subsequent trips to Brazil, Peru, and Chile—with great fondness and spoke warmly of the people she met. She did not cross paths with her former husband on his later travels in South America.[67]

In February 1942 Steward made his second trip to South America, this time on official *Handbook* business. He hoped to recruit more contributors and collect illustrative material. The trip began inauspiciously, he later told Lowie, when the train he took from Washington had a head-on collision near Miami. Several people died, and many others suffered injuries. Steward escaped with only a broken rib, but he missed his flight from Miami and had to wait over for a few days. The trip by air to Belém, Brazil, required two full days since the airplane flew only during daylight hours. Even so, Steward found the "violent speed" impressive as he covered "distances that primitive man never really made in a single voyage, however long." Flying above the clouds for the first time, he felt as if he had entered some other part of the universe. But at last the airplane "suddenly dived down thru the clouds," he wrote, "[and] into the steaming tropics."

Arriving in Belém, he found himself at the gateway of the Amazon River. The city surprised him, both by its large size and by its being "far more civilized" than he had expected, filled with old and stately buildings. His host, Curt Nimuendajú, surprised him as well. An authority on Amazonian Indians, with whom he had worked for almost forty years, Nimuendajú had already published extensively, primarily in German. (Lowie translated several of his articles and monographs into English to make them available to a broader audience, and the two men also published together). Despite his achievements, Nimuendajú had an unassuming air. Steward thought him "a bit on the shy side."[68]

Then nearly sixty years old, Nimuendajú was German by birth but a naturalized citizen of Brazil. Arriving in Brazil in 1903 at the age of twenty, he had soon discovered his lifework as an anthropologist. Lacking any university education, he became an anthropologist by virtue of his years of field experience, not by formal training. In his earliest fieldwork, the Apapócuva-Guaraní held a traditional ceremony and gave him his Indian surname. Eventually Curt Nimuendajú Unckel became simply Curt Nimuendajú. When Steward met him in 1942, he had reputedly spent at least a part of every year since 1905 doing fieldwork in the interior, sometimes supported by grants, but often financing the work himself.[69]

Nimuendajú represented a vanishing breed in anthropology: self-trained, self-financed, an explorer who entered poorly known regions and, once there, mapped them. Besides his abilities as an ethnographer, he had great skill as a cartographer. Based in part on his own travels, he had produced what Steward described as an "unbelievably wonderful" ethnographic map, one that had no counterpart in the United States. Measuring six feet by eight feet, the map showed much of South America. Steward, who had experience in making and using maps, praised Nimuendajú's map for both its artistic and its scientific merits. It could be published, he told Lowie, "just as it stands."

With Nimuendajú as his guide, Steward visited Belém's museum to see its extensive collections of Amazonian material. They selected various specimens to photograph, intending them as illustrations for the *Handbook*. Ever a generous host, Nimuendajú also invited Steward to his house several times and introduced his Afro-Brazilian wife. Steward's surprise at meeting her may have been due to hearing in advance that Nimuendajú had an Indian wife, or it may have reflected his own everyday experience as a white American. Washington was still racially segregated in 1942, and Steward worked for an institution in which staff positions clearly showed an ordering by race as well as gender. In addition, he lived in Virginia, where interracial marriage was illegal. Brazil presented a rather different picture from the United States.[70]

Leaving Belém, Steward flew nearly two thousand miles south to Rio de Janeiro. The landscape, as always, seized his attention. The flight took him first over "solid, flat jungle [that] gradually gave way to broken, bushy land with mesas and deep valleys." Later in the afternoon, the plane crossed the mountains of Minas Gerais, which "culminated in shapely peaks," he observed, "then dropped away to reveal the magnificent bay of Rio." Flying at only eight to ten thousand feet, Steward saw many signs of settlement below, not the unbroken wilderness he had expected.

After spending just one night in Rio de Janeiro, he left Brazil and flew on to Argentina. In Buenos Aires, which he found "quite a bustling center of civilization," he contacted a number of cultural anthropologists and archaeologists, no doubt most of them known to Métraux. They promised to contribute to the *Handbook,* and several eventually did so. Like the archaeologist who failed to submit the pampas article that Willey finally wrote, other would-be contributors did not meet Steward's very firm deadlines. This limited the number of articles by Latin American authors in the *Handbook.*

Following a few weeks in Buenos Aires, Steward planned to visit northern and northwestern Argentina. He had more anthropologists to meet, perhaps in San Miguel de Tucumán, where Métraux had once held a university post. Before continuing on to Chile, he also hoped to have a "glimpse" of Mataco Indians in the arid, thinly populated Gran Chaco region, probably South America's closest counterpart to the Great Basin. Métraux, who must have recommended the Mataco to Steward, had recently published an article on them and was preparing another. He also wrote the *Handbook*'s chapter on the Indians of the Gran Chaco, describing their region as "a dry country" with scattered sources of water, where most river waters "are lost in the sands."[71]

This vast area bordered by mountains and hills, arid and often hot, and characterized by interior drainage, surely struck a chord with Steward. It probably also seemed a likely place to find a patrilineal band, reconstructed through informants' memories. Although he later listed the Gran Chaco as a site of field research, any visit he made there was brief, and no publication resulted from it. Perhaps this had some relation to the fact that Indians of the Gran Chaco "seem to have been strongly matrilineal," as he and a colleague wrote years later. Chaco Indians may have lived in matrilineal bands before contact, they suggested, but by the early colonial period most lived in larger composite (or "multilineage") bands, due to the pressure of conflict with other nomadic Indians and Spaniards.[72]

Matrilineal bands did not engage Steward's interest, although he had listed them as the third type of band—patrilineal, composite, matrilineal—in his 1936 essay. His discussion of that type had consisted, however, of just one sentence: "Matrilineal bands may arise if women are economically of sufficient importance, as for example, in many horticultural societies." He clearly had not expected to find matrilineal bands among hunter-gatherers in the Gran Chaco, and he made no real effort to explain what evidently struck him as an anomaly. Offering several caveats about how little was known about the Chaco Indians before contact, he dropped the matter.[73] In the years following his trip to South America, Steward only occasionally mentioned the patrilineal band in print, but it remained the foundational concept of his thinking. By the mid-1950s, he would finally spell out the specific ecological features that produced the patrilineal band—despite never finding it in his own fieldwork or in travels on two continents.

A few months after returning to Washington, Steward reported that the first volume was nearly finished. Nimuendajú's map had also arrived, and sections of it were to be copied and used in the *Handbook*. "I have proudly shown it to every anthropologist who has visited the Smithsonian Institution," Steward told Nimuenadajú, "and they all agree that it is the finest and most remarkable thing they have seen."[74]

Those anthropologists included Paul Rivet, then in his early sixties and a well-known authority on South American Indians. Métraux had studied with him during his student years in Paris. Rivet, who originally trained as a physician, had spent five years in Ecuador, from 1901 to 1906, where he collected ethnographic and archaeological materials. A militant antifascist and antiracist, and a member of the French Resistance during World War II, he was hunted by the Gestapo and fled to South America, where he lived for the remaining years of the war. Steward provided "lavish entertainment" during Rivet's visit to Washington, hoping to convince him to contribute to the *Handbook*. In New York City, Boas held a lunch in his honor at Columbia University's Faculty Club, but Boas collapsed and died during it. He was eighty-four years old.[75]

Lowie contributed actively to the *Handbook*, writing several articles based on published sources and translating Nimuendajú's work from German into English. He also read many of the manuscripts. Steward sought his advice and help with a wide range of editorial and other professional matters, especially during the three months that Lowie spent at the BAE in fall 1941 at work on the *Handbook*. Kroeber took a much less active part, contributing a few articles and offering advice when consulted. His wartime work in Berkeley, directing a language program for the army, had led him into a bureaucratic morass that left him utterly exhausted. During summer 1943, when he was sixty-seven years old, he suffered a severe heart attack. Although he eventually returned to teaching, he followed his physician's orders and gave up his directorship, and with it the perpetual battle against red tape.[76]

Willey assisted Steward for nearly three years with the *Handbook*. They worked in the Smithsonian's "Old Building," or "Castle" as some call it, a large, reddish, Gothic Revival stone structure, complete with towers. Steward's office was on the fourth floor, in the lower tower at the eastern end of the building.

Willey remembered it as "garret-like" but appealing, with three windows that offered a broad view of the Mall. Both Steward and his secretary had desks in the room. Willey's office was across the hall, and Métraux had an office on the floor below, as did Stirling and some other members of the BAE. The second floor, which held the offices of the Smithsonian's central administration, had gleaming hardwood floors and a more impressive look. A contingent of African American men worked to maintain the quarters occupied by the professional and clerical staffs, mostly comprised of white men and white women, respectively. Some of the African American men also served as receptionists and messengers for the central administration. They wore black suits and ties, Willey remembered, and moved about quietly and with a formal air.

Steward, unlike the young Willey, seemed indifferent to his surroundings. He was engrossed not only in the *Handbook* but in various other projects as well. Still, the *Handbook* consumed a great deal of his time and intellectual energy during these years, even with at least three other people providing full-time assistance. There may have been a fourth as well, Miss Palmer. After he left the BAE, Steward remarked to his former secretary that Palmer had "taken an awful beating on the *Handbook* and yet turned out a superb product." He continued: "Somehow, she has been the forgotten woman, and one of these days I intend to tell the story of the *Handbook,* showing what the insiders, especially you and she, contributed to it." That story, however, remained untold, and the women's labors went unrecognized.

With Métraux, whose temperament Steward thought "volcanic," he sometimes had heated discussions about editorial matters. Occasionally, these erupted into violent disagreements, which ended with Métraux flinging angry words against a wall of silence. While Métraux erupted, Steward simmered, each determined to have his own way. Their arguments often centered on Métraux's corrections of galley proofs. Presented with a clean set of galleys, he would "attack it," Willey recalled, "and bring it back to Julian with so many slips of text addenda glued to both margins that it looked like a centipede." Despite having read and edited at least two previous copies of typed manuscript, Métraux always found more errors and omissions. Sometimes Steward stopped the press, and sometimes he refused.[77]

The first theoretical discussions that Willey had with Steward grew out of efforts to resolve other editorial problems. By 1944 Steward and his coworkers had put most of the first and second volumes in final order. The first volume, *The Marginal Tribes,* covered southern Argentina and Chile, the Gran Chaco, and eastern Brazil. It would have "good routine summaries," he told Kroeber, but would "totally lack flare." That simply reflected the data, he added, "which are pretty drab." The second volume, *The Andean Civilizations,* would have "more punch." While uneven, that volume could boast some excellent articles. As originally planned, the third volume would focus on Indians of the tropical forest. This reflected Cooper's division of South America into three culture areas, then the standard classification. A projected fourth volume would contain topical articles.

As early as 1940, however, Steward told Lowie that the anthropologists he consulted had "totally conflicting" ideas about how to approach the third area. In the same year, he mentioned to Kroeber that he had started to work on the "South American population problem from the point of view of community size rather than density alone." The agricultural terraces and archaeological sites he had seen in Peru two years earlier may have stimulated this line of thought. He had wondered then why population had expanded to a point that made the terraces necessary, and the sheer size of archaeological sites such as Pachacámac had surprised him. As he told Kroeber, the "size, stability, and distribution of communities in relation to general subsistence activities seem to me the crucial basis for understanding major social and political forms."[78]

By 1944 a logistical problem—the bulkiness of the third volume, then in process—led him to propose splitting the material in two, creating separate, conceptually distinct volumes. Steward told Willey over lunch one day that while editing the material for the third volume he realized that the articles dealt with what he referred to as two "culture types." The first represented what they had been calling the "tropical forest tribes." These farming peoples lived in egalitarian and sedentary communities that were larger than the band societies of hunter-gatherers covered in the first volume. They could be distinguished, in turn, from other groups living in tropical lowland areas that constituted a more complex type. Those "Circum-Caribbean tribes," as Steward called them, had more diverse settlement patterns and a social order governed by a hereditary elite, including chiefs. Years later, two of Steward's Columbia University students, Morton Fried and Elman Service, would define the latter type of societies as chiefdoms.[79]

Steward suggested devoting the third volume to the former culture type, the tropical forest tribes, and the fourth volume to the Circum-Caribbean tribes. Neither concept was entirely Steward's creation, but he refined and reworked some ideas then afloat about culture areas, finding in them evidence of different culture types. As he acknowledged a few years later in a (generally overlooked) footnote of a journal article, "The concept of the Circum-Caribbean culture was introduced by Paul Kirchhoff." Kirchhoff, who contributed a number of articles to the *Handbook,* had drawn his evidence from the chronicles of the early Spanish Conquest. Deprived of his German citizenship in 1939, Kirchhoff gained Mexican citizenship in 1941. While he spent most of his career in Mexico, removed from North American anthropology, he influenced Fried and Service quite directly during a visit to New York City. Steward apparently did not act as a mediating figure, as has often been assumed.[80]

Willey listened to Steward's rather persuasive argument that day, but he saw several reasons to argue strenuously against it. The proposed fourth volume violated culture history, linking groups that were not closely related historically (for example, those in lower Central America and in the West Indies). This new

ordering would also shift the *Handbook*'s organization from the culture area–
culture history format of the first two volumes to one based on an "inferred
social typology." And finally, while the groups in the first volume all constituted
one sociopolitical "type," band societies, those in the second volume on the
Andes were not all civilizations.

Steward had seen those problems himself; moreover, the second volume of
the *Handbook* was nearly finished, almost past the point of no return in the
publishing process. He eventually decided to leave it unchanged and proceed
with the third and fourth volumes, organizing them as he had suggested to
Willey. The fifth and sixth volumes contained comparative and topical articles
on subjects ranging from languages to ceramics. (The fifth volume, like the third,
was divided, creating an extra volume.) In its final form, as Willey has pointed
out, the *Handbook* represented a compromise between culture area and culture
type as organizing principles. Steward himself later commented that the *Handbook* "could not depart very much from traditional thinking in anthropology,
[and his] own interpretations of prehistoric and modern South American cultures—especially substitution of the concept of culture type for culture area—
were published much later."[81]

The cultural typology that Steward worked out while editing the *Handbook
of South American Indians* clearly had roots in his earlier North American research. His interest in band societies, and in what he came to call cultural ecology, developed in the Great Basin; his exposure to the Southwest, both its archaeological sites and its existing pueblos, led him to think about culture change
in the direction of greater sociopolitical complexity. The typology that he de-
vised while trying to make sense of South American cultural development was
unmistakably evolutionary, as Willey and others observed, but largely as an
outcome of his interest in social complexity, not in cultural evolution per se.
Steward identified four types of societies based on specific features of economy,
population structure, settlement pattern, and political organization. These were,
in order of increasing complexity: bands of hunter-gatherers, sedentary farming villages, chiefdoms (to use the later term), and civilizations or states.

Future archaeological research would reveal far greater complexity and variation in South American prehistory than Steward could see in the mid-1940s. And
Steward himself would soon refine his own views on cultural evolution, introducing his concept of multilinear evolution. Willey later suggested, "With his deep
understanding of cultural ecology, he saw that the four-fold evolutionary model
of the *Handbook* . . . could not be employed in simplistic unilinear fashion." But
cultural ecology itself would remain in the background until the mid-1950s. A full
fifteen years after the reviewer of *Basin-Plateau* observed that Steward needed to
define his terms and clarify his ideas for his readers, he finally did so.[82]

* * *

Actual publication of the *Handbook of South American Indians* lagged, due to
wartime shortages of paper and other problems. By late 1945, the first two vol-

umes were in page proof, and the others some months away from galley proof stage. The volumes began to appear in print in 1946. With enormous effort, Steward and his coworkers had produced a much larger work than initially planned, one that ran to nearly five thousand pages. Remarkably, they finished preparing the manuscript copy for all six volumes slightly ahead of schedule. Many years later, Willey attributed this to Steward's qualities as editor, both practical and intellectual. Steward had not only recast the book's organization but also had remained attentive to the endless minutiae of editing such a work. As he complained to Kroeber, they even had to get the navy's permission to publish Mishkin's article on the Quechua since he had written it while on duty in the Atlantic.[83]

Besides his editorial work, Steward had a hand in various other projects during the early 1940s, most of them intended to direct federal funds into research opportunities for anthropologists. One of these eventually became the River Basins Archaeological Surveys program, the precursor of federal funding for salvage archaeology. During the early 1940s, Steward and his BAE colleague Frank H. H. Roberts learned that the U.S. Army Corps of Engineers planned to build a series of flood-control dams after the war, creating large reservoirs and thereby flooding archaeological sites. A committee was finally formed, and it eventually persuaded Congress to include funds for archaeologists in these projects. Roberts, an archaeologist, became director of the BAE's River Basin Archaeological Surveys in 1947.[84]

Eight years after joining the BAE, Steward felt spread thin and rather depleted. When Kroeber invited him to Berkeley for several months in 1944 to teach some summer school courses, he declined. A certain amount of prestige and a good salary went along with a summer appointment; the usual idea was to attract senior scholars, to counteract Berkeley's geographic isolation from the eastern academic world. But Steward sent regrets, alluding to "exceedingly strenuous days" at the BAE. "I am deep in obligations," he wrote, "and cannot escape them at present." He cited in particular his duties as editor of the *Handbook* and as director of the Institute of Social Anthropology.[85]

The Institute of Social Anthropology, which he created with support from the State Department in 1943, sent anthropologists and other social scientists to Latin American countries that requested help in developing training and research in social science. Steward characterized his work as the director of the ISA in research terms: "my co-workers and I began to break away from the traditional, limited 'community study' approach," he wrote, "and to see problems in larger dimensions." In the mid-1940s, staff members worked in Mexico, Brazil, Colombia, and Peru. Isabel Kelly, still living and doing research in Mexico, was the only woman on the ISA's field staff, and Steward appears to have hired her largely at Kroeber's urging. "She may have a tiny remnant of her last Guggenheim [fellowship] left," Kroeber told him, "but essentially she must be at loose ends." Eleven years after earning a Ph.D. in anthropology, she remained without regular employment. She was not at all unique among the women trained at Berkeley or elsewhere.[86]

By 1945 Steward's wish to escape the burden of his workload had grown, or perhaps the timing appeared better for finding a full-time academic position, preferably in the West. World War II had ended in September 1945, and returning veterans would soon enter colleges and universities in record numbers, requiring new faculty positions. Steward began an active search, but his interest clearly centered on Berkeley. Kroeber, then seventy years old, would retire during spring 1946, opening a position in anthropology.[87]

As Steward well knew, the department had previously hired two of Kroeber's students, Ronald Olson and Theodore McCown, which obviously provided a precedent for hiring him. He also realized that while he and Kroeber had very different theoretical perspectives, they shared many interests, which now included South American prehistory. This made him a logical successor, as did his status as an academic client and lineage "descendent" of Kroeber. According to Jane Steward, her husband felt an acute, even crushing, sense of disappointment when he realized that he would not be offered Kroeber's position.[88] His eleven-year exile from the West was not to end as he hoped, with a return to Berkeley. Although the exact circumstances remain unclear, Julian Steward always believed that the geographer Carl Sauer had blocked his hiring. He told his wife that Kroeber and Lowie implied that in comments they made privately to him.[89]

By chance, Dorothy Nyswander joined the Berkeley faculty that very year as a full professor in the School of Public Health. She returned to full-time university teaching for the first time since leaving the University of Utah in the 1930s, following her divorce from Steward. As part of her negotiation, she secured a position for her new husband, George Palmer, a public health administrator whom she had married a few years earlier.[90] In an era when nepotism policies prevailed and few women found positions or achieved high academic rank in graduate departments at major universities, this may have been unparalleled.

For his part, Kroeber encouraged Steward to take a university position and leave government service if possible. Steward had complained of going "slightly mad" each day: "Every small thing is done with the most unbelievable complications." Kroeber's own recent experience with the army gave him great sympathy for scholars who were bound, if not gagged, by red tape. "That's how I got my coronary occlusion," he wrote. "Why should you waste yourself? If you get a decent university chance, I hope you take it." No doubt thinking of his own close brush with death, he added, "Living ten years longer is worth more than an Institute of S[ocial] A[nthropology]."[91]

Only a month later, Steward accepted an offer from Columbia University and submitted his resignation to the BAE. Jane Steward happily began to scan the newspapers for housing in New York, something suitable for a family with two children, then seven and nine years old. She welcomed the move from the pressures and frustrations of government service to a position with a university, which she imagined as an oasis of tranquility. In fact, she had actively encouraged her husband to leave the BAE and return to academe. To her great satisfaction, the university professor she had married thirteen years earlier would finally take up a professorship after a long hiatus.[92]

From their first days in Washington, her husband had complained bitterly to her about bureaucratic snarls and internal politics. Jane Steward's entries in their journal during the early months of 1936, when he served as a liaison with the Bureau of Indian Affairs, offer vivid testimony: "It seems an impossible situation to cope with," she wrote, "the angles being devious and the decisions of BIA personnel unstable. J. is a wreck from it. Such phrases as 'a barrel of dynamite, complex but damn interesting' repeated ad nauseam." Ten years later, the ivory tower in the form of Columbia University appeared to offer refuge.[93]

* * *

Despite Julian Steward's complaints, his eleven years at the BAE had provided unusual opportunities for research, writing, and publication, opportunities that few university positions offered. He could now claim a lengthy list of publications and, more important for his future reputation as a theorist, firsthand professional contacts with an array of cultural anthropologists and archaeologists. He had met most of the anthropologists who flooded into Washington during the war years; others who served as fellow officers in professional organizations; still others who worked directly with him at the Institute of Social Anthropology and in related ventures; and dozens who had contributed to the *Handbook*. As editor of the *Handbook,* he had been in a position to dispense patronage. Not only had he given colleagues an opportunity to publish in a major scholarly work but—highly unusual in academic publishing—he had paid them as well, through the largesse of a federal appropriation.

In 1946 Steward left Washington with an extensive network and high visibility in his professional world, a marked change from the mid-1930s, when he published his first theoretical essays. To his mind, those essays had gathered dust for a decade because of their novel, ecological approach, never receiving the recognition that he thought they were due. In fact, however, he had not had the stature at the time that could guarantee them attention. His years in Washington had given him the ways and means to increase his professional stature, thereby creating a larger, more receptive audience for his written work.

At Columbia, where he planned to work solely with a few like-minded graduate students, he would find not only an audience for his materialist "point of view," as he often called it, but also unusually active collaborators.

Alfred L. Kroeber, ca. 1920s.
(Courtesy of the University
of Illinois Archives)

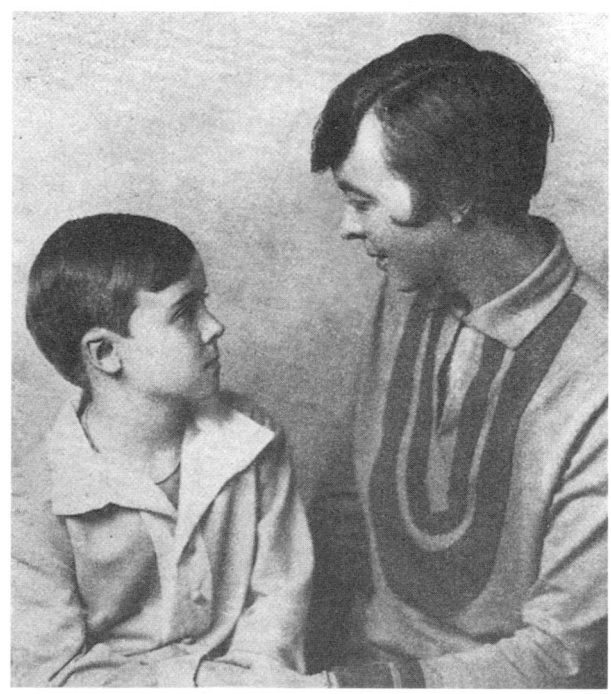

Dorothy Nyswander
and her daughter, Marie,
ca. 1929. (Courtesy of
the University of Utah
Archives)

Jane Cannon, ca. 1927.
(Special Collections,
University of Utah)

Owens Valley Paiute informant Tom Stone with his wife, 1935. (Courtesy of the University of Illinois Archives)

Western Shoshone informant John Shakespeare, Nevada, 1935. (Courtesy of the University of Illinois Archives)

Passport photograph for South America trip, 1938. (Courtesy of the University of Illinois Archives)

LEFT: Jane Steward and Gary Steward, 1938. (Courtesy of the University of Illinois Archives)

BELOW: With a Carrier informant, probably Chief Louis Billy Prince, 1940. (National Anthropological Archives, Smithsonian Institution/56,197)

Robert H. Lowie and
Alfred L. Kroeber, ca.
1950s. (Courtesy of the
University of Illinois
Archives)

Julian Steward soon after arriving
at the University of Illinois, 1952.
(Courtesy of the University of
Illinois Archives)

CHAPTER 10

EAST OF EVERYTHING

Even before he joined the Columbia faculty, Steward had already heard a great deal about it from his old friend and longtime colleague, Strong. Although Strong had resigned from the BAE in 1937 to take a position at Columbia, he returned to Washington during the early 1940s to direct the Ethnogeographic Board, a wartime agency. He and Steward saw each other often, both socially and professionally. His Columbia student, Willey, worked closely with Steward on the *Handbook of South American Indians* during this period, and Strong contributed several chapters.

Among his many colleagues, in the mid-1940s Steward still undoubtedly had the most in common with Strong. The two men had broad interests in natural history, training in the natural sciences, and a 1920s Berkeley education. Even after giving up zoology in favor of anthropology, Strong maintained a deep interest in animal ecology. Remembered as "profoundly a naturalist," an anthropologist who "had the experience of a naturalist wherever he worked," his theoretical orientation was both historical and ecological. He and Steward shared an interest in studying cultural change in an ecological framework, and both men had research programs that embraced archaeology and ethnography.

They also had a long history of formal or informal collaboration, beginning with their joint work on the Columbia River archaeological sites in the mid-1920s and including a more recent interest in South American prehistory. Strong had shifted his attention from Mesoamerica to South America, first excavating there in 1940. In 1946 he was about to undertake archaeological fieldwork in the Virú Valley on the northern coast of Peru, as part of a collaborative project that Steward, Willey, and Wendell Bennett had begun planning informally in 1945. Strong and several other archaeologists soon joined the project as well.[1]

Unlike the others, Steward did not plan to do fieldwork in the Virú Valley. Instead he had two representatives in the field, a social anthropologist, Allan R. Holmberg, and a cultural geographer. Steward obviously had great interest in a project that would study a single valley in depth, documenting cultural development and increasing complexity over a period of thousands of years, and including research on a contemporary community. But eight years after his aborted trip to the Andes, he had no intention of returning to Peru himself. Perhaps following Kroeber's example, he had begun to make a practice of deputizing younger anthropologists for field duty, a practice that he would continue with graduate students at Columbia.[2]

When Ralph Linton resigned from Columbia's anthropology department to accept an offer from Yale in 1946, Strong saw a chance to influence the department's direction. In particular, he had no sympathy with the psychological orientation of some of his colleagues, including Linton, a perspective known as culture and personality. (Its links were with clinical psychology and psychoanalysis, rather than experimental and behaviorist psychology.) He also wanted to reorganize the graduate program to make it more responsive to students. Because they shared theoretical interests and had worked together in the past, Strong thought that he and Steward together could achieve these goals. A twenty-year friendship that had been tested but not broken by professional tensions, as well as the interests and ambitions they held in common, made them natural allies.[3]

It helped enormously that Strong served as chairman of the search committee charged with finding Linton's replacement. The position was not advertised—which was the practice in that era, many years before federal law required it—and Steward visited Columbia while purportedly in New York City on other business. ("I hate being put on display," he explained to Strong in advance.) An offer soon followed for a position with tenure at the highest rank, professor, and with a salary somewhat greater than he had earned at the BAE. Linton, who had backed him for the position, called to tell him of the offer even before it was made formal. "Plenty of people would be quite happy with this job [at the BAE]," he told Linton, "but university life suits my temperament much better." He had attained tenure and the highest academic rank, however, without going through the usual tenure and promotion process, one always fraught with tension and sometimes with bitter conflict.[4]

Just a month before he accepted Columbia University's offer, Steward had told Kroeber that he "long[ed] for the simpler research and teaching niche" of a university position. But his brief academic experience in the 1930s did not prepare him for the postwar world of graduate education at Columbia that he entered in September 1946. He had spent fewer than five years teaching undergraduates at the University of Michigan and the University of Utah, in positions that provided as much time for research as they required for teaching. Apparently, he envisioned a similar position at Columbia, but with the added advantage of having just a few advanced students. Reality proved quite different. "This was not a return to research with limited teaching, which I had expected," he later wrote.[5]

His vision of escape to the ivory tower quickly faded. On a day in late September 1946, as a "student parade" passed through his office on the fourth floor of Schermerhorn Hall, Steward regarded the approach of teaching with a certain dread. Just a month later, he confessed to Ethelwyn Carter, his former secretary, "I am still not sure how I will like Columbia." He found the atmosphere highly competitive, the "lust for status," as he put it, notably stronger than at the Smithsonian, and the political climate very "progressive." A number of the students and faculty were openly leftist and some showed scant regard for middle-class social expectations. Steward, who held liberal political views but was socially conservative, had fit in well in Washington during the years of the Roosevelt administration. He felt at home in the staunchly middle-class social climate of the federal bureaucracy, having grown up in that very setting.[6]

His first months at Columbia had a liminal quality. He had not entirely severed his connection with the Smithsonian or created firm ties with the university. "There is more time for thinking," he conceded, "because I have refused to mix it up politically." As evidence, he considered himself on good terms with Ruth Benedict, despite their very different approaches to anthropology and opposing professional alliances. Of course, Linton's notorious antagonism toward Benedict might have led her to welcome almost anyone who replaced him. Or perhaps her cordiality simply reflected the courtesy and generosity that many students remember as two of her hallmark qualities.[7]

Benedict's presence in the department meant that for the first (and last) time in his career, Steward had a female colleague on almost equal footing with him. (Or this could be construed as the second time, his collaborative research with Nyswander constituting the first.) Benedict's untimely death two years later made it a brief experience, and, in any case, she did not occupy a truly equal place in the academic hierarchy. In 1946 when Steward joined the faculty as a tenured full professor, Benedict, then fifty-nine years old, still held the rank of associate professor. One of a handful of women with tenure at Columbia, she had earned a Ph.D. twenty-three years earlier and had many years of teaching experience and a strong publication record. But as Robert Murphy observed about her situation and the times, "things were bad everywhere for women in academia."[8]

Steward found the Columbia students "earnest," the very term that one of them, Elman Service, later used when recalling his fellow students. But Steward added that "there are many aggressive NY boys, who regard classes as a matter of matching wits with the Prof." As he had quickly learned in a seminar, the students did not hesitate to heckle their instructors, and gaining credibility required winning bouts in the battle of wits. "It's strange how everything in life has to be so calculated," he told Carter, remarking that it left him feeling confused. Near the end of that semester, the four sociology students in the seminar complained about the course in a memorably brutal way. As he recalled many years later, they "announce[d] that I was not as sharp as the students and that because they were wasting their time they quit the seminar." The episode reinforced his long-standing dislike of classroom teaching.[9]

He quickly saw that it would take a few years to learn the rules and play the game well, as he put it, if he cared to do that. During his first semester at Columbia, he retained a strong identification with the Institute of Social Anthropology, despite having resigned as director when he left the Smithsonian. George Foster had succeeded him as director, but Steward struggled to retain some influence over the institute for the next six months. He eventually resigned from his courtesy position at the Smithsonian, as associate in anthropology, and shifted all of his attention and energy to his work at Columbia.[10]

Just a month after joining the Columbia faculty, Steward remarked that "It takes time to re-root, and I feel like a tree not only cut off from nourishment but swaying precariously in the wind." A few weeks later, he quickly accepted an offer to teach two summer school courses at Berkeley, one on South America and the other on the Southwest, which promised to provide a few renewing months in the West. He could escape the concrete canyons of New York City, where he already felt confined and under attack, for the western canyons that always represented freedom and refuge to him. He also saw it, he remarked privately, as a chance "to thumb my nose at Sauer."[11]

To Lowie, he put the best face on his situation at Columbia, praising Lowie's and Kroeber's alma mater as "a grand place." New York City, Steward continued, was a "wonderful place," and he and his wife "expect[ed] to enjoy it enormously." Years later, however, after leaving Columbia, he told Kroeber that he had felt a greater sense of culture shock when he first walked along the streets of New York City than when he arrived in Japan in 1956. In fact, he had made several visits to New York City between the early 1920s and the mid-1940s, and those had not dissuaded him from accepting Columbia's offer. Kroeber had also given him some excellent counsel in advance, as Steward later acknowledged; but just three months into his tenure, he pointed out that his misgivings had been justified. Steward's comments suggest that the milieu at Columbia, more than the city itself, left him feeling uprooted, out of his element, and east of everything.[12]

True to form, he did not live in the city but at a distance, in Demarest, New Jersey, a small community about ten miles north of the George Washington Bridge. Even a bland, domesticated landscape of trimmed lawns and hedges held greater appeal than any cityscape. Replicating his former commute, he again crossed a broad river (this time the Hudson River) that formed a natural boundary between city and countryside, the latter soon to vanish in the face of relentless suburban growth during the postwar years. But he avoided that commute as much as possible, preferring to work at home and venturing into the city only for classes and scheduled meetings. Jane Steward recalled that during the six years of her husband's appointment at Columbia he saw little more of Manhattan than the campus and the American Museum of Natural History. Unlike him, she regretted that her times in New York City proved so rare and fleeting.[13]

As the first semester drew to a close, Steward continued to harbor some doubts about his "reconversion," as he called it, to academic life. The small faculty of anthropologists at Columbia found itself faced with more than a hundred graduate students, many of them returned veterans. Eric Wolf later recalled, "The place was a shambles." Boas had died four years earlier, leaving a void in the department while maintaining something of a presence in it. As Steward noted rather sardonically to an acquaintance, "The ghost of Franz Boas haunts our halls, and I haven't determined whether he is helping or hurting our morale. He is something to live up to, and to live down."[14]

Steward appreciated neither the historicism nor the relativism of the Boasian tradition, which remained strong in Columbia's anthropology department. Only a few years before he died, Boas wrote that "nothing will ever be found [in cultural phenomena] that deserves the name of a law." Steward's idea of a scientific anthropology, in contrast, centered on understanding cause-and-effect relations and formulating cultural laws. Few of his fellow faculty members, aside from Strong, had any sympathy with this view; many, in fact, were Boas's former students.[15]

From the outset of his years at Columbia, Steward had an acute, lingering sense of being an outsider in alien territory, a stranger in a strange land. Any of his previous experiences—his loneliness as a new instructor at Michigan, his social discomfort at the University of Utah, his sense of exile during his travels in Peru—had been either brief or mild in comparison. He seemed to feel that a great gulf separated him from his Columbia colleagues. Many of them were New Yorkers by birth or upbringing, and they were convinced New Yorkers at that; nearly all had trained at northeastern institutions, either Harvard or Columbia; most of them remained Boasian in outlook; and a few of them were women.

* * *

Aside from Benedict, two other women, Gene Weltfish and Marian Smith, regularly taught courses in the department of anthropology in 1946. Both held only temporary appointments. In addition, Margaret Mead and Ruth Bunzel taught on a part-time basis. Mead, who held a full-time position as a curator at the American Museum of Natural History, often worked with Columbia graduate students and occasionally offered courses. Bunzel, who was in her late forties and had no other employment, taught evening courses. In the 1920s she had replaced Esther Goldfrank as Boas's secretary, a job that soon led to fieldwork in the Southwest and eventually to graduate study and a Ph.D. in anthropology. Years after leaving Columbia, Steward recalled seeing her there, but mistakenly—and tellingly—identified her as a student rather than an adjunct faculty member. All of the women had studied anthropology under Boas.[16]

Weltfish, then in her midforties and exactly Steward's age, had ten years' teaching experience at Columbia, but held only the rank of lecturer. Despite the marginal nature of her appointment, Weltfish was remembered by some of her students as an important intellectual influence, albeit "overworked, underpaid, harassed, and somewhat abrupt in manner." Steward, who met her during his brief visit to Columbia in spring 1946, described her as the only person in the anthropology department who did not give him a warm welcome. He did not find her hostile, he said, but instead concluded that she could not afford the hour she spent with him.[17]

Weltfish, a committed activist and scholar, believed in a politically engaged anthropology, one that addressed social problems and took a direct part in trying to solve them. She had published well-regarded works on the Pawnee and a controversial pamphlet on race, coauthored with Benedict in 1943. The pamphlet, purchased in bulk by the federal government for distribution to military officers and instructors, was meant to counter Nazi ideas about racial superiority and inferiority. But controversy over its contents soon erupted. What Weltfish and Benedict wrote about race reflected the perspective of Boasian anthropology, and, by its very nature, challenged the prevailing social order. The U.S. military, like American society in general, remained racially segregated in the early 1940s. Weltfish saw the ensuing war of words, covered by the *New York Times,* as an opportunity to educate Americans and combat racism.[18]

Her colleague Marian Smith, remembered for her warmth, determination, and professional commitment, began teaching at Columbia in 1941. Like Benedict and Weltfish, she bore the Boasian stamp, particularly in the breadth of her interests. Despite a serious disability—a childhood bout with polio had left one leg partially paralyzed, making each step difficult—Smith carried out fieldwork and maintained an active professional life. Throughout her ten years at Columbia, she held the rank of instructor. Steward, who met her briefly before he joined the faculty, found her "cordial."[19]

Strong's private assessment of his female colleagues was that Smith was "o.k. but may turn into a problem." Weltfish, he told Steward, had "her head turned by recent popular acclaim and notoriety but, I hope, is fundamentally o.k." He considered Benedict wholly marginal to the department, in part because of her theoretical interests, which seemed antithetical to the approach he and Steward advocated. "Ruth Benedict (like Ralph [Linton]) is a Prima Donna," he remarked, "and may 'adorn' but will never be an integral part of a Department in the sense we mean when we use that word."[20]

Most of Strong and Steward's male colleagues in the department, in contrast to most of the women, had regular appointments. Charles Wagley, a young cultural anthropologist and Columbia graduate, had just returned to academic life after several years of military service. Before the war, he had carried out fieldwork with Tupi-speaking Indians in Brazil; he also contributed articles to the *Handbook of South American Indians*. George Herzog taught courses in linguistics and ethnomusicology. Like Wagley, he was Boas's former student. Harry Shapiro, Boston-born, Harvard-educated, and a curator at the American Museum of Natural History, held an adjunct position at Columbia. He offered courses in physical anthropology. Strong trained students in archaeology. For four years, between 1948 and 1952, Kroeber had a visiting position in the department, where he, like the majority of Steward's Columbia colleagues, had once studied with Boas.[21]

Many of the graduate students were New Yorkers, and most of them were men who had served in the armed forces during the war. Veterans received educational benefits under the G.I. Bill, and with the government paying their tuition, they enrolled at private, elite universities in record numbers. By 1946 nearly eight thousand of them had crowded into Columbia. Wolf, who began graduate study at Columbia that year, later said that he and many of his fellow veterans in the anthropology program would not have been there but for the G.I. Bill. Sidney Mintz, who entered the graduate program in the same year, recalled that only one of those veterans was a woman.[22]

During the same postwar period, coinciding with Steward's six years on the faculty, the proportion of women in anthropology declined at Columbia. It reached the lowest point ever according to Murphy, who was also a student during that era. No doubt the reasons for this decline were complex, tied in large part to social and political pressures that forced women to surrender positions in the labor market to returning veterans. Steward's own sister, who moved back to Washington in 1943, was twice displaced from positions at the Pentagon by veterans during these years. In any case, enrolling thousands of men at Columbia obviously affected the number of women admitted. Likewise, enrolling so many men in the anthropology program must have limited the number of women offered admission, besides affecting the climate of graduate study in various ways.[23]

The students in Steward's classes included some women. Eleanor Leacock audited a course, and Virginia Heyer (Young), a recent graduate of Sarah Lawrence College, enrolled in two, one on the Southwest and the other on South America. (In Service's memory, classes taught by Benedict were filled with female graduate students; Steward's were not.) Most of the students were men in their mid- or late twenties who grew up during the depression, and many had served in combat zones during the war. Their life experiences inclined them toward materialist approaches to economy and political organization. They had "no trouble understanding the compelling motivations of an empty stomach," according to Murphy, and they had seen authority emerge from the barrel of a gun. Steward's theories resonated with them, he said, and immediately produced a large following.[24]

It does not overstate the case to say that something akin to a division of theory by gender existed in the Columbia department in the 1940s, especially after Steward arrived. Women were not the sole proponents of culture and personality as a theoretical approach, but its leading advocates did include Benedict and Mead. Strong, misspelling Mead's name and appending the surname of her second husband (Reo Fortune), reported to Steward in 1946 that Benedict was not "a great menace now that the Meade-Fortune etc., interests have failed to gain a foothold" in the department. That Mead taught at Columbia only on a part-time basis always limited her influence.[25]

A psychologically oriented approach that focused on emotions, values, and child training obviously had no appeal to Strong and Steward, nor to many of their male students. It did resonate, however, with some of the women in the graduate program (and some of the men). Steward and other critics dismissed culture and personality with contempt as "diaperology." The term is said to have originated when Karl Wittfogel, after listening to Benedict present a paper at a professional meeting, made a scathing comment to the assembled scholars: "'We have just been introduced to a new science of society: diaperology.'"[26]

In his six years at Columbia, Steward worked with dozens of students, nearly all of them men. They included David Aberle, Pedro Carrasco, Stanley Diamond, Clifford Evans, Louis Faron, Morton Fried, Frederic K. Lehman, Robert Manners, Sidney Mintz, Robert Murphy, Raymond Scheele, Elman Service, Elliott Skinner, and Eric Wolf. Service, among others, later remarked that "an extraordinarily large number" of these men attained professional prominence in later years. Most of them eventually held positions at institutions that already had or would develop graduate programs in anthropology. These included Columbia, Berkeley, Yale, the University of Chicago, the University of Michigan, the University of Illinois, Johns Hopkins, and Brandeis, among others.[27]

Steward worked with very few women, and not closely. He served on the committees of several, including Young and Leacock, but made limited comments on their dissertations and did not attend their defenses. After Linton's departure for Yale, Steward agreed to replace him as Ernestine Friedl's dissertation advisor. Friedl remembered that he read and approved the final draft of her dissertation on Chippewa leadership styles and political organization, but he never discussed it with her. Judging by later correspondence, he seems to have maintained a professional relationship only with two of the women who studied at Columbia, Elena Padilla and Vera Rubin. Both eventually managed to establish careers as anthropologists, but only by following indirect routes. The same was true of Leacock. As Stanley Diamond later acknowledged, she struggled with marginal, often part-time positions for years while her male contemporaries took academic posts at leading institutions. Other women who studied at Columbia during the postwar years had similar experiences.[28]

Leacock chose Strong, not Steward, as her dissertation adviser. Although the theoretical argument that she developed in her dissertation took her in a direction that interested Steward, Strong was an appropriate choice for several reasons. While primarily an archaeologist, he contributed to the field of ethnohistory, and he had worked in Labrador, where she did fieldwork. Leacock drew heavily on ethnohistorical sources as well as field research in her dissertation on the Montagnais-Naskapi Indians (now known as the Innu). And Strong apparently did not object to a married woman training in anthropology, even while raising children. In this regard he displayed a tolerance that not all of his colleagues shared.

As the time for her defense approached, Leacock grew increasingly wary of Steward: "I was having my third baby," she wrote, "and it seemed to me that Steward grew more and more negative as I grew bigger." She finally decided to postpone the defense, despite some inconvenience, until after she gave birth. Later she wondered if his antagonism had had more to do with having Strong as her adviser. After Steward's arrival at Columbia, tensions soon appeared between the two men and grew into an open rivalry.[29]

This marked the end of a long friendship and a strong professional alliance, one that had endured for two decades but could not withstand the competitive climate at Columbia. In Jane Steward's memory, the death knell of that friendship was sounded when Strong introduced her husband to a colleague in another department as his "right-hand man." Steward, obviously unwilling to accept the implied role of academic client and junior, bristled in reply, "I'm no one's right-hand man." The awkward moment passed, but feelings of resentment took root and grew.[30]

Before meeting Leacock, Steward had probably never encountered a graduate student who was a married woman, and certainly not one who was pregnant. (Marriage limited a woman's professional chances in anthropology. In the competition for jobs, women's gender constituted the first strike against them; marriage, or even the likelihood of marriage, the second; and children, the third.) Although Steward said nothing directly to Leacock, she remembered that Kroeber pointedly remarked, "My, you *are* prolific," when he saw her with her children. Kroeber also happened to see Young sometime after she finished her doctorate and married in the early 1950s. When he inquired about what she was doing, she told him that she still hoped to find an academic position. She was visibly pregnant, and he asked, "But how could you keep up with your work?" His own wife had given up graduate study in anthropology and any professional ambitions when she married him, waiting until her children were grown to launch a career as a writer.[31]

Years later, some of the men who studied with Steward acknowledged, directly or otherwise, that they had excluded the women in Columbia's graduate program from their professional circle. As Mintz observed with unusual forthrightness, "We were pushing the young women out of the way without even knowing we were doing it." Diamond conceded that Leacock qualified only as "a contemporary, not a colleague" at Columbia. "Although she was very much aware of our cadre of radical young men," he wrote a few years after her death, "we were unaware of her." The postwar "male bonding" that Diamond remembered at Columbia expressed itself in an informal discussion group, the Mundial Upheaval Society, or the M.U.S., which coalesced after several of the members had finished their fieldwork. It took its name from a mock political pamphlet of cartoons drawn by Morton Fried, one of the founding members of the group. All of the members were men. At meetings they read papers and commented on one another's work.[32]

Like Diamond, other members of the M.U.S. do not remember that the group purposely excluded Leacock. Mintz had no memory that Leacock ever inquired about the M.U.S., which he recalled had developed spontaneously and on the basis of shared intellectual interests. "We didn't deny anybody admission," he added. Leacock had allegedly described the M.U.S. as like a "street-corner gang" that brought honor to itself by excluding women, but Service thought that Padilla had been invited to attend the meetings. "So we had nothing against females," he said. "There just weren't many in those early days who were congenial to us and our more or less anti-Benedictian origins." (Mintz did not share that view. He admired Benedict, as his essay about her attests, and he recalled Wolf as an "enthusiastic Benedict student" like himself.) Still, the divisions in the anthropology department did have a strongly gendered quality, even including the notion that Steward did more rigorous, "hard" social science as compared to Benedict's "soft," humanistic approach.[33]

This was the milieu in which Steward taught, and one in which he felt very comfortable in certain respects. In letters to male colleagues, he was consistently positive about his professional situation, and especially about the students. He remarked to Kroeber that "it is a real joy to work with mature students who can take about anything you can give them." He quickly gathered a small group of male students to work on a new project, a study of Puerto Rico that Harry Shapiro invited him to join in 1947. At about the same time, he resigned from his courtesy appointment at the Smithsonian, perhaps seeing the Puerto Rico project as a substitute for the Institute of Social Anthropology and its community studies in Latin America.[34] Steward's interest in collaborative work reflected his wish to work with a small group of like-minded men. The male work group remained highly meaningful to him even thirty years after his experiences on the ranch in Deep Springs Valley.

Almost from the beginning, however, Steward seems to have felt a certain unease with his Columbia students, whose regional background, political sensibilities, and intellectual style differed so much from his own. The labels Steward used, *forester* for himself and *city-slickers* for them, if apt in a mocking way, had a defensive ring. In truth, surrounded by New Yorkers who led such interior lives, in several senses, he felt out of place and anomalous. Some of his students, in turn, thought that he regarded them as "foreigners." The gulf that separated Steward and his Columbia students derived from differences in background and life experience, and probably from divisions within anthropology itself.[35]

At Berkeley and the BAE, most of Steward's fellow students and colleagues were westerners, middle class or working class in origin, and from Anglo-Saxon families long established in America. Before entering anthropology some of the men had lived on ranches or farms or worked as lumberjacks or sailors. As anthropologists, whether archaeologists or ethnographers studying American Indians, their outdoor orientation remained strong. Ralph Beals recalled that they had intellectual debates at Berkeley, but not about philosophical issues. "It never occurred to any of us," he remarked years later, "to worry about whether we were positivists or not." They read extensively in anthropology, in all four subfields; they did not think it necessary to read widely outside anthropology, to ground their work directly and explicitly in the European intellectual tradition.[36]

At Columbia, Steward's tanned hands and the silver-and-turquoise Navajo ring he wore—as well as a detectable indifference to the writings of Karl Marx and a range of European social philosophers—set him apart. In the closing pages of his 1938 monograph on the Great Basin, he had dismissed Marxist thought, writing, "Economic determinism, though resting to an undetermined extent upon substantial truth, is, especially in such extreme interpretations as the Marxian, primarily a philosophy, not a scientifically demonstrable fact." In a sense, he and his students belonged to different bands of anthropologists: the indigenous, long in residence at the BAE; and the European-derived, more recently but firmly established at Columbia.[37]

Years later, Wolf used Steward's terms, *forester* and *city-slicker,* in alluding to the indigenous as opposed to the European roots of American anthropology. The former, he suggested, grew out of research with American Indians, as represented by the work of such men as Lewis Henry Morgan and Henry Schoolcraft. Besides Morgan and Schoolcraft, the roster of indigenous American anthropologists includes Alice Fletcher, Frank Hamilton Cushing, Frederic Ward Putnam, James Mooney, and others. Some had backgrounds in natural history and identified as scientists, and many were affiliated with the BAE. Well known in their day, they were largely overlooked after anthropology also arrived from Europe and graduate training began at Columbia. The European roots of American academic anthropology, according to Wolf, are largely German. "'The model of the American university is really that of the German university,'" he remarked. "'In order to be an intellectual and academic, you have to follow that kind of style.'"[38]

Boas, a European intellectual born and educated in Germany, spent most of his professional life at Columbia University. Steward's graduate teachers shared the same intellectual orientation. Both Lowie and Kroeber spoke German, identified closely with Europe, and cultivated ties with European colleagues. Lowie was born in Europe, and Kroeber, as fate would have it, died there. Lowie spent the first ten years of his life in Vienna and the next twenty-seven years in New York City, where his family lived in German neighborhoods. Kroeber also grew up among New York City's German community. (When the young Kroeber enrolled in a private school for boys in Connecticut, he found himself one of only two "'strange'" boys at the school, being neither Anglo-Saxon nor from New England.) Sauer came from a background somewhat similar to Kroeber's. He was American-born and grew up in a midwestern, German-speaking family, deeply immersed in German cultural tradition.[39]

In terms of his intellectual interests and approach, and his wholly Anglo-American upbringing, Steward actually had little in common with his teachers. Lowie and Kroeber had earned degrees in humanistic fields, the classics and English literature respectively, before entering anthropology. Although they referred to anthropology as a science in their writings, they did not identify anthropology as a science and themselves as scientists with the explicit and self-conscious language that Steward used. Both Kroeber and Lowie, and Sauer as well, showed a strongly humanistic bent in their thinking.[40]

In many respects, Steward followed the model not of Boas and his own teachers at Berkeley, but of John Wesley Powell, the early BAE anthropologists, and other government scientists. His contact, direct and indirect, with some of those men—including his uncle, Edward Garriott, and the fathers of some of his boyhood friends—predated his entry into anthropology. Steward later alluded to them in general terms as professionals whose example led him toward a university education and a profession. More specifically, their example helped to lead him toward a career in science and to shape his identity as a scientist.[41]

Many of Steward's students, however, like his teachers, had strong cultural links with Europe and interests in the humanities. One of them, Wolf, later wrote of anthropology as a bridge discipline, the most humanistic of the sciences and the most scientific of the humanities. Kroeber and Lowie might well have shared this view, while Steward always maintained that anthropology was a social *science*. Wolf himself was Austrian by birth, and some of his fellow students were the children of European immigrants. An ethnically diverse group, most had grown up in or around New York City, the major port of entry for Europeans and the American city with the strongest ties to Europe, intellectually, culturally, and economically. A European-derived intellectual style prevailed in New York, one that Steward found alien. Mintz recalled that he seemed put off by city-wise, articulate New Yorkers, a category that encompassed nearly all of his Columbia students.[42]

Few of them had any acquaintance with the American West, and Mintz had no memory of hearing Steward talk about his Great Basin fieldwork. The students' link with Steward in a geographic sense was mainly Latin America and the Caribbean, where they, but not he, did fieldwork. This perhaps added to his unease. Their own class origins were mixed, but many of the students strongly identified with the working class, for reasons of politics, if not early life experience. As Wolf put it, he and his fellow students were all "some variant of red." The shared experience of war may have helped create their acute political sensibility, which constituted a strong bond among them; war is, after all, politics in its most raw and tangible form. Mintz remembered passionate debates with fellow students on a variety of political issues. He did not recollect ever hearing Steward express political opinions or interest in contemporary politics.[43]

In contrast to his Columbia students, Steward had no direct experience of warfare. Ansel Adams, born the same year as Steward, could speak for him when he wrote, "I never went to war, too young for the First and too old for the Second. The great events of the world have been tragic pageants, not personal involvements." Politically detached for the most part, Steward simply cast his vote each election day. He identified primarily as a scientist and thought that politics belonged outside the classroom and far removed from any research setting. As he told an acquaintance during this period, "my teaching is entirely nonpolitical in every sense." Unlike so many of his students—who saw anthropology as a means to understand political and economic oppression, and who believed that scholarship should be politically engaged—Steward's own commitment was strictly to science, and more specifically to anthropology as science. "I am really a scientist at heart," he wrote soon after arriving at Columbia. "I see now that if anthropology is to do any good, it has got to get back on a decent scientific foundation, and I think I see the answer to that." He added, "This basic loyalty to science, with institutions secondary, really explains my seeming paradoxes."[44]

That commitment, without regard to politics, helps explain his decision some years later to testify for the federal government in the Indian Claims Commission cases. Wolf surmised that Steward's "belief in the truth of science" had led him to it despite a certain sympathy for the Indians. Echoing Steward's own words about his "seeming paradoxes," Wolf characterized his former teacher as "a very contradictory person." His telling words about Steward—"a complex person, in a very American sense"—reveal something about his own perception of their differences, both in background and in outlook.[45]

* * *

The feeling of being out of place, and some doubt about whether he would ever "re-root" in New York City, strengthened Steward's wish to see the West again. He spent part of the summer of 1947, as planned, teaching two courses at Berkeley; he and his family stayed in the Kroebers' house on Arch Street. Sauer also lived on Arch Street, which made him a neighbor, but Steward did not seek him out. Kroeber taught at Columbia that summer, then went on to Harvard to spend a year teaching there. He returned to Columbia in 1948 as a visiting professor.[46]

While he was in Berkeley that summer, Steward happened to meet Nyswander one day while crossing campus. He may have heard about her return to the university through the academic grapevine. She still regarded Lowie as a friend, and, yet another coincidence, she had known Benedict and Du Bois during the years when she lived in New York City. Her enduring memory of the occasion was that Steward seemed excessively "gloomy" and even unwell, which puzzled her. Later she "wondered if he wished he were back in Berkeley too." A letter that he had written to Strong the previous year alluded to the possibility of returning to Berkeley "sometime in the future," a hope that appeared to fade that summer.[47]

In August, when summer school ended, Steward and his wife traveled for a few weeks, leaving their sons at a summer camp in the Southwest. Soon after returning to New York City, he fell ill, missing many of his classes during the fall 1947 semester. That included classes for a training seminar designed to prepare graduate students for field research in Puerto Rico, scheduled to begin in a few months. By spring 1948 he was trying to negotiate a position at Deep Springs for the 1948–49 academic year and redefining his responsibilities for the Puerto Rico project. This came at the same time he learned that his sister, Marion, had requested a transfer from Washington to New Jersey and that his mother planned to move to New Jersey as well. Grace Steward's eyesight had failed so badly by that point that she needed daily care, but Marion's full-time employment precluded her assuming the role of full-time caretaker.[48]

Steward told a longtime acquaintance at Telluride Association that he had worked for nine years without any break and that he had some writing that he wanted to do. Deep Springs represented a refuge to him at the age of forty-six, just as it had earlier in his life. (In many respects, the hours spent in solitude while writing also served this function.) After fewer than two years at Columbia, he was eager to escape to the haven of the high desert: "His inclination is to move far up some canyon in the hills and camp out for a year," the Telluride official reported to a Deep Springs associate. But Steward had also said that he needed to earn money to support four dependents—his wife, two sons, and elderly mother. His affection for Deep Springs, both "as an institution and a geographical location," had led him to consider teaching there for a year, even at a very reduced income. He inquired about schooling for his sons and housing for a family of four.[49]

The official had carefully pointed out to Steward that salaries at Deep Springs were pitifully low. ("I don't like to look at the teaching staff at DS being serfs," he remarked to his associate.) "I painted—but did not overpaint—the dismal budgetary picture," he continued. "I told Steward that he could at least count on a cottage for himself, his wife, and the two boys—and meals for the four either at the Boarding House or at home. (I carefully did not describe to him the horrors of DS coffee.)" Some arrangement could be made for the children's schooling, he added. Clearly anxious to have Steward at the school for a year, he spoke of him as "a man of international professional reputation" and, incorrectly, as the chosen replacement at Columbia for "the late and great" Boas. Steward had in fact filled a position vacated by Linton, who joined the Columbia faculty in 1937, after Boas retired and against Boas's wishes.[50]

A few weeks later, Steward met with a Deep Springs trustee, Carroll N. Whitman, a lawyer from Rochester, New York. The meeting, in his own words "a shocking and staggering experience," left him feeling angry and misunderstood. Whitman, who held deeply conservative political views, subjected Steward to a four-hour diatribe that incorporated the extremist elements of McCarthyism. "You are no doubt quite familiar with the gist of the harangue," Steward wrote to his acquaintance at Telluride Association. "It was directed against communism, liberalism, labor unions, 'mob rule,' majority rule, colored races," and anyone associated with Deep Springs who did not subscribe to Whitman's views.[51]

Steward, simply by virtue of his position at a university in New York City, evidently struck Whitman as highly suspicious and possibly subversive. In the 1930s, remembered by those of Whitman's persuasion as the Red Decade, the publisher William Randolph Hearst had sent agents to various university campuses to search out "red" professors. He evidently thought that they found several at New York University. In the late 1940s, the idea persisted in some quarters that university faculties harbored communists. Later, Steward himself privately referred to Columbia in the 1930s as "a communist cell," but in the context of registering this purely academic complaint: "curiously, many adopted the political and economic orientations [of Marxism] yet remained thoroughgoing relativists [Boasians] in their anthropological work." In the case of Columbia's anthropology department, many of the graduate students in the late 1940s appear to have been more openly leftist than the faculty.[52]

Steward's merely liberal political opinions would undoubtedly have alarmed Whitman, but he said little about them: "it was quite useless to express my own views on things," he explained, "for I have long since learned not to argue with religious people or politically conservative messiahs. On the question of race and civilization, however, I had to let him have it." Experience with his mother had taught Steward the futility of arguing about religion, a topic he usually tried to avoid; his training in anthropology had led him to separate the concepts of race and culture, still a radical idea to many Americans. The public reaction to *The Races of Mankind*, the pamphlet written by Weltfish and Benedict, had already shown that this perspective on race challenged the dominant view.[53]

Steward did not easily give up the idea of teaching at Deep Springs. "I think Deep Springs has something in its small and selected student body, in its unselfish and competent faculty, and in the general setting and regime of life on the ranch," he wrote. "It did a lot for me, and I had some hope that if I could arrange things here I would like to pay back in small part for what I received." (Still a preparatory school in 1948, Deep Springs would soon become a two-year college.) Based on Whitman's remarks, Steward did question whether any semblance of academic freedom prevailed at the school: "I would not give so much as a five minute talk," he declared, "without the absolute guarantee of freedom to say what I believed."

The situation remained unresolved for another month, as some of the concerned parties at Telluride Association and Deep Springs exchanged worried letters and tried to reassure Steward of their goodwill. He responded by conceding that his "rather violent reaction" to the meeting with Whitman might have been "premature." "If I can teach the straight stuff of anthropology without having a trustee down my neck for not supporting racism or something similar," he wrote, "there is still nothing I would rather do than give a year to Deep Springs." While insisting that his teaching was "non-political in every sense," he remained emphatic about his need for academic freedom. Only that would allow him to "give a factual and analytical presentation of race, society, and culture" without any pressure to support any particular "-ism or ideology, whether by a positive or negative approach."

A few weeks later, Steward received a polite letter from a representative of the trustees of Deep Springs, thanking him for his interest in the institution. Financial constraints made it impossible to extend an offer, the representative said, even at the salary level that they had discussed. The letter closed with a bland invitation to visit the school in the future. It came just two weeks after Steward had written, "I am terribly excited about the thought of going to D[eep] S[prings], and it will be a real disappointment if I cannot arrange it somehow." But with the matter irrevocably settled, and no prospect of teaching at Deep Springs in the near future even should the budget improve, he turned his attention back to work at hand.[54]

* * *

Steward left almost immediately for Puerto Rico, where he spent several weeks conferring with the graduate students from Columbia who were carrying out fieldwork.[55] John Murra had been appointed field director. Several months earlier, in January 1948, Diamond, Manners, and Wolf had left New York City for Puerto Rico, traveling by ship. Manners's wife and two children and Wolf's wife later joined them there. Mintz arrived with his wife in late January, and Scheele soon after that.

In mid-February, Diamond left the project and returned to New York City. Murra chose Elena Padilla, a graduate student from the University of Chicago, to replace him. Padilla, who had just completed a master's thesis on Puerto Rican immigration to Chicago and New York City, was from Puerto Rico. The research team also included four Puerto Rican assistants: Delia Ortega, Charles Rosario, Angelina Saavedra de Roca, and Eduardo Seda Bonilla. The presence of three Puerto Rican women (and two Puerto Rican men) transformed the male work group that Steward had assembled in New York City into a more diverse research team. They quickly departed for their chosen research sites, ranging from a sugar plantation to a community of coffee growers.[56]

The Columbia students had prepared for fieldwork in Puerto Rico with a training seminar held in fall 1947. Their training was largely limited to reviewing the literature on the island's history, demography, economy, political relations, and social structure, including race relations. Guest speakers also covered aspects of these topics, and Puerto Ricans living in New York City acted as seminar informants. Steward provided no training in field methods, and, in fact, missed many of the seminar meetings, citing illness.[57]

Years later, Mintz told Steward that the graduate program at Columbia had left him unprepared for fieldwork: "When we all went to Puerto Rico," he wrote, "I had a fair idea of the kinds of goals you were striving for; I found them wholly congenial, and did my best in the field. But Julian, I can hardly tell you how ill-fitted we all were for field work." There followed a list of what Mintz had not learned as a graduate student: how to record a genealogy, do linguistic transcription, carry out a census, and more. "It is true that I had some eye for the big issues," he continued, "but hardly any preparation at all for field procedure."[58]

Steward could have said the same, of course, about his own training for ethnographic research. Kroeber and Lowie had offered their students practically no guidance about field method, although Beals did recall Lowie giving him a crash course on phonetic transcription. But their approach to field research—working intensively with a few informants—also required less preparation than long-term fieldwork in communities. Since Steward had never engaged in the type of field research that his students would undertake, he had no firsthand experience with field methods such as participant observation. He had collected census material, but his method depended on plumbing the memories of one or two elderly informants and had no relevance for his students. Their field research focused on the present, not only the past, and required working in large, complex communities.[59]

In Puerto Rico, Steward thus found himself in the peculiar position of advising a community study project without ever having taken direct part in one himself. Although he had taught a seminar on community studies during his first year at Columbia, he had only administered such projects from a distance, as the head of the Institute of Social Anthropology. Moreover, he still knew rather little about Puerto Rico, having missed so many sessions of the training seminar. And he did not speak Spanish or read it with great ease, which limited his access to published material and his contact with any Puerto Ricans who did not speak English.

This may partly explain why Steward tried to restrict his role almost from the beginning, from director to adviser and fundraiser. His primary interest lay in shaping the theoretical direction of the project, and he spent his time in Puerto Rico in that effort. The eventual result was a framework that reflected his own interests in cause-and-effect relationships and the search for cross-cultural "regularities." It largely overlooked the issues of class power and U.S. control of Puerto Rico that had quickly seized the attention of the students. As Steward described it ten years later, the research in Puerto Rico "helped conceptualize and define the larger territorial and national context within which the several regional subcultures had emerged." But as Mintz well remembered fifty years later, he and his fellow students felt "a certain impatience" with Steward's lack of interest in the political relationship between the United States and Puerto

Rico. (Public awareness of that relationship increased in 1950 when members of a Puerto Rican nationalist group were charged with attempting to assassinate President Truman.)[60]

Tensions within the project and between the project and its sponsors, as well as other complications that typically plague large research ventures, marked the eighteen months of its duration and persisted after it ended. Steward returned to Puerto Rico for a brief visit in February 1949, at which point Murra resigned. The five students ended their fieldwork in summer 1949 and returned to New York City. Padilla did not continue at the University of Chicago, but instead joined her fellow researchers in the doctoral program at Columbia. Over the course of the next two years, the students wrote and defended their dissertations based on the fieldwork in Puerto Rico.[61]

The Puerto Rico Social Anthropology Project, as it was formally known, along with his earlier work at the Institute of Social Anthropology, ushered in the final stage of Steward's long-term research plan. He had begun by studying "the simplest societies," and eventually moved on to complex societies, with the aim of illuminating contemporary social problems. That aim, directly influenced by Nunn, satisfied what he called his "sense of social obligations." He had mentioned this in the mid-1940s to an acquaintance at Telluride Association: "As you perhaps recall," he wrote, "I deliberately chose anthropology in preference to one of the exact sciences for which I had a natural yen because I felt that the latter would always have an adequate following but that the crucial problems of the future would require every possible effort to understand human relationships."[62]

Steward explicitly attributed his own effort to unite science with humanitarian service to Nunn's goal of training public-spirited men who could advance the public good. In twentieth-century America, Steward suggested, scientific training was crucial: "The difficulty with contemporary society," he wrote, "is not too much but too little science, too little knowledge of human relations." He thought that Telluride Association had erred in promoting broad ideals without giving students some direction about how to implement those ideals. "The need in Telluride," he concluded, "[is] to equip the men it trains with techniques for bringing scientific methods to bear on human problems."[63]

Steward conceived of the research in Puerto Rico in just these terms, which he never fully explained to his students: it should help planners and policy makers understand social problems and assess the need for reform. He still thought that his contribution as a scientist lay in providing a range of relevant information, without regard for political currents in policy making—despite the failure of such an approach with the BIA. This element in Steward's research plan, which he would continue to develop during the next decade, came from an early source: his adolescent years at Deep Springs, when he had accepted the high-minded ideal of public service without knowing exactly what it meant or how to carry it out. Even twenty-five years later, the confusion and conflicts created by Nunn's words about "promoting the highest well-being" remained fresh in his mind.[64]

* * *

Steward returned from Puerto Rico to find a letter from J. Alden Mason, editor of the *American Anthropologist,* telling him that his article, "Cultural Causality and Law: A Trial Formulation of the Development of Early Civilizations," had been accepted for publication. The article had grown out of a paper he presented the year before, in 1947, at a conference on Peruvian archaeology sponsored by the Viking Fund (the precursor of the Wenner-Gren Foundation for Anthropological Research) and held in New York City. Steward's appointed task at the conference was to prepare a summary of the other papers, which dealt primarily with Peru. As he had recently done for the *Handbook of South American Indians,* and on an even larger scale in that instance, he searched through a massive amount of empirical data.[65]

His exercise in induction and synthesis had the specific aim of identifying stages of cultural development in Peru and Mesoamerica. It contributed to his long-range research plan, and the goal of studying culture change—especially increasing social and political complexity—in order to "illuminate contemporary affairs," as he later put it.[66] The Puerto Rico project, then in the planning stage, seemed to offer a good opportunity to move on to the study of current social problems, a logical next step after the *Handbook of South American Indians* and the Institute of Social Anthropology projects he had administered in Latin America. But it would present all manner of difficulties as a field project, ranging from the interpersonal to the logistical and methodological.

In producing a paper for the Viking Fund conference, Steward followed a simpler procedure, one in which he had long practice and a record of success. He drew on secondary, published field data independently collected by other scholars, and on his own informal, and unacknowledged, observations. The published data supported, and gave authority to, his generalizing conclusions; but the conclusions themselves resulted from creative leaps based on informal observations and personal memories. The essays that resulted from this approach would make his reputation as a theorist.

Two of the American archaeologists at the conference proposed their own sequences for Peru, evidently following the example of Peruvian archaeologist Rafael Larco Hoyle, who had earlier applied a six-stage sequence to a limited area in northern Peru. Strong and Bennett each presented a different sequence of stages, intended to cover all of Peru. Pedro Armillas suggested four stages for Mesoamerica. Steward, in turn, proposed a sequence that pertained to both areas in the Americas where civilization had first developed. He based the stages on such criteria as subsistence, technology, population density, and the like—elements of what he came to call the "cultural core."[67]

This effort laid the foundation for a much more ambitious paper, "Cultural

Causality and Law." After the conference on Peru and Mesoamerica, Steward had expanded his inquiry to include three other areas where archaeologists thought that civilization had also developed independently: Mesopotamia, Egypt, and China. He concluded that these three areas in the Old World, along with three in the New World (two in Mesoamerica, and one in Peru), had undergone the same sequence of development. Revising his earlier scheme, he proposed a more detailed sequence of stages for the development of early civilizations, still using the same sort of criteria as before. Remarkable for its scope, "Cultural Causality and Law" was perhaps his most notable attempt at synthesis and generalization.

His central argument was that agriculture based on irrigation had developed in the six areas, which were arid or semiarid; and that efforts to control labor for the purpose of building and maintaining irrigation systems and other public works, and efforts to control the distribution of water, had led to increasing stratification, political centralization, and the formation of the state. Steward implicitly drew on what came to be known as Wittfogel's hydraulic theory, but he cited Wittfogel, a specialist in Chinese history, only as a source of empirical data on cultural development in China. In an essay he wrote years later, but which remained unpublished in his own lifetime, he did concede that Wittfogel's "irrigation hypothesis" (not "theory") had "stimulated" his own research on the development of early civilizations.[68]

When Mason returned the manuscript of "Cultural Causality and Law" to Steward, he commended the paper for its boldness, and then cautioned the author about the probable response. "You say well what most of us have felt in the back of our consciousnesses for a long time," he wrote. "But you stick your neck out and will get some hard knocks; I predict you'll come out with a bloody but unbowed head." He enclosed some comments from the reviewer, Frederica de Laguna, who recommended publication and raised a few questions about some technical points. Mason added his own comments and queries and mentioned that he planned to show the manuscript to Linton and to Samuel Kramer, the well-known Near Eastern archaeologist.

Steward wrote a curt reply to each query, and ended his letter by questioning the need for more reviews. "I have no objection to any number of people seeing the manuscript," he said, "but I am puzzled as to why Linton and Kramer should since they are not on the editorial subcommittee. Is it your thought that I should protect myself against as many small matters as possible in advance of publication?" He asserted that many colleagues had already read the paper critically, including Pedro Armillas, Angel Palerm, Strong, Wittfogel, and "a bunch of others."[69]

The unnamed others who had read the manuscript included a number of his graduate students. Steward had made the unusual decision to ask them to read and comment on the paper, and then invited them to his house for an informal discussion. Mintz arrived with his wife, Dorothy Dinnerstein, a psychologist by training, who withstood Steward's rather awkward attempt to shepherd only the men into his study. She insisted on joining the discussion to his evident discomfort. (When she and her husband later separated, Steward took Mintz aside and confided that his first marriage, to a professional woman, had also failed but that his second marriage was very happy. Usually reticent about mentioning his personal life, Steward may have seen an odd number of parallels between his first marriage and his student's. These included the fact that the two Dorothys had each earned a Ph.D. in psychology, and that Dinnerstein, like Nyswander, resisted exclusion by male groups.)[70]

Mintz remembered that he and the other graduate students were "very much in awe" of Steward but liked being asked to read his work and have license to debate issues freely with him. A number of the students, including Mintz and Murphy, remarked that, unlike most of their professors, he listened to them. As Murphy said, he treated his students as if they were full partners in an important venture, "the founding of a true science of society." This represented Steward's vision of anthropology, with the word *science* used in a precise way.[71]

Besides asking his students to read the paper, he seems to have given a copy to Kroeber. "As you see," he commented, "I still can't let go with mere theory, for I don't think it means too much." Strong approved of the paper, Steward said, adding, "I can guess the gist of your reaction." Kroeber does not appear to have responded, at least not in writing. In Wolf's memory, at a meeting where Steward read his paper, "Kroeber reacted to it by not paying attention." It was his usual response to Steward's questions or ideas about causality. Although Steward often attempted to get Kroeber's attention, he seems never to have succeeded, neither by letter nor in person. "There were any number of occasions," Wolf recalled, "when Steward tried to explain to Kroeber what he was about, and Kroeber would continue to talk about theories of pottery on the Peruvian coast."[72]

Undoubtedly with Kroeber in mind, Steward made a sharp distinction between "attacks about small matters" (quarrels about the specific archaeological data he assembled in "Cultural Causality and Law") and "the important attack" (on his central argument). He professed to have no concern about the former, although these seemed to worry Mason. "The important attack," he told Mason, "will come from those who believe that history never repeats itself, and, in traditional manner, they will simply point out that all culture centers are different. There is no answer to this, for it's both true and beside the point."[73]

Kroeber's presence at Columbia may have provoked Steward into taking this strong theoretical position in print. By his own account, he had been reluctant to write theoretical articles because he believed that "they never carried conviction unless supported by substantive material." (Or, as he put it to Strong in 1946, just before joining the Columbia faculty, "theory without supporting fact seems pretty sterile.") That changed, he explained, when Kroeber arrived at Columbia in 1948, "quoting Kluckhohn to the effect that Steward has no theoretical point of view." Kroeber had just left Harvard, where Clyde Kluckhohn was a close colleague. Kluckhohn's goading comment, according to Steward, led him to publish a series of articles in the late 1940s and early 1950s that made his theoretical approach quite clear.[74]

Steward's professional situation, especially in terms of academic clientship, probably also explains the timing. His long years in a patron-client relationship with Kroeber had brought many benefits, but not the long-awaited prize: Kroeber's position at Berkeley when he retired. Steward had accepted the position at Columbia only after realizing that there would be no offer from Berkeley. Verifying that had required some awkward delving, which Steward justified in one revealing sentence: "I just wanted to be sure I wouldn't be jilting my first love." With no prospect of a place at Berkeley, and with a secure and senior position at Columbia, he had little to lose and little to fear if his ideas incurred the disapproval of his senior colleagues. For the first time, he used a very explicit title for a theoretical article, featuring the words *causality* and *law*. He had avoided using the terms *ecological* or *ecology* in titles after having publication problems with his essay on the Southwest; but this time he did not resort to indirect language as he had in choosing titles such as "The Economic and Social Basis of Primitive Bands," or *Basin-Plateau Aboriginal Sociopolitical Groups*.[75]

Steward's persistent, if carefully polite, disagreement with Kroeber had begun nearly twenty-five years earlier, when he asked his teacher when they were going to discuss the causes of cultural phenomena. Kroeber simply dismissed the question, not just once but repeatedly over time. They had a chance to debate each other on this and other points during Kroeber's several years at Columbia in an informal discussion group that met on Saturday mornings. It attracted anthropologists not only from New York City but also from a distance. Willey sometimes traveled with George Foster from Washington to New York City the night before in order to attend, and others came from New Haven and Cambridge. "The discussions," Willey remembered, "would often boil down to arguments between Steward and Kroeber." Kroeber had summed up his position when he said, "'Experience has shown that it is hopeless to storm, by a frontal attack, the great citadels of the causality underlying highly complex groups of facts.'" Nevertheless, at those Saturday morning discussions, Steward did charge the gates. He had not done that quite so openly in the past.[76]

Their disagreement ultimately centered on differing visions of anthropology as a discipline: Kroeber's more humanistic approach versus Steward's commitment to science. When Kroeber good-naturedly labeled Steward a "universalist" during one of the Saturday morning discussions, Steward justified his position by arguing that understanding laws of cultural development allowed better preparation for the future. He evidently did not explain that he viewed anthropology as a vehicle for discovering the laws of culture and culture change, in order to improve understanding of current and future social problems.

Steward appears never to have told Kroeber, nor perhaps any other colleague in anthropology, that he had chosen the field for that very purpose. He usually raised the subject only in correspondence with acquaintances from Deep Springs or Telluride Association. Kroeber, in any case, had a very different view of anthropology. When he presented a paper titled "Have Civilizations a Life History?" at a symposium in Washington, D.C., a member of the audience asked if historians, archaeologists, and other anthropologists had the task of studying the past in order to predict the future. Willey recalled that Kroeber replied flatly, "'I'm not Nostradamus; that's not my game.'"[77]

The "important attack" on "Cultural Causality and Law" that both Mason and Steward had expected never came, and Steward found the postpublication critiques generally positive and constructive. Quite a few colleagues wrote to request reprints, some praising it as "classic" and "the type of thing we have needed for a long time in anthropology." A few months after it appeared in print, Steward remarked that "the older members of [the] profession regard an effort of this kind with horror and say little." Here he undoubtedly alluded to Kroeber, among others. Younger anthropologists, he reported, "are all in favor of it." Requests for reprints came from them, not from senior colleagues.[78]

"Cultural Causality and Law," despite what Steward later saw as its shortcomings, represented a milestone in American anthropology. It signaled an era of increased interest in cultural evolution, appearing in print just six years after Leslie White published his well-known essay "Energy and the Evolution of Culture." Although Steward's own work in the area of multilinear evolution, as he termed it, took him in a different direction from White—or so he always insisted—many younger anthropologists were beginning to turn their attention toward cultural evolution. Years later, Robert Carneiro remembered first reading Steward's article as a student and the strong impression it made on him: "I had barely entered anthropology at that time," he said, "but I could not escape the feeling that something important had occurred."[79]

* * *

Ruth Benedict died unexpectedly in September 1948, soon after belatedly receiving a promotion to the rank of full professor. She had also recently completed an abbreviated term as president of the American Anthropological Association. Benedict was the second woman elected president of the AAA, following Elsie Clews Parsons, who held the office in 1941. Benedict served only a half term, as the last president under the old constitution.[80]

In 1946, then president Linton, her nemesis, had appointed Steward as chair of the AAA's Committee on Reorganization. Despite the opposition of many members, including Kroeber, the committee set about transforming a rather loose scholarly association into a much more cohesive professional organization. Two years later, Steward was nominated for the presidency of the AAA. "Perhaps I am mad," he told a colleague after accepting the nomination. With irreverent humor, he proposed the following platform: "next meetings on a boat to Bermuda, with free beer and babysitters for those who bring families." (The suggestion about child care reflected a strong personal preference for attending conferences in the company of his wife, not a newfound concern about equity and inclusiveness.)[81] He lost the election, according to Willey, because he had irritated so many members of the AAA in the contentious process of reorganization.[82]

Months later, Steward's mother died suddenly at the age of eighty. She was living with his family at the time of her death; they had recently moved from Demarest to nearby Alpine, New Jersey, after buying a house there on Warren Lane. Marion Steward, then working at Fort Monmouth, New Jersey, as an editor of technical reports, had transferred from Washington, D.C., the year before, during the summer of 1948. Grace's presence in her son's household caused a certain strain, which Jane remembered trying to mediate as best she could. Steward had a leave of absence from Columbia in spring 1949 to work for the Social Science Research Council; his project centered on theory and method in area study programs. He finally submitted the report in September, with a comment in passing about "the very sudden death of my mother which stopped my work for a time."[83]

By 1949 Julian Steward had entered what Murphy aptly called "a halcyon period in the life of the middle-class American male that comes at some time between the realization of his ambitions and the start of serious physical decline." As Murphy wrote, "It is a time when his earning potential and position in life are at or near their zenith, but before the triple bypass or the discovery of diabetes." In Steward's case, only months elapsed between publication of "Cultural Causality and Law" and surgery. Instead of teaching scheduled courses during the fall semester of 1949, he spent several months in the hospital, with serious complications resulting from an amoebic infection. Jane Steward later wondered whether the infection he contracted in Ecuador in 1938 had persisted, accounting for the years of chronic health problems that followed that trip. She pointed out that he visited Mexico in the mid-1940s while directing the Institute of Social Anthropology and might have been reinfected there.[84]

Some of Steward's students and colleagues at Columbia seem to have misunderstood his condition in 1949. Many considered his ailment entirely psychosomatic, even after it reached the acute stage, requiring a long stay in the hospital. During the previous three years, their skepticism about his illness had only grown stronger with repeated incidents of canceled classes, interrupted courses, broken appointments, and last-minute absences from scheduled meetings and dissertation defenses. Kirchhoff, according to Wolf, took over one of the abandoned courses; and, in Steward's absence, Scheele apparently substituted as chair of the training seminar for the Puerto Rico project.[85]

The only colleague who seemed not to question his condition was Isabel Kelly. By 1950 she had lived in Mexico for about ten years. "My honest opinion," she wrote, "is that doctors in Mexico are much better equipped to cope with intestinal parasites than is almost anyone in the United States. There, the doctor

wrings his hands and reaches for the new edition of a book on tropical medicine, just to see what to do. Here, however, such afflictions are just routine for
almost every doctor." She encouraged him to seek treatment in Mexico if his
condition failed to improve.[86]

After his release from the hospital, Steward convalesced at home before re-
suming work again. By fall 1950 he reported being "back on the job full-blast
after a rather grisly winter last year spent largely in bed." The number of students finishing doctoral work in anthropology increased sharply after 1950, and
Steward found himself reading more and more dissertations over the next two
years, including those of the five students who had worked on the Puerto Rico
project. He continued with his own writing, but had less time to devote to it.
Graduate students required "an enormous amount of personal attention," he
told an acquaintance.[87]

In addition, he had agreed to serve as an expert witness for the federal government in some of the Indian Claims Commission cases. A law firm had contacted him as they prepared to prosecute on behalf of the Shoshone for lands
taken by the government, but within a few months Steward had agreed to testify for the government, not for the Indians.[88] He may have suspected law firms
of having too strong an interest in financial gain. Perhaps his identification with
government service and government science led him to see the federal government's motives as less suspect. And he probably realized from the outset that
his testimony would not support the argument made by the law firm representing the Shoshone. He always wanted the freedom to state his views as a scientist, which he took to be objective, uncompromised by personal, political, or
other interest. He had taken that stance in the mid-1930s with the BIA, and in
1948 with a Deep Springs trustee—without great success in either case.

Many of his associates at Columbia saw his decision to serve as a government
witness in a different light. Mintz recalled that he and most of his fellow students, along with many other anthropologists, thought that Steward was "on
the wrong side." They believed that he was acting against the interests of American Indians, without regard to the bleak history of federal policies and practices
toward Indians and Indian lands.[89] Some also viewed Steward as making common cause with a government that many academics identified with McCarthyism. As Senator Joseph McCarthy's search for Communists gathered force, universities came under greater scrutiny. In the near future, a Senate subcommittee
would call one of Steward's colleagues in Columbia's anthropology department
for questioning, asking whether she was or ever had been a member of the
Communist party.[90]

* * *

In 1952 Steward accepted a research professorship at the University of Illinois, a
decision that surprised his students and colleagues and one that his wife accepted
with great ambivalence. Jane Steward knew that leaving Columbia would reduce

the strain of his work life and perhaps improve his health. But she did not look forward to following him to a distant and unknown place on the prairie, or to establishing a new life once again. They had crossed the prairie and the plains on their trip to Berkeley in 1947, and she held in memory a picture of a blank and featureless land that seemed almost without limit. (Her husband, who had felt hemmed in and under siege at Columbia, responded differently to the openness, the expansive sense of space, and the endless sky.) The move would also uproot their children, then thirteen and fifteen. They would have to give up the friends they had made after moving from Demarest to Alpine and enter new schools in a faraway place.[91]

Steward had been approached about a position at Illinois by John W. Albig, a sociologist and chairman of the department. The two men may have known each other at the University of Michigan, where both taught in the late 1920s. In any case, Albig visited New York City in spring 1951 and reported spending nine hours with Steward, discussing anthropology, his situation at Columbia, and the prospects for anthropology at Illinois. He told a university administrator that Steward had shown interest in a research professorship, "being especially impressed with the possibility of organizing his time, research, and writing without the intrusion of various duties in which he has become involved at Columbia. Who isn't?" Steward accepted a formal offer from the University of Illinois six months later.[92]

He always said that the offer of a nonteaching, research professorship had drawn him away from Columbia because his position there required so much work with students, deflecting him from his own writing. But he was more than willing, even eager, to leave Columbia and New York City.[93] He did not express his feelings about the university openly to fellow faculty members or to his students. At least one of them, Murphy, understood that Steward had "no stomach," as he put it, for academic politics. It was generally assumed, however, that only the higher salary and promise of generous support for his research—which Columbia reportedly declined to match—had lured him away. In truth, after six years in an atmosphere of intense competition, conflict, and political intrigue, he welcomed the chance to move in a westward direction and to begin again elsewhere.[94]

At the time he accepted the offer from Illinois, Steward had known for more than a year that he had no realistic prospect of ever returning to Berkeley. If he had held out any hope of "inheriting" Lowie's position, his hopes were dashed when Du Bois was offered an appointment with tenure, which she agreed to accept beginning in fall 1951, a year after Lowie retired. She was at least the fourth graduate (following Ronald Olson, Theodore McCown, and Robert Heizer) to receive an offer of a full-time position in the department, and probably the first woman. Another graduate, George Foster, accepted a position at Berkeley in 1953. It appears unlikely that Steward was seriously considered for the post offered to Du Bois. His recent work for the federal government in the Indian Claims Commission cases had not enhanced his collegial relations with several Berkeley faculty members and graduates, who testified on behalf of the Indians. Steward may not have understood this fully since he always contended that his role was neutral and scientific. Many of his colleagues took a different view.[95]

As it happened, Du Bois declined the position at Berkeley when the university insisted that she first sign a loyalty oath. "Quixotically, I publicly refused to accept the appointment," she later wrote, "disregarding Kroeber's advice that such flurries come and go." At that point in her career, Du Bois had spent twelve years working for the federal government, first in the Office of Strategic Services during the war, and then in the State Department. But as McCarthyism emerged in the late 1940s, she found that anthropologists were considered suspect and no longer welcome. She took a leave of absence from the State Department in 1949, without any intention of returning.[96]

At Berkeley, despite its distance from Washington, Du Bois observed a similar atmosphere of silence and fear descending over the university. Some members of the psychology department, including Nyswander's graduate adviser, Edward Chace Tolman, had already refused to sign a loyalty oath. The university dismissed Tolman and about thirty other faculty members. Erik Erikson, a member of the psychology department, soon resigned from Berkeley, having found a position in the East, as did Du Bois in 1954. Nyswander also refused to sign the oath. She was called before a committee, refused once again to sign, submitted her resignation to the dean of the School of Public Health, and left the country to work as a consultant for the World Health Organization. A month or two later, the dean contacted her in Switzerland, and eventually persuaded her to sign the oath in order to protect her department. Even decades later, she regretted her decision and would speak only off the record about some aspects of that period at Berkeley.[97]

A few months after Steward left Columbia, Weltfish was called before a Senate Internal Security subcommittee. Weltfish, an outspoken feminist who supported women's rights, racial equality, and other unpopular causes, had served as president of the Congress of American Women. Her role in that organization, which had been accused of subversive activity, and her active pursuit of social justice made her highly suspect to members of the subcommittee. She invoked the Fifth Amendment and refused to answer whether she had ever belonged to the Communist party. Five months later, Columbia University refused to renew her contract. Administrators insisted that the decision simply reflected a change in policy that made Weltfish, as a temporary member of the teaching staff for seventeen years, ineligible for reappointment.[98]

Strong, then serving as chairman of the department of anthropology, told a *New York Times* reporter that he had tried repeatedly but without success to have her promoted. Although she held what university statutes defined as a part-time position, she in fact carried a full-time teaching load, thirteen hours a week. Weltfish evidently did not blame the department for the loss of her appointment, but rather the "'prejudice against women scholars'" that pervaded universities. Nearly ten years passed before she regained an academic position, teaching undergraduate students in Madison, New Jersey, at a small branch campus of Fairleigh Dickinson University.[99]

Smith had left Columbia in 1951, still at the rank of instructor and without tenure. She taught for a year at the more appropriate rank of associate professor in the Department of State's Foreign Service Institute. In 1952 she began teaching part-time at the London School of Economics. In the same year, she married an English businessman, whom she had met in southern Asia in the late 1940s. The symptoms of the disease that led to her untimely death in 1961, at the age of fifty-three, had already appeared several years before she left Columbia. It was explicitly noted in her obituary that "Marian Smith was not the first distinguished woman anthropologist at Columbia to suffer professional discrimination."[100]

Columbia's graduate program in anthropology appears to have been unique in the 1940s in having any women on the faculty, even in irregular positions (a "temporary" position that lasted for seventeen years, a "part-time" position with a full-time teaching load, an "instructorship" held by a Ph.D. recipient with ten years' teaching experience). Benedict's death in 1948, Smith's departure in 1951, and Weltfish's removal in 1953 left it with a full-time faculty comprised of men.[101] By the early 1950s, mirroring the trend in the larger society, women had been dislodged from the faculty at Columbia; very few held positions in anthropology departments at other American universities.

Their near absence from the professional ranks of academic anthropology corresponded to the way women were still represented in the mainstream of disciplinary thought—which is to say, nearly excluded in an analytic sense. They were represented almost solely as wives and mothers, defined primarily by their relations with men, placed on the social margins, their labor and economic contributions minimized or unrecognized. Steward's concept of the patrilineal band, soon to attract more attention, constituted an apt metaphor for the profession, especially for the placement of men and women within it. This may, in fact, have contributed to the persuasiveness of his theoretical concept, and its acceptance by many of his colleagues. Their own cultural perceptions and social milieu, not the weight of ethnographic evidence, made it believable. The evidence remained remarkably slight.[102]

Two of Steward's former students were among the men hired by Columbia's anthropology department during the early 1950s. Their hiring, and the success of his other male students who found positions in anthropology departments, marked another crucial stage in Steward's career. He had finally "reproduced" in a professional sense, creating his own "sublineage" of men. His former students would help to disseminate some of the theoretical ideas that he had already put into print before arriving at Columbia, as well as others developed during his tenure there. Many of the men who studied with him had a direct stake in those ideas, convinced that they had influenced Steward's thinking just as surely as he had influenced theirs.[103]

CHAPTER 11

AT HOME ON THE PRAIRIE

Steward transplanted easily from the vertical, crowded cityscape of metropolitan New York to the horizontal, open landscape of the Illinois prairie. By coincidence, John Wesley Powell—the exemplar of the explorer/scientist for the young Steward—had known that landscape well during his own days as a professor of geology. Before leaving on his westward journey, he taught briefly at two nearby colleges. The dimensions of land and sky had prepared Powell for the West he would soon see; those same dimensions reminded Steward of the West he had known. The prairie, which had served as Powell's starting point, would be Steward's stopping place, his home for the last twenty years of his life.[1]

Steward and his family arrived in Urbana, Illinois, at the end of the summer. In the first months of fall 1952, Steward found that he liked living in a university town again. With a population of about sixty thousand, Urbana and its twin municipality, Champaign, had an ordered, midwestern look. It seemed mercifully small and compact to Steward in contrast to northern New Jersey and New York, where postwar development and asphalt sprawl were swallowing up the remnants of open land. A ten-minute drive took him from one side of town to the other. From that vantage point, he surveyed an uncluttered expanse of earth and sky, austere in line and color, extravagant in size.[2]

"We enjoy Urbana enormously," he told Wendell Bennett, a midwesterner by birth and upbringing, and one of Steward's few colleagues in the East who had lived in the region. The people he met during his first months there, including fellow faculty, struck Steward as warm and welcoming. He spoke well of the sociologists who made up the majority of his colleagues in a joint department of twenty-one faculty members. All but three of them were men. The several women occupied the lowest ranks, two as instructors and one as assistant professor. The department included two anthropologists, both men, with Steward bringing the number to three.[3]

The only drawback of his situation, as he explained it to Bennett, was the distance from some of the anthropologists he had known in New York City. He alluded here to former students, not to fellow faculty members. Since Steward's new position as research professor provided funds for two research associates, he would soon solve that problem by bringing some of his students from Columbia to Illinois. They would constitute the male work group that Steward always sought out in his professional life and that was so central to his intellectual life, including his thinking about human social groups and cultural development.[4]

Steward and his family moved into a house on Oregon Street in Urbana, a few blocks from the university and his office in the department of sociology and anthropology. The office was located in a corner of Davenport Hall, in a space once occupied by the School of Agriculture. A rambling, three-story brick structure, Davenport Hall looked out on green lawns and tall spreading trees. It stood in a row of academic buildings along one side of a spacious quadrangle and was a short walk from the large Union building.[5]

The department of sociology had expanded just four years earlier, in 1948, when it changed its name and hired a cultural anthropologist, Oscar Lewis, and an archaeologist, John C. McGregor.[6] Steward had first met Lewis during the 1930s when Lewis was a graduate student at Columbia working with Benedict. He received his doctorate in 1940. During the war years, he held several positions with the government, including one that took him, along with his wife and young son, to Mexico for about a year. He used that opportunity to do field research on the side, restudying a peasant community, Tepoztlán, that Robert Redfield had studied about twenty years earlier. This resulted in the first of many books that Lewis would write with his wife's active collaboration, most of them based on fieldwork in Mexico and elsewhere in Latin America.[7] While Jane Steward assisted her husband in various ways, Ruth Lewis contributed far more directly to her husband's research and publication. Her labor went unrecognized during his lifetime.

McGregor, who specialized in midwestern and southwestern archaeology, had earned a master's degree from the University of Arizona in the early 1930s and a Ph.D. from the University of Chicago in 1946. Just three years younger than Steward, he joined the University of Illinois faculty at the rank of associate professor. McGregor helped create the program in anthropology, and he remained responsible for much of the undergraduate teaching, even after Steward's arrival, since Steward's position as research professor did not require any teaching. This disparity did not promote good collegial relations between the two men.[8]

Within months of arriving at the University of Illinois, Steward arranged temporary teaching and research appointments for two Columbia students.

Over the course of a few years, Frederic K. Lehman, Ben Zimmerman, Robert Murphy, and Eric Wolf served as his research associates. Academic positions, once again scarce following the brief postwar expansion, did not materialize for some of those students and others for several years. Their letters to Steward chronicled the instability and insecurity of their work lives, as well as their frustration as they took one temporary position after another. One complained of feeling like "a Syrian peddler, always packing, unpacking, repacking." Another detailed his complicated moving plans, which included collecting belongings stored with various friends in New York City, and then trying to arrange short-term housing nearly a thousand miles away for a job that was guaranteed for only one semester.[9]

Still another former student, having held a series of temporary teaching positions on both sides of the continent, found himself unemployed several years after finishing his degree at Columbia. "It seems absurd that I should find myself in this position," Stanley Diamond wrote. "What the hell is a man supposed to do in order to get the splendid opportunity of supporting his wife and children on a salary of $4500 per year and with some little chance of permanency." He asked sardonically if it required having "a string of brilliant publications, knocked out in your first year of teaching, including summer school."[10]

During that same period, Bernard Mishkin, a recent Columbia graduate when Steward met him in Peru in 1938, gave up on a career in anthropology. His had consisted of a series of fellowships, consultancies, and temporary teaching positions, interrupted by service in the military during the war. After teaching for two years at Brandeis University as a lecturer, still without a permanent academic position fifteen years after earning a Ph.D. in anthropology, he entered the air transport business in 1952. When he died unexpectedly two years later, just forty-one years old, he was working as an executive for the Flying Tigers.[11]

Steward appears not to have told his students about his own wanderings and quest for employment during the depression. Perhaps he was following unwritten rules of the academic world that govern the pursuit of prestige. In any case, like Kroeber and others, he emphasized the successes of his later years and almost never spoke of his early struggles. Many of his students thus assumed that his own career path had been straight and smooth and much easier than their own.[12] This may explain not only the frustration but also the bewilderment that some expressed upon finding themselves unemployed, marginally employed, or temporarily employed and transient. Taking a temporary position, guaranteed for only a semester or a year, could require moving thousands of miles. This had been Steward's own experience when he went to Michigan in 1928 and, for that matter, Kroeber's when he went to San Francisco in 1900.

Like generations of graduate students, Steward's evidently received no formal warning about two of anthropology's occupational hazards: underemployment and dislocation, especially frequent during the early years of a career. Given the length of graduate training, added to several years of military service, his male students were in their thirties—many of them married, a few with children, some the sole providers for their families—when they realized that receiving a Ph.D. in anthropology did not confer security or stability. To the contrary, pursuing their profession could require repeated uprootings and more years of insecurity. Unlike physicians or other professionals who were almost assured of the chance to practice their trade after serving a lengthy apprenticeship, the new anthropologists were not. Even those who found tenure-track positions faced a long probationary period. With it came the possibility of being denied tenure as they approached the age of forty and of having to establish another career. (These circumstances were not unique to the 1950s, but prevailed during most of the twentieth century.)

The students' own subsistence worries, uncertainty, and wanderings in pursuit of a scarce and scattered resource—an academic position in anthropology—may have given even greater personal meaning to Steward's theoretical approach, newly christened cultural ecology. If coming of age during the depression had made them receptive to a materialist perspective that gave attention to work and survival, as Murphy maintained, the early years of their careers certainly reinforced it. Murphy and his fellow students would diverge from Steward in various ways in their research, but most continued to think and write about political and economic issues that articulated in certain ways with their own lives and circumstances.

Following Kroeber's example, Steward tried to provide temporary employment for a number of his male students, along with advice, encouragement, and letters of recommendation. In time, most of them found academic positions in some of the leading programs in anthropology. Belonging to a highly active professional network, comprised of fellow students who had worked with Steward at Columbia and later, also helped them launch successful careers. The competitive struggle and the years of frustration took a toll, however, creating rifts between some of the men and with Steward, much to his disappointment in later years. A small number of his Columbia students left academic life, including the self-styled "Syrian peddler."[13]

Not surprisingly, women with Ph.D.'s in anthropology found it as difficult as ever, or even more difficult, to locate permanent academic positions during this period. Kroeber's depression-era warning to women interested in a career in anthropology, a warning both formal and explicit, appears to have been short-lived and highly unusual in the profession. In the early 1950s, some of them realized only slowly and belatedly that they might not find academic employment. Steward, who worked primarily with men, does not appear to have suggested any women for full-time teaching positions. He rarely recommended a woman for any sort of professional situation.[14]

His own views about women and professional employment had wide currency during the postwar era, inside and outside the academic world. Men had priority, especially married men with dependents, and in the letters they wrote to him, Steward's former students did not hesitate to remind him of their status as providers. Like Steward himself, they seem to have readily identified with the hunters of the patrilineal band. Many of them shared a view of the human social world that placed men and their labor at the center, and women and children, considered nonworking dependents, on the margins.

The men who joined Steward at Illinois as his research associates, nearly all of them easterners, needed the temporary work that he offered but regarded the move to a different region as a kind of exile. They took a dim view of the Midwest even before arriving there. "Most of our New York friends seem to think that we are going into the heart of a dark continent," one wrote shortly before leaving for Urbana. Another alluded to "the wilds of the Corn Belt," and a few months later added, "Write to us and let us know when the corn begins to sprout out in Urbana." Others referred to "corn-fed students" at the university. Corn evidently served as metaphor for all that they found wrong with the Midwest.

Former students who stopped to visit Steward while driving cross-country from the East routinely remarked on the obscurity and remoteness of his new location. Some complained that their maps did not show Urbana. When setting out, they apparently knew only that he lived somewhere in an immense, amorphous region that lay between the Atlantic and Pacific coastlines. Imagining him marooned and entirely alone, many seem to have shared the hope expressed by one, that Steward was not "cut off from any life-lines out in the Mid-West." From their perspective, based on a center/periphery model of North America, Steward had inexplicably chosen to leave the center of intellectual and cultural life to take up residence in an unknown hinterland. Steward, however, never shared the eastern, urban bias of the academic world. In his own view, based on a geographic, East-West model, he lived in a place blessedly distant from the East, if regrettably not quite in the West.[15]

Far from feeling isolated in Urbana, especially once his research associates arrived, Steward rather quickly found town life confining. He and his family had already moved from the house on Oregon Street to a larger house on University Avenue in Champaign. But less than two years after arriving in Illinois, they sold that house and left town entirely, moving about twenty miles east to the hamlet of Fithian. Just as he had left McLean, Virginia, for a house in the country and Demarest, New Jersey, for a more secluded setting in Alpine, he again chose country living. "As in New Jersey," he explained, "we found that life in the midst of the community was not to our liking." In truth, his wife would have happily remained in Champaign. When they had difficulty selling the house, Jane Steward continued living in it during the summer with their two sons, while her husband looked after the house in Fithian. Their older son, Gary, planned to enter college that fall; Mike, then fifteen, would transfer to the local high school.[16]

Perhaps it was no coincidence that the move to Fithian followed a trip Julian Steward made to the Southwest, to the open spaces of New Mexico and Arizona, in summer 1953. Several months after he returned home to Illinois, the search for a country house had begun in earnest, soon leading to the purchase of a large frame house on four acres. Steward described the location as "really rural," adding with unusual warmth, "I love it immensely." The four acres included pasture for a horse (left by the former owners), a barn, a chicken house, sundry other outbuildings, and a large vegetable garden. He told one of his Columbia students jokingly that he had adapted very easily to "the life that I have found to be a distinct rural type, namely, the gentleman peasant type, represented in Illinois and so far as I know in the world by this one case." The allusion was to rural subcultures and types of peasantry in Latin America, an interest that Steward shared with some of his students.[17]

Living in sight of the prairie gave Steward the freeing sense of unbounded space that he had first experienced in the desert West, which was also the only place, up to that point in his life, where he had found it. From Fithian, he could see vast fields of deep black soil stretching out in the distance under an immense, sheltering sky. The prairie lacked his cherished mountains, but it offered views of land and sky as far as the eye could see. "I wish you could come out and stay with us," he wrote to Robert Manners, describing a landscape where "one sees a house several miles away hull down over the horizon with only the upper story or chimney showing." It was a "relief," he added, to have left "town dwelling with its streets, traffic and complications."[18] He was finally at home on the prairie, and would live there for the rest of his life.

* * *

During his first years at Illinois, Steward enjoyed many of the accolades of his profession. Then in his early fifties, he had devoted nearly thirty years of his life to anthropology and had published extensively. He turned down at least one of the honors, editorship of the *American Anthropologist,* citing a lack of time and his probable absence from the country, although he was not teaching and had no immediate plans for foreign travel. But he did have several projects of his own underway, including a collection of essays that would reach print a few years later under the title *Theory of Culture Change.* His experience of editing the *Handbook of South American Indians,* which he continued to describe as a "detour" in his research plan, may explain why he so firmly declined the editorship of the *American Anthropologist.* To his way of thinking, what he privately called "the dirty work of organizing and editing" had rather little intellectual value, although it undeniably offered professional rewards.[19]

A few months later, Steward received an honor in absentia. The Wenner-Gren Foundation awarded him the Viking Fund Medal at the annual meeting of the American Anthropological Association in December 1952.[20] Steward had planned to present a paper, but at the last minute decided not to attend, citing illness. When Fred Eggan, the new president of the AAA, announced Steward's name at the award ceremony, he quoted a press release from Urbana written by a reporter for the Associated Press: "Steward is being honored for research indicating that what happened in one human culture may also be found in others under similar circumstances." The award committee had, in fact, selected him primarily in honor of his work as editor of the *Handbook,* although it also recognized his contributions to the fields of social organization and cultural evolution. (His 1936 essay on bands and 1938 monograph, *Basin-Plateau,* were singled out as major contributions on social organization, offering "a basic analysis and definition of the simplest forms of family and coresidence groups.") It appears that Steward spoke to the reporter and represented his work in terms of the theoretical aim, summarized in one pithy sentence by him or, as likely, the reporter.[21]

A personal letter that he wrote soon after receiving the Viking Fund Medal conveys his view of his place in the profession. He found the award gratifying in an intellectual sense, he said, because it validated his theoretical perspective and showed that fellow anthropologists finally accepted his ideas. "This point of view was seemingly accepted by students [at Columbia]," Steward wrote, "but not by the profession." The very ideas that his senior colleagues had rejected ten years earlier, he thought, had finally begun to receive recognition and approval.[22]

He did not mention here Kroeber's rebuff when he first raised questions about cultural causality in the 1920s, or their Saturday morning debates more than two decades later; the silence that initially greeted his first theoretical papers and Spier's rejection of his article on the Southwest in the 1930s; Linton's dismissive remark in the 1940s, put directly to him, that Steward's ideas amounted to "environmental determinism," which had, of course, been discredited long ago; or Kluckhohn's alleged gibe to Kroeber that Steward had no theoretical perspective. But in the last twenty years of his life, he did often allude to these comments and episodes in language suggesting that the memories still rankled.[23]

Steward's experience, and resentment, were not at all unique, although he did go to unusual lengths to protect himself from critics. Having his ideas treated with indifference, derision, or hostility was simply an unavoidable aspect of academic politics. The silence that greeted his ideas in the 1930s, the lack of acknowledgment, had indicated his marginality as a new member of the profession. The slighting comments, to his face or behind his back, amounted to verbal thrusts in the sparring match for prestige. They were inevitable in a highly competitive profession in which any step up the academic ladder of prestige was considered taken at the expense of someone else. Given that structure, the sparring had as much to do with interpersonal conflicts and resentments as with genuine intellectual disagreements. In the end, it was difficult to separate them. Competitors who gained ground with an opposing intellectual position also encroached on their colleagues' positions in the professional hierarchy.

Almost fifty years after giving a talk to the Anthropological Society of Washington, archaeologist Luther Cressman remembered in painful detail the attack he endured when he presented some new ideas in a public forum. In the course of explaining the findings of his research, he offered a new perspective on the prehistory of the Great Basin, one that departed from orthodox views. During the ensuing discussion, he recalled, an anthropologist who accepted many of the prevailing ideas "practically accused me of falsifying my evidence." Cressman left Washington feeling like an outcast. The episode taught him a "hard lesson about how old theories hate to die," he later wrote, "and the danger inherent in being the cause of their demise."[24]

Those words exactly capture Steward's anxieties about presenting his own theoretical views publicly and in person. Steward had witnessed the results from the firing line when Cressman addressed the Anthropological Society of Washington: he was the hostile critic Cressman remembered. In that instance, however, he had occupied the secure position of defender of majority opinion, which he happened to share. Still, he may have drawn a similar lesson from that episode as well as others he witnessed from the sidelines: not only do "old theories hate to die," but their adherents always outnumber the proponents of any new theory. The new theory, inevitably seen as an attack on the old, nearly always meets with a vigorous counterattack, in this particular case launched by Steward himself.

In publishing and otherwise promoting his own work, Steward proceeded cautiously for years. He always showed more willingness to express and defend his views in writing than in a formal setting and in person. In print he could choose his words carefully and hone his argument, supporting it with a profusion of empirical evidence.[25] Above all, he wanted to avoid being attacked himself, especially publicly and face-to-face. That he rarely attended professional meetings, and that he worked closely with his graduate students rather than with peers, greatly reduced the chance of confrontation. The move to Illinois—where he had only two colleagues in anthropology, both of them junior and one often absent—had the same effect.

His comments later in life suggest that he saw himself as the lonely exponent of an unusual and unaccepted theoretical approach for most of his career. More to the point, he was deeply uncomfortable with his (self-)image as an intellectual black sheep. With the award of the Viking Fund Medal, he felt invited into the fold—but only, as he later confided, for "about ten minutes."[26]

Steward's election to membership in the National Academy of Sciences in 1954, an even greater honor than the Viking Fund Medal, confirmed his status as one of anthropology's dons. He joined a small number of anthropologists so honored by the academy, all of them men. (Some of his predecessors included Powell, elected in 1880, and Boas, elected in 1900. About twenty years later, and not in Steward's lifetime, Margaret Mead and Frederica de Laguna became the first women from his field to gain membership.)[27] Steward suddenly found himself in the company of several men he had long regarded as intellectual adversaries—Kroeber, Spier, and Kluckhohn—and others he also knew well, including Lowie and Shapiro. Linton, another member, had died just months earlier.

They not only welcomed him but also had selected their long-time colleague as a new member of a very small and exclusive club.[28]

His election did not come as a surprise to him. Eight years earlier, Kroeber had written in a letter that Steward would "surely attain election by the National Academy of Sciences by fifty." Steward kept a carbon copy of that letter in his files. He was fifty-two when he received the invitation to join the academy from Alexander Wetmore, whom Steward had known as secretary of the Smithsonian Institution during his years at the BAE. In 1954 Wetmore also served as home secretary for the National Academy of Sciences, and he signed the letter notifying Steward of his election to membership. "The Academy thus desires to express its high appreciation of your services to science," Wetmore wrote.[29]

John Bardeen, a professor of electrical engineering and physics at the University of Illinois, was elected to membership in the same year. Bardeen, who won the Nobel Prize in physics just two years later, had worked as a member of the Bell Laboratories team that invented the transistor in the late 1940s, revolutionizing electronics. (He shared the Nobel Prize again in 1972 for his work on superconductivity.) Owing to the halo effect, Steward's election to the National Academy of Sciences in the same year as Bardeen's increased his stature at the university even more than would otherwise have been the case. He rarely taught during this period, concentrating almost entirely on research and writing.[30]

As a member of the National Academy of Sciences, he also received invitations to present papers at its annual meetings. He accepted one such invitation tentatively, suggesting a paper title but telling Wetmore that it was "not entirely certain" that he would be able to attend. Steward seems to have missed it, just as in previous years he had canceled plans to attend annual meetings of the AAA, usually at the eleventh hour. This happened not only in 1952, when he was awarded the Viking Fund Medal, but also the next year, when a special symposium was devoted to issues raised by his 1949 article, "Cultural Causality and Law." Karl Wittfogel took part, along with Robert McCormick Adams, Pedro Armillas, Ralph Beals, and Donald Collier. Steward, however, failed to appear at the scheduled symposium in Tucson.[31]

The pattern of last-minute cancellations, which had a long history, intensified in the 1950s, even when events took place nearby and he helped plan them. In June 1955 he hosted a small conference in Urbana attended by quite a few of his Columbia students and by Wittfogel and Eggan, among others. Wittfogel and the other participants from New York City had traveled hundreds of miles, and Eggan made a several-hour drive from Chicago, in order to take part. Steward left abruptly on the first day and without saying good-bye to some of them, later explaining that he had felt ill. In Murphy's memory of the event, "Everyone left, mad as hell."[32]

* * *

Theory of Culture Change appeared in print in 1955, published by the University of Illinois Press, which was Steward's last major publisher. The University of California had published his earliest monographs, and many of his midcareer works appeared in print under the auspices of the Smithsonian Institution. Before leaving New York City, he had approached Columbia University Press about the book on Puerto Rico that he and his students were writing, but it finally appeared under the imprint of the University of Illinois Press in 1956. Production costs and other problems led to a long delay in publishing *The People of Puerto Rico.*[33]

Steward was at work on *Theory of Culture Change* in the early months of 1953, just after receiving the Viking Fund Medal and apparently before the metaphorical "ten minutes" had passed. Many of the essays had been previously published, and Steward had long since run out of reprints for them, this in the era before photocopy machines. Making those articles accessible to a larger and younger audience provided one motive for the book. Another was to create a vehicle for several essays, newly written or in process, in which he spelled out his theoretical perspective. Advice that he later gave to one of his Columbia students—to write some short articles dealing with theory ("your professional stock would shoot way up") suggests how clear and conscious his motives were in producing this book, which became his best-known work.[34]

Encouraged by the Viking Fund Medal, Steward decided to include articles that he described as "hardly publishable ten years ago" but finally in demand. He also made passing reference to articles and monographs that he had difficulty publishing in the 1930s. In truth, he revised extensively as he wrote, and he rarely seems to have made significant changes to manuscripts at the request of editors; the article that Spier rejected for the *American Anthropologist* had shortly thereafter appeared in *Anthropos.* His remarks say less about editorial process than about his self-doubt, including chronic anxiety about acceptance or rejection by the profession. As he later admitted privately, receiving the Viking Fund Medal and membership in the National Academy of Sciences gave him a fleeting sense of euphoria. Then he wondered if it was all just a terrible mistake.[35]

Theory of Culture Change, subtitled *The Methodology of Multilinear Evolution,* included an introduction and twelve chapters. Steward divided the chapters into two sections, "Concepts and Methods" and "Substantive Applications." Most of the chapters in the latter section had already appeared in print, but in scattered places and over a period of twenty years. They included his 1937 article on the Southwest and his 1949 article on early civilizations. Steward made minor changes in some articles and altered most of the titles slightly, but he generally avoided adding new citations and material. As he remarked in a footnote, new research might call into question some of the substantive material but not his theoretical point.[36]

He did extensively rework the 1936 paper on bands, dividing it into two chapters and placing the longer essay, "The Patrilineal Band," before "The Composite Hunting Band." Explaining that the patrilineal band constituted a culture type, he argued that its defining features—including patrilineality and patrilocality, exogamy, and land ownership—constituted "a cultural core which recurred cross-culturally with great regularity," while other features varied. Moreover, he suggested that it developed under highly specific ecological conditions: where scattered, nonmigratory game was the main source of food, population density was low, and all transportation was by foot.[37]

Although he had refined his conceptual framework—using new concepts and offering more specifics about ecological factors—he drew on the same ethnographic sources and material on the Ona, Tehuelche, and other hunter-gatherers for illustration and support. He had not refined his argument, in other words, by finding new or more detailed empirical data, provided either by his own fieldwork or by that of others. The patrilineal band had eluded him in North and South America, but he never doubted its existence. Still the foundational concept in his thinking, it had preoccupied him for twenty years; and if the ethnographic data remained sketchy at best, he had nevertheless finally specified the ecological setting in which the patrilineal band developed.

Steward believed that composite bands, which he defined as larger in size and including unrelated families, existed in somewhat different ecological circumstances. Although population density was low, large herds of migratory game provided the major source of food, supporting groups of several hundred people. Or "certain social practices," such as endogamy or matrilocal residence, could produce composite bands among hunters where "patrilineal bands normally occurred," as he put it. Even abundant plant foods, such as the acorns harvested by California Indians, could create composite groups, he concluded. Although he asserted at the outset of the essay that "distinctive cultural ecological processes" produced composite hunting bands, his concept, in fact, seemed something of a catchall, a way of categorizing and explaining groups that deviated from his model of the patrilineal band. As in the original essay, his language and line of argument suggest that Steward saw male-centered groups as normal, predictable, and understandable and other types as far more difficult to predict or explain.[38]

Four of the chapters in *Theory of Culture Change* had not been previously published. Notably, two of them provided formal statements of concepts—"cultural ecology" and "culture type" (in chapters 2 and 5, respectively)—that were largely implicit in some of his earlier work. They had emerged in part from a guiding question about the causes of cultural change, which had directed Steward's research and much of his writing for twenty years. He had also developed other concepts, including what he called the "cultural core" and "levels of sociocultural integration," in the context of empirical research, not in advance of research. Still, his formal statements appeared in print rather late in his career, finally spelled out in some detail in conference papers in the late 1940s and early 1950s. An abiding concern, whether conscious or not, about antagonizing his colleagues—senior ones in general, and Kroeber in particular—probably contributed to the delay.[39]

Perhaps it is no coincidence that one concept he developed in haste resulted from a paper that he wrote at Kroeber's explicit request and under a strict deadline. That paper, on the topic of cultural evolution, soon led Steward to formulate his concept of multilinear evolution. He presented the initial paper at the 1952 Wenner-Gren symposium, held in New York City in June, shortly before he left Columbia for Illinois. "Evolution and Process" appeared in print the next year, in 1953, in a collection of state-of-the-art essays, edited by Kroeber and titled *Anthropology Today*. A revised version of Steward's paper, featuring the term *multilinear evolution* in its title, became the lead chapter of *Theory of Culture Change*, published just two years later, in 1955. It also inspired the book's subtitle, and thus took precedence over cultural ecology, the subject of the second chapter, in a double sense.[40]

Steward defined multilinear evolution as "essentially a methodology based on the assumption that significant regularities in cultural change occur," adding that "it is concerned with the determination of cultural laws." He labeled it "multilinear" to distinguish his approach to cultural evolution from the "unilinear evolution" of nineteenth-century anthropologists such as Lewis Henry Morgan, and what he called the "universal evolution" of Leslie White and the British archaeologist V. Gordon Childe. Years later, Steward told Murphy that he thought he had coined the term.[41] By then he had apparently forgotten about Wittfogel's previous use of it, to say nothing of Lowie's. The words *multilinear evolution* had come to be associated exclusively with Steward, having been featured in the subtitle of his book, but they actually had a complex history.

Steward may not have realized that a sociologist had used the term fifty years before it appeared on the cover of his own book in 1955. He remarked in a footnote in the opening pages that he did not know who had originated the term, and then mentioned that Wittfogel had used it in a way that resembled his own. But he followed that with a pointed reference to a 1951 article in which Wittfogel used other terminology (specifically, "Marx's term, 'pluralism'"), and he neglected to cite publications in which Wittfogel *had* used the words *multilinear evolution*. Even that footnote seems to have faded from conscious memory by the time Murphy inquired about the source of the term.[42]

Murphy, then at work on a biography of Lowie, had found that Lowie referred to multilinear evolution in his book *Social Organization*. That book was published in 1948, five years before Steward used the words *multilinear evolution* in print. Lowie had adopted the term *multilinear* for the view that the course of cultural evolution follows "different routes in diverse areas"; and *unilinear* for the contrasting view that "peoples the world over have traversed the same stages of development." Lowie's concluding words convey the appeal of cultural evolution to Steward, given his overriding interest in causality and cultural law. "Theories of multilinear evolution, in prescribing a fixed order, assume a *law* of sequence just as much as do the unilinear systems," Lowie wrote. "In both theories specific *causes* bring about the alleged modifications." There followed a long cautionary passage, however, in which Lowie emphasized the complexity of cultural phenomena and "the multiplicity of significant antecedent conditions."[43]

By the time Murphy mentioned Lowie's precedent, Steward had largely turned away from cultural evolution. He shrugged off the matter, saying simply that "it makes little difference" who originated the term. But, of course, it did matter. This and other memory lapses, as well as the ambivalent mention of Wittfogel, attest to his deep concern about receiving recognition for original ideas. The profession's reward structure and the prestige gained by creating the appearance of complete originality did not encourage him to acknowledge the highly social nature of his scholarship. For Steward, like many of his colleagues, this led to conflict with competing scholars.[44]

Steward defined cultural evolution in terms compatible with his own general aim, as "a quest for cultural regularities or laws" of cultural change. He thought of multilinear evolution as a methodology, reflecting his long-standing concern with developing concepts and methods to study cultural change empirically. Yet he wrote about it primarily in terms of his concept of culture type, providing ethnographic illustration rather than any concrete guidance about method. That he had begun to think about cultural evolution quite recently perhaps explains the schematic quality of the book's first chapter. He had written its precursor at Kroeber's bidding and in response to a widespread view that his 1949 paper, "Cultural Causality and Law," was a landmark study in cultural evolution. Steward had not chosen to use that term, but he was soon persuaded to reconsider his position.[45]

In the telling, opening words of the first chapter of *Theory of Culture Change*, he commented that cultural evolution, "although long an unfashionable concept," had attracted "renewed interest" in recent years. Riding the crest of that interest—perhaps encouraged by Kroeber's apparent endorsement as well as the attention of younger colleagues—Steward had reexamined his findings on the development of early civilizations. He soon decided that they qualified as "a single case of an undetermined number of evolutionary lines." That "undetermined number" was a defining feature of what he christened "multilinear evolution," to distinguish his approach from White's. Years later, however, referring to "Cultural Causality and Law," he said pointedly that he "did not consider [himself] an evolutionist" when he wrote it—nor, by implication, at the time he made that disclaimer many years later.[46]

The concise, twelve-page essay on cultural ecology that formed the second chapter of *Theory of Culture Change* differed from the first one in several ways. Steward apparently completed it sometime during the first months after his arrival in Urbana, a period of newfound and short-lived solitude. The initial version was written by invitation and for a symposium, "Ecology in Anthropology," a joint session of the Society for American Archaeology and the Central States Anthropological Society. The two societies held concurrent annual meetings in Urbana in May 1953, and the symposium topic was selected as one that intersected with both archaeology and cultural anthropology.[47]

The session, held in the Union, opened with a biologist's paper, "The Concept of Ecology in Biology." Papers by four archaeologists followed. Each of the archaeologists addressed ecological aspects of Plains Indian societies, and at least three of the four had studied with Duncan Strong: John L. Champe, Preston Holder, and Waldo R. Wedel, Strong's student at the University of Nebraska and his associate in pioneering research on the culture history and ecology of Plains Indians. Even the symposium chairman, David A. Baerreis, had worked with Strong, as had Steward himself. The session on ecology thus bore Strong's stamp, but it was Steward's paper, soon published in *Theory of Culture Change,* that would gain him a reputation as *the* architect of cultural ecology. Steward, who warned in advance that his conception of cultural ecology had "little in common" with biologists' conception of ecology, gave the sixth, and last, paper at the symposium.[48]

He had been thinking about what he finally called "the concept and method of cultural ecology" for more than two decades. His ideas about cultural ecology had emerged slowly although they obviously drew directly on his personal memories of the high desert, most notably Deep Springs and Owens Valleys. Over twenty years, he had developed and illustrated his ecological perspective on culture in a number of articles and a monograph. Perhaps what he judged a poor response to that work, or the disappointing results of his study of Carrier ecology, explain why it had less prominence in some publications during the years that followed.

Unlike his ideas on multilinear evolution—which he developed in haste, at the urging of colleagues, and superimposed after the fact on his research—cultural ecology formed an organic part of his intellectual project and field research during the 1930s. It also had deep roots in his own life experience. He consistently spoke of cultural ecology as a lone venture and a "very lonely road," thereby claiming it as his sole invention and implicitly denying any contributions by or influence from Strong or other colleagues.[49] The same could not be said about cultural evolution; undeniably, others had been there well before him.

It is worth remembering here that in 1952 the Viking Fund award committee had cited, among Steward's achievements, his work on cultural evolution, not cultural ecology. This may help to explain his choice of subtitle for *Theory of Culture Change,* and his ordering of the chapters. Having had little success with his efforts to "sell" cultural ecology, to use Steward's own words, he evidently decided to highlight cultural evolution, which was gaining acceptance among American archaeologists and cultural anthropologists after years of disrepute. At that point, it must have seemed a better vehicle, practically speaking, for promoting his theoretical ideas—although his work on cultural evolution was undoubtedly derivative from cultural ecology.[50]

Again in contrast to the content of his first chapter, in the second one, Steward spelled out in concrete terms what he meant by cultural ecology, offering specific guidance about methodology. At the heart of it lay his concept of the cultural core, an idea he later attributed in part to his 1930s work with the culture element lists. Those lengthy lists aimed to be comprehensive and thus included thousands of categories of cultural traits. Steward, pursuing his own, highly focused ecological interests, had found—to his enormous irritation, as recorded in his journal in 1935—that he had to spend a great deal of his time with Paiute and Shoshone informants filling out the lists. Months later he spent more time, with his wife's assistance, putting the lists in shape for Kroeber and eventual publication. But the juxtaposition of these two, contrary tasks evidently led him to separate wheat from chaff, or what he came to distinguish explicitly as the "core" versus the "secondary features" of culture.[51]

Steward's concept of the cultural core was implicit in much of his work from the mid-1930s, both in some concepts he later developed (such as cultural type) and in his well-known works of synthesis (including his articles on band societies, the prehistoric Southwest, and the development of early civilizations). He eventually defined the cultural core in highly abstract terms as "functional interdependency of features in a structural relationship," and more directly as "recurrent constellations of basic features." In his chapter on cultural ecology, he explained the core more tangibly as "the constellation of features that are most closely related to subsistence activities and economic arrangements." "Cultural ecology," he added, "pays primary attention to those features which empirical analysis shows to be most closely involved in the utilization of the environment in culturally prescribed ways."[52]

Steward then outlined the three "fundamental procedures" of cultural ecology, which can be seen as his method for identifying the cultural core in any given case. The first step centered on analyzing the relation between a specific environment and the technology that people use to gain a living from it. In other words, it meant recognizing the important environmental features and the tools used to obtain food, water, and other resources. "The simpler cultures are more directly conditioned by the environment than the advanced ones," Steward remarked. Although he did not elaborate, he had found it easier to establish those links for Northern Paiute of the past than for Puerto Rico in the present, band society and contemporary complex society, respectively.[53]

Steward described the second step as analyzing "the behavior patterns" involved in obtaining food, water, and other resources from a particular place, using a particular technology. Behavior patterns referred, that is, to the organization of productive work. Gathering plant foods was "usually done by women who work alone or in small groups," he remarked, while hunting might require men to work in cooperative groups, depending on such factors as the nature of the prey, the types of weapons, and the terrain. Drawing on his own field experience, but without explicitly mentioning Paiute, Shoshone, or Carrier Indians, he gave examples that related primarily to hunting, fishing, and gathering. None of the examples pertained to the organization of productive work in "advanced" (complex and contemporary) societies, perhaps in part because he had first developed his ideas about cultural ecology with reference to hunter-gatherers.

The third step, as Steward explained it, entailed finding how these "behavior patterns . . . affect other aspects of culture." He wrote, "The third procedure requires a genuinely holistic approach, for if such factors as demography, settlement pattern, kinship structures, land tenure, land use, and other key cultural features are considered separately, their interrelationships to one another and to the environment cannot be grasped." Here Steward specifically cited Western Shoshone and Carrier Indians to illustrate his point, but asserted, "The problem is the same in considering modern industrial civilizations." The aim of his method, he said, was "to determine whether similar adjustments occur in similar environments." The aim, in other words, was to answer questions of cultural causality.[54]

A distinguishing feature of *Theory of Culture Change* was its title, which boldly announced its theoretical content. Steward may have remembered Mead's advice when he chose the title, advice that he must have heard her give at the June 1952 Wenner-Gren symposium at which he presented his paper on cultural evolution. As Mead later reminded Lowie, she had quoted "a remark Boas once made, 'never put a theoretical point in a monograph or no one will recognize it.'" She had elaborated on this point at the symposium, suggesting "'never put a theoretical point anywhere except in an article in an anthropological journal, and for heaven's sake label it THEORY.'" Despite offering this comment to her colleagues, she conceded that she had not "acted upon it very extensively."[55]

Steward, by contrast, acted on Mead's and Boas's advice with great dispatch.[56] While he kept his distance from Mead throughout his career and did not revere Boas, he evidently recognized good counsel when he heard it.[57] Having made a habit of publishing journal articles under titles that did not highlight their theoretical content—apparently for defensive reasons—he finally chose a book title that emphasized it. This removed the need for him to remind anyone, as he had once reminded Willey, about the theoretical nature of his paper on the Southwest or any of the others. *Theory of Culture Change,* by its very title and consolidation of his scattered articles, promoted Steward's position as a theorist as nothing before had done. It underscored that he did indeed have a theoretical perspective—even while he remained wary of having a general theory, which he always equated with dogma.

Steward often spoke of making a "theoretical point," having a "theoretical point of view," and writing "theoretical articles," and he well understood the professional value placed on theory. But he also routinely insisted that cultural ecology is *not* "a theory," but rather "a concept and method." As a title, *Theory of Culture Change* simply attracted more attention to his essays. In Steward's mind, the presence of the word *methodology* in the subtitle made it clear that he was not proposing a grand theory, but methods for achieving a theoretical understanding of something highly specific: particular cases of cultural change. This subtlety, not surprisingly, escaped his readers.

Having given the word *theory* such prominence, Steward would find it necessary again and again in the future to clarify his position, repeating that cultural ecology is not a theory in that it "does not presuppose any conclusions whatsoever."[58] But the confusion would persist, perhaps because he usually issued explicit denials in letters, not in print; perhaps also because he did not clearly distinguish between general theory (which he rejected) and a specific theory (such as a theory about the development of complex society, which he himself had proposed in a landmark essay); and undoubtedly because he welcomed the prestige of being regarded as a theorist, even while he claimed not to have a (general) theory, but a method.

Most of his fellow anthropologists, even Murphy, who heard Steward's denials more than once, took the view that cultural ecology *is* a theory or a theoretical approach. As Murphy later put it, Steward "was not a general theorist in the sense that he looked for some underlying, austerely economical formula that would unify a universe of phenomena." To use Steward's terms, that sort of approach would lead to presupposing certain conclusions. Instead, he attempted to discover rather specific cause-and-effect relationships, in search of general laws, and operating from the premise—not stated by Steward, but by Murphy—that "in a natural order anything that happens can happen again, and, given the same conditions, it probably will."[59]

* * *

When *Theory of Culture Change* appeared in print, Steward's professional prominence guaranteed that his book would be noticed. Cultural ecology, finally labeled and formalized, was at last launched with the publication of that book, which bore the name of a well-known anthropologist as its author. His approach soon attracted the interest of a younger generation, as Steward had hoped. "It was well into the 1950s, perhaps even later," he observed years after his book was published, "that the concept of cultural ecology caught on and came into general use."[60]

By the time of publication in 1955, his professional position, but not his intellectual one, had changed a great deal since the appearance of his earliest theoretical articles in the 1930s. Despite the silence that greeted those first efforts, he continued to publish extensively for the next twenty years. The breadth of his research and writing—ranging from hunter-gatherer societies to early civilizations, covering the Americas but also including the Old World, and encompassing archaeology as well as cultural anthropology—meant that many anthropologists already knew something about his work. His editorship of the *Handbook of South American Indians* had involved firsthand contact with anthropologists and other contributors from a dozen countries. Holding appointments at five universities and the BAE had also given him a broad range of contacts, and through his position at Columbia he had helped train dozens of graduate students, many of whom were establishing themselves in the academic world. And finally, he had just received a number of important awards and honors, which, by increasing his professional visibility, also brought notice to his new book.

Besides his record of publication and his large professional network, Steward's skill in reaping the rewards of academic clientship had contributed to his success. He remained Kroeber's client, and a remarkably active one, for thirty years, carrying on a correspondence with him that in some respect echoes the letters he had once written to his first patrons, the officials of Telluride Association. As their correspondence makes clear, Kroeber primarily served as a patron, not as a mentor. The two men had a major and long-standing intellectual disagreement, but they expressed it quietly in print—so quietly that some of Steward's students failed to detect it or Steward's enduring sense of rivalry with Kroeber. Two monographs and some essays in *Theory of Culture Change* illustrate this well: Steward's 1938 work on the Great Basin and his 1955 essay on cultural ecology, among others; and Kroeber's *Natural and Cultural Areas of Native North America,* which reached print in 1939, apparently after a long delay.[61]

Steward had ended his detailed study of the Great Basin with some thoughts about ecology, observing that the effects of cultural and psychological forces are difficult to assess "if the ecology which conditions and delimits them is unknown." In the case of the Great Basin, he contended, "Even kinship duties and obligations toward different relatives rest ultimately in varying degrees upon ecology." In contrast, Kroeber asserted in the opening statement of his book that "the immediate causes of cultural phenomena are other cultural phenomena." Several hundred pages later, he concluded that the complexity of interaction between culture and environment "makes generalization unprofitable on the whole." As Kroeber so often did, he went not just one step but two or three steps further than others—in this case, including the whole of native North America in his purview. Steward had limited his attention to one area and had found it possible to generalize. Kroeber had not.[62]

Years later, in his 1955 essay on cultural ecology, Steward replied. He wrote pointedly that his approach differed from "relativistic . . . conceptions of culture history" (Kroeber's, among others, although he wisely offered no names). Cultural ecology gives attention to the local environment as "the extracultural factor" that can explain particular cultural features, he explained. It thereby avoids "the fruitless assumption that culture comes from culture." He wrote those words from a protected position, one achieved, ironically, in part as a result of Kroeber's active patronage over a period of decades.[63]

Near the end of his life, when asked about "Kroeber's ecology" and its influence on cultural ecology, Steward flatly denied any. Kroeber remained "antagonistic" to his approach, according to Steward. Moreover, Kroeber's *Natu-*

ral and Cultural Areas of Native North America did not use an ecological approach, he said, but rather the conventional "framework of cultural relativism wherein he compared cultures territorially . . . with emphasis always on characteristic differences[,] especially the humanistic features." Tellingly, Steward added two details that reveal a sense of rivalry: the fact that Kroeber's book had appeared in print in 1939, a year after his own, and that it had never been reprinted. His own 1938 monograph had just been reprinted by a university press.[64]

His words suggest anxiety about his reputation, as do repeated comments that he made in letters during the same period. If Kroeber were seen as his intellectual predecessor, this might diminish Steward's own status as the creator of cultural ecology. Steward had published *Theory of Culture Change* to affirm that status, but remarks about "Kroeber's ecology" seemed to call it into question. He did not want his work to appear merely derivative.

* * *

Theory of Culture Change, which drew together Steward's writings over a period of twenty years, represented one of the final steps in his long-range research plan. By first studying the process of cultural change in the past and in "simpler" societies, Steward had thought he could gain theoretical understandings to apply to the present and to the future. Explaining the course of cultural change in the past, despite the problem of incomplete evidence, seemed a logical first step to understanding change in the contemporary world and predicting its direction in the future. At the University of Illinois, that work came to take precedence. He largely retreated from the subject of cultural evolution in the mid-1950s. His focus on cultural change shifted to the present as he entered the final phase of his research career.[65]

Even before arriving at the University of Illinois, Steward had set to work on what he would eventually name the Studies of Cultural Regularities Project. For nearly fifteen years, from conception to publication, he worked closely with about a dozen younger men, many of them former students from Columbia. With his first five research associates, Steward spent several years planning the project. As he explained to a former student, they had worked at "developing and refining methods and concepts for ascertaining cross-cultural regularities and laying a basis for long range forecasts of cultural change among native peoples under the influence of industrialization."[66] (By the end of the twentieth century, the term *anticipatory anthropology* had come to be used for the sort of predictive research Steward had conceived of earlier in his career and planned with his research associates in the 1950s.)[67]

To an acquaintance at Telluride Association, he explained the project this way: "I am now working on fascinating problems involving changes in native cultures of India, Africa, and Latin America under the impact of western industrial influences—a far cry from the beaten-up Paiute around Deep Springs." His words suggest that he did not connect the political and economic processes that had destroyed the Paiutes' former way of life with those that, in the shape of "western industrial influences," were having a profound effect on native people elsewhere in the world.[68]

Steward had no direct contact with the Paiute and Shoshone during these years, save for his work as an expert witness for the Department of Justice in some of the Indian Claims Commission cases, including *Indians of California v. The United States of America*. Kroeber, Gifford, and Robert Heizer—all from Berkeley's department of anthropology—testified for the plaintiffs in 1954. Two other expert witnesses for the plaintiffs, Homer Barnett and Omer Stewart, were also former students of Kroeber.[69]

An attorney from the Department of Justice who contacted Steward soon after they testified expressed little concern about several of the witnesses. But he added that Kroeber's and Barnett's testimony worried him. They had gone "all out for Indian 'possession' of *all* of the lands in California." Heizer, he said, had finally conceded that the Northern Paiute did not actually use the top of Mount Whitney, while still insisting that it was in their possession, along with desert areas. "Kroeber was not so explicit and admitted," the attorney continued, "that you 'were probably right' when you said that the Shoshone had no concept to ownership of particular tracts—he tried to hedge that you were undoubtedly talking about Shoshone in general, but admitted, on cross[-examination], that you did not except the Panamint from your paper." The attorney suggested that "actual use maps" be drawn for various groups of California Indians, "showing, if it is true . . . that there were significantly large areas which were not used at all."[70]

Although Kroeber and Steward served on opposing sides in the case, they maintained the appearance of cordial relations. (Indeed, after decades of signing his letters to Steward with his surname, Kroeber began to sign them "Alfred.") Kroeber wrote in a conciliatory tone that any conflict between the two groups of anthropologists was "no doubt instigated by the attorneys, to whom as lawyers a trial is a fight." He advised ignoring any animosity among colleagues: "This kind of thing mostly dies down if left alone." And he remarked that the legal proceedings would probably have the effect of stimulating research. "I have two short papers in press as a result, and others begun or planned," he wrote. Kroeber's wife, however, remembered that the land claims case interfered with his research and writing for five years.[71]

Steward devoted far less time to it. It was no doubt unsettling to find Kroeber, along with Barnett, Heizer, and Stewart (in lineage terms, an "elder" and three "younger brothers") making common cause on the opposing side. Not surprisingly, he appears to have felt a strong sense of not belonging, but he tried to make a virtue of his minority status. As he told Isabel Kelly (a rare lineage "sister"), "I would say that most of the saner anthropologists are witnesses for the government." A few months earlier, he had heard about a paper given at the 1954 American Ethnological Society meeting that allegedly referred to expert witnesses for the government as "'on the whole, the minor members of the profession.'" His words to Kelly were a variation on the same theme, in reverse.[72]

Steward spent much of 1956 in Japan. Before leaving he submitted material relating to the Southern Paiute case. He also tried to interest Elman Service in taking his place as a government witness, noting privately in his journal, "I hope this takes me off the hook permanently re: Indian litigation." But in spring 1957, after Steward had returned to the United States, the Department of Justice once again asked him to testify, this time in the Shoshone Bannock land claims case. He declined firmly, saying that he would be out of the country in connection with a research project, although he did not actually leave until five months later. The ongoing professional conflict—and his minority position, which could only have increased his anxiety about public confrontation—probably dissuaded him from testifying. The anger and antipathy did not dissipate as quickly as Kroeber hoped.[73]

Two former students, Murphy and Manners, served in his stead as witnesses for the government. Murphy had already worked on the Northern Paiute case as a graduate student when he was hired to do what Steward called "the dirty work" of library research on the Paiute. (Steward then synthesized the material and wrote a paper.) Several years later, after he and his wife, Yolanda Murphy, returned from fieldwork in Brazil, they carried out fieldwork with Shoshone Indians in Wyoming. Soon after that, in 1957, Murphy told Steward that the Shoshone land claims case was his last. "Let's just say that I am too young and innocent for this sort of thing," he wrote. "Incidentally, the lawyers were absolutely undistinguished on both sides. The Indians should get a good firm of sharp New York lawyers, and the government should lower the retirement age."[74]

* * *

The Stewards left for Japan on a cold January morning in 1956, planning to spend six months there. Kyoto University and Doshisha University had invited Steward to teach anthropology during the spring and direct an American studies seminar during the summer.[75]

They spent about a week in San Francisco and Berkeley, where they looked up old friends and colleagues. Murphy was in the first year of his new position at Berkeley; Steward's old teacher Lowie was one of Murphy's colleagues. Then in his early seventies, Lowie had retired six years earlier but remained active professionally, teaching a seminar now and then. Years later, Steward remembered that he had last seen Lowie in the company of Murphy, walking across campus. The three men, representing three generations of an academic lineage that descended from Boas, met for the last time that day, nine months before Lowie's death from cancer.[76]

Steward also saw some of his old friends from Deep Springs and Telluride Association. Robert Aird, Steward's former roommate who worked with him at his first field site, along the Columbia River, had become a neurologist. He was chairman of the department of neurology at the University of California Medical School in San Francisco. The Stewards had lunch with him one day, along with Henry and Kit Hayes. Henry was an old mountaineering companion from Deep Springs; and twenty years earlier, Henry and Kit had joined Julian and Jane on their weeklong hike through the Sierra high country. Before leaving California, Steward rented a car, and he and his wife spent a day revisiting some of the places he remembered with great affection, from Golden Gate Park to Marin County. They were already thinking about retiring to California, perhaps to Marin County, but not for another twelve years.[77]

The Stewards left San Francisco for Japan on the SS *President Cleveland*, and five days later, the ship put into port at Honolulu for a few hours. The gentle warmth and sunlight proved memorable, in terms of both the grim prairie winter they had left behind and the dreary weather that would greet them at their destination. After another ten days at sea, they reached Japan, where they found leaden skies, a chill winter wind, and the cherry trees bare and brown. Kyoto, known for its ancient Buddhist temples, Shinto shrines, and palaces, was a crowded city of nearly a million people. The "uniform steely gray" of the city, as Steward described it, matched the overcast skies that dispensed drenching rains for days on end. Low mountains cloaked in green were visible in the distance.[78]

Jane Steward had vivid memories thirty years later of the damp and persistent chill, especially in their living quarters, which lacked central heating. They wore the traditional, heavily padded jackets indoors, she recalled, but for the duration of the winter in Kyoto they shivered. The plum blossoms appeared in mid-March as harbingers of spring and the cherry blossoms in mid-April. The trees that immediately took her husband's attention, however, resembled none he had ever seen before and stood only inches tall. Within days of their arrival, he bought a book on the art of bonsai. The self-described forester found the prairie sadly lacking in trees, and he pursued this new interest when he returned, cultivating his own dwarf trees at home in Fithian. Always intrigued by the intersection of nature and culture, he could observe it closely with bonsai and hold a directing hand.[79]

Jane Steward also remembered the courtesy of colleagues at the university and the warm welcome they received. Besides giving a series of formal talks, attended almost exclusively by male students and faculty, her husband worked closely with a small number of men in a research group. The segregated nature of universities in Japan made the presence of women students so rare that he noted the few occasions when they attended his lectures ("45–50, including about 8 girls").[80] Despite the language barrier, he once again found it rewarding to work with a small group of men without any women present. That was more easily accomplished in Japan than in the United States.

Aside from some brief forays into the countryside, Steward spent most of his time in Kyoto conferring with colleagues, lecturing, writing, attending social events, and sightseeing, nearly always in the company of his wife.[81] In contrast to his past travels, he had little to say about the landscape, save for comments about farm fields (*"meticulously* tended fields of rice, vegetables & fruits") and a cryptic remark about the "beauty of scenery," including that most famous peak, Mount Fuji, which he glimpsed from a train window. Rising higher than twelve thousand feet, its symmetrical, snowcapped cone dominated the passing field of view. But most of the land that he saw, under cultivation and densely populated, did not attract his close attention or evoke any deep response. Instead, his six-month sojourn in Japan left him with warm feelings for its people and their way of life.[82]

CHAPTER 12

NOTES FROM THE
NINETIETH MERIDIAN

In the late 1950s, Steward entered the final stage of a long and successful career. He had published what soon became a classic work in anthropology, *Theory of Culture Change,* and he had created his own sublineage, comprised almost entirely of men. Their work and professional prominence would help to perpetuate his own status in the field, and his intellectual legacy. Two of those men, Murphy and Manners, would produce thoughtful essays and whole volumes memorializing Steward's work and providing some of the first commentary on his ideas. Wolf, in a well-known essay on anthropology, would include his former teacher among the field's leaders, and Mintz would contribute a perceptive essay on a distinctive facet of Steward's work in cultural ecology, his attention to water. Willey, an unofficial student who nonetheless regarded Steward as one of his most important teachers, would promote his work among archaeologists, treating Steward's ideas as a theorist in his own writings on method and theory.[1]

During the first five years after his arrival at the University of Illinois, many of Steward's students from Columbia had worked with him there or visited him. Wolf departed after two years to teach at the University of Virginia. He soon moved on to a visiting position at Yale, joining Mintz, who had taught there since 1951; a year later Wolf accepted a position at the University of Chicago and still later moved to the University of Michigan. Lehman stayed at the University of Illinois for a year, after which he finished his graduate work at Columbia; he returned to Illinois as Steward's research associate and later joined the faculty. After two years as a research associate, Murphy accepted a position at Berkeley, but happily returned to Columbia eight years later, in 1963. Steward found this as incomprehensible as it was predictable. "Perhaps we New Yorkers are incorrigible, after all," Murphy explained to him, "for the stink and noise get built in and the violence of the place just adds zest to life."[2]

Service, Mintz, Manners, and Diamond each visited Steward briefly, in some cases taking part in small conferences held in Urbana, in others taking a break in cross-country journeys. Service taught briefly at Columbia before accepting a position in anthropology at the University of Michigan, his undergraduate alma mater. In 1956 Diamond was offered a position at Brandeis University, where he joined Manners as a member of the faculty. Morton Fried, another of Steward's former students, had remained at Columbia as a faculty member in the department of anthropology. All these men found academic positions—and in departments with graduate programs—within five or six years of completing their degrees in anthropology. Some had a period of temporary or otherwise contingent employment, and at least one of them seems not to have had any academic employment for several years, but all eventually found positions and achieved tenure.[3]

A surprising number of Steward's students managed to remain in New York City or, if exiled elsewhere, to return there, as Murphy did. Diamond eventually moved to the New School for Social Research, and Wolf left Michigan to accept a position at the the City University of New York. Aside from the factor of sentiment, so well expressed in Murphy's words of explanation to Steward, the city offered unparalleled professional advantages. New York City had emerged as *the* center of American anthropology by midcentury, with the largest concentration of anthropologists at its many universities and museums.[4]

A few women with Ph.D.'s in anthropology managed to gain a foothold in the profession, if not permanent academic employment, by staying in New York City. Ernestine Friedl, who worked briefly with Steward after her graduate adviser, Linton, left Columbia, was one of a very few women to find a full-time teaching position. She taught at Queens College, where she joined another woman, Hortense Powdermaker, in a small undergraduate program. Powdermaker had established the program when she joined the Queens faculty in 1938, finally obtaining a secure academic position ten years after earning a Ph.D.[5]

Vera Rubin fared less well than Friedl in her search for academic employment. Already in her forties when she completed her graduate training, she succeeded in locating only a temporary appointment at Hunter College. Hunter, a women's college with undergraduate offerings in anthropology, employed several anthropologists, including Ethel Aginsky, whom Rubin replaced for a semester, and Dorothy L. Keur. Keur taught at Hunter for nearly forty years and remembered teaching fifteen to eighteen hours a week, presumably five or six classes a semester; Friedl had a similar schedule at Queens. The heavy teaching load at Hunter and the dismally low salary quickly discouraged Rubin, although she found Hunter pleasant in some ways ("with hardly any of the Columbia tensions," she told Steward). Months later, she applied for a research position with an interdisciplinary social psychiatry project sponsored by Cornell University.[6]

At the Yorkville Project, as it was known, she joined Eleanor Leacock, who had initially been hired as a secretary. "In the end," Leacock later wrote, "I got my first job because I could type." When the project's staff learned about her Ph.D., however, they changed her position from full-time secretary to half-time research assistant. Her salary remained the same. After Yorkville, Leacock taught at the Bank Street College of Education in New York City—still on the distant margins of anthropology but, unusual for the times, holding an academic position.[7] The unwritten rules of the profession and the tenor of the times in America barred her and other women from what remained most scarce and highly valued in anthropology: a full-time, tenured position in an anthropology department, and more specifically, a department with a Ph.D. program. In a metaphorical sense, that was big game, its pursuit reserved for hunters and off-limits to gatherers.

Rubin never established an academic career. Instead, she managed to maintain a presence in her chosen field by creating her own position as director of a research foundation. In the mid-1950s she set up the Research Institute for the Study of Man, financed by her husband, Samuel Rubin, a wealthy businessman. Vera Rubin may have drawn inspiration from the example of Elsie Clews Parsons, a wealthy woman in her own right. For many years before her death in 1941, Parsons offered financial support to anthropologists, including the young Steward, under the auspices of the Southwest Society, which she had founded in 1918. She was just one in a long line of the field's patrons. Anthropology, a young and impoverished discipline, had an established tradition of trying to attract patronage from wealthy women, even before Phoebe Apperson Hearst contributed a small fortune to create the department at Steward's alma mater, Berkeley. Although Steward disliked having women as faculty colleagues, he willingly accepted their financial patronage, as did his associates.[8]

Even before Rubin created the Research Institute for the Study of Man, she had provided anthropologists with funding for research, apparently under the aegis of the Samuel Rubin Foundation. In 1952 Steward asked her to support a research associate position for Elena Padilla. Unlike the other research associates, who worked directly with him at the University of Illinois and were funded by the university, Padilla would work in London. A year or two earlier, under a grant to Steward from the Wenner-Gren Foundation, she had carried out a world survey of areas in which native peoples had recently shifted from a subsistence economy to a peasant or plantation economy. That library-based work helped lay the foundation for his Studies of Cultural Regularities project, indicating possible research sites. Her work in London would focus on the establishment of plantations in British colonies.[9]

Padilla did go to London for about seven months, where she centered her research specifically on plantations established by the British in Africa. The wealth of material that she found there on Africa, both published and unpublished, impressed her, as did the professional ambience in England. It had been a good experience, she said, to meet people who were pursuing research for the sake of learning and not engaging in struggles to gain prestige and an academic post. It appears that the far smaller number of trained anthropologists in England had better employment prospects than their American counterparts. Some worked for the government in the Colonial Office ("in England anthropology is mostly a civil servant's occupation," Padilla remarked); others found positions in universities in England or in colonies or former colonies. This may explain why collegial relations in London differed so visibly from those in New York City.[10]

Obviously aware of her gender-based handicap in the employment contest, Padilla tried to find a position with the United Nations, visiting UNESCO headquarters in Paris soon after she arrived in Europe. Alfred Métraux, a member of UNESCO's Department of Social Science staff since 1950, had told Charles Wagley that there might be a position for Padilla as a research coordinator, working out of Havana, Cuba. This was several years before the Cuban revolution. But nothing materialized for her in Havana, and on her return to New York City, she visited UN headquarters to inquire about positions there. Again, she had no luck. Rubin thought Padilla was highly qualified for such work, but remarked to Steward, "as you know, the same kind of problem exists at the UN as at the university." The United Nations generally excluded women from professional positions, reserving those for men.

Padilla herself later wrote to Steward that she belonged to "the wrong sex to aspire to be an anthropologist." She soon found temporary work with a medical project and taught a seminar on public health, work that at first interested her as a stepping stone to an academic position in anthropology. Despite her long workdays, she tried to keep reading in anthropology, reporting to Steward that she had stayed up late one night studying Shoshone culture element lists (probably Steward's compilation, based on his work for Kroeber in 1935 and 1936). Between 1954 and 1957, Padilla carried out research on Puerto Rican immigrants in New York City, resulting in a book, *Up from Puerto Rico*, that Columbia University Press published in 1958. In the book's preface, she cited Steward's influence on her work, one of his few students to acknowledge it so explicitly.[11]

During the early and mid-1950s, Padilla repeatedly expressed her wish to collaborate with Steward, and especially to do fieldwork in Africa as a part of the project he was planning. Her research in London had been carried out in support of that project, and the months spent poring over books and manuscripts in London's libraries and archives had turned her into "quite an Africanist," according to Rubin. Steward considered her but eventually selected several men to work at various sites in Africa. At that point, Padilla was still involved in research with Puerto Rican immigrants, although it would soon draw to a close.[12] Despite her extensive work on Steward's project, she remained a silent partner in the venture, her research mentioned by him in letters rather than in print. (Padilla later achieved the rank of professor at New York University's Graduate School of Public Administration, where her research centered on health policy and health administration.)[13]

Some of Steward's other students from Columbia showed less interest in collaborating with him, especially those with promising academic positions who soon turned their research in directions that diverged from his. After Wolf and Murphy left Illinois, Charles Erasmus and Louis Faron took their places as research associates and stayed with the Studies of Cultural Regularities project until its completion. Faron had completed graduate study in anthropology at Columbia, and Erasmus had earned a Ph.D. at Berkeley. They carried out research in Peru and Mexico, respectively. Solomon Miller, a graduate student from Columbia, also worked in Peru.

Others who took part in the project included Edward H. Winter, who had received his Ph.D. from Harvard and who went to Tanganyika (known as Tanzania after independence in 1961); and Thomas O. Beidelman, a master's student at the University of Illinois who accompanied Winter. Manners, who had previously taken part in the Puerto Rico project, went to Kenya, and Diamond worked in Nigeria. Three members of the project did research in Southeast Asia: Lehman, in Burma; Richard Downs, an anthropologist who had recently received a Ph.D. from Leiden University, in Malaya (now part of Malaysia); and Jiro Suzuki, also in Malaya.[14] Toshinao Yoneyama, whom Steward had first met in Kyoto, along with Suzuki, did fieldwork in rural Japan, with the assistance of Shuichi Nagata.[15] The goal of the project, as Steward explained, was to analyze changes in "traditional societies" (ranging from tribal groups to peasants and plantation workers in Africa, Asia, and Latin America) that resulted from influences of the "modern industrial world."[16]

The Ford Foundation had awarded Steward $225,000 for the project, then a munificent sum that had few rivals in anthropology. Among those few was Benedict's Research in Contemporary Cultures project, about to begin when Steward arrived at Columbia in 1946, with a far larger budget—almost one hundred thousand dollars a year—than the Puerto Rico study he joined. Benedict's success may have inspired him to aim high when he wrote the proposal and budget for his own project on contemporary cultural change. (Receiving the entire sum surprised him; he exclaimed in his journal, that he had got "the whole $225,000 grant!!!") In any case, he spoke from experience when he later described the Ford Foundation as having "loads of money." The budget not only paid for the eleven fieldworkers' travel and subsistence but also included funds for Steward and his wife to visit the various field sites during the eighteen months of research.[17]

They departed from New York City by ship in 1958, exactly twenty years after an ill-starred trip to South America that began in the same harbor and ended in California. This journey proved strangely similar, cut short by an amoebic infection that alarmed Steward and concerned his wife and the several physicians he consulted from Nairobi and New Delhi to Singapore and Kyoto. The Stewards left Japan by ship in late August and proceeded directly to California, five months earlier than originally planned, bypassing field sites in Peru and Mexico. Once back in California, Steward took the opportunity to visit Deep Springs before returning to Illinois.[18]

* * *

Steward did not attend the annual meeting of the American Anthropological Association, held two months later in November 1958 in Washington, D.C. Instead, he sent a paper that ended up in the hands of Mintz, who agreed to read it, and then wrote to Steward soon afterward to convey some of the comments. A few months later, Steward underwent surgery. Further surgery followed in June 1959 and again in August. He spent several months in the hospital that summer and reported that his room there "was more of an office from which I had to get the new department set up."[19]

Earlier that year, Steward and his colleagues in anthropology had petitioned the dean to form a separate department of anthropology. Internal problems in the joint department may have prompted them to secede at that particular moment; the sociologist Alvin Gouldner, who resigned from his position at about the same time, commented to the dean that he doubted whether there was any department "in worse shape" at the university. Steward assumed the position of acting head of the anthropology department only a few weeks after surgery, with responsibility for overseeing the department and the new Ph.D. program in anthropology.[20]

In November 1959 Steward went to Chicago to take part in the Darwin centennial celebration, where he was scheduled to present a paper. His symposium on cultural evolution included anthropologists and, in Steward's view, "a somewhat strange assortment" of several other scholars, including a plant geneticist. Besides Steward, the anthropologists included Kroeber, White, Kluckhohn, Willey, and Robert McCormick Adams. Steward remarked rather acerbically, but privately, that Kroeber had decided "to substitute 'evolution' for 'history' for this occasion," a comment he repeated many years later in print ("Kroeber took this occasion to honor Darwin largely by substituting the term evolution for history."[21])

Steward attended preliminary sessions on the day before the symposium, and Willey found him in "good combative form." Kroeber, however, actually left a session that day in disgust at the sniping comments of one scholar. The next morning, Jane Steward called Willey from their hotel and asked him to stop by their room to see her husband, who was still in bed when Willey arrived. He complained of an eye problem and said that he had to rest and could not take part in the symposium that evening. Steward later characterized his paper as having "little connection with the views of the other participants," a conclusion he seems to have reached during the contentious preliminary sessions and which may have dissuaded him from presenting it himself. His dislike of public speaking, and anxiety about confrontation and rejection, remained as strong as ever. The paper appeared in print the following year under the title "Evolutionary Principles and Social Types."[22]

Steward had eye surgery a few months later, and in the aftermath found it difficult to read. He had accepted the position of acting head of the department with reluctance, and this disability made the administrative work seem even more onerous. His new secretary, Betty Starr, whom he had recently hired, provided a great deal of help during that difficult year. She brought unusual credentials and experience to the task.[23]

Starr had earned a Ph.D. in anthropology from the University of Chicago in 1951, at the age of forty-five. Previously, she had worked for the *Chicago Daily News* and a publishing company. After finishing her dissertation, based on fieldwork in Veracruz, Mexico, she spent a year working as administrative assistant to Fred Eggan, chairman of the department of anthropology at Chicago. Then, with no prospects for an academic position on the horizon, she returned to Mexico for further fieldwork and to teach for a term at the Escuela Nacional de Antropología e Historia. She arrived back in the United States in 1953, unemployed.

From 1954 to 1959, she worked as assistant to William S. Godfrey, who served as executive secretary of the American Anthropological Association; Godfrey's professional base was the Logan Museum at Beloit College. During her five years at Beloit, Starr continued to look for an academic position. She was recommended for at least one, at the University of Wisconsin, Milwaukee, in 1957, but nothing came of it. In 1959, with the executive secretary's office about to move to Washington, D.C., she began to look for another administrative position and placed a notice in the *American Anthropologist.* Having learned from Godfrey that the new anthropology department at the University of Illinois needed an administrative assistant or secretary, she wrote to Steward, who quickly hired her as department secretary and stenographer. It was one of the most telling statements that could have been made about the place of women in American anthropology.[24]

Other faculty and staff in the new department included longtime members Oscar Lewis and John McGregor, and two visiting faculty members, Morris Siegel and Robert Gray. Donald W. Lathrap, a young archaeologist and South America specialist from Harvard, recommended by Willey, and Howard Maclay, a linguist, joined the faculty as new assistant professors. Two of the three research associates, Lehman and Downs, had worked on the Cultural Regularities project with Steward. The third, Elaine Bluhm, was an archaeologist and a graduate of the University of Chicago, where Starr had been a fellow student.[25]

Joseph B. Casagrande arrived at Illinois the next year, in 1960, as chairman of the department. Steward did not serve on the search committee, but showed particular interest in hiring Casagrande. Then forty-five, Casagrande had earned his Ph.D. from Columbia nine years earlier, before Steward's departure for the University of Illinois. He spent the following years working for the Social Science Research Council in New York City, where he corresponded often with Steward. After being hired in 1960, he began the strenuous task of administering a new department with a new Ph.D. program. His arrival freed Steward from the sorts of academic duties that he always found tedious and time-consuming, privately consigning such "dirty work" to the "locals" of the university world, not to a "cosmo" such as himself. (The terms came from an article by his colleague Gouldner. Steward's allusion was to cosmopolitan scholars, who have such broad horizons that they have neither the time nor the inclination to contribute to local university life. Needless to say, colleagues who bore the burden of teaching and service took a different view.)[26]

Steward departed immediately for California, accompanied by his wife. They lived in Palo Alto, while he spent a year in residence as a fellow at Stanford University's Center for Advanced Study in the Behavioral Sciences. He had angled for a fellowship for some time and had asked Kroeber, himself recently a fellow at the center, for advice and sponsorship. Kroeber once again offered good counsel; he also explained that he had not yet had the chance to inquire "casually" with the director about Steward's prospects. Steward had evidently already written on his own behalf to the center and eventually received a positive reply. "This is about the first time I have been able to go to bat for myself," he noted in his journal. His words convey a sense of dependence and help to explain why successfully promoting his theoretical view, which ran counter to Kroeber's in almost every respect, had taken more than twenty years.[27]

Kroeber's advice in this instance—and a casual inquiry if the chance arose—probably qualified as his last favor for Steward, one of a multitude he bestowed over a period of nearly thirty-five years. He died about a year and a half later. Their long relationship brought Steward many benefits, including funding for his first fieldwork, the opportunity to publish his first monograph, and his first academic position, to say nothing of an impressive flow of invaluable advice and sponsorship for major awards. Theirs was a remarkably active and enduring case of academic clientship, one that proved richly rewarding for Steward, although less obviously beneficial for Kroeber, at least during his lifetime.

While Steward actively sought Kroeber's help over thirty years, he almost never mentioned receiving it. It is not clear whether he did so to conform to an image of the self-made man, standard practice in the academic world, or to obscure his lesser status in the relationship, or for still other reasons. In one instance, he described Kroeber as someone who "generally cut the ties after the diploma was granted," but also conceded that Kroeber "helped many get jobs and grants." The word *many* masked his own status as a major beneficiary of Kroeber's efforts over the course of decades, and especially during the worst years of the depression. (When some of Steward's own students similarly did not acknowledge his help, he seemed puzzled and hurt; but they followed his example, seeking benefits and at the same time seeking to minimize their status as clients.) Although Steward never inherited Kroeber's position at Berkeley, his private goal for many years, by 1960 he no longer appeared to regret that. Berkeley as a place, a locale, had changed in ways that gave him an acute sense of loss.[28]

Steward spent the year in Palo Alto working on an introduction for the three-volume *Contemporary Change in Traditional Societies,* the final product of the Cultural Regularities project. He planned to spell out the theoretical implications of the project in his introduction. Starr, who had honed her editorial skills in her previous career, went over some of the papers that had already been submitted to Steward. He did not acknowledge that work in print, simply thanking her in a letter for doing a "superb job" on one of his own, coauthored papers. Her labor, in this instance and others, remained largely invisible to the profession.[29]

The year also gave Steward the chance to "languish," as he put it, at the center, which made very few demands on him. The mild climate of coastal California added to his pleasure; in mid-February, thinking of the season's piercing chill in other places, he remarked to Starr that he did not miss winter on the prairie. During his sojourn at the center he also avoided what he called "the rat race of [professional] meetings on every conceivable subject," choosing to remain in Palo Alto and not to attend conferences. These would soon include some on ecology and the ecology of hunter-gatherers, whose organizers explicitly cited his work as an influence; but he generally did not attend, sending a paper instead and later reading the conference proceedings.[30]

Steward and his wife spent time revisiting many of his favorite places around the Bay Area. They had already begun to think about retirement, preferably in California. But as Steward later told friends from his student days at Deep Springs, he found the area "teeming with people." California seemed to grow "more horribly congested each year," he complained. Since the years when he had first lived in Berkeley, the population had doubled, and houses and paved streets covered the Berkeley Hills where he had once made field outings for a geography course. What he remembered as open land elsewhere had also vanished beneath the spreading flow of asphalt, concrete, and new construction. When he visited Mill Valley in Marin County, he got "completely lost," he later reported. The state's population had grown from less than four million in the 1920s to nearly sixteen million by 1960 (and in the next forty years it would double).[31]

Even the rapid growth in world population that took place in Steward's lifetime paled beside what he witnessed in California. Seeing the changes in landscape and social life that followed in the wake of population increase and greater density may have helped him to think about the significance of these factors in prehistory. In any case, an awareness of population levels and changes runs through his work from the time of the Great Depression, when dust bowl refugees poured into the state, until the last years of his life, when the state's thriving economy continued to attract new residents. As Theodora Kroeber told him: "About California: It is simply deteriorating faster than other places because people pour in faster."[32]

A book that appeared in print in 1965, soon after Steward wrote to his old friends, chronicled some of the changes he had seen, many of them linked to the explosive population growth. Its title was *The Destruction of California.*[33]

* * *

A few months after Steward arrived in California in 1960, he learned that Kroeber had died in Paris. Then eighty-four, Kroeber had gone to Europe to attend a conference. He had remained at the center of his profession and deeply immersed in its activities until the last days of his long life and his sixty-year career.[34] During the same period, a number of Steward's teachers and senior colleagues died: Lowie, Gifford, and Radin in the late 1950s, then Kroeber and Spier in the early 1960s. Several of his peers also died during these years: Kluckhohn, who was just fifty-five, and Strong, who was sixty-three.

Lowie's death prompted Steward to send a note to his widow, with an expression of sympathy and kind words about his teacher. When Kroeber died three years later, he wrote a lengthy obituary for the *American Anthropologist,* and one for the *Journal of Comparative Sociology;* and he eventually completed a longer biographical work on Kroeber for the National Academy of Sciences. Years later, Steward finally submitted what he called a "long-overdue" biographical memoir about Lowie, also for the academy. His own student, Murphy—Lowie's colleague at Berkeley in the 1950s and, in terms of lineage, an academic "grandson"—published a biography of Lowie soon after that. Still later, he wrote an essay about both Lowie and Steward, and others about Steward only. Full members of an academic lineage, Steward and Murphy thus memorialized their elders.[35]

Betty Starr's untimely death in 1964 elicited a column in the local newspaper; an obituary by Casagrande appeared in the *American Anthropologist* two years later. The local newspaper published the notice of her death under the rather misleading headline, "Dr. Starr of UI Faculty Dies at 58." The text did identify her, however, as the department secretary, while also noting her listing in *Who's Who of American Women.* (In the university's internal correspondence, unlike the newpaper, she was consistently identified as "Miss" Starr.)[36]

If Starr's life had not been cut short she might have finally found a teaching position, as other women did during this period. An unprecedented boom in the academic job market began in the mid-1960s and continued for the rest of that decade. It occurred in response to a sharp increase in the number of students, as the generation born just after World War II began reaching college age. During that brief and unparalleled period, demand for university professors exceeded supply. Even women found full-time and permanent academic positions in anthropology. Few of those, however, were in departments with graduate

programs, where they might have trained another generation of anthropologists, which is to say they might have created sublineages themselves. Leacock
proved to be one of the exceptions. Surveying the employment situation in 1965,
Steward commented, "Illinois has 62 graduate students—today is a seller's
market." (The boom ended abruptly a few years later, ushering in a long period
of retrenchment in academic hiring. Many faculty members who received tenure during the 1960s and early 1970s remained in those positions through the
1990s and into the next century.)[37]

Steward stayed aloof from the department and graduate program in the 1960s.
Many new faculty members arrived during those years, among them Charles J.
Bareis, the department's third archaeologist, and Eugene Giles, a physical anthropologist. Cultural anthropologists, who were hired in greater numbers, included Edward M. Bruner, Clark E. Cunningham, Harold Gould, David O. Plath,
Demitri B. Shimkin, Norman E. Whitten Jr., and R. Tom Zuidema. The first
woman to hold a faculty position, Enid Schildkrout, was finally hired in 1969;
she soon left to take a position with the American Museum of Natural History.[38]

Shimkin had known Steward since the 1930s and had collaborated with him,
and some other faculty members sought him out. But many of them had virtually no contact with him at all. He rarely attended meetings in the department
and, after suffering a stroke in the mid-1960s, almost never visited campus. Jane
Steward stopped by the department to collect her husband's mail on her trips
to town, a practice she had begun even before her husband's health declined,
as he spent nearly all of his time at home in Fithian and avoided the university.[39]

Unlike his experience at Columbia, where he worked with dozens of graduate students, Steward served as adviser to very few at Illinois. William H. Alkire,
who would specialize in Micronesia, and Shuichi Nagata, whom he had recruited
in Japan, were his first two doctoral students. Nagata carried out fieldwork in
the Southwest, focusing his research on what Steward termed "modernization
of the very conservative Hopi." Steward thought of it as an extension of the
Cultural Regularities project, in which Nagata had already taken part in Japan.
Alkire, who was aware of Steward's anxiety about confrontation, remembered
him as supportive of his students, willing to defend them even when it led to
friction with other faculty members.[40]

The few other students who worked closely with Steward included George
L. Hicks, Stephen I. Thompson, and William W. Pilcher. Jane Steward remembered that Pilcher, a former longshoreman from Portland, Oregon, often came
to Fithian to see her husband; he reminisced about his work on the docks, and
the two men discussed how he might study it. Then in his thirties, Pilcher was
older than most of the other students, and his dissertation research on longshoremen—men working together in groups—obviously appealed to Steward.
(After earning a Ph.D. and teaching for a few years, Pilcher returned to Portland and his former occupation.)[41]

Steward also served as graduate adviser to British-born Judith A. Nagata, perhaps his only female doctoral student. She carried out fieldwork in an Amish community in Illinois. The Amish intrigued Steward because they avoid modern technology, from electricity to motor vehicles, and even prosper by doing so. A severe ice storm sometime in 1966 or 1967 showed him that "industrial man can be terribly vulnerable to his environment if something goes wrong." As he later reported, the power lines broke under the weight of the ice, and with the loss of electricity went the lights, heat, and even the water supply, which depended on an electric pump. Telephones remained out of service for days, and the debris of tree limbs and fallen power lines made roads impassable for cars and trucks. But the Amish who lived nearby carried on with their work and daily routine, and even travel, unperturbed by environmental conditions that paralyzed most of the area. Their own technology, unlike that of so many of their neighbors, proved practically weatherproof.[42]

As the 1960s progressed, Steward had less and less contact with graduate students, except for those few who actively sought him out and drove nearly forty miles round-trip to see him in Fithian. He rarely offered courses; when he did teach a small seminar, he held the classes at his house. His virtual absence from the department disappointed many of the students who had been attracted to the University of Illinois when they saw his name on the faculty roster. Even after Steward's retirement in 1969, some students entered the graduate program hoping to work closely with the author of *Theory of Culture Change.* As undergraduates applying for graduate study, they had not noticed his emeritus status. Like the general public, they did not understand the system of academic rank and title; and they had no way of knowing that even in the years before retirement Steward had rarely taught and had largely disengaged from university life. He told an old friend, also recently retired from an academic career, that universities had grown too large and their procedures too complicated: "I am glad to have lived and taught when I did," he concluded, "and to be retiring at the present time."[43]

Ironically, his reputation as a theorist reached a peak during this very period, in part because of the attention Marvin Harris gave to Steward's work in a well-known book, *The Rise of Anthropological Theory.* Harris, a Columbia graduate and faculty member, had entered the anthropology program there shortly before Steward left in 1952. While not actually Steward's student, he had a long and close acquaintance with Steward's approach. His book, which appeared in print in 1968, arguably treated cultural ecology more favorably than any other previous theoretical approach. Steward himself called it a "very charitable presentation" of his ideas.[44]

He increasingly found his work the subject of papers by graduate students, at Illinois and elsewhere. Remarking that he had always benefitted more from interacting with students than with professional colleagues, he told one of them, John K. Chance, that he had read his paper and found it helpful. Steward thought it raised points about theoretical ideas that needed clarification or further development. He implicitly referred to the work of revising *Theory of Culture Change,* which proceeded slowly.[45]

Although he might well have found a position elsewhere, and received offers of visiting appointments from other universities, he stayed at Illinois. As he later warned two of his students, recently embarked on academic careers, they had entered a "snakepit." "I consider practically every university, especially with a graduate department, something of a snakepit," he wrote, "and it is very dubious that one ever gets into a much more pleasant situation by leaving the mess he is now in." Alluding to a colleague who periodically threatened to leave Illinois, but did not, Steward remarked, "Mainly I think it has been fairly clear that bad as things are here, there are few if any places that are better."[46]

During the last ten years of his life, Steward maintained an active correspondence with a few of his former students from Columbia, who were in their turn training another generation of graduate students in anthropology, creating their own sublineages. As Murphy observed, "All of those wise New York kids that you had at Columbia are now full professors and have grey hair, if any, and I hope that it gladdens you to see us turning out our own anthropologists—after all, they are your academic grandchildren." Despite the reference to "all" Steward's students, the comment applied only to some of the men, not the women, as the mention of high academic rank, lineage reproduction, and hair loss makes clear.[47]

A number of the Columbia graduates contributed to a festschrift volume in his honor, edited by Manners and published in 1964. They also assembled in Urbana for a banquet celebrating the book's publication. Mintz, who attended, remembered that Steward appeared to be in poor health. His health was clearly in decline, and his failing vision would make it difficult for him to read and to write during the last years of his life.[48]

Although he did continue to write and to publish, he needed the active assistance of Jane Steward more and more as the years passed. Except for her trips to town, she was his constant companion, as she had been throughout their marriage; only at the BAE had he spent a portion of many workdays out of her presence. His dependence on her, always great, increased as his vision grew worse. She frequently read to him, but he also managed to read by himself with the aid of an elaborate system of lights and magnifying glasses. He typed some of his own letters, often replete with *X*'s crossing out errors, and a word of apology at the end. "Forgive my lousy typing which has gone all to hell with my stroke," he wrote in the closing of a letter to Betty Meggers and Clifford Evans. And a few months later, he added a postscript to his letter to Harris: "Forgive the typing. A stroke of a few years ago raise[s] hell with my coordination."[49]

His physical impairment frustrated him as he tried to complete new works, revise old ones, and, increasingly, defend himself against critics. To his great dismay, those critics included some of his former students, who not only raised questions about his work but did so in print. Steward complained that many of his critics had misunderstood him or had failed to read later works, published after *Theory of Culture Change*, in which he clarified or revised some of his ideas. Murphy commiserated with him but saw generational politics and the structure of the profession as more to the point. "It should be some comfort to you," he wrote, "to realize that young men trying to establish the authenticity and originality of their own contribution to the field of cultural ecology feel that they have to show that their work is different from yours." During this period, a growing number of anthropologists began to use cultural ecology as a framework for research, but, with just one exception, those mentioned by Steward and his correspondents were men. It did not attract many women, perhaps in part because of its masculinist tenor.[50]

The criticism that cut to the quick came from Wolf, whose review of *Contemporary Change in Traditional Societies* appeared in *Science* in 1967. The three-volume work had finally been published after a long delay, and Wolf reviewed it at Steward's invitation before it even reached print. Wolf remarked at the outset of a lengthy review that readers would not get "much theoretical aid from the project organizer." The introduction was rather cursory, he added, because Steward planned to spell out the theoretical basis of the project in a revised version of *Theory of Culture Change*. Wolf proceeded to offer a synopsis of each field study, finding much merit in some but little continuity among them. His closing words troubled Steward even more than the opening remarks. "Finally," Wolf wrote, "there remains the unpleasant ethical question of 'modernization for what?'" Reading the studies, he said, gave him "a profound sense of anguish about a world in which social and cultural arrangements are initiated and carried through with so little concern for attendant human costs."[51]

Steward responded quickly with a letter to the editor of *Science*, giving a spirited defense of unfettered scientific research, detached from ethical questions. "Science must above all remain free," he insisted. "It is not the fault of the nuclear physicist," he wrote, "that enormous new sources of energy are still used largely for potential mass destruction rather than for peaceful purposes." In studying modernization, he argued, the "first and fundamental task is to assess the consequences of policies and decisions—to understand causality in human affairs so as to lay some basis for predictions." (Here he repeated the argument he had made to Kroeber in the Saturday morning discussions at Columbia almost twenty years earlier.) These predictions could help policy makers understand the probable effects of their actions in the future. "It is pointless to stress responsiblity for changes of the past," Steward added.[52] He did not address Wolf's complaint about the lack of a theoretical statement in the introduction, a complaint repeated in many of the reviews.

The reception given *Contemporary Change in Traditional Societies* left him with a feeling of "bitter disappointment," Steward later said. The reviewers, he contended, had failed to see "the obvious comparability, although not similarity, of the different contributions." In truth, Steward had failed to produce for this final project the compelling work of synthesis that had always been his signature as a theorist—that is, the statement that reviewers needed in order to see "the obvious comparability" that he saw. Instead of providing that statement, he mentioned in the introduction that it would appear in print elsewhere, "as a separate book that will enlarge and supersede my *Theory of Culture Change*."[53]

* * *

The first edition of *Theory of Culture Change* went out of print in the late 1960s, although demand had remained rather strong. The University of Illinois Press decided against reprinting it after Steward let it be known that he intended to revise it. In letters written between 1966 and 1970, he referred often to the planned revisions, commenting as the years passed that he found the work "difficult" and that it proceeded "slowly." Although he offered few details, it appears that initially he wanted to rewrite portions of the first section ("Concepts and Methods"), and especially the chapter on multilinear evolution.[54]

As time passed, he decided to make extensive changes in the second section ("Substantive Applications") as well and described the book's revision as "almost total." Steward clearly planned to include the summary and synthesis of field research that he had not managed to produce before *Contemporary Change in Traditional Societies* went to press. Undoubtedly, he also intended to replace the chapter on the Carrier that he had written for *Theory of Culture Change*. In 1960 Steward had published what he called an "entirely new interpretation" of the Carrier in a festschrift volume for Radin. Unlike its predecessors, it illustrated the perspective of cultural ecology in showing how Carrier society had recently changed in response to a change in resources (the growth of the fur trade). Steward probably intended to use the new version, or one based on it, in the second edition of his book.[55]

The new interpretation appeared to echo some of Leacock's ideas about the effects of the fur trade on Montagnais-Naskapi Indians in Labrador. But the 1960 article contained no mention of her name or any refererence to her 1954 monograph. In marked contrast to an earlier, related article that Murphy and Steward had published together in 1956, which cited Leacock extensively (perhaps thanks to Murphy), she was excluded from the text and bibliography of Steward's essay, which reached print five years later: "Murphy and Steward have shown that the Mundurucú of the Amazon and the Montagnais of Labrador . . ." The language in that sentence was misleading in the sense that Murphy had carried out field research with the Mundurucú, while Steward had reading knowledge of both the Montagnais and the Mundurucú. Murphy's name appeared in the list of references, but Leacock's did not.[56]

At the time those words were written, Leacock still had a highly tenuous foothold in the academic world. She taught evening classes at the Brooklyn Polytechnic Institute, where she had virtually no contact with full-time faculty members; and she had not published on the Montagnais for several years, writing instead about mental health issues, an outgrowth of her research at the Yorkville Project. (Two years later, at about the time universities began to expand rapidly, she finally found her first full-time tenure-track position—eleven years after earning a Ph.D.). Her marginality in the profession during the late 1950s and early 1960s made it easy to ignore her even while capitalizing on the results of her labor. Yet as Leacock vividly recalled, during an informal encounter at an AAA meeting, probably in 1955, Steward acknowledged that she had done "the basic work on the hunting territory"—although he did so only in response to direct and persistent prodding by a male colleague. Fortunately for Leacock's intellectual stock, the 1956 journal article found a far wider audience than the 1961 book chapter; and a second edition of *Theory of Culture Change*, which might have contained that chapter, never reached completion.[57]

As he set about making revisions, Steward at first concentrated on reworking his ideas about cultural evolution: "I am attempting to develop the methodology of evolution well beyond what I have previously published, and I am now interested in presenting new ideas rather than explaining again and again what is wrong with [Lewis Henry] Morgan, [Leslie] White, etc." But a few years later, Steward admitted to having "increasing doubts about using the term evolution with reference to culture." He added, as if to underscore the point, "I became classed as an evolutionist in 1952 when Kroeber asked me to give a paper on cultural evolution." His words implied that he had not undertaken the task on his own initiative or with any great enthusiasm, and his writings during the late 1950s and 1960s show that he remained highly ambivalent about contributing to the subject.[58]

He firmly opposed White's approach and did not hesitate to criticize it, either privately or in print. Murphy remembered that Steward often remarked on White's inattention to ecology and local environmental conditions, protesting that his "universal" evolution could just as well take place anywhere in the universe—on Mars as easily as on Earth. The two men exchanged brief and cordial letters now and then and met socially when Steward and his wife visited Ann Arbor, but they did not talk about their differences. When they later reviewed each other's books in journals, however, they did not hesitate to air those differences in print. Despite Steward's comment to White—that although there seemed to be "no point of agreement" in their publications, they might still have a "profitable discussion" of "basic issues"—no such discussion ensued.[59]

According to Service, White confined discussion of his ideas to the classroom and to writing. He refused to discuss his work informally with colleagues or with students outside of class, directing them instead to his publications. Service recalled how this puzzled and annoyed some of White's junior colleagues at the University of Michigan and dismayed students. It did have the effect, however, of protecting White from what he may have considered pointless and distracting debates about his work and misrepresentation of his ideas, which remained highly controversial for many years.[60]

Steward, in contrast, avoided the classroom as well as conferences, fearing public confrontations about his ideas in those formal settings; but he always enjoyed informal discussions with a small number of like-minded men, evidently regarding that as a safe setting. Perhaps he also began asking students to meet at his house because it provided a less formal, safer place for a seminar than a classroom. Jane Steward's presence, her disarming warmth and hospitality, gave these occasions a social aspect, which tempered the academic. It protected against the sort of confrontation that occurred with the sociology students at Columbia, who expressed scorn for his ideas and then dropped his course.

Steward continued to think critically about cultural ecology as well as cultural evolution. "I never intended that an ecological explanation, or any kind of complete correlations between culture and environment would be an undeviating explanation," he wrote in 1970. "It seemed to me more a matter of hypotheses always subject to empirical testing, but in general useful in introducing fairly recognizable causes to much culture change." Years earlier, he had already rejected a central and guiding idea of cultural ecology, the concept of the cultural core as spelled out in 1955 in *Theory of Culture Change*. An essay that he published in 1968 under the same title as the original, "The Concept and Method of Cultural Ecology," bore rather little semblance to the 1955 version. Instead of giving specific guidance about cultural ecology as a method, it offered generalizations about the relation between culture and environment, with no mention of the cultural core.[61]

"Nothing was changed in this article," Steward remarked, a puzzling statement since his revision eviscerated cultural ecology as a methodology. That he made this comment to Murphy, however, helps to explain it. More than twenty years after Steward wrote those words, Murphy laughed when he said that he and Wolf had "talked Steward out of the cultural core" in 1954 or 1955, arguing that it was "too techno-environmental." He laughed not at the ensuing result, which he did not fully recognize, but at the incongruity of it all: the surprising success of two Young Turks who convinced their senior professor of his error.[62]

That very incident may account for the perceptive remark Murphy made to Steward in 1967, about "young men trying to establish the authenticity and originality of their own contribution . . . [by showing] that their own work is different from yours." Murphy, in his forties at the time and with graduate students of his own, spoke from experience. He had once been one of those young men, eager to stake out his own intellectual territory; but, following closely in Steward's footsteps, he now occupied the position of senior professor at Columbia. In fact, he even occupied Steward's old office. Years later, by then in his midsixties, Murphy recalled another young man who had once criticized Steward's ecological ideas, but much more harshly and in print. The critic, who achieved great success as an anthropologist, later said that he regretted his attack on Steward, telling Murphy that he had "'stood on the shoulders of a giant and urinated on his head.'" (The original language may have been slightly more colorful.)[63]

A letter from Murphy to Steward corroborates his memories about the cultural core. Writing in 1964, he referred to "many of the conversations that you, Eric and I had on the subject of core culture and the fact that the only effective way of isolating the key institutions in a society was to see it in the process of change." Steward clearly agreed, as shown by his comment to another colleague: "In fact, I began to think some time ago that the frustrating search for taxonomic criteria for cultural types would be far more readily worked out if the criteria could be seen as the results of processes rather than some static or structural 'core' features." He seems to have begun questioning the concept of the cultural core sometime before the Studies of Cultural Regularities project entered the final planning stage and after *Theory of Culture Change* went to press.[64]

If so, this explains why he soon considered the book "overdue for revision." His concept of the cultural core had held a central place in his thinking about cultural ecology and multilinear evolution. His ideas about culture type had clearly grown out of his concept of the cultural core, and his foundational concept, the patrilineal band. As a culture type, the patrilineal band embraced societies that shared core features: a certain kind of technology, organization of men's labor, kinship system, and rules of postmarital residence, all linked with resources of a particular sort. When Steward abandoned the cultural core, the concept of culture type lost its linchpin, which also compromised his framework for multilinear evolution. And cultural ecology certainly lost focus, although not all meaning.

Steward did not seem to grasp the destruction wrought when he, in his own words, "repudiated" the cultural core. (He wrote the words "now repudiated" in the margins of a manuscript he reviewed in the mid-1960s, which mentioned his concept of the core.) Nor did Murphy, years after the fact, see a connection between Steward's ambivalence about some of his earlier work and his doubts about core culture, which evidently took shape and grew during his conversations with the two younger men. Like many others, Murphy detected a loss of productivity and direction during Steward's last years, which he attributed to advanced age, failing health, and isolation from the eastern academic world. Yet Steward's troubling doubts took root while he was still in his early fifties, before his health declined seriously and while he worked closely with his Columbia associates.[65]

Some of the difficulty Steward experienced in planning the Cultural Regularities project probably stemmed from casting aside a central concept of cultural ecology. The sheer magnitude and complexity of the project, and the active involvement of nearly a dozen men—at varying points in their training or careers, and with wide-ranging, even divergent, interests—also impeded the planning. Both the conceptual and personnel problems help account for Steward's later inability to synthesize the project's findings. At the least, they explain why the findings seemed so disparate to some of the fieldworkers and many reviewers of *Contemporary Change in Traditional Societies*. Steward never completed a final statement, despite the "comparability" that he insisted he saw in the results.[66]

Long before the mid-1960s, Steward had also rejected irrigation as *the* causal factor in the development of early civilizations. He explained his thinking—or rethinking—to Murphy, asserting that "environmental and technological factors are passive features until put into interaction by people." Disparate causal factors, he said, may, in fact, sometimes produce "similar cultural manifestations." "It was a failure to think through these points," he continued, "that made my formulation of early civilizations vulnerable. I assumed that similar manifestations meant the same underlying cause, and I accepted irrigation. This is why [Robert] Braidwood and [Robert McCormick] Adams jumped all over me, insisting on a more empirical approach."[67]

He reported to a number of colleagues that he had "abandoned Wittfogel's irrigation hypothesis," and he made that point in print several times, including his review of Adams's 1966 book, *The Evolution of Urban Societies*. He spelled out some of his reasons in an essay that was published years later, posthumously. Referring to yet another unpublished paper, he told Marvin Harris, "I have gone beyond Adams in attempting to formulate the preconditions in terms of closely placed and interrelated, interdependent microenvironments." Harris, who along with many others thought that the irrigation hypothesis had merit, cautioned against rejecting irrigation too hastily. And Murphy, who also reviewed Adams's book, found it less persuasive than Steward did. "I am still not convinced," Murphy said, "that irrigation follows the state, as he argues." Ironically, he attributed his doubts to research he wrote up in 1954 while working with Steward in Urbana. That paper had remained unpublished.[68]

What Steward saw as rethinking and revision, what he called "modify[ing] my position," many of his colleagues interpreted as recanting and retreat. When Manners asked his permission to reprint the chapter on multilinear evolution in a collection of essays, Steward at first demurred, explaining his reservations about republishing "ancient stuff a second and third time . . . and having to explain that I did not mean this or that the way it sounds." He offered to write something new instead. "Bob Manners wrote back that I was scrapping everything I had stood for," he later told Murphy. "I just don't see this, but I told him to go ahead with the old article."[69]

At the same time, he complained increasingly about being misunderstood and overlooked. The New Ecology, a departure from cultural ecology that emerged in the mid-1960s, struck him as perilously close to biological reductionism, and other variants simply perplexed him. Referring to a well-known anthropologist, he commented, "He is also said to be interested in ecology, but I'm damned if I know any more what most people mean by this." He protested that the New

Ecologists (who came to be called ecological anthropologists) had misinterpreted his early work and failed to read his more recent articles, in which he modified his views or offered new interpretations. And their interest in the concept of ecosystems puzzled him. It struck him as "an a priori attempt to limit by some arbitrary definition" the parameters of study. Cultural ecology, in contrast, "is really a method," he said, "and the relevance of data of any kind is established by [each] particular case."[70]

In Steward's view, the once-unified field of anthropology had, by the mid-1960s, disintegrated into "all manner of splinter groups, each distinguishable by its jargons but not by its ideas." A forty-year career had given him a perspective on fundamental problems that remained "unsolved," he said, while "fads of new methods and new jargon come and go." He conceded that some of the new methods might have merit, but objected that too often their novelty value, rather than any real usefulness, explained their appeal. It troubled him to think that anthropologists faddishly borrowed models and methods from mathematics and the natural sciences in order to create the impression of scientific rigor. He looked askance at the use of game theory, algebraic kinship analysis, componential analysis, and computerization, commenting dryly that "the 'thrust of the dialogue' is demanding a much-needed incredibility gap in knowledge—if I make myself unclear." (Some thirty years after his mention of computers, then in their infancy, a cyber-Steward occupied a site on the Internet.)[71]

He increasingly referred to himself as an "Old Anthropologist." The term alluded in part to his age (mid- to late sixties) and physical condition (he spoke of having "physical handicaps" after suffering a stroke). Primarily, however, Steward used it to affirm his generational status and his support of what he called the "Old Anthropology." The "New Anthropology" ranged from ecological anthropology to Lévi-Strauss's structuralism. "I have grown increasingly unhappy about recent trends in anthropology," he told Murphy. "The trouble is that there are too few left of my generation to perceive the continuities that are being so obscured by verbiage."[72]

He detected few such continuities, however, in the work of French anthropologist Claude Lévi-Strauss, whom he had first known as a refugee scholar during the 1940s. The growing popularity of Lévi-Strauss's competing approach among younger colleagues alarmed him, and he cannot have been pleased to learn in 1966 that his rival was the sole recipient of the Viking Fund Medal that year. When the Smithsonian Institution invited Lévi-Strauss as the main speaker for its centennial celebration in 1968, Steward privately expressed surprise. When he received no invitation to attend, he confessed to feeling hurt. Harris's newly published book on theory would soon bring even more attention to Steward's work in cultural ecology, but he had not yet read it and could not foresee the results. The Smithsonian incident fed a gnawing sense that he was regarded as "passé," and "pushed aside" by most of his profession, an unexpected conclusion to a long and highly successful career.[73]

During the last five years of his life, beginning in the tumult of the late 1960s, Steward also grew increasingly concerned about the changes he saw taking place in the wider world. He and his wife deeply opposed the war in Vietnam and deplored the massive destruction unleashed on the people and the land by means of sophisticated weaponry, including deadly chemicals. "Today, I am sick with apprehension about the course of both domestic and world events," Steward wrote to a colleague. "The consequences of technological change have far outrun our understanding of them and ability to control them. But if anyone is to survive to continue anthropology, an all-out effort is needed, late though it is."[74]

Put in the language of the era's Student Movement, the social sciences no longer seemed quite as "relevant" in a world that killed children with napalm and forests with Agent Orange. "I think it highly improbable that the social sciences can now provide any understandings that will in any way stem or affect the course of events," Steward said. His research project on modernization lay behind him, and the three volumes resulting from it were probably in press when he wrote those words. Even before reading the first critical reviews, he appears to have felt a keen sense of disappointment and pessimism about that project and its purpose.[75]

Reaching the goal he had long ago set for himself as a social scientist—understanding the causes of cultural change in order to predict its future course—suddenly seemed a remote and futile prospect. He no longer believed that he could provide what policy makers and planners needed to make well-informed and rational decisions, or that they, in turn, could affect cultural change. These were perhaps separate matters, the first specific to himself and the highly ambitious project he had directed; but in his darkening mood, his own sense of defeat grew.

As his former optimism about technological change faded, he grew more aware of the ways in which new technologies, including modern techniques for extracting resources, were despoiling the natural world. He and his wife had continued to think about retiring to California, perhaps to Santa Barbara, which he remembered fondly from the 1920s, when he worked there with Ronald Olson at a seaside archaeological site. But an oil spill along the southern California coast in the late 1960s discouraged him, as did the prospect of an ocean view dominated by offshore oil platforms. He increasingly admired the Amish approach to technology during these years, and not only because they weathered ice storms and blizzards with relative ease. Their nonmechanized tools required no petroleum or electricity; they did not lay waste to the land in the name of progress and profit.

Service, who had recently left the University of Michigan for the University of California, Santa Barbara, assured Steward that the offshore oil platforms were "not so visible" as he might think. A letter of inquiry to Beals, soon to retire from a long and highly successful career at UCLA, likewise brought news that most of the drilling platforms could be seen only on clear days. But clear skies and sun were precisely what Steward and his wife sought, and, along with it, natural beauty unmarred by industrial blight. Beals thought that the pollution from the oil spill would no longer be obvious in a year, adding the proviso "if there is no repeat." Steward, immensely saddened by destructive changes to the California landscape, and now to the seascape, finally concluded that the high cost of living and the price of real estate also ruled it out.[76]

During this same period, he received an invitation to teach at Deep Springs, which he declined with regret, citing his failing vision and limited mobility. He expressed a certain resentment toward the end of his life that some of his Deep Springs classmates had not directed their lives toward public service in any obvious way. Having prospered as business executives or lawyers in private practice, they could easily afford to retire wherever they chose. One of them had a winter home in Jamaica, and others traveled widely for pleasure, not under the auspices of a foundation or in the name of science. He wondered why "an astonishing number of Deep Springs [and Telluride Association] graduates . . . went into conventional professions, wherein [Nunn's goal of promoting] the highest well-being somehow got lost—or at least so far as I could understand all of this."[77]

Still hopeful that he might overcome the effects of his stroke, Steward told the director of Deep Springs that he would reconsider the offer in the near future. He added that he had looked forward to retirement as a time when he could volunteer his services to Deep Springs. "Partly I wished to do this because I simply love the place and that part of the world," he explained, "and it is rather depressing to think of remaining in this flat part of the country." Looking at scenes of mountain and desert in the old album of photographs that he had kept since his student days gave him a painfully sharp sense of nostalgia.[78]

Although the horizontal lines of the prairie, and what he called the "bitter" and "endless" winters, wore on him, Steward still drew pleasure from the openness of the landscape and its unpeopled look. "Fithian is about as uncrowded a spot as we know," he remarked, "and it is fine except for its everlasting flatness." To Theodora Kroeber's suggestion that they move to California, he cited as obstacles the "overpopulated and/or contaminated" condition of the Bay Area and Santa Barbara, respectively. "Perhaps we will remain on our four acres in flat Illinois farm country and be content with pictures of the west," he wrote.[79]

When he finally gave up the idea of returning to the West, Steward also stopped looking at pictures that intensified the sense of loss. As it became clear that he had no prospect of returning to Deep Springs, he decided to send his album back to the school as a record of its early years. He remained living near the ninetieth meridian, and within the region of rainfall agriculture, until his final days. The arid West, defined by Powell as land that lay beyond the hundredth meridian, still occupied a place in memory during the last years of Steward's life, but he was never to see it again.[80]

He asked Theodora Kroeber rather wistfully for news about their few remaining friends in Berkeley, after mentioning the names of several who had died in recent years. "Of course, I [still] know a number of people in the department," Steward wrote, "but there was never the warm personal relationship I had with others, even with Ted McCown who unfortunately is gone, too." (McCown had died just months earlier.) He inquired about Lowie's widow and some mutual friends from the 1920s. By the time Theodora Kroeber replied to his letter five weeks later, Lowie's wife had died. Doris Radin, also widowed, had been living with her for the previous two years. But the Lowie house was to be sold, the proceeds going to the department of anthropology, and no provision had been made for Doris Radin. Steward wondered what would become of her. "One thing is sure," he remarked. "Paul did not leave her any property for he never had any. Except his books."[81]

* * *

Oscar Lewis died unexpectedly eight months later, in December 1970. Just fifty-five years old at the time, he was immersed in a study of postrevolutionary Cuba. Steward, then in his late sixties, was shocked by Lewis's untimely death, which interrupted but did not immediately put an end to an impressive flow of publications by his longtime colleague. "It is a pity that he was taken at the peak of his productivity," Steward wrote to Ruth Lewis. "Jane tells me that you are completing some of his manuscripts, each of which will certainly add to the richness of his work."[82]

Ruth Lewis had always worked closely with her husband, even to the point of helping to write text for works published only under his name. The phrase *his manuscripts* was thus inaccurate. In the years after Oscar Lewis's death, Ruth Lewis and a colleague, Susan M. Rigdon, would write three volumes based on the Cuban field research, the first books to carry Ruth Lewis's name as a coauthor. At least one reviewer later said pointedly that these books, written after the senior author's death, were of a piece with the earlier ones. Ruth Lewis's years of unrecognized labor received belated notice as the times changed and the second wave of feminism crested.[83]

Recalling the Lewises' collaborative work, Jane Steward mentioned times when they were so busy that Ruth Lewis had no time to cook. "They'd go to a restaurant for dinner," she added, smiling as she feigned a hint of envy. This led her to recall how their own social life, including dinner parties and restaurant dining, declined even before her husband's health failed, as he began avoiding the university as much as possible. She explained that he refused to go to dinner parties, not knowing who the other guests would be, and preferred instead to invite a few colleagues to their own house. That too diminished over time, at his express wish. (She later attributed this to recurrent but undiagnosed spells of depression, at a time when effective treatment did not yet exist.)[84]

Although Steward's own most productive years lay behind him by 1970, he reported having four books underway, even as his vision continued to deteriorate. He thanked Murphy for sending a copy of his new book, "which I look forward to getting in to as soon as I can get Jane to read it to me." He described his vision problems as cataracts and degeneration of the retina, which would not, however, lead to complete blindness. "This is hereditary," he added, "since my mother's eyes went the same way, and there is nothing I can do about it." But he continued to write. After completing the short biography of Lowie for the National Academy of Sciences in 1971, he worked steadily on a longer biography of Kroeber. Charles Wagley had requested it for the Leaders in Anthropology series, published by Columbia University Press.[85] This was the fourth, final, and lengthiest essay on Kroeber that Steward wrote. Besides biographical detail and commentary, the book included a selection of Kroeber's writings.[86]

Steward's revisions and new chapters for *Theory of Culture Change,* which he planned to give a new title, proceeded slowly, displaced for a time by the Kroeber biography. It had a strict deadline, and he missed his own self-imposed deadline for finishing the revisions. Other requests also distracted him from *Theory of Culture Change,* which he had already worked on sporadically for five years. One of those requests came from Warren d'Azevedo, who was editing a volume on the Great Basin for the *Handbook of North American Indians,* under the general editorship of William Sturtevant. "If I can wind up my obligations to the Kroeber biography for Chuck Wagley," Steward ventured, "perhaps I could write a few pages on the question of basic similarities and differences among the Numic-speaking people." As it turned out, finishing the book left him no time to complete that paper.[87]

Despite giving most of his attention in the final year of his life to the Kroeber biography, Steward continued to insist that completing the revisions of *Theory of Culture Change* remained his primary commitment. He mentioned revising the chapters on cultural evolution, even while questioning the utility of the concept. "My fundamental interest was and continues to be causality," he explained. "I have come . . . to consider what is called evolution as little more than historical transformations." He also questioned whether he had appeared to overemphasize cultural ecology, "to make ecological explanations the only ones," as he put it. The process of writing went slowly, he explained, because of the need to revise so many of the substantive hypotheses. He spoke of doing "'a lot of pondering.'"[88]

Steward planned to rewrite his chapters on bands, saying that recent work on hunter-gatherers and band society had raised many questions and led him to reconsider his past conclusions. "I in no way repudiate what I have done previously," he stressed, pointing out that the "early information [on patrilineal bands] was in many ways incomplete." Instead, he intended to add what he termed "new substantive theory about the explanations of the different kinds of bands." To the end of his life, the patrilineal band remained a pivotal concept for Steward and a subject he returned to again and again with unflagging interest. He continued to see it largely as a male work group, and the men as primary providers. No doubt he identified closely with it, having spent most his own life—from those formative years in adolescence through middle age—working with other men, and in the role of a provider.[89]

His ideas about women's labor remained embryonic and essentialist decades after his encounter with what he called "a woman's economy" in the 1930s. His 1968 essay on cultural ecology contained one line on the subject, under the heading "Biological Factors" (not under "Cultural Variables and Holism"): "Women are food collectors because they must not leave their children, who are their inescapable responsibility. . . ." His own life experience and personal memories, not fieldwork, provided the basis for this interpretive point and for its prescriptive language, that "they must not leave their children."

Julian Steward's own experience had, unhappily for him, diverged from that prescription. Grace Steward had left her children when she left their father, her departure spurred at least in part by her commitment to religious doctrines that her husband did not share. She had taken up paid employment and a new life elsewhere, with painful emotional consequences for her son. Decades later, when Jane Steward expressed interest in earning an income again, years after her children entered school, her husband summarily rejected the idea. In those postwar years, public opinion was on his side, and she did not pursue the matter.[90]

Until the end of his life, Steward thought about cultural ecology in terms of men's labor and the technologies used by men. He also continued to view his ecological approach as a means to an end, a method for achieving theoretical insights about culture and the causes of cultural change. Over the years, he had characterized cultural ecology as a concept, a method, a subject, an approach, but never as a general theory of culture. He had never intended to provide "an undeviating explanation," a grand theory, which, in his eyes, constituted an "-ism." He reserved the right to think, to question, and to change his mind—in other words, to exercise Cartesian doubt. At the same time, his old self-doubts increasingly plagued him, and even the most fleeting feelings of self-confidence eluded him. He found it difficult to defend his ideas or present new ones, as he wanted to do in the revised edition of *Theory of Culture Change*. He confessed to Manners that his self-confidence was in a "somewhat shattered" state.[91]

Steward's distaste for "-ism and ideology"—whether religious or secular, inside or outside science—never wavered. The only ism he ever endorsed was empiricism. Murphy did not exaggerate when he said that Steward was "repelled by ideology" (including Marxism, even though cultural ecology had some common ground). In the last years of his life, Steward worried about anthropology becoming "completely bogged down in various isms." He reserved his greatest scorn for structuralism, privately dismissing Lévi-Strauss as "the present-day Messiah" surrounded by fervent disciples.[92]

At the same time, Steward's position toward religion shifted slightly. He published an article on cultural evolution in *The Christian Century* (a "very ecumenical" journal, he observed with approval, apparently meaning that it promoted open discussion rather than dogmatism), and he made passing reference to religion in some of his writings. Although he still harbored no religious beliefs at all, Jane Steward said that he came to take a certain pride in their ties to Mormonism and Christian Science, which he saw as authentically American in origin. Never a Europhile, ever an Americanist, he pointedly called them "'two native-born American religions.'"[93]

For most of his life he had insisted on keeping science and politics separate, and he remained aloof from political debate and action. But in the last years of his life, he spoke out on various events, especially the war in Vietnam, which he abhorred. He took part in a teach-in sometime in the late 1960s and added his signature to a full-page statement printed in the *New York Times* protesting the war. Student unrest on campus, which Steward viewed from a distance, sometimes perplexed him, but he also conceded that some reforms might be in order. When the decade ended and a new one began, he expressed relief at even a symbolic juncture.[94]

One of his last tasks, although he did not realize how little time remained for it, was to write an autobiographical statement for the National Academy of Sciences. He had made a first attempt soon after his election to membership, but abandoned it—perhaps because of the press of other commitments, or because he was not inclined to engage in self-reflection or examine his past too closely. In a draft that he probably wrote near the end of his life, he denied any family influence on the path he had chosen, citing his years at Deep Springs as the true "turning point."[95]

He never submitted an autobiographical statement to the National Academy of Sciences.[96] A revised version of *Theory of Culture Change* remained far from completion at the time of his death in 1972, and his biography of Kroeber nearly, but not entirely, finished. Before sending the Kroeber manuscript to the publisher, Jane Steward did the final editorial work, not the last of her unacknowledged labor on behalf of her husband's career. But when she looked at his notes for his own book, she could make no sense of them. He had organized them by subject rather than by chapter, "and what he planned to do I don't know," she concluded sadly. "He did want *Theory* revised," she added.[97]

Those notes from the ninetieth meridian contained his last thoughts on cultural ecology, which is also to say his remembrance of places far beyond the hundredth and times long past.

* * *

A year after her husband's death, Jane Steward looked at his notes again, which included some outlines and portions of text. After studying them more carefully, she concluded that no one could complete what he had left unfinished, but she thought that a collection of his later essays might serve as a substitute for the revised *Theory of Culture Change*. She suggested to the University of Illinois Press that it publish a volume of nine essays, eight of them written between the late 1950s and late 1960s, and all in print but scattered and not easily accessible. "Julian had planned to use some of these in his revised [edition]," she explained. For the title, she proposed *Cultural Ecology and Other Essays*, "because Julian invented [the concept of cultural ecology] back in 1937 and used it from then on."[98]

The University of Illinois Press sent the nine essays to a reader for a formal review, and he recommended publication, in part because of their "historic value" in representing Julian Steward's later thinking. But he added that they did not impress him as much as the earlier work, given Steward's obvious pessimism about the limits of theory. A second reader thought these essays far less significant than their predecessors and suggested that republishing some of Steward's highly influential writings would be of greater value to scholars and a greater honor to Steward. *Theory of Culture Change*, which included his best-known essays, had already been brought back into print, and plans for the new collection proceeded. With Jane Steward's advice and approval, Robert Murphy was invited to serve as her coeditor.[99]

The volume of seventeen essays that resulted, designed as a sequel to *Theory of Culture Change*, contained an example of Steward's earliest work as well as some of his last writings. The later writings included a highly critical essay on applied anthropology, based on Steward's experience with the Bureau of Indian Affairs in the 1930s. (Ironically, a tradition of empirical research persisted among applied anthropologists years after Steward's death, even while many other cultural anthropologists began to question empiricism and turn away from it.) A portion of an unpublished paper also appeared in the book, a substitute for the essay of synthesis that Steward never completed for the Cultural Regularities project.[100]

When the book reached print in 1977, it bore the title *Evolution and Ecology: Essays on Social Transformation*, which Murphy had finally suggested and all parties accepted. Simply by virtue of word order it seemed to emphasize cultural evolution; *Theory of Culture Change* had done the same on the basis of its subtitle, *The Methodology of Multilinear Evolution*. The title of the 1977 volume thus obscured Steward's ambivalence about cultural evolution, which had only deepened during the last decade of his life.

Despite the title, an article on cultural ecology served as lead essay, followed by others on cultural evolution, reversing the order used in the previous volume. Steward's original essay on cultural ecology, from *Theory of Culture Change*, was considered, but his later article on that topic, published in 1968 and shorn of the cultural core, won out as the opening essay for *Evolution and Ecology*. In his introduction to the volume, Murphy singled out cultural ecology as Steward's "greatest contribution to anthropology."[101]

Conclusion

Memory, it has been said, is "a kind of homesickness," perhaps especially when it insists on retrieving a place and a time that are irretrievably lost. Julian Steward spent most of his adult life at a distance from the West, single-mindedly pursuing a career in anthropology, but his own words suggest that scenes from the high desert always remained in his mind's eye. As time passed, the images may have lost some clarity and detail, but they stayed emotionally charged and emotionally vivid. Looking at his own photographs of the mountains and desert must have reinforced his memories; even at the end of his life he spoke of feeling homesick and wishing to return.[1]

Steward showed scant interest in examining his personal past closely, in a highly conscious or searching way. Yet he did often reminisce about his student days at Deep Springs, as Dorothy Nyswander and Jane Steward each recalled, and about his graduate years at Berkeley, as some of his graduate students mentioned. Most of his favorite recollections centered on amusing episodes (Mr. McKay, the beleaguered bookkeeper at Deep Springs, shinnying up a pole to escape an angry steer) or on personal achievements (overcoming obstacles in his first foray into archaeological fieldwork, despite having no training in field methods).[2] It was not Julian Steward's recollections of particular episodes such as these, however, but what cognitive psychologists call generic personal memories, memories of repeated experiences, that appear to have inspired cultural ecology. Most of these came from late adolescence: for example, Steward's memories of rounding up cattle with the other students and the ranch hands and repairing the irrigation system to keep the water flowing.[3]

Steward, as a committed empiricist and self-identified scientist, undoubtedly would have claimed that he worked strictly from archaeological and ethnographic data to develop his theoretical ideas. Murphy recalled that one of Steward's favorite aphorisms was, "'There are no theories unless based upon fact, but facts exist only within the context of a theory.'" (Steward obviously referred not to general theory but to a theory about something specific, such as the development of early civilizations.) It would seem to follow that, in Murphy's own words, "most of the theory [of cultural ecology] was emergent from empirical studies," Steward's own and others', which provided the evidence.

But as Murphy himself observed, Steward was a reserved, quiet man who rarely mentioned his personal life or his past, aside from the amusing anecdotes about his student days, and who left much unsaid in his writings. What he left unstated in print included certain points Steward thought too "obvious" to mention (but that led some readers to misconstrue his meaning), as well as exactly what he meant by the word *theory*. A central, underlying premise of his intellectual work—in a natural order, what happens once can happen again and probably will given the same conditions—also remained largely implicit until Murphy's illuminating commentary appeared in print.[4]

Manners described Steward's theoretical work as not only highly empirical but also highly imaginative. As he put it, empiricism, or "fact finding," was no more than a means to an end for Steward. He used the empirical evidence provided by his own research and that of others as "a catalyst for the imaginative leap that might yield an explanation that went beyond the evidence."[5] I would like to suggest instead that autobiographical memory, not empirical data, was the main catalyst for the generalizing and creative—not highly imaginative—leap that took Steward from data to theory. Memory images guided his thinking. His own memories of place provided the primary source for his work as a theorist, including the basic elements and framework for cultural ecology. The published research of other cultural anthropologists and archaeologists constituted secondary sources, literally and metaphorically. His theoretical work was in part a remembrance of the years spent working with other men at a ranch in the West.

For several formative years during adolescence Steward lived in the high desert, an arid and mountainous environment unlike any he had previously known. Six days a week he did manual labor, a very unusual experience for a young man of his social class. In doing this outdoor work, he engaged directly with the natural world: animals, seeds, soil, water. He also learned to use many different tools, from branding irons to blowtorches. More specifically, in this work he was part of a coordinated group of men, which included Indian ranch hands. With them, he used technology to procure food—for example, food for the livestock, which themselves were destined to be food for the table—and to control water. These very elements would be central to cultural ecology: technology, environmental resources (primarily food and water, the basics for survival), and social organization (especially, cooperative work by men to obtain food).

He also saw for the first time that people can subsist in very different ways in the same environment and that their subsistence practices directly affect how they live. During his first year at Deep Springs, he undoubtedly observed, as did students who recorded their memories of Captain Harry and his family, the striking differences between the way Northern Paiute lived and the way the white residents of the ranch lived. Captain Harry and his family knew the high desert intimately, and they knew how to wrest a living from it using a relatively simple technology, tools made with materials the desert provided. They had spent years "living off the country," to use Steward's own phrase, and undoubtedly continued to supplement their small wages by gathering some of their food. Like Owens Valley Paiute during that era, they probably subsisted on a combination of purchased foods and wild foods, and perhaps garden produce as well. Consummate gatherers, they were highly innovative in adapting to ecological change, finding new foods to replace those they had lost and using traditional foods in new ways. Similarly, discarded boards and nails became new resources in their hands, gathered to build and repair their shelter.[6]

The ranch, with its livestock and large workforce and rather elaborate technology, represented an entirely different way of living in the desert. The buildings and the fields around them were meant to be permanent. The technology was used to produce food and to control water, visibly transforming the land in the process. Keeping domesticated animals, especially a herd of grazing livestock, had also altered local ecology in a lasting way. As a community, the ranch had a highly specialized division of labor. All of these are characteristics of food producers, not of food gatherers and hunters.

Hikes in the mountains around the ranch offered contrasts of another order, between nature and culture, a distinction that Steward always drew and that was rooted in his own observations and personal memories of eastern California. From one mountain peak he could see Eureka Valley, which he photographed from afar: vast, waterless, and without people, a true desert wilderness. He lived in view of a natural environment, in other words, that appeared untransformed by human settlement and activity. Not just Eureka Valley but parts of Deep Springs Valley showed him nature without culture. Leaving behind his daily work and routines, he entered a spacious and deeply quiet world that provided a striking counterpoint to the ranch, a compact center of technology and productive labor.

The contrasts, cultural and environmental, that Steward first observed in Deep Springs Valley and its environs left their marks on his later theoretical work. Most impressionably, he saw two radically different ways of adapting to the same environment, one nearly eradicated by the ecological effects of another. In Owens Valley, he saw that even more dramatically illustrated: an entire desert valley devoted to food production, based on the use of irrigation and resulting in the near destruction of a food-collecting way of life. Hundreds of Indians remained in Owens Valley, in contrast to Deep Springs Valley, their presence and cultural practices bearing witness to a different way of living on the land.

His memories of Owens Valley also influenced Steward's thinking in a highly specific way. One of his best-known essays, written in the late 1940s and centering on early civilizations, contains echoes of the valley's complex but brief history. Changes that occurred over the course of millennia in the first centers of civilization, as indicated by the archaeological record, had been compressed into decades in Owens Valley's unique version of the transition from a foraging way of life and band society to food production, complex society, and conquest. Because the process was both brief and recent, Steward had witnessed some of those later changes. As an anthropologist whose research interests embraced archaeology as well as ethnology, he could also see abundant evidence of the preagricultural past, from the obsidian flakes he found along the Owens River to the tools his informants showed him. (Steward probably passed through Owens Valley during summer 1947, when he taught at Berkeley. He submitted his essay for publication just nine or ten months later.)[7]

Many years passed before Steward began to explore the theoretical implications of what he had first observed as a young man in eastern California. Although he apparently never saw the connection between these first observations and his later theoretical ideas, he did occasionally draw on autobiographical memory in a strictly factual way, quite explicitly and in print, even fifty years later. "On the basis of a number of years of travel through the mountains and valleys of this area after 1918," he remarked in a book review when he was in his sixties, "I can say with reasonable confidence that deer did not migrate into the low, arid, and well-grazed valley floors each winter." As he remembered very clearly, during three years in Deep Springs Valley and environs, he had never seen deer below timberline.[8]

Less obviously, but I think unarguably, the school itself provided the template for Steward's patrilineal band, and, in a more general way, it always influenced his thoughts about social organization. The school, in contrast to his model of the patrilineal band, was not actually a kin-based group, yet the people who lived there had obviously served as a surrogate family for the young Steward. His fellow students had become fictive brothers. Nunn, clearly a father figure for him, had some likeness to "the head of the lineage" who, as Steward would one day describe that role, held limited authority. Nunn had curtailed his own authority as well as social hierarchy at the school by making the student body self-governing to an unusual degree. "Centralized control," to borrow Steward's words, was restricted to a few specific domains at the ranch, as it was in his conception of the patrilineal band: the management of cattle and hunting, respectively, to cite two examples.[9]

While not literally kinsmen, the students and older men at Deep Springs formed a group that had many other parallels to the patrilineal band as Steward conceived of it years later. They lived together and claimed a particular place as home; the valley was their "territory." The small community of forty to fifty people ("the band averages fifty individuals") occupied a large area (a band's territory "averages 100 square miles" and "the population is sparse"). In common with the patrilineal band (and especially its "exploitation of a certain restricted territory by small groups of men"), the ranch hands and students worked outdoors each day, usually in small, cooperative groups. Their cooperation promoted group survival, allowing them to live in their arid desert territory.[10]

There were other parallels as well. Relationships between males, both within and across generations, accounted for group composition, structure, and continuity. As in the patrilineal band, nearly all of the women and girls who lived at the school had the status of wives and daughters. Present by virtue of their relationships to men, the women seemed marginal to group life, economically and socially. They did not work alongside the men, or closely with one another, and the products of their labor received little recognition or social reward. Just as men's work in the classroom or at the ranch had greater value than women's cooking or housecleaning, hunting had greater value than gathering in Steward's concept of the patrilineal band. He argued that the "greater economic importance" of men and their work resulted in patrilocality.[11] Something resembling patrilocality also prevailed at Deep Springs, although it was exclusively work-based, not kin-based. Married women followed their husbands, their residence dictated by men's place of work.

As these many parallels illustrate, his personal memories inspired particular details and influenced Steward's thinking in a general way. He had spent years living at a ranch in a region where, crucially, the cowboys were Indians. The same men who rode horses and managed livestock together were also hunters who still sometimes pursued game on foot. In this respect they exactly resembled members of a patrilineal band, although, as Steward had already learned through fieldwork, the immediate ancestors of Owens Valley Paiute had *not* lived in that type of social group. But, in 1934, his memories of the ranch and Deep Springs Valley allowed him to conceive of what was otherwise unknowable, considering the fragmentary published data and his own limited field research with Paiute informants who lived near paved roads and worked for wages in Owens Valley. He envisioned how hunters had lived and worked in remote and wild places.

Put most simply, his personal memories of ranch life in a desert valley metamorphosed into the concept of the patrilineal band. Image- and emotion-laden memories—about working on the land with other men, about living in a place that felt remote—helped him to develop that concept. It was not simply a product of empirical evidence and his powers of reason, although those certainly played a role. His own memories provided a touchstone and obviously made the concept feel very real to him. It is impossible to know with any certainty whether this creative process was highly conscious, although that seems unlikely, or to know exactly when the concept first emerged.

I am not suggesting that the patrilineal band was imaginary, although the supporting ethnographic data were minimal at best. To view it as a mere fiction would simplify, to the point of distortion, theory making as a creative intellectual process—and one with complex cognitive, emotional, and social dimensions, at least in Steward's case. It is fair to say, however, that the patrilineal band had roots in autobiographical memory, in terms of both origin and content, and that it developed within the context of the personal construction of meaning—specifically, the meaning of manhood. Steward's ideas were shaped by emotionally charged interpretations of a range of circumstances, relationships, and events in his own life. Memory images, interpreted in the context of his own personal narrative, gave shape to his concept of the patrilineal band.[12]

The diverse personal sources of cultural ecology included not only what Steward remembered from the distant past but also the recent past, including his ongoing social experiences. Personal circumstances and events during adulthood, not just childhood and adolescence, appear to have had an influence, as did the larger context of his life, the social world in which he lived. Important aspects of this larger context included the gendered structure of his profession, the shape and content of formal disciplinary knowledge, gender-linked social conventions of his profession and class during a particular historic period, and prevailing, unexamined cultural assumptions of the times.[13]

To illustrate, in the mid-1930s he treated patrilocality as the norm, an outcome of biology and the essential nature of men ("innate male dominance") and a practical necessity for many hunters (read: male providers). As he later put it, "the male wishes to remain in the country he knows." He wrote his essay only two years after leaving Utah and an unconventional "matrilocal" marriage and going home to California to live in Berkeley with his new wife, and within weeks or months of undertaking field research in the Great Basin, beginning in eastern California ("men best remain in the territory where they were raised"). In contrast to his previous experience, he had just married a woman who did not outrank him professionally or financially. He thus held "a commanding position," to cite another phrase from his essay, and this change may account for his two assertions about "innate male dominance," which appeared in print during this period. His new wife had willingly left her "territory" in Utah to live in his, first in California and then in Washington, D.C. ("wives come to their [husbands'] territory after marriage"). Whether by chance or not, Steward's preoccupation with patrilocality appeared to wane somewhat at about the time his wife began resisting, very quietly and indirectly, any more dislocation.[14]

In developing his theoretical ideas, beginning with the patrilineal band, Steward consciously drew on a broad range of disciplinary knowledge, published and unpublished. His theory making had a strongly social dimension on both counts. To judge from his later way of working, he probably had informal conversations with colleagues in Berkeley as well as with archaeologists he met on his tour of the Southwest. These informal discussions, almost exclusively with other men, can only be traced, however, through journal entries and letters, which mention names but rarely offer any details about the content of discussion.

The concept of the patrilineal band was also grounded in the published observations of many men, especially his friend and colleague Strong. An emphasis on hunting by men was entirely in accord with the prevailing, dominant cultural view of men and male economic activity as central and important. Steward surveyed dozens of ethnographic accounts of hunter-gatherers living in a range of environments, from tropical to arid, where game was scattered and limited—a setting clearly inspired by his own knowledge of the western Great Basin. Following the conventions of his profession, he cited dozens of published works by men—but almost none by women, a pattern that continued throughout his career, and an exclusionary practice so prevalent and enduring in his profession that it nearly qualified as a convention in twentieth-century American anthropology.[15]

His purpose in writing about the patrilineal band, as he expressed it many years later, was to document "a striking instance in which similar subsistence activities had produced similar social structures." Steward's underlying idea, that subsistence activities have a shaping effect on social structures, was a classic, core insight of cultural ecology. He had first seen tangible, if indirect, evidence in support of that idea at Deep Springs and in Owens Valley among Indians and white ranchers and farmers. Their *different* subsistence patterns correlated with marked differences in social life. Citing published material about other hunter-gatherers, Steward tried to show that similar subsistence patterns resulted in social similarities, even among widely dispersed peoples. Diffusion, in other words, could not explain the patrilineal band; rather, he saw it as rooted in specific ecological conditions. His ideas about the links between subsistence and social structure formed the central theme of most of his written work from the mid-1930s onward and proved useful to generations of archaeologists and cultural anthropologists.[16]

His model of the patrilineal band also resonated with a generation of anthropologists who shared Steward's social experiences as a man in midcentury America and vivid memories of working cooperatively with other men to ensure group survival. Most were veterans of World War II. As it turned out, however, the concept did not hold up in the face of intensive field research with hunter-gatherers in the 1960s and 1970s. A later commentator, in his critical survey of that research, remarked on the "empirically groundless assumptions" of the patrilineal/composite typology of band societies.[17]

Nor did the patrilineal band fare well under the close scrutiny of some women who entered anthropology during the same period. Their own experiences, and the virtual absence of women from graduate faculties, no doubt made them aware of their marginal place in the profession, a subject that began to receive explicit mention in print in the 1960s. Economically active themselves, they had reason to identify with the diligent but disregarded and devalued gatherers. Whether they consciously saw those parallels, their critiques in the 1970s of the "Man the Hunter" model undermined its credibility and, directly or indirectly, Steward's concept of the patrilineal band, which had influenced it.[18]

Steward never renounced the patrilineal band as he did the cultural core. This foundational concept, in many ways more fundamental to his theoretical work than the cultural core, held far greater personal meaning. Even when empirical evidence began to accumulate against it in the 1960s, the concept still felt compellingly real to him. Of course, it *was* real to him: he had spent years living in its prototype, to say nothing of time spent reading, thinking, and writing about the patrilineal band, discussing it with colleagues, actively searching for it in western North America, and making inquiries in western South America.

His own social experience in the professional and academic world must also have reinforced a close, if unconscious, identification with the hunters of the patrilineal band. Steward had entered a male-centered, male-defined social world and work setting first and, most impressionably, at Deep Springs and at the age of sixteen. It offered refuge and security at the very moment when he lost his family home, and this may help to account for his attachment to the concept of the patrilineal band as much as it explains his enduring affection for the school. But he also encountered male-centered groups repeatedly in his later life, beginning with Telluride House at Cornell. His concerted effort to follow his friends to Cornell can be seen as the first of many attempts to recover his place in the protopatrilineal band: a personal quest that in his later professional life he would cast in intellectual terms, and one that would eventually result in the set of ideas he called cultural ecology.

His experience of a male-centered, male-defined work world continued as a member of an academic "patrilineage" at Berkeley, and later at the BAE and the academic departments he joined. Women, while always present in small numbers, occupied socially marginal positions, often consigned to solitary work and tasks that carried little prestige or other reward—analogous to gathering (or housekeeping, for that matter), as Steward and many others then conceived of it. From Anna Gayton in the 1920s to Betty Starr in the 1960s, women and women's labor remained on the periphery, both in his own work experience and in his theoretical approach. Only Dorothy Nyswander was, briefly, a true co-worker, but their collaboration ended badly and no doubt reinforced his preference for working exclusively with men.

In a general sense, his experiences and perspective were not unique. Male work groups, which is also to say groups of male providers, characterized the social world of the educated class of professionals—and more broadly, the middle class—of Julian Steward's day. In an occupationally segregated labor market, white middle-class men held higher-paying, higher-status positions than middle-class women who were employed. (Marion Steward represented the norm and Dorothy Nyswander the exception in this regard.) Married women generally did not work outside the home. (Jane Steward represented the norm and Dorothy Nyswander, once again, the exception.) The ability to act as sole provider, to support a wife and dependent children, was a defining element of middle-class social status and male identity for white American men of his era.

His ongoing experience in this male-centered social world thus reinforced Steward's first experience of it, but he also actively tried to recreate it. He sought out male work groups—and compatible men to work with in a cooperative way—throughout his long career, and he repeatedly created small research groups of men, paralleling his intellectual search for the patrilineal band. Just as he never found the patrilineal band in his fieldwork or travels, Steward seems never to have found a group in his later work life to equal, in an emotional sense, the one he remembered from his student days. The competitive climate of anthropology in America and the hierarchical structure of the academic world simply did not encourage the trust, camaraderie, and cooperation he had once known in a particular time and place.

Steward's materialist perspective just as clearly had its roots in personal circumstance and held personal meaning. It had an obvious connection with his commitment to science, and his training in the natural sciences, which take the material world as their subject of inquiry. At Cornell, his final rejection of religion, which he would always equate with dogma, undoubtedly affected his decision to study science. A strong emotional reaction against his mother's antimaterialism resulted in his firm commitment to empiricism and scientific method and his eventual attempt to create a behaviorist approach for use in ethnographic fieldwork and analysis. He never identified it as behaviorist in origin. Instead, he belatedly called it the method of cultural ecology, a name that obscured, to the point of erasure, the influence of another discipline and of a woman, his former wife.

Many experiences during late adolescence, first at Deep Springs and then at Berkeley and Cornell, also contributed to his materialist perspective and central interest in subsistence. Steward was certainly never poor, but, considering his social background and class origins, he was forced to become self-supporting at an early age and due to circumstances that always troubled him. He had the added problem of having to help support his mother, sporadically and unpredictably, as her financial situation remained in flux throughout these years. The role of male provider was thus imposed on Steward while he was still a student, years before he became a wage-earner. His focus on men working together, implicitly as providers for dependent women, expressed one of his major preoccupations from the age of sixteen.

Not only his financial worries but also his anxiety about attaining a position in the world of educated men—which is to say, maintaining a position in the social world he and his friends came from, the world of the educated, professional middle-class—intensified during his years at Deep Springs. He considered various professions before settling on anthropology for his lifework, not realizing that the new discipline qualified as one of the least secure, with few established positions and a growing number of qualified candidates, including quite a few women. Steward's financial anxieties continued throughout the years of graduate study and loomed large again after his divorce in the early 1930s.

The Great Depression, then in full swing, made finding any employment difficult; but these years proved a fertile time intellectually and, to judge from his own words, perhaps the happiest period in Steward's adult life. He was in his early thirties, back on home territory in California, and accompanied by his new wife. During this time, he charted the direction of his theoretical work, developing a long-term plan for research. He also wrote two classic essays and undertook the fieldwork that provided the empirical foundation for much of his later theoretical work and writing.[19]

What he observed and experienced during the depression reinforced what he already knew—but that period did help create a generation of anthropologists who would be more receptive to his ideas than the men who were his seniors.

* * *

The young man who left the East in 1918—unhappily and bound for an unfamiliar destination—found a new home, entered a new social world, and assumed a new identity in a faraway desert valley in the West. He became, in the words of Jane Steward, a "passionate Westerner." No matter that others often identified him differently. His student Omer Stewart—born and bred in Utah, and a lifelong resident of the West—considered Steward an easterner by virtue of his birth and upbringing in Washington, D.C., and his "correct" way of speaking standard American English. Jane Steward, who shared Stewart's origins in Utah, thought of her husband as an adopted westerner, and, like so many of them, somewhat romantic about the region. But she did not share his passion for its landscape, his deeply aesthetic appreciation of the mountains and deserts.[20]

Julian Steward's identification with the West was primarily with the land rather than the people, whether native or immigrant. His sudden dislocation at the age of sixteen, and the strong emotional reaction that accompanied it, seem to have produced in him a heightened sense of place. Place, along with work, became a central element in his theoretical approach, the two closely linked in his own experience and both imbued with personal meaning. If he arrived in Deep Springs Valley reluctantly, he soon succumbed to what he called the "mystique" of the place, and developed "a great love of the Deep Springs country." Observing it closely for several years, he came to have the intimate knowledge of a particular place that only living there attentively, even devotedly, can provide. That knowledge of place cannot be found in books.[21]

His own words make it clear that the place held far more than scientific interest for him. The sixteen-year-old boy who had so abruptly left city life in the East found his new home in the desert valley both exotic and remote. His telling remark eighteen years later—"Next January we shall go to Fiji, Russia, Deep Springs or some other similar place"—suggests that he regarded these three disparate destinations as equivalent in some important sense: out of the way, recherché, isolated.[22] The high desert did have that look (to city-dwellers and nonwesterners), as the Hollywood directors who shot films in the foothills near Lone Pine and Bishop so well appreciated. But the isolation that Steward experienced at Deep Springs as a student was actually as much a result of school policy as of the rudimentary road that crossed the valley.

During his subsequent travels, Steward had what amounted to passing glances at the surrounding landscapes, and he did not reach any deep understanding of those places *as* places. In truth, he never again knew a place nearly as well as he had once known the mountains and desert of eastern California, even after long residence in other locales. Twenty years of prairie living in later life—but with much of it spent indoors and alone at his typewriter, particularly during the lingering winter months—did not provide ideas about place and work to rival or extend his early insights. Steward always appreciated the openness and the dimensions of the Illinois prairie, the enormity of land and sky, but a century of relentless cultivation had stolen nearly all of its wildness. His own words suggest that he most admired landscapes that appeared "unchanged by civilization" and nearly devoid of human settlement, which is also to say the sorts of places where he expected to find the patrilineal band.[23] He found those only in western North America, despite looking elsewhere and eventually traveling to other continents. The prairie had largely lost what he sought, but its remoteness from the East and metropolitan life, which so dismayed his New York colleagues, pleased him. Working there with a small group of men even had a faint echo of Deep Springs and its protective isolation.

Classic cultural ecology, represented by the essays in *Theory of Culture Change* and written between the 1930s and the early 1950s, gave way during this period to what might be called the "postclassic form." Writings from the late 1950s and 1960s, including those collected in *Evolution and Ecology,* illustrate the transition. His distance, in space and in time, from a place once known so well helps to explain the change in Steward's thinking about cultural ecology, the shift from classic to postclassic. He grew to doubt some of those early insights, living so far from the source of their inspiration and having so little sense of connection with any other place where he lived or traveled after leaving the West. Close and sustained observation of the high desert in California, and his memories of working with men on the land, had given him his most original and distinctive ideas.

* * *

The many connections between Steward's known, outer life and his theoretical work suggest that a social theory can provide a vehicle for ordering life experience, for constructing meaning from personal memories: in short, for creating a past that "makes sense" intellectually and emotionally, while not necessarily doing so in a highly conscious way. Constructing a social theory, at least for Steward, meant drawing on and giving structure to emotionally powerful memories from his early life, but in a seemingly—misleadingly—detached and rational manner. If Steward's cultural ecology did serve as a vehicle for the personal construction of meaning, it also allowed him to avoid troubling memories by directing his attention toward what he valued and remembered in a positive light.[24]

Religion, women and children, matrilocality, and women's work were excluded, essentialized, treated as aberrant, or consigned to a place on the periphery as "secondary" features that could be ignored. This constellation of elements exactly characterized his memories of childhood circumstances he remembered as unhappy: the separation from his father and his childhood home at the age of six, when he lived with his mother "matrilocally," with maternal relatives in St. Louis; his parents' later separation, in part because of religious differences; his mother's chronic financial problems and dependence when her work, first as a clerk and then as a nurse, proved unsuccessful; his first marriage to a woman with a professional career, whose household he joined—again a version of matrilocal residence—and with whom he worked, at great cost to himself as he later saw it. Steward gave precedence and value to a different set of elements, which occupied a place at the center of his theoretical approach, as core features: men's work and the technologies that men use, male-centered groups, patrilocality, and the outdoor, natural world. These were the valued aspects of his life in late adolescence at Deep Springs, a time and place that he remembered in a highly positive, even idealized, way.

To say this in another way, Steward's cultural ecology did emerge, in part, from empirical studies and conscious, logical analysis. But his theoretical approach did double duty, serving not only as the major vehicle for his intellectual project but also as a vehicle for the personal construction of meaning. How else to explain that Steward readily cast aside one of his central theoretical ideas (the cultural core) but believed so deeply in another (the patrilineal band) that he could never question its validity? How else to explain his obvious contempt for a competing theoretical perspective, culture and personality, that did not order the social world as he did, or his outbursts against Lévi-Strauss's structuralism, which he angrily denounced as dogma?

Just as Steward fashioned a theoretical approach that drew on the remembered experiences and preoccupations of his own life, I suspect that choosing a theoretical perspective often rests at least in part on whether it makes sense in terms of one's own social experience and autobiographical memory and helps make sense of them: whether it contributes to the personal construction of meaning. Murphy perhaps alluded to this when he wrote that Steward's students at Columbia had experienced firsthand "the inexorable forces of history" in the form of the Great Depression and World War II, and that "they sought some kind of consistent interpretation of culture that would help them understand their own lives."[25]

As Steward's own response to structuralism illustrates, a theory (or "consistent interpretation of culture") that resonates with one person may feel alien to another. Heated, even passionate, arguments about theory, commonplace in academic life, probably spring from a source other than intellectual disagreements alone. Of course, choosing and using a theoretical perspective is even more complicated than this, often conditioned in part by the pursuit of prestige and academic politics as well. Here again, the personal and the professional intersect in complex ways.

In any case, the markedly masculinist quality of Steward's cultural ecology may help explain why so few women in cultural anthropology adopted it in their research. During his years at Columbia University, in the late 1940s and early 1950s, culture and personality was the competing theoretical perspective in the anthropology program, and Benedict and Mead were two of its leading exponents. Their ideas and presence attracted more women than an approach that centered on men's labor and men's use of technology and promoted essentialist views of men and women as dominant and subordinate, providers and dependents, respectively. Steward's preference for working with male students was undoubtedly a contributing factor at Columbia, and later at the University of Illinois. But that does not explain the same trend elsewhere.

His theoretical perspective—especially the social scenario implied by cultural ecology and spelled out in the patrilineal band—conformed with the life circumstances, both personal and professional, of many men in anthropology. It did not correspond closely to the social experience or the aspirations of many women who were trying to enter the profession. Steward's model did, however, prove eerily predictive of their career paths. They generally found themselves excluded from the center and consigned to the margins, and not simply excluded but rendered invisible by citation practices.[26] Their written work received less recognition in print, although it contributed to the body of disciplinary knowledge, and although other scholars, including Steward, made use of it.

The conservative cast of Steward's model, which conformed to existing social arrangements and prevailing cultural assumptions, made it acceptable (which is also to say, intellectually and emotionally convincing) to many of his colleagues. Given the structure of his social and professional world, he would have faced a far more difficult task in "selling" his theoretical approach had he incorporated ideas about "a woman's economy" into his work. Cultural ecology, as expressed in Steward's writings, drew almost exclusively on male social experience at a time when the social roles of men and women diverged sharply. It was markedly masculinist in conception and its first applications—not by intellectual or empirical necessity, but because of a complex mix of personal memories, emotional conflicts, social conventions, and professional practices. All of these left their marks on his theoretical approach.

So too did his relationships with a multitude of people over the course of his long career affect his theoretical work. The exact influence of other scholars is difficult to judge for a variety of reasons, including the fact that Steward routinely engaged in informal and undocumented discussion that went unacknowledged in print—a common practice at the time. He also cited works by prominent scholars as a matter of academic diplomacy, another standard practice in the academic world. Citations, in other words, provide a poor guide for reconstructing the sources or the course of Steward's intellectual work, in part because of the problem of omissions, a problem not at all unique to him. He simply followed the conventions of his profession.

Tracing Steward's long journey to cultural ecology has led me to think that his ideas are best understood when viewed against the natural and social landscapes he inhabited during the first half of his life, which he always remembered. Autobiographical memory—especially his image- and emotion-laden memories of self in relation to a place and to other people—provided much of the source material for cultural ecology. When I read his essays now, scenes from the high desert often come to mind: arid desert valleys of sagebrush and sand, framed by rugged mountains and a cloudless sky. Owens Valley and Deep Springs Valley have pride of place, along with Wyman Creek, Soldier Pass, Birch Mountain, and many other landmarks in his personal geography.

Images of people enter consciousness as well, especially figures from his early life. Steward knew a few of them only indirectly, others in passing, and still others for most of his career, but all of them remained in memory. Many are familiar to me from photographs, some taken by Steward himself. Several faces remain indistinct because I know them only through words that they wrote, or words that others, sometimes Steward, wrote about them. Two women, Jane Steward and Dorothy Nyswander, I remember very well, and very warmly, as friends.

Leading members of this large cast include a rather distant father who spent his professional career studying new technologies; a distracted mother who unintentionally led her son away from religion and toward science when she sent him west; a maternal uncle who achieved great success as a government scientist; the stern-faced Mr. Nunn, who indirectly inspired the overarching aim of Steward's intellectual project; Professor Srager, whose skepticism and questions helped him see that he could think for himself; the kindly Professor Burr, who argued against dogma; John Wesley Powell, Frederick Coville, and his own kinsman, John F. Steward, well-known and lesser-known explorer/scientists of the arid West; Captain Harry and his family, denizens of the desert; ranch hands and students at Deep Springs, who worked together outdoors and formed the core of the protopatrilineal band; dozens of Owens Valley Paiute, whose ancestral and personal memories came to constitute ethnography; fellow students and faculty at Berkeley—from Duncan Strong and Ralph Beals to Alfred L. Kroeber, Robert H. Lowie, Edward W. Gifford, and others—who talked and listened and became colleagues for life; Carl Sauer and the lesser-known Oskar Schmieder, who showed him the geographer's way of observing the landscape; Dorothy Nyswander, a confident behaviorist who advised greater rigor in ethnographic method; and Jane Cannon Steward, who, in contrast to her husband's former wife, left her own "territory" to spend most of her life in his.

* * *

Julian Steward died in Urbana, Illinois, on a cold winter day in February 1972, a week after celebrating his seventieth birthday. As she had promised, Jane Steward took her husband's ashes home to California. She scattered them in a small lake in the Sierra Nevada, above Owens Valley and due west of Deep Springs, places that Steward regarded with unwavering affection until the end of his life and places that inspired his most distinctive ideas as a theorist.

A few years later, and some twenty years after her first glimpse of Hawaii, Jane Steward moved to Honolulu. She relished city life and the perpetual warmth of the tropics and even felt a slight ancestral connection with the place. Missionary work had drawn her Mormon grandfather to Hawaii in the nineteenth century, but it was light and warmth that drew her back. She died in Honolulu at the age of seventy-nine. Her ashes were scattered in the ocean at Waikiki.

Notes

Abbreviations

ALK	A. L. Kroeber Papers
BAE	Bureau of American Ethnology correspondence
BRMM	University of Utah Board of Regents meetings minutes
DSC	Deep Springs College correspondence and records
HRMF	University of Utah historical records of the members of the faculty
JBC	Joseph B. Casagrande Papers
JHS	Julian H. Steward Papers
JJJS	Journals of Julian and Jane Steward
LF	Livingston Farrand Papers
LLN	L. L. Nunn Papers
MAS	Michigan Academy of Sciences, Arts, and Letters publications
NPRC	Federal employment records, National Personnel Records Center
PPGT	Presidential Papers of George Thomas
RDA	Records of the Department of Anthropology
RHL	Robert Harry Lowie Papers
TA	Telluride Association correspondence and records
UIDA	University of Illinois Department of Anthropology correspondence and records
UICLAS	University of Illinois College of Liberal Arts and Sciences subject file
UIP	University of Illinois Press correspondence and records
UISAF	University of Illinois staff appointments file
WDS	William Duncan Strong Papers

Introduction

1. Mary Austin's (1903) now-classic book about the region, *Land of Little Rain,* drew on her experience of living in Owens Valley.

2. J. H. Steward 1955c:40, 41–42; J. H. Steward to Ford Foundation, re: N. Dyson-Hudson, Dec. 28, 1969, JHS Box 3; Murphy 1981:180.

3. J. H. Steward 1938a:260.

4. *Theory of Culture Change* went out of print briefly in the late 1960s while Steward worked on a revised version, which he never completed (see chap. 12). The book remains in print today.

5. J. H. Steward 1955c:94; J. H. Steward to William Speth, May 4, 1971, JHS Box 3.

6. J. H. Steward 1955c:125, 156.

7. See Murphy (1977:16–18) on Steward's "concepts and premises."

8. Murphy interview; Murphy 1977:21. Textbooks on theorists in anthropology also routinely include Steward (e.g., J. D. Moore 1997).

9. J. H. Steward, "Autobiographical Appraisal," n.d., JHS Box 16; J. H. Steward 1936a; Lee and DeVore 1968:7–8; Murphy 1977:24. For some of the early critical commentary on the "Man the Hunter" model, see, among others, Leacock (1972), Martin and Voorhies (1975:chap. 7), and Slocum (1975). See also Lutz (1995) on gender and the anthropological canon, and the "masculinizing of theory."

10. For published commentary on Steward's work, see, among others, Shimkin (1964), Harris (1968), Manners (1973, 1976), Carneiro (1974, 1979), Murphy (1977, 1980, 1981), Mintz (1979), D. H. Thomas (1983), Willey (1988:218–41), Patterson (1987), Blackhawk (1997), Crum (1999), Kerns (1999), and other contributors to Clemmer, Myer, and Rudden (1999).

11. J. H. Steward 1933d:239, 241–46; J. H. Steward to A. L. Kroeber, May 3, 1935, RDA Box 141.

12. For example, the extensive bibliography of Steward's (1936a) essay included only one reference to an ethnographic work by a woman, Isabel Kelly, a Berkeley-trained anthropologist whom he knew well. He removed that reference from *Theory of Culture Change* and failed to cite Kelly's (1934) paper, "Southern Paiute Bands," in both his original essay and in the revised version. This was not an isolated instance (see chap. 12) or specific to his work in ethnology (see Reyman [1992:76] for an example involving archaeology). On the erasure of women's writings more recently in sociocultural anthropology, see Lutz (1990).

13. See, for example, Harris (1968:662), Lukermann (1977:562), Murphy (1980), Orlove (1980:237), Bohannon and Glazer (1988:319), and Shimkin (1964:2). Lowie (1959:170) made this assertion in a memoir about his career, written years after Boas's death.

14. Murphy interview; Murphy 1977:6.

15. Sydel Silverman (1981:ix–x) made this point about the process of theory making twenty years ago.

16. J. H. Steward to Alexander Wetmore, n.d. [ca. 1954], JHS Box 6. This is a draft, probably the first, of an autobiographical statement that Steward prepared at the request of the National Academy of Sciences after he was elected to membership.

17. This is William F. Brewer's (1986:33) definition of autobiographical memory. He distinguishes two forms of personal memories, both experienced as mental images: memories of single events, and memories of a repeated set of experiences, the latter producing a "generic image" (Brewer 1986:26, 30; 1996:19). His essays and others in the collections edited by David C. Rubin (1986, 1996) provide excellent overviews of research by cognitive psychologists on this topic. See also the conclusion.

18. For nine of the ten years between 1915 and 1924, coinciding with Steward's adolescence, a book by Zane Grey appeared among the top ten on the best-seller list (Gruber 1970:13, 15; see also Kimball 1993:239).

19. On the Owens Valley–Los Angeles water dispute, see Kahrl (1976a, 1976b, 1982) and Wood (1972a, 1972b); see Mulholland (2000) for a contrasting perspective. See also chap. 4.

20. Wood 1972a:2; Nyswander interview, 1996; JJJS I, May 2, 1935.

21. J. C. Steward interview.

22. On the importance of autobiographical memories of adolescence, see Fitzgerald (1996). See also the conclusion, n.3.

23. Nyswander interviews, 1996, 1997. Her father was general manager of a ranch owned by the Rickey Land and Cattle Company. He did no manual labor, suggesting that social class as well as gender affected his daughter's experience of ranch work. Any white women who did outdoor labor at the time usually worked with their husbands on small and marginal ranches, sometimes as tenants (e.g., see Doig 1978:52).

24. For life stories of ranch women who qualify as cowgirls, see Jordan (1982). By her defini-

tion, cowgirls routinely work outside, not just when the ranch is short-handed (Jordan 1982:xxv–xxvi). The cases she profiles suggest that such women remain highly unusual, to the point of being seen as socially deviant, and that they work alone or with men, not primarily with peers (other women). In those important social respects they are *not* "a full-fledged counterpart to the cowboy."

25. J. H. Steward to Wetmore, n.d. [ca. 1954], JHS Box 6; J. C. Steward interview.

26. Dorothy Nyswander trained as an educational psychologist and later worked in the field of public health education, holding both academic posts and research positions (Nyswander interviews, 1996, 1997; Nyswander 1994). Certain features of Steward's research and writing are difficult to explain without reference to her (see chaps. 4 and 6).

27. For a critique of poststructuralist views of the self as destabilized, fragmented, and shifting, see Chodorow (1999).

28. J. C. Steward, Nyswander, and D. Fowler interviews. For the list of interviews with friends, colleagues, and students of Steward, see the list of references cited. Important published sources include the remembrances of Ralph Beals (1979), Robert Murphy (1977, 1981), and Gordon Willey (1988:218–41). Elman Service's (n.d.) recollections, recorded late in life, also proved helpful. I thank Robert Carneiro for bringing them to my attention, and Helen Service for providing me with a transcript.

29. For a very succinct statement of his own view about scientific evidence, see J. H. Steward (1955b:300–301). On the personal construction of meaning, see Chodorow (1999) and the conclusion. On the posited link between identity formation, self-definition, and autobiographical memory, see Fitzgerald (1996).

30. See Brewer (1996:27–29) on memory images and images of imagination.

31. Bennett (1998:xi) defines the "Classic anthropology era" as the forty years from 1915 to 1955. The major portion of Steward's career falls into the last thirty years of this period, from 1925, when he began graduate study, to 1955, when *Theory of Culture Change* appeared in print. On anthropology as a "guild occupation," see Geertz (1995:132–33).

32. J. H. Steward to Herbert Reich, Nov. 25, 1969, JHS Box 3.

Chapter 1: An Eastern Childhood

1. Stegner 1954:54–111; Worster 2001:155–202.

2. Stegner 1954:96–110, 224, 240; Worster 2001:354–60, 384, 396–99; Hinsley 1981:147; Fowler and Fowler 1971. The BAE was founded in 1879, with Powell (1834–1902) as its first director.

3. Rowe 1962:397; [McGee] 1903:191–92; Stocking 1960:12; Mark 1980:5. By 1915 American universities had awarded about thirty-three Ph.D.'s in anthropology (Stocking 1960:16n.10).

4. Mark 1980:5–6; D. Cole 1999:104; J. H. Steward 1973:6.

5. Mark 1980:9–11, 62–95; 1988. Besides Alice Fletcher (1838–1923), 39 men were invited to attend the founding meeting of the American Anthropological Association. Of the 175 people who joined the new association, 16 were women. If Boas had succeeded in limiting the group to professional anthropologists and keeping out "interested amateurs whose main contribution was financial" (Stocking 1960:9), many of the women probably would have been excluded. One of them, Phoebe Apperson Hearst, provided the funding to set up a museum and a department of anthropology, as well as hire Kroeber, at the University of California, Berkeley (Mark 1980:42–43).

6. Wister 1902; Tompkins 1992.

7. Marquis 1910:1835–36 (entry for Thomas G. Steward); J. H. Steward, "Autobiographical Appraisal," n.d., JHS Box 16. I have reconstructed Steward's family background by piecing together the documentary evidence, which is fragmentary and scattered, to verify and amplify what I learned from Jane Steward and Dorothy Nyswander. The most useful sources include censuses, city directories, family genealogical material, and employment records.

8. I have reconstructed the work histories of Thomas and Grace G. Steward and her brother by

using federal employment records from the National Personnel Records Center (U.S. Office of Personnel Management) and city directories of the period.

9. J. H. Steward, "Autobiographical Appraisal," n.d., JHS Box 16; Willey 1988:221; Shimkin 1964:1.

10. Marquis 1910:1835–36; J. H. Steward, "Autobiographical Appraisal," n.d., JHS Box 16.

11. Marquis 1910:1835–36; genealogical material, JHS Box 17; Dumas 1936, 18:1; Ozanne 1968:59–60.

12. Marquis 1910:1835–36; Ozanne 1968:23–25.

13. Marquis 1910:1835–36; J. Matthew Gaglione, registrar, George Washington University, personal communication, Mar. 25, 1994; Kayser 1970:148, 290. Thomas Steward may have earned his engineering degree from the Columbian University, an institution largely founded and controlled by Baptists in the nineteenth century. The Columbian University later shed its sectarian ties and assumed a new name, George Washington University.

14. Stevens 1983:85n.14. Many of the students who attended the Columbian University Law School in 1895 claimed that "they had come to Washington in the federal service in order to go to law school" (Stevens 1983:85n.16). More than fifty years later, in the late 1940s, the student bodies of universities in Washington, D.C., had diversified; but most of them, including the law school of National University, remained racially segregated and did not admit African American students (Green 1963:499).

15. Marquis 1910:1835–36; Jones 1971:14, 197.

16. Qtd. in Jones 1971:23.

17. The Patent Office remained in a building on F Street from 1840 until 1932. Later occupants included the National Portrait Gallery, among others (Jones 1971:16–17; Federal Writers' Project 1937:976).

18. Pryor 1987:57; Mark 1980:135.

19. J. C. Steward interview.

20. 1890 census, Washington, D.C.; Marquis 1910:717; genealogical material, JHS Box 17; Edward B. Garriott, official personnel folder, NPRC.

21. J. H. Steward, "Autobiographical Appraisal," n.d., JHS Box 16; Edward B. Garriott, official personnel folder, NPRC; obituary, *New York Times,* May 14, 1910; Whitnah 1965.

22. G. G. Steward, official personnel folder, NPRC; 1890 census, Washington, D.C. Most of the 1890 census records for Washington, D.C., were destroyed in a fire, but a portion of the census form for Edward Garriott's household survives: the second page, which lists Edward's mother and his sister Grace.

23. Aron 1981:847; McMillin 1938:4. Grace Steward stated in her employment records in 1919 that she earned a salary of twelve hundred dollars in the 1890s (official personnel folder, NRPC). During roughly the same period, public school teachers earned on average $392 a year, while the average federal employee in an executive department earned $1072 (Derks 1999:74). According to Aron (1987:45), many of the women applying for federal positions in the late nineteenth century were "refugees from the teaching profession," dissatisfied with both their low salaries ("'almost starvation,'" as one applicant put it) and their working conditions.

24. Aron 1981:836; McMillin 1938:4, 5.

25. McMillin 1938:10; Jones 1971:16.

26. McMillin 1938:10–11; Pryor 1987:59.

27. Aron 1981:839–42, 1987:47; G. G. Steward, official personnel folder, NPRC.

28. 1890 census, Washington, D.C.; Marquis 1910:717; Edward B. Garriott, official personnel folder, NPRC. According to later employment records, Edward helped support his parents; his records before the late 1890s are lost. See n.22 on his household in 1890.

29. Aron 1981:848; McMillin 1938:2; 1900 census, Washington, D.C.

30. McMillin 1938:2; G. G. Steward, official personnel folder, NPRC; Aron 1981:844.

31. J. C. Steward interview; Nyswander interview, 1996; Stegner 1987:60. Jane Steward remembered her mother-in-law as having an "almost Victorian" aesthetic sensibility about landscape.

32. Murphy interview; Murphy 1977:1; Willey 1988:222; J. C. Steward interview; Boy Scouts of America, personal communication, Jan. 10, 1994.

33. Clark interview.

34. Washburn 1978:15; Stegner 1954:242; Worster 2001:437–38; Mark 1980:144.

35. Washburn 1978:23–24, 84; Worster 2001:437–39. The Cosmos Club is now located at 2121 Massachusetts Avenue, NW, having moved from its quarters in the Dolly Madison House in the 1950s.

36. By the time the club celebrated its centennial in 1978, its membership had grown from less than a hundred men to more than three thousand (Washburn 1978:149) The Cosmos Club was racially segregated until the 1960s, when the journalist Carl Rowan became its first African American member. Women have been admitted as members since the late 1980s (Clark interview).

37. Green 1963:97; Washburn 1978:103.

38. Hurston 1984:156; Hemenway 1977. As Mikell (1989:164) comments, Hurston's career "sheds light on the difficulty that creative women in general and black women in particular had in academia and the professions during the 1920s and 1930s."

39. J. H. Steward, "Autobiographical Appraisal," n.d., JHS Box 16; Telluride Association Historian's Record for Steward, n.d. [ca. 1921], TA; city directories, Washington, D.C., 1908–10. Thomas Steward's widowed mother lived with him during at least part of this period (1910 census records, Washington, D.C.).

40. Genealogical material, JHS Box 17; obituary, M. Garriott, *St. Louis Post-Dispatch*, July 9, 1909, 14; obituary, Edward B. Garriott, *New York Times*, May 14, 1910; Virginia S. Harris, clerk, First Church of Christ, Scientist, personal communication, Dec. 17, 1990; R. D. Thomas 1994:290.

41. Marquis 1910:1836; Harris, personal communication, Dec. 17, 1990. At its founding in the mid-nineteenth century, the Republican party strongly opposed slavery.

42. R. D. Thomas 1994:127.

43. Laird 1975:81–82; Hough 1931:94. J. Walter Fewkes (1850–1930) and his wife evidently agreed to disagree; they remained married. In her writings, Eddy also used the phrases "the Science of Life," "the Science of Mind," and "Christ Science," thus distinguishing the religion from what she called "material science."

44. Cather and Milmine 1993:480; R. D. Thomas 1994:300–306. The book first appeared in serial form in *McClure's* magazine in 1907–8. Cather's role in writing it has only recently come to light. Mary Baker Eddy (1821–1910) has been the subject of many, often highly partisan, biographies by adherents or critics of Christian Science.

45. Cather and Milmine 1993:209–10, 469. On Grace Steward's work as a Christian Science nurse, see chap. 2.

46. Jane Steward and Dorothy Nyswander (interviews) each told me about this episode with the microscope. See also, among others, Gordon (1990:4, 13–14) on cultural notions that then prevailed about the separate spheres of men and women, and Keller (1985), Schiebinger (1989:9), and Noble (1992:281) on the linking of science with the masculine.

47. Nyswander interviews; Eddy 1906:468.

48. Eddy 1906:62.

49. Hussey interview.

50. Specifically, such a child might interpret his mother's behavior as neglect or abandonment, possibly as life-threatening. This is my inference based on Jane Steward's and Dorothy Nyswander's comments in their interviews about several episodes that Julian Steward recalled from early life. My inference here is also influenced by Bowlby (1969–80, 1979), among others, and by Simmons's (1991) recollections of an episode of illness during childhood.

51. I believe that these feelings and preoccupations sometimes surfaced years later in his published writing: for example, in his assertion that women "must not leave their children, who are their inescapable responsibility" (J. H. Steward 1968b:340, 1977:48). See chap. 12.

52. J. H. Steward, "Autobiographical Appraisal," n.d., JHS Box 16.

53. Ibid.; J. H. Steward to Wetmore, n.d. [ca. 1954], JHS Box 6; J. H. Steward to Deep Springs, May 17, 1961, DSC. Steward's own frank words, and the circumstances surrounding his acceptance at Deep Springs, do not support the prevailing idea that he was recognized as a gifted student (e.g., Willey 1988:222).

54. City directories, Washington, D.C., 1907–13; Laura M. Patterson, registrar, University of Michigan, personal communication, Dec. 15, 1993; J. C. Steward interview; J. H. Steward to Wetmore, n.d. [ca. 1954], JHS Box 6; J. H. Steward, "Autobiographical Appraisal," n.d., JHS Box 16.

55. In his twenties and thirties, he painted during fieldwork and other travels in the West, sometimes making gifts of his paintings (J. C. Steward interview; Nyswander interviews; JJJS I, 1934–36).

56. J. H. Steward to Wetmore, n.d. [ca. 1954], JHS Box 6; J. H. Steward, "Autobiographical Appraisal," n.d., JHS Box 16.

57. J. H. Steward to F. C. Noon, Mar. 31, 1918, TA.

58. J. H. Steward, "Autobiographical Appraisal," n.d., JHS Box 16; Patterson, personal communication, Dec. 15, 1993; M. Steward, official personnel folder, NPRC. Although most of Thomas Steward's employment records are lost, newspaper clippings and letters in his file state that he "tendered his resignation," not that he retired (official personnel folder, NPRC). Grace Steward's position, at first temporary, soon became permanent. She earned eleven hundred dollars a year at the Department of Agriculture in 1918 (official personnel folder, NPRC).

59. Eddy 1906:59–60; R. D. Thomas 1994:122. Eddy divorced her second husband several years after he left her. She was forty-six and had no means of financial support, but she later prospered along with her church. Eddy's experience may have served to encourage Grace Steward as she gave up the financial security of her own marriage.

60. Jane Steward (interview) mentioned the settlement but knew no details. A letter from the early 1920s refers to bonds in Steward's name that had been signed over to his mother (see chap. 3).

61. J. H. Steward to Noon, Jan. 7, 1918, TA.

62. The surnames of most of the early students at Deep Springs were British, with German surnames a distant second in frequency. One student was Catholic, but most appear to have been Protestant. The school's religious services followed an Episcopalian format (Aird, in "Alumni of Deep Springs and Telluride Association Oral History Project," Chris Breiseth and Brad Edmonston, interviewers, Sept. 1987:148, TA). Jewish students were not admitted until the 1940s, at which time the trustees established a quota of two (Etnier 1981:7). A picture in Steward's photograph album (DSC) of the students in costume for a party shows him in blackface, a vivid reminder of the racial order during that era.

63. Hovey 1988:5.

64. J. H. Steward to Noon, Jan. 7, 1918, TA.

65. Washburn 1978:94; Coville, in Breiseth and Edmonston, 1987:246, TA; Orville Sweeting, untitled ms. about Nunn, n.d.:239, LLN Box 23; Stegner 1954:273; Dumas 1936, 19:327–29; Bailey 1933:19. On Charles D. Walcott (1850–1927) and his work in paleontology, see Gould (1988).

66. Sidney Walcott appears to have been one of the original members of Telluride Association (Convention Minutes, 1912, TA; see also Coville, in Breiseth and Edmonston 1987:249, TA).

67. Convention Minutes, vol. 1, 1923, TA.

68. Noon to J. H. Steward, Mar. 23, 1918, TA; J. C. Steward interview.

69. J. H. Steward, information form, May 31, 1918, TA; J. C. Steward interview.

70. G. G. Steward, official personnel folder, NPRC.

71. Ibid. Jane Steward (interview) told me about her mother-in-law's excellent health, contrasting it with Julian Steward's erratic health.

72. Divorce was extremely uncommon during that period, as evidenced by the absence of the term on federal employment forms. Grace Steward's supervisor at Klamath Agency first listed her

marital status as "married," and later as "widow." Thomas Steward was very much alive at the time; he died in 1936 (see chap. 8).

73. G. G. Steward, official personnel folder, NPRC; M. Steward, official personnel folder, NPRC. According to records in her file, initially Grace Steward's salary dropped from eleven hundred dollars to nine hundred dollars when she went to Oregon.

74. Eddy saw fear as an obstacle to health (Amy Richmond, First Church of Christ, Scientist, personal communication, Apr. 21, 2000). "Fear is a fountain of sickness," she wrote, also advising, "We should master fear instead of cultivating it" (Eddy 1906:197, 391).

75. J. H. Steward to Wetmore, n.d. [ca. 1954], JHS Box 6.

76. Stegner 1987:78. See also Tompkins (1992:4, 137).

Chapter 2: West to Deep Springs

1. J. H. Steward, information form, May 31, 1918, TA. The *Slim Princess* ceased operation in about 1960. Its rails were only three feet apart; standard-gauge rails are more than four feet apart (Hungerford 1961). In the late 1990s, the engine and a few cars remained on permanent display in a railroad museum in Laws, California.

2. On Owens Valley during this period, see Wood (1972a, 1972b), Southern Inyo Chapter (1977), and Kahrl (1982).

3. The first two plates (facing 16) in Steward's (1938a) monograph, *Basin-Plateau,* show the Sierra Nevada, looking west across Owens Valley, as well as a scene in the White Mountains, both of which he initially saw in 1918.

4. Reich interview; Reich 1974:1; Mansfield, in "Alumni of Deep Springs and Telluride Association Oral History Project" (typescript), Chris Breiseth and Brad Edmonston, interviewers, 1987:295, TA.

5. Dunn, n.d., untitled ms., DSC; F. C. Noon, Chancellor's Report, LLN Box 13; Bailey 1933:102–3; Orville Sweeting, unpublished ms. on Nunn, n.d., LLN Box 23.

6. On the isolation policy, see F. C. Noon, Chancellor's Report, LLN Box 13; master plan, n.d., DSC; Nunn to Dunn and Sweeney, May 15, 1917, LLN Box 13. Sixty years later, Dunn, an early student, bluntly explained one practical reason for the school's isolation policy: "[Nunn had] bad experiences with . . . a few pregnancies where he had to pay them off to get the kid [student] off the hook." Former students have speculated for many years about how Nunn regarded women and whether he was homosexual (J. C. Steward interview; see the comments of Dunn, Aird, Coville, Ashley, and Northrup, in Breiseth and Edmonston 1987:128, 146, 189, 230, 267, TA).

7. F. C. Noon, chancellor's report, 1917, LLN Box 13.

8. Master plan, n.d., DSC; Newell interview. According to Bailey (1933:102–3), Nunn was "dissatisfied with the location of Claremont, largely because of its lack of isolation." A report on Deep Springs in 1923 noted that "there is practically nothing to interfere with the isolation of Deep Springs and the resulting opportunity for continuity of study and effort" (Convention Minutes, vol. 1, 1923, TA).

9. See Rountree (1990) and Isaac (1982:11–15).

10. Plate B, facing 17 in Steward's (1938a) monograph, shows Deep Springs Valley as he would have seen it in 1918, entering from Westgard Pass and Owens Valley.

11. Fiero 1986; Trimble 1989.

12. J. H. Steward 1938a:58, 60; Delacorte 1990:12, 22–25; Convention Minutes, vol. 1, 1923, TA.

13. Delacorte 1990; master plan, n.d., DSC.

14. Dunn, n.d., untitled ms., DSC; Reich interview; Reich 1974:1–3; Convention Minutes, vol. 1, 1923, TA.

15. Reich interview; Reich 1974:1–3; Dunn, n.d., untitled ms., DSC.

16. Reich 1974:2, 3; Dunn n.d., untitled ms., DSC; Reich, in Breiseth and Edmonston 1987:163,

164, TA. Steward (1933:234) first used the name Indian Harry (recalled from his student days at the ranch) and later Captain Harry (1938a:67, 314). His informant "MH" was Mary Harry (J. H. Steward 1938a:314–15). Paiute women commonly worked as laundresses in Owens Valley during this period, as did Northern Paiute, Western Shoshone, and Washo women elsewhere in the Great Basin (Crum 1994:63; Wheat 1967:19; Nyswander interview, 1996; Southern Inyo Chapter 1977:15, 19). On Northern Paiute, see C. S. Fowler 1986a.

17. Reich interview; Convention Minutes, vol. 1, 1923, TA. The school does not have early employment records for staff members (L. Jackson Newell, personal communication, June 27, 1998), including the ranch hands, most of whom were probably Northern Paiute (Nyswander interviews; Kahrl 1982:354; Crum 1994:187).

18. On place-names, see J. H. Steward (1938a:57).

19. Ibid., 7, 314–15.

20. Ibid., 7, 8, 14, 65–67, 249, 315. Steward (ibid., 7) noted that because of the effects of white settlement, after the 1870s, "most Shoshoni remained near their native haunts, gradually abandoning their native economy and attaching themselves to ranches or mining towns."

21. Dunn, n.d., untitled ms., DSC; Reich, in Breiseth and Edmonston 1987:163, TA; master plan, n.d., DSC; J. H. Steward 1938a:315.

22. [Reich], "Indian Harry," n.d., DSC. This is one of two unsigned, undated short essays about the family that I found at Deep Springs College. Reich (interview) later told me that he wrote the essays for a course in composition, probably in about 1919. See also Reich, in Breiseth and Edmonston 1987:164, TA.

23. J. H. Steward 1933:264–65, 343, plate 3c, 1938a:19–20, 314. See Wheat (1967:103–11) on construction materials and techniques.

24. Reich interview; Reich 1974:2, 3; in Breiseth and Edmonston 1987:161, TA; inventory of furnishings, LLN Box 13.

25. Reich interview; Reich 1974:2.

26. Dunn, n.d., untitled ms., DSC; Reich 1974:3; Reich, in Breiseth and Edmonston 1987:162, TA; J. H. Steward photograph album, DSC. The Fresno scraper was probably used primarily to level the roads at the ranch. The swimming pool eventually became a reservoir known as the "lower reservoir."

27. Reich 1974:3; J. C. Steward interview. Many of the workmen quit to join the armed services after the United States entered the war (see Coville, in Breiseth and Edmonston 1987:251, TA).

28. Coville, in Breiseth and Edmonston 1987:252–53, TA; J. C. Steward interview. The closest physician was many miles away in Big Pine or Bishop.

29. Master plan, n.d., DSC; Telluride Association 1928:22; Reich interview; Newell 1982:122

30. Faculty reports, Nov. 1919 to May 1920, addenda, vol. 3, DSC; Reich, in Breiseth and Edmonston 1987:163, TA; Newell 1982:123. Whether Coville was the first labor commissioner is unclear (see Coville and Aird, in Breiseth and Edmonston 1987:141, 254, 255–56, TA).

31. Master plan, n.d., DSC; Newell 1980, "Among the Few: A Study of Deep Springs College Alumni, 1917–1980," DSC; Newell 1982:122.

32. Bailey 1933; Sweeting, n.d., untitled ms., LLN Box 23; master plan, n.d., DSC.

33. Master plan, n.d., DSC; Aird, in Breiseth and Edmonston 1987:147–48, TA; Newell 1980:2–3, DSC; Dunn, n.d., untitled ms., DSC.

34. Aird, in Breiseth and Edmonston 1987:147, TA. Dunn (n.d., untitled ms., DSC), who worked at a remote power plant in Utah in 1915, recalled, "We were so isolated we could literally study around the clock."

35. Master plan, n.d., DSC; Bishop 1962:56, 57, 126–28.

36. Aird, in Breiseth and Edmonston 1987:139, TA. Dunn (n.d., untitled ms., DSC) noted the shift to younger students and Nunn's concerns about the war. Reich (interview) recalled that none of the students smoked or drank (see also Reich, in Breiseth and Edmonston 1987:164, TA).

37. Aird, in Breiseth and Edmonston 1987:147, 148, TA; J. H. Steward, alumnus questionnaire,

May 17, 1961, DSC. Nearly all sources agree that Nunn was an unabashed elitist, but one who also believed in "talent" (e.g., Newell 1980:2, DSC; Newell 1982:121). As explicitly stated in a 1923 report on the school, "Given men of equal purpose and power—equal character and ability—the one of greater financial resources is preferred" (Convention minutes, vol. 1, 1923, TA).

38. By 1922 eleven of the twenty-one students were from the East, four were from the Midwest, and only six were from the West (Convention minutes, vol. 1, 1923, TA). Figures in Newell's (1980:22, DSC) alumni study suggest that easterners predominated only through the 1920s and that over time the student body achieved greater regional balance.

39. Mansfield and Coville, in Breiseth and Edmonston 1987:246–48, 295, TA. Frederick Coville (1867–1937) was a graduate of Cornell (Marquis 1918:623), and one of his sons and Sidney Walcott were fellow students there. The two families thus had ties.

40. Coville, in Breiseth and Edmonston 1987:246–47, TA; F. V. Coville 1892:3511; J. H. Steward 1938a:73n.8, 1941b:236, 237.

41. Coville, in Breiseth and Edmonston 1987:248–49, TA; Convention minutes, 1923, TA.

42. J. H. Steward photograph album, DSC. The album contains some photographs taken by other students, but the great majority were taken by Steward.

43. Reich interview; Reich 1974:3; "Faculty Report to the Student Body," Mar. 5, 1920, Faculty reports, Nov. 1919 to May 1920, addenda, vol. 3, DSC.

44. Reich to J. H. Steward, Dec. 7, 1969, JHS Box 3.

45. See Fiero (1986:152) on mining in the Tonopah district.

46. Master plan, n.d., DSC; J. H. Steward 1929b; Cadbury interview. The ruins of White Mountain City remain one of the valley's landmarks.

47. J. H. Steward 1928c, 1938a:58. For recent archaeological work in Deep Springs Valley, see Delacorte (1990).

48. J. H. Steward 1938a:64–66, 314; [Reich], "Indian Harry," n.d., DSC. See Steward's (1938a:34) comments on coyotes and several other carnivorous species that "were not greatly valued" by Paiute and Shoshone.

49. [Reich], n.d., "Indian Harry," and "Old Mary and Young Mary," DSC; Reich interview. I assume that the unidentified woman in the photograph, shown with a baby, was Captain Harry and Mary's daughter, who reportedly had a child and whose husband worked as a ranch hand.

50. Women's use of technology remained a neglected topic for decades. It is largely through the efforts of archaeologists, including Rita P. Wright (1996a, 1996b) and contributors to her edited volume, *Gender and Archaeology,* that it has recently emerged as a subject of serious study in anthropology. See McGaw (1996) for a historian's approach to technologies associated with women and Wajcman (1991) on the identification of technology with masculinity.

51. Willey 1988:236.

52. Mansfield, in Breiseth and Edmonston 1987:322, TA.

53. Reich, in Breiseth and Edmonston 1987:162, TA; Reich interview. The gopher holes were probably made by pocket gophers, a type of burrowing rodent that the Shoshone and Northern Paiute hunted (J. H. Steward 1938a:40).

54. See Mintz (1979) on Steward's attention to water and water scarcity in his published writings.

55. J. C. Steward interview; J. H. Steward to alumni committee, March 3, 1946, JHS Box 6. He expressed the same thought to friends (e.g., Aird 1977:4), in correspondence, and in autobiographical statements.

56. J. H. Steward, alumni questionnaire, March 17, 1961, DSC; J. C. Steward interview. The "moralistic philosophy" he referred to derived from Nunn (see Hovey 1988).

57. J. C. Steward interview; Aird 1977:4; J. H. Steward, academic records, DSC; Newell 1980:7, DSC; Newell 1982:124.

58. J. H. Steward to alumni committee, Mar. 3, 1946, DSC; Thornhill to J. H. Steward, July 28, 1921, TA; Faculty reports, Nov. 19 to May 1920, addenda, vol. 3, DSC. Steward's dislike of public

speaking perhaps stemmed from its being a highly competitive, highly social event at Deep Springs, with an audience made up of all the students and faculty and often some of the ranch hands and visitors. Public speaking remains a community event at the school (Newell 1980:7, DSC; Newell 1982:124).

59. Erik K. Reed, who had attended the same high school as Steward in Washington, D.C., specialized in southwestern archaeology. He earned a Ph.D. in anthropology and worked for the National Park Service (*Telluride News Letter*, 1959, 46[1]: 1, TA; Jacques Cattell Press 1968:1310). Lloyd Fallers (1925–74) spent a year at Deep Springs before entering the University of Chicago and eventually earning a Ph.D. An obituary in the London *Times* mentioned that his unusual practical skills, including carpentry and car repair, served him well in his fieldwork in East Africa (*Deep Springs Newsletter*, 1974, 20:6, DSC). Steward acquired the same useful skills at the school.

60. Of nine men who attended Deep Springs between 1917 and 1919 and responded to an alumni survey, one became an engineer, another entered public service, three were academics, and four had careers in business (Newell 1980:67, DSC; see also J. H. Steward to H. E. Kirby, May 15, 1961, DSC).

61. J. H. Steward to Noon, July 16, 1919, TA; Noon to J. H. Steward, July 30, 1919, TA. Some of the buildings still stood at the site in the late 1990s. Rachel Carson (1962:45) mentioned the Klamath Basin and its transformation in her classic book *Silent Spring*.

62. J. H. Steward to Noon, July 16, 1919, TA.

63. Ibid.; Aird, in Breiseth and Edmonston 1987:145, TA. The opening of the tribal forestlands to commercial logging provided revenue, undermining incentives to earn income by raising cattle or by other pursuits. The Klamath reservation no longer exists; the land was sold in the 1960s and 1970s and the proceeds distributed among the Klamath Indians who had formerly lived there (Stern 1998:462). Most of the land now lies within a national forest.

64. Keeping detailed financial records became a lifelong habit for Steward, as illustrated by the accounts found in some of his journals. Nunn regarded financial responsibility as an important personal quality, and one essential for public leaders (J. C. Steward interview).

65. G. G. Steward, official personnel folder, NPRC.

66. Ibid. A Christian Science nurse provides bedside care and spiritual support but not conventional medical treatment. Anyone using the system of prayer-based healing taught by Eddy may consult a practitioner, obtain care from a Christian Science nurse at home, or enter a Christian Science care facility (Hussey interview). The first nursing care facility in San Francisco operated by the Mother Church, the First Church of Christ, Scientist, opened in May 1930 (Donna Read, manager, church records dept., the First Church of Christ, Scientist, personal communication, Apr. 20, 2000).

67. Jane Steward (interview) identified the baskets in the photograph. Grace Steward had moved to San Rafael by July 1920 (J. H. Steward, information form, July 15, 1920, TA).

68. J. H. Steward 1933:234, 1938a:50, 315. Steward gave the date as 1920 in the earlier publication and 1919 in the later one. Paiute in western Nevada burned a shelter when someone died in it; they also burned the deceased person's possessions to prevent the spirit from returning for any belongings (Wheat 1967:8).

69. J. H. Steward to Thornhill, July 21, 1921, TA.

70. Schoenherr 1992:1–2, 12, 82.

71. J. H. Steward 1923:312. Temple Crag had been previously named Mount Alice, and the name change may explain the long-ago confusion about the first recorded ascent. Adding to the confusion, another peak in the Sierra is now called Mount Alice. Jane Steward told me about the photograph of (the first) Mount Alice—the name her husband always used—but could not recall its significance to him. Later, I happened across the following reference in a guidebook: "This mountain was first scaled June 24, 1921, by W. B. Putnam and Julian H. Steward" (Rider 1927:383). Julian Steward (1923:312) noted that there was "no indication of the summit having been visited before."

Currently, the Sierra Club credits a U.S. Geological Survey party with the first recorded ascent, in 1909 (Ellen Byrne, Sierra Club, personal communication, June 17, 1998).

72. J. H. Steward 1923. Sierra Club publications give Mount Humphreys's summit a class 4 rating, meaning that ropes should be used and some technical skills are necessary.

73. Chalfant 1933:337; Baugh 1937:23, 26, 29; Kahrl 1982:223. For valley residents' memories of that time, see Wood (1972a, 1972b), Inyo County Board of Supervisors (1966:65, 78, 79), and Southern Inyo Chapter (1977:111).

74. Their climb was reported in the *Sierra Club Bulletin*, following Steward's (1923) description of the Temple Crag ascent. John Muir (1838–1914) wrote about his ascent in *The Mountains of California* (Muir 1894).

75. Murphy 1977:15; Faculty reports, Nov. 1919 to May 1920, addenda, vol. 3, DSC; J. H. Steward to Wetmore, n.d. [ca. 1954], JHS Box 6.

76. J. C. Steward interview. The teacher's comment in 1920 about "pessimism and gloom" suggests that Steward experienced spells of depression following his parents' separation (if not earlier).

Chapter 3: *University Years, East and West*

1. J. H. Steward to Thornhill, July 21, 1921, TA; Starr 1996:100–101. Starr's (1996:100) telling words about the city and especially the waterfront—"Male, volatile, close to a frontier life of men in groups"—suggest why Steward, never a city lover, always had a certain affection for San Francisco.

2. J. H. Steward to Thornhill, July 21, 1921, TA. Nunn had bought the house in Pasadena the year before, in 1920 (Bailey 1933:110). Marion Steward's salary of more than thirteen hundred dollars as a federal employee fell to less than eleven hundred dollars (official personnel folder, NPRC).

3. Secretary, Telluride Association to J. H. Steward, June 30, 1920, TA; J. H. Steward to Thornhill, July 21, 1921, TA; University of California 1926b:98. The said "shortcomings" or his close friendship with Putnam may explain why Steward did not receive a full scholarship. Putnam and Nunn allegedly had some sort of "confrontation" in 1921 (Aird, in Breiseth and Edmonston 1987:145), and Putnam was not elected into membership in Telluride Association until several years later.

4. J. H. Steward to E. A. Thornhill, July 21, 1921, TA; J. H. Steward to Noon, Oct. 5, 1921, TA; J. H. Steward, information form, July 15, 1920, TA.

5. J. H. Steward to Thornhill, n.d. [Aug. 1921]; J. H. Steward to Noon, Oct. 5, 1921, TA; J. H. Steward transcript, 1921–22 (with the permission of Jane Steward, courtesy of the Office of Admissions and Records, University of California, Berkeley).

6. J. H. Steward to Noon, Oct. 5, 1921, TA; J. H. Steward to Thornhill, Nov. 13, 1921, TA.

7. See Gordon (1990:52–84) on these and other experiences of the second generation of women college students (1890–1920) at the University of California, Berkeley.

8. Nerad 1987a, 1987b, 1999; Mark 1980:60n.99; T. Kroeber 1970:60–62; Gordon 1990:56–59; Paul 1971. Phoebe Apperson Hearst (1842–1919) became a regent in 1897. In 1898 the university appointed Mary Bennett Ritter as a physician and a part-time lecturer in hygiene. According to Gordon (1990:62), the first woman to hold a faculty position was Jessica Peixotto, appointed instructor in political economy in 1904 (see also Nerad 1999:36–40). By 1915 women comprised 6 percent of the faculty and nearly half of the student body. In 1916 the university established the department of home economics, "and with it the manifest ghetto of women at Berkeley was created" (Nerad 1987b:73–78). See also Gordon (1990:68).

9. J. H. Steward to E. A. Thornhill, Nov. 13, 1921, TA.

10. J. H. Steward to Wetmore, n.d. [ca. 1954], JHS Box 6; J. H. Steward, "Autobiographical Appraisal," n.d., JHS Box 16; J. H. Steward to Alumni Committee, Deep Springs Student Body, Mar. 3, 1946, JHS Box 6. See also Aird (in Breiseth and Edmonston 1987:148, TA) and Hovey (1988).

11. J. H. Steward, "Autobiographical Appraisal," n.d., JHS Box 16; J. H. Steward to Thornhill, Nov.

13, 1921, TA; J. H. Steward transcript, 1921–22, University of California, Berkeley; University of California 1921:33.

12. Rowe 1962:395, 397; J. H. Steward 1973:6; A. L. Kroeber 1901, 1915; Mark 1980:51; Lowie 1959:176. Murphy (1977:2), among many others, refers to Kroeber as the department's "founder," which is an error. Frederic Ward Putnam (1839–1915) served as founding chairman of the advisory committee that directed the department during its first years (University of California 1902:28; see also Mark 1980:43–51). Kroeber held the rank of instructor and was not a member of the committee.

13. Caffrey 1989:103; A. L. Kroeber 1922, 1923, 1925. On Alfred L. Kroeber's life (1876–1960) and career, see T. Kroeber (1970) and J. H. Steward (1973).

14. Rowe 1962:400; Lowie 1920, 1924; Lowie, "Biographical Data for National Academy of Sciences," April 19, 1944, JHS Box 1. On Robert H. Lowie's life (1883–1957) and career, see his own account (Lowie 1959), published posthumously, and Murphy (1972).

15. On Edward W. Gifford (1887–1959), see Foster (1960).

16. J. H. Steward to Thornhill, April 6, 1922; J. H. Steward to Noon, May 15, 1922, TA. Steward's own words during this period do not support the idea that he was committed to anthropology after taking his first course, or that he chose another major at Cornell "almost by default" (Manners 1973:889, 1996:326; Murphy 1977:2).

17. J. H. Steward to Noon, May 15, 1922; J. H. Steward to Thornhill, May 15, 1922, TA.

18. J. H. Steward to Noon, May 15, 1922; Reich interview.

19. J. H. Steward to Thornhill, May 15, 1922; J. H. Steward to Noon, May 15, 1922; "Scholastic Record of Julian H. Steward," June 19, 1922, TA; J. A. Boshard to J. H. Steward, July 25, 1922; M. Steward, official personnel folder, NPRC; Derks 1999:139.

20. *Telluride News Letter* 1922, 8(5): 15, TA; Reich interview; Emma Schroeder to J. H. Steward, Jan. 1942, JHS Box 17.

21. Reich interview.

22. Bishop 1962:410; J. H. Steward to Wetmore, n.d. [ca. 1954], JHS Box 6.

23. Aird, in Breiseth and Edmonston 1987:143, TA; Bainton 1943:134.

24. J. H. Steward to Deep Springs student body, Mar. 3, 1946, JHS Box 6.

25. J. H. Steward to Noon, Oct. 7, 1922, TA; J. H. Steward to Wetmore, n.d. [ca. 1954], JHS Box 6; Bishop 1962:452. Given Steward's tendency to think in polarities, sometimes gender linked, I think it is no stretch to suggest that for him eastern landscapes had gendered, female associations, just as western landscapes had male associations.

26. Bishop 1962:453; Delacorte 1990:16.

27. Jane Steward (interview) mentioned that *The Last of the Mohicans* and Cooper's other novels about the American frontier, along with Zane Grey's, were favorites of her husband. Julian Steward shared this enthusiasm with Lowie (1959:1), who, in the opening sentence of his memoir, recalled reading Cooper as a child in Vienna.

28. On Lewis Henry Morgan (1818–81), see Tooker (1983); on the League of the Iroquois, see Fenton (1998). The Onondaga Indian Reservation, one of a number of reservations in the state, and located north of Ithaca, was the closest.

29. J. H. Steward to Broshard, Sept. 27, 1922, TA; J. H. Steward transcript, 1922–25 (with the permission of Jane Steward, courtesy of the Office of the Registrar, Cornell University); J. H. Steward to Wetmore n.d. [ca. 1954], JHS Box 6; J. C. Steward interview.

30. Bainton 1943:3–4, 50–51, 130, 132–34; MacCurdy 1919:51; J. H. Steward to Noon, Mar. 6, 1924, TA. George Lincoln Burr (1857–1938) spent time in the mid-1930s at Deep Springs. He died a few years later in Ithaca (Bainton 1943:141–42). Jane Steward (interview) told me that her husband turned entirely away from religion during his undergraduate years.

31. J. H. Steward to Broshard, July 24, 1923; J. H. Steward to Noon, July 25, 1923, TA.

32. San Francisco city directory, 1923; J. H. Steward to Noon, July 25, 1923, TA.

33. J. H. Steward transcript, 1922–25, Cornell University.

34. By 1915 women comprised 44 percent of the student body at the University of California (Nerad 1987b:75). They did not exceed 25 percent of the student population at Cornell until the 1960s (Conable 1977:111). Other universities that limited the admission of women were the University of Michigan, where Steward later taught, and Stanford (Gordon 1990:43).

35. Conable 1977:110–13, 116, 139–40; Bishop 1962:143–52, 448. Cornell was the first major institution in the East to accept women along with men, but some universities in the Midwest had already established the practice (Conable 1977:8, 62). Bishop (1962:151) refers to "anticoedism" as "the ugliest of Cornell traditions." See Conable (1977:116–20) for specific examples, ranging from insulting songs to ostracizing practices. Women finally gained access to the food service areas of the student union in the mid-1930s and to most other areas of the building during the 1940s (Conable 1977:140).

36. Conable 1977:126–29; Bishop 1962:337–38, 380. The board of trustees supported establishing a home economics department but initially refused to grant faculty status to the two women hired to develop the department (Conable 1977:127).

37. J. H. Steward to Wetmore, n.d. [ca. 1954], JHS Box 6. Anna B. Comstock (1854–1930) taught for many years without faculty rank and did not become a full professor until 1920 (Conable 1977:91, 127; Jacklin 1971:368). Her *Handbook of Nature Study* (1911) is in its twenty-fourth edition and has been widely translated. On Comstock and the nature study movement, see Henson (1997). See Lear (1997:13–15) with specific reference to Rachel Carson (1907–64).

38. J. H. Steward to Noon, Mar. 6, 1924, TA; Gould 1988:16.

39. J. H. Steward to Noon, Mar. 6, 1922, TA; J. C. Steward interview. San Francisco city directories verify what Jane Steward recalled: that Grace and Marion Steward lived together at times, and apart at times, throughout the 1920s.

40. Noon to J. H. Steward, Apr. 9, 1924, TA. George R. Mansfield held a Ph.D. in geology from Harvard and spent most of his career as a government scientist (Marquis 1932:1499).

41. Coville, in Breiseth and Edmonston 1987:247–48, TA.

42. I first found mention of John F. Steward (1841–1915) while reading about the second Powell expedition (Stegner 1954:125, 137; Dellenbaugh 1926 [1908]). His surname prompted me to learn more about him. For a photograph of John F. Steward, see D. D. Fowler (1972:18); for his journal and a brief biography, see Darrah (1947–48). See also Worster (2001:219, 232–33).

43. Noon to J. H. Steward, Apr. 9, 1924, TA; Aird 1977:4.

44. J. H. Steward to W. L. Biersach, Dec. 7 and 8, 1924, Jan. 27, 1925, TA; M. Steward, official personnel folder, NPRC.

45. The first such facility opened five years later (see chap. 2, n.67), when Grace Steward was sixty-one; she appears not to have been employed during the 1930s or later. Christian Science doctrine permits vision correction and standard dental care, although the healing of vision problems and dental conditions is also sought through prayer (Hussey interview).

46. Bishop 1962:452; Farrand to A. L. Kroeber, Feb. 6, 1925, RDA Box 55; J. H. Steward to Biersach, Oct. 13 and Nov. 10, 1925; J. H. Steward to O. B. Suhr, May 1, 1926, TA.

47. J. H. Steward to Wetmore, n.d. [ca. 1954], JHS Box 6; J. H. Steward, "Autobiographical Appraisal," n.d., JHS Box 16; J. H. Steward, Deep Springs alumnus questionnaire, May 17, 1961, DSC. See also J. H. Steward to alumni committee, Deep Springs student body, Mar. 3, 1946, JHS Box 6.

48. Darrah 1947–48:175–76. On International Harvester and the Steward family, see chap. 1.

49. Stegner 1954; Hinsley 1981:147–82; Fowler and Fowler 1971:1–22.

50. Marquis 1942:886; D. Cole 1999:251; Bishop 1962:450; Mark 1980:40; Farrand to Lowie, Feb. 17, 1925, RDA Box 55. Livingston Farrand (1867–1939) was not formally trained in anthropology; he had not "taken his degree in the subject under Boas at Columbia," as Murphy (1977:2) and many others report.

51. Bishop 1962:450; A. L. Kroeber 1918, 1919.

52. Farrand to A. L. Kroeber, Feb. 6, 1925, RDA Box 55.

53. J. H. Steward transcript, 1922–25, Cornell University; J. H. Steward to department of anthropology, University of California, Apr. 20, 1925, RDA Box 141; J. H. Steward to alumni committee, Deep Springs student body, Mar. 3, 1946, DSC.

54. Convention minutes, 1926, TA.

55. J. H. Steward to Lowie, May 11, 1925; Lowie to J. H. Steward, May 21, 1925, RDA Box 141.

56. J. H. Steward to Biersach, Aug. 11, 1925, TA; Reich interview.

57. Biersach to J. H. Steward, July 21, 1925; J. H. Steward to Biersach, Aug. 11, 1925, TA.

58. Larson 1997:3, 7–8, 191.

59. Nyswander (interview, 1997) remembered specific instances in the early 1930s when her husband expressed deep exasperation about the financial decisions his mother made. Steward's journal from the mid-1930s contains comments in a similar vein (JJJS I).

60. J. C. Steward interview.

Chapter 4: Berkeley and Beyond

1. San Francisco city directory, 1925; J. H. Steward to Biersach, Sept. 15, 1925, TA; University of California 1926b:96, 99. According to Jane Steward (interview), he had a difficult relationship with his sister as well as with his mother and found living with either of them a strain.

2. City directory, 1925; J. H. Steward to Biersach, Oct. 13 and 28, 1925, TA. Grace Steward advertised in the *Christian Science Journal* for a year, beginning late in 1925. I am grateful to Virginia S. Harris, then clerk of the Mother Church, for bringing this to my attention (personal communication, Dec. 17, 1990).

3. J. H. Steward to O. B. Suhr, Dec. 16, 1925, DSC. The University of California waived the tuition fee for state residents and for graduate students who were nonresidents and enrolled in programs other than those in the professional schools (such as law and medicine). The only fee, just fifty dollars a year, guaranteed them medical treatment (University of California 1926b:98). Steward was one of a legion of students who managed graduate study in anthropology only by virtue of its modest cost at the University of California (see, e.g., Howell 1998:33).

4. J. H. Steward to Strong, Aug. 14, [1926], WDS Box 14; J. H. Steward, expense records, 1927, RDA Box 141. Ferries provided transportation from San Francisco to the East Bay and to Marin County before 1937, when the Bay Bridge and Golden Gate Bridge were completed (WPA 1939:276, 287). Jane Steward (interview) mentioned her husband's mechanical competence, including his skill with cantankerous cars, which he attributed to his years at Deep Springs.

5. J. H. Steward to Biersach, Oct. 28, Nov. 10, 1925, TA.

6. Beals 1979:13–14. Dorothy Nyswander (interviews 1996, 1997), in contrast, remembered his health as normal during this period and later.

7. Beals (1979:14) referred to Steward's last term at Berkeley, in spring 1928. A year earlier, Steward had mentioned to Strong that his work might be "held up for a couple of weeks in May because I will have to have another operation" (J. H. Steward to Strong, Mar. 29, [1927], WDS Box 14).

8. Letters that Julian Steward wrote to his friend Strong during the late 1920s, peppered with the very expletives that would have most offended his highly religious mother, give some sense of his religious sensibilities. He may have avoided that language in her presence, but as Jane Steward (interview) remembered from the 1930s, he and his mother did argue, sometimes vigorously, about religion and other issues.

9. Beals 1979:3, 14. Nyswander (interview, 1996), who met Steward during this period, described him as extremely attractive to women, a quality that she initially found suspect.

10. J. H. Steward to Stirling, Dec. 21, 1957, JHS Box 15; Willey 1988:247–49. On Matthew W. Stirling (1896–1975), see Collins (1976) and Willey (1988:242–64). Steward's encounter with Stirling apparently took place in 1927, when Stirling returned from New Guinea, and a year before his appointment as director of the BAE at the age of only thirty-two (Collins 1976:886).

11. Rowe 1962:397; Mark 1980:43; McCown 1969:86.

12. J. H. Steward 1961b:1045; Beals 1979:3–4; Drucker 1981:606; T. Kroeber 1970:62–65; Foster 1976:9–10. It was also known as the "tin building" and the "tin tank." The department occupied it for nearly sixty years.

13. Beals 1979:3–4, 1982:4; list of graduate students, RDA Box 1b. On Ronald Olson (1895–1979), see Drucker (1981) and Winters (1991:521–22). Lloyd Warner (1898–1970), who had earned a bachelor's degree at Berkeley in 1925 soon left for graduate study at Harvard (Winters 1991:739–40). William Duncan Strong (1899–1962) departed for a position at the Field Museum within a year (see Solecki and Wagley 1963; Willey 1988:74–96). On Ralph Beals (1901–85), see Goldschmidt (1986) and Winters (1991:41–42). The several women in the graduate program are discussed below.

14. Strong to A. L. Kroeber, July 2, 1922, RDA Box 141; Rowe 1962:401. Max Uhle (1856–1944) began excavating sites in Peru in the 1890s. He was employed by the University of California from 1901 to 1903 (Winters 1991:712).

15. Strong to A. L. Kroeber, July 2, 1922; A. L. Kroeber to Strong, July 3, 1923, RDA Box 141. Parezo (1993:37n.23) is one of the few to acknowledge the "years of poverty and years of subordination" that characterize graduate training in anthropology. Few students seem to be forewarned about this aspect of professional training; as Kroeber's comments make clear, it has a long history.

16. Rowe 1962:395–96; J. H. Steward 1973:9, 11; T. Kroeber 1970:53–58, 101–7; Kroeber-Quinn 1982:75.

17. Deacon 1997:211.

18. D. Cole 1999:165–66.

19. Beals 1979:10; Murphy 1972:32.

20. Paul Radin (1883–1959) moved from one temporary position to another for most of his career, with spells of unemployment or marginal employment between them. Some of these do not seem to have been voluntary, but for "a figure both widely known and mysterious, even impenetrable" (Diamond 1981:69), it is difficult to say. He sometimes lived in Berkeley, where his brother Max Radin, a prominent legal scholar, taught (Hoijer 1959; Diamond 1981). Loeb (see below) was not steadily employed by the university (Toffelmier 1967:201). On Isabel Kelly (1906–83), Anna Gayton (1899–1977), and Lila O'Neale (1886–1948), see Knobloch (1989), Rowe (1978), and Schevill (1989), respectively.

21. A scarcity of academic positions for anthropologists characterized most of the twentieth century except for two brief periods: the years following World War II, when the G.I. Bill allowed many veterans to attend college (see chap. 10); and again in 1960s (see chap. 12), when the number of students increased dramatically for demographic reasons, as the baby boom generation reached college age.

22. J. H. Steward to Biersach, Jan. 14, 1926, TA.

23. J. H. Steward to Suhr, Dec. 16, 1925, Jan. 25, 1926, DSC.

24. J. H. Steward transcript, 1925–29, University of California, Berkeley, JHS Box 13; University of California 1925:40–41. Upper-division courses were open to both undergraduates who had taken the two introductory courses and graduate students.

25. J. H. Steward transcript, 1925–29; program of dissertation defense, Sept. 10, 1929; J. H. Steward, curriculum vitae, n.d. [ca. 1928], JHS Box 13. Later in life, Steward wrote, "I have never done any [research in] linguistics, nor found a need for such studies in my own problems" ("Autobiographical Appraisal," n.d., JHS Box 16).

26. J. H. Steward 1961b:1047; Kroeber-Quinn 1982:68, 94, 97–98, 100, 102; Buzaljko 1989:188, 189; T. Kroeber 1970:76–80, 123–26, 129–33. After her children were grown, Theodora Kroeber (1897–1979) began to write, producing several books on California Indians for a general audience (Buzaljko 1989:192).

27. J. H. Steward, "The Distribution and Use of the Tambourine in Shamanism," 1–3, 51–53, JHS Box 11.

28. Memo to the dean of the graduate division, Feb. 19, 1926, RDA Box 141; J. H. Steward to Suhr, May 1, 1926, DSC.

29. Nyswander interview, 1996; Goldfrank 1978:90.

30. Nyswander interviews, 1996, 1997; Tolman 1932:354–56. See also Nyswander 1926, 1994:52–54.

31. Nyswander interview, 1996; Nyswander 1994:55; Kroeber-Quinn 1982:65; Murphy 1972:34. In 1933, at the age of fifty, Lowie married Luella Cole, a psychologist (Lowie 1959:177; Murphy 1972:35–36).

32. Beals 1979:9; Murphy interview; Murphy 1972:72; Murphy 1977:4. Lowie had some interest in psychology during this period, but his 1924 book, *Primitive Religion,* stressed individual differences in visionary experiences (Lowie, "Biographical Data," Apr. 19, 1944, JHS Box 1).

33. J. H. Steward, "Autobiographical Appraisal," n.d., JHS Box 16; J. H. Steward 1973:20. Kroeber's resistance to generalization and questions of causality forms a central theme of Steward's (1973) biography of Kroeber.

34. Nyswander 1994:277; MacKenzie 1972:225. On John B. Watson (1878–1958), see K. W. Buckley (1989). Edward Chace Tolman (1886–1959) achieved great prominence in academic psychology, and recognition during the McCarthy era for his opposition to mandatory loyalty oaths (see chap. 10).

35. Edward L. Thorndike (1874–1949), visiting Berkeley from Columbia University, had already published the work for which he is best known (Karier 1986:93–94): the three-volume *Educational Psychology,* "the bible of the student who aspired to be an educational psychologist," as Nyswander (1994:277) put it.

36. The Rickey Land and Water Company comprised more than twenty-two thousand acres in Inyo and Mono Counties (Mulholland 2000:109, 123–24).

37. Nyswander interview, 1996; Nyswander 1994:21, 273. True to her convictions, Nyswander left a major portion of her estate to an organization that promotes education of American Indians. The Progressive Era (1890–1920) was a period of optimism about the prospects for social reform: "Progressives exuded confidence that human beings could ameliorate the deficiencies of the national life" (Gordon 1990:3).

38. Nyswander interviews, 1996, 1997. See also Nyswander 1994:18–21, 60. On T. B. Rickey, see Kahrl (1982:42).

39. Convention minutes, vol. 1, 1926:3, 27–28, TA.

40. Aird 1977:4; Beals 1979:9; J. H. Steward, "Autobiographical Appraisal," n.d., JHS Box 16; J. H. Steward to Strong, Aug. 14, [1926], WDS Box 14. In the mid-1920s, William Egbert Schenk (1884–1956) held the position of honorary assistant curator at the Museum of Anthropology, University of California; Sara Moffatt Schenk took courses in the department (Gifford 1957; Kroeber-Quinn 1982:66–67, 447).

41. J. H. Steward, "Autobiographical Appraisal," n.d., JHS Box 16. Training in ethnographic field methods remained minimal at Berkeley—as Du Bois (Seymour 1989:74), Foster (1976:17), and Omer Stewart (Howell 1998:34) recalled—and elsewhere for many years. On Kroeber's work in archaeology, see Rowe (1962) and T. Kroeber (1970:143–54). Kroeber worked most intensively in archaeology during the 1920s (T. Kroeber 1970:144), the very years when Steward studied at Berkeley.

42. J. H. Steward to Gifford, July 16, 1926, RDA Box 141.

43. Strong, Schenk, and Steward 1930:1; Rowe 1962:404; J. H. Steward to Strong, Aug. 14, [1926], WDS Box 14. During the two previous summers, in 1924 and 1925, Strong had carried out survey work and directed excavations in the same area with Schenk. The idea that Strong and Steward worked at the site at the same time (Solecki and Wagley 1963:1103; Beals 1979:5) appears to be mistaken.

44. J. H. Steward to Strong, Aug. 14, [1926], WDS Box 14.

45. Strong, Schenk, and Steward 1930; J. H. Steward to Strong, Aug. 14, [1926], WDS Box 14; J. H. Steward 1927a; see also J. H. Steward (1928b). Steward referred to Herbert W. Krieger (1889–1970), a curator at the Smithsonian's U.S. National Museum (Winters 1991:364).

46. J. H. Steward 1927a:260; J. H. Steward to Tax, Feb. 11, 1966, JHS Box 6.

47. J. H. Steward 1927b; Beals 1979:9; J. C. Steward interview. *Touring Topics* was the precursor of *Westways*, the magazine of the Automobile Club of Southern California (Hart 1987:27).

48. J. H. Steward, "Autobiographical Appraisal," n.d., JHS Box 16; M. Steward 1924, 1925. Edward Garriott published on such topics as long-range weather forecasting, cold waves in the United States, and hurricanes in the West Indies.

49. Solecki and Wagley 1963:1103; Rowe, 1962:404; Lowie, "Biographical Data," Apr. 19, 1944, JHS Box 1; University of California 1926a:40–41; J. H. Steward transcript, 1925–29, JHS Box 13. They worked at Lodi, at a site Steward described as "[E. J.] Dawson's mound" (J. H. Steward to Strong, Oct. 1, [1926], WDS Box 14; see also Lowie [1933:159–60]). On Nordenskiöld (1877–1932) and his career, see Lowie (1933) and Winters (1991:510–12).

50. Lowie, "Biographical Data," Apr. 19, 1944, JHS Box 1; 1959:125. Beals (1979:4) implied that Lowie already had great interest in South American ethnography when Nordenskiöld visited Berkeley, but, according to Lowie's own account of his career, this was not the case.

51. University of California 1926a:41, 269; Beals 1979:9; J. H. Steward transcript, 1925–29; program of dissertation defense, Sept. 10, 1929, JHS Box 13. Steward may have selected his minor with Kroeber's active encouragement. Beginning in 1925, Kroeber began to form a collaborative relationship with the geographer Carl Sauer (MacPherson 1987:75).

52. Beals 1979:4, 8. On Edwin Loeb (1894–1966), see Toffelmier (1967).

53. J. H. Steward, "Primitive Religion," JHS Box 10. See Sered (1994) on religions dominated by women; she includes Christian Science as one of them.

54. Beals (1979:6–7) recalled this course as a year-long, upper-division course on social organization, but Lowie presumably covered much of the same material in the graduate seminar on theory. See Murphy (1972:43–56) on Lowie's views about cultural evolution and diffusion.

55. J. H. Steward transcript, 1925–29, JHS Box 13; University of California 1926a:115; Parsons 1979:11; D. Stanislawski 1975; J. H. Steward to Strong, Mar. 29, [1927], WDS Box 14

56. J. H. Steward transcript, University of California, Berkeley, 1925–29, JHS Box 13; Leighly 1979:6.

57. Parsons 1979:9, 14; Bushong 1981:209; Speth 1981. See also Leighly (1976) on Carl O. Sauer (1889–1975).

58. Parsons 1979:10, 13; MacPherson 1987:75; Beals 1979:4, 6; Shimkin interview, 1989. On Sauer's Germanic worldview, see Speth (1987). Toffelmier (1967:200) characterized Loeb not as an anthropogeographer but as "an anthropologist first and always."

59. Leighly 1979:7, 8; MacPherson 1987:75; University of California 1927:117; Speth 1981:225; J. H. Steward, "Autobiographical Appraisal," n.d., JHS Box 16. Steward took this seminar, on cultural geography, during fall 1927.

60. J. H. Steward to Pres. George Thomas, Jan. 9, 1930, PPGT Box 53; J. H. Steward to A. L. Kroeber, n.d. [ca. June 1927], RDA Box 141.

61. A. L. Kroeber to Rosenberg, Oct. 28, 1929, RDA Box 127; convention minutes, vol. 1, 1927, TA; Boshard to J. H. Steward, July 27, 1927; A. L. Kroeber to Parsons, Jan. 3, 1928, RDA Box 118. According to Theodora Kroeber, Rosenberg made a trip to Mexico with Kroeber and helped finance some of his research; in later years he set up a foundation (Kroeber-Quinn 1982:85).

62. San Francisco city directory, 1927; M. Steward, official personnel folder, NPRC. Grace Steward apparently did not receive a federal pension; as a divorced wife rather than widow, she presumably had no rights to a portion of Thomas Steward's pension.

63. J. H. Steward to Strong, Mar. 29, [1927], WDS Box 14.

64. Nyswander interview, 1997; J. H. Steward to Lowie, July 25, 1927; department of anthropology, July 12, 1927; J. H. Steward to A. L. Kroeber, July 14, 1927, RDA Box 141. On Erna Gunther (1896–1982), see Amoss (1989); on Leslie Spier (1893–1961) at Berkeley, see Beals (1979:4).

65. J. H. Steward to Strong, Oct. 1, [1926], Nov. 5, [1926], WDS Box 14.

66. J. H. Steward 1928c, 1929b, 1930, 1933, 1934.

67. A. L. Kroeber to Strong, Jan. 25, 1927, RDA Box 141; J. H. Steward photograph album, DSC.

68. J. H. Steward to A. L. Kroeber, July 14, [1927], RDA Box 141; Kahrl 1982:376.

69. Kahrl 1982:287–88, 292, 312; Ryan 1968:181–85; Mulholland 2000:296. Hundreds of western films, and countless television productions and commercials, have been made in the Alabama Hills, not far from the town of Lone Pine.

70. J. H. Steward to A. L. Kroeber, July 14, 1927, RDA Box 141; J. H. Steward 1933:234.

71. J. H. Steward to A. L. Kroeber, July 21, 1927; A. L. Kroeber to J. H. Steward, July 21, 1927, RDA Box 141.

72. Kahrl 1982:308–9; Ryan 1968:185; Wood 1972a:4–5. Wood witnessed the events of 1927. Steward's (1933:233) later estimate, that he spent "about six weeks" in Owens Valley and vicinity in summer 1927, appears to be an overestimate, and only a portion of that time was devoted to ethnographic research.

73. J. H. Steward to Lowie, July 25, 1927, RDA Box 141.

74. Liljeblad and Fowler 1986:460. The 1890 Ghost Dance spread widely and culminated in the massacre of Sioux Indians by the U.S. cavalry at Wounded Knee, South Dakota. Kehoe (1999) suggests that Steward overlooked recent history, and thus Wovoka, because he wanted to reconstruct the aboriginal way of life, a "primitive" one untouched by "civilization." It can also be argued, however, that he ignored Wovoka because he consistently avoided the topic of religion.

75. Parsons to Lowie, Nov. 12, 1927, RDA Box 118; Deacon 1997:244–45.

76. For example, Alice Fletcher's career in anthropology was largely financed by Mary Copley Thaw. Some years before Hearst paid the salary of the first woman to hold a faculty position at Berkeley, Thaw established a fellowship for Fletcher at Harvard's Peabody Museum. Fletcher thus became the first woman to hold an official, paid position at Harvard (Mark 1980:73, 1988:203–5; Temkin 1989:97).

77. Deacon 1997:34, 46; Friedlander 1989:283; Parsons to Lowie, Nov. 12, 1927, RDA Box 118. On Elsie Clews Parsons's (1874–1941) life and career, see Zumwalt (1992) and Deacon (1997).

78. Beals 1979:14.

79. Lowie to Parsons, Dec. 5, 1927; A. L. Kroeber to Parsons, Jan. 3, 1928, RDA Box 118.

80. J. H. Steward to Hubbell, Jan. 31, 1928; Hubbell to J. H. Steward, Feb. 4, 1928. I am grateful to Theodore Reinhart for bringing this correspondence to my attention and for providing me with copies. The documents are found in the Hubbell Collection (Boxes 14 and 105) at the University of Arizona Library. Edward T. Hall met Hubbell and Corrigan at the trading post a few years after Steward's visit; for his memories of that time and place, see Hall (1994:31–45).

81. Frigout 1979:564.

82. J. H. Steward 1931:68n.48; J. H. Steward to A. L. Kroeber, Feb. 11, 1928; Lowie to J. H. Steward, Feb. 13, 1928, RDA Box 141.

83. J. H. Steward to A. L. Kroeber, Feb. 11, 1928, RDA Box 141. The Hopi-Tewa, who are Tewa-speaking, live in two settlements at First Mesa. Their ancestors, refugees from the Pueblo Revolt of 1680, arrived at First Mesa by about 1700 (M. B. Stanislawski 1979:587, 600).

84. J. H. Steward to Thornhill, n.d. [ca. Apr. 1928], TA; Lowie to J. H. Steward, Mar. 12, 1928, RDA Box 141. A letter from Fletcher Corrigan, a clerk at Lorenzo Hubbell's trading post, to Steward, dated Feb. 25, 1928 (Hubbell Collection, Box 105, University of Arizona Library), suggests that he had already left by that date. Steward's later statement that he spent six weeks in "observations on the Powamu ceremony and following ceremonies" is an overestimate (J. H. Steward to Thomas, Jan. 6, 1930, PPGT Box 53).

85. A. L. Kroeber to Parsons, Mar. 13, 1928, RDA Box 118.

86. Beals 1979:11. A major detail that Nyswander (interview, 1998) remembered about the visit in spring 1928 was the privacy of their engagement. As a woman with a professional career, and who was divorced, she undoubtedly understood the importance of protecting herself from gossip about her personal life.

87. Hentoff 1968:58; Tolman 1932:42n.5.

88. Brodie 1981:86. I am grateful to Kirk Baddley, Archivist, University of Utah, for bringing Brodie's essay to my attention.

89. On race and culture in the history of anthropology, and Boas's writings, see Stocking (1969). Lowie published an article on eugenics in 1921 and one on racism years earlier (see Murphy 1972:34).

90. Parsons to A. L. Kroeber, Nov. 27, 1928, A. L. Kroeber to Parsons, Dec. 10, 1928, RDA Box 118; J. H. Steward 1931.

91. Virginia Heyer Young (interview), who had courses with Steward at Columbia University, found the data in the article very detailed and of high quality, but she regarded the topic as a rather surprising choice for him. Nyswander (interview, 1996) had no clear memory of Steward's work with the Hopi. That she had some influence is my own inference, based on her interests at the time and that others in his academic circle did not share them.

92. A. L. Kroeber to Strong, May 25, 1928, RDA Box 141.

93. J. H. Steward to Gifford, June 15, 1928, RDA Box 141; Service to J. H. Steward, Feb. 23, 1969; J. H. Steward to Beals, Mar. 11, 1969, JHS Box 3.

94. Cressman 1988:421. Cressman began to include women in his field crews in the late 1940s, when the presence of married women students (wives of returning war veterans) solved the problem of chaperonage. Cordell (1993:204) has suggested that "the problem of the mixed [gender] dig was not solely one of propriety," and that some excavation leaders excluded women in order to avoid assigning them supervisory positions in the field. See also Gero (1985).

95. J. H. Steward to A. L. Kroeber, June 30, 1928, RDA Box 141; Kahrl 1982:309. Supporters of the Watterson brothers regarded them as casualties of the water war, not criminals seeking illegal financial gain.

96. J. H. Steward to A. L. Kroeber, July 26, 1928, RDA Box 141; J. H. Steward 1933:341, plates 1e, 5g. For informants' names and ages, see J. H. Steward (1933:233–34). Two of the men, Tom Stone and Andrew Glenn, served again as informants in Steward's 1935 fieldwork (see chap. 8). Captain Harry seemed very old to the students at Deep Springs, but his age may have been less than ninety (see n.97 below). Mary Harry's age is also open to question. Steward estimated it as eighty-five both in 1928 (J. H. Steward 1933:234) and seven years later (JJJS I, May 13, 1935).

97. J. H. Steward to Gifford, July 18 and 24, 1928, RDA Box 141; J. H. Steward 1934:423. Some of Steward's age estimates appear unusually high. He was trying to reconstruct life as it existed before contact in about 1861 and preferred to work with informants born before that time.

98. J. H. Steward 1934:423–24, 432. Life histories had grown rather popular in the 1920s; see Langness and Frank (1981:18–20) and Du Bois (1960:xii).

99. J. H. Steward to A. L. Kroeber, July 26, 1928, RDA Box 141.

100. J. H. Steward to A. L. Kroeber, July 26, 1928; A. L. Kroeber to J. H. Steward, July 31, 1928, RDA Box 141. See also J. H. Steward (1930).

101. J. H. Steward to A. L. Kroeber, July 26, 1928; A. L. Kroeber to J. H. Steward, July 31, 1928, RDA Box 141; Kroeber 1928:377.

102. Beals 1982:6–7. To a limited degree, Steward had also used observation in his previous research, at First Mesa, when he attended public performances of Powamu.

103. Murphy interview; Murphy 1977:24–25; J. H. Steward 1953a:318.

104. J. H. Steward 1933:325–30. Steward is still recognized as "principal ethnographer of the Owens Valley Paiute" (Liljelbad and Fowler 1986:412).

105. J. H. Steward 1934:424, 426n.2.

Chapter 5: From Far West to Midwest

1. Beals 1979:10; A. L. Kroeber to E. T. Hiller, Mar. 4, 1929, RDA Box 70. Forrest Clements (1900–1970) later taught at the University of Oklahoma, but eventually left the academic world to work as a consultant (Jacques Cattell Press 1968:281; Social Security Death Index).

2. Rowe 1978:655. The department's first master's degree was awarded to a woman, Louisa McDermott, in 1904 (Rowe 1962:397). According to Rowe (1978:653), before 1928 only four women had earned doctorates in anthropology. In that year, however, at least four more American women received Ph.D.s in the field: Anna Gayton (1899–1977) at Berkeley (Rowe 1978:655); Charlotte D.

Gower (1902–82) at the University of Chicago; (Winters 1991:105; Lepowsky 2000:130); Erna Gunther (1896–1982) at Columbia (Winters 1991:255); and Hortense Powdermaker (1896–1970) at the London School of Economics (Silverman 1989:292). Margaret Mead (1901–78) earned a doctorate from Columbia a year later, in 1929 (Jacques Cattell Press 1968:1075).

3. A. L. Kroeber to Frank R. Lillie, National Research Council, Aug. 8, 1928, RDA Box 112.

4. Griffin 1958:1477, 1976:170. Carl Eugen Guthe (1893–1974) earned his Ph.D. in 1917. He accepted a position with the University of Michigan in 1922 and spent most of his career there. Guthe helped to organize both the Society for American Archaeology and its journal, *American Antiquity*. He became director of the New York State Museum in 1944 (Griffin 1976:168, 172).

5. Gayton to Gifford, Aug. 11, 1928, A. L. Kroeber to Gayton, Sept. 7, 1928, RDA Box 59; A. L. Kroeber to Lillie, Aug. 8, 1928; Edith Elliott to A. L. Kroeber, Aug. 28, 1928, RDA Box 112.

6. J. H. Steward to A. L. Kroeber, Oct. 6, 1928; J. H. Steward to Lowie, Oct. 11, 1928, RDA Box 141. Beals (1979:10, 11) and others mistakenly give 1927 as the year Steward began teaching at the University of Michigan.

7. Leacock and Rothschild 1994:1, 7.

8. J. H. Steward to Strong, Sept. 28, [1928], WDS Box 14.

9. J. H. Steward to A. L. Kroeber, Oct. 6, 1928, A. L. Kroeber to J. H. Steward, Dec. 4, 1928, RDA Box 141; employment records, JHS Box 13.

10. J. H. Steward to A. L. Kroeber, Oct. 6 and Dec. 11, 1928, RDA Box 141; J. C. Steward interview. Omer Stewart remembered Steward, his teacher in the early 1930s at the University of Utah, as having "the ability to lecture as if from edited text" (Howell 1998:164). Columbia students also recalled him as a skilled speaker (Murphy interview; Mintz interview).

11. J. H. Steward to A. L. Kroeber, Oct. 6, 1928, RDA Box 141. Guthe (1951:440), in a later, official account of the department's origins, referred to failed attempts in the mid-1920s to organize a department. Given his record of success in professional organizing, it seems unlikely that the department's creation was in any sense unintended.

12. Mark 1980:43–51; A. L. Kroeber 1915; Rowe 1962:395–97. See also chap. 3, n.12 on the structure of the department.

13. T. Kroeber 1970:105–7; Winters 1991:364–65; Rowe 1962:397, 409. Kroeber underwent psychoanalysis during a year he spent in New York City and then maintained a practice as a lay psychoanalyst in San Francisco for a few years. He finally gave up his practice in favor of anthropology because he "was hard-headed enough to realize that without being an M.D. he wouldn't have real control, and that the subject he really controlled was anthropology" (Kroeber-Quinn 1982:91).

14. Kroeber-Quinn 1982:150, 174–75, 193. Hearst reportedly found Kroeber very difficult and expressed dissatisfaction about him to Putnam (Mark 1980:45). Kroeber was about twenty-six at the time; Theodora Krakow Brown met him when he was about fifty.

15. A. L. Kroeber to J. H. Steward, Oct. 11, 1928, RDA Box 141; Murphy interview.

16. A. L. Kroeber to J. H. Steward, Oct. 11, 1928, RDA Box 141.

17. Ibid.; J. H. Steward to Lowie, Oct. 11, 1928, RDA Box 141. Gayton has received credit as a pioneer in the "transition from a cultural to an ecological approach to Native American political organization" (Vincent 1990:180). Between 1930 and the 1940s, she published a series of works that, in Vincent's (1990:181–85) view, contributed to this transition. Gayton was not employed during most of this period, which put her in a kind of professional limbo. This may help to explain why she has not generally received recognition for her contributions.

18. A. L. Kroeber to Gayton, Sept. 7, 1928, RDA Box 59; Amoss 1989:134. Gayton's fellowship from the National Research Council supported her research on the Yokuts of the San Joaquin Valley, California. She did not seek an academic position for years after marrying Spier (Rowe 1978:653, 654).

19. Lila Morris O'Neale (1886–1948) taught in the department of household art, later named the department of decorative art, from the 1930s until her death (Harrison 1948; Schevill 1989:278). She was well known as the leading expert on prehistoric textiles of the Americas. Gayton also had

the respect of her colleagues. Shimkin (interview, 1989), who earned a Ph.D. in anthropology from Berkeley in the 1930s, remarked, "For overall creativity and intellectual ability, she was the best." He added, by way of explaining her professional situation at Berkeley, "That was a time when women were relegated to home economics." Gayton taught not in art history (e.g., Vincent 1990:180) but in decorative art.

20. J. H. Steward to Lowie, Oct. 11, 1928; J. H. Steward to Gifford, Oct. 13, 1928, RDA Box 141.

21. Lowie to J. H. Steward, Oct. 18, 1928; J. H. Steward to Gifford, Nov. 16, 1928; J. H. Steward to A. L. Kroeber, Nov. 25, 1928, RDA Box 141. Whether Steward chose this topic himself or, like Du Bois (Seymour 1989:73), had a dissertation topic assigned to him, is unclear.

22. J. H. Steward to A. L. Kroeber, Nov. 25, 1928; J. H. Steward to A. L. Kroeber, Dec. 1, 1928, RDA Box 141. Guthe worked with Kidder and Morley for several years after earning his Ph.D.; he had carried out ethnoarchaeological work at Kidder's Pecos, New Mexico, site several years earlier (Griffin 1976; R. H. Thompson 1991:18).

23. J. H. Steward to A. L. Kroeber, Jan. 14, 1929, RDA Box 141; J. H. Steward to Strong, Dec. 8, [1928], Jan. 13, 1929, WDS Box 14.

24. J. H. Steward to A. L. Kroeber, Jan. 14, 1929, RDA Box 141; J. H. Steward 1929a:493.

25. J. H. Steward to A. L. Kroeber, Dec. 11, 1928; J. H. Steward to Lowie, n.d. [ca. Apr. 15, 1929], RDA Box 141; J. H. Steward to Strong, Dec. 8, [1928], Apr. 17, 1929, WDS Box 14. On Lowie and diffusionist explanation, see Murphy (1972:48–49).

26. J. H. Steward to Strong, Dec. 8, [1928], Apr. 17, 1929, WDS Box 14; J. H. Steward 1929a. He considered "The Economic and Social Basis of Primitive Bands" (J. H. Steward 1936a) his "first major theoretical work" ("Autobiographical Appraisal," n.d., JHS Box 16). See chap. 8.

27. A. L. Kroeber to J. H. Steward, July 31, 1928, RDA Box 141; J. H. Steward 1930:153–55, 1933:248–50.

28. J. H. Steward 1938a:53. His 1949 article on the development of early civilizations argued for the repeated, independent invention of agriculture and irrigation in widely separated areas of the world (J. H. Steward 1949a). See chap. 10.

29. J. H. Steward 1930:152, 1970:123 (reprinted in J. H. Steward 1977:377); A. L. Kroeber to J. H. Steward, July 31, 1928, RDA Box 141. I am grateful to Catherine S. Fowler (interview) for explaining current views on irrigation by Owens Valley Paiute, especially in terms of the origins question. See also Liljeblad and Fowler (1986:417–18).

30. J. H. Steward, "Hunting as a Factor in the Evolution of Social Structures," n.d. [ca. 1966], typescript, JHS Box 6.

31. See, for example, Carneiro (1979:291–94) and Service (n.d.:25–26) on Steward's wavering position on state formation. Shimkin (interview) emphasized Steward's "thoroughgoing honesty" as a scholar, as did Murphy (1977:16; interview), who spoke of his having "a kind of old-fashioned honesty" about him. Steward's testimony in Indian Claims Commission cases later in his career angered many anthropologists, but most called it "misguided" rather than false (see chaps. 10 and 11). One of his greatest opponents recalled Steward saying in court that he had "changed his mind" about Indian territories (Howell 1998:165).

32. J. H. Steward to Lowie, Feb. 4, 1929, RDA Box 141.

33. Lowie to J. H. Steward, Apr. 29, 1929, RDA Box 141; program of dissertation defense, Sept. 10, 1929, JHS Box 13. Jane Steward (interview) emphasized Lowie's greater intellectual influence on her husband (see also Murphy 1980). In terms of Steward's career, however, the importance of Kroeber's patronage and counsel cannot be overestimated.

34. A. L. Kroeber to J. H. Steward, Apr. 30, 1929, RDA Box 141.

35. Drucker 1981:606; Gunther to J. H. Steward, Mar. 31, 1929, JHS Box 10; R. L. Olson 1933; J. H. Steward 1937b.

36. Gunther to J. H. Steward, Mar. 31, 1929, JHS Box 10.

37. J. H. Steward to A. L. Kroeber, May 5, 1929; J. H. Steward to Lowie, May 5, 1929, RDA Box 141.

38. Reich to J. H. Steward, Dec. 7, 1969, JHS Box 3; Reich interview.

39. Program of dissertation defense, Sept. 10, 1929, JHS Box 13. Steward variously referred to his trip in summer 1929 as a "collecting expedition to the Creek, Seminole and Choctaw Indians of Oklahoma" (J. H. Steward to Thomas, Jan. 9, 1930, PPGT Box 53) or to Cherokee and Seminole (J. H. Steward, record of research, 1926–36, JHS Box 13).

40. J. H. Steward to Miss Harris, n.d. [ca. June 1929], RDA Box 141; Nyswander interview, 1996.

41. Nyswander interview, 1997.

42. J. H. Steward to Strong, Oct. 30, 1929, WDS Box 14; program of dissertation defense, Sept. 10, 1929, JHS Box 13; Speth 1981:225; West 1979:25n.1. On the department of social institutions and Hodgen, see Nisbet (1981:75, 83). Hodgen, trained as an economist, joined the Berkeley faculty in 1925 (*Daily Californian,* Aug. 19, 1925, 1) and spent her career there.

43. Beals 1977:57–58. See Hooson (1981) on Sauer's scholarship and perspective, and Speth (1987) on the opposition between historicism and positivism.

44. J. H. Steward, "Autobiographical Appraisal," n.d., JHS Box 16; Manners 1973:889.

45. Samuel A. Barrett (1906), J. Alden Mason (1911), Strong (1926), Gayton (1928), and Clements (1928) earned the first five Ph.D.'s in anthropology awarded by the university.

46. J. H. Steward to A. L. Kroeber, Oct. 23, 1929, RDA Box 141; Nyswander to Thomas, July 6, 1929, PPGT Box 54; Nyswander interview, 1996; J. H. Steward, extension course, 1929, JHS Box 11.

47. McElvaine 1984:46–48.

48. J. H. Steward, n.d. [ca. 1937], U.S. Civil Service Commission records, JHS Box 13; J. H. Steward, HRMF; J. H. Steward to A. L. Kroeber, Jan. 14, 1929, RDA Box 141.

49. A. L. Kroeber to J. H. Steward, Jan. 25, 1929, RDA Box 141; J. H. Steward to Strong, Feb. 25, 1929, WDS Box 14.

50. Solecki and Wagley 1963:1103; Willey 1988:79; Strong to J. H. Steward, Feb. 27, 1929, JHS Box 10.

51. Carlisle 1983; Willey 1988:79; Solecki and Wagley 1963:1106. Loren Eiseley (1907–77) studied at the University of Pennsylvania and spent most of his career there. Waldo R. Wedel (1908–96) had a career with the Smithsonian Institution (Willey 1988:79; Jacques Cattell Press 1968:1692; Social Security Death Index).

52. Winters 1991:672–73; Strong 1933.

53. J. H. Steward to Strong, Feb. 25, 1929, WDS Box 14; J. H. Steward to Lowie, Mar. 16, 1929, RDA Box 141.

54. J. H. Steward to A. L. Kroeber, Nov. 21, 1929, RDA Box 141. Andrew Affleck Kerr (1877–1929) had earned a Ph.D. from Harvard in 1921 (Kerr, HRMF). On Edgar L. Hewett (1865–1946), see Walter (1947).

55. Hewett to Thomas, Nov. 3, 1929; Thomas to Hewett, Nov. 6, 1929, PPGT Box 53.

56. J. H. Steward to Thomas, July 2, 1930, PPGT Box 56; Knobloch 1989:176. The notice appeared in 1930 in the *American Anthropologist* 32:588.

57. Nyswander interview, 1996. See also Nyswander (1994:76–77, 80–81).

58. J. H. Steward to A. L. Kroeber, Nov. 21, 1929, RDA Box 141.

59. A. L. Kroeber to J. H. Steward, Nov. 26, 1929, RDA Box 141.

60. Amoss 1989:134. Spier taught at the University of Oklahoma for two years, from 1927 to 1929 (Basehart and Hill 1965:1259; Winters 1991:658). Correspondence suggests that he then struggled with unemployment and marginal employment for several years (e.g., A. L. Kroeber to Stirling, Feb. 5, 1931, RDA Box 142). Obituaries and biographical profiles of Spier are generally silent about this.

61. Nyswander, official personnel folder, NPRC.

62. A. L. Kroeber to J. H. Steward, Nov. 26, 1929, RDA Box 141.

63. Thomas to J. H. Steward, Dec. 6, 1929; J. H. Steward to Thomas, Dec. 11, 1929; Thomas to J. H. Steward, Dec. 21, 1929, PPGT Box 53.

64. J. H. Steward to Thomas, Dec. 30, 1929, PPGT Box 53; J. H. Steward to Lowie, Apr. 27, [1930], RDA Box 141. His twelve-hour course load at Michigan was not unusual for the times.

65. Thomas to J. H. Steward, Jan. 21, 1930, PPGT Box 53.

66. Thomas to J. H. Steward, Feb. 11, 1930, J. H. Steward to Thomas, Feb. 16, 1930, PPGT Box 53; A. L. Kroeber to J. H. Steward, Nov. 26, 1929, RDA Box 141; board of regents to J. H. Steward, June 19, 1930, JHS Box 13; Rowe 1962:397; Nyswander, HRMF. The fact that Dorothy Nyswander had just been promoted to full professor in 1929 may also have influenced the rank given to her new husband.

67. Beals 1979:11.

68. Lowie to J. H. Steward, Feb. 21, 1930, RDA Box 141.

69. J. H. Steward to Lowie, Apr. 12, 1930, RDA Box 141.

70. J. H. Steward to Lowie, Apr. 27, [1930], RDA Box 141. Kelly, Gayton, Clements, Strong, and Theodora Brown (Kroeber) had earned their undergraduate degrees at Berkeley. O'Neale and Olson held bachelor's degrees from, respectively, Stanford University and the University of Washington.

71. On fears of feminization in academia and attempts to segregate women, see Rosenberg (1982), Fitzpatrick (1990), and Nerad (1999).

72. I am not suggesting that this was a conscious ploy, but that these practices did evolve in response to a perceived problem. The pattern itself is clear in records that I have examined and in career trajectories as reported in biographical profiles.

73. Kroeber-Quinn 1982:66–67, 99; J. H. Steward 1961b:1047.

74. Steward's correspondence contains negative comments about Mead, made by him and by male colleagues. Given the highly competitive structure of academic anthropology, backbiting remarks are rather common in professional correspondence. Mead, however, was one of the few women prominent enough in the field to attract even that sort of notice from her male peers.

75. See Parezo (1993) on anthropology's reputation as a "welcoming science" for women.

76. Cole, Dixon, and Kidder 1929a, 1929b.

77. I am grateful to Willow Powers, Laboratory of Anthropology, for providing copies of this correspondence between Parsons and Kroeber in spring 1929. These letters, and related ones by other parties, are quoted in some detail by Deacon (1997:262–64).

78. J. H. Steward to Lowie, Apr. 27, [1930], May 15, 1930, RDA Box 141. According to William Peace (n.d.:12), the university almost hired Charlotte Gower, although administrators disliked the prospect of having a woman in a full-time faculty position. On Gower, see n.2 above.

79. J. H. Steward to Lowie, Apr. 27, [1930], May 15, 1930, RDA Box 141; Griffin 1976:171. Leslie White (1900–1975) remained at Michigan for forty years, from 1930 until his retirement in 1970 (Service 1976:612). On White's political views and activities, see Peace (1993).

80. Years later, Steward wrote that he "gave the first courses in anthropology" at Michigan ("Autobiographical Appraisal," n.d., JHS Box 16; see also Manners 1973:889 and Murphy 1977:5). Steward apparently taught the first regularly scheduled courses in ethnology. The university offered instruction in archaeology as early as 1892 (Griffin 1958:1476). In the early 1920s, a Colonel Thomas Callan Hodson held a one-year appointment as special lecturer in anthropology, and taught courses in ethnology, as well as general anthropology ("Supplementary Announcement, 1923–24," UM Box 1). I am grateful to Tom Hyry (Bentley Library, University of Michigan, personal communication, Jan. 9, 1997) for bringing Hodson's appointment to my attention, and to Catharine Dann for assistance with research on Steward's years at Michigan.

81. Program, annual meeting of the Michigan Academy of Science, 1929, MAS Box 7; J. H. Steward to Lowie, Mar. 16, 1929; Lowie to J. H. Steward, Mar. 21, 1929, RDA Box 141. On Sapir's (1884–1939) life and career, see Darnell (1990).

82. J. H. Steward 1929a, 1929b, 1930; J. H. Steward to A. Wetmore, n.d. [ca. 1954], JHS Box 6; J. H. Steward to John Chance, Mar. 23, 1969, JHS Box 3.

83. J. H. Steward to Lowie, Apr. 27, [1930]; J. H. Steward to A. L. Kroeber, n.d. [June 1930], RDA Box 141. Nyswander (interview, 1996) remembered the Dodge, a step up from the Chevrolet Steward drove in Berkeley, as a joint purchase and also an extravagance, given their academic salaries.

Chapter 6: The Utah Years

1. Nyswander interview, 1996; Salt Lake City directory, 1930, 1931.

2. Beals 1977:76, 1979:11; Benson 1996:44–49; Brodie 1981; Howell 1998:29. Steward later complained about the Mormon influence on university life (J. C. Steward interview), but Nyswander (personal communication, Oct. 20, 1996) denied that it ever constrained her or her former husband: "We had all the freedom we wanted to do our work," she said.

3. J. H. Steward to A. L. Kroeber, n.d. [June 1930], RDA Box 141; J. H. Steward to Pres. George Thomas, June 2, 1930, PPGT Box 56.

4. J. H. Steward to Thomas, July 2, 1930; Thomas to C. G. Abbot, July 2, 1930, PPGT Box 56.

5. Abbot to Thomas, July 8, 1930; Thomas to Abbot, n.d. [ca. May 1931], PPGT Box 56; J. H. Steward to A. L. Kroeber, n.d. [June 1930], RDA Box 141.

6. J. H. Steward, "Archaeological Reconnaissance by the University of Utah, 1930 Field Season," n.d. [ca. Jan./Feb. 1931], PPGT Box 56.

7. Program of Uintah Basin Indian Conference, Aug. 6–8, 1930; Marshall to Thomas, June 24, 1931, PPGT Box 63.

8. Hentoff 1968:59. Marie Nyswander (1919–86) was widely recognized for her pioneering use of methadone in treating heroin addiction (see Hentoff 1968; Kolbert 1986). On women's education and social activism during the Progressive Era (1890–1920), see Gordon (1990).

9. J. H. Steward to A. L. Kroeber, n.d. [June 1930], J. H. Steward to A. L. Kroeber, Oct. 3, 1930, RDA Box 141; Nyswander interviews, 1996, 1997.

10. Hentoff 1968:59; Nyswander interview, 1997.

11. Nyswander interview, 1997. Marie Nyswander died in New York City of cancer in 1986. In her last conversation with her mother, she recalled that desert scene.

12. Nyswander interviews, 1996, 1997, 1998; Nyswander, personal communication, June 30, 1996.

13. J. H. Steward to A. L. Kroeber, Oct. 3, 1930, RDA Box 141; Nyswander, personal communication, Aug. 7, 1996.

14. Domhoff 1986:36, 39–40; Howell 1998:28; Nyswander interview, 1998.

15. *Utah Chronicle,* Feb. 13, 1931, 1.

16. Howell 1998:28–29. Omer Stewart (1908–91) later earned a Ph.D. in anthropology at Berkeley. For his memories of the Promontory Point excavation, see Howell (1998:28–29). Some of the dates he mentions in reference to Steward and the excavation are incorrect. See Janetski (1999) for an appraisal of Steward's archaeological work in Utah. See also J. H. Steward 1955a.

17. J. H. Steward, "Archaeological Reconnaissance by the University of Utah, 1930 Field Season," n.d., [ca. Jan./Feb. 1931], PPGT Box 56; J. H. Steward to A. L. Kroeber, Oct. 3, 1930, RDA Box 141; *Utah Chronicle,* Feb. 17, 1930, 3.

18. J. H. Steward to A. L. Kroeber, Oct. 3, 1930, RDA Box 141; J. H. Steward, "Archaeological Reconnaissance by the University of Utah, 1930 Field Season," n.d. [ca. Jan./Feb. 1931], PPGT Box 56.

19. J. H. Steward to A. L. Kroeber, Oct. 3, 1930; J. H. Steward to Gifford, Mar. 18, 1931, RDA Box 141; J. H. Steward 1937b. On his 1934 travels, see chap. 7.

20. J. H. Steward to A. L. Kroeber, Dec. 10, 1930, RDA Box 141.

21. Ibid.; J. H. Steward, "Archaeological Reconnaissance by the University of Utah, 1930 Field Season," n.d. [ca. Jan./Feb. 1931], PPGT Box 56. According to records of the Utah Museum of Natural History in Salt Lake City, Neil Judd (1887–1976) carried out archaeological research in Utah from 1907 until about 1920.

22. J. H. Steward to A. L. Kroeber, Dec. 10, 1930, RDA Box 141; *Utah Chronicle,* Feb. 17, 1931, 3.

23. J. H. Steward, "Archaeological Reconnaissance by the University of Utah, 1930 Field Season," [ca. Jan./Feb. 1931], PPGT Box 56; J. H. Steward to A. L. Kroeber, Dec. 10, 1930, RDA Box 141.

24. *Utah Chronicle,* Feb. 13, 1931, 1; *Salt Lake Tribune,* June 1, 1931.

25. Thomas to C. G. Abbot, Mar. 17, 1931; W. A. C. Rammel to Thomas, Mar. 26, 1931, PPGT, Box 56; J. H. Steward to Gifford, Mar. 18, Apr. 17, 1931, RDA Box 141.

26. J. C. Steward interview; Nyswander interview, 1996.

27. Salt Lake City directory, 1931; J. C. Steward interview; registrar, University of Utah, personal communication, Aug. 13, 1993.

28. Salt Lake City directory, 1930, 1931, 1932; Poll 1978:206, 309; J. C. Steward interview.

29. J. C. Steward interview; J. H. Steward 1932; *Utah Chronicle,* Apr. 14, 1931, 3.

30. *Utah Chronicle,* Apr. 14, 1931, 3; University of Utah, Museum Accession Records, vol. 2, Whiterocks, Mar. 1931 (courtesy of Anne Hannibal, curator, Utah Museum of Natural History); J. H. Steward 1932.

31. Nyswander (interview, 1996) remembered visiting the reservation at least three times in Steward's company.

32. Thomas to John H. Edwards, Apr. 29, 1931, PPGT Box 56; *Salt Lake Tribune,* June 1, 1931.

33. J. H. Steward to Gifford, Apr. 17, 1931; A. L. Kroeber to J. H. Steward, June 15, 1931, RDA Box 141; Buzaljko 1989:189; T. Kroeber 1970:139–40.

34. Thomas to Peterson, June 25, 1931, PPGT Box 63; Strong to A. L. Kroeber, July 2, 1931, RDA Box 141; Beals 1979:9–10; Nyswander, personal communication, Aug. 25, 1996.

35. Nyswander, personal communication, Aug. 25, 1996.

36. J. H. Steward to A. L. Kroeber, July 7, 1931, RDA Box 141; J. H. Steward 1937a:3; Janetski 1999:25; Thomas to Abbot, Mar. 17, 1931, PPGT Box 56.

37. J. H. Steward to Gifford, Nov. 5, 1931; J. H. Steward to A. L. Kroeber, Nov. 27, 1931, RDA Box 141; Nyswander, personal communication, June 30, 1996. Her words about boundaries were not inspired in hindsight by postmodernist trends in social science, but rather recalled her long experience of collaborating with colleagues in other disciplines.

38. Nyswander interview, 1996; Nyswander, personal communication, June 29, 1996.

39. Caffrey 1989; Du Bois 1980:2; L. J. Friedman 1999; J. H. Steward to Gifford, Nov. 5, 1931, RDA Box 141.

40. Thomas to Duncan, Oct. 8, 1931, PPGT Box 60; J. H. Steward to A. L. Kroeber, Nov. 27, 1931, RDA Box 141.

41. J. C. Steward interview; Beals 1979:11.

42. The monograph on mythology (J. H. Steward 1936b) finally reached print six years after he first submitted it. The "objectivist" shift is not entirely clear in Steward's publication record because of such delays.

43. Nyswander interview, 1996. As she put it, in research with human subjects "the quality of the data may depend on the quality of the personal inter-relationships," and not only on the rigor of methodology (Nyswander 1994:281).

44. J. H. Steward to Gifford, Nov. 5, 1931; J. H. Steward to A. L. Kroeber, Nov. 27, 1931, RDA Box 141; J. H. Steward to Suhr, Nov. 16, 1931, DSC.

45. J. H. Steward to Suhr (enclosure), Nov. 16, 1931, DSC.

46. J. H. Steward to A. L. Kroeber, Jan. 13, 1932; A. L. Kroeber to J. H. Steward, Jan. 15, 1932, RDA Box 141.

47. Later correspondence alludes to their conversation at Ogden (e.g., J. H. Steward to R. L. Olson, Feb. 10, 1932, J. H. Steward to A. L. Kroeber, June 21, 1932, RDA Box 141).

48. J. H. Steward to E. M. Johnson, n.d. [Feb. 1932]; Johnson to J. H. Steward, Mar. 11, 1932; J. H. Steward to Johnson, May 21, 1932, TA; *Telluride News Letter* 17, no. 6 (1932): 1, 7; J. C. Steward interview.

49. K. W. Buckley 1989. On Alexander Goldenweiser's employment problems, see Deacon (1997:432n.13).

50. J. H. Steward to R. L. Olson, Feb. 10, 1932; R. L. Olson to J. H. Steward, Mar. 30, 1932, RDA Box 141; Drucker 1981; Amoss 1989:134.

51. Nyswander interviews, 1996, 1997; Nyswander, personal communication, June 30, 1996.

52. J. C. Steward interview. Despite the Mormon prohibition of alcohol, and legal prohibition during this period, speakeasies flourished in Salt Lake City as in other large American cities. Wallace Stegner's father bootlegged and ran a speakeasy from home during the 1920s (Benson 1996:15).

53. J. C. Steward interview.

54. J. H. Steward to A. L. Kroeber, June 21, 1932, RDA Box 141.

55. Beals 1977:76; Howell 1998:31–33.

56. Rowe 1978:654. Unpublished letters provide evidence of Spier's employment problems during the 1930s; published sources simply list his academic affiliations. Kroeber wrote to many colleagues on Spier's behalf (see, for example, Kroeber to Stirling, Feb. 5, 1931, RDA Box 142). Boas also recommended him for a position in 1931 (Parezo 1993:36n.16). Spier obtained a permanent position at the University of New Mexico in 1939 (Basehart and Hill 1965:1259).

57. On Marshall Saville (1867–1935) and George Heye (1874–1956), see Willey (1988:198) and Lothrop (1957). On Samuel K. Lothrop (1892–1965), see Willey (1988:194–216) and Winters (1991:424–25). Saville was appointed Loubat Professor at Columbia in 1903 (McVicker 1992:149; D. Cole 1999:232–33). He was on the staff of the Museum of the American Indian, Heye Foundation, from 1918 to 1932 (Cattell and Cattell 1933:975; Marquis 1942:1082).

58. J. H. Steward to A. L. Kroeber, June 21, 1932, RDA Box 141.

59. J. H. Steward to Strong, Jan. 24, 1933, WDS Box 14.

60. J. C. Steward interview.

61. Nyswander interviews, 1996, 1997.

62. J. C. Steward interview; Nyswander interview, 1996; J. H. Steward to A. L. Kroeber, June 21, 1932, RDA Box 141.

63. J. H. Steward, "An Archaeological Reconnaissance of Glen Canyon on the Colorado River," n.d. [1932], JHS Box 10. Steward identified the river as the Fremont. Maps today show the place where he began his river journey as the confluence of the Dirty Devil and the Colorado Rivers, with a tributary called the Fremont River flowing into the Dirty Devil.

64. J. H. Steward, "An Archaeological Reconnaissance of Glen Canyon on the Colorado River," n.d. [1932], JHS Box 10; J. H. Steward 1941a:282. Nyswander (personal communication, Aug. 7, 1996) remembered Kelly as the owner of a printing company and a "Mormon-hater [who] wrote books expressing it." She found much to admire about Mormon family life and avoided discussing Mormons or Mormonism with him.

65. J. H. Steward, "An Archaeological Reconnaissance of Glen Canyon on the Colorado River," n.d. [1932], JHS Box 10. The Capitol Reef region is now a national park.

66. Ibid.

67. Steward and his companions thought that Glen Canyon should be made a national park (ibid.) Instead, Lake Powell, 186 miles in length, and the land immediately surrounding it are now designated the Glen Canyon National Recreation Area. See Worster (1985:272–74) on dams and the "death of the Colorado River."

68. Thomas to secretary of the interior, May 31, 1932, PPGT Box 60; J. H. Steward 1941a:282. *Riders of the Purple Sage* is believed to have been set in the area east of Kanab, Utah (see May 1997; Kimball 1993).

69. J. H. Steward to A. L. Kroeber, June 21, 1932, RDA Box 141; *Telluride News Letter* 9, no. 3 (Dec. 1932): 1; Nyswander, personal communication, June 29, 1996.

70. Jenson 1901, 1:50, 51; Jardine 1967:321, 325, 337; J. C. Steward interview. According to Jenson, George Q. Cannon had four wives and twenty-four children; Jardine, a descendant, set the number at five wives and thirty-three children. Joseph J. Cannon, Jane Steward's father, was born to the second wife. He was listed in the Salt Lake City directory as editor of the *Deseret News* from 1931 through 1934.

71. J. C. Steward interview; R. Cannon 1981. Ramona W. Cannon (1887–1979) seemed to have a gift for offering good advice in troubling circumstances; after her children were grown she wrote a very popular advice column for the *Deseret News* for nearly thirty years. She also published

magazine articles on a variety of topics. I am grateful to Kirk Baddley for providing me with copies of her writings.

72. J. H. Steward to Strong, Jan. 24, 1933, WDS Box 14. Radin may have supported himself by tutoring students in German, as he did before and after this period (Du Bois 1960:xiii; Howell 1998:34). At this very point in time, Kroeber sent a formal statement to applicants for graduate study, warning them about the very poor employment prospects (see chap. 7).

73. McElvaine 1984:93–94, 134; J. H. Steward to Thomas, Nov. 17, 1932, PPGT Box 64; J. H. Steward to Strong, Jan. 24, 1933, WDS Box 14; M. Steward, official personnel folder, NPRC; Nyswander interview, 1996. Marion Steward worked on a temporary basis for Remington Rand and other employers during the next two years.

74. J. H. Steward to Thomas, Oct. 20, 1932, PPGT Box 64.

75. J. H. Steward to Strong, Jan. 24, 1933, WDS Box 14.

76. Thomas to J. H. Steward, Oct. 27, 1932, PPGT Box 64. Both Nyswander (interview, 1996) and Jane Steward (interview) recalled that Steward simply never mentioned his father.

77. Nyswander to Thomas, Nov. 10, 1932, PPGT Box 64; Nyswander interview, 1996; Nyswander, personal communication, Aug. 25, 1996; Hentoff 1968:60–61.

78. J. H. Steward to Thomas, Nov. 17, 1932; Thomas to J. H. Steward, Dec. 27, 1932; J. H. Steward to Thomas, Jan. 5, 1933, PPGT Box 64. Nyswander told me that she knew nothing about the president's letter to Steward urging a reconciliation or his decision to force the resignation (personal communication, Aug. 7, 1996).

79. J. H. Steward to A. L. Kroeber, Jan. 31, 1933; A. L. Kroeber to J. H. Steward, Feb. 7, 1933; A. L. Kroeber to fellowship committee, Aug. 21, 1932; A. L. Kroeber to William J. Robbins, Mar. 17, 1933, RDA Box 141.

80. J. H. Steward to A. L. Kroeber, Mar. 21, 1933; A. L. Kroeber to J. H. Steward, Apr. 5, 1933, RDA Box 141.

81. Student petition re: J. H. Steward, Apr. 14, 1933, BRMM; Thomas to J. H. Steward, June 8, 1933, PPGT Box 64.

82. J. H. Steward to A. L. Kroeber, Apr. 21, 1933, RDA Box 141; J. H. Steward to Thomas, June 7, 1933, PPGT Box 64.

83. A. L. Kroeber to J. H. Steward, May 5, 1933, RDA Box 141. Rosenberg may also have been a benefactor of Marion Steward. She worked for the firm of Rosenberg Brothers on a temporary basis in 1929 or 1930, after losing a secretarial position due to the stock market crash (M. Steward, official personnel folder, NPRC).

84. J. H. Steward to Thomas, June 7, 1933; Thomas to J. H. Steward, June 8, 1933, PPGT Box 64. Elmer Smith (1909–60), an archaeologist who had trained at the University of Utah under Kerr and Steward, was hired in 1937, four years after Steward resigned (Dibble 1960:1047).

85. J. H. Steward to Thomas, June 23, 1933, PPGT Box 64.

86. Nyswander interviews, 1996, 1998; Nyswander, personal communication, Aug. 25, 196; Nyswander 1994:257; Nyswander, official personnel folder, NPRC; McElvaine 1984:255, 265.

87. Nyswander, HRMF; Nyswander interview, 1996.

88. Published reports on his Utah research include J. H. Steward (1936c, 1937a, 1941a). Steward occupied an unusual bridge position in midcentury anthropology (Willey 1988:219), as shown by his inclusion in Willey's collection of biographical profiles of Americanist archaeologists.

89. Nyswander interviews, 1996, 1997.

90. Nyswander interview, 1996; Nyswander, personal communication, Aug. 7, 1996. She was agnostic during those years; later in life she attended a Unitarian church.

91. Steward once mentioned his first marriage to his student Sidney Mintz (see chap. 10), but cast himself as the injured party who paid a high price for marrying a professional woman. Neither Steward's official records nor his obituaries contain any mention of his first marriage ("Dr. Julian Steward, Anthropologist, 70," *New York Times*, Feb. 8, 1972, 36; J. H. Steward obituaries, JHS Box 16).

Chapter 7: Southwestern Sights

1. J. C. Steward interview. In official records, Steward listed only his October 1933 marriage.

2. A. L. Kroeber to J. H. Steward, July 18, 1933; J. H. Steward to A. L. Kroeber, Oct. 3, 1933; A. L. Kroeber to J. H. Steward, Oct. 5, 1933, RDA Box 141.

3. J. C. Steward interview.

4. J. H. Steward to Elmer Johnson, Nov. 6, 1933; Breiseth and Edmonston 1987:257, DSC; Hart 1987:126. Albert Mussey Johnson (1872–1948) served as president and chairman of the board of the National Life Insurance Company (Marquis 1950:282). Evidently, Johnson and Walter Scott (1872–1954) hoped to convince investors that gold could be mined around Scotty's Castle. The structure, which still stands, is a well-known tourist site in Death Valley.

5. J. H. Steward to Johnson, Nov. 6, 1933, TA.

6. [A. L. Kroeber] to SSRC, Dec. 28, 1933; A. L. Kroeber to Donald Young, SSRC [Jan. 1934], RDA Box 141; A. L. Kroeber to J. H. Steward, Apr. 30, 1937, JHS Box 13. Kroeber probably alluded to his published, but brief, comments on the importance of giving attention to ecology (A. L. Kroeber 1928:377). An undated and typed copy of those comments is filed among Steward's papers (JHS Box 7).

7. J. H. Steward, "Autobiographical Appraisal," n.d., JHS Box 16. For later references to his research plan, see J. H. Steward to Strong, Feb. 3, [1946], WDS Box 14; J. H. Steward to Grant Cannon, Apr. 1, 1953, JHS Box 13.

8. J. H. Steward 1928a.

9. Willey 1988:239; Willey interview.

10. J. C. Steward interview. She could not say exactly when this incident took place, but Steward's own reference to it suggests that it dated from his years in graduate school (J. H. Steward to Speth, Sept. 8, 1970, JHS Box 3).

11. Mount Tamalpais, the tallest summit in the area, rises to about twenty-six hundred feet, a mere hill in comparison to the towering Sierra peaks that Steward knew so well. As I saw in the late 1990s, much of the once open land has been swallowed up by development, and air quality has declined so much that the Sierra Nevada is often not visible.

12. J. C. Steward interview; Solecki and Wagley 1963:1105, 1106.

13. J. C. Steward interview; J. C. Steward to Elizabeth [Cannon] and Frank Haymond [1934], JHS Box 10; record of research, JHS Box 13.

14. JJJS I, Apr. 29, 1934 (entry by J. H. Steward); J. C. Steward interview. Wages for CWA workers averaged about fifteen dollars a week (McElvaine 1984:153–54), or less than forty cents an hour.

15. J. C. Steward interview. On Hall, see Christenson (1987:4) and Rider (1927:382–83).

16. JJJS I, May 1, 1934; J. C. Steward interview. Because of limitations of space, this chapter provides only a summary account of Steward's travels in the Southwest.

17. Winters 1991:129–30; JJJS I, May 7–13, 1934; Willey 1988:3; J. H. Steward, "Autobiographical Appraisal," n.d., JHS Box 16. Byron Cummings (1860–1954) taught at the University of Utah from 1893 to 1915 (Cummings, HRMF), and then at the University of Arizona.

18. JJJS I, May 13–14, 1934. On Colton (1881–1970), see "Dr. Harold Sellers Colton, 1881–1970" (1971:146–47) and Judd (1968:129).

19. JJJS I, May 14, 1934 (entry by J. C. Steward); Dick and Schroeder 1968:3.

20. Elliott 1995:200–203; Hargrave 1935:20. In the early 1930s, Lyndon L. Hargrave (1896–1978) served as chief archaeologist for the Rainbow Bridge/Monument Valley expedition (see below), organized by Hall (Christenson 1987:19; Howell 1998:30; Dick and Schroeder 1968:3; Social Security Death Index).

21. Elliott 1995:200–203; J. H. Steward, "A Study of Ute Economic Life," Mar. 28, 1935, JHS Box 13; J. H. Steward 1938a:2, 260; Dick and Schroeder 1968:4. Steward used the term *human ecology* in his proposal and in publications (e.g., J. H. Steward 1940:445) but eventually dropped it, later ex-

plaining that sociologists had already used it in a different sense (e.g., J. H. Steward to Speth, Sept. 8, 1970, JHS Box 3).

22. JJJS I, May 23, 1934; J. H. Steward to Stirling, Jan. 24, 1933, BAE Box 83; see also J. H. Steward to Strong, Jan. 24, 1933, WDS Box 14. By 1934 he had collected for three university museums (California, Michigan, and Utah); he later collected for the Heye Foundation, Harvard's Peabody Museum, and the BAE (see chaps. 8 and 9).

23. JJJS I, May 23–27, 1934 (entries by J. C. and J. H. Steward).

24. JJJS I, May 28 and May 31, 1934 (entries by J. C. Steward). On Alfred V. Kidder (1885–1963), see Givens (1992). Jesse L. Nusbaum (1887–1975) served as the first director of the Laboratory, from 1931 to 1935 (Toulouse 1981:12, 13). See also Stocking (1981).

25. JJJS I, June 2–3, 1934 (entries by J. C. Steward); Judd 1968:119, 125. Earl H. Morris (1889–1956) spent most of his career at the University of Colorado Museum (Winters 1991:485–86). For a summary of his work at Aztec Ruin, see Elliott (1995:56–77).

26. JJJS I, June 3–4, 1934 (entries by J. C. Steward); Elliott 1995:15, 16.

27. JJJS I, June 4, 1934.

28. Arrington 1986:248–49, 252; J. C. Steward interview.

29. Wolf based that statement on his experience of working with Steward in the late 1940s and early 1950s. Specifically, he doubted that Steward ever read Marx (J. Friedman 1987:110). Conversations with students who did so, however, may have had some influence on Steward's thinking.

30. JJJS I, June 5–8, 1934.

31. JJJS I, May 12–13, 1934; J. C. Steward interview. The Kroebers' house, constructed in 1906, was one of many in the Berkeley Hills designed by architect Bernard Maybeck, who helped shape the Bay Area architecture tradition. Built of untreated redwood, the house remained Kroeber's prized possession from the 1920s until his death in 1960 (T. Kroeber 1970:136; Keeler 1976:viii).

32. M. Steward, official personnel folder, NPRC; JJJS I, Apr. 29, 1934 (entry by J. H. Steward), June 15, 1934 (entry by J. C. Steward); J. C. Steward interview.

33. JJJS I, June 16–20, 1934 (entries by J. C. Steward); Nyswander interview, 1996.

34. J. H. Steward 1936a; J. H. Steward, "Autobiographical Appraisal," n.d., JHS Box 16; "Ecological Aspects of Shoshoni Society," n.d. [1935], RDA 141). On the revised 1955 version of his 1936 essay, see chap. 11. As Bennett (1998:xiii) points out, the essay did not receive a great deal of attention until the late 1950s and 1960s.

35. Commentary on Steward's work usually contains only passing, if any, mention of the patrilineal band. See, for example, Murphy (1977).

36. J. H. Steward 1936a; Strong 1927, 1929; A. L. Kroeber 1925; Gifford 1918.

37. J. H. Steward 1936a:331, 334.

38. Ibid., 348n.3. On Koppers and the cultural-historical school, see below.

39. Ibid., 331, 333, 343.

40. Ibid., 338.

41. Ibid., 338, 342. See Kuper (1988) on well-known anthropologists—from Morgan in the nineteenth century to Lévi-Strauss in the twentieth—who created such theories. Steward's essay is not treated.

42. J. H. Steward 1936a:335, 336, 337, 344. Later research showed, for example, that some of the hunter-gatherers he classified as patrilineal and patrilocal were not (see Barnard 1983:196). Moreover, except for groups living in the subarctic and Arctic, most depended more heavily on plant foods, generally gathered by women, than on the animals hunted by men (see, for example, Lee 1979).

43. J. H. Steward 1936a:333, 1937b:90.

44. J. H. Steward to Strong, Jan. 24, 1933, WDS Box 14.

45. JJJS I, June 14–23, 1934 (entries by J. C. Steward); Willey 1988:223.

46. JJJS I, June 24, July 1 and 4, 1934 (entries by J. C. Steward); McElvaine 1984:226–27; J. C. Steward interview.

47. McElvaine 1984:227.

48. JJJS I, July 12–15, 1934 (entries by J. C. Steward).

49. JJJS I, July 15, 1934.

50. McElvaine 1984:176–78, 225; J. C. Steward interview.

51. J. C. Steward to Elizabeth [Cannon] and Frank Haymond, n.d. [1934], JHS Box 10; J. C. Steward interview.

52. J. C. Steward to Elizabeth [Cannon] and Frank Haymond, n.d. [1934], JHS Box 10; J. H. Steward to Johnson, Aug. 25, 1934, TA.

53. "World Ethnography" notes, 1934, JHS Box 10; Borgoras 1929. On Waldemar Borgoras (1865–1936), see Winters (1991:71–72).

54. JJJS I, Mar. 26, 1935 (entry by J. H. Steward); Howell 1998:38; J. C. Steward interview. On Olson, see Drucker (1981:606) and Heizer (1970:208). The well-known animosity between Stewart and Steward in later years may have had as much or more to do with these circumstances, and Stewart's perceived rejection (Howell 1998:26), than with their intellectual differences (Ronassen, Clemmer, and Rudden 1999:174). As Steward confided, he was trying to "keep my personal affairs under my hat" (J. H. Steward to Strong, Jan. 24, 1933, WDS Box 14).

55. J. C. Steward interview.

56. JJJS I, Mar. 26, 1935 (entry by J. H. Steward); M. Steward, official personnel folder, NPRC; Bauman and Coode 1988:181.

57. "Anthropological Examination," [Jan. 1935], JHS Box 10; "A Proposal for Research Concerning the Present Status of Indians," [1935], JHS Box 10; Nyswander interview, 1996; Nyswander, personal communication, June 29, 1996.

58. JJJS I, Mar. 26, 1935 (entry by J. H. Steward); "Anthropological Examination," Jan. 10, 1935, JHS Box 10; Lowie to SSRC, Jan. 24, 1935; Lowie to ACLS, Jan. 30, 1935; A. L. Kroeber to ACLS, Jan. 31, 1935, RDA Box 141.

59. JJJS I, Mar. 26, 1935 (entry by J. H. Steward); "49 Scholars Get Research Grants-in-Aid," *New York Herald Tribune,* Apr. 14, 1935.

60. J. H. Steward 1973:14; T. Kroeber 1970:165; Myers 1999. As Steward (1961b:1057) later described Kroeber's project, it "included 254 tribes and tribal subdivisions west of the Rocky Mountains. The lists ranged from 3,000 to 6,000 elements, the presence and absence of which were recorded for each local group." Steward's participation in the project appears to have been voluntary, though motivated by pressing financial need.

61. JJJS I, Mar. 26, 1935 (entry by J. H. Steward); "An Archaeological Reconnaissance of Glen Canyon on the Colorado River," JHS Box 10; Willey 1988:5.

62. Christenson 1987:4–6; Howell 1998:29–30, 33. The expedition ended after six field seasons, in summer 1938.

63. JJJS I, Mar. 26, 1935; J. C. Steward interview.

64. J. H. Steward, "A Study of Ute Economic Life," Mar. 28, 1935, JHS Box 13. See also J. H. Steward, "A Proposal for the Investigation of Pueblo Economic Culture," 1935, JHS Box 10.

65. Willey 1988:227, 236–37; J. H. Steward, "Ecological Aspects of Shoshoni Society," n.d., [1935], RDA Box 141; Shimkin 1964:4; Murphy 1977:5.

66. J. H. Steward 1937b, 1955c:151–72.

67. J. H. Steward 1937b:88, 1955c:155; R. L. Olson 1933; Lowie 1924; Lowie, "Biographical Data," Apr. 19, 1944, JHS Box 1. Hanc (1981:9) remarks on the "distant, coldly analytic voice" in Steward's writing. Steward's own comments in correspondence make it clear that he tried to achieve what he regarded as a scientific style.

68. J. H. Steward to Strong, Jan. 24, 1933, WDS Box 14. Heizer (1970:208) also remembered Kroeber as "difficult of access" during this period, but recalled that Olson "genuinely liked students" and spent time talking with them. On Spier's approach, see Basehart and Hill (1965:1269) and W. Taylor (1963:379–80).

69. J. H. Steward to Lowie, Apr. 20, 1935, and May 18, 1935, RHL Box 13; Lowie 1959:189, 190; J. H. Steward 1936a:348n.3, 1937b:90n.23, 1955c:156n.4. Wilhelm Koppers (1886–1961), a Roman Catholic priest and anthropologist, taught at the University of Vienna at the time (Winters 1991:359). He was a close associate of Wilhelm Schmidt (1858–1954), who was also a Roman Catholic priest (Winters 1991:619).

70. Steward reportedly told Manners (1973:890) and other students that several journals rejected this paper and the one on bands "'because of their novelty.'" I have not found documentary evidence of multiple submissions.

71. Goldschmidt 1986:949; Beals 1982:8–11.

72. Knobloch 1989:173–74.

73. Howell 1998:31. The aspiring student was Omer Stewart.

74. Kroeber's statement is reproduced in Howell (1998:32–33). A copy is in the Omer C. Stewart Collection, housed at the University of Colorado Archives, but its location in his papers is currently uncertain. Only a preliminary finding guide is available (David M. Hays, archivist, University of Colorado Archives, personal communication, Apr. 11, 2000).

75. For example, Stewart received a copy of the statement in January 1933 (Howell 1998:31) and was not dissuaded from entering the graduate program.

76. JJJS I, Mar. 26, 1935.

77. J. C. Steward interview. On the Christian Science view of fear and illness, see chap. 1, n.74.

78. J. C. Steward interview; JJJS I, Mar. 26, 1935 (entry by J. H. Steward); M. Steward, official personnel folder, NPRC; Dorothy Nyswander, official personnel folder, NPRC.

79. According to McElvaine (1984:183), "Women lost proportionately fewer jobs than men precisely because their types of employment were *not* considered interchangeable." Positions held almost exclusively by women—in primary education, domestic service, and the clerical and secretarial sector—remained available to them "regardless of how many men were out of work." See also Himmelberg (2001:70), who notes that the number of employed women actually increased as the need for clerical workers grew.

80. McElvaine 1984:183; M. Steward, official personnel folder, NPRC.

81. J. C. Steward interview; McElvaine 1984:153–54; JJJS I, June 24, 1934, Mar. 26, 1935; M. Steward, official personnel folder, NPRC.

82. Jane Steward and her husband both cast "Marion's problem" in strictly emotional terms. A close examination of the material dimensions—Marion Steward's employment history, summarized above—led me to the conclusion that the emotional *and* financial difficulties she faced as a single woman and provider, during the depression and for much of her working life, were inseparable and mutually reinforcing.

83. J. C. Steward interview; JJJS I, Mar. 26, 1935 (entry by J. H. Steward).

Chapter 8: Return to the High Desert

1. JJJS I, Apr. 13, 1935 (entry by J. H. Steward); J. H. Steward 1933. I have reconstructed Jane and Julian Steward's 1935 journey by drawing on their journal and letters written during those months; Jane Steward's memories (interview); my own observations at some of the sites they visited in eastern California, Nevada, and Utah; and descriptions of those sites provided by Julian Steward (1938a) and others who saw them in the 1930s (e.g., WPA 1939, 1940, 1941; Chalfant 1933; Baugh 1937). Due to space limitations, I can provide only an abbreviated account of Steward's Great Basin fieldwork in this chapter.

2. J. H. Steward to A. L. Kroeber, July 26, 1928, RDA Box 141; J. H. Steward 1941b:210; J. H. Steward to Murphy, Mar. 31, 1967, JHS Box 6.

3. Kahrl 1982:314; Chalfant 1933:406; Baugh 1937.

4. The school did not necessarily employ any women as cooks during this period; men and stu-

dents sometimes made up the kitchen staff. As traditionally defined in anthropology, the postmarital residence pattern at Deep Springs would be termed "neolocal," but that obscures an important feature, its male-centered quality.

5. JJJS I, Apr. 14–25, 1935; J. H. Steward to Lowie, Apr. 20, 1935, RHL Box 13; J. C. Steward interview. One of the first-year students in 1935 was Charles C. Collingwood (1917–85), who became a well-known foreign correspondent and broadcast journalist (J. C. Steward interview; Social Security Death Index).

6. JJJS I, Apr. 26–27, 1935. Steward (1941b:213, 214, 1938a:92) identified Hunter as "JH" and Patterson as "WP." All age estimates for informants are Steward's (1941b:212–14), as are spellings of names, unless the spelling in his journal differs from that in a published source (the latter taking precedence). For his specific comments about these two men and his other informants, identified only by their initials, see Steward (1941b:212–14). For a reexamination of Steward's data from Death Valley and surrounding areas, see Fowler et al. (1999).

Although anthropologists have traditionally tried to protect their informants' privacy by using pseudonyms (or initials, as Steward did), this practice has changed in some cases. Following the recommendation of Catherine S. Fowler (interview), I am providing the full names of informants as recorded in Steward's journal.

To avoid confusion, I use the same cultural names—such as "Northern Paiute"—that appear in the publications I cite by Steward and other twentieth-century scholars writing in English (e.g., see D'Azevedo 1986; see also Goss 1999 for a critique of naming practices by outsiders to the region).

7. J. H. Steward to A. L. Kroeber, Apr. 27, 1935, RDA Box 141. Steward purchased hand game bones and other items from Patterson. On specimens collected, see Steward (1941b:250); see also Thomas, Pendelton, and Cappannari (1986:275). On Heye, see chap. 6, n.59.

8. JJJS I, Apr. 26, 1935; J. H. Steward to A. L. Kroeber, Apr. 27, 1935, RDA Box 141.

9. JJJS I, Apr. 27, 1935. On using English and interpreters in fieldwork, see Lowie (1959:12).

10. JJJS I, Apr. 28, 1935; J. H. Steward 1941b:213; WPA 1939:520. Steward (1941b:213, 214, 1938a:94) identified Hanson as "GH" and his niece as "MHa." Indian Ranch was a reserve from 1928 to 1958, when along with about forty others in California it was slated for termination. It was officially terminated in 1963 (Crum 1994:75, 144). A photograph of Hanson, who died in 1943, appears in Thomas, Pendelton, and Cappannari (1986:278).

11. JJJS I, Apr. 28, 1935 (entry by J. H. Steward); Kahrl 1982:376; WPA 1939:520.

12. WPA 1939:520; JJJS I, Apr. 29, 1935; J. H. Steward 1938a:52. The spellings of place-names are Steward's (1938a); in some cases his renderings are inaccurate (Fowler et. al 1999:58). Steward (1941b:213, 1938a:73) identified Gregory as "GG." Harold Driver (1907–92) spent his career at Indiana University (Winters 1991:1159–61; Social Security Death Index).

13. J. H. Steward to A. L. Kroeber, May 3, [1935], RDA Box 141; JJJS I, Apr. 26–29, 1935 (entries by J. H. Steward); J. C. Steward interview; WPA 1939:520.

14. JJJS I, Apr. 30, 1935 (entry by J. H. Steward); J. H. Steward 1941b:210.

15. JJJS I, May 1, 1935; J. H. Steward to A. L. Kroeber, May 3, [1935], RDA Box 141.

16. JJJS I, May 2, 1935 (entry by J. H. Steward).

17. J. H. Steward 1933:237; Southern Inyo Chapter 1977:15, 19; Wheat 1967:19; Kahrl 1982:354. According to Bauman and Coode (1988:184), relief payments were not uniform during the depression; ethnic minorities received lesser amounts.

18. Jane Steward (interview) also commented that in many cases the Paiute and Shoshone seemed "better off" than poor whites during the depression. Specifically, she implied that they had greater food security because of their skill in hunting and gathering, not that they had a higher income level or standard of living.

19. JJJS I, May 2, 1935 (entry by J. H. Steward), May 3, 1935 (entry by J. C. Steward); J. H. Steward to A. L. Kroeber, May 3, [1935], RDA Box 141. Steward identifed Spratt as "TSp"; he described him

as one-quarter Shoshone and one-quarter Kawaiisu (1941b:214), but elsewhere (1938a:71n.7) mentioned his white ancestry as well.

20. J. H. Steward 1938a:xi.

21. J. H. Steward to A. L. Kroeber, May 3, [1935], RDA Box 141; J. C. Steward interview; JJJS I, May 27, 1935; J. H. Steward 1941b:210, 1973:46.

22. JJJS I, May 16 and 27, 1935: Howell 1998:36–37, 50; Shimkin interview, 1989.

23. J. H. Steward 1941b:210, 1973:59; J. H. Steward to A. L. Kroeber, May 3, [1935], RDA Box 141. See T. Buckley (1982:54–55) on Kroeber's neglect of ethnographic data on menstrual shelters and ritual observances.

24. J. H. Steward 1938a:20–33 (on plant foods), 33–44 (on animal foods), 1941b:218–31. A number of journal entries suggest that he worked with women as a last resort, if men were unavailable or could not answer his questions. See the case of Susie Shepherd and Patsie Wilson, below and n. 33. Language barriers do not explain this since he willingly used interpreters with men. When he worked with married couples—as in the case of George Gregory and his wife—he routinely named the man as his informant, both in print (J. H. Steward 1938a, 1941b) and elsewhere (J. H. Steward, expense account, Apr. 23–May 30, 1935, RDA Box 141).

25. Anthropologists began to publish extensively on women's work in the 1970s, after Steward's death. See H. Moore (1988:42–72) for some of the findings and debates in this literature.

26. J. H. Steward 1938a:52; JJJS I, May 4, 1935.

27. Southern Inyo Chapter 1977:53–54, 235–36; Kahrl 1982:321–22. *Chinatown*, a feature film made about forty years later, also drew very loosely on events surrounding Los Angeles's quest for water (see, e.g., Mulholland 2000:4). In the 1930s Mount Whitney qualifed as the highest mountain in the forty-eight states.

28. JJJS I, May 5, 1935; J. H. Steward 1933:234; Southern Inyo Chapter 1977:225. Glenn reportedly lived by the creek until his death in the early 1970s (Southern Inyo Chapter 1977:17, 225). Steward (1933:234, 1938a:56, 1941b:213) identified him as "AG." On Owens Valley Paiute, see Liljeblad and Fowler (1986).

29. JJJS I, May 5, 1935. Steward (1933:234, 1938a:54, 1941b:214) identified Stone as "TS." See also chap. 4, n.95.

30. JJJS I, May 6, 1935; J. H. Steward to Mrs. Chilcote, May 6, 1935, RDA Box 141; J. H. Steward 1938a:51; J. H. Steward to Lowie, May 6, [1935], RHL Box 13.

31. JJJS I, May 6–7, 1935 (entries by J. H. Steward); J. H. Steward 1938a:51; Kahrl 1982:353; WPA 1939:518.

32. JJJS, May 4–7, 1935 (entries by J. H. Steward); J. H. Steward 1938a:51, 1941b:213. Steward (1941b:213, 1938a:55) identified Robinson as "GR."

33. JJJS I, May 8, 1935 (entry by J. H. Steward). Steward (1941b:214, 1938a:71), identifying Shepherd as "SS," mainly noted her skill as a basket weaver. Wilson was identified as "PW" by Steward (1941b:214). He commented that she was "not used as informant [for the culture element lists], but is willing and well informed and would probably be excellent. . . ."

34. JJJS I, May 8–9, 1935; J. H. Steward 1943b.

35. JJJS I, May 9, 1935.

36. J. H. Steward, expense account, Apr. 23–May 30, 1935, RDA Box 141; J. H. Steward to Strong, July 2, 1935, WDS Box 14; Howell 1998:33, 40). To put this stipend in perspective, Jane and Marion Steward earned 50 percent more as SERA employees, even at the lower rates that work relief programs paid to women.

37. JJJS I, May 10, 1935.

38. JJJS I, May 11–12, 1935 (entries by J. H. Steward); J. H. Steward 1941b:214; WPA 1939:518. Steward (1933:234, 1938a:62; 1941b:214) identified Mary Harry as "MH."

39. JJJS I, May 8–16 (entries by J. H. Steward), May 17 and 20, 1935 (entries by J. C. Steward); J. H. Steward 1938a:61–68, 314–15.

40. JJJS I, May 18, 1935; J. H. Steward 1933:233, 1938a:50; Chalfant 1933; Mulholland 2000:270–71. To judge from his publications, Willie A. Chalfant (1868–1943) specialized in California history.

41. JJJS I, May 21, 1935 (entry by J. H. Steward); J. H. Steward, expense account, Apr. 23–May 30, 1935, RDA Box 141.

42. JJJS I, Apr.28, May 18–19, 1935; J. H. Steward to Lowie, May 18, [1935], RHL Box 13.

43. JJJS I, May 22, 1935 (entry by J. H. Steward); A. L. Kroeber to J. H. Steward, May 20, 1935, RDA Box 141.

44. J. H. Steward to Lowie, May 18, 1935, RHL Box 13; J. H. Steward 1938a:50.

45. JJJS I, May 23–24, 1935; J. C. Steward interview.

46. JJJS I, May 25, 1935.

47. J. H. Steward to A. L. Kroeber, May 30, 1935, RDA Box 141.

48. JJJS I, June 5, 1935; A. L. Kroeber to J. H. Steward, May 27, 1935; Strong to A. L. Kroeber, June 4, 1935, RDA Box 141.

49. JJJS I, May 17, 1935 (entry by J. C. Steward); J. H. Steward 1938a:70. Steward (1941b:214, 1938a:70) identified Shakespeare as "JS." His daughter, identified as "ES," appears in Steward's (1941b:213) list of informants. Cow Camp is located near Silver Peak in Clayton Valley (J. H. Steward 1941b:214, 1938a:69).

50. JJJS I, June 20–21, 1935; WPA 1940:217–18, 224. Despite taking this legal precaution, they always listed October 13, 1933, as the date of their marriage.

51. JJJS I, June 22–26, 1935 (entries by J. C. Steward); J. H. Steward 1941b:213, 1938a:110. On the lack of detailed maps, see J. H. Steward (1938a:100).

52. JJJS I, June 21–27, 1935 (entries by J. C. Steward).

53. JJJS I, June 27–30, 1935 (entries by J. C. Steward); T. Kroeber 1970:139–40; Kroeber-Quinn 1982.

54. JJJS I, July 1–8, 1935 (entries by J. C. Steward).

55. JJJS I, July 14–20, 1935 (entries by J. C. Steward); J. C. Steward interview.

56. JJJS I, July 21–22, 1935; WPA 1940:244. The area around Duckwater where Steward worked in 1935 is now the Duckwater Indian Reservation.

57. J. C. Steward interview.

58. Ibid.

59. JJJS I, July 24[–Aug. 2], 1935 (entry by J. C. Steward); WPA 1940:249–51; Crum 1994:30, 74; J. H. Steward 1938a:121.

60. JJJS I, Aug. 3–11, 1935; J. H. Steward 1938a:21, 1933:233. Steward probably met Walter P. Cottam (1894–1988) in 1931, when Cottam joined the University of Utah faculty. He became a well-known Great Basin ecologist and conservationist (*Deseret News,* Dec. 24, 1988, B5; *Salt Lake Tribune,* Dec. 14, 1988, E3).

61. WPA 1940:121; J. H. Steward 1938a:155. A 1935 photograph of the Indian colony in Elko appears in Thomas, Pendelton, and Cappannari (1986:269).

62. JJJS I, Aug. 12–13, 1935.

63. JJJS I, Aug. 15–16, 1935.

64. J. C. Steward interview; J. H. Steward to Strong, July 2, 1935, WDS Box 14.

65. JJJS I, Aug. 12–16, 1935 (entries by J. C. Steward); J. H. Steward to Strong, Jan. 24, 1933, WDS Box 14; J. C. Steward interview.

66. JJJS I, Aug. 14, 18, 19, 1935. Steward (1941b:213, 1938a:157) identified Gibson as "BG." Gibson's advocacy of Western Shoshone treaty rights (see Crum 1994:67–68) no doubt had a bearing on his unusual interest in history.

67. JJJS I, Aug. 19, 31 1935 (entries by J. C. Steward); Helen Olmstead to J. H. Steward, Aug. 31, 1935, JHS Box 13; Murphy 1972:35–36; Du Bois 1960:xiii; A. L. Kroeber to J. H. Steward, Sept. 26, 1935, RDA Box 141. "Career advice" is Willey's (1988:188) term, and he counted himself a fortunate recipient of Kroeber's excellent counsel. Steward often sought, but did not often acknowledge, support from Kroeber (see chap. 12).

68. JJJS I, Sept. 4[–Oct. 3], 1935; J. H. Steward to Strong, July 2, 1935, WDS Box 14.

69. J. H. Steward 1938a:144, 145, 1941b:213–14, 215; JJJS I, Sept. 4[–Oct. 3], 1935; J. H. Steward to Lowie, Sept. 17, [1935], RDA Box 141. Jane Steward wrote only one journal entry for September and did not record informants' names.

70. JJJS I, Sept. 4[–Oct. 3], 1935 (entry by J. C. Steward); J. H. Steward to Lowie, Sept. 17, [1935], RDA Box 141; WPA 1940:170. The current name is the Duck Valley Indian Reservation (Thomas, Pendelton, and Cappannari 1986:264). For its history, see Crum (1994:43–57).

71. J. H. Steward to Lowie, Sept. 17, [1935], RDA Box 141; JJJS I, Sept. 4[–Oct. 3], 1935. The names of his Owyhee informants do not appear in the journal entry for September 1935.

72. J. H. Steward 1941b:209, 213, 320–22, 1943a:263.

73. JJJS I, Sept. 3[–Oct. 3], 1935; J. H. Steward to Lowie, Sept. 17, [1935], RDA Box 141; J. H. Steward 1939b. On John K. Hillers (1843–1925), see D. D. Fowler 1972.

74. JJJS I, Oct. 10–18, 1935 (entries by J. C. Steward); J. C. Steward interview.

75. JJJS I, Oct. 20–21, 1935.

76. JJJS I, Oct. 21 and Nov. 15, 1935 (entries by J. C. Steward); J. H. Steward to Lowie, Oct. 23, 1935, J. H. Steward to A. L. Kroeber, Oct. 23, 1935, Nov. 12, [1935], RDA, Box 141. On John Peabody Harrington (1884–1961), see Stirling (1963) and Laird (1975). Truman Michelson (1879–1938) was an Algonquian specialist (Cooper 1939:281). John R. Swanton (1873–1958), an ethnologist and ethnohistorian, specialized in southeastern Indians (Winters 1991:680; J. H. Steward 1960c). Archaeologist Frank H. H. Roberts (1897–1966) would later serve as director of the BAE, following the retirement of Stirling in the late 1950s (Winters 1991:589).

77. JJJS I, Dec. 15, 1935[–Feb. 1936] (entry by J. C. Steward); J. C. Steward interview; Collier to Stirling, Dec. 26, 1935, JHS Box 10.

78. JJJS I, Dec. 15, 1935[–Feb. 1936]; A. L. Kroeber to J. H. Steward, Oct. 16, 1935; J. H. Steward to A. L. Kroeber, Nov. 12, [1935], RDA Box 141; J. C. Steward interview.

79. J. H. Steward to A. L. Kroeber, Feb. 3, 1936; A. L. Kroeber to J. H. Steward, Feb. 10, 1936, RDA Box 141; JJJS I, Mar. 1936. In her brief journal entry for March 1936, Jane Steward mentioned that they conceived their first child during the first week of March.

80. J. H. Steward to A. L. Kroeber, Feb. 17 and 29, 1936; A. L. Kroeber to J. H. Steward, Feb. 27, 1936, RDA Box 141; J. C. Steward interview. Steward (1943a:263) did later acknowledge the assistance of WPA personnel. By the time he accepted that assistance, his wife had given birth to their first son, at which point she concluded that child care took precedence over typing.

81. A. L. Kroeber to J. H. Steward, Feb. 27, 1936; J. H. Steward to A. L. Kroeber, Feb. 29, 1936, RDA Box 141; J. C. Steward to A. L. Kroeber, Mar. 10, 1936, A. L. Kroeber to J. C. Steward, Mar. 27, 1936, RDA Box 141; J. H. Steward 1941b, 1943a.

82. J. C. Steward interview; JJJS I, Dec. 15, 1935[–Feb. 1936].

83. JJJS I, Mar. and Apr. 18, 1936.

84. J. H. Steward, "Shoshonean Tribes: Utah, Idaho, Nevada, Eastern California" n.d. [1936], JHS Box 10; J. C. Steward interview. On the Indian Reorganization Act, the Western Shoshone, and Steward's role as consultant, see Crum (1994:85–86, 115–16); Blackhawk (1997); and Russo (1999). See also J. H. Steward (1969b).

85. JJJS I, Apr. 18 and May 1936 (entries by J. C. Steward); J. H. Steward to A. L. Kroeber, May 12, 1936, RDA Box 141.

86. JJJS I, June and July 1, 1936 (entries by J. C. Steward); Maurice Howe to George Thomas, Feb. 15, 1936, PPGT Box 76; J. H. Steward to A. L. Kroeber, Aug. 12, 1936, RDA Box 141.

87. JJJS I, Aug. 1936 (entry by J. C. Steward); J. H. Steward to A. L. Kroeber, June 9 and July 23, 1936, RDA Box 141; Mekeel to J. H. Steward, Sept. 11, 1936, JHS, Box 10. The BIA paid for his expenses through mid-August, and the BAE paid for the remainder of the period (J. H. Steward, field expenses, June–Oct. 1936, JHS Box 10). Steward (1938a:ix) collected data "during a trip of four months"; about half of it was devoted to fieldwork. *Couvade* refers to a variety of practices by the father of an unborn or newborn child that in some way parallel the experience of pregnancy or childbirth.

88. J. H. Steward, field expenses, June–Oct. 1936, JHS Box 10; J. H. Steward 1938a:198, 1943a:264.

89. JJJS I Sept. 1936 (entry by J. C. Steward); J. H. Steward, field expenses, June–Oct. 1936, JHS Box 10; WPA 1941:294–95; J. H. Steward 1938a:186–87, 259. On the Northern Shoshone and Bannock, see Murphy and Murphy (1986) and Walker (1999).

90. J. H. Steward 1938a:152, 181, 200, 201; Thomas, Pendelton, and Cappannari 1986:263. On the introduction of the horse, see Shimkin (1986).

91. JJJS I, Sept. 1936; J. H. Steward, field expenses, June–Oct. 1936; Steward 1938a:222; J. H. Steward, "Shoshonean Tribes: Utah, Idaho, Nevada, Eastern California," [1936], JHS Box 10.

92. J. H. Steward to A. L. Kroeber, July 3, 1936, RDA Box 141; WPA 1941:351–52; J. H. Steward, "Shoshonean Tribes: Utah, Idaho, Nevada, Eastern California," [1936], JHS Box 10; J. H. Steward 1943a:264.

93. J. H. Steward, field expenses, June–Oct. 1936, JHS Box 10; J. H. Steward 1938a:218, 219–20; J. H. Steward 1943a:264, 265.

94. J. H. Steward 1938a:7, 18, 238. Crum (1994:18–19) mentions bands that formed in response to white aggression in northern Nevada during the mid-nineteenth century. See also Walker (1999:71–72) on warfare.

95. JJJS I, June and Aug. 1, 1936 (entries by J. C. Steward); J. C. Steward interview.

96. JJJS I, Aug. and Sept. 1936 (entries by J. C. Steward); J. H. Steward to A. L. Kroeber, Sept. 25 and Oct. 26, 1936, RDA Box 141; J. H. Steward 1938a:134.

97. J. H. Steward 1943a:265; J. H. Steward, field expenses, June–Oct. 1936, JHS Box 10; J. H. Steward 1938a:136. Steward (1943a:265, 1938a:135, 137) identified Moody as "M" and Bonamont as "FB" and "FBo." Stewart remembered collecting a culture element list on a Gosiute reservation in fall 1937. He mistakenly recalled that Steward had worked there during summer or fall 1937, but Steward was actually there in 1936. The passage of time—a full year—may help to explain what Steward did or did not see and why he failed to report the use of peyote (see Howell 1998:77–78). Steward's lack of interest in religion, which bordered on wholesale avoidance, may also have contributed.

98. J. H. Steward, field expenses, June–Oct. 1936, JHS Box 10; WPA 1941:384; J. H. Steward 1938a:134, 137.

99. He identified his informant in print as "ChB" (J. H. Steward 1938a:184), but listed him only as "Informant 1 day at Las Vegas" when he submitted his expense report (J. H. Steward, field expenses, June–Oct. 1936, JHS Box 10). On Las Vegas in the 1930s, see WPA (1940:182ff.).

100. Worster 1985:272–75.

101. J. H. Steward, field expenses, June–Oct. 1936, JHS Box 10; JJJS I, passim. On the surveying and exploring tradition, see Hinsley (1981:152).

102. J. H. Steward to Murphy, Mar. 31, 1967, JHS Box 6; J. H. Steward 1938a.

103. J. H. Steward, field expenses, June–Oct. 1936, JHS Box 10.

Chapter 9: *Washington Ways and Means*

1. J. H. Steward to A. L. Kroeber, Jan. 21, 1937, RDA Box 141; J. H. Steward to Lowie, Jan. 21, 1937, RHL Box 13.

2. J. H. Steward 1938a:246; J. H. Steward, "Shoshonean Tribes: Utah, Idaho, Nevada, Eastern California," [1936], JHS Box 10; J. C. Steward interview. Future scholars would stress the complexity of the subsistence pattern (see Thomas, Pendelton, and Cappannari 1986:265–68; C. S. Fowler 1986b).

3. J. H. Steward, "Shoshonean Tribes: Utah, Idaho, Nevada, Eastern California," [1936], JHS Box 10.

4. Collier, "Memorandum for Dr. Mekeel (COPY)," Dec. 22, 1936, JHS Box 11; J. H. Steward, "Shoshonean Tribes: Utah, Idaho, Nevada, Eastern California," [1936], JHS Box 10. On Collier, see L. Kelly (1983).

5. Collier, "Memorandum to Dr. Mekeel (COPY)," Dec. 22, 1936, JHS Box 11.

6. Bowler to Collier, Mar. 7, 1937, JHS Box 10. Bowler had been superintendent for less than three years and was the first woman to hold that position in the BIA (Crum 1994:92).

7. Mekeel to J. H. Steward, Mar. 27, 1937, JHS Box 10; J. H. Steward to A. L. Kroeber, Jan. 21, 1937, RDA Box 141.

8. Both the title and the contents of the play undoubtedly would have offended many people then, as today. The title, "Anthropology Inaction or Another Redskin Bit the Dust" (n.d. [ca. Mar. 1937], JHS Box 11), expresses Steward's view that assimilation was well underway, and that a staff of applied anthropologists could not preserve what had already been lost.

9. J. H. Steward to Lowie, Jan. 21, 1937, RHL Box 13; Solecki and Wagley 1963:1103. Frances T. Densmore (1867–1957) had a long association with the BAE (Frisbie 1989:52), which extended through the years of Steward's tenure there; however, she did not have a permanent, salaried position as he did, and she spent much of her time in the field, doing research and collecting.

10. Lamb 1906:664; Worster 2001:439; J. H. Steward to Lowie, Jan. 21, 1937, RHL Box 13; J. H. Steward 1936a, 1937b. Nyswander (interview; 1996, 1994:78) recalled giving a series of six lectures in Salt Lake City and elsewhere in Utah. Those lectures were yet another competing interest that had drawn her attention away from her husband.

11. "Notes and News," *American Anthropologist* 42, no. 2 (1940): 372–73; "Notes and News," *American Anthropologist* 42, no. 3 (1940): 552–53.

12. On Father John M. Cooper (1881–1949), see Winters (1991:125–26) and Flannery (1950).

13. Lowie, "Biographical Data for the National Academy of Sciences," JHS Box 1; J. H. Steward, "Autobiographical Appraisal," n.d., JHS Box 16; J. H. Steward 1946:1.

14. J. H. Steward to A. L. Kroeber, May 28, 1936, and Feb. 24, 1937, RDA Box 141.

15. J. H. Steward to Lowie, Feb. 6, 1936, RHL Box 13; J. H. Steward 1936a:337, 1955c:132–33.

16. J. H. Steward 1936a:337, 1955c:132–33; J. H. Steward to Lowie, Mar. 21, 1938, RDA Box 141; Winters 1991:359. Gusinde later taught at Catholic University in Washington, D.C.

17. J. H. Steward 1936a:337–38, 1955c:132–33, 135.

18. J. H. Steward to Kelly, Jan. 7, 1947, JHS Box 4; J. H. Steward to Lowie, Mar. 21, 1938, RDA Box 141.

19. J. H. Steward to Lowie, Feb. 6, 1938, RHL Box 13; J. H. Steward to Lowie, Mar. 21, 1938, RDA Box 43; Collins 1976:887; Willey 1988:252.

20. J. H. Steward to Lowie, Feb. 6, 1938, RHL Box 13.

21. J. H. Steward to Lowie, Mar. 21, 1938, RDA Box 141. Cooper (1946) later wrote about the Pehuenche for the *Handbook*. See Steward and Faron (1959:408–10) on the Puelche.

22. Secretary of Smithsonian Institution to secretary of state, Mar. 28, 1938; Stirling to J. H. Steward, Apr. 7 and July 1, 1938, BAE Box 83.

23. J. H. Steward to Lowie, Mar. 21, 1938, RDA Box 141; J. C. Steward interview; secretary of Smithsonian Institution to secretary of state, Mar. 28, 1938; secretary of Smithsonian Institution to Friends of Smithsonian Institution, Mar. 28, 1938, BAE Box 83; J. H. Steward, academic records, DSC.

24. J. H. Steward to Lowie, Mar. 21, 1938, RDA Box 141.

25. Stirling to J. H. Steward, Apr. 7, 1938, BAE Box 83; JJJS II, Apr. 23 and Apr. 30, 1938 (entries by J. H. Steward); Solecki and Wagley 1963:1103. Due to limitations of space, this account of Steward's 1938 travels is highly abbreviated.

26. J. C. Steward interview; R. Cannon 1926a, 1926b. Ramona Cannon briefly taught Spanish at the University of Utah after the family returned from South America (R. Cannon, HRMF).

27. JJJS II, May 9–23, 1938 (entries by J. C. and J. H. Steward). The amoebic parasite *Entamoeba histolytica* is usually transmitted through contaminated food or water.

28. JJJS II, June 6, 1938 (entry by J. C. Steward).

29. JJJS II, June 30–July 8, 1938. On Wendell C. Bennett (1905–53), see Willey (1988:122–45) and

Kidder (1954). On Herbert Spinden (1879–1967), see Winters (1991:659–60). On Julio C. Tello (1880–1947), see Lothrop (1948), Willey (1988:179–80), and Daggett (1992). On Luis E. Valcárcel (1891–1987), see Winters (1991:719–20).

30. JJJS II, July 2–10, 1938: J. H. Steward 1939a:113 (fig. 120), 116.

31. JJJS II, Aug. 18–19, 1938. On Bernard Mishkin (1913–54), see Wagley (1955).

32. JJJS II, Aug. 21–28, 1938; J. H. Steward 1939a:115 (figs. 121 and 122), 116.

33. JJJS II, Aug. 21 and Aug. 24, 1938.

34. JJJS II, Aug. 26, 1938.

35. JJJS II Sept. 7–16, 1938 (entries by J. H. Steward), and [Apr. 3, 1939] (entry by J. C. Steward).

36. JJJS II, Jan. 1938 and n.d. [Apr. 3, 1939] (entries by J. H. and J. C. Steward); M. Steward, official personnel folder, NPRC.

37. JJJS II, Nov. 1, 1938 (entry by J. H. Steward) and n.d. [Apr. 3, 1939] (entry by J. C. Steward).

38. J. H. Steward to Elmer Johnson, Oct. 28, 1936, TA; J. C. Steward interview; Wolf 1988:306.

39. Fenton interview; Willey 1988:231; J. H. Steward 1939b; J. H. Steward to A. L. Kroeber, Feb. 18, 1939, RDA Box 141; Ruth Bryan to J. H. Steward, Mar. 1, 1940, JHS Box 9.

40. J. H. Steward 1938a; Turney-High 1940. The University of Utah Press reprinted *Basin-Plateau* in 1970.

41. J. H. Steward to Elmer Johnson, Oct. 21, 1937, TA.

42. JJJS II, Jan. 1939 (entry by J. H. Steward); J. H. Steward to A. L. Kroeber, Feb. 18, 1939, RDA Box 141; J. C. Steward interview.

43. J. H. Steward to A. L. Kroeber, Feb. 18, 1939, RDA Box 141; J. C. Steward interview. According to Beals (1977:142), the initial plans for the *Handbook* called for him to be editor. By the time the project received funding, Beals held a full-time teaching position at the University of California, Los Angeles, and Steward had joined the BAE. According to Mintz (interview), Métraux was also a contender for the position.

44. JJJS II, Feb.–Nov. 1939 (entries by J. H. Steward); J. H. Steward to Lowie, Sept. 13, 1940, Jan. 28, 1942, and Feb. 17, 1941 [1942], RDA Box 141.

45. J. H. Steward to Lowie, Sept. 13, 1940, RDA Box 43; J. H. Steward, "Autobiographical Appraisal," n.d., JHS Box 16; J. H. Steward to A. L. Kroeber, Feb. 24, 1937, RDA Box 141; J. H. Steward 1946–59. The *Handbook*'s small, seventh volume was an index.

46. J. H. Steward to Stirling, Dec. 21, 1957, JHS Box 15; J. H. Steward 1941c.

47. JJJS II, Sept. 7, 1938; J. H. Steward, "Autobiographical Appraisal," n.d., JHS Box 16; J. H. Steward 1936a:338, 340, 1955c:148, 175; J. H. Steward to A. L. Kroeber, Apr. 9, 1940, RDA Box 141. Diamond Jenness (see below) recommended the Carrier. His Mar. 5, 1940, letter to Steward is found in Manuscript 703 (J. H. Steward field notes and other material, ca. 1940), National Anthropological Archives, Smithsonian Institution.

48. J. H. Steward to Stirling, June 5, [1940], BAE Box 83; J. H. Steward 1941c:83, 86.

49. J. H. Steward to Stirling, June 5 and June 15, [1940], BAE Box 83; J. H. Steward 1941c:86. On the cultural core, see chaps. 11 and 12.

50. J. H. Steward to Stirling, June 5 and June 15, [1940], BAE Box 83. On Diamond Jenness (1886–1969), see Winters (1991:324–25).

51. A. L. Kroeber to J. H. Steward, Apr. 16, 1940, RDA Box 141. The list, collected by Verne Ray, was not cited. Willey (1988:129), among others, mentions Kroeber's words about publication.

52. J. H. Steward to Stirling, June 15, [1940], BAE Box 83; J. H. Steward 1941c:88, 1955c:175. The dates on correspondence suggest that Steward worked with Prince for a maximum of five weeks, not eight (J. H. Steward 1941c:86).

53. Wetmore to J. H. Steward, July 9, 1940, JHS Box 11; Steward 1941c:88. See also J. H. Steward (1961c) and J. H. Steward and Murphy (1956).

54. "Autobiographical Appraisal," n.d., JHS Box 16; J. H. Steward to A. L. Kroeber, [Feb. 1946], JHS Box 13.

55. J. H. Steward 1936a:331, 342, 1955c:148. Steward (1955c:139) did make mention of matrilineal

moieties among some northern Australian Aborigines, but he could only explain these as having "probably diffused from Melanesia."

56. J. H. Steward to Stirling, June 15, [1940], BAE Box 83.

57. Since Steward's health did not prevent him from later undertaking long trips with his wife, it probably did not constrain further fieldwork.

58. J. H. Steward to Johnson, Sept. 16, 1940, TA; J. C. Steward interview. Some anthropologists of Steward's era who had families did take them to the field (see, e.g., Willey 1988:149).

59. J. H. Steward, "Autobiographical Appraisal," n.d., JHS Box 16.

60. J. H. Steward 1946:5–6; Steward to Strong, Feb. 3, [1946], WDS Box 14. In his letter to Strong, Steward's reference was to his summary in the fifth volume (J. H. Steward 1949b).

61. J. H. Steward to Lowie, Feb. 17, 1941 [1942], RDA Box 141.

62. J. H. Steward 1946:9. Alfred Métraux (1905–63) eventually took a position with UNESCO in Paris, where he later died (Wagley 1964:603–5; Winters 1991:475–76). One biographical profile, written by Rhoda Métraux, his colleague and former wife, explicitly refers to him as "co-editor" of the *Handbook* (Winters 1991:475).

63. Willey 1988:86–90, 219, 225–26. Willey (interview) recalled that the designated Argentinean author, "an archaeologist who was pro-German," actually refused to write the chapter.

64. J. H. Steward to Lowie, Feb. 17, 1941 [1942], RDA Box 141.

65. J. H. Steward to A. L. Kroeber, Mar. 11, 1944, RDA Box 141; J. H. Steward to Lowie, Feb. 17, 1941 [1942], RDA Box 141. For Steward's later view of Lévi-Strauss's work, see chap. 12.

66. J. H. Steward, "Autobiographical Appraisal," n.d., JHS Box 16; J. H. Steward 1946:2; West 1982:6n.2; J. H. Steward, "Design of the Institute of Social Anthropology," n.d. [May 1967], JHS Box 3.

67. Nyswander interviews, 1996, 1997; Nyswander 1994:115–21, 171–85.

68. J. H. Steward to Lowie, Mar. 15, 1942, RDA Box 141.

69. On Curt Nimuendajú (1883–1945), see Baldus (1946) and Winters (1991:507–8).

70. J. H. Steward to Lowie, Mar. 15, 1942, RHL Box 13. Murphy (1972:38) mentioned Nimuendajú's Indian wife in print. Neither woman received mention in Nimuendajú's obituary in the *American Anthropologist* (Baldus 1946).

71. J. H. Steward to Lowie, Mar. 15, 1942, RHL Box 13; Métraux 1946:197–99.

72. J. H. Steward, typed biographical entry for *International Directory of Anthropologists*, 3d ed., 1950, UISAF. On matrilineal bands, the Gran Chaco, and Mataco Indians, see Steward and Faron (1959:384–85, 413–20).

73. J. H. Steward 1936a:343, 1955c:122–42. For caveats, see Steward and Faron (1959:385, 417). In teaching, Steward would later cite the Sirionó of Bolivia as a "matrilineal hunting and gathering band" (Anthropology 461 syllabus, fall 1959 [from the personal files of William H. Alkire]).

74. J. H. Steward to Nimuendajú, Sept. 10, 1942, RDA Box 141.

75. Wagley 1964:603; Caffrey 1989:314. Paul Rivet (1879–1958) returned to France after the war ended (Winters 1991:585).

76. J. H. Steward to Lowie, Dec. 29, 1942, and Sept. 23, 1943; Lowie 1959:177; J. H. Steward to A. L. Kroeber, Mar. 11, 1944, RDA Box 141; T. Kroeber 1970:179–89.

77. Willey 1988:223–25, 233–35; J. H. Steward to Carter, Jan. 6, 1947, JHS Box 4; J. C. Steward interview; J. H. Steward, "Autobiographical Appraisal," n.d., JHS Box 16.

78. Willey 1988:227–28; J. H. Steward to Lowie, Sept. 13, 1940; J. H. Steward to A. L. Kroeber, Jan. 13, 1940, and Mar. 11, 1944, RDA Box 141; JJJS II, July 6 and July 8, 1938; Cooper 1942.

79. J. H. Steward 1947:85–86; Willey interview; Willey 1988:228.

80. J. H. Steward 1947:95n.10. Service (n.d.:57–60) recalled the contact that he and Fried had with Kirchhoff in New York City. On Paul Kirchhoff (1900–1972), see Winters (1991:348–49). According to William Peace (personal communications, Apr. 15, 2000, and Oct. 22, 2001), the FBI compiled files on a number of anthropologists, including Steward; Steward's file is quite small.

81. Willey 1988:228–30; J. H. Steward, "Autobiographical Appraisal," n.d., JHS Box 16. In this draft

of his autobiographical essay, Steward cited his book with Faron as the work in which he substituted culture type for culture area (see Steward and Faron 1959).

82. Willey 1988:230–31; Turney-High 1940:137.

83. J. H. Steward to contributors, Dec. 10, 1945; J. H. Steward to A. L. Kroeber, June 6, 1944, and March 3, 1946, RDA Box 141; Willey 1988:226.

84. J. H. Steward, "Autobiographical Appraisal," n.d., JHS Box 16; Willey 1988:235; Stephenson 1967:89–90.

85. J. H. Steward to A. L. Kroeber, June 6, 1944, RDA Box 141.

86. Willey 1988:234–35; J. H. Steward to A. L. Kroeber, [Feb. 1946], and J. H. Steward to Linton, Mar. 19, 1946, JHS Box 13; J. H. Steward, "Autobiographical Appraisal," n.d., JHS Box 16; Institute of Social Anthropology, Sept. 20, 1946, JHS Box 4; J. H. Steward, research proposal, JHS Box 2; A. L. Kroeber to J. H. Steward, Nov. 23, 1943, RDA Box 141. The employment histories of Anna Gayton, Laura Maud Thompson, and Charlotte Gower (Chapman), among others, are instructive (Rowe 1978; Winters 1991:105–6, 695–96; see also chap. 10).

87. Events of the previous year may also have encouraged Steward to search for an academic position. He had learned that he was under consideration for the chairmanship of the department of anthropology at the University of Michigan, a position in which he had no interest. Leslie White, who had an embattled relationship with the university administration in part because of his radical political beliefs, was eventually named chairman of the department (Peace n.d.:19).

88. J. C. Steward interview; J. H. Steward 1973:10. Steward knew Theodore McCown (1908–69) when McCown was an undergraduate at Berkeley. He trained as a physical anthropologist and joined the department faculty ten years later, in 1938 (McCown 1969; Kennedy 1997).

89. J. C. Steward interview; A. L. Kroeber to J. H. Steward, Jan. 30, 1946, JHS Box 3. Jane Steward did not know whether Sauer served on a selection committee or interfered in the hiring process in an informal but decisive way. Kroeber had not yet retired when the hiring decision was made, but he obviously did not intervene. Murphy, who later taught at Berkeley for eight years, heard nothing there about the episode and chose not to mention it in his account of Steward's career (Murphy 1977; Murphy to J. C. Steward, June 27, 1975, JHS Box 7).

90. Nyswander interview, 1996; Nyswander 1994:258.

91. J. H. Steward to A. L. Kroeber, n.d. [Feb. 1946], ALK Box 28; A. L. Kroeber to J. H. Steward, Feb. 12, 1946, JHS Box 3. More than one anthropologist with experience at the BAE has suggested to me, either informally or in an interview, that the stated problem had more to do with unrealistic expectations than with the BAE itself.

92. J. H. Steward to Fackenthal, Mar. 19, 1946; J. H. Steward to Strong, Mar. 19, 1946, JHS Box 13; J. C. Steward interview. Steward accepted the position at Columbia while implying to Strong that Berkeley had not yet made a final decision. The body of evidence suggests that this was a face-saving remark. Perhaps as a result of having called Lowie he apparently knew that the offer would go to someone else (J. H. Steward to A. L. Kroeber, n.d. [Feb. 1946], ALK Box 28).

93. J. H. Steward to Linton, Mar. 19, 1946, JHS Box 13; JJJS I, Dec. 15, [1935–Feb. 1936]; J. C. Steward interview.

Chapter 10: *East of Everything*

1. Solecki and Wagley 1963:1103–5; Willey and Sabloff 1974:148–52, 1988:92, 132–33, 236. Other archaeologists who joined the project included Clifford Evans (1920–81) and James A. Ford (1911–68); both earned Ph.D.s in anthropology at Columbia in the late 1940s (Marquis 1981:184; Winters 1991:206). Donald Collier (1911–95) also took part (Winters 1991:120–21; Social Security Death Index), as did Junius Bird (1907–82), then a curator of South American archaeology at the American Museum of Natural History (Willey 1988:147–68).

2. Willey and Sabloff 1974:152. The geographer was F. W. McBryde. Allan R. Holmberg (1909–

66) later taught at Cornell and became well known for his applied research on social change (Winters 1991:300).

3. Strong to J. H. Steward, Apr. 23, 1946, WDS Box 14. On Ralph Linton (1893–1953), see Linton and Wagley (1971) and Winters (1991:413–15).

4. J. H. Steward to Strong, Feb. 3, [1946], WDS Box 14; J. H. Steward to Linton, Mar. 19, 1946; J. H. Steward to Strong, Mar. 19, 1946; Frank D. Fackenthal to J. H. Steward, Mar. 14, 1946, JHS Box 13.

5. J. H. Steward to A. L. Kroeber, n.d. [Feb. 1946], JHS Box 13; J. H. Steward, "Autobiographical Appraisal," JHS Box 16.

6. J. H. Steward to Kelly, Sept. 24, 1946; J. H. Steward to Carter, Sept. 24, [1946], and Oct. 26, [1946], JHS Box 4.

7. J. H. Steward to Carter, Sept. 24, [1946], and Oct. 26, [1946], JHS Box 4; Ghani 1987:357; Mintz 1981:157, 161; Murphy 1977:10.

8. Murphy 1977:10n.3; Murphy interview. For perspectives on Ruth Benedict's (1887–1948) life and career in anthropology, see Babcock (1993), Caffrey (1989), Lapsley (1999), Mintz (1981), and Modell (1983, 1989).

9. J. H. Steward to Carter, Oct. 26, [1946], JHS Box 4; J. H. Steward to Manners, Apr. 3, 1970, JHS Box 3. Murphy (interview; 1977:8, 1981:179), among other Columbia students, remembered Steward as a skilled lecturer.

10. J. H. Steward to Carter, Oct. 26, [1946], and Dec. 15, 1946; J. H. Steward to Wetmore, Mar. 23, 1947, JHS Box 4.

11. J. H. Steward to Carter, Oct. 26, [1946], and Dec. 15, 1946, JHS Box 4; J. H. Service 1988:149; J. H. Steward to Monroe Deutsch, Nov. 26, 1946; J. H. Steward to Lowie, Nov. 26, 1946; Lowie to Steward, Dec. 2, 1946, JHS Box 9. Steward confined candid remarks about Columbia to his letters to Ethelwyn Carter, his former secretary and confidante at the Smithsonian.

12. J. H. Steward to Lowie, Nov. 26, 1946; J. H. Steward to A. L. Kroeber, Dec. 22, 1946, JHS Box 9; J. H. Steward to A. L. Kroeber, Feb. 20, 1956, ALK Box 28. "West of Everything," as Tompkins (1992) uses the phrase, reflects an (unself-conscious) eastern sensibility, in keeping with her own regional origins. The reverse conveys Steward's differing regional identity and his sense of complete alienation from New York City and Columbia University.

13. J. C. Steward interview.

14. J. H. Steward to A. L. Kroeber, Dec. 22, 1947, JHS Box 9; J. H. Steward to Elmer Johnson, Feb. 19, 1947, TA; J. Friedman 1987:108. Steward's estimates of the number of graduate students generally ranged from more than 80 to about 100; former students put the number between 100 and 150 (Service 1988:149; Murphy 1977:8). About Boas's persisting influence on graduate students at Columbia in the late 1940s, Diamond (1993:112) remarked, "More than a method, or vision, Boas left behind a spirit of freedom and intellectual independence, which we all share."

15. Boas 1940:311. See also Lesser (1981:9–10) and Stocking (1974).

16. J. H. Steward to Anthony Leeds, Dec. 4, 1971, JHS Box 3; Lapsley 1999:307. Ruth Bunzel (1898–1990) spent her working life at Columbia but never held a tenured position there (Fawcett and McLuhan 1989:29, 32; Social Security Death Index).

17. Murphy interview; Murphy 1977:8; Leacock 1993:12–13; J. Friedman 1987:108; J. H. Steward to Strong, Apr. 10, [1946], WDS Box 14. For a summary of Gene Weltfish's (1902–80) long and complex career, see Parks and Pathé (1985) and Pathé (1989).

18. Weltfish and Benedict 1943; Parks and Pathé 1985:62–63.

19. Murphy interview; Murphy 1981:178; Leacock 1993:12; De Laguna 1962:567. Marian Wesley Smith (1907–61) carried out fieldwork in the Pacific Northwest and southern Asia (De Laguna 1962:567; Winters 1991:645).

20. Strong to J. H. Steward, Apr. 23, 1946, WDS Box 14.

21. T. Kroeber, 1970:213; J. Friedman 1987:108. Wagley spent most of his professional career at

Columbia, later moving to the University of Florida (Winters 1991:737–38). George Herzog (1901–84) left for Indiana University in 1948 (McAllester 1985:87). Harry Shapiro (1902–90) taught at Columbia on a part-time basis for more than thirty years and held a full-time, permanent position at the American Museum of Natural History (Howells 1990:499).

22. K. W. Olson 1974:51, 69; Wolf 1988:306; Service n.d.:40; Mintz interview.

23. Murphy 1981:178; Mintz 1981:156–57; Caffrey 1989:340; Service 1988:151; M. Steward, official personnel folder, NPRC.

24. Young interview; Service n.d.:42; Murphy interview; Murphy 1977:9; Murphy 1981:177, 178, 181.

25. Strong to J. H. Steward, Apr. 23, 1946, WDS Box 14. Service (n.d.:28) recalled that "the students tended to line up by gender," the women with Benedict and Mead, while "more of the men tended to lean toward Steward's kind of philosophy, if they thought of it as a philosophy yet." Among the exceptions to this tendency were Leacock (1993:14), who had no interest in culture and personality, and Victor Barnouw (1915–89) (Graber and Silverberg 1990:492).

26. Goldfrank (1983:6) attributed the first use of the term *diaperology* to her husband, Wittfogel. Steward used it more than once in correspondence with like-minded colleagues.

27. Manners 1973:893; Service 1988:149.

28. Young interview; Leacock 1993:14, 21; Hollingshead 1989:103–4; Diamond 1993:113. Jane Steward (interview) remembered that he also served on the dissertation committee of archaeologist Betty Meggers.

29. Leacock 1993:19–20; Solecki and Wagley 1963:1102–3; J. C. Steward interview. Eleanor Burke Leacock's (1922–87) memoir includes her recollections about Columbia and her long search for academic employment (Leacock 1993; see also Gailey 1989 and Sutton and Lee 1993). The antagonism she detected probably had more to do with her pregnancy (see below) than with her status as Strong's student. Steward's assertions in print about women's responsibilities for children (see chap. 12) suggest that he regarded any competing interest as tantamount to child neglect—perhaps reflecting his own emotional history.

30. Service (n.d.:40) thought that Strong and Steward maintained a friendship until Steward left for Illinois, when it "thereupon dissolved," but Leacock's (1993:20) and Jane Steward's (interview) comments suggest otherwise.

31. Leacock 1993:19–20, 21; Young interview. As Young commented, "If you married, they didn't have to find a job for you. It was assumed that you were comfortably taken care of." The fact that women usually had to choose between marriage and a career in anthropology must have discouraged some from continuing in the field, thereby reducing their numbers. Most of the (very few) women with academic positions were unmarried. Steward's female colleagues at Columbia were single (Benedict and Weltfish were divorced, and Smith had not yet married).

32. Mintz interview; Mintz 1994; Diamond 1993:111, 113; Wolf 1987:109; Ghani 1987:355; Service 1988:149, n.d.:41–43; Lauria-Perricelli 1989:206n.243. Wolf recalled Leacock "wheeling all of her babies" in May Day parades (J. Friedman 1987:109). Besides Diamond, Wolf, and Fried, the group included Mintz, Service, and Manners.

33. Service n.d.:42, 1988:149; Mintz, personal communication, Aug. 15, 2001; Mintz 1981.

34. J. H. Steward to A. L. Kroeber, Dec. 22, 1946, JHS Box 9; Lauria-Perricelli 1989:108.

35. Wolf 1988:306; Ghani 1987:353–54; Mintz interview. Steward used the terms *forester* and *city slicker* in letters to some of his former students during the 1950s.

36. On the Berkeley students, see Beals (1982:3–4). Steward's BAE colleagues with strong links to the West—by birth and upbringing, or by years spent living and working there—included Stirling, Strong, Harrington, and Roberts.

37. Beals 1982:3–4; Murphy interview; Mintz interview; J. H. Steward 1938a:260. Steward's personal library (purchased by Southern Methodist University after his death) largely comprised books and journals in anthropology. It did not include works by Marx (library, JHS Box 16; J. C. Steward interview).

38. Ghani 1987:253–54. On four of these "indigenous" American anthropologists, see Mark (1980,

1988). On James Mooney (1861–1921), see Moses (1984). Berkeley's Gifford might also be considered as belonging to the indigenous line in American anthropology.

39. Radin 1958:358; Murphy 1972:10; T. Kroeber 1970:5–30; Kenzer 1987. Kroeber died in Paris in 1960. Steward's graduate teachers included two Europeans, Oskar Schmieder and Nordenskiöld.

40. Murphy 1972:10; T. Kroeber 1970:44; Speth 1987. One of Sauer's students, James Parsons, recalled (1979:13), "We didn't think of ourselves as social scientists. 'Culture history' was the preferred term."

41. J. H. Steward, "Autobiographical Appraisal," n.d., JHS Box 16.

42. Wolf 1964:88; Ghani 1987:346–47; Mintz interview. Steward's Columbia students, in keeping with the multiethnic character of New York City, represented a broad range of backgrounds, from Jewish and Irish to Anglo-Saxon and Hispanic.

43. J. Friedman 1987:109; Mintz interview; Murphy 1981:177; Diamond 1993:113.

44. Adams 1985:9; J. C. Steward interview; J. H. Steward to Bonham Campbell, Apr. 28, 1948, JHS Box 6; J. H. Steward to Carter, Jan. 6, 1947, JHS Box 4.

45. J. Friedman 1987:110; Ghani 1987:353.

46. J. C. Steward interview; J. H. Steward to A. L. Kroeber, Jan. 31, 1947, JHS Box 9; J. Parsons 1979:10; T. Kroeber 1970:207; Rowe 1962:397.

47. Nyswander interview, 1996; J. H. Steward to Strong, Mar. 19, 1946, JHS Box 13; J. H. Steward to A. L. Kroeber, July 28, [1947], ALK Box 28.

48. J. C. Steward interview; Fried to J. H. Steward, Oct. 16, 1947, JHS Box 1; J. H. Steward to Greg Votaw, Aug. 7, 1947, JHS Box 6; Lauria-Perricelli 1989:120. Grace Steward lived with relatives in East St. Louis, Illinois, in the early 1940s (M. Steward, official personnel folder, NPRC), apparently until her health declined.

49. Johnson to J. H. Steward, Mar. 28, 1948, JHS Box 6; Johnson to Bonham Campbell, Mar. 29, 1948, TA.

50. Johnson to Bonham Campbell, Mar. 29 and Apr. 21, 1948, TA; Johnson to J. H. Steward, Mar. 28, 1948, JHS Box 6; Johnson to J. H. Steward, Apr. 21, 1948, TA; Linton and Wagley 1971:48; Caffrey 1989:276–77.

51. J. H. Steward to Johnson, Apr. 15, 1948, TA.

52. McElvaine 1984:203; J. H. Steward to Harris, Mar. 8, 1969, JHS Box 3.

53. Johnson to Bonham Campbell, Mar. 29, 1948; J. H. Steward to Johnson, Apr. 15, 1948; Johnson to Campbell, Apr. 21, 1948, TA; Johnson to J. H. Steward, Mar. 28, 1948, JHS Box 6; J. C. Steward interview; Pathé 1989:377.

54. J. H. Steward to Johnson, Apr. 28, 1948, J. H. Steward to Campbell, Apr. 28, 1948, Campbell to J. H. Steward, May 19, 1948, JHS Box 6; J. H. Steward to Johnson, May 1, [1948], TA.

55. The following brief summary does not do justice to the intricacies of the project, including Steward's role in it. Such an account is beyond the scope of this book. See Lauria-Perricelli's (1989) full-length study, which provides depth and detail as well as important commentary.

56. Lauria-Perricelli 1989:141–45. Several months into the project, Murra chose two other graduate students from the University of Chicago to take part in it. Both left the project before the end of 1948 (Lauria-Perricelli 1989:162). According to Service (n.d.:29–30), Steward initially asked him to serve as his "lieutenant" (evidently, field director) in the project. Service declined and went to Paraguay to do fieldwork for his dissertation.

57. Fried to J. H. Steward, Oct. 16, 1947, JHS Box 1; Lauria-Perricelli 1989:120; Mintz interview. As Lauria-Perricelli points out (1989:113n.92), the use of Puerto Ricans as seminar informants was an "interesting echo of the 'culture at a distance' methodology used by Benedict's Research on Contemporary Cultures program to which Steward was antagonistic."

58. Mintz to J. H. Steward, June 27, 1957, JHS Box 2.

59. J. H. Steward, "Autobiographical Appraisal," n.d., JHS Box 16; Beals 1982:6–7.

60. Lauria-Perricelli 1989, 1996; J. H. Steward, proposal for sabbatical leave [1959], JHS Box 2; Mintz interview.

61. Lauria-Perricelli 1989:108n.88, 139, 141n.139, 173, 185n.210, 194.

62. J. H. Steward, "Autobiographical Appraisal," n.d., JHS Box 16; J. H. Steward to Johnson, Feb. 13, 1945, TA.

63. J. H. Steward to [*Telluride News Letter*] Ed., typescript, n.d. [ca. 1945], TA.

64. As Lauria-Perricelli (1989:196) notes, "For Steward, somehow being useful to planners and legislators in assessing social reform in Puerto Rico was a legitimate—or at least necessary—end of the study." This was due not so much to the influence of the New Deal era (ibid.:197n.227) as to that of Nunn.

65. Mason to J. H. Steward, June 30, 1948, JHS Box 8; J. H. Steward 1948; Willey 1988:237.

66. J. H. Steward, "Autobiographical Appraisal," n.d., JHS Box 16.

67. J. H. Steward 1948. Willey (1988:94–95, 138–40) mentions Rafael Larco Hoyle (1901–66), "a devoted amateur archaeologist" and businessman, whose family hosted a 1946 conference on Virú Valley archaeology at their estate in the Chicama Valley (see also Winters 1991:382–83).

68. J. H. Steward 1949a. For other commentary, see Carneiro (1974:92–94; 1979:289–90) and Murphy (1977:27–29; 1981:195–96). Carneiro (1974:94), Murphy (1977:28), and Goldfrank (1978:188–92), among others, have noted Steward's debt to Wittfogel. Murphy, not Steward himself, included the unpublished paper on Wittfogel in a collection of his essays (J. H. Steward 1977:87–99). See also chap. 11.

69. Mason to J. H. Steward, June 30, 1948; J. H. Steward to Mason, Aug. 5, 1948, JHS Box 8. His paper appeared as the lead article in a 1949 issue of the *American Anthropologist,* and with some slight revision in *Theory of Culture Change* (J. H. Steward 1949a, 1955c:178–209).

70. Mintz interview. Mintz recalled that Steward described his first marriage as a "dreadful experience" that led to the loss of his position at the University of Utah. This was the only instance in which Mintz remembered Steward speaking about his personal past. Dinnerstein (1976) was the author of a well-known feminist work, *The Mermaid and the Minotaur,* in which she theorized about the development of gender identity and the roots of gender relations.

71. Mintz interview; Murphy interview; Murphy 1977:9. Service (n.d.:49) recalled that "it was just as though he were one of us. . . ." See also Service (1988:149).

72. J. H. Steward to A. L. Kroeber, Mar. 4, [ca. 1948], ALK Box 28; Wolf 1981:52, 63.

73. J. H. Steward to Mason, Aug. 5, 1948, JHS Box 8.

74. J. H. Steward to Padilla, Nov. 15, 1954, JHS Box 2; J. H. Steward to Strong, Feb. 3, [1946], WDS Box 14. Clyde K. M. Kluckhohn (1905–60) did not himself develop a firm, easily identified theoretical position. Unlike Steward, he had an eclectic, humanistic perspective and a deep interest in cultural values (Parsons and Vogt 1962:142–43; see also Winters 1991:353–54).

75. J. H. Steward to A. L. Kroeber, n.d. [Feb. 1946], ALK Box 28.

76. Willey 1988:185–86. After Kroeber's death, Steward (1973:27) wrote, "Kroeber did not deal in causes or explanations, of which he was always suspicious, although he was interested in any attempts by others in this direction." The Kroeber-Steward correspondence gives little evidence of such interest.

77. Willey 1988:186; Willey interview. Kroeber presented the paper in 1948; it was published two years later (A. L. Kroeber 1950).

78. Marvin K. Opler to J. H. Steward, Feb. 15, 1949; Goldschmidt to J. H. Steward, Feb. 21, 1949; Eggan to J. H. Steward, Feb. 24, 1949; William A. Ritchie to J. H. Steward, Mar. 28, 1949; Edward T. Hall to J. H. Steward, Aug. 31, 1949, JHS Box 8; J. H. Steward to R. L. Kirkpatrick, May 31, 1949, JHS Box 2.

79. White 1943; Carneiro 1979:298n.3; Carneiro interview.

80. Caffrey 1989:333; Mintz 1981:144; Modell 1983:301; Zumwalt 1992:322. Benedict's term ran from January to May 1947. According to Jane Steward (interview), her husband supported Benedict's promotion to professor.

81. J. H. Steward to Bennett, Oct. 10, 1948, JHS Box 4. Decades later, concerns about equity and inclusiveness did lead some professional organizations to offer child care services at meetings.

82. Willey 1988:235. Beals (1982:15; 1977:104) remembered the reorganization as "bitter," with

some members accusing Steward of being "power hungry," and he thought that afterward Steward refused nomination for any elective office in the AAA. A. Irving Hallowell served as president of the AAA in 1949, and Beals in 1950.

83. J. C. Steward interview; M. Steward, official personnel folder, NPRC; J. H. Steward to Pendleton Herring, Sept. 5, 1949, JHS Box 4; see also Patterson and Lauria-Perricelli (1999). Marion Steward transferred back to Washington, D. C., after her brother left Columbia; she died in 1979 (Social Security Death Index).

84. Murphy 1987:9; J. C. Steward interview.

85. Ghani 1987:109; Lauria-Perricelli 1989:141n.139. Wolf recalled, "Steward gave courses where he would teach the first four lectures and then fall ill—he had a general tendency to withdraw from the world by getting a stomach ailment" (J. Friedman 1987:109; see also Wolf 1981:62). Physicians attributed the 1949 illness to a lingering amoebic infection (J. C. Steward interview); his 1938 trip to South America predated the development of highly effective drugs to treat such infections.

86. Kelly to J. H. Steward, Mar. 17, 1950, JHS Box 4.

87. J. H. Steward to Johnson, Apr. 28 and Oct. 29, 1950, TA. By one estimate, Steward supervised thirty-five doctoral dissertations during his six years at Columbia (Murphy 1977:9).

88. Ernest L. Wilkinson to J. H. Steward, Apr. 4, 1950; J. H. Steward to A. Devitt Vanech, Apr. 26, 1949, JHS Box 4. See also Rosenthal (1990).

89. Mintz (interview) and Sturtevant (interview) used the same words to describe how Steward was regarded in this instance by many of his colleagues. Diamond (Ghani 1987:110) and Omer Stewart (Howell 1998) were among the most outspoken critics. See Ronaasen, Clemmer, and Rudden (1999) on Steward's testimony to the Indian Claims Commission.

90. On McCarthyism's effect on universities, see Schrecker (1986).

91. J. C. Steward interview.

92. Albig to Dean Henning Larsen, May 7, 1951; J. H. Steward to Albig, Nov. 24, 1951, UISAF. John William Albig (1899–1963) taught at the University of Michigan from 1927 to 1929 and joined the University of Illinois faculty in 1930 (Cattell 1956:7; Social Security Death Index). On his 1951 trip, he also tried to recruit well-known Columbia sociologist Kingsley Davis.

93. J. H. Steward to Suzuki, Dec. 13, 1957, JHS Box 2; J. C. Steward interview; Murphy 1977:11. In his letter to Suzuki, Steward alluded to the "interpersonal tensions" that he had found difficult.

94. Murphy interview; Murphy 1977:15; Service n.d.:40. The salary offer, eleven thousand dollars, exceeded what he earned at Columbia and was magnified by the lower cost of living in the Midwest (J. C. Steward interview; University of Illinois, Transactions of the Board of Trustees, 1950–52, 1337).

95. Du Bois 1980:2; Heizer 1970; Winters 1991:212. Heizer, Kroeber, and Gifford were among those who testified on behalf of the Indians (see chap. 11).

96. Du Bois 1980:2–3; Seymour 1989:74.

97. L. J. Friedman 1999:245–46, 251, 253–54; Nyswander 1994:151–54. Nyswander chose early retirement from Berkeley a few years later. Erikson's complicated case is detailed by Lawrence J. Friedman (1999:245–52). In 1954 Du Bois accepted a tenured position specifically designated for "a woman scholar," the Radcliffe Zemurray Professorship. She was affiliated with the department of anthropology and the department of social relations at Harvard, apparently the only woman to have an affiliation with their faculties.

98. Schrecker 1986:255–57; Lissner 1953.

99. Lissner 1953; Parks and Pathé 1985:62–63.

100. Winters 1991:645; De Laguna 1962:568–69.

101. Bunzel may have had a part-time position during these years, teaching evening courses (Fawcett and McLuhan 1989), and Mead may have taught courses occasionally, as an adjunct.

102. How ethnographers of Steward's era represented women could be the subject of an entire volume, or several. See H. Moore (1988:1–11) on some of the feminist critiques published during the 1970s and 1980s that addressed questions of representation during the preceding period.

103. Murphy interview; Mintz interview; Service 1988:149, 151, n.d.:33, 49; J. Friedman 1987:110.

Chapter 11: At Home on the Prairie

1. Stegner 1954:17; Worster 2001:114–17.

2. J. H. Steward to Bennett, Nov. 12, 1952, JHS Box 1; Andriot 1983:189, 194.

3. University of Illinois 1952:428–29.

4. J. H. Steward to Bennett, Nov. 12, 1952, JHS Box 1; Provost Coleman R. Griffith to Albig, Dec. 20, 1951, UISAF.

5. J. H. Steward to Bennett, Nov. 12, 1952, JHS Box 1.

6. Albig to Stoddard, June 14, 1948; Albig to Henning Larsen, June 17, 1948, UICLAS, Box 35. In 1929 and in 1946 Kroeber had recommended Steward for a position at Illinois (A. L. Kroeber to Hiller, Mar. 4, 1929, RDA Box 71; A. L. Kroeber to Albig, Feb. 28, 1946, JHS Box 13).

7. J. H. Steward to Ruth Lewis, Jan. 11, 1971, JHS Box 3; Lewis interview. On Oscar Lewis (1914–70), see Rigdon (1988). The last books to carry Lewis's name were written by his wife and Rigdon; see chap. 12.

8. John C. McGregor (1905–92) used the phrase "prehistoric human ecology," not "cultural ecology," perhaps because he had previously worked with Lyndon Hargrave (see chap. 7) at the Museum of Northern Arizona (Jacques Cattell Press 1973:1571; Social Security Death Index). University catalogs from the 1950s show that McGregor taught a wide variety of courses. Some of his colleagues recalled in interviews that collegial relations between McGregor and Steward never improved.

9. Zimmerman to J. H. Steward, Feb. 13, 1953; Wolf to J. H. Steward, Sept. 13, 1953, JHS Box 2.

10. Diamond to J. H. Steward, Nov. 27, 1954, JHS Box 1. Diamond found employment (once again, temporarily) when Steward offered him a research position.

11. Wagley 1955:1033–35.

12. Some of his former graduate students and associates implied or said this directly in interviews. Omer Stewart shared that view (see Howell 1998:26).

13. Julian Steward's correspondence contains references to various frictions and animosities that reportedly grew over time. Jane Steward (interview) mentioned some of these, as well as her husband's disappointment that relationships with several former students approached estrangement in his later years. Murphy (interview) spoke about the value of having a recommendation from Steward and recognition by a strong network of peers (including citation of one's published work).

14. Fifteen years later, during the unprecedented hiring boom in the late 1960s, he did recommend a woman (a former student) for a position at a Canadian university (J. H. Steward to Cyril Belshaw, Oct. 19, 1969, JHS Box 3). Steward refused to recommend Ruth Bunzel even for a visiting position at the University of Texas: "Since my point of view differed completely from Ruth's I can hardly recommend her, though I must say that I have heard nothing about her for many years" (J. H. Steward to Anthony Leeds, Dec. 4, 1971, JHS Box 3).

15. Wolf to J. H. Steward, Jan. 6, 1953; Murphy to J. H. Steward, Dec. 11, 1952, Feb. 26, 1953; Service to J. H. Steward, May 15, 1953, JHS Box 2; Rubin to J. H. Steward, [ca. June 1953], JHS Box 4. Letters from other students written during the early 1950s express the same view.

16. J. H. Steward to Manners, Sept. 27, 1954; J. H. Steward to Service, July 7, 1954, JHS Box 2; J. H. Steward to Fried, Sept. 8, 1954, JHS Box 1; J. C. Steward interview.

17. Zimmerman to J. H. Steward, Aug. 10, 1953, JHS Box 1; J. H. Steward to Manners, Sept. 27, 1954, JHS Box 2; J. H. Steward to Fried, Sept. 8, 1954; J. C. Steward interview.

18. J. H. Steward to Manners, Sept. 27, 1954, JHS Box 2.

19. Bennett to J. H. Steward, Oct. 31, 1952; J. H. Steward to Bennett, Nov. 12, 1952, JHS Box 1; J. H. Steward to Joe and Grant [Cannon], Apr. 1, 1953, JHS Box 13.

20. Steward was among three scholars who received the award in 1952, six years after Kroeber received it, and five years after Lowie ("Viking Fund Medal and Award," *Current Anthropology* 7, no. 2 [1966]: 111).

21. J. H. Steward 1955c:78n.1; J. H. Steward to David B. Stout, Jan. 20, 1953; J. H. Steward to Wenner-Gren Foundation, Jan. 19, 1953, JHS Box 2; Eggan, "Presentation of the Viking Award Medalist," [Dec.] 1952, TA. Fred Eggan (1906–91) taught at the University of Chicago (Winters 1991:174–75) and was probably Steward's closest colleague—in terms of geography and shared interests—when Steward arrived at the University of Illinois.

22. J. H. Steward to Joe and Grant [Cannon], Apr. 1, 1953, JHS Box 13.

23. Willey 1988:185–86; J. H. Steward to Marvin Harris, Mar. 8, 1969, Box 3; J. H. Steward to Padilla, Nov. 15, 1954, JHS Box 2; J. H. Steward to Mintz, Jan. 7, 1953, JHS Box 2.

24. Cressman 1988:388.

25. According to Cressman (1988:388), Steward followed up those first critical comments with others in print.

26. J. H. Steward to Harris, Mar. 8, 1969; J. H. Steward to Murphy, July 4, 1971, Box 5; Manners to J. H. Steward, Mar. 24, 1970, JHS Box 3.

27. Cochrane 1978:615, 625; Worster 2001:384; Woodbury 1989:5; Belmonte 1985:640. Steward was one of only thirty anthropologists elected to membership in the academy during the century following its founding in 1863.

28. Cochrane 1978:621, 622, 626. Linton long served as chairman of the anthropology division in the National Academy of Sciences. He died in December 1953 (Winters 1991:413, 414).

29. A. L. Kroeber to Albig, Feb. 28, 1946, JHS Box 13; Wetmore to J. H. Steward, Apr. 27, 1954, JHS Box 2.

30. Wilford 1991; J. C. Steward interview. University catalogs for the period list Steward as a faculty member but not a course instructor.

31. J. H. Steward to Wetmore, Jan. 31, 1955, JHS Box 1. On the 1953 symposium, see Goldfrank (1978:188) and Steward et al. (1955).

32. Wittfogel to J. H. Steward, Oct. 28, 1955; J. H. Steward to Vera Rubin, June 20, 1955, JHS Box 2; Murphy interview.

33. Henry Wiggins to J. H. Steward, Jan. 25, 1954, JHS Box 2; Lauria-Perricelli 1989:206–19; Steward et al. 1956.

34. J. H. Steward to Joe and Grant [Cannon], Apr. 1, 1953, JHS Box 13; J. H. Steward to Manners, Dec. 11, 1968, JHS Box 3.

35. J. H. Steward to Joe and Grant [Cannon], Apr. 1, 1953, JHS Box 13; Manners to J. H. Steward, Mar. 24, 1970, JHS Box 3; M. Steward interview. Steward's repeated complaints about publishing problems, and rejected manuscripts in particular, are not supported by extant records.

36. J. H. Steward 1955c:151n.1.

37. Ibid., 122–24.

38. Ibid., 143–44, 150.

39. Chapter 2, "The Concept and Method of Cultural Ecology" grew out of a 1953 conference paper (see below) and drew on a 1948 paper for a symposium sponsored by the Ecological Society of America ("Cultural Ecology," Sept. 10, 1948, JHS Box 5). Chapter 5, "Culture Area and Cultural Type in Aboriginal America," was a revised version of a paper intended for the 1952 annual meeting of the AAA, which he did not attend (J. H. Steward 1955c:78n.1). Chapters 4 and 10 were also previously unpublished.

40. J. H. Steward to Preece, May 25, 1970, JHS Box 3; J. H. Steward 1953a, 1955c:11n.1.

41. J. H. Steward 1955c:18; J. H. Steward to Murphy, July 4, 1971, JHS Box 5. On Vere Gordon Childe (1892–1957), see Peace (1995).

42. J. H. Steward 1955c:4n.2. According to Carneiro (1974:101n.26), sociologist Edward A. Ross had previously used the term in print, in 1905.

43. Murphy 1977:30; J. H. Steward 1953a; Lowie 1948:33, 34, 35–37. See also Murphy (1980).

44. J. H. Steward to Murphy, July 4, 1971, JHS Box 5.

45. J. H. Steward 1955c:14. Carneiro (1974:94) and others identify Steward's 1949 paper as "a landmark in the study of evolutionism."

46. J. H. Steward 1955c:11; J. H. Steward to Preece, May 25, 1970; "Comments on Colin Renfrew by Julian Steward," [ca. 1968], JHS Box 3; J. H. Steward 1969a. See Carneiro (1974, 1979) for detailed summaries and trenchant commentary on Steward's approach to cultural evolution. Steward's schematic comments about multilinear evolution as a methodology led to a certain amount of confusion and protest over the years. See, for example, Carneiro's (1974:101) comments on "confound[ing] the *object* of study with the *method* of study."

47. Collier to J. H. Steward, Jan. 28, 1953, JHS Box 8.

48. Joint session program, JHS Box 8; J. H. Steward to Collier, Feb. 3, 1953, JHS Box 8; Solecki and Wagley 1963:1106. The other participant was Donald Collier (see chap. 10, n.1), an archaeologist at the Field Museum who had trained at the University of Chicago and worked in the Virú Valley in Peru (Winters 1991:120). John L. Champe (1895–1978), a former insurance company executive, earned a Ph.D. at Columbia in 1946; he was on the faculty of the University of Nebraska (Cattell 1956:114; Social Security Death Index). Baerreis also earned a Ph.D. in anthropology at Columbia in 1949 (Cattell 1956:26); he taught at the University of Wisconsin.

49. Examples include J. H. Steward to Tax, Feb. 11, 1966, JHS Box 6; J. H. Steward to Harris, Mar. 8, 1969; J. H. Steward to Speth, Sept. 8, 1970, and May 4, 1971, JHS Box 3; J. H. Steward to Murphy, July 4, 1971, JHS Box 5.

50. J. H. Steward to Harris, Mar. 8, 1969, JHS Box 3. When Steward remarked in 1969 that cultural ecology "took years to sell," it had finally come into its own; this was not the case in the early 1950s.

51. J. H. Steward to Tax, Feb. 11, 1966, JHS Box 6; J. H. Steward 1955c:37.

52. J. H. Steward 1955c:6, 37, 94.

53. Ibid., 40.

54. Ibid., 40–42.

55. Mead to Lowie, Apr. 8, 1956, RHL Box 12. Mead mistakenly referred to the date of the symposium as 1951. See Lutz (1995:252) on the "self-labeling" of theory.

56. I encountered Mead's words while searching Lowie's correspondence. The connection between what she said in 1952 and Steward's subsequent choice of title is my own inference. Her comments may have affected the content, not only the title, of *Theory of Culture Change*, leading him to think about republishing some of his more important journal articles as a collection, under a more strategic title. Steward had already written a lengthy manuscript that addressed "factors in culture change," including "the ecological factor" ("Culture Dynamics," JHS Box 7), but it was superseded by his writings in the early 1950s.

57. Steward's reference to "St. Boas" (J. H. Steward to Murphy, Mar. 31, 1967, JHS Box 6) is telling, as are his occasional comments about Mead in letters.

58. J. H. Steward to Speth, May 4, 1971, JHS Box 3.

59. Murphy 1977:17, 21; Murphy interview. Steward's premise, which provided the rationale for his focus on causality, derived from the natural sciences (Murphy 1977:17).

60. J. H. Steward to Speth, Sept. 8, 1970, JHS Box 3.

61. Wolf (1981:62, 63) noticed the conflicts and intellectual differences far more than Murphy did (Murphy interview; Murphy to J. H. Steward, Sept. 22, 1957, JHS Box 2). The Kroeber-Steward correspondence, which has an almost uniformly respectful tone, reveals little about their differences.

62. J. H. Steward 1938a:260, 261; A. L. Kroeber 1939:1, 205.

63. J. H. Steward 1955c:36.

64. Speth to J. H. Steward, Aug. 26, 1970; J. H. Steward to Speth, Sept. 8, 1970, and May 4, 1971, JHS Box 3. The University of Utah Press reprinted *Basin-Plateau* in 1970.

65. J. H. Steward 1967b:v. See Carneiro (1979:297–98) on Steward's retreat from the study of cultural evolution (see also Carneiro, in Murphy 1981:201). Steward published occasionally on the topic during the late 1950s and early 1960s (e.g., J. H. Steward 1960b; Steward and Shimkin 1961;

see also J. C. Steward 1973) and reviewed works by Childe and White (J. H. Steward 1953b, 1960d). Increasingly, however, he questioned the meaning of the term and denied interest in the subject (see chap. 12).

66. J. H. Steward to Fried, Sept. 8, 1954, JHS Box 1. Elena Padilla also contributed to the planning of this project, but she received no acknowledgment in print (see chap. 13).

67. Anticipatory anthropology, as now defined, uses "anthropological perspectives, theories, models and methods in an anticipatory mode. Such contributions will allow citizens, leaders and governments to make informed policy choices, and thereby improve their society's or community's chances for realizing preferred futures and avoiding unwanted ones" (*Anthropology News*, Dec. 1999, 36).

68. J. H. Steward to Elmer Johnson, [spring 1953], TA.

69. T. Kroeber 1970:221–23. Homer Barnett (1906–85), then a faculty member at the University of Oregon, had worked with Yurok Indians in the 1930s (Stern 1987:702). Alfred L. Kroeber (1925) had published the authoritative work on California Indians. Robert Heizer (1915–79) had carried out archaeological work throughout California (Baumhoff 1980).

70. Ralph A. Barney to J. H. Steward, July 3, 1954, JHS Box 1; T. Kroeber 1970:221–23.

71. A. L. Kroeber to J. H. Steward, Oct. 25, 1955, JHS Box 1; T. Kroeber 1970:222.

72. J. H. Steward to Kelly, Jan. 31, 1955, JHS Box 4; Manners to J. H. Steward, May 1, 1954, JHS Box 2.

73. Japan diary, Dec. 9 and Dec. 20, 1955, JHS Box 6; Steward to John Jones, Apr. 20, 1951; J. H. Steward to Leland Yost, Apr. 20, 1951; Yost to J. H. Steward, May 28, 1951, JHS Box 4; J. H. Steward to Barney, May 24, 1957, JHS Box 1; J. H. Steward to Suzuki, Dec. 13, 1957, JHS Box 2.

74. Murphy 1977:5–6; Murphy and Murphy 1986; Murphy to J. H. Steward, Sept. 22, 1957, JHS Box 2. On the complex history of the Indian Claims Commission and Shoshone land claims, see Crum (1994:123–47, 176–83).

75. Japan diary, Jan. 6, Jan. 18–19, and Jan. 24, 1956, JHS Box 6; J. H. Steward to Lowie, Dec. 30, 1955, RDA Box 141; J. C. Steward interview. Richard K. Beardsley (1918–78), a Berkeley-trained anthropologist and Japan specialist at the University of Michigan, originally contacted Steward about going to Japan (Japan diary, Oct. 13, 1955, JHS Box 6; Jacques Cattell Press 1968:93; Social Security Death Index).

76. Japan diary, Jan. 21–28, 1956, JHS Box 6; J. H. Steward to Murphy, July 4, 1971, Box 5; Murphy to J. H. Steward, Sept. 22, 1957, JHS Box 2.

77. Japan diary, Jan. 26–27, 1956, JHS Box 6.

78. Japan diary, Jan. 29–Feb. 13 and Feb. 28, 1956, JHS Box 6; J. H. Steward to Johnson, Feb. 1, 1956, TA.

79. Japan diary, Feb. 17, JHS Box 6; J. C. Steward interview; see also Murphy 1981:170.

80. J. C. Steward interview; Japan diary, Apr. 19, 1956, JHS Box 6.

81. Japan diary, Feb.–Aug. 1956, JHS Box 6.

82. Japan diary, Feb. 17, 1956, JHS Box 6; J. C. Steward interview.

Chapter 12: Notes from the Ninetieth Meridian

1. Manners 1964, 1973, 1996; Murphy 1977, 1981; J. H. Steward 1977; Wolf 1964:55; Mintz 1979; Willey and Phillips 1958; Willey 1988.

2. Murphy to J. H. Steward, Sept. 27, 1965, JHS Box 3; Murphy interview; Murphy 1977:12, 1981:205; Lehman interview; Mintz interview; Mintz 1981:167; Wolf 1981:65.

3. Correspondence with Steward, as well as entries in such works as *American Men and Women of Science*, document their careers.

4. Diamond 1981:98; Service to J. H. Steward, Apr. 27, 1953, July 5, 1954, and Oct. 11, 1955, JHS Box 2; Wolf 1981:65.

5. Hollingshead 1989:104. On Powdermaker, see Silverman (1989) and chap. 5, n.2.

6. James 1989:183; Rubin to J. H. Steward, n.d. [spring 1953], JHS Box 4; Rubin to J. H. Steward, Oct. 1, 1953, JHS Box 2.

7. Leacock 1993:22–23.

8. Saunders 1989:317; Zumwalt 1992:270–72, 279n.153.

9. J. H. Steward to Rubin, Sept. 12, 1952; Padilla to J. H. Steward, Nov. 29, 1953; J. H. Steward to Samuel Rubin Foundation, Sept. 13, 1952; J. H. Steward to Wagley, Dec. 3, 1952, JHS Box 2. Steward later offered her a research associate position at Illinois, but she declined, citing her husband's illness (Padilla to J. H. Steward, July 6, 1953, JHS Box 2).

10. Padilla to J. H. Steward, Oct. 18, 1952, Feb. 2, 1953, Apr. 1 and Apr. 23, 1953, JHS Box 2. Throughout most of the twentieth century, American graduate programs in anthropology trained Ph.D. students in numbers that exceeded the few academic positions available in that field.

11. Padilla to J. H. Steward, Oct. 18, 1952, Apr. 1 and Apr. 23, 1953; Rubin to J. H. Steward, n.d. [ca. spring 1953]; Padilla to J. H. Steward, n.d. [ca. 1954]; "Tuesday," [ca. Dec. 1953]; "Thursday," [ca. 1953], and "Sunday," [ca. 1954], JHS Box 2; Wagley 1964:605; Padilla 1958:vii.

12. Rubin to J. H. Steward, n.d., JHS Box 4.

13. J. H. Steward to Albig, May 21, 1952, UISAF; J. H. Steward 1967b:vi.

14. Wolf to J. H. Steward, Feb. 18, 1957, JHS Box 2; J. H. Steward 1967b:vi, 1967c; Lehman interview; Beidelman 1998:278–81. Beidelman continued graduate study, entering Oxford University after the fieldwork in Tanganyika. Suzuki did not contribute a chapter to the publication that resulted from the project (J. H. Steward to Suzuki, Aug. 12, 1959, JHS Box 2).

15. J. H. Steward, Japan diary, Mar. 15 and Apr. 5, 1956, JHS Box 6; J. H. Steward 1967b:vi.

16. J. H. Steward, "Research Proposal," 1959, JHS Box 2.

17. Caffrey 1989:329; J. H. Steward, Japan diary, Mar. 20, 1956, JHS Box 6; Murphy 1977:13.

18. World trip diary, Jan.10–Aug. 27, 1958, JHS Box 6; J. H. Steward to Suzuki, Dec. 13, 1957, Apr. 27, July 6, 1958, Nov. 2, 1958, and Jan. 22, 1959, JHS Box 2; Strong to J. H. Steward, Sept. 10, 1958, JHS Box 4; J. H. Steward to [Louella] Cy Lowie, Oct. 1, 1957, RHL Box 13; J. C. Steward interview.

19. Mintz to J. H. Steward, Nov. 27, 1958, JHS Box 15; J. H. Steward to Manners, Sept. 20, 1959; J. H. Steward to Tax, Sept. 25, 1959, JHS Box 2; J. H. Steward to Diamond, July 29, 1959, JHS Box 1; J. C. Steward interview. A portion of Steward's colon was removed during the second surgery.

20. Petition of "The Anthropology Committee," Feb. 3, 1959; Gouldner to Dean Lyle Lanier, May 13, 1959, UICLAS Box 43.

21. J. H. Steward to White, Nov. 13, 1959, JHS Box 2; Willey 1988:190; J. H. Steward 1973:16.

22. Willey 1988:190, 240; Alkire interview; T. Kroeber 1970:230; J. H. Steward 1973:16, 1960b.

23. J. H. Steward to Sarah Dees, Mar. 30, 1960, JHS Box 2; J. C. Steward interview; Alkire interview. Steward had surgery for a detached retina.

24. This account of Betty Starr (1906–64) draws on documents in the Joseph Casagrande Papers, JBC Box 3; Starr's personnel file, UIDA; internal documents of the university (UICLAS Box 44); and Casagrande (1966). In conversations and interviews with anthropologists who knew Starr in the 1960s, I was twice told that she had injured her leg in Mexico and that this prevented her from doing further fieldwork. Both men thought that this disability explained her job as secretary. Another anthropologist who knew Starr years before that, however, remembered that she walked with a noticeable limp; it did not prevent her from doing fieldwork in Mexico (Constance Sutton, personal communication, Mar. 17, 1997). Starr's 1959 notice appeared in the back pages of vol. 61, no. 2 of the *American Anthropologist*. (The bound volumes found in some library collections do not include these back pages, which consist of advertisements.)

25. "Department of Anthropology," [ca. fall 1959], JBC Box 1; Lehman interview; Bareis interview; Alkire interview.

26. S. I. Thompson 1985; J. H. Steward to White, Nov. 13, 1959, JHS Box 2; J. C. Steward interview; Gouldner 1957. In interviews, Steward's colleagues invariably brought up his virtual absence from the department, which they interpreted in various ways.

27. A. L. Kroeber to J. H. Steward, Oct. 25, 1955, and Jan. 19, 1959, JHS Box 1; World trip diary, Feb. 3, 1959, JHS Box 6.

28. J. H. Steward to Vera Rubin et al., June 3, 1955, JHS Box 2; J. H. Steward to Manners, Jan. 28 and May 22, 1970, JHS Box 3. I do not use the phrase "self-made man" in a generic way; the academic model of success was male defined in every sense.

29. J. H. Steward, "Research Proposal," 1959, JHS Box 2; Shimkin interview, 1991; J. H. Steward to Starr, Feb. 14, 1961, UIDA. The draft of the introduction he worked on at Stanford remained unpublished during his lifetime. An edited version appears in a posthumous collection (J. H. Steward 1977:297–330).

30. J. H. Steward to Starr, Feb. 14, 1961, UIDA. David Damas and Richard Lee were among those who cited his influence in letters and in print (e.g, Damas to J. H. Steward, Feb. 17, 1970, JHS Box 3; Lee to J. H. Steward, Feb. 18, 1966, and Jan. 20, 1967, JHS Box 6).

31. J. H. Steward to Johnson, Dec. 7, 1960, TA; J. H. Steward to Aird, Mar. 3, 1964, JHS Box 5; J. H. Steward to Louise Lacey, Oct. 14, 1969, JHS Box 3; Andriot 1983:62, 66.

32. Kroeber-Quinn to J. H. Steward, Mar. 28, 1970, JHS Box 3. She had recently remarried, hence the change in surname.

33. Dasmann 1965.

34. T. Kroeber 1970:276–86; J. H. Steward 1961b.

35. J. H. Steward to [Louella] Cy Lowie, Oct. 1, 1957, RHL Box 13; J. H. Steward 1961a, 1961b, 1962; J. H. Steward to Faron, June 5, 1970, JHS Box 3; Murphy 1972, 1980. The bibliography compiled by Jane Steward (1973), which accompanied her husband's obituary (Manners 1973), did not include several posthumously published works, the Lowie biography among them (J. H. Steward 1974).

36. According to Starr's obituary in a local newspaper, the *News-Gazette*, the cause of death was a brain tumor. She died on December 18, 1964.

37. J. H. Steward to Barney Childs, Aug. 24, 1965, DSC. For example, Ruth Landes (1908–91) found an academic position in 1965, at the age of fifty-seven and nearly thirty years after she carried out fieldwork in Brazil (Landes 1986; S. Cole 1995).

38. Listings of faculty, which appear in university course catalogs published during this period, document the growth of the department.

39. Shimkin interview, 1989; J. C. Steward interview.

40. Alkire interview; J. H. Steward to Belshaw, Dec. 26, 1968, JHS Box 3; World trip diary, Aug. 20–21, 1958, JHS Box 6; S. Nagata 1970; J. H. Steward 1967b:vi, 52. Alkire spent most of his career at the University of Victoria, and Nagata at the University of Toronto.

41. J. C. Steward interview; Pilcher 1972; Alkire interview. George L. Hicks (1935–98) taught at Brown University from 1967 until his death (*Anthropology Newsletter*, Sept. 1998). Thompson spent his career at the University of Oklahoma.

42. J. H. Steward to Belshaw, Oct. 19, 1969, JHS Box 3; J. H. Steward to Murphy, Mar. 31, 1967, JHS Box 6. Jane Steward (interview) recalled that the Amish hitched their horses to sleighs and traveled off the road as necessary after the ice storm. See also J. A. Nagata (1989). Judith A. Nagata has spent her career at York University.

43. Bareis interview; J. H. Steward to Reich, Nov. 25, 1969, JHS Box 3. I also draw here on conversations with former students who entered the program in the late 1960s and early 1970s. Steward officially retired in September 1969, citing health reasons; this was about six months before the then mandatory retirement age of sixty-eight (J. H. Steward to Louise Lacey, Oct. 14, 1969, JHS Box 3; J. H. Steward to Randall C. Reid, Nov. 25, 1969, DSC).

44. Harris 1968; Murphy 1977:35; Murphy interview; J. H. Steward to Harris, Mar. 23, 1969, JHS Box 3.

45. J. H. Steward to John K. Chance, Mar. 23, 1969, JHS Box 3; Chance, "Julian Steward's Evolution," 1968, JHS Box 6.

46. J. H. Steward to Judith and Shuichi Nagata, Oct. 19, 1969, JHS Box 3.

47. Murphy to J. H. Steward, Nov. 11, 1964, JHS Box 3.

48. Manners 1964; Mintz interview.

49. J. C. Steward interview; J. H. Steward to Scheele, Aug. 28, 1969; J. H. Steward to Betty Meggers and Clifford Evans, Nov. 18, 1968; J. H. Steward to Harris, Mar. 8, 1969, JHS Box 3.

50. Murphy to J. H. Steward, Apr. 7, 1967; J. H. Steward to Manners, Sept. 30, 1966, JHS Box 3; J. H. Steward to Tax, Feb. 11, 1966, JHS Box 6. June Helm was the exception; her name appears several times in Steward's correspondence.

51. J. H. Steward to Manners, Jan. 28, 1970, JHS Box 3; J. H. Steward 1967b; Wolf 1967:759, 761.

52. J. H. Steward 1968c:147.

53. J. H. Steward to Manners, Dec. 11, 1968; J. H. Steward to Manners, Jan. 28, 1970, JHS Box 3; J. H. Steward 1967b:ix.

54. Donald Jackson, interoffice memo, July 19, 1968, UIP; J. H. Steward to Manners, Sept. 30, 1966, Jan. 9, 1968, and Jan. 28, 1970; J. H. Steward to Damas, Mar. 2, 1970; J. H. Steward to T. Kroeber, Apr. 3, 1970, JHS Box 3; J. H. Steward to Tax, Feb. 11, 1966, JHS Box 6. I am grateful to Elizabeth G. Dulany for providing copies of correspondence from the files of the University of Illinois Press.

55. Miodrag Muntyan to Richard Wentworth, May 15, 1970, UIP. The inclusion of Steward's (1960a) article on the Carrier in a posthumous collection of his essays also suggests that this was Steward's intention (J. H. Steward 1977:188–200).

56. Murphy and Steward 1956; Leacock 1954; J. H. Steward 1960:742; J. H. Steward 1977:198.

57. Leacock 1993:20, 24.

58. J. H. Steward to Manners, Sept. 30, 1966; J. H. Steward to Preece, May 25, 1970, JHS Box 3.

59. Murphy interview; Murphy 1977:31; J. H. Steward 1960d; White 1957; J. H. Steward to White, Nov. 13, 1959, JHS Box 2. Steward visited Ann Arbor in 1955 before leaving for Japan (Japan diary, Dec. 7, 1955, JHS Box 6).

60. Service n.d.:65–67. See also Peace (1993, 1998, n.d.).

61. J. H. Steward to Damas, Jan. 27, 1970, JHS Box 3; J. H. Steward to Tax, Feb. 11, 1966, JHS Box 6; J. H. Steward 1968b.

62. J. H. Steward to Murphy, Mar. 31, 1967, JHS Box 6; Murphy interview. Murphy used the phrase "too techno-environmental" after the fact, not in the mid-1950s. He thought that the concept of core culture leaned too far in the direction of the approach that Harris advocated, cultural materialism (Harris 1979).

63. Murphy interview; Murphy to J. H. Steward, Apr. 7, 1967, JHS Box 3. Murphy attributed these words to Roy Rappaport (1926–97). The comment was made in reference to a manuscript that caused Steward great distress. Rappaport knew this because Sol Tax, then editor of *Current Anthropology,* sent the two authors a copy of Steward's comments. Steward argued rather bitterly that they had misrepresented his ideas (see below). The article appeared in print in an edited collection two years later (Vayda and Rappaport 1968).

64. Murphy to J. H. Steward, Nov. 11, 1964, JHS Box 3; J. H. Steward to Lee, July 21, 1966, JHS Box 6.

65. Vayda and Rappaport, "Ecology, Cultural and Non-cultural," n.d. [1966], JHS Box 6; Murphy interview; Hanc 1981:159–61. When Murphy told me about the role he and Wolf played, he made no connection between the loss of that concept and the direction—or rather the uncertainty about direction—that characterized some of Steward's later work. I did not clearly see the connection myself until I wrote this chapter, years after Murphy's death and months after Wolf's.

66. Wolf 1967:762; Beidelman 1998:281. The essay about this project published after his death (J. H. Steward 1977:297–330) was intended as an introduction; it was not a statement of summation and synthesis.

67. J. H. Steward to Murphy, Mar. 31, 1967, JHS Box 6.

68. J. H. Steward to Harris, Mar. 8, 1969; Harris to J. H. Steward, Mar. 19, 1969; Murphy to J. H. Steward, Apr. 7, 1967, JHS Box 3; J. H. Steward 1966, 1977:87–99, 1978.

69. J. H. Steward to Manners, Sept. 30, 1966, JHS Box 3; J. H. Steward to Murphy, Mar. 31, 1967, JHS Box 6.

70. J. H. Steward to Tax, Feb. 11, 1966; J. H. Steward to Murphy, Jan. 24, 1967, and July 10, 1970, JHS Box 3; J. H. Steward to Murphy, Mar. 31, 1967, JHS Box 6.

71. J. H. Steward to Manners, Jan. 9, 1968 [1969]; J. H. Steward to Murphy, Jan. 24, 1967, JHS Box 3; J. H. Steward to Murphy, Mar. 31, 1967, JHS Box 6. Graduate students at the University of Illinois founded a journal in Steward's honor in the late 1960s. The *Journal of the Steward Anthropological Society* posted Steward's photograph and a brief biographical profile at its Web site in the 1990s.

72. J. H. Steward, Deep Springs alumnus supplementary questionnaire, May 28, 1970, DSC; J. H. Steward to Manners, Dec. 11, 1968, JHS Box 3; J. H. Steward to Murphy, Mar. 31, 1967, JHS Box 6.

73. J. H. Steward to Manners, Dec. 11, 1968, and Jan. 9, 1968 [1969]; J. H. Steward to Meggers and Evans, Nov. 18, 1968, JHS Box 3; "Viking Fund Medal and Award," *Current Anthropology* 7, no. 2 (1966): 111.

74. J. C. Steward interview; J. H. Steward to Foster, May 14, 1967, JHS Box 3.

75. J. H. Steward to Foster, May 14, 1967; J. H. Steward to Mark L. Berman, Mar. 23, 1969, JHS Box 3.

76. J. C. Steward interview; Service to J. H. Steward, Feb. 23, 1969; J. H. Steward to Beals, Mar. 11, 1969; Beals to J. H. Steward, Apr. 4, 1969, JHS Box 3.

77. Randall C. Reid to J. H. Steward, Nov. 14, 1969; J. H. Steward, Deep Springs alumnus questionnaire, May 17, 1961, DSC. Windsor Putnam, as reported in the *New York Times* (May 13, 1976, 38), died at his home in Jamaica after retiring from a New York City law firm at which he was a partner. See also chap. 2, n.60.

78. J. H. Steward to Reid, Nov. 25, 1969, DSC. Steward received another invitation in 1971 (Reid to J. H. Steward, Feb. 4, 1971, DSC), which he also had to decline. On Deep Springs in the 1990s, see Doherty (1995).

79. J. H. Steward to Manners, Jan. 28, 1970; J. H. Steward to T. Kroeber, Feb. 19, 1970; J. H. Steward to Scheele, Aug. 28, 1969, JHS Box 3.

80. Stegner 1954; J. C. Steward interview. To be precise, Urbana lies east of the ninetieth meridian. Geographers later adjusted the borderline slightly, using the ninety-eighth meridian instead (Worster 2001:355).

81. J. H. Steward to Kroeber-Quinn, Feb. 19, 1970; Kroeber-Quinn to J. H. Steward, Mar. 28, 1970; J. H. Steward to Kroeber-Quinn, Apr. 3, 1970, JHS Box 3; Kennedy 1997. Doris Radin (1901–91) died in California some twenty years later (Social Security Death Index).

82. J. H. Steward to Ruth Lewis, Jan. 11, 1971, JHS Box 3.

83. Rigdon 1988:18; Lewis, Lewis, and Rigdon 1977–78; Shimkin interview, 1991. I recall reading this review in the late 1970s, but I have not been able to locate it. The reviewer implied that Ruth Lewis must have had an active hand in the previous publications. Years after her husband's death, the University of Illinois acknowledged her work by awarding her an honorary doctorate.

84. J. C. Steward interview.

85. J. H. Steward to Murphy, June 23, 1971, JHS Box 5; J. H. Steward to Scheele, Aug. 28, 1969, JHS Box 3; Wagley to J. H. Steward, Feb. 24, 1970, JHS Box 5; J. H. Steward 1974.

86. J. H. Steward 1961a, 1961b, 1962, 1973.

87. Muntyan to Wentworth, May 15, 1970, UIP; J. H. Steward to Murphy, June 23, 1971, JHS Box 3; J. H. Steward 1970. Steward's death, just months later, prevented him from completing his paper for the Great Basin volume (D'Azevedo 1986). During his final illness, he dictated a portion of it, but the manuscript remained incomplete (J. C. Steward to D'Azevedo, May 14, 1972, JHS Box 16).

88. J. H. Steward to Faron, June 5, 1970; J. H. Steward to Murphy, July 10, 1970; J. H. Steward to Preece, May 25, 1970; J. H. Steward to Damas, Mar. 2, 1970, JHS Box 3; Muntyan to Wentworth, May 15, 1970, UIP.

89. J. H. Steward to Damas, Jan. 27, 1970; J. H. Steward to Harris, Mar. 23, 1969, JHS Box 3: J. H. Steward 1968a:332–33.

90. J. H. Steward 1968b:340, 1977:48; J. C. Steward interview. Michael Steward (interview) commented that his mother spent most of her adult life as "Mrs. Julian Steward," but finally became "Jane Steward" after she took up a new life in Honolulu in the late 1970s. That new life included working at a shelter for battered women and later volunteering at a suicide prevention center.

91. J. H. Steward to Damas, Jan. 27, 1970; J. H. Steward to Wenner-Gren Foundation, Jan. 12, 1972; J. H. Steward to Manners, Mar. 3, 1970, JHS Box 3.

92. Murphy 1977:36; J. H. Steward to Beals, Mar. 11, 1969, JHS Box 3; J. H. Steward to Judith and Shuichi Nagata, Oct. 19, 1969, JHS Box 3. Steward (1938a:260) termed Marxism a "philosophy" at a time, in the 1930s, when many intellectuals—including colleagues such as White—viewed it as a "science" (see Peace 1993:128). Steward's comments in correspondence suggest no change in his view later in life.

93. J. H. Steward 1967a; J. H. Steward to Manners, Sept. 30, 1966, JHS Box 3; J. C. Steward interview. Steward perhaps overstated the case when he said that he could offer "scores of references" in which he included religion as a factor in "the ecological picture" (J. H. Steward to Tax, Feb. 11, 1966, JHS Box 6).

94. J. H. Steward 1977:345; J. C. Steward interview. Steward expressed support for the civil rights movement, but extreme skepticism about curricular reforms such as the creation of "Afro-American culture courses" that covered only the United States (J. H. Steward to Scheele, Aug. 28, 1969, JHS Box 3; Alkire interview).

95. J. H. Steward, "Autobiographical Appraisal," n.d., JHS Box 16. In a previous publication (Kerns 1999), I dated this statement ca. 1954, which is probably incorrect. He may have started writing the incomplete draft that he titled "Autobiographical Appraisal" in 1969 (see J. H. Steward to Barry Nadler, Apr. 6, 1969, JHS Box 3).

96. Jane Steward sent a draft of her husband's statement to Manners for his use in preparing an obituary (J. C. Steward to Manners, n.d. [ca. Mar. 1972], JHS Box 3). The words quoted in the obituary (Manners 1973) show that she sent another draft, probably a later one.

97. J. C. Steward to Manners, n.d. [ca. Mar. 1972], HS Box 3; J. C. Steward interview. Other tasks included gathering her late husband's papers for deposit in the University of Illinois Archives and answering inquiries, including my own, about his work. She did gain formal recognition as the coeditor of the last collection of his essays (J. H. Steward 1977).

98. J. C. Steward to Manners, n.d. [ca. Mar. 1972], JHS Box 3; J. C. Steward to Muntyan, July 14, 1973; J. C. Steward to Wentworth, Jan. 1, 1978, UIP.

99. Harold M. Ross to Wentworth, Nov. 2 and Nov. 14, 1973, UIP. Ross was the first reader and Norman E. Whitten Jr. was the second. If sales figures are any indication, scholars have agreed with Whitten. *Evolution and Ecology* has sold less than four thousand copies since its publication in 1977, and *Theory of Culture Change* has sold more than seventeen thousand copies since being reprinted in 1972 (Dulany, University of Illinois Press, personal communication, Feb. 28, 2000).

100. Murphy 1977:14; J. H. Steward 1977:297–330, 333–46. See also n.66 above.

101. J. H. Steward 1977; Murphy 1977:21; Murphy to Wentworth, July 22, 1975, UIP. Wolf and Fried read and commented on a draft of Murphy's introduction (Murphy to J. C. Steward, May 26, 1974, UIP). Jane Steward did not correct a few errors, perhaps for reasons of academic diplomacy: for example, the idea that Kroeber and Lowie "guided his thinking" in equal measure (Murphy 1977:4).

Conclusion

1. Doig 1978:239; J. H. Steward to Reich, Feb. 25 1969, JHS Box 3.

2. J. C. Steward interview; Nyswander interview, 1996; Murphy interview; Murphy 1977:1; J. H. Steward to H. E. Kirby, Feb. 12, 1962, DSC.

3. Brewer (1996) now uses the term "recollective memories" for memories of a single specific event (e.g., McKay's escape). "Generic personal memories" result from "repeated exposure to a

set of related experiences" (Brewer 1986:30–31). The importance of Steward's memories from adolescence and early adulthood is not uncommon. Research by cognitive psychologists with American subjects indicates that personal memories from this period tend to be regarded as more vivid and important than those from earlier and later ones (see Fitzgerald 1996).

4. Murphy interview; Murphy 1977:1, 9, 16–21, 21n.6; J. H. Steward to Manners, Mar. 3 and Apr. 3, 1970, JHS Box 3.

5. Manners 1973:897, 1996:333.

6. J. H. Steward 1938a:8. Mixing wheat with wild seeds, mentioned in chapter 8, is an example of using the traditional (gathered, wild foods) and the new (purchased, cultivated foods).

7. J. H. Steward 1949a, 1955c:178–209, 1941b:235. See table 5, with a chronology of stages that culminate in "Cyclical Conquests" (J. H. Steward 1955c:190).

8. J. H. Steward 1967d:251.

9. J. H. Steward 1955c:126.

10. Ibid., 125, 136. At least forty people lived at Deep Springs around 1918, including students, the faculty and their families, the cooks, a few construction workers, the ranch manager and ranch hands, some of their family members, a bookkeeper, and Nunn. The valley itself is about fifty square miles, but Steward and his fellow students also explored adjacent, uninhabited areas.

11. Ibid., 125, 137.

12. I believe this definition of the personal construction of meaning is in keeping with Chodorow's (1999) use of the term. The meaning emerges most clearly in her case examples (see Chodorow 1999:78–91).

13. See Chodorow (1999) with reference to the complex relationship of personal meaning and cultural meaning, and the personal construction of meaning as an ongoing process in the subjective life of the individual.

14. J. H. Steward 1936a:333, 1937b:90, 1955c:125, 136, 137, 156. Steward obviously did not change his ideas about patrilocality and male dominance, as the language in the 1955 version of his essays indicates.

15. On the failure to cite publications by women in sociocultural anthropology, see Lutz (1990); on women scholars' "lack of visibility" in anthropology, see Parezo (1993:28–29).

16. J. H. Steward to Speth, May 4, 1971, JHS Box 3.

17. Barnard 1983:196. Barnard's comments were directed at what he labeled the "Steward-Service typology of band societies," and its "fatal flaw, the supposed widespread existence of the 'patrilineal' or 'patrilocal' band" (Barnard 1983:195). Service (1962) used the term *patrilocal band.*"

18. On critical commentary, see the introduction, n.9. Fischer and Golde (1968) wrote directly about gender discrimination in the profession (see also De Laguna's [1962:568] pointed remark about women at Columbia).

19. J. H. Steward 1936a, 1937b, 1938a. Letters and journal entries suggest that the years between 1933 and 1938 were a particularly happy period in Steward's adult life.

20. Howell 1998:26; J. C. Steward interview.

21. J. H. Steward to Aird, Mar. 3, 1964, DSC; J. H. Steward to alumni committee, Mar. 3, 1946, DSC.

22. J. H. Steward to Johnson, Aug. 25, 1934, TA.

23. See, for example, J. H. Steward 1941c:83.

24. In the language of psychoanalysis, "the anthropologist's transferences"—or "resonant creations of personal meaning" (Chodorow 1999:208)—were at work here, greatly influencing where Steward directed his attention and how he interpreted what he saw.

25. Murphy 1977:9; Murphy interview. See also Wolf (2001:10).

26. See Lutz (1990, 1995).

References Cited

Documentary Sources and Manuscript Collections

A. L. Kroeber Papers, MSS C-B 925, Bancroft Library, University of California, Berkeley

Board of regents meetings minutes, accession 139, University of Utah Archives, Salt Lake City

Deep Springs College, correspondence and records

Federal employment records, National Personnel Records Center, U.S. Office of Personnel Management, St. Louis

General Correspondence, 1909–50, Records of the Bureau of American Ethnology, National Anthropological Archives, Smithsonian Institution

Historical records of the members of the faculty, accession 78–79, University of Utah Records Center, Salt Lake City

Joseph B. Casagrande Papers, record series 15/2/22, University of Illinois Archives, Urbana

Julian H. Steward Papers, record series 15/2/21, University of Illinois Archives, Urbana

Journals of Julian and Jane Steward, I:1934–36, II:1938–39

Livingston Farrand Papers, Department of Manuscripts and University Archives, Cornell University

L. L. Nunn Papers, Department of Manuscripts and University Archives, Cornell University

Michigan Academy of Sciences, Arts, and Letters publications, Bentley Library, University of Michigan

Presidential Papers of George Thomas, accession 17, University of Utah Archives, Salt Lake City

Records of the Department of Anthropology, CU-23, University Archives, Bancroft Library, University of California, Berkeley

Robert Harry Lowie Papers, MSS C-B 927, Bancroft Library, University of California, Berkeley

Telluride Association, correspondence and records, Ithaca, New York

University of Illinois, Department of Anthropology, correspondence and records, Urbana, Illinois

University of Illinois, College of Liberal Arts and Sciences subject file, record series 15/1/1, University Archives, Urbana, Illinois

University of Illinois Press, correspondence and records, Urbana, Illinois

University of Illinois, staff appointments file, record series 2/5/15, University Archives, Urbana, Illinois

William Duncan Strong Papers, National Anthropological Archives, Smithsonian Institution, Washington, D.C.

Interviews

William H. Alkire, October 26, 2001, telephone interview

Charles J. Bareis, July 25, 1991, Urbana, Illinois

Joel Cadbury, June 20, 1989, Ithaca, New York
Robert Carneiro, July 28, 1998, Williamsburg, Virginia
Margaret Clark, Cosmos Club, August 21, 1990, Washington, D.C.
William Fenton, Nov. 13, 1988, Williamsburg, Virginia
Catherine S. Fowler, July 28, 1998, Williamsburg, Virginia
Don Fowler, July 28, 1998, Williamsburg, Virginia
Eva Boone Hussey, Coordinator of Nursing Services, Mother Church of Christ, Scientist, August 22, 2000, telephone interview
Frederick K. Lehman, August 3, 1989, Urbana, Illinois
Ruth M. Lewis, August 7, 1989, Urbana, Illinois
Sidney W. Mintz, July 20, 1998, telephone interview
Robert F. Murphy, August 24, 1989, Leonia, New Jersey
L. Jackson Newell, June 22, 1988, Salt Lake City, Utah
Dorothy B. Nyswander, June 24, 1996, June 4, 1997, and July 7, 1998, Kensington, California
Herbert R. Reich, May 19–21, 1989, Groveland, Massachusetts
Demitri B. Shimkin, July 31, 1989, July 22 and July 24, 1991, Urbana, Illinois
Jane Cannon Steward, March 6–12, 1988, Honolulu, Hawaii
Michael G. Steward, March 12, 1988, Honolulu, Hawaii
William Sturtevant, July 29, 1998, Williamsburg, Virginia
Gordon R. Willey, October 4, 2001, telephone interview
Virginia Heyer Young, December 5, 1989, Charlottesville, Virginia

Published Sources

Adams, Ansel, with Mary Street Alinder. 1985. *Ansel Adams: An Autobiography.* Boston: Little, Brown.
Aird, Robert. 1977. "A Few Informal Recollections." *Deep Springs Newsletter* 25:4.
Amoss, Pamela. 1989. "Erna Gunther, 1896–1982." In *Women Anthropologists: Selected Biographies.* Ed. Ute Gacs, Aisha Khan, Jerrie McIntyre, and Ruth Weinberg. 133–39. Urbana: University of Illinois Press.
Andriot, John L., ed. 1983. *Population Abstract of the United States.* Vol. 1. McLean, Va.: Andriot Associates.
Arkush, Brooke S. 1999. "Numic Pronghorn Exploitation: A Reassessment of Stewardian-Derived Models of Big-Game Hunting in the Great Basin." In *Julian Steward and the Great Basin: The Making of an Anthropologist.* Ed. Richard O. Clemmer, L. Daniel Myers, and Mary Elizabeth Rudden. 35–52. Salt Lake City: University of Utah Press.
Aron, Cindy S. 1981."'To Barter Their Souls for Gold': Female Clerks in Federal Government Offices, 1862–1890." *Journal of American History* 67 (4): 835–53.
———. 1987. *Ladies and Gentlemen of the Civil Service: Middle-Class Workers in Victorian America.* New York: Oxford University Press.
Arrington, Leonard J. 1986. "Utah's Great Drought of 1934." *Utah Historical Quarterly* 54 (3): 245–64.
Austin, Mary. 1903. *Land of Little Rain.* Boston: Houghton Mifflin.
Babcock, Barbara A. 1993. "'Not in the Absolute Singular': Rereading Ruth Benedict." In *Hidden Scholars: Women Anthropologists in the Native American Southwest.* Ed. Nancy J. Parezo. 107–28. Albuquerque: University of New Mexico Press.
Bailey, Stephen A. 1933. *L. L. Nunn: A Memoir.* Ithaca, N.Y.: Cayuga Press for Telluride Association.
Bainton, Roland H. 1943. *George Lincoln Burr: His Life.* Ithaca, N.Y.: Cornell University Press.
Baldus, Herbert. 1946. "Curt Nimuendajú, 1883–1945." *American Anthropologist* 48 (2): 238–43.
Barnard, Alan. 1983. "Contemporary Hunter-Gatherers: Current Theoretical Issues in Ecology and Social Organization." *Annual Review of Anthropology* 12:193–214.

Basehart, Harry, and W. W. Hill. 1965. "Leslie Spier, 1893–1961." *American Anthropologist* 67 (5): 1258–77.

Baugh, Ruth E. 1937. "Land Use Changes in the Bishop Area of Owens Valley, California." *Economic Geography* 13 (1): 17–34.

Bauman, John F., and Thomas H. Coode. 1988. *In the Eye of the Great Depression: New Deal Reporters and the Agony of the American People.* De Kalb: Northern Illinois University Press.

Baumhoff, M. A. 1980. "Robert Fleming Heizer, 1915–1979." *American Anthropologist* 82 (4): 843–47.

Beals, Ralph. 1977. *Anthropologist and Educator: Ralph L. Beals.* Oral history compiled by Diane L. Dillon. Berkeley: Regional Oral History Office, Bancroft Library, University of California.

———. 1979. "Julian Steward: The Berkeley Days, A Personal Recollection." *Journal of the Steward Anthropological Society* 11 (1): 3–16.

———. 1982. "Fifty Years in Anthropology." *Annual Review of Anthropology* 11:1–23.

Beidelman, T. O. 1998. "Marking Time: Becoming an Anthropologist." *Ethnos* 63 (2): 273–96.

Belmonte, Thomas. 1985. "Alexander Lesser, 1902–1982." *American Anthropologist* 87 (3): 637–44.

Bennett, John W. 1998. *Classic Anthropology: Critical Essays, 1944–1996.* New Brunswick, N.J.: Transaction.

Benson, Jackson J. 1996. *Wallace Stegner: His Life and Work.* New York: Viking.

Bishop, Morris. 1962. *A History of Cornell.* Ithaca, N.Y.: Cornell University Press.

Blackhawk, Ned. 1997. "Julian Steward and the Politics of Representation." In *Julian Steward and the Great Basin: The Making of an Anthropologist.* Ed. Richard O. Clemmer, L. Daniel Myers, and Mary Elizabeth Rudden. 203–18. Salt Lake City: University of Utah Press.

Boas, Franz. 1940. *Race, Language, and Culture.* New York: Macmillan.

Bohannon, Paul, and Mark Glazer, eds. 1988. *High Points in Anthropology.* 2d ed. New York: Alfred A. Knopf.

Borgaras, W. G. 1929. "Elements of the Culture of the Circumpolar Zone." *American Anthropologist* 31 (4): 579–601.

Bowlby, John. 1969–80. *Attachment and Loss.* 3 vols. New York: Basic Books.

———. 1979. *The Making and Breaking of Affectional Bonds.* London: Tavistock.

Brewer, William F. 1986. "What Is Autobiographical Memory?" In *Autobiographical Memory.* Ed. David C. Rubin. 25–49. New York: Cambridge University Press.

———. 1996. "What Is Recollective Memory?" In *Remembering Our Past: Studies in Autobiographical Memory.* Ed. David C. Rubin. 19–66. New York: Cambridge University Press.

Brodie, Fawn M. 1981. "It All Happened Very Quietly." In *Remembering the University of Utah.* Ed. Elizabeth Haglund. 85–95. Salt Lake City: University of Utah Press.

Buckley, Kerry W. 1989. *Mechanical Man: John Broadus Watson and the Beginnings of Behaviorism.* New York: Guilford Press.

Buckley, Thomas. 1982. "Menstruation and the Power of Yurok Women: Methods in Cultural Reconstruction." *American Ethnologist* 9 (1): 47–60.

Bushong, Allen D. 1981. "Geographers and Their Mentors: A Genealogical View of American Academic Geography." In *The Origins of Academic Geography in the United States.* Ed. Brian W. Blouet. 193–219. Hamden, Conn.: Shoe String Press.

Buzaljko, Grace Wilson. 1989. "Theodora Kracaw Kroeber, 1897–1979." In *Women Anthropologists: Selected Biographies.* Ed. Ute Gacs, Aisha Khan, Jerrie McIntyre, and Ruth Weinberg. 187–93. Urbana: University of Illinois Press.

Caffrey, Margaret M. 1989. *Ruth Benedict: Stranger in This Land.* Austin: University of Texas Press.

Cannon, Ramona Wilcox. 1926a. "A Narrow Neck of Land." *Children's Friend* (June): 235–37.

———. 1926b. "A New Home in an Ancient Land." *Children's Friend* (Oct.): 392–93.

———. 1981. "One Cannot Live Long Enough to Outgrow a University." In *Remembering the University of Utah.* Ed. Elizabeth Haglund. 3–19. Salt Lake City: University of Utah Press.

Carlisle, E. Fred. 1983. *Loren Eiseley: The Development of a Writer.* Urbana: University of Illinois Press.

Carneiro, Robert L. 1974. "The Four Faces of Evolution." In *Handbook of Social and Cultural Anthropology.* Ed. John J. Honigmann. 89–110. Chicago: Rand McNally.

———. 1979. "Julian Steward and the Evolution of Culture." *Reviews in Anthropology* 6 (3): 287–300.

Carson, Rachel. 1962. *Silent Spring.* Greenwich, Conn.: Fawcett.

Casagrande, Joseph B. 1966. "Betty Warren Starr, 1906–1964." *American Anthropologist* 68 (1): 128–31.

Cather, Willa, and Georgine Milmine. 1993. *The Life of Mary Baker G. Eddy and the History of Christian Science.* Lincoln: University of Nebraska Press.

Cattell, Jacques, ed. 1956. *American Men of Science.* 9th ed. Vol. 3. New York: R. R. Bowker.

Cattell, J. McKeen, and Jacques Cattell, eds. 1933. *American Men of Science.* 5th ed. New York: Science Press.

Chalfant, W. A. 1933. *The Story of Inyo.* Rev. ed. Bishop, Calif.: Chalfant.

Chodorow, Nancy J. 1999. *The Power of Feelings: Personal Meaning in Psychoanalysis, Gender, and Culture.* New Haven, Conn.: Yale University Press.

Christenson, Andrew L. 1987. "The Last of the Great Expeditions: The Rainbow Bridge/Monument Valley Expedition, 1933–38." *Plateau* 58 (4): 3–32.

Clemmer, Richard O., L. Daniel Myers, and Mary Elizabeth Rudden, eds. 1999. *Julian Steward and the Great Basin: The Making of an Anthropologist.* Salt Lake City: University of Utah Press.

Cochrane, Rexmond C. 1978. *The National Academy of Sciences: The First Hundred Years, 1863–1963.* Washington, D.C.: National Academy of Sciences.

Cole, Douglas. 1999. *Franz Boas: The Early Years, 1859–1906.* Seattle: University of Washington Press.

Cole, Fay-Cooper, R. B. Dixon, and A. V. Kidder. 1929a. "Anthropological Scholarships." *Science* 69 (1789): 394.

———. 1929b. "Anthropological Scholarships." *American Anthropologist* 31 (3): 572–73.

Cole, Sally. 1995. "Ruth Landes and the Early Ethnography of Race and Gender." In *Women Writing Culture.* Ed. Ruth Behar and Deborah Gordon. 166–85. Berkeley: University of California Press.

Collins, Henry B. 1976. "Matthew Williams Stirling, 1896–1975." *American Anthropologist* 78 (4): 886–88.

Comstock, Anna Botsford. 1911. *Handbook of Nature Study.* Ithaca, N.Y.: Cornell University Press.

Conable, Charlotte Williams. 1977. *Women at Cornell: The Myth of Equal Education.* Ithaca, N.Y.: Cornell University Press.

Cooper, John M. 1939. "Truman Michelson." *American Anthropologist* 41 (2): 281–85.

———. 1942. "Areal and Temporal Aspects of Aboriginal South American Culture." *Primitive Man* 15 (1–2): 1–38.

———. 1946. "The Patagonian and Pampean Hunters." In *Handbook of South American Indians.* BAE Bulletin 143. Vol. 1. Ed. Julian H. Steward. 127–68. Washington, D.C.: Government Printing Office.

Cordell, Linda S. 1993. "Women Archaeologists in the Southwest." In *Hidden Scholars: Women Anthropologists and the Native American Southwest.* Ed. Nancy J. Parezo. 202–20. Albuquerque: University of New Mexico Press.

Coville, Frederick V. 1892. "The Panamint Indians of California." *American Anthropologist* 5 (1): 351–61.

Cressman, Luther S. 1988. *A Golden Journey: Memoirs of an Archaeologist.* Salt Lake City: University of Utah Press.

Crum, Steven J. 1994. *The Road on Which We Came (Po'i Pentun Tammen Kimmappeh): A History of the Western Shoshone.* Salt Lake City: University of Utah Press.

———. 1999. "Julian Steward's Vision of the Great Basin: A Critique and Response." In *Julian Steward and the Great Basin: The Making of an Anthropologist.* Ed. Richard O. Clemmer, L. Daniel Myers, and Mary Elizabeth Rudden. 117–27. Salt Lake City: University of Utah Press.

Daggett, Richard E. 1992. "Tello, the Press, and Peruvian Archaeology." In *Rediscovering Our Past: Essays on the History of American Archaeology.* Ed. Jonathan Reyman. 191–202. Brookfield, Vt.: Ashgate.

Darnell, Regna. 1990. *Edward Sapir: Linguist, Anthropologist, Humanist.* Berkeley: University of California Press.

Darrah, William Culp. 1947–48. "John F. Steward, 1841–1915." *Utah Historical Quarterly* 16–17:175–79.

———, ed. 1947–48. "Journal of John F. Steward, May 22–November 3, 1871." *Utah Historical Quarterly* 16–17:180–251.

Dasmann, Raymond F. 1965. *The Destruction of California.* New York: Macmillan.

D'Azevedo, Warren, vol. ed. 1986. *Great Basin: Handbook of North American Indians.* Vol. 11. Ed. William C. Sturtevant. Washington, D.C.: Smithsonian Institution.

Deacon, Desley. 1997. *Elsie Clews Parsons: Inventing Modern Life.* Chicago: University of Chicago Press.

Delacorte, Michael G. 1990. "The Prehistory of Deep Springs Valley, California: Adaptive Variation in the Western Great Basin." Ph.D. diss., University of California, Davis.

De Laguna, Frederica. 1962. "Marian Wesley Smith, 1907–1961." *American Antiquity* 27 (4): 567–70.

Dellenbaugh, Frederick S. 1926 [1908]. *A Canyon Voyage: The Narrative of the Second Powell Expedition Down the Green-Colorado River from Wyoming, and the Explorations on Land, in the Years 1871 and 1872.* New Haven, Conn.: Yale University Press.

Derks, Scott, ed. 1999. *The Value of a Dollar: Prices and Incomes in the United States, 1860–1999.* Lakeville, Conn.: Grey House.

Diamond, Stanley. 1981. "Paul Radin." In *Totems and Teachers: Perspectives on the History of Anthropology.* Ed. Sydel Silverman. 67–97. New York: Columbia University Press.

———. 1993. "Eleanor Leacock's Political Vision." In *From Labrador to Samoa: The Theory and Practice of Eleanor Burke Leacock.* Ed. Constance Sutton. 111–14. Arlington, Va.: Association for Feminist Anthropology/American Anthropological Association.

Dibble, Charles E. 1960. "Elmer R. Smith, 1909–1960." *American Anthropologist* 62 (6): 1047–49.

Dick, Herbert W., and Albert H. Schroeder. 1968. "Lyndon Lane Hargrave: A Brief Biography." In *Collected Papers in Honor of Lyndon Lane Hargrave.* Ed. Albert H. Schroeder. 1–8. Papers of the Archaeological Society of New Mexico. Vol. 1. Santa Fe: Museum of New Mexico Press.

Dinnerstein, Dorothy. 1976. *The Mermaid and the Minotaur: Sexual Arrangements and Human Malaise.* New York: Harper and Row.

Doherty, Jim. 1995. "The Cattle Ranch That Doubles as a School for Doers." *Smithsonian Magazine* 26 (1): 114–25.

Doig, Ivan. 1978. *This House of Sky: Landscapes of a Western Mind.* New York: Harcourt Brace Jovanovich.

Domhoff, G. William. 1986. *The Mystique of Dreams: A Search for Utopia through Senoi Dream Theory.* Berkeley: University of California Press.

"Dr. Harold Sellers Colton, 1881–1970." 1971. *Plateau* 43 (4): 146–47.

Drucker, Philip. 1981. "Ronald Leroy Olson, 1895–1979." *American Anthropologist* 83 (3): 605–7.

Du Bois, Cora. 1960. "Paul Radin: An Appreciation." In *Culture in History: Essays in Honor of Paul Radin.* Ed. Stanley Diamond. ix–xvi. New York: Columbia University Press.

———. 1980. "Some Anthropological Hindsights." *Annual Review of Anthropology* 9:1–13.

Dumas, Malone, ed. 1936. *Dictionary of American Biography.* New York: Charles Scribner's Sons.

Eddy, Mary Baker. 1906. *Science and Health: With Key to the Scriptures.* Boston: Published by the Trustees under the Will of Mary Baker G. Eddy.

Elliott, Melinda. 1995. *Great Excavations: Tales of Early Southwestern Archaeology, 1888–1939.* Santa Fe, N.M.: School of American Research.

Etnier, Carl. 1981. "Harvey Mansfield on the Jewish Quota." *Deep Springs Newsletter* 33:7.

Fawcett, David M., and Teri McLuhan. 1989. "Ruth Leah Bunzel, 1898–." In *Women Anthropologists: Selected Biographies.* Ed. Ute Gacs, Aisha Khan, Jerrie McIntyre, and Ruth Weinberg. 29–36. Urbana: University of Illinois Press.

Federal Writers' Project (Work Projects Administration). 1937. *Washington: City and Capital.* Washington, D.C.: Government Printing Office.

Fenton, William N. 1998. *The Great Law and the Longhouse: A Political History of the Iroquois Confederacy.* Norman: University of Oklahoma Press.

Fiero, Bill. 1986. *Geology of the Great Basin.* Reno: University of Nevada Press.

Fischer, Ann, and Peggy Golde. 1968. "The Position of Women in Anthropology." *American Anthropologist* 70 (2): 337–44.

Fitzgerald, Joseph M. 1996. "Intersecting Meanings of Reminiscence in Adult Development and Aging." In *Remembering Our Past: Studies in Autobiographical Memory.* Ed. David C. Rubin. 360–83. New York: Cambridge University Press.

Fitzpatrick, Ellen. 1990. *Endless Crusade: Women Social Scientists and Progressive Reform.* New York: Oxford University Press.

Flannery, Regina. 1950. "John Montgomery Cooper, 1881–1949." *American Anthropologist* 52 (1): 64–74.

Foster, George M. 1960. "Edward Winslow Gifford, 1887–1959." *American Anthropologist* 62 (2): 327–29.

———. 1976. "Graduate Study at Berkeley, 1935–1941." *Anthropology UCLA* 8:9–18.

Fowler, Catherine S. 1986a. "Northern Paiute." In *Handbook of North American Indians.* Ed. William C. Sturtevant. Vol. 11, *Great Basin,* edited by Warren D'Azevedo. 435–65. Washington, D.C.: Smithsonian Institution.

———. 1986b. "Subsistence." In *Handbook of North American Indians.* Ed. William C. Sturtevant. Vol. 11, *Great Basin,* edited by Warren D'Azevedo. 64–97. Washington, D.C.: Smithsonian Institution.

Fowler, Catherine S., Molly Dufort, Mary K. Rusco, and Pauline Esteves. 1999. "In the Field in Death Valley: Julian Steward's Panamint Shoshone Fieldwork." In *Julian Steward and the Great Basin: The Making of an Anthropologist.* Ed. Richard O. Clemmer, L. Daniel Myers, and Mary Elizabeth Rudden. 53–59. Salt Lake City: University of Utah Press.

Fowler, Don D., ed. 1972. *Jack Hillers's Diary of the Powell Expeditions, 1871–1875.* Salt Lake City: University of Utah Press.

Fowler, Don D., and Catherine S. Fowler, eds. 1971. "Anthropology of the Numa: John Wesley Powell's Manuscripts on the Numic Peoples of Western North America, 1868–1880." *Smithsonian Contributions to Anthropology* 14:1–307.

Friedlander, Judith. 1989. "Elsie Clews Parsons, 1874–1941." In *Women Anthropologists: Selected Biographies.* Ed. Ute Gacs, Aisha Khan, Jerrie McIntyre, and Ruth Weinberg. 282–90. Urbana: University of Illinois Press.

Friedman, Jonathan. 1987. "An Interview with Eric Wolf." *Current Anthropology* 28 (1): 107–18.

Friedman, Lawrence J. 1999. *Identity's Architect: A Biography of Erik H. Erikson.* New York: Scribner.

Frigout, Arlette. 1979. "Hopi Ceremonial Organization." In *Handbook of North American Indians.* Ed. William C. Sturtevant. Vol. 9, *Southwest,* edited by Alfonso Ortiz. 564–76. Washington, D.C.: Smithsonian Institution.

Frisbie, Charlotte J. 1989. "Frances Theresa Densmore, 1867–1957." In *Women Anthropologists: Selected Biographies.* Ed. Ute Gacs, Aisha Khan, Jerrie McIntyre, and Ruth Weinberg. 51–58. Urbana: University of Illinois Press.

Gailey, Christine Ward, ed. 1989. "Eleanor Burke Leacock, 1922–1987." In *Women Anthropologists:*

Selected Biographies. Ed. Ute Gacs, Aisha Khan, Jerrie McIntyre, and Ruth Weinberg. 215–21. Urbana: University of Illinois Press.

Geertz, Clifford. 1995. *After the Fact: Two Countries, Four Decades, One Anthropologist.* Cambridge, Mass.: Harvard University Press.

Gero, Joan. 1985. "Socio-Politics and the Woman-at-Home Ideology." *American Antiquity* 50 (2): 342–50.

Ghani, Ashraf. 1987. "A Conversation with Eric Wolf." *American Ethnologist* 14 (2): 346–66.

Gifford, Edward W. 1918. "Clans and Moieties in Southern California." *University of California Publications in American Archaeology and Ethnology* 14:155–219.

———. 1957. "William Egbert Schenk, 1884–1956." *American Anthropologist* 59 (2): 326–27.

Givens, Douglas R. 1992. *Alfred Vincent Kidder and the Development of Americanist Archaeology.* Albuquerque: University of New Mexico Press.

Goldfrank, Esther. 1978. *Notes on an Undirected Life: As One Anthropologist Tells It.* Queens College Publications in Anthropology No. 3. Flushing, N.Y.: Queens College Press.

———. 1983. "Another View: Margaret and Me." *Ethnohistory* 30 (1): 1–14.

Goldschmidt, Walter. 1986. "Ralph Leon Beals, 1901–1985." *American Anthropologist* 88 (4): 947–53.

Gordon, Lynn. 1990. *Gender and Higher Education in the Progressive Era.* New Haven, Conn.: Yale University Press.

Goss, James A. 1999. "The Yamparika—Shoshones, Comanches, or Ute—or Does It Matter?" In *Julian Steward and the Great Basin: The Making of an Anthropologist.* Ed. Richard O. Clemmer, L. Daniel Myers, and Mary Elizabeth Rudden. 74–84. Salt Lake City: University of Utah Press.

Gould, Stephen Jay. 1988. "A Web of Tales." *Natural History* 97 (10): 16–23.

Gouldner, Alvin W. 1957. "Cosmopolitans and Locals: Toward an Analysis of Latent Social Rules, I." *Administrative Science Quarterly* 2:281–306.

Graber, Robert Bates, and James Silverberg. 1990. "Victor Barnouw, 1915–1989." *American Anthropologist* 92 (2): 492–94.

Green, Constance McLaughlin. 1963. *Washington: Capital City.* Vol. 2: *1879–1950.* Princeton, N.J.: Princeton University Press.

Griffin, James B. 1958. "The Museum of Anthropology." In *The University of Michigan Encyclopedia Survey.* Vol. 4. Ed. Walter A. Donnelly. 1476–81. Ann Arbor: University of Michigan Press.

———. 1976. "Carl Eugen Guthe, 1893–1974." *American Antiquity* 41 (1): 168–177.

Gruber, Frank. 1970. *Zane Grey: A Biography.* New York: New American Library.

Guthe, Carl E. 1951. "The Department of Anthropology." In *The University of Michigan Encyclopedic Survey.* Vol. 2. Ed. Wildred B. Shaw. 440–441. Ann Arbor: University of Michigan Press.

Hall, Edward T. 1994. *West of the Thirties: Discoveries among the Navajo and Hopi.* New York: Doubleday.

Hanc, Joseph Robert. 1981. "Influences, Events, and Innovations in the Anthropology of Julian H. Steward: A Revisionist View of Multilinear Evolution." Master's thesis, University of Chicago.

Hargrave, Lyndon L. 1935. *Report on Archaeological Reconnaissance in the Rainbow Plateau Area of Northern Arizona and Southern Utah.* Berkeley: University of California Press.

Harris, Marvin. 1968. *The Rise of Anthropological Theory.* New York: Crowell.

———. 1979. *Cultural Materialism: The Struggle for a Science of Culture.* New York: Random House.

Harrison, Margaret. 1948. "Lila Morris O'Neale, 1886–1948." *American Anthropologist* 50 (4): 657–65.

Hart, James D. 1987. *A Companion to California.* Rev. ed. Berkeley: University of California Press.

Heizer, Robert F. 1970. [Untitled essay]. In *There Was Light: Autobiography of a University—Berkeley, 1868–1968.* Ed. Irving Stone. 207–13. New York: Doubleday.

Hemenway, Robert E. 1977. *Zora Neale Hurston: A Literary Biography.* Urbana: University of Illinois Press.

Henson, Pamela M. 1997. "'Through Books to Nature': Anna Botsford Comstock and the Nature

Study Movement." In *Using Nature's Language: Women Engendering Science, 1690–1800.* Ed. Barbara T. Gates and Ann B. Shteir. 116–43. Madison: University of Wisconsin Press.

Hentoff, Nat. 1968. *A Doctor among the Addicts.* New York: Rand McNally.

Himmelberg, Robert F. 2001. *The Great Depression and the New Deal.* Westport, Conn.: Greenwood Press.

Hinsley, Curtis M. 1981. *Savages and Scientists: The Smithsonian Institution and the Development of American Anthropology, 1846–1910.* Washington, D.C.: Smithsonian Institution Press.

Hoijer, Harry. 1957. "Paul Radin, 1883–1959." *American Anthropologist* 61 (5): 839–43.

Hollingshead, Lynne M. 1989. "Ernestine Friedl, 1920–." In *Women Anthropologists: Selected Biographies.* Ed. Ute Gacs, Aisha Khan, Jerrie McIntyre, and Ruth Weinberg. 102–8. Urbana: University of Illinois Press.

Hooson, David. 1981. "Carl O. Sauer." In *The Origins of Academic Geography.* Ed. Brian W. Blouet. 165–74. Hamden, Conn.: Shoe String Press.

Hough, Walter. 1931. "Jesse Walter Fewkes, 1850–1930." *American Anthropologist* 33 (1): 92–97.

Hovey, Kenneth A. 1988. "The Intellectual Origins of L. L. Nunn." *Deep Springs Newsletter* 47:5–9.

Howell, Carol L., comp. and ed. 1998. *Cannibalism Is an Acquired Taste and Other Notes from Conversations with Anthropologist Omer C. Stewart.* Niwot: University Press of Colorado.

Howells, W. W. 1990. "Obituary: Harry Lionel Shapiro, 1902–1990." *American Journal of Physical Anthropology* 83 (4): 499–500.

Hungerford, John B. 1961. *The Slim Princess: The Story of the Southern Pacific Narrow Gauge.* 4th ed. Reseda, Calif.: Hungerford Press.

Hurston, Zora Neale. 1984. *Dust Tracks on a Road: An Autobiography.* 2d ed. Urbana: University of Illinois Press.

Inyo County Board of Supervisors. 1966. *Inyo, 1866–1966.* Bishop, Calif.: Chalfant Press.

Isaac, Rhys. 1982. *The Transformation of Virginia, 1740–1790.* Chapel Hill: University of North Carolina Press.

Jacques Cattell Press, ed. 1968. *American Men of Science.* 11th ed. Vols. 7 and 8. New York: R. R. Bowker.

———. 1973. *American Men and Women of Science.* 12th ed. Vol. 2. New York: R. R. Bowker.

Jacklin, Kathleen. 1971. "Anna Botsford Comstock." In *Notable American Women.* Ed. Edward T. James. Vol. 1. 367–69. Cambridge, Mass.: Harvard University Press, Belknap Press.

James, Alice. 1989. "Dorothy Louise Strouse Keur, 1904–." In *Women Anthropologists: Selected Biographies.* Ed. Ute Gacs, Aisha Khan, Jerrie McIntyre, and Ruth Weinberg. 181–86. Urbana: University of Illinois Press.

Janetski, Joel C. 1999. "Julian Steward and Utah Archaeology." In *Julian Steward and the Great Basin: The Making of an Anthropologist.* Ed. Richard O. Clemmer, L. Daniel Myers, and Mary Elizabeth Rudden. 19–34. Salt Lake City: University of Utah Press.

Jardine, Winnifred Cannon. 1967. "Life on the Cannon Farm." In *Cannon Family Historical Treasury.* Ed. Beatrice Cannon Evans and Janath Russell Cannon. 321–38. Salt Lake City: George Cannon Family Association.

Jenson, Andrew. 1901. "George Quayle Cannon." *Latter-day Saint Biographical Encyclopedia.* Vol. 1. 43–51. Salt Lake City: Andrew Jenson Historical Company.

Jones, Stacy V. 1971. *The Patent Office.* New York: Praeger.

Jordan, Teresa. 1982. *Cowgirls: Women of the American West.* Garden City, N.Y.: Anchor Press.

Judd, Neil. 1968. *Men Met along the Trail.* Norman: University of Oklahoma Press.

Kahrl, William. 1976a. "The Politics of California Water: Owens Valley and the Los Angeles Aqueduct, 1900–1927—Part 1." *California Historical Quarterly* 55 (1): 2–25.

———. 1976b. "The Politics of California Water: Owens Valley and the Los Angeles Aqueduct, 1900–1927—Part 2." *California Historical Quarterly* 55 (2): 98–120.

———. 1982. *Water and Power: The Conflict over Los Angeles' Water Supply in the Owens Valley.* Berkeley: University of California Press.

Karier, Clarence J. 1986. *Scientists of the Mind: Intellectual Founders of Modern Psychology.* Urbana: University of Illinois Press.

Kayser, Elmer Louis. 1970. *Bricks without Straw: The Evolution of George Washington University.* New York: Appleton-Century-Crofts.

Keeler, Charles. 1976. *The Simple Home.* Santa Barbara, Calif.: Peregrine Smith.

Kehoe, Alice. 1999. "Where Were Wovoka and Wuzzie George?" In *Julian Steward and the Great Basin: The Making of an Anthropologist.* Ed. Richard O. Clemmer, L. Daniel Myers, and Mary Elizabeth Rudden. 164–69. Salt Lake City: University of Utah Press.

Keller, Evelyn Fox. 1985. *Reflections on Gender and Science.* New Haven, Conn.: Yale University Press.

Kelly, Isabel. 1934. "Southern Paiute Bands." *American Anthropologist* 36 (4): 548–60.

Kelly, Lawrence. 1983. *The Assault on Assimilation: John Collier and the Origins of Indian Policy Reform.* Albuquerque: University of New Mexico Press.

Kennedy, K. A. R. 1997. "Theodore D. McCown, 1908–1969." In *History of Physical Anthropology.* Ed. Frank Spencer. Vol. 2. 627–29. New York: Garland.

Kenzer, Martin S. 1987. "Like Father, like Son." In *Carl O. Sauer: A Tribute.* Ed. Martin S. Kenzer. 40–65. Corvallis: Oregon State University Press for the Association of Pacific Coast Geographers.

Kerns, Virginia. 1999. "Learning the Land." In *Julian Steward and the Great Basin: The Making of an Anthropologist.* Ed. Richard O. Clemmer, L. Daniel Myers, and Mary Elizabeth Rudden. 1–18. Salt Lake City: University of Utah Press.

Kidder, Alfred V. 1954. "Wendell Clark Bennett, 1905–1953." *American Anthropologist* 56 (2): 269–73.

Kimball, Arthur G. 1993. *Ace of Hearts: The Westerns of Zane Grey.* Fort Worth: Texas Christian University Press.

Knobloch, Patricia J. 1989. "Isabel Truesdell Kelly, 1906–1983." In *Women Anthropologists: Selected Biographies.* Ed. Ute Gacs, Aisha Khan, Jerrie McIntyre, and Ruth Weinberg. 175–80. Urbana: University of Illinois Press.

Kolbert, Elizabeth. 1986. "Dr. Marie Nyswander Dies at 67: Expert in Treating Drug Addicts." *New York Times,* April 21, B-8.

Kroeber, Alfred L. 1901. "Decorative Symbolism of the Arapaho." *American Anthropologist* 3 (2): 308–36.

———. 1915. "Frederic Ward Putnam, 1839–1915." *American Anthropologist* 17 (4): 712–18.

———. 1918. "The History of Philippine Civilization as Reflected in Religious Nomenclature." *Anthropological Papers of American Museum of Natural History* 19 (2): i–ii, 35–67.

———. 1919. "Peoples of the Philippines." *American Museum of Natural History Handbook.* Series No. 8. New York.

———. 1922. *Three Essays on the Antiquity and Races of Man.* Berkeley: University of California Press.

———. 1923. *Anthropology.* New York: Harcourt Brace.

———. 1925. *Handbook of the Indians of California.* Bureau of American Ethnology Bulletin No. 78. Washington, D.C.: Government Printing Office.

———. 1928. "Native Culture of the Southwest." *University of California Publications in American Archaeology and Ethnology* 23:375–98.

———. 1939. *Cultural and Natural Areas of Native North America.* Berkeley: University of California Press.

———. 1950. "Have Civilizations a Life History?" In *American Association for the Advancement of Science Centennial: Collected Papers.* 9–13. Washington, D.C.: American Association for the Advancement of Science.

Kroeber, Theodora. 1970. *Alfred L. Kroeber: A Personal Configuration.* Berkeley: University of California Press.

Kroeber-Quinn, Theodora. 1982. "Timeless Woman: Writer and Interpreter of the California Indian World." Oral history compiled by Anne Brower, 1976–78. Regional Oral History Office, Bancroft Library, University of California, Berkeley.

Kuper, Adam. 1988. "The Invention of Primitive Society: Transformations of an Illusion." New York: Routledge.

Laird, Carobeth. 1975. *Encounter with an Angry God: Recollections of My Life with John Peabody Harrington*. Banning, Calif.: Malki Museum Press.

Lamb, Daniel S. 1906. "The Story of the Anthropological Society of Washington." *American Anthropologist* 8 (3): 564–79.

Landes, Ruth. 1986. "A Woman Anthropologist in Brazil." In *Women in the Field: Anthropological Experiences*. 2d ed. Ed. Peggy Golde. 117–39. Berkeley: University of California Press.

Langness, L. L., and Gelya Frank. 1981. *Lives: An Anthropological Approach to Biography*. Novato, Calif.: Chandler and Sharp.

Lapsley, Hilary. 1999. *Margaret Mead and Ruth Benedict: The Kinship of Women*. Amherst: University of Massachusetts Press.

Larson, Edward J. 1997. *Summer for the Gods: The Scopes Trial and America's Continuing Debate over Science and Religion*. New York: Basic Books.

Lauria-Perricelli, Antonio. 1989. "A Study in Historical and Critical Anthropology: The Making of *The People of Puerto Rico*." Ph.D. diss., New School for Social Research.

———. 1996. "The Social Anthropology of a Colonized Nation: *The People of Puerto Rico* after Half a Century." Paper presented at the New York Academy of Sciences, March 25.

Leacock, Eleanor B. 1954. *The Montagnais "Hunting Territory" and the Fur Trade*. Memoir No. 78. Washington, D.C.: American Anthropological Association.

———. 1972. Introduction to *The Origin of the Family, Private Property, and the State*, by Frederick Engels. Ed. Eleanor B. Leacock. 7–67. New York: International Publishers.

———. 1993. "Being an Anthropologist." In *From Labrador to Samoa: The Theory and Practice of Eleanor Burke Leacock*. Ed. Constance Sutton. 1–31. Arlington, Va.: Association for Feminist Anthropology/American Anthropological Association.

Leacock, Eleanor B., and Nan A. Rothschild, eds. 1994. *Labrador Winter: The Ethnographic Journals of William Duncan Strong, 1927–1928*. Washington, D.C.: Smithsonian Institution Press.

Lear, Linda. 1997. *Rachel Carson: Witness for Nature*. New York: Henry Holt.

Lee, Richard B. 1979. *The !Kung San: Men, Women, and Work in a Foraging Society*. New York: Cambridge University Press.

Lee, Richard B., and Irven DeVore, eds. 1968. *Man the Hunter*. Chicago: Aldine Atherton.

Leighly, John. 1976. "Carl Ortwin Sauer, 1889–1975." *Annals of the Association of American Geographers* 66 (3): 337–48.

———. 1979. "Berkeley: Drifting into Geography in the Twenties." *Annals of the Association of American Geographers* 69 (1): 4–9.

Lepowsky, Maria. 2000. "Charlotte Gower and the Subterranean History of Anthopology." In *Excluded Ancestors, Inventible Traditions: Essays toward a More Inclusive History of Anthropology*. History of Anthropology, vol. 9. Ed. Richard Handler. 123–70. Madison: University of Wisconsin Press.

Lesser, Alexander. 1981. "Franz Boas." In *Totems and Teachers: Perspectives on the History of Anthropology*. Ed. Sydel Silverman. 1–33. New York: Columbia University Press.

Lewis, Oscar, Ruth M. Lewis, and Susan M. Rigdon. 1977–78. *Living the Revolution: An Oral History of Contemporary Cuba*. 3 vols. Urbana: University of Illinois Press.

Liljeblad, Sven, and Catherine S. Fowler. 1986. "Owens Valley Paiute." In *Handbook of North American Indians*. Ed. William C. Sturtevant. Vol. 11, *Great Basin*, edited by Warren D'Azevedo. 412–34. Washington, D.C.: Smithsonian Institution.

Linton, Adelin, and Charles Wagley. 1971. *Ralph Linton*. New York: Columbia University Press.

Lissner, Will. 1953. "Columbia Is Dropping Dr. Weltfish, Leftist." *New York Times*, April 1, L-1, 19.

Lothrop, Samuel K. 1948. "Julio C. Tello, 1890–1947." *American Antiquity* 14 (1): 50–56.

———. 1957. "George Gustav Heye, 1874–1956." *American Antiquity* 23 (1): 66–67.

Lowie, Robert H. 1920. *Primitive Society*. New York: Boni and Liveright.

————. 1924. *Primitive Religion.* New York: Boni and Liveright.

————. 1933. "Erland Nordenskiöld." *American Anthropologist* 35 (1): 158–64.

————. 1948. *Social Organization.* New York: Rinehart.

————. 1959. *Robert H. Lowie, Ethnologist: A Personal Record.* Berkeley: University of California Press.

Lukermann, Fred E. 1977. "In the Cause of Science." *Reviews in Anthropology* 4 (4): 561–66.

Lutz, Catherine. 1990. "The Erasure of Women in Sociocultural Anthropology." *American Ethnologist* 17 (4): 611–27.

————. 1995. "The Gender of Theory." In *Women Writing Culture.* Ed. Ruth Behar and Deborah A. Gordon. 249–66. Berkeley: University of California Press.

MacCurdy, George Grant. 1919. "The Academic Teaching of Anthropology in Connection with Other Departments." *American Anthropologist* 21 (1): 49–60.

MacKenzie, Brian D. 1972. "Behaviorism and Positivism." *Journal of the History of the Behavioral Sciences* 8 (2): 222–31.

Macpherson, Anne. 1987. "Preparing for the National Stage: Carl Sauer's First Ten Years at Berkeley." In *Carl O. Sauer: A Tribute.* Ed. Martin S. Kenzer. 69–89. Corvallis: Oregon State University Press.

Manners, Robert A. 1973. "Julian Haynes Steward, 1902–1972." *American Anthropologist* 75 (3): 886–97.

————. 1996. "Julian Haynes Steward, January 31, 1902–February 6, 1972." *Biographical Memoirs, National Academy of Sciences* 69:324–37.

————, ed. 1964. *Process and Pattern in Culture: Essays in Honor of Julian H. Steward.* Chicago: Aldine.

Manners, Robert A., and David Kaplan, eds. 1968. *Theory in Anthropology: A Source-book.* Chicago: Aldine.

Mark, Joan. 1980. *Four Anthropologists: An American Science in Its Early Years.* New York: Science History Publications.

————. 1988. *A Stranger in Her Native Land: Alice Fletcher and the American Indians.* Lincoln: University of Nebraska Press.

Marquis, Albert Nelson, ed. 1910. *Who's Who in America.* Vol. 6: 1910–11. Chicago: A. N. Marquis Co.

————. 1918. *Who's Who in America.* Vol. 10: 1918–19. Chicago: A. N. Marquis Co.

————. 1932. *Who's Who in America.* Vol. 17: 1932–33. Chicago: A. N. Marquis Co.

————. 1942. *Who Was Who in America.* Vol. 1. Chicago: A. N. Marquis Co.

————. 1950. *Who Was Who in America.* Vol. 2. Chicago: A. N. Marquis Co.

————. 1981. *Who's Who* in America. Vol. 7. Chicago: Marquis Who's Who.

Martin, M. Kay, and Barbara Voorhies. 1975. *Female of the Species.* New York: Columbia University Press.

May, Stephen J. 1997. *Zane Grey: Romancing the West.* Athens: Ohio University Press.

McAllester, David P. 1985. "In Memoriam: George Herzog, 1901–1984." *Ethnomusicology* 29 (1): 86–87.

McCown, Theodore. 1969. "Teaching Anthropology at Berkeley." *Kroeber Anthropological Papers* 40:82–92.

McElvaine, Robert S. 1984. *The Great Depression: America, 1929–1941.* New York: Times Books.

McGaw, Judith A. 1996. "Reconceiving Technology: Why Feminine Technologies Matter." In *Gender and Archaeology.* Ed. Rita P. Wright. 52–75. Philadelphia: University of Pennsylvania Press.

[McGee, W. J.]. 1903. "The American Anthropological Association." *American Anthropologist* 5 (1): 178–92.

McMillin, Lucille Foster. 1938. *Women in the Federal Service.* Washington, D.C.: Government Printing Office.

McVicker, Donald E. 1992. "The Matter of Saville: Franz Boas and the Anthropological Definition of Archaeology." In *Rediscovering Our Past: Essays on the History of American Archaeology.* Ed. Jonathan E. Reyman. 145–59. Brookfield, Vt.: Ashgate.

Métraux, Alfred. 1946. "Ethnography of the Chaco." In *Handbook of South American Indians.* BAE Bulletin No. 143. Vol. 1. Ed. Julian H. Steward. 197–370. Washington, D.C.: Government Printing Office.

Mikell, Gwendolyn. 1989. "Zora Neale Hurston, 1903–1960." In *Women Anthropologists: Selected Biographies.* Ed. Ute Gacs, Aisha Khan, Jerrie McIntyre, and Ruth Weinberg. 160–66. Urbana: University of Illinois Press.

Mintz, Sidney W. 1979. "The Role of Water in Steward's Cultural Ecology." *Journal of the Steward Anthropological Society* 11 (1): 17–32.

———. 1981. "Ruth Benedict." In *Totems and Teachers: Perspectives on the History of Anthropology.* Ed. Sydel Silverman. 141–66. New York: Columbia University Press.

———. 1994. "An Impartial History of the Mundial Upheaval Society." *AnthroWatch* (newsletter of the Columbia University Graduate Anthropology Alumni Association) 2 (3): 19–20.

Modell, Judith Schacter. 1983. *Ruth Bendedict: Patterns of a Life.* Philadelphia: University of Pennsylvania Press.

———. 1989. "Ruth Fulton Benedict, 1887–1948." In *Women Anthropologists: Selected Biographies.* Ed. Ute Gacs, Aisha Khan, Jerrie McIntyre, and Ruth Weinberg. 1–7. Urbana: University of Illinois Press.

Moore, Henriett. 1988. *Feminism and Anthropology.* Minneapolis: University of Minnesota Press.

Moore, Jerry D. 1997. *Visions of Culture: An Introduction to Anthropological Theories and Theorists.* Walnut Creek, Calif.: AltaMira Press.

Moses, L. G. 1984. *The Indian Man: A Biography of James Mooney.* Urbana: University of Illinois Press.

Muir, John. 1894. *The Mountains of California.* New York: Century Co.

Mulholland, Catherine. 2000. *William Mulholland and the Rise of Los Angeles.* Berkeley: University of California Press.

Murphy, Robert F. 1972. *Robert H. Lowie.* New York: Columbia University Press.

———. 1977. "Introduction: The Anthropological Theories of Julian H. Steward." In *Evolution and Ecology: Essays on Social Transformation.* Ed. Jane C. Steward and Robert F. Murphy. 1–39. Urbana: University of Illinois Press.

———. 1980. "Robert Lowie, Julian Steward, and Neo-Evolutionism." *Journal of the Steward Anthropological Society* 11 (2): 141–63.

———. 1981. "Julian Steward." In *Totems and Teachers: Perspectives on the History of Anthropology.* Ed. Sydel Silverman. 170–204. New York: Columbia University Press.

———. 1987. *The Body Silent.* New York: Henry Holt.

Murphy, Robert F., and Yolanda Murphy. 1986. "Northern Shoshone and Bannock." In *Handbook of North American Indians.* Ed. William C. Sturtevant. Vol. 11, *Great Basin*, edited by Warren D'Azevedo. 284–307. Washington, D.C.: Smithsonian Institution.

Murphy, Robert F., and Julian H. Steward. 1956. "Tappers and Trappers: Parallel Process in Acculturation." *Economic Development and Cultural Change* 4:335–55.

Myers, L. Daniel. 1999. "A Frame for Culture: Observations on the Culture-Element Distribution of the Snake River Shoshone." In *Julian Steward and the Great Basin: The Making of an Anthropologist.* Ed. Richard O. Clemmer, L. Daniel Myers, and Mary Elizabeth Rudden. 128–43. Salt Lake City: University of Utah Press.

Nagata, Judith A. 1989. *Conformity and Change among the Old Order Amish of Illinois.* New York: AMS Press.

Nagata, Shuichi. 1970. *Modern Transformations of Moenkopi Pueblo.* Urbana: University of Illinois Press.

Nerad, Maresi. 1987a. "Gender Stratification in Higher Education: The History of Home Economics at the University of California, 1912–1962." *Women's Studies International Forum* 10 (2): 157–64.

————. 1987b. "The Situation of Women at Berkeley between 1870 and 1915." *Feminist Issues* 7 (1): 67–80.

————. 1999. *The Academic Kitchen: A Social History of Gender Stratification at the University of California, Berkeley.* Albany: State University of New York Press.

Newell, L. Jackson. 1982. "Among the Few at Deep Springs College: Assessing a Seven-Decade Experiment in Liberal Education." *Journal of General Education* 34 (2): 120–34.

Nisbet, Robert A. 1981. "Teggart of Berkeley." In *Masters: Portraits of Great Teachers.* Ed. Joseph Epstein. 69–87. New York: Basic Books.

Noble, David W. 1992. *A World without Women: The Christian Clerical Culture of Western Science.* New York: Knopf.

Nyswander, Dorothy B. 1926. "Recency, Frequency, and Pattern Factors in Learning." Ph.D. diss., University of California, Berkeley.

————. 1994. "Professor and Activist for Public Health Education in the Americas and Asia." Oral history compiled by Harriet Nathan, 1993–94. Regional Oral History Office, Bancroft Library, University of California, Berkeley.

Olson, Keith W. 1974. *The G.I. Bill, the Veterans, and the Colleges.* Lexington: University Press of Kentucky.

Olson, Ronald L. 1933. "Clan and Moiety in Native America." *University of California Publications in American Archaeology and Ethnology* 33 (4): 351–422.

Orlove, Benjamin. 1980. "Ecological Anthropology." *Annual Review of Anthropology* 9:235–73.

Ozanne, Robert. 1968. *Wages in Practice and Theory: McCormick and International Harvester, 1860–1960.* Madison: University of Wisconsin Press.

Padilla, Elena. 1958. *Up from Puerto Rico.* New York: Columbia University Press.

Parezo, Nancy J. 1993. "Anthropology: The Welcoming Science." In *Hidden Scholars: Women Anthropologists and the Native American Southwest.* Ed. Nancy J. Parezo. 3–37. Albuquerque: University of New Mexico Press.

Parks, Douglas R., and Ruth E. Pathé. 1985. "Gene Weltfish, 1902–1980." *Plains Anthropologist* 30 (107): 59–64.

Parsons, James J. 1979. "The Later Sauer Years." *Annals of the Association of American Geographers* 69 (1): 9–15.

Parsons, Talcott, and Evon Vogt. 1962. "Clyde Kay Maben Kluckhohn, 1905–1960." *American Anthropologist* 64 (1): 140–61.

Pathé, Ruth E. 1989. "Gene Weltfish, 1902–1980." In *Women Anthropologists: Selected Biographies.* Ed. Ute Gacs, Aisha Khan, Jerrie McIntyre, and Ruth Weinberg. 372–81. Urbana: University of Illinois Press.

Patterson, Thomas C. 1987. "Development, Ecology, and Marginal Utility in Anthropology." *Dialectical Anthropology* 12:15–31.

Patterson, Thomas C., and Antonio Lauria-Perricelli. 1999. "Julian Steward and the Construction of Area-Studies Research in the United States." In *Julian Steward and the Great Basin: The Making of an Anthropologist.* Ed. Richard O. Clemmer, L. Daniel Myers, and Mary Elizabeth Rudden. 219–40. Salt Lake City: University of Utah Press.

Paul, Rodman Wilson. 1971. "Phoebe Apperson Hearst." In *Notable American Women.* Vol. 2. Ed. Edward T. James. 171–73. Cambridge, Mass.: Harvard University Press, Belknap Press.

Peace, William J. 1993. "Leslie White and Evolutionary Theory." *Dialectical Anthropology* 18:123–51.

————. 1995. "Vere Gordon Childe and the Cold War." In *Childe and Australia: Archaeology, Politics, and Ideas.* Ed. Peter Gathercole, T. H. Irving, and Gregory Melleuish. 128–43, 231–35. St. Lucia: University of Queensland Press.

————. 1998. "Bernhard Stern, Leslie White, and an Anthropological Appraisal of the Russian Revolution." *American Anthropologist* 100 (1): 84–93.

————. n.d. "Academic Threats to White's Career." Ms.

Pilcher, William W. 1972. *The Portland Longshoremen: A Dispersed Urban Community.* New York: Holt, Rinehart and Winston.

Poll, Richard D., ed. 1978. *Utah's History.* Provo, Utah: Brigham Young University Press.

Pryor, Elizabeth Brown. 1987. *Clara Barton: Professional Angel.* Philadelphia: University of Pennsylvania Press.

Radin, Paul. 1958. "Robert H. Lowie, 1883–1957." *American Anthropologist* 60 (2): 358–75.

Reich, Herbert. 1974. "Early Recollections of Deep Springs." *Deep Springs Newsletter* 19:1–3.

Reyman, Jonathan E. 1992. "Women in American Archaeology: Some Historical Notes and Comments." In *Rediscovering Our Past: Essays on the History of American Archaeology.* Ed. Jonathan E. Reyman. 69–80. Brookfield, Vt.: Ashgate.

Rider, Fremont, ed. 1927. *Rider's California.* 2d ed. Vol. ed. Frederic Taber Cooper. New York: Macmillan.

Rigdon, Susan M. 1988. *The Culture Facade: Art, Science, and Politics in the Work of Oscar Lewis.* Urbana: University of Illinois Press.

Ronaasen, Sheree, Richard O. Clemmer, and Mary Elizabeth Rudden. 1999. "Rethinking Cultural Ecology, Multilinear Evolution, and Expert Witnesses: Julian Steward and the Indian Claims Commission Proceedings." In *Julian Steward and the Great Basin: The Making of an Anthropologist.* Ed. Richard O. Clemmer, L. Daniel Myers, and Mary Elizabeth Rudden. 170–202. Salt Lake City: University of Utah Press.

Rosenberg, Rosalind. 1982. *Beyond Separate Spheres: Intellectual Roots of Modern Feminism.* New Haven, Conn.: Yale University Press.

Rosenthal, Harvey. 1990. *Their Day in Court: A History of the Indian Claims Commission.* New York: Garland.

Rountree, Helen. 1990. *Pocahontas's People: The Powhatan Indians of Virginia through Four Centuries.* Norman: University of Oklahoma Press.

Rowe, John Howland. 1962. "Alfred Louis Kroeber, 1876–1960." *American Antiquity* 27 (3): 395–415.

———. 1978. "Anna Hadwick Gayton, 1899–1977." *American Anthropologist* 80 (3): 653–56.

Rubin, David C., ed. 1986. *Autobiographical Memory.* New York: Cambridge University Press.

———. 1996. *Remembering Our Past: Studies in Autobiographical Memory.* New York: Cambridge University Press.

Rusco, Elmer R. 1999. "Julian Steward, the Western Shoshones, and the Bureau of Indian Affairs: A Failure to Communicate." In *Julian Steward and the Great Basin: The Making of an Anthropologist.* Ed. Richard O. Clemmer, L. Daniel Myers, and Mary Elizabeth Rudden. 85–116. Salt Lake City: University of Utah Press.

Ryan, Marian L. 1968. "Los Angeles Newspapers Fight the Water War, 1924–1927." *Southern California* 50 (2): 177–90.

Saunders, Lucie Wood. 1989. "Vera Dourmashkin Rubin, 1911–1985." In *Women Anthropologists: Selected Biographies.* Ed. Ute Gacs, Aisha Khan, Jerrie McIntyre, and Ruth Weinberg. 316–21. Urbana: University of Illinois Press.

Schevill, Margot Blum. 1989. "Lila Morris O'Neale, 1886–1948." In *Women Anthropologists: Selected Biographies.* Ed. Ute Gacs, Aisha Khan, Jerrie McIntyre, and Ruth Weinberg. 275–81. Urbana: University of Illinois Press.

Schiebinger, Londa. 1989. *The Mind Has No Sex?: Women in the Origins of Modern Science.* Cambridge, Mass.: Harvard University Press.

Schoenherr, Allan A. 1992. *A Natural History of California.* Berkeley: University of California Press.

Schrecker, Ellen W. 1986. *No Ivory Tower: McCarthyism and the Universities.* New York: Oxford University Press.

Sered, Susan Starr. 1994. *Priestess, Mother, Sacred Sister: Religions Dominated by Women.* New York: Oxford University Press.

Service, Elman R. 1962. *Primitive Social Organization.* New York: Random House.

———. 1976. "Leslie Alvin White, 1900–1975." *American Anthropologist* 78 (3): 612–17.

———. 1988. "Morton Herbert Fried, 1923–1986." *American Anthropologist* 90 (1): 148–52.

———. n.d. "Segment of Oral History and Cultural Anthropology: With Special Emphasis on the Formation of Schools of Thought." Ms.

Seymour, Susan. 1989. "Cora Du Bois, 1903–." In *Women Anthropologists: Selected Biographies*. Ed. Ute Gacs, Aisha Khan, Jerrie McIntyre, and Ruth Weinberg. 72–79. Urbana: University of Illinois Press.

Shimkin, Demitri. 1964. "Julian H. Steward: A Contributor to Fact and Theory in Cultural Anthropology." In *Process and Pattern in Culture: Essays in Honor of Julian H. Steward*. Ed. Robert A. Manners. 1–17. Chicago: Aldine.

———. 1986. "Introduction of the Horse." In *Handbook of North American Indians*. Ed. William C. Sturtevant. Vol. 11, *Great Basin*, edited by Warren D'Azevedo. 517–24. Washington, D.C.: Smithsonian Institution.

Silverman, Sydel. 1981. Introduction to *Totems and Teachers: Perspectives on the History of Anthropology*. Ed. Sydel Silverman. ix–xv. New York: Columbia University Press.

———. 1989. "Hortense Powdermaker, 1896–1970." In *Women Anthropologists: Selected Biographies*. Ed. Ute Gacs, Aisha Khan, Jerrie McIntyre, and Ruth Weinberg. 291–96. Urbana: University of Illinois Press.

Simmons, Thomas. 1991. *The Unseen Shore: Memories of a Christian Science Childhood*. Boston: Beacon Press.

Slocum, Sally. 1975. "Woman the Gatherer: Male Bias in Anthropology." In *Towards an Anthropology of Women*. Ed. Rayna R. Reiter. 36–50. New York: Monthly Review Press.

Solecki, Ralph, and Charles Wagley. 1963. "William Duncan Strong, 1899–1962." *American Anthropologist* 65 (5): 1102–11.

Southern Inyo Chapter (AARP), comp. 1977. *Saga of Inyo County*. Covina, Calif.: Taylor Publishing.

Speth, William W. 1981. "Berkeley Geography, 1923–33." In *The Origins of Academic Geography in the United States*. Ed. Brian W. Blouet. 221–44. Hamden, Conn.: Shoe String Press.

———. 1987. "Historicism: The Disciplinary World View of Carl O. Sauer." In *Carl O. Sauer: A Tribute*. Ed. Martin S. Kenzer. 11–39. Corvallis: Oregon State University Press.

Stanislawski, D. 1975. "Carl Ortwin Sauer, 1889–1975." *Journal of Geography* 74 (9): 548–54.

Stanislawski, Michael B. 1979. "Hopi-Tewa." In *Handbook of North American Indians*. Ed. William C. Sturtevant. Vol. 9, *Southwest*, edited by Alfonso Ortiz. 587–602. Washington, D.C.: Smithsonian Institution.

Starr, Kevin. 1996. *Endangered Dreams: The Great Depression in California*. New York: Oxford University Press.

Stegner, Wallace. 1954. *Beyond the Hundredth Meridian: John Wesley Powell and the Second Opening of the West*. Boston: Houghton Mifflin.

———. 1987. *The American West* as Living Space. Ann Arbor: University of Michigan Press.

Stephenson, Robert L. 1967. "Frank H. H. Roberts, Jr., 1897–1966." *American Antiquity* 32 (1): 84–94.

Stern, Theodore. 1987. "Homer Garner Barnett, 1906–1985." *American Anthropologist* 89 (3): 701–3.

———. 1998. "Klamath and Modoc." In *Handbook of North American Indians*. Ed. William C. Sturtevant. Vol. 12, *Plateau*, edited by Deward E. Walker. 446–66. Washington, D.C.: Smithsonian Institution.

Stevens, Robert. 1983. *Law School: Legal Education in America from the 1850s to the 1980s*. Chapel Hill: University of North Carolina Press.

Steward, Jane C., comp. 1973. "Bibliography of Julian H. Steward." *American Anthropologist* 75 (3): 897–903.

Steward, Julian H. 1923. "Temple Crag (13,016 Feet), Mount Humphreys (13,972 Feet), Mount Ritter (13,156 Feet)." *Sierra Club Bulletin* 11 (3): 312–13.

———. 1927a. "A New Type of Carving from the Columbia Valley." *American Anthropologist* 29 (2): 255–61.

———. 1927b. "Words Writ on Stone." *Touring Topics* (May): 18–20, 36, 38.

———. 1928a. "The Paiute Indians." *Telluride Association and Deep Springs Work* 4:13–15.

———. 1928b. "A Peculiar Type of Stone Implement." *American Anthropologist* 30 (2): 314–16.

———. 1928c. "Pottery from Deep Springs Valley, Inyo County, California." *American Anthropologist* 30 (3): 348.

———. 1929a. "Diffusion and Independent Invention: A Critique of Logic." *American Anthropologist* 31 (3): 491–95.

———. 1929b. "Petroglyphs of California and Adjoining States." *University of California Publications in American Archaeology and Ethnology* 24:47–238.

———. 1930. "Irrigation without Agriculture." *Papers of the Michigan Academy of Science, Arts, and Letters* 12 (1929): 149–56.

———. 1931. "Notes on Hopi Ceremonies in Their Initiatory Form in 1927–1928." *American Anthropologist* 33 (1): 56–79.

———. 1932. "A Uintah Ute Bear Dance, March, 1931." *American Anthropologist* 34 (2): 263–73.

———. 1933. "Ethnography of the Owens Valley Paiute." *University of California Publications in American Archaeology and Ethnology* 3:233–350.

———. 1934. "Two Paiute Autobiographies." *University of California Publications in American Archaeology and Ethnology* 33:423–38.

———. 1936a. "The Economic and Social Basis of Primitive Bands." In *Essays on Anthropology in Honor of Alfred Louis Kroeber*. Ed. Robert Lowie. 311–50. Berkeley: University of California Press.

———. 1936b. "Myths of the Owens Valley Paiute." *University of California Publications in American Archaeology and Ethnology* 34:355–439.

———. 1936c. "Pueblo Material Culture in Western Utah." *University of New Mexico Bulletin* (Anthropological Series 1, No. 3) 287:1–64.

———. 1937a. *Ancient Caves of the Great Salt Lake Region.* BAE Bulletin No. 116. 1–131. Washington, D.C.: Government Printing Office.

———. 1937b. "Ecological Aspects of Southwestern Society." *Anthropos* 32:87–104.

———. 1938a. *Basin-Plateau Aboriginal Socio-Political Groups.* BAE Bulletin No. 120. 1–346. Washington, D.C.: Government Printing Office.

———. 1938b. "Panatubiji, an Owens Valley Paiute." In *Anthropological Papers No. 6.* BAE Bulletin No. 119. 185–95. Washington, D.C.: Government Printing Office.

———. 1939a. "Anthropological Reconnaissance in South America." In *Explorations and Field-Work of the Smithsonian Institution in 1938.* 111–16. Washington, D.C.: Government Printing Office.

———. 1939b. "Notes on Hillers' Photographs of the Paiute and Ute Indians Taken on the Powell Expedition of 1873." *Smithsonian Miscellaneous Collections* 98 (18).

———. 1940. "Native Cultures of the Intermontane (Great Basin) Area." In *Essays in Historical Anthropology of North America.* Ed. Julian H. Steward. Smithsonian Miscellaneous Collections 100:445–502. Washington, D.C.: Smithsonian Institution.

———. 1941a. "Archaeological Reconnaissance of Southern Utah." In *Anthropological Papers No. 18.* BAE Bulletin No. 128. 277–356. Washington, D.C.: Government Printing Office.

———. 1941b. "Culture Element Distributions: XIII—Nevada Shoshoni." *Anthropological Records* 4:208–359.

———. 1941c. "Recording Cultural Changes among the Carrier Indians of British Columbia." In *Explorations and Field-Work of the Smithsonian Institution in 1940.* 83–90. Washington, D.C.: Government Printing Office.

———. 1943a. "Culture Element Distributions: XXIII—Northern and Gosiute Shoshoni." *Anthropological Records* 8:263–392.

———. 1943b. "Some Western Shoshoni Myths." *Anthropological Papers No. 31.* BAE Bulletin No. 136. 249–99. Washington, D.C.: Government Printing Office.

———. 1946. Introduction to *Handbook of South American Indians.* Ed. Julian H. Steward. BAE Bulletin No. 143. Vol. 1. 1–15. Washington, D.C.: Government Printing Office.

———. 1947. "American Culture History in the Light of South America." *Southwestern Journal of Anthropology* 3:85–107.

———. 1948. "A Functional-Developmental Classification of American High Cultures." *American Antiquity* 13 (4), pt. 2:103–4.

———. 1949a. "Cultural Causality and Law: A Trial Formulation of the Development of Early Civilizations." *American Anthropologist* 51 (1): 1–27.

———. 1949b. "South American Cultures: An Interpretative Summary." In *Handbook of South American Indians.* Ed. Julian H. Steward. BAE Bulletin No. 143. Vol. 5. 669–772. Washington, D.C.: Government Printing Office.

———. 1950. "Area Research: Theory and Practice." *Social Science Research Council Bulletin* 63:1–164.

———. 1953a. "Evolution and Process." In *Anthropology Today.* Ed. A. L. Kroeber. 313–25. Chicago: University of Chicago Press.

———. 1953b. "Review of *Social Evolution,* by V. Gordon Childe." *Sociologia* 17:428–30.

———. 1955a. "Review of *Archeological Survey of Western Utah* by Jack R. Rudy." *American Antiquity* 21 (1): 88–89.

———. 1955b. "Theory and Application in a Social Science." *Ethnohistory* 2 (4): 292–302.

———. 1955c. *Theory of Culture Change: The Methodology of Multilinear Evolution.* Urbana: University of Illinois Press.

———. 1960a. "Carrier Acculturation: The Direct Historical Approach." In *Culture in History: Essays in Honor of Paul Radin.* Ed. Stanley Diamond. 732–44. New York: Columbia University Press.

———. 1960b. "Evolutionary Principles and Social Types." In *Evolution after Darwin.* Ed. Sol Tax. Vol. 2. 169–86. Chicago: University of Chicago Press.

———. 1960c. "John Reed Swanton, 1873–1958." *Biographical Memoirs, National Academy of Sciences* 34:329–49.

———. 1960d. "Review of *The Evolution of Culture,* by Leslie A. White." *American Anthropologist* 62 (1): 144–48.

———. 1961a. "Alfred Louis Kroeber." *International Journal of Comparative Sociology* 2:88–106.

———. 1961b. "Alfred Louis Kroeber, 1876–1960." *American Anthropologist* 63 (5): 1038–87.

———. 1962. "Alfred Louis Kroeber." *Biographical Memoirs, National Academy of Sciences* 36:192–253.

———. 1966. "Review of *The Evolution of Urban Societies: Early Mesopotamia and Prehispanic Mexico,* by Robert McC. Adams." *Science* 153 (3737): 729–30.

———. 1967a. "Cultural Evolution Today." *Christian Century* 54 (7): 203–7.

———. 1967b. Foreword to *Contemporary Change in Traditional Societies.* Ed. Julian H. Steward. Vol. 1. v–x. Urbana: University of Illinois Press.

———. 1967c. "Perspectives on Modernization: Introductions to the Studies." In *Contemporary Change in Traditional Societies.* Ed. Julian H. Steward. Vol. 1. 1–55. Urbana: University of Illinois Press.

———. 1967d. "Review of *Rock Art of Owens Valley, California,* by Jay C. Von Werlhof." *American Antiquity* 32 (2): 250–51.

———. 1968a. "Causal Factors and Processes in the Evolution of Prefarming Societies." In *Man the Hunter.* Ed. Richard B. Lee and Irven DeVore. 321–34. Chicago: Aldine.

———. 1968b. "Cultural Ecology." In *International Encyclopedia of the Social Sciences.* Vol. 4. 337–44. New York: Macmillan.

———. 1968c. "Scientific Responsibility in Modern Life" (letter to the editor). *Science* 159 (3811): 147–48.

———. 1969a. "Comments on *Trade and Culture Processes in European Prehistory*, by Colin Renfrew." *Current Anthropology* 10:164–65.

———. 1969b. "Limitations of Applied Anthropology: The Case of the American Indian New Deal." *Journal of the Steward Anthropological Society* 1 (1): 1–17.

———. 1970. "The Foundations of Basin-Plateau Shoshonean Society." In *Languages and Cultures of Western North America: Essays in Honor of Sven S. Liljeblad.* Ed. Earl H. Swanson Jr. 113–51. Pocatello: Idaho State University Press.

———. 1973. *Alfred L. Kroeber.* New York: Columbia University Press.

———. 1974. "Robert Harry Lowie, June 12, 1883–September 21, 1957." *Biographical Memoirs, National Academy of Sciences* 44:175–83.

———. 1977. *Evolution and Ecology: Essays on Social Transformation.* Ed. Jane C. Steward and Robert F. Murphy. Urbana: University of Illinois Press.

———. 1978. "Initiation of a Research Trend: Wittfogel's Irrigation Hypothesis." In *Society and History: Essays in Honor of Karl August Wittfogel.* Ed. G. L. Ulman. 3–14. The Hague: Mouton.

———, ed. 1946–59. *Handbook of South American Indians.* Vols. 1–7. BAE Bulletin No. 143. Washington, D.C.: Government Printing Office.

———. 1967. *Contemporary Change in Traditional Societies.* 3 vols. Urbana: University of Illinois Press.

Steward, Julian H., Robert M. Adams, Donald Collier, Angel Palerm, Karl A. Wittfogel, and Ralph L. Beals. 1955. *Irrigation Civilizations: A Comparative Study.* Social Science Monographs No. 1. Washington, D.C.: Pan American Press.

Steward, Julian H., and Louis Faron. 1959. *Native Peoples of South America.* New York: McGraw-Hill.

Steward, Julian H., Robert A. Manners, Eric R. Wolf, Elena Padilla Seda, Sidney W. Mintz, and Raymond L. Scheele. 1956. *The People of Puerto Rico: A Study in Social Anthropology.* Urbana: University of Illinois Press.

Steward, Julian H., and Demitri B. Shimkin. 1961. "Some Mechanisms of Sociocultural Evolution." *Daedalus* 90:477–97.

Steward, Marion. 1924. "The Sweet Singer of Israel." *Christian Science Journal* 42 (6): 314.

———. 1925. "Seeds of Truth." *Christian Science Journal* 43 (2): 80.

Stirling, Matthew. 1963. "John Peabody Harrington, 1884–1961." *American Anthropologist* 65 (2): 370–81.

Stocking, George W., Jr. 1960. "Franz Boas and the Founding of the American Anthropological Association." *American Anthropologist* 62 (1): 1–17.

———. 1969. *Race, Culture, and Evolution: Essays in the History of Anthropology.* New York: Free Press.

———. 1974. "Introduction: The Basic Assumptions of Boasian Anthropology." In *The Shaping of American Anthropology, 1883–1911: A Franz Boas Reader.* Ed. George W. Stocking Jr. 1–20. New York: Basic Books.

———. 1981. "Anthropological Visions and Economic Realities in the 1930s Southwest." *El Palacio* 87 (3): 14–17.

Strong, William Duncan. 1927. "An Analysis of Southwestern Society." *American Anthropologist* 29 (1): 1–69.

———. 1929. "Aboriginal Society in Southern California." *University of California Publications in American Archaeology and Ethnology* 26:1–358.

———. 1933. "The Plains Culture Area in the Light of Archaeology." *American Anthropologist* 35 (2): 271–87.

Strong, William Duncan, W. Egbert Schenk, and Julian H. Steward. 1930. "Archaeology of the

Dalles-Deschutes Region." *University of California Publications in American Archaeology and Ethnology* 29:1–154.

Sutton, Constance R., and Richard Lee. 1993. "Eleanor Burke Leacock, 1922–1987." In *From Labrador to Samoa: The Theory and Practice of Eleanor Burke Leacock.* Ed. Constance R. Sutton. 131–39. Arlington, Va.: Association for Feminist Anthropology/American Anthropological Association.

Taylor, Walter W. 1963. "Leslie Spier, 1893–1961." *American Antiquity* 28 (3): 379–81.

Telluride Association. 1928. *Telluride Association and Deep Springs: An Account of Their Origin and Plan.* Malden, Mass.: Dunbar-Kerr.

Temkin, Andrea S. 1989. "Alice Cunningham Fletcher, 1838–1923." In *Women Anthropologists: Selected Biographies.* Ed. Ute Gacs, Aisha Khan, Jerrie McIntyre, and Ruth Weinberg. 95–101. Urbana: University of Illinois Press.

Thomas, David Hurst. 1983. "On Steward's Model of Great Basin Shoshonean Sociopolitical Organization: A Great Bias in the Basin?" In *The Development of Political Organization in Native North America.* Ed. Elizabeth Tooker and Morton H. Fried. 59–67. Washington, D.C.: American Ethnological Society.

Thomas, David Hurst, Lorann S. A. Pendelton, and Stephen C. Cappannari. 1986. "Western Shoshone." In *Handbook of North American Indians.* Ed. William C. Sturtevant. Vol. 11, *Great Basin,* edited by Warren D'Azevedo. 262–82. Washington, D.C.: Smithsonian Institution.

Thomas, Robert David. 1994. *With Bleeding Footsteps: Mary Baker Eddy's Path to Religious Leadership.* New York: Knopf.

Thompson, Raymond H. 1991. "Shepard, Kidder, and Carnegie." In *The Ceramic Legacy of Anna O. Shepard.* Ed. Ronald L. Bishop and Frederick W. Lange. 11–41. Niwot: University Press of Colorado.

Thompson, Stephen I. 1985. "Joseph Bartholomew Casagrande, 1915–1982." *American Anthropologist* 87 (4): 883–88.

Toffelmier, Gertrude. 1967. "Edwin Meyer Loeb, 1894–1966." *American Anthropologist* 69 (2): 200–203.

Tolman, Edward Chace. 1932. *Purposive Behavior in Animals and Men.* New York: Century Co.

Tompkins, Jane. 1992. *West of Everything: The Inner Life of Westerns.* New York: Oxford University Press.

Tooker, Elizabeth. 1983. "The Structure of the Iroquois League: Lewis H. Morgan's Research and Observations." *Ethnohistory* 30 (3): 141–54.

Toulouse, Betty. 1981. "The Laboratory's Early Years, 1927–1947." *El Palacio* 87 (3): 6–13.

Trimble, Stephen. 1989. *The Sagebrush Ocean: A Natural History of the Great Basin.* Reno: University of Nevada Press.

Turney-High, Harry Holbert. 1940. "Review of Basin-Plateau Aboriginal Sociopolitical Groups." *American Anthropologist* 42 (1): 136–38.

University of California. 1902. *Announcement of Courses, 1902–1903.* University of California Bulletins 4, no. 2. Berkeley: University of California Press.

———. 1921. *Announcement of Courses of Instruction for the Academic Year 1921–22.* University of California Bulletin, 3d ser., 15, no. 1. Berkeley: University of California Press.

———. 1925. *Announcement of Courses of Instruction Primarily for Students in the Departments at Berkeley for the Academic Year 1925–26.* Berkeley: University of California Press.

———. 1926a. *Announcement of Courses, 1926–27, Primarily for Students in the Departments at Berkeley.* University of California Bulletin, 3d ser., 20, no. 1. Berkeley: University of California Press.

———. 1926b. *Register of the Academic Year 1925–1926.* Part 1. University of California Bulletin, 3d ser., 20, no. 6. Berkeley: University of California Press.

———. 1927. *Announcement of Courses of Instruction, 1927–28, Primarily for Students in the De-*

parmtents at Berkeley. University of California Bulletin, 3d ser., 21, no. 1. Berkeley: University of California Press.

University of Illinois. 1952. *Undergraduate Study Catalog, 1952–53.* Urbana: University of Illinois.

Vayda, Andrew P., and Roy A. Rappaport. 1968. "Ecology, Cultural and Non-cultural." In *Introduction to Cultural Anthropology.* Ed. James A. Clifton. 476–98. Boston: Houghton Mifflin.

Vincent, Joan. 1990. *Anthropology and Politics: Visions, Traditions, and Trends.* Tucson: University of Arizona Press.

Wajcman, Judy. 1991. *Feminism Confronts Technology.* University Park: Pennsylvania State University Press.

Wagley, Charles. 1955. "Bernard Mishkin, 1913–1954." *American Anthropologist* 57 (4): 1033–35.

———. 1964. "Alfred Métraux, 1902–[1963]." *American Anthropologist* 66 (3): 603–13.

Walker, Deward E., Jr. 1999. "A Revisionist View of Julian Steward and the Great Basin Paradigm from the North." In *Julian Steward and the Great Basin: The Making of an Anthropologist.* Ed. Richard O. Clemmer, L. Daniel Myers, and Mary Elizabeth Rudden. 60–73. Salt Lake City: University of Utah Press.

Walter, Paul A. F. 1947. "Edgar Lee Hewett, 1865–1946." *American Anthropologist* 49 (2): 260–71.

Washburn, Wilcomb E. 1978. *The Cosmos Club of Washington: A Centennial History, 1878–1978.* Washington, D.C.: Cosmos Club.

Weltfish, Gene, and Ruth Benedict. 1943. *The Races of Mankind.* New York: Public Affairs Committee.

West, Robert C. 1979. *Carl Sauer's Fieldwork in Latin America.* Dellplain Latin American Studies No. 3. Ann Arbor: University Microfilms International.

———, ed. 1982. *Andean Reflections: Letters from Carl O. Sauer While on a South American Trip under a Grant from the Rockefeller Foundation, 1942.* Dellplain Latin American Studies No. 11. Boulder, Colo.: Westview Press.

Wheat, Margaret M. 1967. *Survival Arts of the Primitive Paiutes.* Reno: University of Nevada Press.

White, Leslie. 1943. "Energy and the Evolution of Culture." *American Anthropologist* 45 (3): 335–56.

———. 1957. "Review of *Theory of Culture Change: The Methodology of Multilinear Evolution,* by Julian H. Steward." *American Anthropologist* 59 (3): 540–42.

Whitnah, Donald R. 1965. *A History of the United States Weather Bureau.* Urbana: University of Illinois Press.

Wilford, John Noble. 1991. "Dr. John Bardeen, 82, Winner of Nobel Prize for Transistor, Dies." *New York Times,* Jan. 31, B-9.

Willey, Gordon R. 1988. *Portraits in American Archaeology: Remembrances of Some Distinguished Americanists.* Albuquerque: University of New Mexico Press.

Willey, Gordon R., and Philip Phillips. 1958. *Method and Theory in American Archaeology.* Chicago: University of Chicago Press.

Willey, Gordon R., and Jeremy A. Sabloff. 1974. *A History of American Anthropology.* San Francisco: W. H. Freeman.

Winters, Christopher, ed. 1991. *International Dictionary of Anthropologists.* New York: Garland.

Wister, Owen. 1902. *The Virginian: A Horseman of the Plains.* New York: Macmillan.

Wolf, Eric. 1964. *Anthropology.* Englewood Cliffs, N.J.: Prentice-Hall.

———. 1967. "Review of *Contemporary Change in Traditional Societies,* ed. Julian H. Steward." *Science* 158 (3802): 759–62.

———. 1981. "Alfred Kroeber." In *Totems and Teachers: Perspectives on the History of Anthropology.* Ed. Sydel Silverman. 35–64. New York: Columbia University Press.

———. 1988. "Reply [to Alan Beals]." *Current Anthropology* 29 (2): 306–7.

Wolf, Eric, with Sydel Silverman. 2001. *Pathways of Power: Building an Anthropology of the Modern World.* Berkeley: University of California Press.

Wood, Coke. 1972a. "Owens Valley as I Knew It, Part 1." *Pacific Historian* 16 (2): 2–9.

———. 1972b. "Owens Valley as I Knew It, Part 2." *Pacific Historian* 16 (3): 3–11.

Woodbury, Nathalie F. S. 1989. "Past Is Present—Anthropology in the Academy, Part 3: The Academicians." *Anthropology Newsletter* 30 (9): 5.

Work Projects Administration (WPA). 1939. *California: A Guide to the Golden State*. New York: Hastings House.

———. 1940. *Nevada: A Guide to the Silver State*. Portland, Ore.: Binfords and Mort.

———. 1941. *Utah: A Guide to the State*. 2d ed. New York: Hastings House.

Worster, Donald. 1985. *Rivers of Empire: Water, Aridity, and the Growth of the American West*. New York: Pantheon.

———. 2001. *A River Running West: The Life of John Wesley Powell*. New York: Oxford University Press.

Wright, Rita P. 1996a. "Introduction: Gendered Ways of Knowing in Archaeology." In *Gender and Archaeology*. Ed. Rita Wright. 1–19. Philadelphia: University of Pennsylvania Press.

———. 1996b. "Technology, Gender, and Class: Worlds of Difference in Ur III Mesopotamia." In *Gender and Archaeology*. Ed. Rita Wright. 79–110. Philadelphia: University of Pennsylvania Press.

Zumwalt, Rosemary Lévy. 1992. *Wealth and Rebellion: Elsie Clews Parsons, Anthropologist and Folklorist*. Urbana: University of Illinois Press.

Index

VIRGINIA KERNS is the author of *Women and the Ancestors: Black Carib Kinship and Ritual* and the coeditor of *In Her Prime: New Views of Middle-Aged Women.* She is a professor of anthropology at the College of William and Mary.

The University of Illinois Press
is a founding member of the
Association of American University Presses.

———————————————————

Composed in 10.5/12.5 Adobe Minion
with Copperplate Gothic 33bc display
by Barbara Evans
at the University of Illinois Press
Designed by Dennis Roberts
Manufactured by Thomson-Shore, Inc.

University of Illinois Press
1325 South Oak Street
Champaign, IL 61820–6903
www.press.uillinois.edu